Thrifty
and
Thriving

Thrifty and Thriving

Illustrations by Emily Doheny.
Cover design by Jennie Lodien.

Printed in the United States of America

Dedicated to Marlys, the thriftiest mother
a girl ever had.

Contents

PART 4: How to be Thrifty & Thriving: 10 Simple Strategies

PART 5: Rewards for the Thrifty

Acknowledgements

*"How can I ever thank you?"**

(*excluding time or money)

The problem is where to start. It would be easier to list people I don't want to thank, ha ha, because life consists of thousands of little encounters with people that shape the way you think.

It all began with great parents that showed me how to live responsibly. I watched them plan and save and live with contentment. They only bought things they could pay for. On the spot. I assumed everyone lived like that. Thanks for the great example!

My 'Mr. Fixit' husband has given his blessing on my need to try new things, start little home businesses, and plan various events. He is a master at all-things-maintenance and squeezes more life out of a car or appliance than any human I know. Thanks for being the best partner I could ask for.

Thanks to Chris Payne for his insight and encouragement as I endeavored to write a book. I don't know why I wanted to try, I just did. He had an enormous amount of patience to coach this novice. I have learned so much and grown to love the process. I would have quit for sure without you, Chris.

And to Lynn Huyck, who seemed way more excited about this little book than I was, your energy picked me up when I was losing inertia. We make a great team and I can't wait to work on more projects together.

Thanks to John Swanson, my dream graphic design client and friend. You hung with me through toddlers and diapers and homework and moving. You were my lifeline to the work I loved, and I am forever grateful for the day we met.

Of course, my 3 children have been on the receiving end of all this and still love me. Thank you, and love you back.

There are so many moms (and dads) we have lived life with and learned by their example to make the most of our time, our talents, and our resources: Jody and David, Susan, Brenda, Lori, Dawn, Lynn, Sherri, Carrie Jo, Debi, Noelle, Amy and Steve, Kate, Marjorie, Carole, Rachael, Audra, Gracia, Lisa and Scott, Jennifer, Wendy, Emily, Bruce, Janet, Bea, Suzanna, Linda (and I am only stopping, because I am out of room). Your thrift and generosity and friendship have made a big impact on me. Thank you.

Foreword

*"These days, you've gotta
milk a dollar out of every dime."*
— *Gayle Forman*

I am one of the Survivors of Jennie's Thrifty College Haircuts. (See Part 4, page 67)

Actually, she cut quite well.

While I took out loans and had a few grants, Jennie was wise. She was creatively entrepreneurial and made enough money to go overseas on the same Denmark study program I did, but she walked away without debt. My husband helped pay off my $4,000 loan a few years later.

Jennie and I go way back together. As in 36 years back. We met in college, studied and traveled in Europe, started our young married life and raised children together. Both of our families decided to homeschool when it was not mainstream. We learned cooking skills together, shared ideas on housekeeping and good books to read aloud. Steve and Jennie were instrumental in changing our parenting method and how to live more responsibly with what we had. It was not in words so much as by example.

They exuded a fun, never boring, content and hard working aura that was hard not to get caught up in. Not once, ever, have I heard Jennie complain about too little money. Instead, what I witnessed was a determined and joyful willingness to be creative, learn, and seek out ways to be financially wise.

No matter what your monetary situation is, you can learn to be more thrifty and have a ton of free fun while doing it.

Jennie is, and as long as I've known her to be, engaging, energetic, entertaining, and a Truly Nice Minnesotan.

This book IS her heart, through and through. She lives, eats, breathes, and I'm pretty sure prays in Thriftiness.

Read, think, laugh and learn from a Lifelong Thrifter. Pour yourself that self-made cup of coffee or tea or kombucha and meet a new friend.

Lynn Huyck
P.S. Jennie I am sooooo proud of you!

Introduction

I am guessing if you picked up this book, you are ready for a change. Do you wish you had more money left over at the end of the month? Do you find yourself stressing over surprise expenses? Would you love to take a vacation without charging it to a credit card? I am sure you know people who live this way, but you can't figure out how they do it.

If only there was a magic pill to make money worries go away. Spending money can feel like a quick fix, but spending carelessly can rob you of the things you care about most — like your peace of mind, enjoying your children, reliable transportation, a little extra to share, time with your spouse, or retiring well. Take heart!

Anyone can make little changes that can add up to a big difference. My drumbeat is "spend less on what you don't care about so you can spend more on what you do care about." You will hear it throughout this book, because my hope is to start you down the path of being thrifty and really thriving! Let's get started.

Why We Resist Being Thrifty

Why We Resist Being Thrifty

"He that goes a borrowing goes a sorrowing."
— *Ben Franklin*

Over the years I have had friends in all economic levels, and I assure you the ability to manage money does not correlate with how much you earn. As incredible as it seems, I know people with 8 children who make under $40,000 a year, but they live well, have great kids, and always have food and fellowship to share. Others that earn well over 6 figures can't even make their minimum credit card payments. Be encouraged that living within your means is not dependent on how much you make, but how much you spend.

For 15 years I homeschooled our 3 kids while freelancing a bit as a graphic designer. When women asked me what I did, their knee-jerk reaction was often, "Oh, I could never afford to do that!" Never? Really, never? I bet if it was do-or-die, they would figure out a way. Now, I do tend to take things more literally than I should, but I always 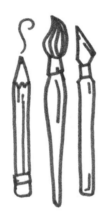 thought that these women gave themselves way too little credit. It boils down to analyzing what you care about most and figuring a workable way to get it. After all, this is America and we have options! For our family, having time together was a priority so we gave up a few extras like eating out, nice carpet, and fancy vacations. Totally worth it to us. Your 'must haves' may look very different from ours, but that is okay! Figure out what you really care about and let go of things you don't.

I have observed people on both ends of the spectrum; people who spend wildly and people who manage money beautifully. Inability to manage money seems to fall into 3 categories:

1. *Misconceptions about thrift.* Often, people seem to have negative stereotypes regarding thrift.

2. *Poor imitation.* Sometimes we lack models of good habits from people who manage money well and instead copy people who don't manage their money well.

3. *Missing guidelines.* We may struggle to create guidelines that help us with the myriad of buying choices we face every day.

So don't just skip to the 'how to' part of this book. Take some time to consider your mindset and the very real benefits that come with financial control. Your efforts might start strong but fizzle out unless you are convinced of the *why*. Take time to look at what really matters to you. You might be surprised — and relieved! Let's look at some of the common hurdles to intentional spending.

Why Do We Overspend?

There is a whole laundry list of reasons and excuses for spending. I can spot my weaknesses. What are yours?

We want to impress others
Will Rogers said it best: "We buy things we don't need with money we don't have to impress people we don't like." Ouch. I have done that.

We are unwilling to wait
We don't like to wait. It is hard. Sometimes it seems unbearable. It may feel unfair, but waiting is actually a necessary

ingredient to enjoying what you have.

I received a text from my friend Kate the other day. "Hey, my frugal friend. I'm glad you found a way to treat yourself."  And what a treat when you have waited 20 years. I happily plunked down $115 for a haircut. Sounds like a huge extravagance, but I paid it with no guilt at all. You have to realize that I cut my family's hair (4 people) x 4 times a year x 20 years for an approximate savings of at least $5,000. I know people need to get their hair cut somehow. Not everyone can cut hair reasonably well, but since I can, I just did it myself. I prop up a couple of mirrors and go at it. Getting my own hair professionally done was not a priority in the busy years of raising kids, but now that I work in an office, I like having a 'big girl' cut. My turn has come.

The point of this story (and there is one), is that I probably enjoyed that trip to the salon more than any woman in there because it was new and special and I had gone without. It's great to have something to look forward to.

Anticipation can double or triple the value of a purchase or event. We took our kids on a field trip to Israel with a student group. We waited and planned and saved for a year and a half. It was the best trip of my life — and all the more memorable because of the buildup. Delaying adds an enjoyment that impulsive consuming can't give. Waiting makes it all the sweeter: an anniversary cruise, new shoes, finishing a college degree, etc. Don't give in to the idea that you should grab everything you want when you want it. Waiting is an exercise in self-control, and you will multiply your thankfulness and enjoyment if you have to wait a while.

In 2013, the *Journal of Consumer Research* published a study which found that when it comes to shopping, wanting things makes people happier than actually having them. Researchers analyzed the emotional state of consumers before and after making a significant purchase.

Most people anticipated future purchases with strong, positive emotions. They felt joy, excitement, optimism, and peacefulness when they thought of their future purchase, which they also believed would improve their relationships, boost their self-esteem, enable them to experience more pleasure, and be more efficient.

But after the purchase was made and the anticipation faded into reality, what followed was what the researchers called 'hedonic decline.' Happy feelings dissipated. Consumers were left wanting more. Apparently, we are happier longing than getting.

We have not learned to manage a budget
This is very common. For some reason, even though this will

affect every single day of your life, it is not considered a routine part of a complete education. If budgeting wasn't modeled in your home, you may not understand how it works and how to set up a budget.

Debt seems normal and credit is readily available
Are you old enough to remember when you needed cash to buy things? The availability of credit has almost wiped out the idea that you do not want to buy things you don't have the money to pay for.

The *Book of Proverbs* has a ton of common sense concerning money. In verse 22:7 it tells us, "The rich rule over the poor, and the borrower is slave to the lender." That is a scary warning, and yet it can be way too easy to borrow against what we hope to earn in the future.

We fail to plan ahead
I kick myself when I have to run to the grocery store for one ingredient, because I never come out with just one item. Rush charges, expedited shipping, or late fees at the bank or credit card company result from failing to plan. Do you buy in bulk when consumables are on sale, or just enough to get by? Do you regularly buy toilet paper at a convenience store?

Failing to plan is planning to fail. Stocking up, planning ahead, and staying on top of bills are all key to avoid paying too much. Lack of planning is very expensive.

We allow impulse buying

The more time you spend in retail outlets or shopping online, the more opportunity you have to spend just to spend. When I go to a mall, I always discover all kinds of things I didn't even know I wanted. Do you have that same experience?

And how about those infomercials? I am extremely gullible, and if I can't sleep at night there could be 4 new purchases from late night television before my husband wakes up.

We are embarrassed to look 'less than'

Well, here's some good news. First, when you live in a wealthy country, you can look great in someone else's 'seconds'. I have more beautiful clothes from thrift stores than I could ever need. We fixed up our house with refurbishing and do-it-yourself projects and, all in all, it looks pretty good.

Sadly, trying to impress others as a way to get into social circles can backfire. More importantly, it can hinder making friends. A recent study was titled *Forget the Bling: High Status-Signaling Deters New Friendships*. When it comes to making new friends, status symbols actually repel people from making friends with us, according to research published in the journal *Social Psychological and Personality Science*.[2]

"Often we think that status symbols — whether a luxury

car like a BMW, a brand-name purse like Prada, or an expensive watch like Rolex — will make us look more socially attractive to others," says Stephen Garcia (University of Michigan). "However, our research suggests that these status signals actually make us look less socially attractive, not more."

The scientists conducted a series of 6 tests in which participants either presented themselves as potential friends or evaluated those they would want to be their friends. Throughout the tests, people presenting themselves to a new group chose higher-status items. Yet the people asked about who they would want to be friends with tended to prefer people with lower or neutral status symbols.

To control for the possibility that a luxury good might play a role in people's reactions, the researchers conducted a study in which they asked participants which of 2 plain t-shirts they would choose to wear to a picnic in their effort to make new friends. One t-shirt had 'Walmart' written on it in plain script, and the other t-shirt had 'Saks Fifth Avenue' written on it in plain script. While neither shirt was, in itself, a luxury item, 76% of the participants who presented themselves as new friends chose to wear the t-shirt that said 'Saks Fifth Avenue' whereas 64% of the would-be friends chose the person wearing the 'Walmart' t-shirt.

"At a societal level, we may be wasting billions of dollars on expensive status symbols that ultimately keep others from wanting to associate with us," says Kimberlee Weaver Livnat

(University of Haifa). "And to the extent that close friend-ships are important to well-being, we may be inadvertently hurting ourselves."

Hmmmm. Something to think about.

We lack confidence

Nobody wants to appear strange, but if you want to get off the 'never-enough-money-at-the-end-of-the-month' merry-go-round, you will have to try something different. And that might seem strange to your friends and family. You wonder if people can tell you are wearing secondhand clothes. Will they know you went canoeing instead of cruising to stay on budget? Can you tell that Girl Scout 'no' to her cookies? When you begin to choose different entertainment or vehicles or clothing you might stick out. It can be difficult to explain to friends and family. Some people will understand, but some might not. Change can be uncomfortable — even good change.

We splurge on special occasions

This is like being on your best eating behavior 11 months of the year and keeping the weight off, but putting 20 pounds on be-tween Thanksgiving and Christ-mas. You can undo so much work in such a short time by

rationalizing splurges that you can't afford.

I see friends starting to do this with their children's weddings. I think a wedding should be lovely and special and meaningful, but I don't think an $80,000 wedding is 10 times more wonderful than an $8,000 wedding. And it isn't about the price tag; it is the cost to your family. If you can truly afford $80,000 without debt, without drawing out all your life savings, mortgaging your house and pulling out your retirement account, go for it! But we so easily get caught up in some notion of 'once in a lifetime' or 'princess for a day' while lining someone else's pockets and ruining our future.

We can't bear to see our kids unhappy
This is a killer. Even the strictest parents want to shower their

children with good things and advantages and fun. We want them to like us. This can often be more for our benefit than for their well-being.

Here is a little story to illustrate how it won't ruin your kids to say no. We still laugh about the Paul Bunyan story. We live in Minnesota where Paul Bunyan, with his blue ox Babe, is a legendary lumberjack. There are big statues of him in little towns all over northern Minnesota. When our children were very small, we took them to see Paul in Brainerd, where he has sat since I was a small girl. This statue of Paul was my favorite, because when I approached it, my dad would whisper my name to the 'man behind the curtain' so it seemed as if Paul was greeting me in his booming voice as I ran up to touch his big foot.

When we took our children to see him, we didn't realize that an amusement park had been built up around Paul and admission was now $8 per person for the whole day. We just weren't prepared to spend the time or money. We quickly discussed it with the aunts and uncles, walked the children up to the chain-link fence, pointed and said, "Well, look, there is Paul Bunyan! Wasn't it fun to see him? Get in the car, kids, we are going to get an ice cream cone." They were slightly confused, but not too put out. We saved our money and set aside a whole day the next summer to go to Paul Bunyan Land, and it was all the more fun because we looked forward to it all year.

Kids are resilient. Teach them to do with, and teach them to do without.

We practice retail therapy
Sometimes, we use shopping as a diversion from being bored, angry, sad, or lonely. Buying can give you a quick high followed by the crash of bills and dissatisfaction. Shopping for entertainment can create strong temptation to spend money on what you don't need, want, or can afford.

We don't want to feel deprived
No one wants to look around and feel like they are being left out. Left out of vacations and concerts and clothes and cars and second houses and horseback riding lessons and fill-in-the-blank. It is so easy to look at what we are missing (glass-half-empty or half-full?)

The list can go on and on. Powerful emotions can drive us to spend money — even money we don't have.

Why We Are Resistant to Thrifting

It may seem daunting to spend carefully, wait for things, plan ahead, and set goals, but if you are daring, give it a try. Just because everyone else seems to be in debt, living on monthly payments, and renting rather than owning does not mean it is the superior way to live. Let me try to change your mind about what thrifty is and what thrifty is not.

Thrifty (def.) adverb: 1. using money and other resources carefully and not wastefully.

The thrifty want to use their money thoughtfully. They demand value, and when they see it, happily plunk down their money. Unfortunately, it is easy to throw money at things that give very little value in return. This may surprise you, but the goal is to spend wisely, not just avoid spending. It's smart to spend less on what you don't care about, so you can spend more on what you do care about. (There's that drumbeat again.) Let me correct some common misconceptions about the thrifty:

- **BEING THRIFTY ≠ STINGY.** Stingy means "unwilling to give or spend; ungenerous." You will never thrive if your objective is to simply hang on to your money and resent anything that takes it away from you. Stingy people do not enjoy spending on themselves or on others. I don't want to be that way and I don't think you do either.

- **BEING THRIFTY ≠ CHEAP.** Cheap implies constant haggling for the bottom-of-the-barrel price, but price should never be the only factor in making a purchase. Sometimes paying more will give better long-term value. (Do you see the theme developing?) Buying cheap products can be expensive. Sometimes, I even pay a premium to support a business or cause I care about.

When we first got married, my whole criterion for shopping was price. Cheap, cheap, cheap. My husband had a different perspective, which won out after the demise of our seventh used vehicle. This led to our first — you guessed it — *new* minivan! None of our cars at that point had been less than 10 years old or cost more than $2,000. With small children to haul around, Steve decided it was the right time to get a reliable vehicle. A brand-spanking-new Mazda MPV. For $22,000. I couldn't breathe. I couldn't even wrap my head around the amount. We argued and debated and crunched numbers, and we bought that van.

I warned our 8-year-old to go easy on that van, because he was going to drive it to college. He did. So did child No. 2. Would you believe that 17 years later, the baby of the family is driving it to her nursing clinicals during college? That van was well maintained (by hubby) and actually cost us much less over the course of these years than a series of old beaters would have. I might even get my van back next year.

I was starting to get on board with the idea of looking at the bigger value and the hidden costs behind the price tag, and this has really helped us spend less to get more.

Here is another lesson I learned about being cheap. I was printing worksheets for a class, but the toner was low and was leaving white streaks across the pages. I usually give it a good shake and try to get 20–30 more pages printed, but I broke down and put in the new cartridge. After finishing that project, I had the brilliant idea to pop the old one back in and squeeze out a few more pages on personal stuff.

A couple of days later, I realized I hadn't sent in the old cartridge for recycling, but was not certain if I had swapped the old one back in. My memory isn't what it used to be, and you guessed it, I packaged up and sent the brand-new toner back in for recycling! Ugh. Sometimes, I can take cheap too far.

- **BEING THRIFTY ≠ UNGENEROUS.** In the beloved Charles Dickens novel *A Christmas Carol,* Ebenezer Scrooge scrimped and saved and pinched pennies, never sharing or enjoying any of his wealth. Thankfully, he saw the light. (A must-read.) For us, spending less on consumables and services has given us a little cushion to share with others, which adds greatly to our enjoyment.

  And being generous is not limited to giving money. When we aren't stretched to our limit financially, we have the time and freedom to bring meals to a family with sick children or share our house with an exchange student. I do graphic design work for charities and ministries;

my husband helps older neighbors with house and car maintenance. We can respond to the needs of people around us when we have a little cushion.

- **BEING THRIFTY ≠ BORING.** If you are bored by the challenge of learning new skills, hunting up deals, sharing with your neighbors, getting more physical activity and watching your savings grow, then I hope I can change your mind. Please, don't say it is boring until you give it a try.

Developing your 'thrift' muscles is not unlike working out at the gym. It requires effort. It requires a decision. It requires discipline. But once you get going and start seeing results, you want to do more, and it starts to get easier. You get stronger and more confident, plus you start seeing the payoff. You will be surprised at the things you can do, from brewing your own kombucha to changing oil in the car, cutting hair, preparing your own taxes, teaching a class, building a shed, writing a book (hahaha) or designing a website. "Necessity is the mother of invention," said Ben Franklin, and he was right. You will find creative ways to travel, invest, barter, and who knows what else. Not. Boring.

Finding Contentment

The world tells us we need more . . . of everything. Our American culture has convinced us that the main goal in life is acquiring. Acquiring what? Anything and everything. We work to buy more stuff, to store it, fix it, haul it, organize it, drown in it. Every purchase comes with a commitment and the stress that comes with paying for that commitment. This kind of treadmill can be tough to jump off.

And he said to them, "Take care, and be on your guard against all covetousness, for one's life does not consist in the abundance of his possessions."

LUKE 12:15

Are you a glass-half-empty or glass-half-full person?

Last week I was visiting a friend whose family had just moved into their first house after years in an apartment. She was telling me how thrilled she was when they first moved in and how wonderful it all seemed. But as she grew accustomed to it, she began wishing it was a little bigger, had a better kitchen, was a little closer to the school, etc. She was almost yelling, "I have to stop this, because I am already ungrateful for this perfect little house." We always assume more is better.

Do you remember studying the Law of Marginal Utility in economics class? It attempts to define the additional satisfaction a consumer gains from consuming one more unit of a good or service. My son will never forget this concept. He volunteered to demonstrate this principle for a class. The tutor handed him a bag of marshmallows and told him he was free to eat as many as he liked. And he liked marshmallows. He said the first 10 were delicious. The next 5 were okay, but at 22 he was begging to stop. He realized that each 'unit' did not deliver equal satisfaction. He enjoyed the first units by far the most. This idea can help us understand we can have great pleasure without extreme consumption.

More stuff is not the magic ingredient to happiness. And we all know people who are proof of that. Have you noticed that happy people are happy independent of their circumstances? My mail delivery lady was a great example. She was one of the most cheerful, friendly people I have ever known. I loved seeing her mail truck come down the street. She was like sunshine at your door and, because she was a talker, I knew her life wasn't all roses. She was proof that, in spite of the constant message that possessions make us happy, it is not true. Possessions can add convenience but not create contentment.

What if we stepped back and explored goals that did not involve material possessions? What if we learned to be grateful with much or little?

I think of friends I want to emulate. What is so attractive about their lives? It isn't the clothes they wear or the car they drive. I am drawn to people who are happy, hospitable, thoughtful, active, loyal, and fun to be around. You can show up at their house and know you are welcome. Do I care how big or clean or decorated their house is? No, I just love putting my feet up, sharing a meal, playing with the kids, and spending time together. We could eat grilled cheese sandwiches. And this kind of happy home is possible to achieve regardless of your income. Why do we let the pursuit of 'stuff' crowd out the enjoyment of 'now'?

At the root of excessive buying is a lack of clear goals. Stephen Covey, in his fantastic book *The 7 Habits of Highly Effective People,* says to begin with the end in mind. At the end of your life, you aren't going to care much about all your stuff, so give some thought to that now. Consuming to 'fill our emotional tank' can leave us disappointed and dissatisfied as we look to the next purchase. Inevitably, people realize that friends and family are what matters most. By looking at what is in the glass (half full) you can be thankful and start enjoying the people around you, instead of spending all your energy trying to fill the other half of the glass.

My dad grew up in the Great Depression, without a father or 2 nickels to rub together, yet he is the most content guy I know. I asked him to explain this. He answered, "I never expected to have anything, so everything seems like a bonus." Glass overflowing. Another person in his circumstances could find a list as long as your arm of reasons to be disgruntled. Which will you be?

I love going to garage sales here in Minnesota in the summer. People drag their stuff out on the driveway or into the garage and try to get other people to buy it. It's like a local archeological dig. Visit 5 sales and you will get a picture of all the stuff we buy and are soon trying to give away. If buying all that throwaway stuff is making your household suffer, then it is time for a change. How different would it feel to pass up buying all the stuff you won't care about in one month, so when opportunities come that you really care about, you will have the means to grab it?

Practice being grateful. Practice lowering your expectations. Viewing your possessions as opportunities to share just increases joy and contentment. Contentment comes when we hold our things with open hands instead of hanging on with tight fists.

Keep your lives free from the love of money and be content with what you have, because God has said, "Never will I leave you; never will I forsake you."

HEBREWS 13:5

Watch Your language

I need a new dishwasher. I need a better car. I need to get my ankle tattooed.

Did I mention that I am very literal? It's true. I am a stickler for language. When we get sloppy with words, we get

sloppy with ideas and even decisions. I did a little experiment when my kids were little. I told my 3 small children I would give them a quarter for each time they caught me saying "I need . . ." Out of the 26 times I said it over 3 days, only 2 were legitimate needs such as "I need to take my insulin shot." I really don't *need* a scoop of ice cream or to sit in the hot tub. I realized how casually I claimed I *needed* something. When I boiled it down, there were very few things that I could not live without, but tons of extras that I would like to have. Claiming I need it makes it easier to rationalize getting what I want.

So now I try to tell my husband, "I would be more productive if . . ." or "It would save me a lot of time if . . .", "I would love to have . . ." because the truth is I don't need a new couch or another sweater or a cabin up north. Once my genuine needs are met (food, clothes, shelter), we can start sorting out the next priorities. Remember, we want to spend less on what we don't care about and more on what we do care about.

The High Cost of Living Beyond Your Means

Spending more than you make does not work long-term. Eventually, it catches up with you. The momentary thrill is replaced with the stress of debt, sometimes bill collectors, and tax audits. There might be a temporary thrill in buying a pair of shoes or taking that cruise, but it is usually short-lived. And the deeper you go in the hole, the harder it is to dig out.

Beyond your personal distress, it can take a big toll on your family and friendships. It's hard to relax and enjoy events and people when you are worried about money. I had a cousin who always cancelled coming to my house because she didn't have $10 to throw gas in the tank. It felt like I wasn't worth $10 to her. Money starts becoming the focus, not people.

Overspending robs you of peace and contentment — such a terribly high price tag, and for what? A bunch of stuff you are going to sell at a garage sale in 10 years.

There must be a better way . . .

The Goal of the Thrifty

The Goal of The Thrifty

"A budget is telling your money where to go instead of wondering where it went."
— *Dave Ramsey*

Jamie and her husband recently bought the lake home they have been dreaming of and saving to buy for 10 years.

The Whitneys saved for a month-long European vacation, with 3 of their 9 children, to visit a son stationed in Germany. Memories for a lifetime.

Very good friends of ours (to remain unnamed) simplified their life so they can donate upwards of 40% of their income to charities they care about.

Change the Paradigm

Wouldn't you like to sleep at night and wake up without dreading the coming day? Maybe it is time for a paradigm shift. A paradigm is the lens through which you see the world. Maybe your whole perspective has been that consuming is the highest achievement. I like to imagine picking up that paradigm, like a small globe, and looking at it from a variety of angles. There may be new perspectives to consider.

Maybe you don't want to be labeled 'thrifty,' but the merits are worth considering if your current plan is not working. My friend Jane always said, "If the horse is dead, dismount." Doing more of the same will not get different results. If overspending has not created the contentment, opportunities, and good relationships you hope for, it is time for a change.

There is one thing we can agree on: living in debt, or paycheck to paycheck, is a miserable way to live. We all want to afford the things that really mean the most.

Here's how I sum it up:

> *Spend less on what you don't care about*
> *and more on what you do.*

Our culture tells us that the main objective in life is acquiring, and many follow along blindly. Is it true? Is spending money the only way to get what you want?

I would argue that 'possessing' can take many forms. I used to assume that you earned money and then spent it to get the lifestyle you wanted, but that is not always the path. I see that in our friends, Scott and Lisa. They were typical suburbanites until they were asked to take over management of a small Bible camp. They packed up their 4 small boys and headed to northern Minnesota. They don't earn much, but their life is overflowing in the blessings of a small community, life on a lake, and plenty of meaningful work for growing boys. Plus, they are loved beyond measure by hundreds of campers. These are benefits they could not have purchased but enjoy as the result of their work and commitment to the camp.

Earn, spend, earn, spend, rinse, repeat. As you ponder a different paradigm, consider that there are many worthy objectives besides just earning and spending and different paths to reach those goals. Let's look at a few of the thought processes the thrifty use to evaluate wise handling of money and whether it is achieving the end they desire.

Demand Value

Thrifty people are looking to find the very best value they can get. This boils down to crunching a few numbers or, as we call it in science class, a Cost/Benefit Analysis. How does this work in practical terms?

Stretch a Dollar

Often, my husband and I know what we need — snow tires, for example — and know the brand we want to buy. Then I will go on a quest to find the best price for that specific tire. Other times, we set a budget and then see how much we can get for that allotment. This is a slightly different challenge.

On our last anniversary, we set aside $125 to celebrate. The question was, how much fun can we squeeze out of our $125? Here are a few options it opens up:

1) *dinner for 2 in an exclusive restaurant*
2) *dinner for 2 in a mid-priced restaurant and 2 tickets to a high school play*
3) *half day bike trip with a gourmet picnic lunch and new kayak paddles*
4) *a free art show, lunch and a new painting to commemorate the anniversary*

Then we get to decide which option will give us the most enjoyment for the money invested. For me, eating is just eating, so I would always take less expensive food, so as to have dinner and a movie for the cost of just dinner. By the way, I would vote for option 3.

This scenario played out in textbook fashion for our son. After college, he got an apartment by himself (which he loved), but it cost *a lot*. When he found a different place to rent with a bunch of great guys, he got a big roomy bedroom, use of the house kitchen, a garage and all his groceries for the same price as just his previous apartment. He spent the same amount but got so much more for his dollar. That is sssstttreetcchiinnggggg a dollar. It freed him to start saving for his next car.

Calculate Your Savings

I still remember reading this in *The Tightwad Gazette* 20 years ago. The author, Amy Dacyczyn, described calculating her hourly wage for different tasks such as washing sandwich bags or pureeing her own pumpkin for pie.

It may seem insignificant, but all those little tasks add up to money you do not need to earn and pay tax on. I recently made a birthday card. It took me 10 minutes and would have cost $3. I could make 6 in an hour for a cost savings at the rate of $18/hour. I would much rather make the card than go to work to pay for it.

Sewing on a button, shoveling snow, or changing the oil in your car are all services that can be purchased. Think about the trade-off of your time and money next time you want to use a disposable turkey roaster.

Trade Up

Amy Dacyczyn tells another great story in *The Tightwad Gazette*. She desperately wanted a large cast-iron cookstove to adorn her New England farm house. But instead of buying the stove they really wanted, they were offered a smaller version for $100 in desperate need of a good cleaning and stove blacking. They decided to try it, but when they set it up, they realized it didn't really fit the space. Getting the perfect stove would require a strategy called 'trading up.' I have a co-worker who did this with cars. He bought a fixer-upper, fixed it up and sold it at a profit to buy 2 more fixer-uppers. Eventually, for a $1200 investment, a lot of labor and some spare parts, he had a $20,000 muscle car.

Anyway, Amy and her husband sold that cleaned-up stove for $500, then proceeded to find a $500 stove in need of a little elbow grease. They sold that one also, and eventually they were able to own a stove worth over $800 for the initial investment of $100, plus the cost of a fire brick and stove blacking.

This can work for real estate, vehicles, furniture, or almost anything that might need some restoring and is in demand. Not a bad way to earn your way to a great acquisition.

Compare Benefit to Cost

Finally, compare the use and enjoyment of your various options. Will a $1,000 cruise yield 10 times the enjoyment of $100 camping trip? Maybe yes, maybe no. Will the highest-speed Internet (3 times the cost and 10,000 times faster) make your experience 3 times better? Maybe yes, maybe no. I find this very, very

helpful when I am tempted to upgrade. We try to carefully consider whether the benefit is so compelling that we are willing
to give up other things to gain it. Most of the time, we settle
for the economy version with no great loss.

Learn Love Languages

We all give and receive love differently. This idea is well
illustrated in Gary Chapman's book, *The 5 Love Languages.*
Chapman boils down the 5 main categories whereby people
give and receive love:

- *Acts of service*
- *Quality time*
- *Words of affirmation*
- *Touch*
- *Gifts*

If you think about it, only one love language involves material
objects, but we are told over and over that *if* you really love
someone, you will give them gifts.

There are 2 people in my family that rank gifts as their No.
1 love language — my husband and my son. I admit it is at the
bottom of my list, and I was annoyed that I would have to
spend money if I wanted to speak their 'language,' but surprisingly, it takes very little. Sometimes a pack of gum from the
grocery store or a new pair of socks or huge cardboard sheeting
from a dumpster (my husband needs it to cover flooring at

work) is enough to convey that I am thinking of them enough to bring home a small token to show it.

On the flip side, people who want time, service, touch, or encouraging words merely need us to intentionally make room for that (and stop just throwing stuff their way). My dear husband, who prefers tangible gifts, routinely offers to walk in the nature preserve with me because, not only do I love the fresh air, I love his time and attention. He could not buy me a more precious gift. But just for the record, he did buy me a kayak for Christmas one year — which was the best Christmas gift ever! — and then immediately had to buy himself one so I had a buddy to take on outings. Good thing he is a lot of fun to bring to the lake.

I am sure that what you care about most will look different than what I care about, and that is okay! Once you decide what you care about most, it is easier to let other things fall away. My hope is to give you a glimpse of how to:

Spend less on what you don't care about and more on what you do

Habits of the Thrifty

Habits of the Thrifty

"Beware of little expenses.
A small leak will sink a great ship."
— Benjamin Franklin

What the Thrifty Are Doing Right

When you think of the thrifty people you know, I bet you will find these common threads. These are the distinguishing qualities that let them get control of their money instead of money controlling them.

- *They spend less than they make.*

Sometimes a lot less.

Life is a great big word problem — just like math class, except it matters that you get this one right. First, add up all your income (actual take-home pay) to determine how much you make each month. Next, add up all your expenses. This includes monthly expenses such as a mortgage payment, insurance, groceries, entertainment, clothing, savings, etc. Add up your yearly expenses, such as Christmas gifts, vacations, sports fees, etc. Divide these by 12 (months) and add the result to your monthly expenses.

When you subtract your spending from your earning, you must have something left over, or you are heading for disaster. You can solve this problem 2 ways: 1) make more money 2) spend less. Almost anyone can look at their expenses and cut back immediately. If you want to get ahead and enjoy the rewards of financial stability, you must consistently spend less than you make. If you need help learning to budget, I recommend Dave Ramsey's *EveryDollar* budgeting tool.

- *They spend as little as possible on consumables.*
Less really is more.

People who manage their money well watch what they spend on food, clothes, and cars. These items lose their value. And, really, a $60 pair of jeans works as well as a $350 pair. They spend less on the things that get used up.

- *They save on autopilot and begin investing early.*
  It is so easy now to set up automatic savings with online banking. Set it and forget it. Recurring payments can be directed to different savings, retirement, or investment accounts. Review and adjust them once or twice a year.

- *They demand the best value (not just best price).*
  A price tag is one factor, but savvy consumers look at quality, durability, fixability, and flexibility (does it have more than one use?) This could be calculated by cost per month, cost per use, or looking at a total cost (costs beyond the price tag).

  Consider a cellphone. There is the one-time cost of buying it. There is the cost of a monthly service plan (lots of different options). There is a cost to fix it if it breaks. There is a cost to insure it against theft (optional). Somewhere between the bottom and the top-dollar option, there is a good value. Thrifty buyers take time to figure that out.

- *They use it up, wear it out, make do or do without.*
  I always hear this idea credited to the Amish. They were

the original 'green' consumers before recycling was even a word. Who says you can't wear a great coat for 15 years? Is there a rule somewhere?

- *They avoid clutter.*
  These people can find their hammer, packing tape, camping tent, spare batteries, or Christmas dishes when they want to use them. They aren't buying duplicates of what they already have.

- *They carefully invest in tools and education.*
  This does not mean just a college education, though that could be a great investment. There is so much to learn about finance, owning property, running a business, maintaining your car, etc. Thrifty people spend money to make themselves more valuable.

How to be Thrifty and Thriving

How to Be
Thrifty and Thriving
10 Simple Strategies

*"We make a living by what we get,
but we make a life by what we give."*
— Winston Churchill

Here are the strategies we use to trim our budget. Sometimes the savings are small, some are big, but it all adds up.

1. Shift (to cheaper versions)

We can't stop buying things, but we can shift our buying on

essentials such as food, gas, cars, and clothes. Shifting can involve less expensive stores, some DIY, changing the schedule, or buying in bulk. Keep a lookout for less-expensive but acceptable alternatives. Let's look at how this works with food.

Groceries

Everyone needs to eat, but not everyone needs to walk into a high-end grocery store and plunk down top dollar. Since food is an ongoing expense, the smarter you shop (or garden or can or swap) the more the savings rack up. I plan our grocery budget by the month. We consider eating out as entertainment dollars — not grocery dollars. We try to decide just how much fun we will have eating out when we could eat well at home for much less.

Our family of 5 spent $400/month on groceries all the time the kids were growing up. I know families that spend even less than that and families that spend $1,500/month. If you can eat healthy and tasty for less, why not save your dollars for something you really want?

You must be willing to alter some of your eating habits. Taste is acquired. It seems reasonable, when babies all over the world learn to eat and like whatever food they are fed. If children are expected to try and eat new things or even food they don't like — gasp! — they discover they can eat foods they do not want to eat and even grow to like them. Of course there are exceptions, but you get the idea. It is a basic part of training a child (or spouse) to require them to eat food that is good for them. That said, be brave and make changes.

Here are ways of keeping food costs down:

- **I only go to the grocery store every 2 weeks.** Seriously. Our family would scrape the bottom of the refrigerator clean before I went shopping. This resulted in 3 things:

  1) *We didn't waste food; we all know the 'fun' food gets eaten first*

  2) *When I came home with new groceries, they would rise up and call me blessed — see Proverbs 31*

  3) *It eliminated impulse buying*

  It is impossible to run into the grocery store for one thing and come out with one thing, especially if it is Costco! By not running to the store several times a week, I drastically reduced our grocery spending. One trick I used was freezing gallons of milk. If you take it out in the morning, give it 24 hours to thaw and shake it well, you can hardly tell the difference. Again, I think it builds some resilience to eat things a little out of our preferences. Moms tell me their kids would never drink unfrozen milk, but I think we should give kids more credit and less choice. And the earlier you start, the better!

- **I buy my meat from a local farmer.** About every 10 months I order a quarter cow, because that works for us.

I divide the cost by 10 and factor it into my monthly grocery spending. Because I get *all* the cuts at the same price (about $4/pound) we enjoy steaks and roasts and ribs, and it is grass-fed, no-hormones — the whole deal. I have friends who buy farm-raised chickens or go fishing in North Dakota, where there is no walleye fishing limit. Meat is a huge budget expense. Explore ways to stock up and spend less.

- **I grow a small garden** for fresh tomatoes, cucumbers, green peppers, and zucchini. Even if you just have small potted herbs, such as basil or cilantro, you not only save a little money but eat better. Any time we can eat food less processed or fresh, we are better off. Check out the *Square-foot Gardening* book.

- **We have a meatless dinner each week.**

- **I plan several days of meals around a meat.** If I cook a ham, we can have ham and potatoes, then ham and bean soup, ham and french toast, ham sandwiches, then ham fried rice. Larger quantities are usually cheaper, so there is less waste and cooking takes less time.

- **We pack our own lunches.** Yes, this is a chore, but everyone helps on a rotating basis. My husband sets a great example by taking a good lunch with him to work every day. Without exception. Without a fuss. Everyone is better off because there is less temptation to grab fast food. Eat better *and* save money.

- **I had to learn to cook.** I did not have cooking skills when we got married. So I read cookbooks, watched my friends cook, and then practiced and practiced. My dear husband never complained as long as there was food on the table, but he ate a lot of terrible dinners. His patience paid off, and now I am quite good. With acquired skill and my pantry basics on hand, I can make fast, easy meals any time without running to the store.

- **I shop at a discount grocery store** and adjust meals to items available at that store. Clipping and filing coupons is very time-consuming, plus much of the food sold with coupons is overprocessed and overpriced. It is much easier to go where everything is cheaper. I love Aldi stores the best.

- **I shop to stock the pantry, not for specific recipes.** When I was a new cook, I selected recipes and made a list of ingredients, then went to the store in search of that list of special items. As I got a better handle on coordinating a meal, I realized that if I stock the basics (cheese, veggies, fruit, rice and grains, butter, eggs, oils, along with meat, pastas, seasonal or sale items) I can always pull together a meal. For example, I keep a head of green cabbage on hand. It keeps a long time and I can add it to a stew, make kielbasa + cabbage + apples, or chop it up for coleslaw salad. Stock your pantry and you won't be running to the store repeatedly.

You don't need to copy what I do, but I hope it will give you ideas that can work with your family. These ideas apply to cellphone service, clothing, home and car insurance, garbage service, etc. Keep your eyes open for acceptable alternatives and you could start shifting today.

2. Scrounge (from thrift stores, cast-offs, family, etc)

Keep your eyes and ears open, because you never know what might float your way. Pop into thrift stores and garage sales. Carry a notebook with pant/waist sizes, shoe sizes or room dimensions, so you can grab a bargain if you see one. I have found my best deals when I was not looking for anything specific, just scanning for what I would need in the future. For example, because we live in Minnesota, I knew the kids would need bigger snow boots and snow pants each winter (minus whatever got passed down). Since I kept a lookout, I never had to pay full price at the beginning of winter for winter clothing.

Instead of hunting for a specific item (gray, wool-flannel armchair) think in more general terms such as 'chair' or 'something to sit on.' You can often find interesting and cheap items that will work. Be sure to mention whatever you are looking for to everyone you see, because someone always knows someone who knows someone who is trying to get rid of something. If I walk all around my house I see many items I brought home, then discovered a way to make them fill a hole.

One of my favorite furniture finds was a low bedroom dresser that we painted for our living room. It works as a sideboard right at the top of the stairs, with lots of storage drawers. Each drawer face is a slightly different color from the frame. Once it was painted, no one suspected it had been intended for a bedroom. Now it is even chic to use dressers as vanities in bathrooms. Keep an open mind and look at things for their possibilities.

Never refuse, always accept hand-me-downs or 'goodie bags.' Accept anything you are offered unless you seriously can't fit it into your house, and then use it, fix it up, sell it, or

donate it right away. I will take 4 bags of girls' clothes to sort through, even if I find just one great pair of pants, then happily donate the rest. Amy Dacyczyn, author of *The Tightwad Gazette*, encouraged readers to calculate the return on their time. If I can whip through 4 bags of clothes in 15 minutes and find one $40 pair of pants that we need and will use, that's equivalent to earning $160 per hour. It feels great.

Breeze through sale racks routinely — don't even look at the front of the store, just make a beeline for the back, where the marked-down items are.

Consider the dumpster dive (with permission). My husband works in construction, so after a tear-out there are often good appliances, light fixtures, sinks, etc., being thrown away. A year ago he brought home a high-end toilet (goodie!). It sat in our shed awaiting our bathroom remodel. In the meantime, our dear friends with 4 small boys (and 1 on the way) moved into their first house. The lower-level bathroom desperately needed a new toilet, so we decided to give them the shed toilet (Steve even in-stalled it). And do you know, 3 weeks later he picked up another toilet to bring home? And would you believe our friends decided to change the upstairs toilet, too? So we gave it to them. They were very grateful.

The point is, save it to use it, not just fill your shed. If an item has good life left and can be reused, then money can be spent on something else — like a giant swing set for the backyard for those 5 little boys! That's much more satisfying. Again, spend less on what you don't care about, so you can spend more on the things you do care about.

3. Simplify (less stuff, less services, less to take care of)

It may seem unrelated, but having too much stuff carries a high price tag. Ever had to go buy something you know you have but couldn't find? If that happens routinely, you have more stuff than you can manage. I know people save stuff because they think they will use it in the future, but be honest: most of our stashed stuff never sees the light of day.

We had a rule for our kids: if you can't tidy your room in 10 minutes, you have more stuff than can be easily managed. We worked on choosing things to pass on to other boys and girls to enjoy. More is not always more. By practicing this as a family, we kept our whole house pared down and manageable.

Have a zero sum gain mentality. If you bring something in, take something out. This is especially important around birthdays and holidays. It is so easy to accumulate — keep a thrift store box in some closet to throw items in as soon as you realize you won't be needing them, and teach your kids to do the same.

Love collecting? Try selling collectibles instead of just acquiring them. You can turn a passion into a small business, instead of just filling up your house.

Develop a wardrobe 'uniform.' This idea came from Kathi Lipp in her book *Clutter Free*. Determine the look you need for your lifestyle and buy fewer pieces, but ones that mix and match within a color scheme. Try not to buy that strange blouse that requires specific pants and shoes and accessories. The more your clothes mix together, the less you need to buy and still look put-together.

Simplify gift-giving by keeping a box of items to pull out (bought on sale, of course). This works especially well for baby shower gifts and hostess gifts. My mom is really good about stocking up on greeting cards for various occasions. Simplify potlucks by bringing the same thing each time. My deviled eggs are always a hit, and I always have the ingredients on

hand (eggs, mayo, mustard). Fewer decisions, less running around. Done.

4. Sort (your mail immediately)

When you carry in the mail, don't set it down! I watched my mother do this for years. I can still see her coming in with the mail, standing over the garbage can, tossing all the junk mail, setting bills or action items on her writing desk, and opening letters and cards to read. Done.

The advantages are numerous, but this is by far the best way to avoid late bills, late fees, and missed notices. I have paid fees I could have avoided and am sure you have, too.

5. Step Up (and learn to fix your own toilet handle)

There are so many simple skills that can save lots of time and lots of money. In the old days we had to find someone to show us how or go find a book in the library, but with YouTube I think you could even learn to do brain surgery if pressed.

In college, I had the chance to learn to cut hair. I bought a nice pair of scissors and a Wahl clipper. I had watched my dad cut my brother's hair and had seen my mom cut her own bangs, so I figured with a little trial and error I could figure it out. Plus, I had a whole dorm full of financially strapped college students willing to let me practice. As a result, my own kids never went to a salon until they were old enough to pay for it themselves, and my husband hasn't been to a barber since we got married.

Even if you can learn just a couple of things, it builds your confidence and puts a little money back in your pocket. Here are some ideas:

- *Learn to cook.*
- *Practice planning your meals.* They can be simple and

repetitive, but it's the key to avoid wasting food, or panicking when everyone is hungry and rushing out to eat.

- *Learn to sew* — or at least sew on a button. I have bought many shirts at the thrift store that were just missing a button. You can pick up a sewing machine — someone may even give you an old one if you ask — and learn to sew a simple straight line to fix a rip or shorten your pants. There are lots of great video tutorials on the Internet.

  My daughters received so many beautiful clothes from their very tall cousin. I shortened lots of pants, which were then greatly enjoyed and cost us nothing. If you get good at altering, you could even have a little side gig doing it for others.

- *Learn simple car maintenance,* such as changing the oil and checking the tire pressure.

- *Learn to sell on Amazon.*

- *Learn to do your taxes* with a great software such as *TurboTax.* For simple returns, this is a no-brainer.

- *Learn to build websites* if you are techy. The demand for this will only keep growing.

- *Learn to garden.*

- *Learn to roll your own sushi.*

- *Learn to speak a foreign language.*

Between YouTube and the public library, there is more skills training available than you can learn in a lifetime. Pick something that suits you and start learning.

6. Swap (skills, tools, knowledge, time...)

Instead of looking at what you don't have (money), look at what you do have. When our children were very little, my husband worked in radio and we were barely scraping by. We had no family nearby and couldn't afford to pay a sitter, so I asked a friend (who also had 3 small children and was likewise strapped) if her family would like to swap date nights. They did! So every Thursday we either watched their kids, which was a treat for our children, or we got to go out. I was able to plan ahead and keep a lookout for restaurant coupons or free museum passes, or we would plan a bike ride or walk downtown by the river. Just the anticipation was worth half of the outing.

You may think you have nothing to trade, but can you watch a dog, water plants during a vacation, pick up mail, or vacuum a living room? You would be surprised how many ways you can offer services to  friends and neighbors and both come out ahead. Give it a try!

7. Share (with like-minded people)

There are items in life that are very useful but are needed infrequently. Living in Minnesota, we need the whole range of lawn and garden and tree care in addition to snow removal.

Look for neighbors, friends, or family who would be willing to pitch in and share certain items. This works best with items that are not used often. For example, I love edging our sidewalk. This involves cutting the grass back along the sidewalk. It looks so neat and trim, but it only needs to be done once a year. We borrow our neighbor Keith's edger, and since he owns every tool under the sun, we return the value in other ways, such as lending him our kayaks for an afternoon or sending over a pack of steaks.

In our part of the city, there is a strong tradition of giving an outdoor open house for graduating high school seniors. This strikes terror into the hearts of most parents, as they try to envision 200 people eating and playing at a house designed for 6.

Of course, none of us have 2 yard tents, 12 tables, 100 folding chairs and 2 roaster ovens lying around, but I do have a couple of thrifty friends. We started picking up items at yard sales. We pitched in to buy tents on sale, then planned our parties so they weren't at the same time. We even had a little calendar. One year we were at the end of 3 different parties that we wrapped up by taking down the tents, chairs, tables and loading them up to go to the next house. Genius!

I have a classic memory of my frugal mother and her 2 sisters. They invested in a crystal punch bowl, ladle and 16 crystal cups. You know, the kind you can't give away today. That bowl appeared in at least 6 wedding showers, 8 baby showers, a 50th wedding anniversary, and at least a couple of birthday parties. When it was sitting in the pile by the door to go to Auntie Marilyn, I knew there was a party in the works.

Speaking of my mother and her identical twin sister, here is the ultimate in swapping. About 10 years ago they discovered they sometimes sent the same birthday card more than once to each other without realizing it. As a joke, they both (without telling each other) saved the card they received from each other in 2009, added a note and sent it back the following year. They thought this was so funny, they have continued to use the same 2 cards ever since. Yes, twins actually do a lot of the same things without talking it over. And don't even get me started talking about their clothes.

Here are a few guidelines for helping everyone stay on the same page before you start the give-and-take:

- *Test people out by first offering to loan an item.* If they want to 'play,' they will reciprocate by offering something back at a later date. Don't push if they are not interested. Keep asking and you will find those kindred spirits.

- *Items should be returned in the same condition they were borrowed.* If that rake gets bent, it should be replaced. If a neighbor isn't willing to honor the commitment to replacing damaged or broken items, best to find different swappers.

- *It is generally best to have single ownership, not pool the money and have joint ownership.* For example, instead of 3 families pitching in $150 for a snowblower, one family should buy and share the snowblower; one could buy and share a table saw; and one could maintain a small trailer for sharing. Then if someone moves or decides to stop sharing, there is no messy division.

- *Have a set borrowing time, like the library.* Mention a specific time right at the beginning. Don't assume everyone has the same sense of timing. "Here you go. Could you get that back by Wednesday evening?" or "I plan to use this tomorrow, can I return it this weekend?" Three days should be enough unless other arrangements are made.

- *Be willing to ask for your item back, but also be willing to let it go if it never comes back and move on a little wiser.*

- *It's great if you can share and reciprocate with something you needed to buy anyway.* That's a win-win.

In general, this has built goodwill and closer interaction with our neighbors, and we are glad for that. Have grace for people that disappoint and just move on.

8. Schedule

Here's an idea to throw in your hopper — *schedule it, and they will come*. After 15 years of organizing student activities, I concluded I could create a sensation with just 3 things:

- *an activity or idea*
- *another mother to help lead*
- *a date on the calendar*

Parents pay hundreds and even thousands of dollars to put their kids in organized activities. If you want group experiences for your children, there is a Do-It-Yourself option (oh, boy!).

Here is how it worked for us. My eldest daughter received a coveted invitation to attend a 6-week book club at Mrs. Whitacker's house. They met once a week for an hour and a half. She thoughtfully put together a half-hour of discussion, a related craft, and something to bake in the kitchen. It was the highlight of Brooke's week.

When my youngest turned 10, I realized most of her time was spent being schlepped to her big brother and sister's activities, so I decided I would try organizing a small book club. If it lasted only 6 or 7 weeks, I could untangle myself at the end if it was a disaster or too demanding. She was a reluctant reader, so I hoped this would provide positive peer pressure to read and think about books.

My beautiful, artistic friend Rachael jumped right in. She was the 'face' of the club, meaning I found a book, broke it into

7 weeks, made a simple workbook, and planned a craft and cooking activity for each week. Then I gathered the materials and Rachael led the class time, while I was there to help with crowd control and cleanup.

It was a success. We had 10 girls sign up immediately, and those 10 stayed together for the next 8 years. They formed such good friendships it led to many other shared classes and activities. We even took them on a yearly overnight outing at a donation-based retreat center (making sure to leave a good donation).

You might be thinking, "I couldn't do that; it is too much work," or "I am not creative," or "I don't know any other families." Those may be valid objections, but they can be overcome. Most things worth doing are hard — especially at first (try writing a book!). Sure, I could have taken a job and then paid other people to entertain my kids. Sometimes I did. But the best memories, the best friendships, and the life skills that came out of that book club were priceless.

And here is the fruit of doing this with your kids. My eldest daughter started her own craft club to earn money for her year on Rotary Youth Exchange. She had 14 girls come for 10 weeks in 2 separate groups. She taught watercolor journaling. She was 17 at the time and the girls were 9–12 years old, and boy, did they think she was special. She charged $6/girl per week and the mothers were happy to pay it. You can do the math.

If you decide to start a club, for example a boys' woodwork-

ing club, you don't need to reinvent the wheel. Go to Home Depot, Pinterest, or Google and search for woodcrafts for boys. Use ideas that work with your space and tools and budget.

We have friends who live on a lake. They have a standing boot hockey pickup game every Sunday afternoon at 4 pm, December through February. With a little work to keep the ice clean, we have entertainment, exercise and fellowship. Excellent return on investment, simply by putting it on the calendar.

Do you know something about sewing? Start a small sewing class. You can easily pick up 4 sewing machines for almost nothing. Set a time to work together and help new sewers build skills, get past tough spots, and make new friends.

This could work for adult activities as well as kids. Start a biking club or Bible study. A lady in our church meets with 3 other women each week. Their year-long project is collecting items to pack in shoeboxes to ship to kids around the world with Samaritan's Purse (called Operation Christmas Child).

Test it and see — you will be amazed.

9. Shop (and stock up on bargains)

Thrifty people are happier saving money than spending it, but the reality is that we buy and acquire things on a constant basis. Since we need to shop, be as smart and prepared as possible to take advantage of deals. This means being on the lookout and having cash available to jump on a good value. Caution: the key is to only buy items you would have purchased anyway. Don't become the yard sale hoarder who can't pass up a bargain just because it is a bargain. You haven't gained value if you pay for something that you don't need. This is why I generally don't use coupons, because they convince me to buy things I wouldn't buy otherwise, and that is a waste of good money.

My husband and I grooved this idea into our thinking early on, after watching each other come home with 'great bargains.' He would spot very different things than I would. For example, he would come home with 4 jars of sidewalk salt (to melt ice) at 85% off in July. It wasn't on my radar, but it made great sense when I thought about it: 1) we would use it; 2) it was not perishable; 3) we got 4 jars in July for less than the price of 1 in December. Gold star for Steve!

I hate spending money on toilet paper. I have been on a 20-year quest to find the absolute least amount we can spend on toilet paper. At one point I was convinced that the 1-ply, 20-roll pack gave the lowest cost per square. And then the 20-pack went on sale. I came home with 10 (yes, 10!) packs of 20. Where does one put 200 rolls of toilet paper, and why? As dubious as my husband was, he had to admit that $.30 a roll compared to $1.25 for the name brand 2-ply cushy stuff was a much better value. Over the course of the year, that freed up about $75 toward the electric bill.

Steve started stocking up on other nonperishable stuff. When oil was on sale (of course he changes all the oil in our cars) he'd grab a couple of cases and even more if there was a rebate.

These days, I buy 10 boxes of lasagna noodles at a time because I can't get them at the discount store and I want to minimize trips to the expensive store.

We also try to keep our eyes open for items we will need in the future that are very specific, such as winter boots, paper for the printer, thank-you cards, canned tomatoes, tea candles, paper towels. You get the idea. I know a local soap maker that will sell me unscented castille soap at wholesale cost. I buy the entire batch, cut but unwrapped, for $1 bar. It is wonderful, creamy soap from just olive oil, palm oil and coconut oil. It would sell for about $6 a bar retail.

Our local discount outlet store sells flats of berries super cheap in season. We wash and freeze them for smoothies all winter. In addition, I buy 2 or 3 50-pound bags of wheat berry once a year for about $30 each. I grind it in my Whisper Mill and make a loaf of bread a week. Mmmm, can't you just smell it baking?

Here is another trick I use to help keep our food budget lower. I buy a few treats at the grocery store so the family doesn't feel deprived or run to the store to get overpriced candy or pop (that means soda, in Minnesotan). You can buy a

5-quart pail of ice cream for the cost of one large Dairy Queen Blizzard. My goal isn't to make everyone miserable but to maximize our enjoyment for the least cost.

Here is another version of 'plan ahead.' My husband works in construction and wears through the toes of his shoes  quickly, so we always take a quick scan down the shoe aisle in any thrift store. Once in a while he gets a barely worn pair of leather shoes for a fraction of the cost of brand-new work boots.

I am sure there are many ways your family can shop smart, stock up, and save when the deals are good. If you can't remember prices for comparing, keep a small notebook for recording grocery prices and other details, including the shoe and pant sizes of all the people in your family. If you love to shop, make this your new challenge.

10. Spend (YES! on tools and education)

There is a time and a place to plunk down your money. Two of the best reasons are investing in tools and what I call 'life's tuition'. This can be formal or informal education, but it makes you more valuable and more versatile. Keep your eyes open for some of these different possibilities:

- *Invest in tools*

Back in the early '90s, we took the plunge and bought an Apple LC computer so I could freelance as a typesetter from our house. Almost no one had home computers at that point, and it seemed extravagant. But that computer more than paid for itself in jobs and kept me learning new software and developing my graphic design skills. The computer was an essential tool, and the bonus was a computer for our family to use.

Another great purchase was our Vitamix (a blender on steroids). We use it to make smoothies, soups, and gravy, and to puree pumpkin and tomatoes. It gets used every day. You can't always know if a tool will work well for your family. Do as much research as you can, and then you just have to try it. If you find you bought something you really don't use — sell it and move on. My husband will tell you that most things boil down to having the right tool for the job.

- *Invest in sports and recreation equipment*
  Buy good quality first- or second-hand sports equipment for hours and hours of recreation and exercise. Once you are properly outfitted, you can use your items at very little or zero ongoing expense. We used our first bikes for 20 years and put hundreds and hundreds of miles on them. Our favorite items include our bikes with baby trailers (Minneapolis is one of the top 10 cities in the world for bike trails), our kayaks and my walking shoes. These items have

paid for themselves over and over again.

- *Buy non battery-operated toys*
  Legos, Duplos, dress-up clothes, puzzles, and board games give such great value, in addition to contributing to brain development and social skills.

- *Learning — life's tuition*
  Sometimes it is worth paying to learn from an expert. For a monthly subscription, *Lynda.com* will train you at home on almost any software on the planet. Night school, conferences, community college, apprenticeships, or coaching can mean a substantial increase in your earning power over the years.

  I paid good money to have Christopher John Payne coach me through writing this book. (It is actually my second because the first one was so bad I had to scrap it.) It has been a lot of work with a steep learning curve, and I could not have done this without his help and encouragement. His expertise was an investment in a goal I wanted to achieve, and what I gained is invaluable. Now I know how to tackle other writing project ideas.

Remember, don't just look at a price tag; look at the value, the savings, the benefits, and how much a purchase may improve your position. You can happily spend on these things that really add to the quality of life.

Now we have looked at the 10 Simple Strategies that can drastically cut your expenses. Don't get overwhelmed by the sheer volume of ideas. Any change begins with small steps. Remember the movie *What About Bob?* It comically portrays the idea that change begins with baby steps, and that is so true.

Instead of aiming for saving $X, let me encourage you to just change one thing today, then calculate what you saved. It could be swapping with a neighbor or visiting a discount grocery store. Pick a strategy instead of a dollar amount. Once it starts becoming a routine and you see how much less you are spending, add another strategy. Remember: it all adds up, and soon you will see that you are spending less on what you don't really care about and have more to spend on what you do.

Rewards for the Thrifty

Rewards for the Thrifty

"The habit of saving is itself an education; it fosters every virtue, teaches self-denial, cultivates the sense of order, trains to forethought, and so broadens the mind."
— *T. T. Munger*

Now we get to the 'thriving' part. Thriving means looking forward to things you have planned, not living in fear of bills. It means enjoying your friends and family, and having time and space to be creative. You may not even notice it is happening, but at some point, you look back and realize you are doing great. Some of the very best things in life can't be bought.

Here are some things to look forward to — the list could go on and on.

Expand Your Creativity

At its core, creativity is problem-solving. Working within tight limits can really stretch your imagination. I had a friend who was a fantastic cook but spared no expense on ingredients — and you could taste it. However, I was coordinating a weekend retreat for 10 6th-grade girls and asked her to make a dinner for $10. She thought I meant $10 each. No. $10 total. Well, she was sure that wasn't possible, but I told her it was all we had budgeted. You know what she came up with? The best macaroni and cheese casserole you ever tasted. Two dollars' worth of pasta and 8 dollars worth of real cheese. Yum. Forced creativity with great results.

Practice Sharing

If 'necessity is the mother of invention' (thank you, Ben Franklin), then exploring ways to give and take can be fun, frugal, and yes, sometimes frustrating. The more affluent we become, the less we practice sharing, but can set out to retrain friends and neighbors and hopefully build some goodwill.

We all have things around our house that we use once a year, maybe more, maybe less. What if you shared that punch bowl or weed trimmer or set of folding chairs? Start by offering to loan small items and see who reciprocates. After a while, you will find like-minded friends who will loan, borrow, and return in a timely way. Let go of those who don't choose to 'play.' This shared cooperation can build some good friendships and help us not hang on so tightly to our stuff.

Forced Exercise

Think of all the exertion you will make when you don't pay others to do things for you — walk your own dog, paint your living room, clean your house, mow the lawn, bag your groceries, plant your flowers . . . the list is endless. It is a great side benefit and pays off in health and well-being. Why pay for a gym membership if you are moving all day long? Some of the most inexpensive entertainment involves activity.

When I was homeschooling our young children, I had a rule that I would never sit and watch if it was an option for me to join in. So, during swim lessons, I swam laps while they were in class. I skied with them (instead of sitting in the chalet); we biked to the library instead of taking the car. If there was a kickball game, I was all in. Once I was in the habit, I did it without thinking. Imagine all the exercise I got without really trying to find it. Walking, biking, swimming, hiking, skating, and jogging are basically free, with a small investment

in equipment, and pay high dividends in wellness and well-being (and can be a lot of fun!).

Enjoy Contentment

> *"Who is rich? He that rejoices in his portion."*
> — *Benjamin Franklin*

Believe it or not, researchers in one study found that people rate their happiness the highest when they are earning about $70,000 a year. Enough, but not too much. I remember, clear as a bell, reading the classic novel *Robinson Crusoe* out loud to our children and marveling at the wisdom Daniel Defoe wrapped into this novel from the 1700s. In the very first chapter, his father is exhorting young Crusoe to be grateful for a middle class life.

> *My father, a wise and grave man, gave me serious and excellent counsel against what he foresaw was my design. He called me one morning into his chamber, where he was confined by the gout, and expostulated very warmly with me upon this subject. He asked me what reasons, more than a mere wandering inclination, I had for leaving father's house and my native country, where I might be well introduced, and had a prospect of raising my fortune by application and industry, with a life of ease and pleasure. He told me it was men of desperate fortunes on one hand, or of aspiring, superior fortunes on the other, who went abroad upon adventures, to rise by enterprise, and make them-*

selves famous in undertakings of a nature out of the common road; that these things were all either too far above me or too far below me; **that mine was the middle state, or what might be called the upper station of low life, which he had found, by long experience, was the best state in the world,** *the most suited to human happiness, not exposed to the miseries and hardships, the labour and sufferings of the mechanic part of mankind, and not embarrassed with the pride, luxury, ambition, and envy of the upper part of mankind. He told me I might judge of the happiness of this state by this one thing — viz. that this was the state of life which all other people envied; that kings have frequently lamented the miserable consequence of being born to great things, and wished they had been placed in the middle of the 2 extremes, between the mean and the great; that the wise man gave his testimony to this, as the standard of felicity, when he prayed to have neither poverty nor riches . . .*

Ah, to be satisfied with life in the middle class. Of course, he ignored his father and went to sea anyway, and that did not end well. Read it for yourself and consider.

Less Stuff

If you have never lived in a clutter-free house, you are in for a real treat.

Less Stress

Less stuff, less pressure to maintain all the stuff, less income to live well, more time for people. All good stuff.

More Options

My son was recently asked to go on a band tour for one month. He works at a day job and lives with a bunch of guys. I am always harping on him to 'expect the unexpected' and save accordingly.

To my surprise (and delight), he had stashed a bit of money aside and could take a leave from his job for this once-in-a-lifetime experience. Way to go! Leaving a little margin in your life lets you take advantage of unexpected opportunities when you least expect it!

Defined Priorities

Making time to look at your buying choices forces you to decide what is most important and is the start of making it happen. "I could never do what you do." You don't need to. You get to figure out what is important in *your* family, and don't let other things crowd it out.

Better Relationships

Money is one of the most common topics that cause marital friction. As you gain control over your spending and start working in your family toward common goals, there is less fighting over where the resources go.

In addition, working together to creatively save and earn money can be great for bonding. My husband knows how much it endears me to hear he remembered to use the AAA discount at the auto parts store. Treating your money carefully becomes a team effort, and teams root for each other and stick together. Even the kids feel like they can contribute when there are clear boundaries and goals to achieve together (can you say Disney World?).

Financial Security

You may never be a millionaire or live in Beverly Hills, but if you can pay your bills, help a neighbor in need, handle reasonable emergencies, take care of your children, or pay off your mortgage, you will be putting yourself in a better and better financial situation instead of falling further behind. That's a great feeling.

These are just a few of the benefits you will reap. And, of course, you will spend less on what you don't care about and more on what you do — *yeah!*

A Final Word

I have to give a shout out to Amy Dacyczyn, a.k.a. The Frugal Zealot. I began reading her newsletter, *The Tightwad Gazette*, as a young mother (maybe like you are now). She seemed like a good friend, reassuring me that thrifty living could be fun and rich and rewarding. She was right.

Don't get overwhelmed. I have given lots of ideas. Pick the few that make sense and will provide the biggest difference right away. For example, this could be trimming your grocery budget, dropping your gym membership to take up cycling, or selling a brand-new vehicle for a pre-owned one. Review the strategies again later and implement something else. It is a constant learning process. Trust me, I am always gleaning new ideas and tips that work for us.

Using your resources thoughtfully (instead of carelessly) is an idea intended to give you more peace and freedom and choice. Don't turn it into a chore or punishment. We all have means to live within, so do it well and be proud. Spend less on what you don't care about and more on what you do. My prayer is that you will have room in life for fun with your children, time with your spouse, sharing a meal with a sick neighbor, fresh air, and the things that mean the very most to you.

About the Author

Please think of me as a friend down the street hoping to share what I have learned.

As we raised our 3 children, we chose to homeschool and my husband worked as a tile setter. We have college degrees but gave up my income to allow me to stay home. Most years we have been self-employed without most common job benefits. We live simply, enjoying frugal things such as the public library, bike rides, thrift stores, repairing our own cars, great friends, swimming in the lake, cooking from scratch and mending clothes — just like the pioneers. (Well, not really, haha!) But we had more time together and more control over our time.

Yes, we need income, but we found we could live on much less than one would think and still look like everyone around us. I did some freelance graphic design work. We learned skills and how to make our own fun. It forced our kids to find meaningful work for pocket money and creative ways to pay for their education. Our 7-year-old got her 9-year-old sister to help write a contract offering to walk the neighbor's dog. She was hired on the spot and walked that dog 6 days a week for the next 7 years!

As an empty-nester, I have re-entered the work world and am enjoying this new season of life. And I have been shocked to learn that many of my double-income co-workers have less money saved than we did earning half as much.

So, I decided to share some of the things I have learned through watching others and practicing. Maybe someone out there is curious enough to consider doing the same. I talk with women who tell me, "Oh, I could never live on one income." I just want to say, "Friend, you don't give yourself enough credit. I am nothing special. You *can* do it, too."

It's never too late to start rowing the other direction! It will be worth every stroke. I assure you, the payoff is greater than anything money can buy.

— *Jennie Lodien*

"The world of the generous

gets larger and larger;

the world of the stingy

gets smaller and smaller.

The one who blesses others

is abundantly blessed;

those who help others are helped."

PROVERBS 11:24-25

(Mostly) Free Ideas

Ways to Save Money this Week

- Eat one meatless meal.
- Reduce your internet service to economy speed — most likely you won't even notice the difference.
- Check your cable subscription so you are only paying for channels you want to watch (or drop it all together).
- Stop paying fees at your bank. Insist they find you accounts without fees or change banks.
- Never carry a credit-card balance. Pay it off every month.
- Invite friends over instead of going out.
- Mend your clothes instead of donating or tossing.
- Drink more water and use a refillable bottle.
- Make your own cup of coffee.
- Shop yard sales, but only buy what you really need.
- Find a discount grocery store (did someone say Aldi?)
- Cancel a club membership unless you get really good value from it.
- Buy used when you can.

- Donate your time instead of money.
- Avoid the mall. Stay away from the mall. Don't go near the mall.
- Swap babysitting with a friend.
- Volunteer so you get free entrance (museum, concerts, zoo, etc).
- Pack a lunch.
- Dress simply in mix-and-match.
- Invest in a chest freezer — this will revolutionize your food budget and cooking.
- Consider moving to a cheaper place.
- Try to fix things yourself — YouTube is amazing for instructional videos.
- Have a thrift-store Christmas. This has been surprisingly fun and the kids have come home with some really creative finds on a budget.
- Stage your own yard sale and turn junk into cash.

Ways to Have Fun
- My best advice is to read books together. I cannot overstate the value of reading out loud with your kids. You will share

stories and experiences in a way that leaves a bigger impact than anything else. My favorite list of read-aloud books is called *Hand that Rocks the Cradle,* by Nathaniel Bluedorn. He recounts listening to his mother read to his siblings with such clarity and affection it will make you want to run to the library. Even if you only read the introduction, it is worth the price of the book. This treasure is available for free to anyone with a library card.

- Walk with a friend.
- Visit local museums on 'free' days.
- Pop over to the library and check out a movie.
- Attend free concerts.
- Bike somewhere new.
- Start a book club on a theme you love.
- Find a book on urban foraging, then go out and practice identifying plants.
- Plant a garden on the cheap (put the word out you want seeds and clippings).
- Swim at the local beach.
- Braid a rag rug from old t-shirts.
- Exchange recipes and put together a personal recipe book.
- Have an ugly cake contest.
- Play board games.
- Volunteer at a local food packing charity (such as Feed My Starving Children).

- Volunteer at banquets and galas.
- Help an elderly neighbor.
- Organize a family talent show.
- Plan your own Amazing Race contest.
- Cook a creative meal.
- Try on new outfit combinations.
- Rearrange your furniture.
- Visit your grandparents and play Scrabble.
- List things you don't want on Craigslist and watch them go out the door.
- Paint the bathroom — changing color gives a real boost.
- Pack a picnic and head to a local park.
- Learn a new skill on YouTube (how to apply makeup for women over 50?)
- Invite family to a backyard potluck and beanbag toss tourney.

Great Resources

Here are a few of the books that made a big impact on me. Don't neglect your education!

The Tightwad Gazette I, II & III by Amy Dacyczyn

I learned more about economics from Amy than I ever did in my college classes. She started a newsletter in the '90s that was smart and fun and full of inspiration. She didn't just give tips on saving money; she delved into the decision-making and cost/benefit analysis processes that make you a smart consumer. All this, and she is very funny. Plus, she is a graphic designer (like me), and back then I didn't know anyone else who was a graphic designer. I loved the layout of her books as much as the content. I recommend anything she has written.

Clutter Free: Quick and Easy Steps to Simplifying Your Space by Kathi Lipp

> Written in an easy, encouraging tone with tons of practical ideas for tackling your piles. I never get tired of gleaning tips, and this book is a treasure.

Financial Peace by Dave Ramsey

> If you need to start at the beginning with money management, he is one of the best to help you reset from out-of-control debt.

How to Manage Your Money by Larry Burkett

> A look at biblical money principles from a financial pioneer. Did you know Jesus talked more about money than just about anything else?

The 7 Habits of Highly Effective People by Stephen Covey

> It seems so obvious once you have read it, but this is a powerful book to help you clarify your goals and values.

Margin: Restoring Emotional, Physical, Financial, and Time Reserves to Overloaded Lives by Richard Swenson

> Wow, this book hits the nail on the head. Because handling money flows into all areas of life. Which is the good news and the bad news.

For the Children's Sake by Susan Schaeffer Macaulay
Rethink what constitutes an education. We gave up an income to educate our own kids and gained all the things we cared about.

More with Less by Doris Longacre
A Mennonite cookbook that shows how to make simple, inexpensive and often meatless meals from the perspective of good stewardship.

Speed Cleaning by Jeff Campbell
As a young mom, my homemaking skills were pretty bad. He convinced me to clean faster and more efficiently. His mottos are "If it isn't dirty, don't clean it" and "Top to bottom."

Are You Next? by Christopher John Payne
I hope so! Thank you to my wonderful mentor and coach Chris Payne. I will always be grateful for the encouragement he gave me to write this book.

All Creatures Great and Small by James Herriott
This book encapsulates a simpler way of life, with rich relationships, and the challenges that are part of it. One of my absolute favorite memories is listening to my dad laugh out loud in the living room while he was reading it. Herriott is one of the most gifted storytellers ever.

Book of Proverbs
There is no greater wisdom for dealing with people and money than the Bible.

Hand That Rocks the Cradle: Good Books to Read Aloud to Children by Nathaniel Bluedorn
One of my most favorite lists for read-aloud books, because it is a collection put together by the grown children. Many lists are geared toward girls, but Nathaniel's list contained books that were enjoyed immensely by our whole family.

The Treasure Principle by Randy Alcorn
There is more to do with money than just spending it. This tiny volume made a big impact on me.

Whatever Happened to Penny Candy? by Richard J Maybury
Economics simply explained.

Squarefoot Gardening by Mel Bartholomew
Squarefoot gardening is the most practical, foolproof way to grow a garden, whether you live in an apartment or have an entire backyard. Mel developed his techniques back in the early 1980s and has been teaching them around the world ever since. In the process, he has made improvements and refinements, and has continually adapted his practices to keep pace with modern times.

The 5 Love Languages by Gary Chapman

A great insight into the different ways people give and receive love. He has online tests to help you understand the love languages of everyone in your family and express your love more effectively.

References

Page 21

1. Marsha L. Richins, *Journal of Consumer Research*
    Vol. 40, No. 1 (June 2013), pp. 1-18

Page 23

2. Journal Reference: Stephen M. Garcia, Kimberlee
    Weaver, Patricia Chen. The Status Signals Paradox.
    Social Psychological and Personality Science, 2018

Printed in Great Britain
by Amazon

FRANCE by TROLLEYBUS

Published by Trolleybooks Joint Publications Panel
52 Claudius Way, Witham, Essex CM8 1PZ

Printed by B.T.S. Printing, Reading, Berkshire

Martin Nimmo

ISBN 0 904235 11 4

COVER PHOTOGRAPH

STAS (St. Etienne) 427, of the second (Alsthom-motored) batch of ER100s, turns at Bellevue before setting off for the long interurban run to Firminy.

Photo: M.P.M. Nimmo

Contents

Acknowledgements

It would have been difficult to produce this book without the assistance I have received over the past few years from many people, including the Marketing Departments and other staff of SEMITAG, TCRL, CGFTE (Nancy), RTM and STAS, and from the Directeur Général of TCL (Limoges) and members of his staff.

I should also like to thank Alan Murray, John Priestley, Denis Syddall and John Whitehead for assistance of various kinds.

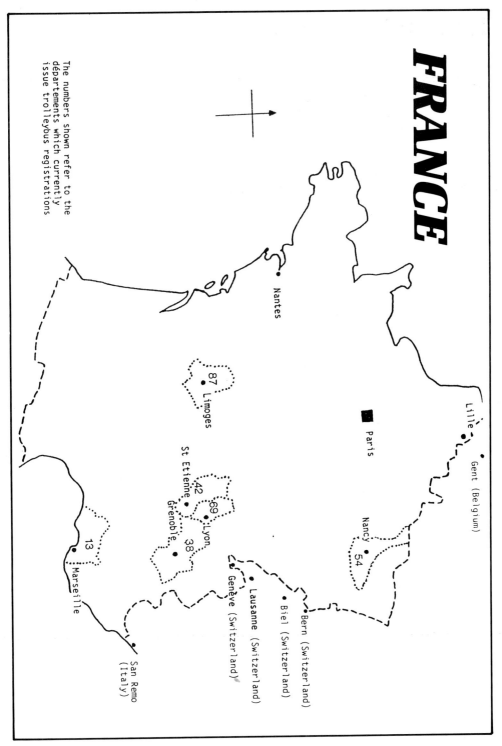

FRANCE

The numbers shown refer to the
départements which currently
issue trolleybus registrations

87 • Limoges

Nantes •

Paris ■
•

Lille •
• Gent (Belgium)

Nancy •
54

St Etienne
42
• 69
Grenoble • Lyon.
• 38

13
• Marseille

Genève (Switzerland)
• Lausanne (Switzerland)
• Biel (Switzerland)
• Bern (Switzerland)

• San Remo
(Italy)

5

Introduction

With Germany, Austria and Italy, France was a pioneer of railless electric traction at the beginning of the twentieth century, when inventor Lombard-Gerin developed a method of propulsion using a "trolley automoteur". Current was passed from overhead wires through a trolley running on top of the wires, propelled by a small electric motor, and along a flexible cable to the vehicle itself. More conventional vehicles with rigid trolleypoles were also used, on the engineer Nithard's system at Charbonnières-les-Bains in 1901 — 1907.

Several small systems in urban, suburban and rural locations were constructed but none survived the first World War. During the 1920s a revival of interest saw the trolleybus as an alternative or substitute for light railway lines, freight traffic usually being an important consideration. It was not until the middle of the next decade that the first urban routes were inaugurated in Rouen and Lyon, but little had been achieved by 1939.

Wartime fuel shortages stimulated developments which continued until the 1950s. No new system opened after Perpignan (1952), but existing networks such as Lyon and Marseille continued to expand. Decline set in during the 1960s in particular, and it was not until Lyon and Grenoble encouraged Berliet to produce an electric version of their successful PR100 motorbus that the whole picture changed. The opening of an entirely new trolleybus system at Nancy in 1982 — the first such event in Western Europe for 16 years — was another highly significant step.

Now trolleybuses again form the backbone of some of France's largest urban transport networks outside the Parisian metropolis and they have been joined by revived interest in tramways, driverless VAL métros and the silent rubber-tyred métros. There is no doubt that past government policy and local opinion have combined to favour electric transport. Certainly the future of the majority of the systems currently operated looks extremely good in a country which has seen fit to develop nuclear power in order to compensate for its lack of natural fuel resources.

This booklet aims to give sufficient detail to the visiting enthusiast for him to be able both to understand each system and enjoy his holiday! Tramway operators have been included, although no attempt has been made to go into detail of track layout. Motorbuses and métro systems are, regrettably, beyond the scope of the booklet. I apologise for any inaccuracies given in this account, and hope that any such will be brought to the attention of the author, c/o the publishers.

Martin Nimmo
Bromley.
May 1988.

Notes

Registration numbers

There is no universal rule in France as to the registration of trolleybuses. The majority of systems, when they operated vehicles without auxiliary petrol or diesel engines, did not seem to have to register them. Today only St. Etienne 401 — 425 seem to fall into this category. Other systems did not have to register trolleybuses at first, but then had to register the entire fleet (e.g. Marseille).

Registration (immatriculation) in France is done separately by each départe-ment. The registration number (numéro minéralogique*) is allocated in the form of up to four numbers, followed by one or two letters, and finally the departmental number. The latter are allocated (initially alphabetically) to each département. Those which currently register trolleybuses are 13 (Bouches-du-Rhône), 38 (Isère), 42 (Indre et Loire), 54 (Moselle et Meurthe), 69 (Rhône) and 87 (Vienne). These cover, respectively, Marseille, Grenoble, St. Etienne, Nancy, Lyon and Limoges. The number therefore appears as this example — 6046 AD 13 (Marseille 304). All vehicles must be re-registered upon change of owner even when in the same départment.

The RATP has never had to register its vehicles (and still does not register its diesel buses) as it is exempt as a Government-owned authority.

Neither buses nor trolleybuses in France carry licences (vignettes).

Before a vehicle is registered it may be given a temporary number in the "W" series, and these may be regarded as the equivalent of British trade plates. St. Etienne 136 latterly carried the plate (plaque) 1901 W 92, as it was owned and operated as a test bed by Alsthom — whose headquarters are in Hauts de Seine département — although kept at St. Etienne.

*the term "minéralogique" is used because it is the Service des <u>Mines</u> which has the responsibility for vehicle registration and testing in France.

Ownership and operation of trolleybuses and trams

The current operators of the systems covered are shown below. In some cases the operators are also the owners of the vehicles (e.g. SEMITAG), but in others (e.g. CGFTE) the actual vehicles are owned by the local authority. In the case of TCL (Limoges) the older stock was owned by the Compagnie des Trolley-bus and passed to TCL, whilst the new stock is owned by the local authority.

System	Operator	System	Operator
Grenoble	SEMITAG	Marseille	RTM
Lille	TCC	Nancy	CGFTE
Limoges	TCL	Nantes	SEMITAS
Lyon	TCL	St. Etienne	TRAS

7

Ticketing

Information on individual systems is included with each. In general, individual tickets may be brought on the bus, but must also be cancelled immediately in a machine. Books (carnets) or pages (planches or plaquettes) of tickets, costing much less per ticket, are usually sold at métro stations (Lyon, Marseille) and some tabacs. Except in Lyon, carnets or plaquettes are not sold on the vehicles.

Certain systems (Lyon, Grenoble, Nancy) offer tourist cards, which are usually sold at enquiry bureaux, and may need to be cancelled on entry to the first vehicle entered (only). Multi-lingual instructions are given in all cases. Grenoble and Nantes offer a one-day ticket, as does Lyon (on Saturdays only).

Most systems allow a free transfer on an individual ticket to a second (or third) vehicle travelling in the same direction (but on a different route). Except in Lyon and Lille the ticket should not be re-cancelled. The transfer is usually limited to one hour from first cancellation. Break of journey is not permitted, nor is return on the same ticket. In Marseille and Grenoble, carnets include "talons" or "contre-marques" (counterfoils) which must be kept to present in case of inspection.

No tickets are sold on tramcars, except in Lille, but individual tickets may be bought at automatic machines at stops (St. Etienne, Marseille, Grenoble and Nantes), and must be cancelled before boarding the tramcar — in fact the machines in St. Etienne cancel the ticket for you when you pay.

After each fares rise (usually once a year), six months' grace is given to passengers to use up any tickets prepaid at the old rate. You risk prosecution if you use tickets of a previous series on a subsequent visit to a system. On the spot fines range from F60.00 to F100.00, and these increase vastly if not paid at the time. "Contrôleurs" (inspectors) will also levy fines if a ticket has not been cancelled.

System guides and maps

Grenoble publishes a free system map and individual route timetable leaflets. Limoges produces a free fold-out map and guide. Lyon has a free diagrammatic map and individual route timetables, but also sells a comprehensive bus and métro guide, as does Marseille. Nancy and St. Etienne publish free guides with maps, and Nantes sells a timetable and map.

Sunday and evening working

Most systems operate a much reduced service after about 7 p.m. and on Sundays. In Limoges there are no trolleybuses at all in the evenings (or on Sundays), and in Grenoble, Marseille and St. Etienne the last vehicles run in to depot by 9.30 — 10.30 p.m. Later services operate in Lyon, Nancy, Nantes and Lille (and Marseille trams). Sunday services in St. Etienne are often motorbus-operated.

During school holidays reduced timetables are introduced. In August major roadworks are often begun, resulting in motorbus substitution on all or some routes on several systems.

Photography

Whilst there is in general no objection to street scenes or vehicles being photographed, shots taken in depots or bus stations or on vehicles need (usually written) permission. It is against the law to take photographs of individuals without their agreement.

GRENOBLE

On 29 June 1947 the first trolleybuses in Grenoble opened route 12 from the station to La Tronche. The system expanded steadily until 1953, when routes were extended to Sassenage and Montfleury. During the 1950s the Grenoble system received refugees from Bordeaux, Strasbourg and the Aix-Marseille route, but it was the arrival of 38 Vétra VBF vehicles from Paris in the mid-1960s which enabled the survival of the system until the advent of the Berliet ER100 ten years later.

Between 1975 and 1985, the trolleybus route mileage doubled, with the opening of new routes to Meylan and Eybens, and the extension of others beyond the existing termini. Fifty ER100 vehicles arrived in 1977 — 8 to replace the ex-Paris stock, and six PER180 articulated vehicles arrived in mid-1984. The latter followed the brief demonstration of a Nancy vehicle to SEMITAG in early 1983, and an earlier demonstration of a Hungarian-built Ikarus articulated trolleybus (1980).

In 1987, a new tramway opened on 5 September (commercial traffic began on 3 August), serving the main route between Grand'Place (Eybens) and Fontaines. Although this means that all motorbuses are now kept out of the centre, it has also meant that the trolleybus routes have been recast. In January and February 1986 routes 4 and 12 (partially) were abandoned, and most of the remaining routes (with compensational mileage covering part of the old motorbus route 10) combined to produce two semi-circular routes, 31 and 32. Route 1 continues, slightly abridged at the city end.

Unfortunately, the six PER180H trolleybuses do not at present seem to fit into the scheme of things, and their future in Grenoble must be in some doubt. They were bought for route 4, and intended for transfer to route 8, which has not, after all, been converted.

Of the remaining routes, probably the most interesting is that towards Montfleury (32), but the area round Grand'Place (including the depot) will show the most activity. A tramway terminal opened there in 1987, and the trolleybus routes 31 and 32 have already been linked up. Route 31, in this area, passes through two blocks of flats, and also (thanks to deep and wide pits set into the road) has what amounts to some reserved track. Since 3 August 1987 all route 31 vehicles pass through Grand'Place on their way to Eybens.

Montfleury nestles under the mountains, and the route from the town centre crosses the Isère, climbing through narrow streets and then descending a wooded avenue to the terminus. The remaining routes are rather flat and straight! The SEMITAG depot at Eybens is intended to be all-electric from the inauguration of the second line of tramway in about 1990.

Livery: red and white, applied either as stripes (horizontal), or, with a narrow yellow stripe as well, partly swept up over the front of the vehicle. Newer repaints have red lower panels with a gradual change to white, using speckles; the general appearance is that of a vehicle which has just gone through a blood-bath! Trams are metallic grey with bands in light and dark blue.

Depot: Rue de l'Industrie, Eybens (there is a separate motorbus garage at Sassenage), route 31.

Tickets: A one-, two- or three-day "Visibus" tourist ticket may be bought at kiosks (Gare SNCF, Maison du Tourisme, Grand'Place), as may carnets (10). The "Visibus" ticket must be cancelled on the first vehicle boarded. Ticket cancellers show the date, time and the fleet-number of the vehicle boarded — solid evidence of having travelled by trolleybus!

At tram stations, single tickets, carnets and one-day "Visibus" tickets may be obtained from the machines. Tickets must be cancelled at stations, not on the tramcars.

Grenoble: Trolleybus and Tram Routes (see map)

1   Grenoble Centre (pl V. Hugo) — Le Rondeau — Echirolles (La Luire)

31   Meylan (Les Béalières) — Grenoble Centre (Maison du Tourisme) — Grand'Place — Eybens

32   Corenc Montfleury — Grenoble Centre (Maison du Tourisme) — Cité Paul Mistral — Grand'Place

A   *(tram route)* Fontaines (la Poya) — Gares — Grenoble Centre — Grand 'Place — Alpexpo *(Alpexpo first used 31 October 1987 — for exhibitions only)*. (Standard gauge)

[Tramway opened to commercial traffic between Grand'Place and Gares on 3 August 1987 — official opening on 5 September 1987 — when the service was extended to Fontaines (Louis Massonat). The final extension to Fontaines terminus took place in December 1987.]

B   *(tram route)* A second route, branching off route A at Maison du Tourisme, to the Hospitals and the University, is to be built over two years from late 1988.

Grenoble: Fleet List

TROLLEYBUSES

701 — 750   Berliet ER100R. 701 — 720 are 11.52m long x 2.5m wide, weighing 10.66 tonnes. They have dual-doorway layout with a capacity of 32 seated/66 standing, but were originally 31 seats with a seated conductor. Nos. 721 — 750 weigh 10.77

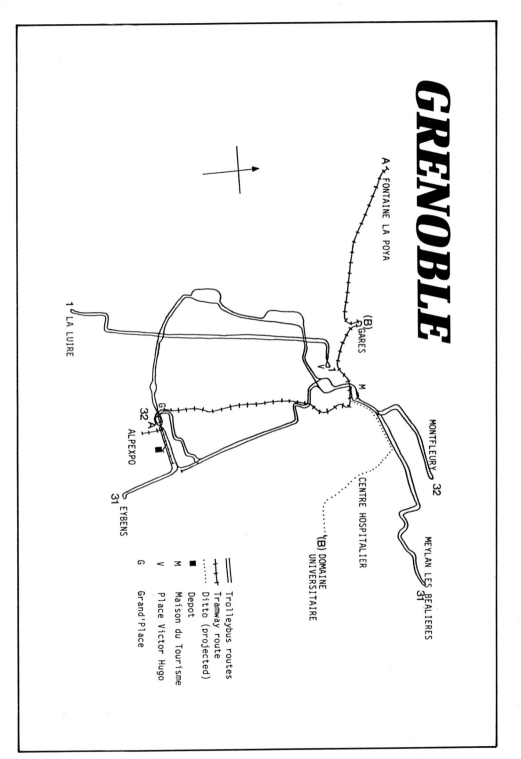

GRENOBLE

A — FONTAINE LA POYA

1 — LA LUIRE

(B) GARES

M

MONTFLEURY 32

MEYLAN LES BEALIERES 31

CENTRE HOSPITALIER

(B) DOMAINE UNIVERSITAIRE

32 A

ALPEXPO

31 EYBENS

══		Trolleybus routes
┼┼┼		Tramway route
⋯⋯		Ditto (projected)
■		Depot
M		Maison du Tourisme
V		Place Victor Hugo
G		Grand'Place

tonnes with a capacity of 31/70. Chopper **control** equipment was fitted to 729 circa 1982, making it an ER100H. Built 1977/8. Total in service: 43. All have TCO traction equipment and auxiliary diesel engines.

701	9200 UN 38	718	9211 UN 38	735	2598 UT 38
702	9201 UN 38	W719	9212 UN 38	736	9457 UW 38
703	1495 UN 38	720	9213 UN 38	737	9458 UW 38
W704	1494 UN 38	721	2601 UT 38	738	9454 UW 38
W705	932 UN 38	722	2587 UT 38	739	9450 UW 38
706	9199 UN 38	723	2604 UT 38	740	9447 UW 38
W707	9202 UN 38	724	2589 UT 38	741	9445 UW 38
S708	9203 UN 38	725	2600 UT 38	742	9440 UW 38
709	3719 UN 38	726	2592 UT 38	743	9437 UW 38
W710	9204 UN 38	727	2602 UT 38	744	9429 UW 38
711	3718 UN 38	728	2588 UT 38	745	9433 UW 38
712	9205 UN 38	729	2594 UT 38	746	9410 UW 38
W713	9206 UN 38	730	2591 UT 38	747	9413 UW 38
714	9207 UN 38	731	2593 UT 38	748	9417 UW 38
715	9208 UN 38	732	2605 UT 38	749	9419 UW 38
716	9209 UN 38	733	2599 UT 38	750	9424 UW 38
717	9210 UN 38	734	2595 UT 38		

704/5/7/10/3/9, marked W, were sold in February 1987 to St. Etienne. 708, marked S, was scrapped in 1986. Chassis nos. of 701 – 720 were 10E.0001 – 0020 and 721 – 750 are 10E.0156 – 0185, all in order. The ER100R demonstrator was temporarily numbered 700, but was never owned by SEMITAG.

801 – 806   Renault PER180H. 801 – 806 have a passenger capacity of 46 seated/95 standing and carry TCO traction equipment. The chopper control gear is air-cooled (rather than freon-cooled). In applying the undertaking's livery of red and white, imaginative use has been made of vertical yellow and red bands. The vehicles are 17.792m long x 2.5m wide and weigh 18 tonnes unladen. They have triple-doorway layout. Built 1983/4. Since the conversion of route 4 in 1986, these vehicles have usually been used as diesel buses.

801	4993 WP 38	803	5001 WP 38	805	5004 WP 38
802	5006 WP 38	804	4997 WP 38	806	5005 WP 38

Chassis numbers of 801 – 806 are VF6PUO2A.4PT100.059 – 064, in order.

TRAMS (Current collection by pantograph)

2001 – 2020   Built by Alsthom-Francorail at Aytre (near La Rochelle) in 1986/7. Double-articulated, with low floor for wheelchair access. Centre bogie has no motor, to allow for low floor. Roof-mounted electrical equipment. Seating capacity 54 plus 120 standing in a total length of 29.4m. Unladen weight is 44.2 tonnes.

2001	2006	2011	2016
2002	2007	2012	2017
2003	2008	2013	2018
2004	2009	2014	2019
2005	2010	2015	2020

A further twelve tramcars will be required for 1990 delivery for route B.

LILLE

Although Lille once boasted two extensive tram systems, one on standard gauge and the other on metre gauge, only one Y-shaped route of the metre gauge system remains of the whole network. It is, unfortunately, envisaged that Line 2 of the VAL métro may replace the tramway in the mid-1990s. Today ex-German articulated and rigid trams, built by Düwag, run frequently and quickly to Tourcoing or Roubaix from Lille (Gares), where there is an underground interchange with the automated VAL métro system.

Until a very short time ago, the ELRT (Electrique Lille Roubaix Tourcoing) was the province of twenty-eight bogie cars of the famous 500-series, built in 1949 (to an immediate pre-war design) by Brissoneau et Lotz of Creil. These have now been scrapped, sold to Hanoi (Vietnam), or sold for preservation.

In 1979, the undertaking saw the need for updating the whole route, and six bogie cars were bought from the Vestische Strassenbahnen in 1980. These were extensively refurbished and placed in service. A study showed that the purchase of further second-hand stock was a good alternative to buying new (French) trams, and it became the undertaking's policy to buy twenty-one cars of articulated six-axle design from the Vestische as they became available. Two of these cars were heavily accident-damaged, and three similar articulated cars (originally Mönchengladbach 36 — 8) were supplied as "runners", the damaged cars having been thrown-in at scrap value.

The town terminus at Lille was moved to the underground interchange on 16 May 1983, to coincide with the opening of the VAL. This terminus will be slightly altered with the building of VAL Line 1B in 1988.

The ELRT is often known as the "Mongy", a reference to the engineer Alfred Mongy who developed the scheme for a high-speed tramway in 1904 and was the founding father of the company.

Livery: Red and white, using diagonal stripes.

Depot: Marcq (tram stop Brossolette).

Tickets: Tickets are available in carnets or singly from machines, or singly on trams.

Lille: Tram Routes (see map)

Lille (Gares) — Croisé Laroche — Tourcoing (T). (Metre gauge)

Lille (Gares) — Croisé Laroche — Roubaix (R)

LILLE

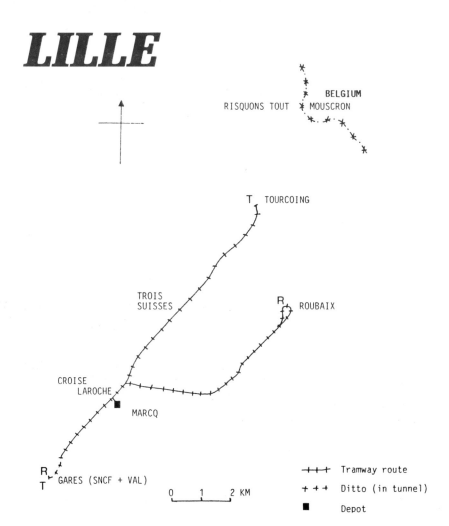

BELGIUM

RISQUONS TOUT ✳ MOUSCRON

T TOURCOING

TROIS
SUISSES

R
ROUBAIX

CROISE
LAROCHE

■ MARCQ

R
T GARES (SNCF + VAL)

0   1   2 KM

┼┼┼ Tramway route

+ + + Ditto (in tunnel)

■ Depot

16

Lille: Fleet List

TRAMS (Current collection by pantograph)

352 — 367 Düwag rigid bogie cars, built 1954/5, and originally similarly numbered in the Vestische Strassenbahnen (Germany) fleet. Bought by ELRT in 1979/80. Entered service from 12/80 onwards.

352	362	365	367
353	363		

369 — 391 Düwag articulated six-axle cars, built 1957/8, and originally similarly numbered in the Vestische Strassenbahnen (Germany) fleet. Bought by the ELRT in 1982. Entered service 1982/3. Kiepe electrical equipment. Unladen weight 20.7 tonnes. Seating capacity 44 plus 117 standing.

369	375	381	387
370	376	382	388
371	377	383	389
372	378	385	390
373	379	386	391
374	380		

392 — 394 Düwag articulated six-axle cars, built 1958 – 60. Originally Mönchengladbach 36 – 8, then Vestische 401 – 403. Monomotor trucks, but otherwise similar to the above batch. Bought by Lille 1982, and originally numbered 401 – 403 in this fleet.

392	393	394

395 — 399 Düwag articulated six-axle cars, built 1962 (395 – 397) or 1957/8 (398/9). Originally Bochum 30 – 2 and 278/296. Details similar to main batch above.

395	397	398	399
396			

Lille has also bought the three remaining cars of the Genève 795 – 799 batch (795/7 – 8), ex-Aachen (originally Mönchengladbach) Düwag articulated cars of 1958, bought by Genève in 1975. These cars seated 39 in Genève with 122 standing, and are 21.1m long and 2.2m wide, weighing 21 tonnes with two 100kw motors. Bought by Lille in 1987, but none in service by 4/88.

There are also several preserved cars and works cars owned.

LIMOGES

For a last chance of riding on vehicles up to forty years old, a trip to Limoges is essential. Often portrayed as the "Worthing" of France, as Limoges is a popular retirement retreat, the city has a hilly centre ideally suited to trolley operation.

During the Second World War, the lack of fuel gave an impetus to trolleybus development. Limoges had intended to open a system during the late 1930s, but bureaucratic delays postponed the inauguration until 1943. As luck would have it, the French trolleybus constructor, Vétra, was evacuated to Limoges, and the fleet was therefore built in the undertaking's own workshops. This also meant that a large quantity of parts was still available when, in the early 1970s, it became essential to rebuild the majority of the native fleet for further service and for one-man operation. By this method, several Vétra CTL CB60 trolley-buses served Limoges for 44 years.

In 1966 — 7, twenty-four ex-Paris Vétra VBRh vehicles were bought for service (others were used for spare parts), and routes have been extended on a regular basis over the years. 1983 saw the delivery of fifteen Renault ER100H vehicles which have replaced some of both the native and Parisian trolleys. Ten further vehicles replaced most of the remaining CB60s in 1987, the last of the latter being withdrawn officially in early 1988.

The trunk routes (1/9, 2/3, 4/7) are through-operated, but (as shown on the map) have nominal terminals either side of the town centre. If travelling the full length of the route, a second ticket must be cancelled.

Route 1/9 is probably the most interesting, as it includes a long run at its southern end, a climb across the town centre and a very low bridge and a wind-ing climb towards its northern terminus. Route 6 is remarkable for the number of railway bridges encountered (no possibility of double-deckers here!). The depot, near the western terminus of route 2/3, consists of a large open-ended barn, restricted entirely to trolleybuses. The works are very comprehensive and spares for the older generation of vehicles are actually produced there. Most of the rush-hour extras are performed by ex-Paris vehicles, which usually spend the intervening hours parked at the outer termini, with their booms left up, off-wire and slewed to the roadside!

Livery: Red and cream.

Depot: Clos Moreau (route 2/3).

Tickets: Tickets are available in carnets (ten) from most tabacs. On the vehi-cles, small "Solomatic" type tickets are issued. No transfers are permitted, and combined routes (e.g. 1/9, 2/3) require two tickets for a full terminus to terminus journey. Carnet tickets must be stamped on the bus when you board.

Resting at Meylan, Les Béalières, terminus in September 1987, Grenoble 745 faces the long run back to Eybens.

Photo: David Stuttard

Grenoble tram 2014 waits to reverse at Louis Massonat terminus the morning of the official opening in September 1987.

Photo: M.P.M. Nimmo

Grenoble tram 2006 and trolleybus 703 side by side at the Maison du Tourisme on the day before the official opening of the tramway in September 1987.

Photo: M.P.M. Nimmo

Lille 383 inbound from Roubaix at Croisé Laroche.

Photo: M.P.M. Nimmo

Limoges: Trolleybus Routes (see map)

1/9   Route de Lyon — Hôtel de Ville — Porte de Louyat

2/3   Pierre Curie (Bel Air) — Place Carnot — La Bastide

4/7   Montjovis — Place Denis Doussoubs — G. Pompidou

5   Jean Gagnant — François Perrin

6   Armand Dutreix — Aristide Briand

N.B.   No trolleybuses operate on Sundays in Limoges.

Limoges: Fleet List

TROLLEYBUSES

251 — 274   Vêtra-Berliet VBRh. Built 1949/50/4. Ex-RATP (Paris) 1966, entering service 1966 — 72. Seating capacity 26 plus 55 standing. Very variable unladen weights are recorded. Eighteen vehicles of this batch survived in late-1987.

251	784 GA 87	259	506 HJ 87	268	882 KD 87
252	125 GL 87	262	274 HZ 87	270	138 KM 87
253	238 GQ 87	264	940 JL 87	271	414 KR 87
255	760 GV 87	265	547 JR 87	272	613 KX 87
256	890 GY 87	266	962 JW 87	273	312 LD 87
258	250 HE 87	267	715 KA 87	274	820 LP 87

These vehicles originally had auxiliary petrol engines (under the driver's seat position), but none now does so.

401 — 415   Renault ER100R. Built 1983. 401 — 415 have a capacity of 27 seated/64 standing and an unladen weight of 11.69 tonnes. They carry TCO traction equipment incorporating type 4ELC2330T traction motors of 125kw (170CV) rating and Deutz type KHD-F3L-912 auxiliary diesel engines rated at 43kw.

401	6875 QS 87	406	9413 QS 87	411	1032 QT 87
402	9414 QS 87	407	2064 QT 87	412	5877 QT 87
403	9415 QS 87	408	1033 QT 87	413	7713 QT 87
404	8038 QS 87	409	9416 QS 87	414	7712 QT 87
405	1034 QT 87	410	2219 QT 87	415	7711 QT 87

Chassis numbers of 401 — 415 are VF6PSO6A1PE10.0285 — 0299, in order.

416 — 425   Renault ER100.2H. Built 1987. Seating capacity 27 plus 61 standing, with chopper equipment and Alsthom motors. Unladen weight is 12.16 tonnes. Alsthom electrical equipment, with auxiliary diesel engines.

416	9439 RD 87	420	9445 RD 87	423	9449 RD 87
417	9440 RD 87	421	9446 RD 87	424	9450 RD 87
418	9442 RD 87	422	9448 RD 87	425	9451 RD 87
419	9444 RD 87				

Chassis numbers of 416 — 425 are PE100.300 — 309, in order.

Further vehicles of the ER100.2H type will replace Vêtras of the 251 — 274 batch in 1988 —9.

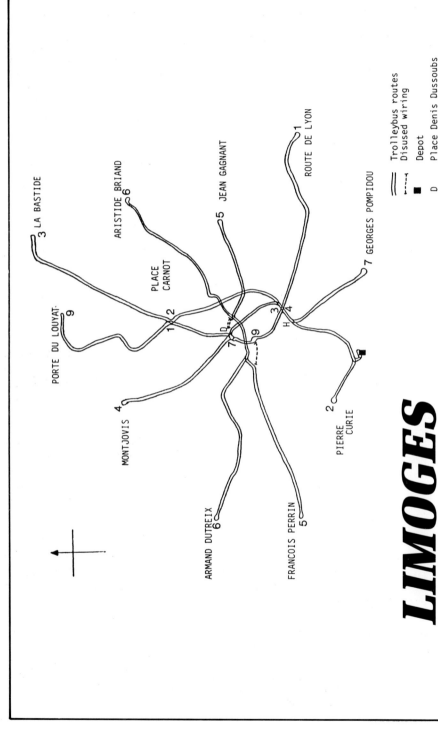

LIMOGES

Although route termini are shown, routes 1/9, 2/3 and 4/7 are run as through routes.

3 LA BASTIDE

ARISTIDE BRIAND
6

5 JEAN GAGNANT

1 ROUTE DE LYON

7 GEORGES POMPIDOU

PLACE
CARNOT

PORTE DU LOUVAT-
9

1 2

3 4

D

7

9

H

2

PIERRE
CURIE

MONTJOVIS
4

ARMAND DUTREIX
6

FRANCOIS PERRIN
5

Trolleybus routes
Disused wiring
Depot
D Place Denis Dussoubs
H Hôtel de Ville

LYON

It was with the inauguration of the Lyon system in 1935 that the main impetus was given to the development of the French trolleybus. Although by no means the first system (in fact the first French trolleybus route of any longevity was opened at Charbonnières in the Lyon area in 1901), Lyon was the first large city to develop the use of this type of vehicle, and only the second — Rouen was the first — to build an urban system with the intention of tramway replacement.

The system developed rapidly, especially in the immediate post-war years, and reached a peak of development in the late 1950s when the backbone of the fleet was the Vétra VA3B2, a three-axle vehicle capable of absorbing 125 people (most standing!). Two of these are now preserved.

Route closures characterised the 1960s and early 1970s, but the oil crisis of 1973 galvanised the transport authority into slowing down the conversion scheme and into opening discussions with Berliet and other trolleybus operators about the possibility of developing a new electric vehicle. The ER100 resulted, and 110 were delivered in 1978 — 9 followed by 26 more in 1981 — 2, replacing the last VA3B2s.

Future plans include the possible conversion of motorbus routes 9, 39 and 53 to trolleybuses, and the extension southwards of route 18. The most recent route is the 23, opened in October 1984. Seven of the VBH85 vehicles of 1963 — 4 (short two-axle trolleys) have been completely rebuilt and painted in pre-war OTL livery to operate route 6 from Hôtel de Ville to Croix Rousse, re-entering service in 1984 — 5.

Route 6 is certainly not to be missed on any visit to Lyon. Not only does it have the attraction of the "trolleys-rétro" in the old livery, but these small vehicles weave a tortuous path in their climb up the steep slope of the Croix Rousse. One great loop encircles a Roman amphitheatre, huge flights of steps criss-cross the trolley's path, and (on the way back down) there is even a short stretch of reserved track, partly through a block of flats.

Route 3 is a fast and frequent route with heavy loadings throughout its length. Eventually the Renault ER100H vehicles which form the backbone of this service may be replaced by articulated trolleybuses, and possibly displaced to the quieter route 9 if converted. Like route 44, route 3 runs alongside the river Saône for part of its northern leg.

Worthy of note is the use of two bus stations by trolleybuses. Routes 3 and 11 share part of the modern station at Laurent Bonnevay with motorbuses and the métro (line A), and routes 4 and 44 use the bus station at the SNCF railway station at Perrache, where massive concrete rotundas with bracket arms liberally mounted are probably the biggest traction poles in the world.

Livery: Orange (molybdenum red), chocolate brown and white. (1701 – 7 maroon and white with gold lining-out.)

Depots: Parmentier, St. Simon, Caluire, la Soie.

Tickets: Carnets (6 tickets) may be bought at Métro stations and TCL kiosks, or plaquettes (cards of tickets) may be bought on the buses, as may single tickets. 2- or 3-day tourist cards are available from kiosks, and on Saturdays an all-day "Samedi Bleu" ticket may also be bought. All tickets must be cancelled on the first vehicle (bus, trolleybus or Métro) used and transfers are effected with ordinary tickets by re-cancelling in subsequent vehicles.

Lyon: Trolleybus Routes (see map)

3   Gorge de Loup – Villeurbanne – Place Laurent Bonnevay
     (some journeys operate from Gare St. Paul to Laurent Bonnevay)

4   Perrache – Parc de la Tête d'Or

6   Terreaux (Hôtel de Ville) – Croix Rousse

11   Bellecour – Grandclément – Cimetière de Cugeot – Place Laurent Bonnevay

13   Bellecour – Terreaux – Croix Rousse – Montessuy

18   Gerland – Cimetière Croix Rousse

23   Place des Cordeliers – Rond-Point de Parilly

44   Perrache – La Duchère – Les Sources

The Undertaking's Annual Report for 1983/4 indicated that the following routes were still projected for eventual conversion from motorbus to trolleybus:

(i)   9 – Gare St. Paul – C.H. de Grange Blanche
(ii) 39 – Perrache – C.U. Bron-Parilly
(iii) 53 – Perrache – Rond-Point de Parilly

Lyon: Fleet List

TROLLEYBUSES

10   Vétra-Berliet VBBhf (ELR100C). Built 1960. Ex-Marseille in 1977, and used for driver-training only. Never used in service in Lyon.
                10   8230 GN 69

1701 – 1707 Vétra-Berliet VBH-85. Built 1963/4. Originally part of batch 451 – 471. Totally rebuilt 1984/5. Seating capacity 22 plus 55 standing, triple-doorway layout.

24

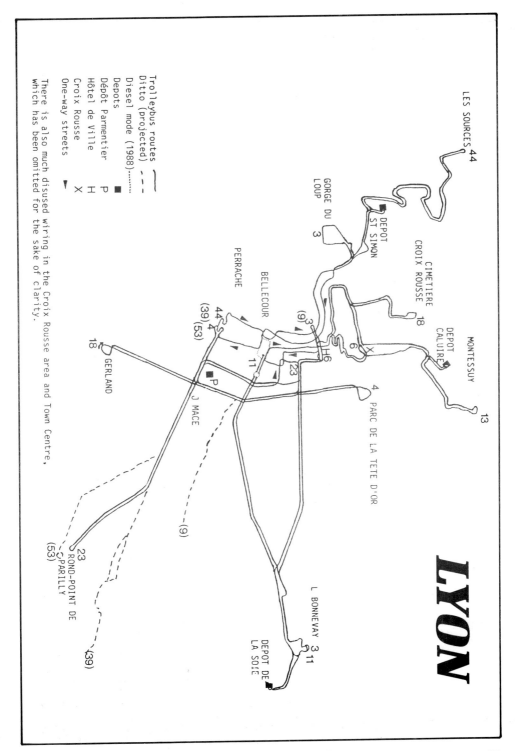

LYON

LES SOURCES 44

GORGE DU LOUP 3

DEPOT ST SIMON

CIMETIERE CROIX ROUSSE

MONTESSUY

DEPOT CALUIRE

18

PERRACHE

BELLECOUR

(9) 3

6

X

H6

23

44 (39) (53) 4

11

P

J MACE

GERLAND 18

4

PARC DE LA TETE D'OR

(9)

23 ROND-POINT DE (53) PARILLY

(39)

L BONNEVAY 3 11

DEPOT DE LA SOIE

Trolleybus routes ⎯⎯
Ditto (projected) ⎯ ⎯ ⎯
Depots ■
Diesel mode (1988)········
Dépôt Parmentier P
Hôtel de Ville H
Croix Rousse X
One-way streets ▼

There is also much disused wiring in the Croix Rousse area and Town Centre, which has been omitted for the sake of clarity.

25

Unladen weight 9.375 tonnes, length 9.8m.

1701	2602 LD 69	1704	7830 LG 69	1706	4394 LR 69
1702	7832 LG 69	1705	4396 LR 69	1707	7396 LR 69
1703	7825 LG 69				

1901 — 1912
2901 — 2929
3901 — 3969

All Berliet ER100R. Delivered 1977/8.

1901 – 1912. Triple double-width doorway layout with capacity of 30 seated/ 50 standing; 11.52m long x 2.5m wide: TCO SCR contactor control: Alsthom 100CV secondhand traction motors of unspecified type. Auxiliary diesel engine developing 58CV. Unladen weight 11.160kg. Entered service 1977. Chassis numbers 10E.0021 – 0032, in order.

1901	1118 GY 69	1905	1133 GY 69	1909	1144 GY 69
1902	1121 GY 69	1906	1136 GY 69	1910	1147 GY 69
1903	1127 GY 69	1907	1138 GY 69	1911	1150 GY 69
1904	1131 GY 69	1908	1140 GY 69	1912	1154 GY 69

2901 – 2929. Triple double-width doorway layout with capacity of 30 seated/ 50 standing; 11.52m long x 2.5m wide: TCO SCR contactor control: Alsthom 160CV secondhand traction motors of unspecified type. Auxiliary diesel engine developing 58CV. Unladen weight 11.160kg. Entered service 1978. Chassis numbers 10E.0033 – 0061, in order.

2901	3007 GZ 69	2911	3062 GZ 69	2921	3103 GZ 69
2902	3010 GZ 69	2912	3065 GZ 69	2922	3106 GZ 69
2903	3016 GZ 69	2913	3071 GZ 69	2923	3111 GZ 69
2904	3023 GZ 69	2914	3074 GZ 69	2924	3115 GZ 69
2905	3029 GZ 69	2915	3078 GZ 69	2925	3120 GZ 69
2906	3033 GZ 69	2916	3081 GZ 69	2926	3122 GZ 69
2907	3038 GZ 69	2917	3085 GZ 69	2927	3124 GZ 69
2908	3045 GZ 69	2918	3091 GZ 69	2928	3129 GZ 69
2909	3053 GZ 69	2919	3095 GZ 69	2929	3133 GZ 69
2910	3058 GZ 69	2920	3097 GZ 69		

3901 – 3969. Triple double-width doorway layout with a capacity when new of 31 seated/50 standing; 11.52m long x 2.5m wide: TCO SCR contactor control: Alsthom 130CV traction motors of unspecified type. Auxiliary diesel engine developing 58CV. Unladen weight 11.160kg. Entered service 1978. Chassis numbers 10E.0062 – 0130, in order.

3901	340 HB 69	3924	8981 HB 69	3947	3221 HE 69
3902	341 HB 69	3925	8985 HB 69	3948	3222 HE 69
3903	342 HB 69	3926	8988 HB 69	3949	3223 HE 69
3904	343 HB 69	3927	8992 HB 69	3950	3224 HE 69
3905	344 HB 69	3928	8996 HB 69	3951	3225 HE 69
3906	345 HB 69	3929	8976 HB 69	3952	3226 HE 69
3907	346 HB 69	3930	8979 HB 69	3953	3227 HE 69
3908	347 HB 69	3931	8986 HB 69	3954	3228 HE 69
3909	348 HB 69	3932	8989 HB 69	3955	3229 HE 69
3910	349 HB 69	3933	8993 HB 69	3956	3230 HE 69
3911	350 HB 69	3934	8997 HB 69	3957	3231 HE 69
3912	351 HB 69	3935	8982 HB 69	3958	3232 HE 69
3913	352 HB 69	3936	8984 HB 69	3959	3233 HE 69
3914	353 HB 69	3937	8987 HB 69	3960	3234 HE 69
3915	354 HB 69	3938	8990 HB 69	3961	3235 HE 69
3916	355 HB 69	3939	8995 HB 69	3962	3236 HE 69
3917	8977 HB 69	3940	8998 HB 69	3963	3237 HE 69
3918	8980 HB 69	3941	9002 HB 69	3964	3238 HE 69
3919	8983 HB 69	3942	9003 HB 69	3965	3239 HE 69
3920	8991 HB 69	3943	9001 HB 69	3966	3240 HE 69
3921	8994 HB 69	3944	3218 HE 69	3967	3241 HE 69
3922	8999 HB 69	3945	3219 HE 69	3968	3242 HE 69
3923	8978 HB 69	3946	3220 HE 69	3969	3243 HE 69

Several vehicles of this last batch, at least, have different seating capacities from that specified.

1801 — 1826 Renault ER 100H. Triple doorway layout with a passenger capacity when new of 27 seated/60 standing; 11.52m long x 2.5m wide: TCO freon-cooled chopper control. Traction motor make, type and rating not yet recorded. Auxiliary diesel engine details also not yet recorded. Unladen weight 11,800kg. Entered service 1981. Chassis numbers VF6PSO6A.1PE10.0234 – 0259, in order.

1801	6381 JP 69	1810	6421 JP 69	1819	8476 JP 69
1802	6380 JP 69	1811	6423 JP 69	1820	8469 JP 69
1803	6386 JP 69	1812	6426 JP 69	1821	8475 JP 69
1804	6393 JP 69	1813	6430 JP 69	1822	8477 JP 69
1805	6398 JP 69	1814	6436 JP 69	1823	8468 JP 69
1806	6403 JP 69	1815	6441 JP 69	1824	8471 JP 69
1807	6407 JP 69	1816	6445 JP 69	1825	8472 JP 69
1808	6411 JP 69	1817	8470 JP 69	1826	8474 JP 69
1809	6417 JP 69	1818	8473 JP 69		

MARSEILLE

With its cluster of routes around Notre Dame de la Garde, plus one longer route, the Marseille system is but a shadow of its former self today. Even so, one further route was added in March 1988, which links the tramway (68) to the trolleybus network.

Like Lyon, the Marseille area had a pioneer route early in the century. In 1902 a pair of cars using the Lombard-Gérin method of current collection opened a short route at Allauch (pronounced "allo"). This method involved the use of a self-propelled collector, under-running, which was connected to the car by a cable. The resemblance to the organ-grinder's monkey was obvious, and the collectors were nicknamed "les singes" (monkeys). A model of one of these vehicles is displayed at Noailles métro station.

Whilst this early system was soon discontinued, another suburban route was inaugurated in 1927 between Aubagne and Gémenos, extended in 1928 to Cuges-les-Pins. This was operated by five primitive-looking trolleybuses with equipment mounted under the bonnet. All five survived unaltered until the mid-1930s, and three were reconstructed in 1938 — 40 into forward-control vehicles when the route was absorbed by OTM. One of these survives as a museum piece with RTM.

Hit by requisitions of motorbuses, a shortage of oil and a ban on tramway extensions, Marseille tramways inaugurated its first trolleybus route in April 1942, and, by liberation in August 1944, five routes operating 28 Vetra CS60s (but with *Berliet* chassis) were open.

The replacement of tram routes continued through the post-war years, the network reaching its maximum extent in 1955 with 181 vehicles. From 1956 onwards there was a gradual move towards trolleybus abandonment, which gathered momentum in the 1960s and early 1970s.

Today, the remaining routes all operate from Dépôt Catalans, which lies on the coast road overlooking the Mediterranean. The longest route is the 81, Pharo to Métro St. Just, which traverses Marseille's main street, La Canebière, on its way. Most other routes start at Joliette, beside the modern port, and proceed via the Vieux Port towards Notre Dame, the basilica which lies high above the southern part of the city. The most impressive climb is on route 57, which climbs most of the way up to the basilica, turning by reverser in a side-street. Reversers may also be found at Bompard and Eglise d'Endoume.

The trip to Roucas Blanc is recommended, as not only does the trolleybus pass the foot of Notre Dame, but winds its way along narrow streets with typically Provençal architecture. The village of Roucas Blanc still retains its small-town atmosphere, and the terminal loop gives a picturesque view back towards Notre Dame de la Garde.

Limoges 401 crosses Place Léon Betoulle inbound from Route de Lyon on 6 April 1985.

Photo: M.J. Russell

Ex-Paris Limoges 265 picks up passengers in place Winston Churchill en route for the Armand Dutreix in August 1985.

Photo: M.P.M. Nimmo

Lyon 1703 is one of seven Vétra VBH-85 vehicles, now over twenty years old, reconstructed in 1985 to run route 6 up the steep slopes of the Croix Rousse.

Photo: M.J. Russell

Lyon 3965 rewiring itself automatically during metro works near Guillotière in February 1985.

Photo: M.P.M. Nimmo

One of the famous Lyon VA3B2s of thirty years ago, shown in its final condition, converted for Self-Service.

Photo: T. C. L., Lyon

Marseille 213 on the reverser at Bompard in 1985.

Photo: M.J. Russell

Marseille TB17 leads TA04, to which it is coupled, on the short stretch of street tramway between the reserved track and St. Pierre depot and terminus.

Photo: M.P.M. Nimmo

Nancy 617 waits at Champ le Boeuf in July 1985.

Photo: J. Priestley

Livery:	Mid-blue and cream, now changed on repaint to a darker blue and white, with a thin green line. All trams are in the latter livery.
Depot:	Catalans (tram depot — St. Pierre) at route 54 terminus.
Tickets:	Carnets may be bought at Métro stations, at kiosks and at some tabacs. Individual tickets may be bought on-board vehicles. Carnets and plaquettes include "contre-marques" or control tickets, which must be presented with the cancelled ticket if required for inspection. Tickets must be cancelled on boarding, and transfers are permitted.

Marseille: Trolleybus and Tram Routes (see map)

54	Catalans — Place Castellane — St. Pierre
55	Joliette — Cours J. Ballard — Roucas Blanc
55 barré	Cours J. Ballard — Roucas Blanc
57	Joliette — Cours J. Ballard — Vauban
57 barré	Cours J. Ballard — Vauban
61	Joliette — Cours J. Ballard — Bompard
61 barré	Cours J. Ballard — Bompard
63	Vieux Port (Cours J. Ballard) — Eglise d'Endoume
81	Pharo — Métro St. Just

Routes 55, 57 and 61 do not operate on Sundays, but are replaced by the 55 barré, 57 barré and 61 barré. Route 54 does not operate at all on Sundays.

Vehicles operate on auxiliary engines in Place Castellane on route 54.

T68	*(tramway)* Noailles — St. Pierre *(projected for extension in 1988/9 to Les Caillols).* (Standard gauge)

Marseille: Fleet List

TROLLEYBUSES

201 — 248 Berliet ER100. They have two double-width doorways and a capacity of 33 seated/67 standing (although 201 indicates only 65 standing). They are 11.272m long x 2.5m wide and are fitted with TCO SCR contactor control gear and TCO type 4ELC2330T traction motors rated at 125kw (170CV). Unladen weight is 10.82 tonnes.

201	6940 HU 13	217	4056 JE 13	233	512 JG 13
202	8319 JD 13	218	474 JF 13	234	513 JG 13
203	8321 JD 13	219	472 JF 13	235	510 JG 13

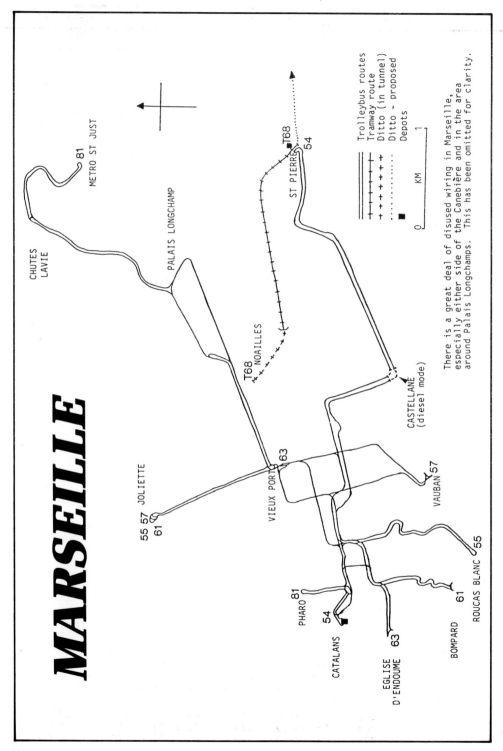

MARSEILLE

CHUTES LAVIE

METRO ST JUST

81

PALAIS LONGCHAMP

T68 NOAILLES

ST PIERRE T68

54

CASTELLANE
(diesel mode)

VAUBAN 57

63 VIEUX PORT

55 57 JOLIETTE
61

ROUCAS BLANC 55

BOMPARD 61

EGLISE
D'ENDOUME 63

CATALANS 54

PHARO 81

0 KM 1

Trolleybus routes
Tramway route
Ditto (in tunnel)
Ditto - proposed
Depots

There is a great deal of disused wiring in Marseille,
especially either side of the Canebière and in the area
around Palais Longchamps. This has been omitted for clarity.

204	8311 JD 13	220	464 JF 13	236	509 JG 13
205	8320 JD 13	221	461 JF 13	237	508 JG 13
206	8316 JD 13	222	487 JF 13	238	507 JG 13
207	8312 JD 13	223	485 JF 13	239	506 JG 13
208	460 JF 13	224	484 JF 13	240	505 JG 13
209	8309 JD 13	225	482 JF 13	241	504 JG 13
210	4052 JE 13	226	480 JF 13	242	503 JG 13
211	4053 JE 13	227	478 JF 13	243	523 JG 13
212	4055 JE 13	228	475 JF 13	244	522 JG 13
213	4054 JE 13	229	7419 JF 13	245	521 JG 13
214	4059 JE 13	230	7417 JF 13	246	519 JG 13
215	4058 JE 13	231	7416 JF 13	247	518 JG 13
216	4057 JE 13	232	511 JG 13	248	515 JG 13

Chassis numbers of 201 — 248 are 10E.0186 — 0233, in order.

TRAMS (Current collection by pantograph)

TA01 — TA16
TB17 — TB19
PCC-type cars built 1969 (TA01 — 16), 1983 (TB17 — 19), the earlier cars completely rebuilt in 1983/4. Originally ran as individual (double-ended) cars, but now run as twin sets. TA01 — 16 were formerly cars 2012/0/5, 2009/6/13/1, 2005/1/7/8/14, 2004/16, 2003/2 respectively. Seating capacity 16, plus 83 standing (each car).

TA01	TA06	TA11	TA16
TA02	TA07	TA12	TB17
TA03	TA08	TA13	TB18
TA04	TA09	TA14	TB19
TA05	TA10	TA15	

Six similar cars are to be built in 1988/9 for the extension to Les Caillols.

NANCY

Of the six trolleybus systems in France today, that of Nancy has the shortest history. In fact, until 1982 there were no trolleybuses; the last tram had run in 1958 and was replaced by motorbuses. Over the years the town centre became rapidly more congested and polluted, so much so that by 1977 it was decided to set up a commission to report on future strategy for traffic and public transport.

The findings were published in 1979, and as part of the proposed traffic management scheme the transport authority examined various bus and tram options. The vote in March 1980 was for a previously untried option, the articulated bi-mode trolleybus, to provide the backbone of the system. After some thirty months' preparation and testing, the official opening of the first route (19) took place in November 1982, the other two trunk lines following during the next ten months.

Today there are forty-eight Renault PER180H vehicles, with the possibility of some additions eventually if plans for the conversion of another trunk route materialise. The trolleybuses are the property of the district council, but are operated by the CGFTE, an arrangement often found in France. Although trolleybuses with auxiliary diesel engines may be found on all French systems, and even the wartime and post-war Paris vehicles had small Peugeot engines, the bi-mode trolleybus is capable of complete autonomy under full diesel power. Part of the idea is that route extensions and variations may be diesel operated, and in Nancy there are two such extensions beyond the Essey terminus of route 3.

Visitors will find no difficulty in picking up any of the three main routes (3, 4 and 19) outside the station; if arriving from Paris turn right as you leave the station buildings, then left (follow the trolleybus wires) for 200 metres to reach Place Maginot where there is a kiosk which sells one-day tourist tickets (Carte Portes d'Or) and will supply maps, timetables and copies of the local transport newspaper, *Lignes*. Taking a 19 on the same side of the square, back past the station, will eventually give you an exhilarating climb up to the Haut du Lièvre, or a 4 the other way from Place Maginot will produce a really steep sweep up to the plateau on the way to CHU Brabois, with high views over the city.

Photographers will find a wealth of photogenic situations on all routes, especially on the 4 and 19, but photography in the centre tends to be disappointing. The fleet numbers are also difficult to spot in photographs, and of course the vehicles are all virtually the same, though one thing to look for is the "F"-plate on the rear of 610 from its visits to Blackpool in November 1983 and Gent in 1985. The depot is not on a trolleybus route, or even (at the time of writing) on a bus route! With bi-mode vehicles it is not necessary to wire it, though there is a short test-track at the rear.

Nancy is also an extremely interesting town, with a wealth of historic buildings. These include the palace of King Stanislas (1737 — 1766), the last of the Dukes of Lorraine, and museums. It lies in the heart of Lorraine, close to the Vosges mountains.

Livery: Ivory, black and grey, with red and gold bands.

Depot: Rue Marcel Brot (easiest access by motorbus route 1 to Carnot, then five minutes' walk).

Tickets: Carte Portes d'Or (one-day tourist ticket) from kiosks at Place Maginot or central market (Couarail). Carnets from kiosks or most tabacs, and individual tickets from drivers. Ordinary tickets must be stamped in a canceller on the first bus boarded, but may be used for transfer to other vehicles in the same direction within one hour; they should not be stamped again. The tourist ticket is validated for the same or next day at the kiosk of sale, as required.

Nancy: Trolleybus Routes (see map)

3   Laxou Provinces — Centre Ville — Essey
     [— Pulnoy (33); — Seichamps (43): diesel-mode extensions]

4   Nancy Beauregard — Centre Ville — C.H.U. Brabois

19   Champ le Boeuf — Ile de Corse

It is expected that route 40 will be converted to trolleybus in the medium term

40   Champ le Boeuf — Nancy Oberlin

Nancy: Fleet List

TROLLEYBUSES

603 — 650 Renault PER180H. Built 1982/3. All vehicles have a passenger capacity of 41 seated/103 standing (delivered as 46 plus 95), and whether TCO or Alsthom-equipped, have an unladen weight of 18.09 tonnes. Those fitted with TCO traction equipment have electro-magnetic contactors and type 4EXD2538 traction motors rated at 185kw. Alsthom-equipped vehicles have thyristor control and type TAO682A1 motors rated at 198kw.

*603	3072 TB 54	*619	7309 SX 54	†635	8990 SX 54
†604	1912 SZ 54	*620	7301 SX 54	†636	7245 SY 54
*605	8993 SX 54	*621	7302 SX 54	†637	7243 SY 54
*606	4084 SW 54	*622	7303 SX 54	†638	7244 SY 54
*607	8173 SW 54	*623	8997 SX 54	†639	7242 SY 54
*608	8176 SW 54	*624	7306 SX 54+	†640	7241 SY 54
*609	8179 SW 54	*625	7308 SX 54	†641	7240 SY 54
*610	4067 SX 54@	*626	8967 SX 54	†642	7238 SY 54
*611	1922 SX 54	*627	8976 SX 54	†643	7236 SY 54
*612	1931 SX 54	†628	8980 SX 54	†644	7307 SY 54

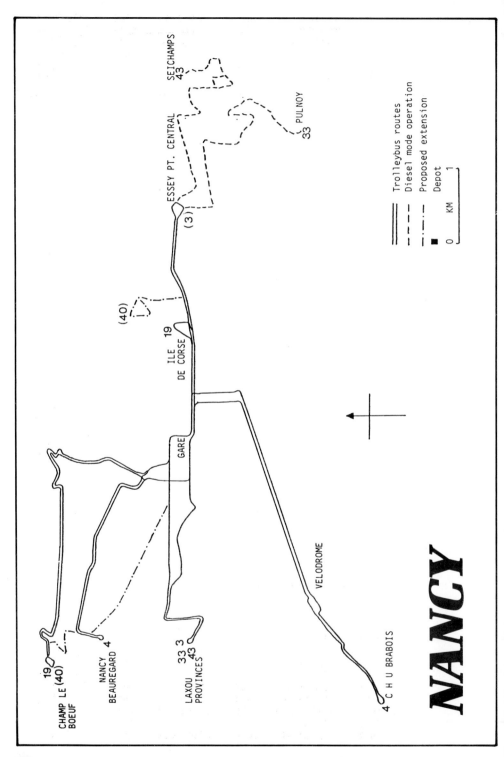

NANCY

SEICHAMPS
43

PULNOY
33

ESSEY PT. CENTRAL

(3)

(40)

ILE
DE CORSE
19

GARE

VELODROME

C H U BRABOIS
4

CHAMP LE (40)
BOEUF
19

NANCY
BEAUREGARD 4

LAXOU
PROVINCES
33 3
43

Trolleybus routes
Diesel mode operation
Proposed extension
■ Depot

0 KM 1

*613	1930 SX 54	†629	8984 SX 54	†645	7320 SY 54
*614	1929 SX 54	†630	8991 SX 54	†646	7319 SY 54
*615	1926 SX 54	†631	8996 SX 54	†647	7312 SY 54
*616	4066 SX 54	†632	8999 SX 54	†648	7306 SY 54
*617	1925 SX 54	†633	8983 SX 54	†649	1910 SZ 54
*618	1932 SX 54	†634	8987 SX 54	†650	1907 SZ 54

*TCO equipment; † Alsthom equipment; @ 610 visited Blackpool in 1983 and Gent (Belgium) in 1985; + 624 was exhibited at the Paris Motor Show, 1982.

Chassis numbers of 603 − 650 are 4PT100.003 − 050, in order.

NANTES

When Nantes' last tram ran on 25 January 1958, it could not be foreseen that a new tramway would open twenty-seven years later, on 7 January 1985.

France's first new tram system for more than thirty years, and indeed, the first new tramcars built to the specification of the "tramway standard français" (developed during the 1970s as a standard design in the expectation of tramway renewal), has been a bold experiment which seems to be paying off.

As with Nancy's trolleybus system, a major enquiry had been conducted to find the most suitable transport solution for Nantes, and the tramway was seen as an ideal solution. Costing a great deal less than a heavy Métro system, but having considerably greater capacity than trolleybuses, the tramway project was given the official go-ahead in March 1981.

Despite a brief set-back in mid-1983, when the local elections returned a different party to office, the tramway was officially inaugurated on time at the beginning of 1985, with the western section from Commerce to Bellevue following in April 1985.

Future plans involve a short extension of the existing line (opening planned for May 1989), and the probable construction of a second line from Commerce to Château de Rezé on the south side of the Loire.

Livery: White and green.

Depot: Dalby (close to Hôpital Bellier stop).

Tickets: Tickets are sold at automatic machines at tram stops.

Nantes: Tram Routes (see map)

1   Haluchère — Commerce — Bellevue *(extension proposed from Haluchère to Parc de la Beaujoire).* (Standard gauge)

A second route is proposed from Commerce to Château de Rezé

Nantes: Fleet List

TRAMS (Current collection by pantograph)

301 — 320	Built by Alsthom Atlantique 1984/5. Length 28.5m, width 2.3m. Articulated
321 — 326	with three bogies. Unladen weight 40.1 tonnes. Seating capacity 60 plus 108 standing.

Nantes 320 is the last of the first batch of trams, and was used for prototype work on the low-floor vehicles for Grenoble. It is shown at Bellevue terminus.

Photo: M.P.M. Nimmo

Two of STAS's PER100H articulated vehicles (103 nearest camera) wait at Métare terminus of route 6.

Photo: M.P.M. Nimmo

STAS 519 (now 19) is one of the 1959 PCC-type single-ended cars, shown at Bellevue. The old sub-station behind the car is still in use.

Photo: M.P.M. Nimmo

St. Etienne 462, seen here at Firminy terminus, is one of six ER100 vehicles bought from Grenoble in early 1987 (ex-Grenoble 705).

Photo: M.P.M. Nimmo

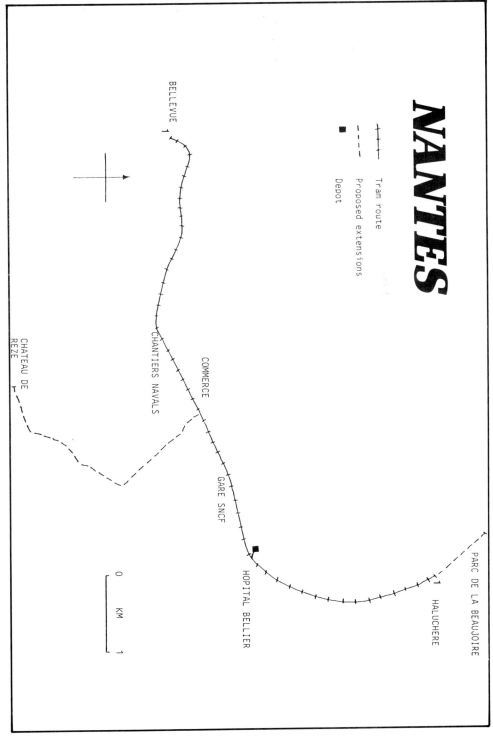

NANTES

Tram route

Proposed extensions

Depot

BELLEVUE

CHANTIERS NAVALS

COMMERCE

CHATEAU DE
REZE

GARE SNCF

HOPITAL BELLIER

PARC DE LA BEAUJOIRE

HALUCHERE

0   KM   1

43

301	306	311	316
302	307	312	317
303	308	313	318
304	309	314	319
305	310	315	320

Six similar cars are due for delivery in 1988.

| 321 | 323 | 325 | 326 |
| 322 | 324 | | |

ST. ETIENNE

In November 1940, the CFVE (Chemins de Fer à Voie Etroite) replaced its first narrow-gauge tram route with trolleybuses. With the declaration of war, the delivery of its vehicles was held up until 1942, so for the first two years several vehicles intended for Poitiers were used, the latter town having trolleybuses available but no overhead completed owing to wartime difficulties.

In postwar years, expansion of the system was rapid. The most important substitution was on suburban line 1, where the single-line tramway from Bellevue to Firminy, nearly 10km long, was converted. By 1954 all the trams had been replaced except for the north — south main line between La Terrasse and Bellevue. This last line was not converted owing to both the density of traffic (70,000 passengers a day) and the narrowness of the streets. In 1958 — 9 the tram fleet was entirely replaced by modern PCC-type cars, later joined by some articulated cars. One of these was rebuilt in 1982 — 3 to provide the prototype of a new tram for the twenty-first century. The tram route was extended from Bellevue to Solaure in 1983.

St. Etienne has developed its trolleybus system methodically over the years. During the 1960s it took advantage of abandonment or vehicle replacement elsewhere to buy large numbers of young Berliet ELR two-axle vehicles from Marseille, Nice and Toulon, together with a batch of three-axle VA3B2 vehicles from Marseille. In 1978 — 82 these vehicles were replaced by new Berliet or Renault ER100 vehicles, and the most recent vehicles delivered are articulated PER180H vehicles for route 6 (La Métare). All vehicles, buses, trolleybuses and tramcars, have "piped" local radio.

Routes have also been refined and extended, the most recent extension being that to La Cotonne from Tardy (one of the original termini of 1940) in early 1986. As St. Etienne is the centre of a major coal-mining area, the connection between industry and electric transport is obviously important for local politics, but the majority of routes is well suited to trolleybuses (or trams) in any case.

From Gare Châteaucreux a trip on route 10 to La Cotonne is a very good introduction to the system. At the latter terminus a very steep twisting climb leads to an excellent viewpoint over the town. High speeds may be experienced on route 1, the interurban from Bellevue to Firminy, and while at Bellevue the depot may be seen; an old tram depot with entrances and exits directly onto the street, with both trams and trolleybuses running into and out of service throughout the day. There is also a short length of tram and trolleybus combined reserved track at Bellevue, which may occasionally be shared by that very rare type of bus (in France at least), the Leyland National.

Tenders have recently been invited for the replacement, rather than rebodying, of the tram fleet by new trams.

Livery:	Pistachio green and broken white (applied in horizontal stripes). The unrebuilt articulated trams remain in cream and pale green.
Depot:	Bellevue (tram route 4, trolleybus routes 1 and 7). Small overnight depot at Firminy terminus as well.
Tickets:	Carnets may be bought at kiosks, and individual tickets on trolleybuses or from machines at tram stops. Carnet tickets may be used for two journeys, cancelling the relevant end on each journey; these journeys do not have to be in continuation of each other. Each end of a carnet ticket is regarded separately.

St. Etienne: Trolleybus and Tram Routes (see map)

1   Bellevue — Firminy

3   Dorian — Terrenoire

5   Hôtel de Ville — Michon

6   Dorian — la Métare

7   . Châteaucreux — Bellevue

8   Dorian — Rivière

10   Le Soleil — Tardy — La Cotonne (alternate journeys usually short-worked from Soleil to Tardy)

.4   (tramway) Solaure — Terrasse (Metre gauge)

St. Etienne: Fleet List

TROLLEYBUSES

401 — 425   Berliet ER100. Built 1978/9. Two-door layout, seating 33 with 67 standing when delivered. Unladen weight 10.380 tonnes, with TCO motors and equipment. No auxiliary diesel engines and, therefore, no registrations are carried. All vehicles carry "STAS Tr4.." on their number plates. A recent change of operating authority may change this to "TRAS Tr4.."

401	410	418
402	411	419
403	412	420
404	413	421
405	414	422
406	415	423
407	416	424
408	417	425
409		

Chassis numbers of 401 – 425 are 10E. 0131 – 0155, in order.

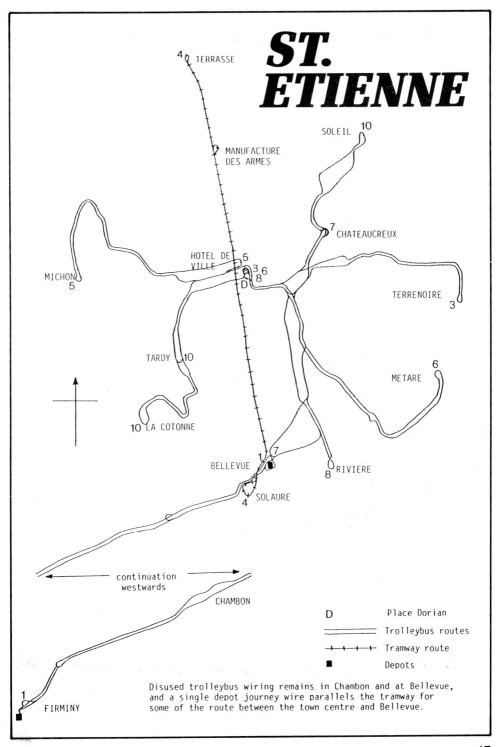

ST. ETIENNE

4 TERRASSE

SOLEIL 10

MANUFACTURE
DES ARMES

7 CHATEAUCREUX

HOTEL DE 5
VILLE
3 6
D 8

MICHON
5

TERRENOIRE
3

TARDY 10

METARE 6

10 LA COTONNE

1 7

BELLEVUE

8 RIVIERE

4 SOLAURE

continuation
westwards

CHAMBON

D	Place Dorian
─────	Trolleybus routes
+++++	Tramway route
■	Depots

1

FIRMINY

Disused trolleybus wiring remains in Chambon and at Bellevue,
and a single depot journey wire parallels the tramway for
some of the route between the town centre and Bellevue.

47

426 — 450 Renault ER100H. Built 1981/2. Alsthom electrical equipment and motors, with auxiliary diesel engines. Two-door layout, with variable seating capacities, both 27/68 and 33/65 having been noted within the batch, and equally variable unladen weights.

426	626 SL 42	435	6024 SL 42	443	1541 SM 42
427	610 SL 42	436	7007 SL 42	444	1538 SM 42
428	4673 SL 42	437	7017 SL 42	445	1542 SM 42
429	4674 SL 42	438	7008 SL 42	446	3959 SM 42
430	4672 SL 42	439	7009 SL 42	447	3958 SM 42
431	6043 SL 42	440	7006 SL 42	448	3971 SM 42
432	6045 SL 42	441	1539 SM 42	449	3972 SM 42
433	6071 SL 42	442	1540 SM 42	450	3960 SM 42
434	6025 SL 42				

Chassis numbers of 426 – 450 are 1PE100.260 – 284, in order.

461 — 466 Berliet ER100. Built 1977. Ex-Grenoble in 1987. TCO electrical equipment, and auxiliary diesel engines. Ex-Grenoble numbers 704/5/7/10/3/9; order of numbering at St. Etienne retained. Seating capacity remains at 32 plus 66 standing, and the unladen weight at 10.66 tonnes. Hopper windows and short roof shrouds distinguish these vehicles from native vehicles when observed from a distance.

461	2343 TP 42	463	2345 TP 42	465	2349 TP 42
462	2347 TP 42	464	2348 TP 42	466	2350 TP 42

Chassis numbers of 461 – 466 are 10E.004/5/7/10/3/9, in order.

101 — 108 Renault PER180H. Built 1983. Articulated bi-mode trolleybuses. TCO equipment and motors. Length 17.792m, weight 18.150 tonnes. Seating capacity is 46 plus 95 standing.

101	1722 SS 42	104	1715 SS 42	107	1711 SS 42
102	1721 SS 42	105	1714 SS 42	108	1712 SS 42
103	1710 SS 42	106	1713 SS 42		

Chassis numbers of 101 – 108 are 4PT100.051 – 058, in order.

TRAMS (Current collection by trolleypole)

01 — 30 PCC-type, single-ended bogie cars, built 1958. Length 14.247m, width 2.020m, with triple doorways. Constructed at Strasbourg from plans by La Brugeoise, the batch is similar to the 7000-series of Brussels trams. Seating capacity is 26 plus about 85 standing. Renumbered from 501 – 530 in 1987.

01	09	17	24
02	10	18	25
03	11	19	26
04	12	20	27
05	13	21	28
06	14	22	29
07	15	23	30
08	16		

51 — 55 PCC-type articulated bogie cars, built 1969. Length 20.651m, width 2.020m, with four doorways. Seating capacity 33 plus about 150 standing. Renumbered from 551 – 555 in 1987.

51	52	54	55

001 Originally number 553 of the articulated series, rebodied in 1982/3 by Heuliez as a prototype "Tram 2000" for the system. Inaugurated the Solaure extension on its first day in service, 17 February, 1983. Despite a number "clash" with 01 above, it had not been renumbered by May 1988.

001

Tenders are currently being invited for a dozen replacement tramcars (of an eventual 25) for delivery in 1990. Both Alsthom-Francorail and B.N. Constructions Ferroviaires Métalliques S.A. (Belgium) have shown interest, and Alsthom and ACMV Vevey are reported to be in the process of setting up a consortium to build a single-articulated version of Bern's latest low-floor cars.

The Future

The former right-wing government of M. Chirac has unfortunately checked expansion somewhat of both trolleybus and tramway systems. Only those schemes which had already been agreed and financed have been permitted to proceed, and authorities have been requested to recost or reschedule much other major expenditure.

The first casualty of this policy has been the RATP tramway between St. Denis and Bobigny, which is unlikely now to open until 1990. One extra cost of this project has been that the intended rolling-stock can no longer be bought in continuation of the Grenoble batch, so that complete re-tooling will be required at Alsthom Atlantique unless construction follows Grenoble's second batch.

Marseille has (1988) finally proceeded with the conversion of route 54 to trolleybus, but is likely to expand only its métro system and tramway in the near future. Route 68 (tramway) is to be extended to Les Caillols in 1988 − 9, and six further cars purchased. It is intended to extend Métro line 1 from Castellane to La Timone, and line 2 from Bougainville (extension opened February 1987) to Madrague Ville, and (at its southern end) towards St. Loup. A suburban railway line from Hyères to Salins d'Hyères may also be converted to light rail, taking perhaps three cars of the Marseille tramway pattern to be built in continuation of the RTM's batch.

Nancy intends to convert route 40 (Nancy-Oberlin to Champ le Boeuf) to trolleybuses. Whilst it uses much of the same wiring as route 19, it includes a long climb up avenue de Boufflers to the plateau. No date has yet been set for conversion, owing to financial stringency.

Grenoble has received permission to begin construction in late 1988 of a second tram route, from the University campus to the station. Conversely, the long-term future for the trolleybus looks insecure, and the opportunity to scrap the existing routes may well be taken when the ER100 vehicles become due for replacement after the next few years.

Despite having the largest trolleybus fleet in France, the Lyon system cannot yet be regarded as totally safe. The conversion of routes 9, 39 and 53 to electric traction has been policy since at least 1981, but by mid-1987 nothing had been done. It partly depends on the availability of articulated trolleybuses; with the RVI factory within the conurbation, Lyon cannot look elsewhere, but RVI have made it clear that they are not proposing to produce an articulated version other than the PER180H. Lyon feels that the additional cost of fully bimode vehicles cannot be justified.

The existing Lyon fleet is due for renewal in stages from the early 1990s, and it is to be hoped that suitable replacements can be found, possibly by the adaptation of the new RVI series-312 motorbus.

St. Etienne, meanwhile, has expanded its fleet by purchasing six ex-Grenoble ER100s, and extended one route substantially in 1986. Here both trolleybus and tramway seem secure, and both systems may possibly be further expanded in the next few years. Tenders are currently being invited for new tramcars.

The success of Nantes' first tram route, opened in 1984, has brought proposals for a second route, as in Grenoble. Lille, however, intends to scrap the "Mongy" when route 2 of the VAL network opens in the mid-1990s. Despite the clampdown on capital expenditure, Reims, Toulouse, Strasbourg and Bordeaux are all looking at rapid transit systems. Reims proposes 7.4km of tramway with 19 stations, whilst Strasbourg (9.7km), Toulouse (9.8km) and Bordeaux are all contemplating métros, of which at least Strasbourg will be of the VAL type.

Vehicle Notes

Renault vehicles (ER100/PER180)

All modern vehicles in use are of Berliet (and, after the takeover by Renault, RVI) manufacture. Two basic types are available; the two-axle rigid ER100 and the articulated (three-axle) PER180.* Differences occur between different batches in doorway specification and seating plan and capacity. The Marseille vehicles have full-height sliding windows. Where chopper equipment is fitted, the designation has an "H" suffix (e.g. ER100H), otherwise an "R" suffix is added (H — hacheur = chopper).

ER100 vehicles may be supplied with or without auxiliary Deutz diesel engines, which are used as diesel-electric sets. The PER180 is not currently available except as a dual-mode vehicle, with a diesel engine producing full power.

Seating capacities (usually given on a plate above the driver's seat) often include the driver. On the outside of the vehicle, a plate declares the unladen weight (PV) in tonnes, the maximum laden weight (PTC), the length and width (L x l) in metres and the inside floor area (surface) in square metres.

A full batch list, with chassis numbers, is given below:

ER100	Fleet Nos	Chassis Nos	Equipment
Grenoble	701 — 720†	1 — 20	TCO
Lyon	1901 — 1912	21 — 32	TCO
Lyon	2901 — 2929	33 — 61	TCO
Lyon	3901 — 3969	62 — 130	TCO
St. Etienne	401 — 425	131 — 155	TCO
Grenoble	721 — 750	156 — 185	TCO
Marseille	201 — 248	186 — 233	TCO
Lyon	1801 — 1826	234 — 259	TCO
St. Etienne	426 — 450	260 — 284	ALSTHOM
Limoges	401 — 415	285 — 299	TCO
Limoges	416 — 425	300 — 309	ALSTHOM

There was also an experimental ER100 demonstrator, never sold to an operator, whose chassis was not numbered in this series. This vehicle was scrapped in 1986. It had TCO equipment.

* *These are based on the PR100 and PR180 motorbuses, and have most parts in common.*

† *Certain vehicles from this batch are now St. Etienne 461 — 466.*

PER180H	Fleet Nos	Chassis Nos	Equipment
Demonstrators+		1 — 2?	TCO?
Nancy	603 — 650	3,5 — 27	TCO
		4,28 — 50	ALSTHOM
St. Etienne	101 — 108	51 — 58	TCO
Grenoble	801 — 806	59 — 64	TCO

The ER100 vehicles have chassis numbers in the series 10E0001 — 0233 (Berliet) and VP6PSO6A1PE100234 onwards, whilst the PER180H vehicles have numbers in the series beginning VF6PUO2A1PT100001 onwards.

TCO = Traction C. E. M. — Oerlikon.

ALSTHOM was formed from the Alsace-Lorraine Company and the Thompson Houston Company.

+ *Demonstrators for RVI are at least one PER180H, last heard of in the USA at Seattle, but probably now returned to France, and an ER180H, an all-electric bi-mode vehicle.*

Vétra – The Classic French Trolleybus

Details of the modern generation of French trolleybuses will be found under the respective systems, but it is worth sketching briefly the particulars of older types, some of which are to be found in museum collections.

French trolleybuses in the past achieved a degree of standardisation not found in Britain for, apart from small numbers of vehicles produced by Somua or Jacquemond, none of which survives, a lone example by Isobloc and a handful of Chausson trolleybuses and motorbus conversions, nearly every trolleybus was supplied by Vétra.

Vétra, a contraction of "Société des Véhicules et Tracteurs Electriques", was a subsidiary of Alsthom, set up to supply "electrobus", as the first passenger trolleybuses were described, as well as freight vehicles. Between 1925 and 1966 nearly 2,000 trolleybuses were built, about one-third going for export to north Africa, Spain, Switzerland, West Germany, eastern Europe and as far as Brazil and Chile. Vétra did not, however, build trolleybuses; it designed standard models for which the chassis, bodywork and electrical equipment were subcontracted.

Some early examples bore type classifications which related to nominal capacity, but later different codes were applied to the same model. The trolleybus based on the Berliet PLR motorbus is known by Berliet as an ELR, but vehicles also carried Vétra VBBh type plates. In the post-war period, four standard models were devised:

Type	Length (m)	Width (m)	Capacity	Notes
A	12.0	2.5	32 + 88	Three-axle
B	10.0	2.5	28 + 52	
C	9.0	2.38	21 + 39	
D	8.7	2.15	19 + 26	

Additional letters in the type classification include B (Berliet), F (Franco-Belge), R (Renault), S (Renault-Scémia) and h (high floor). Not all type classifications carried the chassis manufacturer's code, some are misleading, while latterly the designation reflected the motorbus from which the trolleybus was derived. The commonest types of trolleybus were: CS60, CB60, VCR, VBR, VBRh, VBB, VA3, VA3B2 and VBBh/ELR.

Museums

AMTUIR, St. Mandé, Paris (métro Port Dorée)

The Paris transport museum includes many trams (including Glasgow Standard car 488) and trolleybuses from Le Havre, Perpignan (ex-Marseille), Grenoble (ex-Paris), Limoges, Poitiers, St. Etienne, and, as a bonus, London. A Marseille vehicle is also owned, but not currently displayed. The museum is open weekends, from 15 April to 31 October, 1430 — 1800 hours.

Le Havre 15	Vétra VBRh	Poitiers 21	Vétra CS35
Perpignan 124	Vétra VA3	St. Etienne 65	Vétra VCR
	(ex-Marseille)		
Grenoble 637	Vétra VBF (ex-Paris)	(Marseille 53	Vétra CB60)
Limoges 10	Vétra CTL CB60	London 796	Leyland/MCW
			(H1 Class)

Museum address:

> Musée des Transports Urbains
> 60 ave Sainte Marie
> 94160 Saint Mandé

National Railway Museum, Mulhouse

The railway museum has one "trolleybus" in its collection, but it is not usually on display. The museum is, however, well worth a visit. The opening hours are 1000 — 1700, every day of the year except 1 January and 25/26 December.

Paris 2728 (Renault TN6C2 motorbus conversion to "bi-mode trolleybus" — both petrol and electric drives — for use on the pioneer route at Vitry in 1934/5).

Museum address:

> Musée du Chemin de Fer Français
> 2 rue Alfred de Glehn
> 68200 Mulhouse

Musée de la Barque, La Barque-Fuveau

The Musée de la Barque (the Provençal Museum of Urban and Rural Transport) is the home of three trolleybuses. They are Toulon 85, a Chausson-Vétra VBC-APU of 1955, Marseille 239, a Vétra VBRh of 1952, and Aix-Marseille 17, a Vétra type VBR of 1949. These are static exhibits, but there is a narrow-gauge railway and a number of railway and tramway vehicles is also preserved, as are several motorbuses. The museum is at the SNCF station of La Barque-Fuveau, on the RN96 not far from Toulon. It is open from 1000 till 1800 hours every Sunday and on (French) bank holidays throughout the year.

Museum address:

> Musée Provençal des Transports Urbains et Ruraux
> Gare SNCF de la Barque
> 13710 Fuveau (Bouches-du-Rhône)

Musée Henri Malartre, Rochetaillée

This small motor museum, on the outskirts of Lyon, contains two Lyon trolleybuses; one of the original "Boîtes à Savon" (soapboxes), or Vétra CS60 "Francheville" vehicles which opened the Lyon system in 1935, and one of the famous three-axle VA3B2 vehicles of the 1950s. Opening hours are 0800 — 1200 and 1400 — 1800 (1900 from 15 March to 14 September), every day except 1 January and 25 December. TCL bus 40 passes nearby (some journeys). Regrettably, neither trolleybus has been on display for some time.

Lyon 1	Vétra CS60 "Francheville"
Lyon 728	Vétra VA3B2

Museum address:

> Musée Henri Malartre
> Château de Rochetaillée
> 69 Rochetaillée-sur-Saône

Trolleybuses from Grenoble, Lyon, St. Etienne, Nice and Marseille are kept on the premises of those undertakings, though not necessarily in their ownership. These include:

Grenoble:	662 (Vétra VBF — ex-Paris)
Lyon:	830 (Vétra VA3B2), 20 (Vetra CS60 "Francheville")
Marseille:	304 (OTM2, rebuilt from Aubagne-Cuges no. 3), 316 (Vetra-Berliet ELR) and several trams, two of which are displayed at the Transport Gallery at Noailles tramway station, plus one actually in the station. The Transport Gallery is open Tuesday to Saturday, from 1030 to 1730 hours.
Nice:	25 (Vétra-Berliet ELR)
St. Etienne:	72 (Vétra VCR), 126 (Vétra-Berliet ELR), 151 (Vétra VA3B2 — ex-Marseille) and trams H2 (1907) and J74 (1938)

Ex-Grenoble 633 and 653 (Vétra VBF — ex-Paris) are preserved at the Deutsches Strassenbahn Museum at Wehrningen, near Hanover.

Limoges 20 and 23 (Vetra CTL CB60) are both to be preserved, one at a museum in Albi, the other by "Sauvabus", a preservation organisation. It is hoped that Limoges 5 will eventually operate at Sandtoft Transport Centre (U.K.).

The above is not an exhaustive list, even of some of the undertakings listed, but it must be remembered that most of these vehicles are not currently on public display, even where owned by the undertaking.

Modern Tramway publishes a regularly up-dated feature on tramway museums, and much more detail may be gleaned from those columns. There are several museums with tramway exhibits in France, which are not listed above. These are at:

> Froissy (Somme)
> Lamastre (Ardèche)
> Lille
> Valmondois

Some Vocabulary
(not usually found in phrase-books!)

le trolleybus	=	trolleybus
la perche	=	trolley-boom
la tête de trolley	=	trolley-head
le saut de perches	=	dewirement
l'emperchage, le dépercharge	=	rewiring, depoling
la ligne aérienne	=	overhead line
le hâcheur	=	chopper
le moteur de traction	=	traction motor
la puissance	=	power
l'alimentation électrique	=	electricity supply
le feeder, la borne	=	feeder
le poteau, le support	=	traction pole
le sous-station	=	substation
le (cable) transversal	=	span-wire
l'aiguillage (m)	=	frog
l'isolateur (m)	=	insulator
la ratrappe-trolley	=	trolley retriever
l'ancrage (en facade) (m)	=	(wall) rosette
le matériel roulant	=	rolling-stock
le parc	=	fleet
l'affichage (des destinations) (f)	=	destination screen
la girouette	=	destination blind
l'oblitérateur (m)	=	ticket canceller/validator
l'emetteur de tickets (m)	=	ticket machine
la cabine	=	cab
le parcours, la ligne	=	route
le réseau	=	network
le couloir à contre-sens	=	contra-flow lane
la porte à quattre battants	=	four-section (folding) door
férrailler	=	to scrap
réformer, déclasser	=	to withdraw (a vehicle, etc.)
supprimer	=	to close down (a route, etc.)
l'emperchoire (f)	=	rewiring pan
le coeur	=	crossing centre
le souris	=	skate (literally "a mouse"!)
la clochette	=	gong
la pince de jonction	=	splicing ear
la croisement talonnée	=	trailing frog
le coup'secteur	=	section insulator
le dispositif d'accrochage	=	hanger
le hauban	=	bracket arm
la griffe d'alignement	=	offset hanger
la croisement	=	crossing
la mitraille, la ferraille	=	scrap
la voiture échelle	=	tower-wagon
le passionné (des trolleybus)	=	(trolleybus) enthusiast

57

Abbreviations commonly encountered

GRENOBLE
TAG = Tramway de l'Agglomération Grenobloise
SEMITAG = Société Mixte des Transports de l'Agglomération Grenobloise (sometimes abbreviated further to TAG)

LILLE
ELRT = Eléctrique Lille Roubaix Tourcoing ("Mongy")
SNELRT = Société Nouvelle de l'ELRT
TCC = Transports Collectifs de la Communauté Urbaine de Lille
COTRALI = Compagnie des Transports de la Communauté Urbaine de Lille
COMELI = Compagnie du Métro de Lille
VAL = Véhicule Automatique Léger

LIMOGES
TCL = Transports en Commun de Limoges
CTL = Compagnie des Trolleybus de Limoges

LYON
TCL = Transports en Commun de Lyon
STCRL = Syndicat des Transports en Commun de la Région Lyonnaise (sometimes abbreviated further to TCRL)
COURLY = Communauté Urbaine de Lyon
MAGGALY = Métro Automatique à Grand Gabarit de l'Agglomération Lyonnaise
OTL = Omnibus et Tramways de Lyon
SEMALY = Société d'Economie Mixte du Métropolitain de l'Agglomération Lyonnaise
SYTRAL = Syndicat Mixte des Transports pour le Rhône et l'Agglomération Lyonnaise

MARSEILLE
OTM = Omnibus et Tramways de Marseille
RATVM = Régie Autonome des Transports de la Ville de Marseille
RTM = Régie des Transports de Marseille

NANCY
CGFTE = Compagnie Génerale Française de Transports et d'Entreprises

NANTES
SEMITAN = Société d'Economie Mixte des Transports en Commun de l'Agglomération Nantaise

ST. ETIENNE
CFVE = Chemins de Fer à Voie Etroite de Saint-Etienne, Firminy, Rive-de-Gier et Extensions
STAS = Société des Transports de l'Agglomération Stéphanoise

SIOTAS = Syndicat Intercommunal pour l'Organisation des Transports Collectifs de l'Agglomération Stéphanoise
TRAS = Société des Transports Urbains de l'Agglomération Stéphanoise

GENERAL

SNCF = Société Nationale des Chemins de Fer
TGV = Train à Grande Vitesse
UTP = Union des Transports Publics
RATP = Régie Autonome des Transports Parisiens
RVI = Renault Véhicules Industriels
RER = Réseau Exprès Régional
TCO = Traction CEM-Oerlikon
CEM = Compagnie Electro-Méchanique
PV = Poids à Vide
PTC(PTAC) = Poids total (à) Complet
SACM = Société Alsaciénne de Constructions Méchaniques
VETRA = Société des Véhicules et Tracteurs Electriques
EDF = Electricité de France
CHU = Centre Hospitalier Universitaire
ZAC = Zone d'Aménagement Concerté

Bibliography

Chemins de Fer Régionaux et Urbains	*FACS (Paris)*
Modern Tramway	*LRTA (London)*
Trolleybus	*BTS (Reading)*
Trolleybus Magazine	*TMC (London)*
New Scientist	*(London)*
La Vie du Rail	*(Paris)*
Connaissance du Rail	*(Bellenares)*
Transport Public	*UTP (Paris)*
En Ligne Directe	*TCL (Lyon)*
L'Echo du Rail	*(Breil-sur-Roya)*
Transports Urbains	*GETUM (Courbevoie)*
Lignes	*CGFTE (Nancy)*
Dépêche Sioky	*STAS (St. Etienne)*

Plan d'Entreprise 1984 — 1988	*TCL (Lyon)*
Cent Ans de Transports en Commun 1879 — 1979	*TCL (Lyon)*
75 ans d'Autobus en France	*Coullaud & Tilliet (EPA-Paris)*
Les Trolleybus Français	*Courant & Bejui (PEF-Grenoble)*
Les Transports à Lyon	*Borgé & Clavaud (Honoré-Lyon)*
Le Trolley à Nancy	*reprint from Le Moniteur (District Urbain de Nancy)*
Histoire des Transports dans les Villes de France	*Robert (Robert-Paris)*
Rapports d'Activité	*TCL/RTM/CGFTE*
Fiches Techniques (ER100H/R, PER180H)	*RVI (Suresnes)*
Le Réseau Bus-Métro de l'Agglomération Lyonnaise	*TCL (Lyon)*
Du Tram au TAG	*Guétat, Lachenal, Muller (La Vie du Rail-Paris)*

MUSIC
TAIZE

VOLUME I
Conceived and edited by Brother Robert
Composed by Jacques Berthier

PEOPLE'S EDITION

COLLINS

MUSIC FROM TAIZÉ — VOLUME I
is available in three editions

Vocal edition   ISBN 0 00 599720 8
Instrumental edition   ISBN 0 00 599721 6
People's edition   ISBN 0 00 599952 9

Also available
MUSIC FROM TAIZÉ — VOLUME II

Vocal edition   ISBN 0 00 599863 8
Instrumental edition   ISBN 0 00 599883 2
People's edition   ISBN 0 00 599884 0

Recordings: available as records or cassettes
from Christian booksellers

CANTATE!

CANONS ET LITANIES

RESURREXIT

HarperCollins*Religious*
a division of HarperCollins*Publishers*
77–85 Fulham Palace Road
Hammersmith, London W6 8JB

Collins Dove
PO Private Bag 200, Burwood
Victoria 3125, Australia

First published, this edition, 1986
Reprinted 1992

Made and Printed in Great Britain
by Bell & Bain Ltd, Glasgow

FOREWORD

Hidden away in the hills of Burgundy, in the eastern part of France, is an ecumenical community of brothers whose prayer is at the heart of their life. Founded in 1940, this community made up of Protestants and Catholics, from some 20 different countries, has become host to thousands of young people who visit Taizé, entering into the prayer and spirit of the community.

With the growing number of young people from all over the world coming to Taizé, a form of song that could enable people with no common langauge to participate in the community's prayer had to be developed. With the help of Jacques Berthier, musician and friend of Taizé, different methods were tested, and a solution found in the use of repetitive structures—short musical phrases with singable easily memorized melodies—and some very basic Latin texts. To this was added verses for cantor in numerous living languages. The experiment proved to be an overwhelming success, as one can easily verify by listening to either of the two recordings made during the actual prayer services—one at Taizé and one during the pilgrimage to Rome.

The present American edition of the MUSIC FROM TAIZÉ retains the beautiful Latin refrains, which because of the natural "color" of the language, bear up under constant repetition better than any vernacular. In this edition, however, all verses have been translated and adapted into English.

The people's melodies contained in this edition, are in the form of responses, litanies, acclamations and canons (rounds). Added to these are numerous choral harmonies, secondary refrains or canons, and a delightful array of instrumental solos and accompaniments for various instruments. This material is found in the Vocal and Instrumental Editions.

The Music of Taizé is performable by small groups with a simple guitar or keyboard accompaniment, or larger groups of hundreds or even thousands accompanied by choir, brass, strings, woodwinds, organ and percussion.

For a more thorough introduction to the music and its origin, see the foreword to the Vocal and Instrumental Editions.

TABLE OF CONTENTS

I. OSTINATO RESPONSES AND CHORALES (1)

II. LITANIES AND OTHER TEXTS WITH REFRAINS (40)

III. ACCLAMATIONS (72)

IV. CANONS (82)

Beatitudes

BEATI

3

Happy they who dwell in God's house.

Principal Ostinato Response

Calmly

Be - a - ti   in do - mo   Do - mi - ni   Be -

Secondary Ostinato (Unison or Canon)

Be - a - ti   Be - a - ti   Be - a - ti   Be -

a - ti   Be - a - ti   Be - a - ti   Be -

BEATI PACIFICI

5

Blest are the peacemakers, and blest the pure in heart, for they shall see God.

Ostinato Chorale

Calmly

Be - a - ti pa - ci - fi - ci   Be - a - ti mun - do cor - de

quo - ni - am i - psi De - um   i - psi De - um   vi - de - bunt.

5

6

CRUCEM TUAM

We adore your cross, O Lord, and we praise your resurrection.

Ostinato Chorale

Cru-cem tu - am a-do-ra-mus Do-mi - ne, re-sur-rec-ti-o-nem

tu-am lau-da-mus Do-mi - ne. Lau-da-mus et glo - ri - fi - ca - mus.

(Fine)

Re-sur-rec-ti-o-nem tu-am lau-da - mus Do-mi - ne. Cru-cem tu -

7

GLORIA I

Glory to God in the highest.

Ostinato Response

Joyfully

Glo - ri, Glo - ri, Glo - ri - a in ex - cel - sis De - o.

8

HOW BLESSED ARE YOU

Chorale *p*

How blessed are you who are poor; the

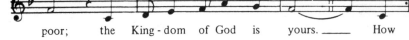

King-dom of God is yours, how blessed are you who are

(Fine)

poor; the King - dom of God is yours. ___ How

6

JESUS, REMEMBER ME

9

Je - sus, re - mem - ber me when you come in - to your King - dom. Je - sus, re - mem - ber me when you come in - to your King - dom.

LAUDATE DOMINUM

10

Praise the Lord, all you peoples.

Chorale

Lau - da - te Do - mi - num, Lau - da - te Do - mi - num om - nes gen - tes, Al - le - lu - ia. Al - le - lu - ia.

LAUDATE OMNES GENTES

12

All peoples, praise the Lord.

Ostinato Chorale

Lau - da - te om - nes gen - tes, lau - da - te Do - mi - num. Lau - da - te om - nes gen - tes, lau - da - te Do - mi - num! Lau -

7

13   **MANDATUM NOVUM**

I give you a new commandment, says the Lord: Love one another as I have loved you.

Theme (Ostinato Response or Canon)

Man - da - tum no - vum do___ vo - bis, di - cit Do - mi -
nus, di - cit Do - mi - nus._____

18   **MISERERE MEI**

Turn to me, have mercy on me, for I am alone and poor.

Ostinato Response

Mi - se - re - re me - i Do - mi - ne mi - se - re - re.

20   **MISERERE NOBIS**

Ostinato Response   *Have mercy on us, O Lord.*

Mi - se - re - re no - bis Do - mi - ne, mi - se - re - re no - bis.

Mi - se - re - re no - bis Do - mi - ne, mi - se - re - re no - bis.

21   **MISERICORDIAS DOMINI**

Ostinato   *p*   *For ever will I sing the mercy of the Lord.*

Mi - se - ri - cor - di - as Do - mi - ni in ae - ter - num can - ta - bo.

Canticle of Simeon
NUNC DIMITTIS   22
Now, Lord, you can let your servant go in peace according to your promise.

Chorale

Lento

Nunc di - mit - tis ser-vum tu - um Do- mi - ne,   se -

cun - dum ver-bum tu - um in   pa - ce.   Nunc di -

Lord's Prayer
PATER NOSTER   23

Ostinato Response

(Fine)

Pa - ter no - ster qui es in coe - lis Pa - ter

Magnificat II
SANCTUM NOMEN DOMINI   25
My soul magnifies the holy name of the Lord.

Ostinato Chorale

San - ctum no-men Do-mi - ni   ma-gni - fi - cat __ a - ni - ma me - a.

San-ctum no-men Do-mi - ni   ma-gni- fi-cat a - ni - ma me - a.

9

28   # UBI CARITAS

Where charity and love are found, God himself is there.

Ostinato Response

U - bi ca - ri - tas et a - mor,

U - bi ca - ri - tas De - us i - bi est.

36   # VENI SANCTE SPIRITUS

Come, Holy Spirit

Ostinato Response

Ve - ni San - cte Spi - ri - tus. ____

42   # ADORAMUS TE DOMINE I

We adore you, O Lord.

Refrain

A - do - ra - mus te, A - do - ra - mus te, Do - mi - ne.

44   # ADORAMUS TE DOMINE II — GLORIA

We adore you, O Lord. — Glory to God in the highest.

Refrain

A - do - ra - mus te Do - mi - ne.

10

Alternate Refrains

Lord, we wor-ship you.

Glo-ri-a! Glo-ri-a! Glo-ri-a!

CREDO I 47

We believe in one God, in one Lord, in one Spirit.

Refrain

Cre-do in u-num De-um, cre-do in u-num *Do-mi-num.

* 1st time: Dominum; 2nd time: Spiritum.   Spi-ri-tum.

DOMINE MISERERE I-II 49

Lord, have mercy on us.

Domine Miserere 1- Refrain

Do - mi - ne mi - se - re - re.

Domine Miserere 2- Refrain

Do - mi - ne, Do - mi - ne mi - se - re - re.

EXAUDI NOS 50

Refrain   *Hear us*

Ex - au - di - nos; ex - au - di - nos.
Lord, hear our prayer, Lord, hear our prayer.

11

51

GLORIA TIBI DOMINE

Glory to you, O Lord.

Refrain

Glo-ri - a ti - bi Do - mi - ne.

Canon

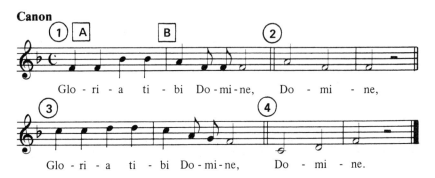

Glo - ri - a ti - bi Do - mi - ne, Do - mi - ne,

Glo - ri - a ti - bi Do - mi - ne, Do - mi - ne.

53

JESU CHRISTE MISERERE

Jesus Christ have mercy on us.

Refrain

Je - su Chri - ste mi - se - re - re.

55

KYRIE ELEISON I-X

Lord, have mercy.

Kyrie 1

Ky - ri - e, Ky - ri - e, e - le - i - son.

Kyrie 2

Ky - ri - e, e - le - i - son.

Kyrie 3

Ky - ri - e   e - le - i - son,   E - le   -   i - son.

Kyrie 4

Ky - ri - e   e - le - i - son,   e - le - i - son.

Kyrie 5

Ky - ri - e   e - le - i - son,   e   le - i - son.

Kyrie 6

Ky - ri - e   e - le - i - son,   Ky - ri - e   e - le - i - son.

Kyrie 7

Ky - ri - e   e - le - i - son,   Ky - ri - e   e   - le - i - son.

Kyrie 8

Ky - ri - e   e   - le - i - son,   Ky - ri - e   e   - le - i - son.

13

Kyrie 9

Kyrie 10

60   LIBERA NOS DOMINE

Deliver us, O Lord.

MARANATHA! ALLELUIA! I

62

Come soon! Alleluia!

Refrain 1. Choir 2. All

Ma - ra - na - tha, Ma - ra - na - tha!

Refrain 1. Choir 2. All

Al - le - lu - ia, al - le - lu - ia!

MEMENTO NOSTRI DOMINE

63

Remember us, O Lord.

1 *Calmly*

Me - men - to no - stri Do - mi - ne.

2

Me - men - to no - stri Do - mi - ne.

3

Me - men - to no - stri Do - mi - ne.

4

Me - men - to no - stri Do - mi - ne.

Mo - men - to no - stri Do - mi - ne.

Me - men - to no - stri Do - mi - ne.

Me - men - to no-stri Do - mi - ne. Me-men - to no - stri Do - mi - ne.

66   ## O CHRISTE AUDI NOS
O Christ, hear us.

Refrain

O   Chri - ste   au - di - nos.
Hear   us,   O   Christ, Our Lord.

66   ## TE ROGAMUS AUDI NOS
We ask you to hear us.

Refrain

Te ro - ga - mus au - di nos,   te ro - ga - mus au - di nos,

VENI CREATOR SPIRITUS

Come, Creator Spirit

68

Ve - ni Cre - a - tor Spi - ri - tus.

VENI LUMEN CORDIUM I-II

Come, light of our hearts. Come, Holy Spirit.

71

Veni Lumen Cordium 1

Ve - ni lu - men cor - di - um.

Veni Lumen Cordium 2

Ve - ni lu - men cor - di - um.

ALLELUIAS I-VI

73

Alleluia 1

Al - le - lu - ia, al - le - lu - ia!

Al - le - lu - ia, al - le - lu - ia!

17

Alleluia 2

Al - le - lu - ia, al - le - lu - ia.

Alleluia 3

Al - le - lu - ia, _____ Al - le - lu - ia! _____

Alleluia 4

Al - le - lu - ia, al - le - lu - ia, al - le - lu - ia!

Alleluia 5

Al - le - lu - ia, al - le - lu - ia. Al - le -

lu - ia, al - le - lu - ia!

Alleluia 6

Al - le - lu - ia, Al - le - lu - ia,

Al - le - lu - ia! ia!

18

Amen 1

A - men, A - men.

Amen 2

A - men, A - - men.

Amen 3

A - men, A - men, A - men,

A - men, Al - le - lu - ia. Al - le - lu - ia.
A - men, A - men.

HOSANNA FILIO DAVID 78

Hosanna to the Son of David.

Ho - san -na Fi - li - o Da -vid Ho - san -na

Fi - li - o Da - vid Ho - san -na Fi - li - o Da - vid.

MARANATHA — ALLELUIA II 78

Come soon! Alleluia!

Ma - ra - na -tha, Al - le - lu - ia, al - le -lu - ia.

79   # MARANATHA — VENI DOMINE

Come soon. Come, Lord, and do not delay.

Ma-ra-na-tha, ma-ra-na-tha, Ve-ni Do-mi-ne, No-li tar-da-re.

79   # MYSTERIUM FIDEI

The mystery of faith. Savior of the world, save us. By your cross and your resurrection you have delivered us.

Mys-te-ri-um fi-de-i, mys-te-ri-um fi-de-i.

80   # SANCTUS DOMINUS

Holy Lord

San-ctus, San-ctus, San-ctus Do-mi-nus.

80   # TU SOLUS SANCTUS I-II

You alone are Holy, you alone are Lord, you alone, O Jesus Christ, are Most High.

Tu Solus Sanctus 1

Tu so-lus san-ctus, Tu so-lus Do-mi-nus, Tu so-lus al-tis-si-mus.

Tu Solus Sanctus 2

Tu so-lus san - ctus, Tu so-lus Do - mi-nus, Tu so-lus al -

tis - si - mus Je - su Chri - ste.

UNUM CORPUS 81

One Body and one Spirit.

U - num Cor - pus et u - nus Spi - ri - tus.

AGNUS DEI 85

Lamb of God, you take away the sins of the world, have mercy on us; grant us peace.

Canon

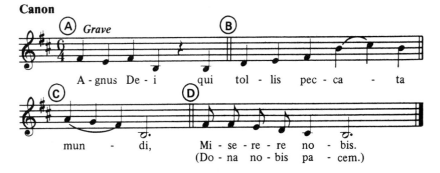

A - gnus De - i qui tol - lis pec - ca - ta

mun - di, Mi - se - re - re no - bis.
(Do - na no - bis pa - cem.)

21

86 **ALLELUIA**

Canon

Al - le - lu - ia, Al - le - lu - ia, Al - le - lu - ia, Al - le - lu - ia.

Coda

A - men! A - men! A - men! A - men! A - men! A - men!

87 **BENEDICITE DOMINO**

Bless the Lord, all you works of the Lord.

Canon

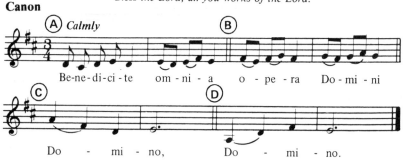

Be - ne - di - ci - te om - ni - a o - pe - ra Do - mi - ni

Do - mi - no, Do - mi - no.

88 **BENEDICTUS**

Blessed is he who comes in the name of the Lord.

Principal Canon

Be - ne - di - ctus qui ve - nit, Be - ne - di - ctus qui ve - nit, in

no - mi - ne, in no - mi - ne, in no - mi - ne Do - mi - ni.

CANTATE DOMINO

(Four canons on the same harmonic pattern using the same accompaniments)

1. Cantate Domino

Sing to the Lord, rejoice in God.

Can - ta - te Do - mi -no. Al - le - lu - ia, al - le -

lu - ia! Ju - bi - la - te De - o.

2. Glory to the Father

Glo - ry to the Fa - ther al - might - y,

glo - ry to his Son, Je - sus Christ, glo - ry to the

Spir - it of life, now and for ev - er. A - men.

3. Gloria II (for Christmas)

Glory to God in the highest, and peace to his people on earth.

Rhythmically

Glo- ri - a, Glo- ri - a, in ex - cel - sis De - o,

softly

Glo -ri - a, Glo-ri -a, al -le- lu - ia! Et in ter-ra pax ho -

23

mi - ni - bus   bo - nae vo - lun - ta - tis.

4. Veni Creator Spiritus (for Pentecost)

Come, Holy Spirit

Ve - ni   Cre - a - tor,   Ve - ni   Cre - a - tor,

Ve - ni   Cre - a - tor   Spi - ri - tus.

91   CHRISTUS VINCIT — JUBILATE COELI

Christ conquers, Christ reigns, Christ rules.
Heaven and earth rejoice for Jesus Christ is truly risen.

Double Canon (2nd canon ad lib.)

Chris-tus, Chris-tus vin - cit.   Chris-tus, Chris-tus reg - nat, __
Ju - bi - la - te coe - li,   Ju - bi - la - te mun-di, __

(rat.)   Chris-tus, Chris-tus vin - cit,   Chris-tus, Chris - tus
(*re.*)   *Ju - bi - la - te coe - li,   Ju - bi - la - te*

Chris - tus,   Chris - tus,   Chris - tus im - pe - rat.
Chris - tus   Je - sus   Sur - re - xit ve - re.

reg-nat.   Chris - tus,   Chris - tus,   Chris-tus, im - pe -
mun-di, __   Je - sus   Chris - tus   sur - re - xit ve -

CREDO II

We believe in one God, one Lord and one Spirit.

93

Ostinato Response (in Canon)

Cre-do in u-num De-um, Cre-do in u-num Do-mi-num,

Cre - do in u-num De - um, Cre-do in u-num Spi-ri-tum.

DA PACEM DOMINE

Give peace, O Lord.

94

Ostinato

Da pa - cem Do - mi - ne, Da

FOR YOURS IS THE KINGDOM

96

Canon

For yours is the King-dom, for yours is the power,

for yours is the King - dom, for yours is the power,

for yours is the glo - ry, for ev - er, A - men!

for yours is the glo - ry, for ev - er, A - men!

97

GLORIA IIı

Glory to God in the highest. Alleluia!
Christ is born today, the Savior has appeared.

Principal Canon

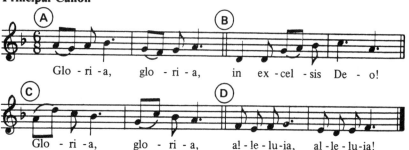

Glo - ri - a,   glo - ri - a,   in ex - cel - sis De - o!

Glo - ri - a,   glo - ri - a,   al - le - lu - ia,   al - le - lu - ia!

99

HOSANNA

Hosanna in the highest.

Canon

Ho - san - na, ho - san - na, ho - san - na in ex - cel - sis. Ho -

100

JUBILATE DEO

Rejoice in God.

Canon (Praetorius)

Ju - bi - la - te De - o, Ju - bi - la - te De - o, A - le - lu - ia.

JUBILATE, SERVITE

101

Rejoice in God all the earth. Serve the Lord with gladness.

Canon

Ju - bi - la - te De - o om - nis ter - ra.

Ser - vi - te Do - mi - no in lae - ti - ti - a.

Al - le - lu - ia, al - le - lu - ia, in lae - ti - ti - a.

Al - le - lu - ia, al - le - lu - ia, in lae - ti - ti - a!

LAUDAMUS TE

103

We praise you, Lord.

Canon

Lau - da - mus te Do - mi - ne, lau - da - mus te Do - mi -

ne, lau - da - mus te Do - mi - ne.

104 MAGNIFICAT

Principal Canon

My soul magnifies the Lord.

Ma - gni - fi - cat, Ma - gni - fi - cat, Ma - gni - fi - cat a - ni - ma me - a Do - mi - num.

Ma - gni - fi - cat, Ma - gni - fi - cat, Ma - gni - fi - cat a - ni - ma me - a!

105 OSTENDE NOBIS

Lord, show us your mercy. Amen! Come soon!

Principal Canon

Os - ten - de no - bis Do - mi - ne, mi - se - ri -

cor - di - am tu - am. A - men! A - men! Ma - ra - na -

tha! Ma - ra - na - tha! Os - ten - de. - tha.

107 PATER SANCTE

Canon

Holy Father, listen to our pleading.

Pa - ter san - cte, - Pa - ter san - cte, ex -

au - di de - pre - ca - ti - o - nem no - stram.

PER CRUCEM

109

By your cross and passion, and by your holy resurrection, deliver us, O Lord.

Canon

Per cru - cem et pas - si - o - nem tu - am

Li - be - ra nos Do - mi - ne, li - be - ra nos Do - mi - ne,

li - be - ra nos Do - mi - ne, Do - mi - ne.

Per cru - cem et pas - si - o - nem tu - am.

Li - be - ra nos Do - mi - ne, li - be - ra nos Do - mi - ne,

li - be - ra nos Do - mi - ne, Do - mi - ne.

Per sanc - tam re - sur - rec - ti - o - nem tu - am.

29

Li - be - ra nos Do - mi - ne, li - be - ra nos Do - mi - ne,

li - be - ra nos Do - mi - ne, Do - mi - ne.

110 SALVATOR MUNDI

Principal Canon *Savior of the world, save us, free us.*

Sal - va - tor mun - di sal - va nos. Sal - va - tor mun - di sal - va nos.

Sal - va nos, sal - va nos. Sal - va - tor mun - di sal - va nos.

112 SANCTUS

Canon *Holy Lord, God of hosts.*

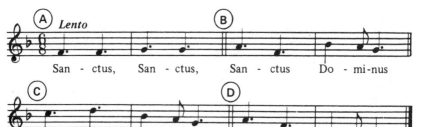

San - ctus, San - ctus, San - ctus Do - mi - nus

De - us Sa - ba - oth, De - us Sa - ba - oth.

30

SURREXIT DOMINUS VERE II

The Lord is truly risen! Christ is risen today!

Canon

Sur - re - xit Do - mi - nus ve - re.

Al - le - lu - ia, Al - le - lu - ia,

Sur - re - xit Chris - tus ho - di - e,

Al - le - lu - ia, Al - le - lu - ia.

114

TIBI DEO

To you, God the Father, through the Son and in the Holy Spirit,
be all honor and glory for ever and ever. Amen.

Canon

Ti - bi De - o Pa - tri, per Fi - li - um, in Spi - ri - tu

om - nis ho - nor et glo - ri - a, per sae - cu - la. A - men!

115

INDEX

French

FOR

DUMMIES®

PORTABLE EDITION

French FOR DUMMIES®

PORTABLE EDITION

by Dodi-Katrin Schmidt, Michelle M. Williams, Dominique Wenzel and Zoe Erotopoulos

WILEY

A John Wiley and Sons, Ltd, Publication

French For Dummies® Portable Edition

Published by
John Wiley & Sons, Ltd
The Atrium
Southern Gate
Chichester
West Sussex
PO19 8SQ
England
www.wiley.com

For general information on our other products and services, please contact our Customer Care Department within the U.S. at 877-762-2974, outside the U.S. at 317-572-3993, or fax 317-572-4002.

For technical support, please visit www.wiley.com/techsupport.

Wiley publishes in a variety of print and electronic formats and by print-on-demand. Some material included with standard print versions of this book may not be included in e-books or in print-on-demand. If this book refers to media such as a CD or DVD that is not included in the version you purchased, you may download this material at http://booksupport.wiley.com. For more information about Wiley products, visit www.wiley.com.

British Library Cataloguing in Publication Data: A catalogue record for this book is available from the British Library

ISBN 978-1-119-94561-1 (pbk); ISBN 978-1-119-94021-0 (ebk); ISBN 978-1-119-94022-7 (ebk); ISBN 978-1-119-94023-4 (ebk)

Printed and bound in Great Britain by TJ International Ltd

10 9 8 7 6 5 4 3 2 1

MIX
Paper from
responsible sources
FSC® C013056

About the Authors

Dodi-Katrin Schmidt has been a writer, translator, and editor for over a decade. Aside from translating German, French, and English texts of various kinds, including linguistic handbooks, film reviews, travel guides, and children's books, she has also been involved in developing language textbooks, language courses, teachers' handbooks, and grammar companions for video language courses.

Michelle M. Williams is an editor at a major educational publisher. A former French teacher, she taught students in both the public and private sectors. She is a firm believer in making the language fun and accessible to all who want to learn.

Dominique Wenzel was a freelance teacher of French and a translator for 15 years. Born and raised in France, she received a Master's degree from the University of Paris-Sorbonne and studied at the University of Chicago on a postgraduate Fulbright scholarship.

Dr Zoe Erotopoulos holds an MA, MPhil, and PhD in French and Romance Philology from Columbia University in New York, NY. Dr. Erotopoulos has also studied in Aix-en-Provence, at the Sorbonne, and at the École Normale Supérieure in Paris. Her teaching experience in French ranges from elementary to advanced level courses, including literature and theater. Dr. Erotopoulos is the author of *French Verbs For Dummies*.

Berlitz has meant excellence in language services for more than 120 years. At more than 400 locations and in 50 countries worldwide, Berlitz offers a full range of language and language-related services, including instruction, crosscultural training, document translation, software localization, and interpretation services. Berlitz also offers a wide array of publishing products, such as self-study language courses, phrase books, travel guides, and dictionaries. The world-famous Berlitz Method® is the core of all Berlitz language instruction. From the time of its introduction in 1878, millions have used this method to learn new languages. For more information about Berlitz classes and products, please consult your local telephone directory for the Language Center nearest you or visit the Berlitz website at www.berlitz.com, where you can enroll in classes or shop directly for products online.

Publisher's Acknowledgments

We're proud of this book; please send us your comments at http://dummies.
custhelp.com. For other comments, please contact our Customer Care Department
within the U.S. at 877-762-2974, outside the U.S. at 317-572-3993, or fax 317-572-4002.

Some of the people who helped bring this book to market include the following:

*Acquisitions, Editorial and Vertical
Websites*

Project Editor: Rachael Chilvers

Commissioning Editor: Mike Baker

Assistant Editor: Ben Kemble

Production Manager: Daniel Mersey

Publisher: David Palmer

Cover Photos: ©iStock/David Freund

Cartoons: Rich Tennant
(www.the5thwave.com)

Composition Services

Project Coordinator: Kristie Rees

Layout and Graphics: Carrie A. Cesavice,
Lavonne Roberts, Christin Swinford

Proofreaders: Rebecca Denoncour,
Susan Moritz

Indexer: Potomac Indexing, LLC

Publishing and Editorial for Consumer Dummies

Kathleen Nebenhaus, Vice President and Executive Publisher

Kristin Ferguson-Wagstaffe, Product Development Director

Ensley Eikenburg, Associate Publisher, Travel

Kelly Regan, Editorial Director, Travel

Publishing for Technology Dummies

Andy Cummings, Vice President and Publisher

Composition Services

Debbie Stailey, Director of Composition Services

Contents at a Glance

Table of Contents

Introduction

● ●

*A*s society becomes increasingly more international and as we seek to become global citizens, knowing how to say at least a few words in other languages becomes more and more useful. The European Union is a great example of global citizenry as borders between the member countries become easier to cross. Furthermore, global business environments necessitate overseas travel. Thanks to numerous travel websites, finding a package deal for airfare and hotel stays makes travel abroad easier and more convenient than ever before. Moreover, the Internet allows us to have contact with people all over the world, making learning a foreign language a great asset.

Whether you are traveling overseas on business, exploring a different culture, or even connecting with your heritage, learning a little bit of the language has many advantages. Whatever your reason for wanting to learn some French, *French For Dummies* can help. It gives you the skills you need for basic communication in French. We're not promising fluency here, but if you need to greet someone, purchase a ticket, ask for directions, make a hotel reservation, or order off a menu in French, you need look no further than this book.

Remember that everyday French is like everyday English. It makes use of simplified lingual forms which, although perfectly correct, avoid and ignore certain complicated verb tenses and moods such as, say, the future perfect or the subjunctive. In everyday French, you can express yourself adequately by following just a few easy-to-understand grammar rules and by knowing a minimum number of words. So you should find the lessons in this book to be fun and not the least bit overwhelming.

Now is playtime: **C'est la récréation** (seh lah rey-krey-ah-syohN).

About This Book

French For Dummies isn't like a class that you have to drag yourself to twice a week for a specified period of time. You can use this book however you want to, whether your goal is to learn some words and phrases to help you get around when you visit France or a francophone country, or you just want to be able to say 'Hello, how are you?' to your French-speaking neighbor. Go through this book at your own pace, reading as much or as little at a time as you like. You don't have to trudge through the chapters in sequential order, either; just read the sections that interest you.

Conventions Used in This Book

To make this book easy to navigate, we've set up some conventions:

- French terms are set in **boldface** to make them stand out.

- Pronunciation, set in parentheses, follows the French terms. Hyphens connect syllables in the same word as well as words that are linked by the French liaison (which you can find out all about in Chapter 3).

- Translation of the French terms is set in *italic* and follows the pronunciation.

- Because French nouns are typically preceded by an article, we include those articles in the word lists throughout this book, even though the English translation may not use the article. Furthermore, because articles indicate a noun's gender, they're helpful bits of information when you're learning a language. When the article is abbreviated (l'), however, you can't tell the gender. In those instances, we add a gender designation: (m) for masculine and (f) for feminine.

- Verb conjugations (lists that show you the forms of a verb) are given in tables in this order:
  - The 'I' form
  - The 'you' (singular, informal) form

- The 'he/she/it/one' form
- The 'we' form
- The 'you' (plural, and singular, formal) form
- The 'they' form.

Pronunciations follow in the second column. The example shown uses the verb **parler** (pahr-ley) (*to speak*). The conjugation starts with the French equivalent of *I speak* or *I am speaking*; *you speak,* or *you are speaking,* and so on.

Conjugation	*Pronunciation*
je parle	zhuh pahrl
tu parles	tew pahrl
il/elle/on parle	eel/ehl/ohN pahrl
nous parlons	nooh parh-lohN
vous parlez	vooh parh-ley
ils/elles parlent	eel/ehl parhl

Also note that, because each language has its own way of expressing ideas, the English translations that we provide for the French terms may not be exactly literal. We want you to know the gist of what's being said, not just the words that are being said. For example, the phrase **C'est normal** (seh nohr-mahl) can be translated literally as *It's normal,* but the phrase really means *It's no big deal.* This book gives the second translation.

Foolish Assumptions

To write this book, we had to make some assumptions about who you are and what you want from a book called *French For Dummies.* Here are the assumptions that we've made about you:

- You know no or very little French – or if you took French back in school, you don't remember much of it.

- You're not looking for a book that will make you fluent in French; you just want to know some words, phrases, and sentence constructions so that you can communicate basic information in French.

✔ You don't want to have to memorize long lists of vocabulary words or a bunch of boring grammar rules.

✔ You want to have fun and learn a little bit of French at the same time.

If these statements apply to you, you've found the right book!

How This Book Is Organized

This book is divided by topic into parts and then into chapters. The following sections tell you what types of information you can find in each part.

Part I: Getting Started

This part lets you get your feet wet by giving you some French basics: how to pronounce words, what the accents mean, and so on. We even boost your confidence by reintroducing you to some French words that you probably already know. Finally, we outline the basics of French grammar that you may need to know when you work through later chapters in the book.

Part II: French in Action

In this part, you begin learning and using French. Instead of focusing on grammar points as many language textbooks do, this part focuses on everyday situations, such as asking for directions, dining, and making small talk.

Part III: French on the Go

This part gives you the tools you need to take your French on the road, whether you're going to a local French restaurant or to a museum in France. This part covers all aspects of travel in French-speaking parts of the world, and it even has a chapter on how to handle emergencies.

Part IV: The Part of Tens

If you're looking for small, easily digestible pieces of information about French, this part is for you. Here you can find ten useful French expressions to know and ten phrases that make you sound French.

Part V: Appendixes

This part of the book includes important information that you can use for reference. Appendix A is a mini-dictionary in both French-to-English and English-to-French formats. If you encounter a French word that you don't understand or you need to say something in French that you can't find quickly elsewhere in the book, you can look it up here. Appendix B features verb tables, which show you how to conjugate regular verbs and then how to conjugate those verbs that stubbornly don't fit the pattern.

Icons Used in This Book

You may be looking for particular information while reading this book. To make certain types of information easier to find, we've placed the following icons in the left-hand margins throughout the book:

This icon highlights tips that can make learning French easier.

This icon points out interesting information that you ought not forget.

To help you avoid linguistic, grammatical, and cultural faux pas, we use this icon.

Languages are full of quirks that may trip you up if you're not prepared for them. This icon points to discussions of these peculiar grammar rules.

If you're looking for information and advice about culture and travel, look for this icon. It draws your attention to interesting tidbits about the countries in which French is spoken.

Where to Go from Here

Learning a language is all about jumping in and giving it a try (no matter how bad your pronunciation is at first). So make the leap! Start at the beginning or pick a chapter that interests you. Before long, you'll be able to respond **Oui!** (wee!) (*Yes!*) when people ask **Parlez-vous français?** (pahr-ley vooh frahN-seh?) (*Do you speak French?*).

Note: If you've never been exposed to French before, you may want to read the chapters in Part I before you tackle the later chapters. Part I gives you some of the basics that you need to know about the language, such as how to pronounce the various sounds, some basic expressions and words, and the fundamentals of French sentence structure.

Part I
Getting Started

The 5th Wave

By Rich Tennant

"There are many French phrases that we all use every day. You're no doubt familiar with the term 'à la mode.'"

In this part . . .

You have to start somewhere, but we bet that you know a lot more French than you think. Don't think so? Then check out Chapter 1 and see how many French words and idioms you already use. Chapters 2 and 3 provide some basic background on French grammar and pronunciation, while Chapters 4 and 5 get you talking about yourself and your family. So get started and don't worry – we make it fun!

Chapter 1

The French You Already Know

In This Chapter

▶ French words that are identical or similar to their English counterparts

▶ French words to watch out for

▶ Idioms and popular expressions you may already know

*L*earning a new language can be challenging. Not only do you need to know a whole new vocabulary, but you also need to twist your head around different grammar rules and your tongue around different pronunciation rules. But here's a little news that may make the task seem a little less daunting: You already know quite a few French words and expressions. How? Because the English language, being the borrower that it is, contains many French words and expressions, and French has absorbed some English words, too.

In this chapter, you get to explore some French words and phrases without having to know pronunciation or grammar rules (that info comes in Chapters 2 and 3). Here, we include French words that are spelled the same and mean the same as their English counterparts, as well as words that are close in meaning and spelling. But because not every French word that resembles an English word shares its meaning, we also tell you what words to watch out for. In addition, we include some French expressions that you probably already know and understand. By the end of this chapter, you may discover that you actually know more French than you previously thought.

The French You're Familiar With

With just a narrow stretch of water between them, the English and the French have historically been pretty close, even if they haven't always been the friendly allies they are today. In fact, French was the language of the English court for a very long time – a fact that many people tend to forget. (The Normans who invaded England in 1066 with William the Conqueror were French, as were some of the most prominent people in English history).

What does this have to do with your learning French? Well today, about 35 percent of English vocabulary is of French origin. That being the case, you already know an impressive amount of French, whether you realize it or not. The only pitfall you have to watch out for is that sometimes the English words have a different meaning from their French counterparts, and they almost certainly have a different pronunciation.

French nouns are preceded by either definite or indefinite articles. The definite articles are **le** (masculine), **la** (feminine), **l'** (an abbreviation of either **le** or **la**), and **les** (plural); these are the equivalent to the English word *the.* The indefinite articles are **un** (masculine)**, une** (feminine), **des** (plural); these are all equivalent to the English words *a, an,* or *some.* As you learn French, knowing which articles go with what nouns helps you identify the noun's gender; that's why we include the articles with the nouns in the lists throughout this book. Because the abbreviated article **l'** obscures the noun's gender, we added the gender in parentheses. Finally, because the articles are not always used in English transla- tions, we don't include them in the translations of the word lists: **l'université** (f) (lew-nee-vehr-see-tey) (*university*) and **le kiosque** (luh kyohhsk) (*kiosk*), for example.

Friendly allies – bons alliés

Several French words are spelled the same and have the same meaning as their English counterparts. The only thing that may be different is the pronunciation (for more on pronuncia- tion guidelines, head to Chapter 3). Take a look at these **bons alliés** (bohN-zah-lyey) (*friendly allies*):

- l'**art** (m) (lahr)
- **brave** (brahv)
- le **bureau** (luh bew-roh)
- le **client** (luh klee-yahN)
- le **concert** (luh kohN-sehr)
- la **condition** (lah kohN-dee-syohN)
- **content** (kohN-tahN)
- le **courage** (luh kooh-rahzh)
- le **cousin** (luh kooh-zaN)
- la **culture** (lah kewl-tewr)
- **différent** (dee-fey-rahN)
- **excellent** (ehk-seh-lahN)
- le **garage** (luh gah-rahzh)
- le **guide** (luh geed)
- **important** (aN-pohr-tahN)
- le **journal** (luh zhoohr-nahl)
- la **machine** (lah mah-sheen)
- le **message** (luh mey-sahzh)
- le **moment** (luh moh-mahN)
- la **nation** (lah nah-syohN)
- la **nièce** (lah nyehs)
- l'**orange** (f) (loh-rahNzh)
- le **parent** (luh pah-rahN)
- **possible** (poh-see-bluh)
- **principal** (praN-see-pahl)
- **probable** (proh-bah-bluh)
- la **question** (lah kehs-tyohN)
- la **radio** (lah rah-dyoh)
- le **restaurant** (luh rehs-toh-rahN)
- la **rose** (lah rohz)

✔ **rouge** (roohzh)

✔ **la route** (lah rooht)

✔ **la science** (lah syahNs)

✔ **le secret** (luh suh-kreh)

✔ **le service** (luh sehr-vees)

✔ **le signal** (luh see-nyahl)

✔ **le silence** (luh see-lahNs)

✔ **la solitude** (lah soh-lee-tewd)

✔ **le sport** (luh spohr)

✔ **la station** (lah stah-syohN)

✔ **la statue** (lah stah-tew)

✔ **la suggestion** (lah sewg-zheh-styohN)

✔ **la surprise** (lah sewr-preez)

✔ **la table** (lah tah-bluh)

✔ **le taxi** (luh tah-ksee)

✔ **le tennis** (luh tey-nees)

✔ **le train** (luh traN)

✔ **urgent** (ewr-zhahN)

✔ **violet** (vyoh-leh)

✔ **le voyage** (luh voh-yahzh)

✔ **le zoo** (luh zooh)

Kissing cousins

Some French words, while not identical in spelling to their English counterparts, look very similar. These words also have similar meanings. Table 1-1 shows words that fit into this category.

Table 1-1 — **Words Similar in Meaning, Slightly Different in Spelling**

French	English	French	English
l'acteur (m) (lahk-tuhr)	actor	l'hôtel (m) (loh-tehl)	hotel
l'adresse (f) (lah-drehs)	address	le kiosque (luh kyohhsk)	kiosk
l'aéroport (m) (lah-eyr-oh-pohr)	airport	la lampe (lah lahmp)	lamp
l'allée (f) (lah-ley)	alley	la lettre (lah leh-truh)	letter
l'Américain (m)/ l'Américaine (f) (lah-mey-ree-kaN/lah-mey-ree-kehn)	American	la mémoire (lah mey-mwahr)	memory
l'âge (m) (lahzh)	age	le miroir (luh mee-rwahr)	mirror
l'artiste (m/f) (lahr-teest)	artist	la musique (lah mew-zeek)	music
la banque (lah bahNk)	bank	la nationalité (lah nah-syoh-nah-lee-tey)	nationality
la cathédrale (lah kah-tey-drahl)	cathedral	nécessaire (ney-sey-sehr)	necessary
le chèque (luh shehk)	check	ordinaire (ohr-dee-nehr)	ordinary
la classe (lah klahs)	class	le papier (luh pah-pyey)	paper
la chambre (lah shahN-bruh)	chamber, bedroom	le poème (luh poh-ehm)	poem
la comédie (lah koh-mey-dee)	comedy	potentiel (poh-tahN-syehl)	potential
le congrès (luh kohN-greh)	congress	le problème (luh proh-blehm)	problem

(continued)

Table 1-1 *(continued)*

French	English	French	English
la crème (lah krehm)	*cream*	**le professeur** (luh proh-feh-suhr)	*teacher/ professor*
la démocratie (lah dey-moh-krah-see)	*democracy*	**le sénateur** (luh sey-nah-tuhr)	*senator*
le développe-ment (luh dey-vlohp-mahN)	*development*	**le succès** (luh sew-kseh)	*success*
la famille (lah fah-meey)	*family*	**la terrasse** (lah teh-rahs)	*terrace*
la géographie (lah zhey-oh-grah-fee)	*geography*	**la tragédie** (lah trah-zhey-dee)	*tragedy*
le gouverne-ment (luh gooh-vehr-nuh-mahN)	*government*	**l'université** (f) (lew-nee-vehr-see-tey)	*university*
l'histoire (f) (lee-stwahr)	*history*	**la visite** (lah vee-zeet)	*visit*

False friends – faux amis

Some French words are **faux amis** (foh-zah-mee) (*false friends*). They look similar to English words, but they don't have the same meaning. Misusing these words can be quite confusing. For example, if you tell someone that your young adult son or daughter is in a **collège** (koh-lehzh), they'd probably look at you – or your child – strangely because the French word **collège** means *middle school*, not *university*. The following list shows some of these easy-to-confuse words:

- ✔ **actuellement** (ahk-tew-ehl-mahN): This word means *now*, not *actually*. The French word for *actually* is **en fait** (ahN feht).

- ✔ **assister à** (ah-sees-tey ah): This word means *to attend*, not *to assist*. The French word for *to assist* is **aider** (ey-dey).

✔ **attendre** (ah-tahN-druh): This word means _to wait for,_ not _to attend._ The French word for _to attend_ is **assister à** (ah-sees-tey ah).

✔ **la bague** (lah bahg): This word means _ring_ (the kind you wear on your finger), not _bag._ The French word for _bag_ is **le sac** (luh sahk).

✔ **blesser** (bleh-sey): This word means _to wound_ or _to hurt._ The French word for _to bless_ is **bénir** (bey-neer).

✔ **la cave** (lah kahv): The French word **cave** means _cellar_ in French. The word for _cave_ is **la grotte** (lah grohht) in French.

✔ **le collège** (luh koh-lehzh) means _middle school;_ use the French word **l'université** (f) (lew-nee-vehr-see-tey) when you want to say _college._

✔ **formidable** (fohr-mee-dah-bluh): This word means _wonderful_ or _tremendous,_ not _fearsome_ or _daunting._ To say _formidable_ in French, you use the word **redoutable** (ruh-dooh-tah-bluh).

✔ **la lecture** (lah leh-ktewr): This word means _a reading,_ as in a reading of Balzac's novels. The word for _lecture_ is **la conférence** (lah kohN-fey-rahNs).

✔ **la librairie** (lah lee-brey-ree): This word means _bookstore,_ not _library._ The French word for _library_ is **la bibliothèque** (lah bee-blee-oh-tehk).

✔ **la place** (lah plahs): This word means _square, seat at the theater,_ or _seat on the bus,_ not _place._ The French word for _place_ is **le lieu** (luh lyuh) or **l'endroit** (m) (lahN-drwah).

✔ **rester** (rehs-tey): This word means _to stay_ or _to remain,_ not _to rest._ The French word for _to rest_ is **se reposer** (suh-ruh-poh-zey).

✔ **sympathique** (saN-pah-teek): This word means _nice._ To say _sympathetic_ in French, you say **compatissant(e)** (kohN-pah-tee-sahN[t]).

✔ **la veste** (lah vehst): This word means _jacket_ in French, not _vest_ or _waistcoat._ The French word for _vest_ is **le gilet** (luh zhee-leh).

Borrowed English words

The preceding sections note quite a few English words that have been borrowed from French and that have retained their French meaning, even though the pronunciation is different.

But English isn't the only language that's nicked a few words. French has also borrowed many words from English and continues to do so in spite of the loud protest by purists who condemn this trend as a sign of cultural contamination and name it **franglais** (frahN-gleh): Here is a list of some of the terms borrowed from English and absorbed into the French language. Note the different pronunciation:

- ✔ **le budget** (luh bewd-zheh)
- ✔ **le business** (luh beez-nehs)
- ✔ **le camping** (luh kahN-peeng)
- ✔ **le chewing-gum** (luh shweeng-gohhm)
- ✔ **les chips** (ley sheep[s])
- ✔ **le coca** (luh koh-kah)
- ✔ **cool** (koohl)
- ✔ **le fast food** (luh fahst foohd)
- ✔ **le hamburger** (luh ahm-boohr-guhr)
- ✔ **le jet set** (luh jeht seht)
- ✔ **le manager** (luh mah-nah-jehr)
- ✔ **le marketing** (luh mahr-kuh-teeng)
- ✔ **le parking** (luh pahr-keen)
- ✔ **le rock** (luh rohk) (as in rock music)
- ✔ **le shopping** (luh shoh-peeng)
- ✔ **le steak** (luh stehk)
- ✔ **le chat** (luh chaht)
- ✔ **le tunnel** (luh tew-nehl)
- ✔ **le week-end** (luh wee-kehnd)

Quebec is pure French

The rules of good and pure French speech are especially enforced in Quebec. People in Quebec will easily understand your **franglais**, but you may be taken aback when you hear Quebeckers talk about the following, where the French use the English word:

- ✔ **la fin de semaine** (lah faN duh suh-mehn) (*weekend*)

- ✔ **un hambourgeois** (uhN ahN-boohr-zhwah) (*hamburger*)

- ✔ **le magasinage** (luh mah-gah-zee-nazh) (*shopping*)

- ✔ **la mise en marché** (lah mee-zahN mahr-shey) (*marketing*)

- ✔ **le stationnement** (luh stah-syoh-nuh-mahN) (*parking*)

Quebec's purism is easily explained:

- ✔ The proximity of the United States south of its border, plus the English-speaking majority in Canada threatens the French cultural identity of Quebec's 7.5 million inhabitants. For Quebeckers, their language constitutes a rampart against the all-powerful presence of the English – spoken by 300 million people – surrounding them.

- ✔ People who lived mostly in rural isolation for 300 years are now living in modern cities like Montreal, Quebec, Sherbrooke, and a few others where cable TV is constantly bombarding them with American commercials, movies, and a variety of shows. These people are trying to preserve the French lanuage.

Although protective of their language, French-Canadians are an extremely friendly people.

Idioms and Popular Expressions

French, like English, has many *idioms* (unusual ways of expressing feelings and ideas). You may find the meaning of these expressions puzzling if you try to translate them word for word.

These fixed forms of expression belong specifically to the language in question. If you walk up to a French person and say **Il pleut des chats et des chiens** (eel pluh dey shah ey dey shyaN) (*It's raining cats and dogs*), he or she would question your sanity. On the other hand, you may find yourself wondering what a French speaker means when she says **Il tombe des cordes** (eel tohNb dey kohrd), whose literal translation is *Ropes are falling,* but it's roughly equivalent to *It's raining cats and dogs.*

Apart from those idioms, which take a long time to comprehend and belong specifically to a culture, every language has many expressions and phrases that, although they cannot be translated word for word, can easily be learned and used. Here are a few of the useful expressions you frequently hear in French:

- ✔ **À la vôtre!** (ah lah voh-truh!) (*Cheers!*)

- ✔ **À mon avis** (ah mohN-nah-vee) (*in my opinion*)

- ✔ **À tes/vos souhaits!** (ah tey/voh sweh!) (*Bless you!/ Gesundheit!*)

- ✔ **Allez! Un petit effort!** (ah-ley! uhN puh-tee-teh-fohr!) (*Come on! Try a little!*)

- ✔ **Bien sûr.** (byaN sewr.) (*Of course.*)

- ✔ **Bon appétit!** (bohN-nah-pey-tee!) (*Enjoy your meal!*)

- ✔ **Ça vaut la peine/le coup.** (sah voh lah pehn/luh kooh.) (*It's worth it.*)

- ✔ **D'accord.** (dah-kohr.) (*Okay.*)

- ✔ **De rien.** (duh ryaN.) (*Don't mention it.*)

- ✔ **Jamais de la vie!** (zhah-meh duh lah vee!) or **Pas question!** (pah kehs-tyohN!) (*No way!*)

- ✔ **Revenons à nos moutons.** (ruh-vuh-nohN ah noh mooh-tohN.) (*Let's get back to the subject at hand.*)

- ✔ **Tant mieux.** (tahN myuh.) (*So much the better.*)

- ✔ **Tant pis.** (tahN pee.) (*Too bad.*)

- ✔ **Tout à fait.** (tooh-tah feh.) (*Quite.*)

- ✔ **Un coup d'oeil** (uhN kooh duhy) (*a glance, a quick look*)

Chapter 2

Laying the Foundation: Basic French Grammar

In This Chapter

▶ Getting familiar with nouns, articles, pronouns, adjectives, and adverbs

▶ Understanding gender and agreement

▶ Introducing regular and irregular verbs

▶ Constructing simple sentences

*I*n your native language, you instinctively know how to form sentences and ask questions that make sense. However, when learning a new language, you need to learn that language's grammar because it lays the foundation for communicating correctly and effectively. This chapter simplifies French grammar, introducing you to the parts of speech and telling you how to construct grammatically correct sentences and questions. As you read this material, you'll be amazed to discover that learning basic French grammar is easy and completely painless. The key to success is to remain cool and patient. Little by little – and before you know it – you'll be able to speak French.

Key Parts of Speech

Words are classified based on their part of speech – verbs, nouns, pronouns, adjectives, adverbs, prepositions, conjunctions, and interjections – depending on how they are used. In this section, we concentrate on a few key parts of speech you need to know in order to form and understand basic French sentences: nouns, articles, pronouns, adjectives, and adverbs.

You can check out verbs in the later section 'Cavorting with Verbs.'

Naming things with nouns

Nouns name things: people, objects, places, concepts, and so on. *House* is a noun. So is *Mary* or *truth* or *Sandusky*. There are a few key differences between French and English nouns, however, as the next sections explain.

That whole gender thing

Unlike English nouns, all French nouns have a gender: They are either grammatically masculine or feminine. Knowing whether a noun is masculine or feminine is very important because it has an impact on the sentence construction. For example, if the noun is feminine, the articles and adjectives that modify that noun must also be feminine.

But how do you know whether a noun is masculine or feminine? Of course, if you are talking about the sex of a person or an animal, the gender is obvious. But if the noun is a thing or an idea, how do you determine its gender? For the most part, just look at the word's ending. With a few exceptions, the ending of a noun is a rather good indication of its gender. Table 2-1 shows common masculine and feminine endings.

Table 2-1	Common Masculine and Feminine Noun Endings		
Masculine Endings	*Example*	*Feminine Endings*	*Example*
–eur (uhr)	l'auteur (loh-tuhr) (*author*); le bonheur (luh boh-nuhr) (*happiness*)	–ade (ahd)	la promenade (lah prohm-nahd) (*walk*); la limonade (lah lee-moh-nahd) (*lemonade*)
–eau (oh)	le chapeau (luh shah-poh) (*hat*); le manteau (luh mahN-toh) (*coat*)	–ance/–ence (ahNs)	la naissance (lah neh-sahNs) (*birth*); la différence (lah dee-fey-*rahNs*) (*difference*)

Masculine Endings	Example	Feminine Endings	Example
–isme (eez-muh)	le capitalisme (luh kah-pee-tah-leez-muh) (*capitalism*); le féminisme (luh fey-mee-neez-muh) (*feminism*)	–oire (wahr)	la mémoire (lah mey-mwahr) (*memory*); la victoire (lah veek-twahr) (*victory*)
–ment (mahN)	l'appartement (lah-pahr-tuh-mahN) (*apartment*); le logement (luh lohzh-mahN) (*lodging, place of residence*)	–sion/tion (syohN)	l'impression (laN-prey-syohN) (*impression*); la condition (lah kohN-dee-syohN) (*condition*)
–ail (ahy)	le travail (luh trah-vahy) (*work*); le détail (luh dey-tahy) (*detail*)	–son (zohN)	la saison (lah seh-zohN) (*season*); la maison (lah meh-zohN) (*house*)
Final vowels other than –e	le cinéma (luh see-ney-mah) (movies); le piano (luh pyah-noh) (*piano*); le genou (luh zhuh-nooh) (*knee*)	–té, –ée (tey, ey)	la liberté (lah lee-behr-tey) (*freedom*); l'égalité (ley-gah-lee-tey) (*equality*); l'idée (lee-dey) (*idea*); la pensée (lah pahN-sey) (*thought*)
-al (ahl)	le journal (luh zhoohr-nahl) (*newspaper*); le festival (luh feh-stee-vahl) (*festival*)	–ie (ee)	la boulangerie (lah booh-lahN-zhree) (*bakery*); l'épicerie (ley-pees-ree) (*grocery store*)

In addition, certain occupations are always masculine in French, even though both men and women work in them. Some examples include

- ✔ **un professeur** (uhN proh-feh-suhr) (*teacher, professor*)
- ✔ **un architecte** (uhN-nahr-shee-tehkt) (*architect*)
- ✔ **un chef** (uhN shehf) (*chef*)
- ✔ **un ingénieur** (uhN-naN-zhey-nyuhr) (*engineer*)
- ✔ **un agent** (uhN-nah-zhahN) (*agent*)
- ✔ **un médecin** (uhN meyd-saN) (*doctor*)
- ✔ **un auteur** (uhN-noh-tuhr) (*author*)

Similarly, some nouns are always feminine, even when they refer to a male. Here they are:

- ✔ **une vedette** (ewn veh-deht) (*movie star*)
- ✔ **une personne** (ewn pehr-sohhn) (*person*)
- ✔ **une victime** (ewn veek-teem) (*victim*)

If you come across a noun that does not follow any of these patterns, simply consult a French dictionary.

Making singular nouns plural

In French, as in English, nouns are either singular or plural. The French say they have a *number*. To make nouns plural, you simply add an *s* to most of them, just like in English. **La maison** (lah meh-zohN) (*house*) is singular while **les maisons** (ley meh-zohN) (*houses*) is plural.

However, if a noun ends in **–ou**, **–eu**, or **–eau**, you add an *x* instead of an *s* to make it plural: The singular **le bureau** (luh bew-roh) (*office, desk*) becomes the plural **les bureaux** (ley bew-roh) (*offices, desks*).

If a noun already ends in an **–s**, **–z**, or **–x**, you don't add anything to it. In these instances, the article (and the context) makes clear that the noun is plural):

Singular	*Plural*
un fils (uhN fees) (*son*)	**des fils** (dey fees) (*sons*)
un nez (uhN ney) (*nose*)	**des nez** (dey ney) (*noses*)
un époux (uhN-ney-pooh) (*spouse*)	**des époux** (dey-zey-pooh) (*spouses*)

Keeping an eye on articles

Unlike English nouns, which don't necessarily need articles (the words *the, a,* and *an*), French nouns are almost always preceded by articles. In English, for example, you say *France,* but in French, you say **la France** (lah frahNs) (*France*). The same convention applies to plural nouns: *mountains* in English becomes **les montagnes** (ley mohN-tah-nyuh) (*mountains*) in French. Another difference between English and French articles is that French articles mark the gender and the number of nouns.

When you learn the gender of a noun, try to learn the article that goes with it. Instead of memorizing **table** (tah-bluh) (*table*), for example, memorize **la table** (lah tah-bluh) (*the table*) or **une table** (ewn tah-bluh) (*a table*). Instead of **livre** (lee-vruh) (*book*), think **le livre** (luh lee-vruh) (*the book*) or **un livre** (uhN lee-vruh) (*a book*).

Table 2-2 lists the variations of definite, indefinite, and partitive articles in French. For details on how these articles are used, keep reading.

Table 2-2	Definite, Indefinite, and Partitive French Articles			
Type of Article	*Masculine*	*Feminine*	*Preceding a Vowel or Mute H*	*Masculine and Feminine Plural*
Definite (*the*)	**le** (luh)	**la** (lah)	**l'** (see note)	**les** (ley)
Indefinite (*a, an, some*)	**un** (uhN)	**une** (ewn)	**un** (uhN), **une** (ewn)	**des** (dey)
Partitive (*some, any*)	**du** (dew)	**de la** (duh lah)	**de l'** (see note)	**des** (dey)

Note: **L'** (ehl ah-pohs-trohf) means *l apostrophe* and **de l'** (duh ehl ah-pohs-trohf) means *de l apostrophe.* These abbreviations are used when these articles are followed by a vowel or a mute h.)

Defining definite articles

The definite article refers to a specific noun and has only one form in English, even when used in the plural: *the.* In French, because nouns have a gender, the article has to take the gender of the noun as well as its number, singular or plural. Here are the definite articles in French:

- **le** (luh) (*the*) – masculine definite article, singular

- **la** (lah) (*the*) – feminine definite article, singular

- **l'** (ehl ah-pohs-trohf) (*the*) – masculine and feminine definite article, singular, used in front of nouns that start with a vowel or mute h.

- **les** (ley) (*the*) – masculine and feminine definite article, plural

For example, the word **nuage** is masculine singular; therefore, you add a masculine, singular article in front of it: **le nuage** (luh new-ahzh) (*the cloud*). You follow the same pattern for a feminine singular noun: Simply add the feminine singular article **la** in front of **maison,** for example, and you have **la maison** (lah meh-zohN) (*the house*). If the noun is plural, regardless of whether it's masculine or feminine, the article is always **les**. For example, **les nuages** (ley new-ahzh) (*the clouds*) or **les maisons** (ley meh-zohN) (*the houses*).

If a masculine or feminine noun begins with a vowel or a mute h (more on the mute h in Chapter 3), then you drop the *e* in **le** and the *a* in **la** and you add an apostrophe, **l'**. If nouns beginning with a vowel or a mute h are plural, just use **les** (ley). Here are some examples:

l'idée (f) (lee-dey) (*idea*)

les idées (ley-zee-dey) (*ideas*)

l'hôtel (m) (loh-tehl) (*hotel*)

les hôtels (ley-zoh-tehl) (*hotels*)

French also uses definite articles after verbs of preference, such as **aimer** (eh-mey) (*to like, to love*), **détester** (dey-tehs-tey) (*to hate*), and **préférer** (prey-fey-rey) (*to prefer*). (You can check verbs of preference out in Chapter 6). For example: **J'aime le café** (zhehm luh kah-fey) (*I like coffee*).

Using the indefinite article

When referring to undetermined objects, you use indefinite articles, equivalent to the English words *a* and *an*. In French, the indefinite articles are:

✔ **un** (uhN) (*a, an*) – masculine indefinite article, singular

✔ **une** (ewn) (*a, an*) – feminine indefinite article, singular

✔ **des** (dey) (*some, any*) – masculine and feminine indefinite article, plural

You use French indefinite articles the same way you use English indefinite articles. Check out the following examples:

✔ **Paris est une grande ville.** (pah-ree eh-tewn grahNd veel.) (*Paris is a big city.*)

✔ **Je voudrais un café.** (zhuh vooh-dreh-zuhN kah-fey.) (*I would like a coffee.*)

✔ **Il y a des maisons dans la rue.** (eel ee ah dey meh-zohN dahN lah rew.) (*There are houses on the street.*)

Choosing the partitive

The French language has a specific article that refers to a part of something as opposed to the whole. You can sometimes translate this article as *some* or *any*, but it is frequently omitted in English.

As you may guess, the article has a masculine form, **du** (dew); a feminine form, **de la** (duh lah); and a plural form, **des** (dey). There is also a singular form when the noun that follows starts with a vowel or a mute h, **de l'** (duh ehl ah-pohs-trohf). Here are a few examples:

Je voudrais du pain et du fromage. (zhuh vooh-dreh dew paN ey dew froh-mahzh.) (*I would like [some] bread and [some] cheese.*)

Si tu as soif, bois de l'eau! (see tew ah swahf, bwah duh loh!) (*If you are thirsty, drink* [*some*] *water!*)

Il mange souvent de la salade. (eel mahNzh sooh-vahN duh lah sah-lahd.) (*He often eats* [*some*] *salad.*)

Meeting subject pronouns face to face

Pronouns replace nouns, enabling you to avoid clumsy repetition when you write or speak. In French, pronouns change, depending on their role (subject, direct object, indirect object, or to show possession) in a sentence. Fortunately, you don't need to worry about all those different forms at this point. Instead, this section focuses on French *subject pronouns,* those that function as subjects. (The other pronouns are covered in various chapters throughout the book.)

In a sentence, the *subject* indicates who or what is performing the action. In the sentence 'John plays tennis,' *John* is the subject. You can replace *John* with the pronoun *he,* and the sentence becomes 'He plays tennis.' In this case, the pronoun *he* is the subject. Here are the French subject pronouns with their English translations:

Singular	*Plural*
je (zhuh) (*I*)	nous (nooh) (*we*)
tu (tew) (*you*)	vous (vooh) (*you*)
il/elle/on (eel/ehl/ohN) (*he/she/it, one*)	ils/elles (eel/ehl) (*they*)

Taking a closer look at 'je'

Unlike the English *I,* **je** is not capitalized in French, unless it begins the sentence. Also, if the verb that follows **je** begins with a vowel or a mute h (head to Chapter 3 for more on the mute h), the –e is dropped and an apostrophe added. This doesn't happen with any other subject pronoun. Here's an example:

J'aime le français. (zhehm luh frahN-seh.) (*I like French.*)

More on 'il,' 'elle,' 'ils,' and 'elles'

As mentioned previously, French nouns are either feminine or masculine. The same is true of French pronouns. Therefore, **il** refers not only to a person, meaning *he*, but also to a masculine singular object, meaning *it*. For example, **il siffle** (eel see-fluh) could mean *he is whistling* or *it is whistling*, depending on the context of the sentence. The same thing applies to **elle**. **Elle est belle** (ehl eh behl) could mean *she is beautiful* or *it is beautiful*. Of course, **ils** and **elles**, the masculine and feminine third person plurals, have only one meaning, *they*, regardless of whether they refer to people or things.

It's 'you,' you know: The tu/vous issue

Both **tu** and **vous** mean *you*, but you need to be aware of a fundamental difference between them. **Tu** is always singular, whereas **vous** can be singular or plural.

Vous is both singular and plural, yet even when it refers to one person, you always conjugate the verb in the plural. So start practicing your greetings using **vous** and the corresponding verb form ending **–ez** (except for three irregular verbs), whether you're addressing one person or more.

How you address someone in French depends on how well you know them. If the person is a family member, a peer, or a child, you use **tu**, which is an informal way of speaking to someone. You need to use the more polite and respectful form of the English *you*, **vous**, in these situations:

- ✔ When you meet someone for the first time (unless that person is a child)
- ✔ When you're talking to someone older than yourself
- ✔ When you're talking with someone with authority, like your teacher or your supervisor
- ✔ When you are referring to two or more people

Go to Chapter 3 for more information about using **tu** and **vous**.

In France, using **tu** to address a stranger or a new acquaintance would sound strange at best and impolite at worst. However, if you go to Quebec, you may soon discover that the familiar **tu** is much more liberally used at all times.

Using 'on' for all

On, a very versatile subject pronoun, has several meanings: *one*, *we*, *they*, and *people*. The sentence **On parle français au Québec** (ohN pahrl frahN-seh oh key-behk), for example, can mean *One speaks French in Quebec* or *We/they/people speak French in Quebec*.

On can also be used when you want to repeat something that you heard without revealing your source: **On m'a dit qu'on vous a renvoyé.** (ohN mah dee kohN vooh-zah rahN-vwah-ey.) (*Someone told me that you got fired.*)

Pretty handy pronoun, right? Remember that whether **on** refers to a singular or a plural subject, its verb conjugation is always third person singular. (See the verb conjugations later on in this chapter)

Getting descriptive with adjectives

Adjectives describe nouns. Because French nouns have both gender and number, any adjectives have to match the nouns they modify in gender and number.

Changing adjective endings to specify gender

You can change the ending of an adjective so that it agrees in gender and number with the noun. Table 2-3 shows the masculine and feminine singular and plural forms, as well as examples using these endings.

Table 2-3	Endings of French Adjectives		
Masc., Sing	*Fem. Sing.*	*Masc. Plural*	*Fem. Plural*
−e: calme (kahlm) (*calm*)	−e: calme (kahlm)	−es: calmes (kahlm)	−es: calmes (kahlm)
−é: fatigué (fah-tee-gey) (*tired*)	−ée: fatiguée (fah-tee-gey)	−és: fatigués (fah-tee-gey)	−ées: fatiguées (fah-tee-gey)
−consonant: **grand** (grahN) (*big, tall*)	−consonant + e: **grande** (grahNd)	−consonant + s: **grands** (grahN)	−consonant + es: **grandes** (grahNd)

Masc., Sing	Fem. Sing.	Masc. Plural	Fem. Plural
–eux: heu-reux (uh-ruh) (*happy*)	–euse: heu-reuse (uh-ruhz)	–eux: heureux (uh-ruh)	–euses: heureuses (uh-ruhz)
–eur: travail-leur (trah-vah-yuhr) (*hard working*)	–euse: tra-vailleuse (trah-vah-yuhz)	–eurs: tra-vailleurs (trah-vah-yuhr)	–euses: trav-ailleuses (trah-vah-yuhz)
–teur: conser-vateur (kohN-sehr-vah-tuhr) (*conservative*)	–trice: con-servatrice (kohN-sehr-vah-trees)	–teurs: con-servateurs (kohN-sehr-vah-tuhr)	–trices: conserva-trices (kohN-sehr-vah-trees)
–f: sportif (spohr-teef) (*athletic*)	–ve: sportive (spohr-teev)	–fs: sportifs (spohr-teef)	–ves: sportives (spohr-teev)
–ien: cana-dien (kah-nah-dyaN) (*Canadian*)	–ienne: ca-nadienne (kah-nah-dyehn)	–iens: ca-nadiens (kah-nah-dyaN)	–iennes: ca-nadiennes (kah-nah-dyehn)
–on: bon (bohN) (*good*)	–onne: bonne (bohhn)	–ons: bons (bohN)	–onnes: bonnes (bohhn)
–er: fier (fyehr) (*proud*)	–ère: fière (fyehr)	–ers: fiers (fyehr)	–ères: fières (fyehr)

A few adjectives have very irregular forms in the feminine singular:

- ✔ **beau/belle** (boh/behl) (*beautiful*): **un beau garçon** (uhN boh gahr-sohN) (*a beautiful [handsome] boy*) and **une belle fille** (ewn behl feey) (*a beautiful girl*)

- ✔ **nouveau/nouvelle** (nooh-voh/nooh-vehl) (*new*): **un nou-veau manteau** (uhN nooh-voh mahN-toh) (*a new coat*) and **une nouvelle robe** (ewn nooh-vehl rohhb) (*a new dress*)

- ✔ **vieux/vieille** (vyuh/vyehy) (*old*): **un vieux bureau** (uhN vyuh bew-roh) (*an old desk*) and **une vieille maison** (ewn vyehy meh-zohN) (*an old house*)

Putting the adjective in the right place

Most French adjectives are placed after the noun they describe, which is the opposite from English. Whereas in English you say *an interesting trip*, for example, in French you say **un voyage intéressant** (uhN voh-yahzh aN-tey-reh-sahN). However, this rule changes when the adjectives relate to any of the following. In these cases, the adjective goes in front of the noun:

- **Beauty**: Adjectives in this category include **beau/belle** (boh/behl) (*beautiful*) and **joli/jolie** (zhoh-lee) (*pretty*)

- **Age:** The category includes words like **jeune** (zhuhn) (*young*), **vieux/vieille** (vyuh/vyehy) (*old*), and **nouveau/ nouvelle** (nooh-voh/nooh-vehl) (*new*).

- **Numbers**: Words in this group include **premier/première** (pruh-myey/pruh-myehr) (*first, premiere*), **dernier/ dernière** (dehr-nyey/dehr-nyehr) (*last*), **deux** (duh) (*two*), **trois** (trwah) (*three*), and so forth.

- **Goodness (or lack of it):** Words like **bon/bonne** (bohN/ bohhn) (*good*), **mauvais/mauvaise** (moh-veh/moh-vehz) (*bad*), and **gentil/gentille** (zhahN-tee/zhahN-teey) (*nice*) are in this group.

- **Size:** This category includes words like **grand/grande** (grahN/grahNd) (*big, tall*), **petit/petite** (puh-tee/puh-teet) (*small, little*), and **gros/grosse** (groh/grohs) (*large, fat, thick*).

To help you remember that these categories of words precede the noun, think **B-A-N-G-S**: **B**eauty, **A**ge, **N**umbers, **G**oodness, **S**ize).

Some adjectives are a little tricky because they can change meaning according to whether they are placed before or after the noun. Check out the following list:

- **ancien/ancienne** (ahN-syaN/ahN-syehn): Before the noun, it means *former*; after the noun it means *ancient* or *old*.

- **cher/chère** (shehr/shehr): Before the noun, it means *dear*; after the noun, it means *expensive*.

- **pauvre** (poh-vruh): Before the noun, it means *unfortunate*, and after, it means *penniless*.

- **propre** (proh-pruh): Before the noun, it means *own*; after the noun, it means *clean*.

Here's a way to remember the different meanings of these adjectives: When placed before the noun, the meaning is figurative. When placed after the noun, the meaning is literal. Here are some examples:

> **un ancien collègue** (uhN-nahN-syaN koh-lehg) (*a former colleague*) versus **un bâtiment ancien** (uhN bah-tee-mahN ahN-syaN) (*an old building*)

> **un pauvre garçon** (uhN poh-vruh gahr-sohN) (*an unfortunate boy*) versus **un enfant pauvre** (uhN-nahN-fahN poh-vruh) (*a poor or impoverished child*)

Getting creative with adverbs

An adverb is a word that modifies (describes) a verb, an adjective, or another adverb. In English, many adverbs end with *–ly: quickly, nervously, slowly,* and so on. In French, most adverbs end in **–ment,** and they usually follow the verb. Here are the rules:

- ✔ To the feminine form of an adjective, add **–ment: lente** (lahNt) (*slow*) becomes **lentement** (lahNt-mahN) (*slowly*), and **active** (ahk-teev) (*active*) becomes **activement** (ack-teev-mahN) (*actively*).

- ✔ To the masculine form of an adjective that ends in a vowel, add **–ment: vrai** (vreh) (*true*) becomes **vraiment** (vreh-mahN) (*truly, really*), and **absolu** (ahb-soh-lew) (*absolute*) becomes **absolument** (ahb-soh-lew-mahN) (*absolutely*).

- ✔ To the masculine form of an adjective that ends in **–ent** or **–ant**, drop the **nt** and add **–mment: constant** (kohN-stahN) (*constant*) becomes **constamment** (kohN-stahN-mahN) (*constantly*), and **évident** (ey-vee-dahN) (*evident*) becomes **évidemment** (ey-vee-dah-mahN) (*evidently, obviously*).

The adverbial forms of good and bad are irregular in French. The adjective *good* – **bon** (bohN) – becomes the adverb **bien** (byaN) (*well*) and **mauvais** (moh-veh) (*bad*) becomes **mal** (mahl) (*badly*).

Most adverbs in French come right after the verb:

Parlez lentement, s'il vous plaît. (pahr-ley lahNt-mahN, seel-vooh-pleh.) (*Speak slowly, please.*)

Les petits oiseaux chantent joyeusement. (ley puh-tee-zwah-zoh shahNt zhwah-yuhz-mahN.) (*The little birds sing happily.*)

Cavorting with Verbs

A verb expresses an action or a state of being. In French as in English, the verb form that is not conjugated and has no marking to indicate a subject or a tense (past, present, future) for the action is called the *infinitive form.* English infinitives begin with *to,* as in *to go* or *to speak.* In French, infinitives have special endings, such as **–er, –ir,** or **–re:**

- ✔ **aller** (ah-ley) (*to go*)
- ✔ **parler** (pahr-ley) (*to speak*)
- ✔ **finir** (fee-neer) (*to finish*)
- ✔ **être** (eh-truh) (*to be*)

In addition, verbs can be regular or irregular. Regular verbs have the same stem throughout the conjugation, while the stems on irregular verbs change. (The *stem* is the main part of the verb before you add the endings.) For example, in English, the verb *to love* is a regular verb because it has the same stem whoever the subject is: I love, you love, he/she/it love**s,** we love, you love, they love. But the verb *to be* is irregular because it doesn't have a common stem throughout the conjugation. The form of the verb depends on the subject: I am, you are, he/she/it is, we are, you are, they are.

Just as in English, French verbs must match the subject (you don't say, for example, 'The children sings'). In French, the verb has a special ending for each subject (*I, you, she, we,* and so on). The following sections have the details.

Regular verbs

In French, regular verbs – those that follow a set pattern – belong to three large groups, which are determined by the ending of the verb's infinitive:

✔ The largest group whose infinitive ends with **–er**:
Examples include **chanter** (shahN-tey) (*to sing*), **parler**
(pahr-ley) (*to speak*), and **donner** (dohh-ney) (*to give*).

A simple way to conjugate this category is to first drop
the **–er** from the infinitive and add the following endings:
–e, –es, –e, –ons, –ez, and **–ent**. Here is the present tense
conjugation of **parler**:

Conjugation	*Pronunciation*
je parle	zhuh pahrl
tu parles	tew pahrl
il/elle/on parle	eel/ehl/ohN pahrl
nous parlons	nooh parh-lohN
vous parlez	vooh parh-ley
ils/elles parlent	eel/ehl parhl

Don't be lulled into thinking that all verbs ending in **–er**
are regular. **Aller** (ah-ley) (*to go*), for example, is an irregular verb.

✔ The group whose infinitive ends in **–ir,** such as **finir** (fee-
neer) (*to finish*) and **choisir** (shwah-zeer) (*to choose*).

To conjugate these verbs, first drop the **–r** from the
infinitive and add the following endings: **–s, –s, –t, –ssons,
–ssez**, and **–ssent**. Here is the present tense conjugation
of **finir** (fee-neer) (*to finish*):

Conjugation	*Pronunciation*
je finis	zhuh fee-nee
tu finis	tew fee-nee
il/elle/on finit	eel/ehl/ohN fee-nee
nous finissons	nooh fee-nee-sohN
vous finissez	vooh fee-nee-sey
ils/elles finissent	eel/ehl fee-nees

✔ The smaller but important group whose infinitive ends
in **–re,** such as **attendre** (ah-tahN-druh) (*to wait*) and
vendre (vahN-druh) (*to sell*).

To conjugate this category of verbs, just drop the **–re** from the infinitive and add **–s**, **–s**, nothing, **–ons**, **–ez**, and **–ent**. Consider the present tense conjugation of **vendre**:

Conjugation	Pronunciation
je vends	zhuh vahN
tu vends	tew vahN
il/elle/on vend	eel/ehl/ohN vahN
nous vendons	nooh vahN-dohN
vous vendez	vooh vahN-dey
ils/elles vendent	eel/ehl vahNd

Irregular verbs

Irregular verbs are verbs that don't follow a regular pattern throughout the conjugation. Although the irregular verbs can present a bit of a challenge, you can master them with some practice and a little memorization. The most important ones are the following:

✔ **être** (eh-truh) (*to be*)

The following table shows the present tense conjugation of **être:**

Conjugation	Pronunciation
je suis	zhuh swee
tu es	tew eh
il/elle/on est	eel/ehl/ohN eh
nous sommes	nooh sohm
vous êtes	vooh-zeht
ils/elles sont	eel/ehl sohN

✔ **avoir** (ah-vwahr) (*to have*)

The following table shows the present tense conjugation of **avoir:**

Conjugation	Pronunciation
j'ai	zhey
tu as	tew ah
il/elle/on a	eel/ehl/ohN ah
nous avons	nooh-zah-vohN
vous avez	vooh-zah-vey
ils/elles ont	eel-/ehl-zohN

Not only are **être** and **avoir** used in many expressions, but they also serve as helping verbs or auxiliaries in making up past compound tenses as we explain in Chapter 9.

✔ **faire** (fehr) (*to do, to make*)

The following table shows the present tense conjugation of **faire:**

Conjugation	Pronunciation
je fais	zhuh feh
tu fais	tew feh
il/elle/on fait	eel/ehl/ohN feh
nous faisons	nooh fuh-zohN
vous faites	vooh feht
ils/elles font	eel/ehl fohN

✔ **aller** (ah-ley) (*to go*)

The following table shows the present tense conjugation of **aller:**

Conjugation	Pronunciation
je vais	zhuh veh
tu vas	tew vah
il/elle/on va	eel/ehl/ohN vah
nous allons	nooh-zah-lohN
vous allez	vooh-zah-ley
ils/elles vont	eel/ehl vohN

For more irregular verbs, refer to Appendix B.

Verbs tenses

Verb tense simply means time. To express an action or a state of being taking place in the present, you use the present tense. If the action hasn't happened yet, you use the future tense. And if it took place in the past, you use a past tense.

Speaking in the present

When something is happening now, use the present tense. Here's what a simple sentence in the present looks like in French: **Les enfants chantent.** (ley-zahN-fahN shahNt.) (*The children sing/are singing/do sing*).

The French present tense can be translated in three different ways, as the preceding example shows. Although you can use these translations interchangeably, you need to decide which is the better translation for the context of the sentence. For the conjugation of the present tense of regular and irregular verbs, refer to the preceding two sections.

A quick look at past tense

You can express past tense in French in several ways, but the simplest and the most common is **le passé composé** (luh pah-sey kohN-poh-zey) (*the compound past*). This tense is made up of more than one component: an auxiliary verb (**avoir** or **être)** conjugated in the present tense and the past participle of the desired verb (the form which in English would often end with –*ed*). Here are some examples:

> **J'ai travaillé.** (zhey trah-vah-yey.) (*I worked.*)

> **Il est entré.** (eel eh-tahN-trey.) (*He entered.*)

To give you an idea of what a regular verb looks like in past tense, here's how you conjugate the verb **parler** (pahr-ley) (*to speak*):

Conjugation	Pronunciation
j'ai parlé	zhey pahr-ley
tu as parlé	tew ah pahr-ley
il/elle/on a parlé	eel/ehl/ohN ah pahr-ley
nous avons parlé	nooh-zah-vohN pahr-ley
vous avez parlé	vooh-zah-vey pahr-ley
ils/elles ont parlé	eel-/ehl-zohN pahr-ley

Peeking into the future

To make the future tense, you use the present tense conjugation of **aller** followed by an infinitive. Here's an example: **Demain, Sylvie va voyager** (duh-maN, seel-vee vah voh-yah-zhey) (*Tomorrow, Sylvie is going to travel.*)

This future form – **aller** (ah-ley) + the infinitive – is called the *immediate* or *near future* because it expresses events that will take place soon or fairly soon. French has another future tense, called the *simple future,* which translates to *will* in the English. The simple future and immediate future are often interchangeable. For example, you can say *Sylvie will travel* (simple future) or *Sylvie is going to travel* (immediate future). To find out more about the simple future tense, head to Chapter 10.

To get an idea of how to construct the immediate future with all the subject pronouns, look at the following example that uses the verb **parler** (pahr-ley) (*to speak*):

Conjugation	Pronunciation
je vais parler	zhuh veh pahr-ley
tu vas parler	tew vah pahr-ley
Il/elle/on va parler	eel/ehl/ohN vah pahr-ley
nous allons parler	nooh-zah-lohN pahr-ley
vous allez parler	vooh-zah-ley pahr-ley
ils/elles vont parler	eel/ehl vohN pahr-ley

Forming Sentences and Questions

A simple sentence construction (in French or in English) consists of at least a subject and a verb. Beyond that, it may include an object noun, an adjective, and an adverb. The sentence **Elle porte une jolie robe** (ehl pohr-tewn zhoh-lee rohhb) (*She is wearing a pretty dress*) has a subject (**elle**), a verb (**porte**), a feminine singular indefinite article (**une**), an adjective (**jolie,** in its feminine form), and an object noun (**robe**).

The English translation of a French sentence may not follow the same order of the sentence components because, as mentioned earlier, French adjectives can go before or after the noun. In the sentence, **Charles est un garçon intelligent** (shahrl eh-tuhN gahr-sohN aN-teh-lee-zhahN) is translated as *Charles is an intelligent boy,* even though the adjective (**intelligent**) comes after the noun (**garçon**) in the original sentence.

Believe it or not, some grammar issues in French are easier than in English. A good example of this is the way you can form questions:

- ✔ Use intonation by raising your voice at the end of your statement: **Vous avez un ticket?** (vooh-zah-vey-zuhN tee-keh?) (*Do you have a ticket?*)

- ✔ Add **est-ce que** (ehs-kuh) to the beginning of the phrase: **Est-ce que vous avez un ticket?** (ehs-kuh vooh-zah-vey-zuhN tee-keh?) (*Do you have a ticket?*)

If a word beginning with a vowel follows **est-ce que** (ehs-kuh), it becomes **est-ce qu'** (ehs-kuh). For example: **Est-ce qu'elle a un ticket?** (ehs-kehl-ah uhN tee-keh) (*Does she have a ticket?*)

These easy forms of questioning are valid no matter what the tense of the verb is: present, past, or future.

Chapter 3

Getting Started with Pronunciation and Basic Expressions

*W*henever anyone hears a foreign language spoken or sung at normal speed, the words – which don't make sense to begin with – create a muddle of sounds impossible to reproduce. So one of the hardest parts of learning any language – including French – is overcoming your fear of not sounding French. Once you overcome this fear of sounding 'funny,' however, everything else is fun and easy. To that end, this chapter includes all the information you need to know to pronounce French correctly.

The world has over 200 million *francophones* (people who speak French), and as you can imagine, the French accent varies in the different parts of the world. This book concentrates on the Parisian accent, which is considered the standard French accent.

The French Alphabet

The French alphabet has the same 26 letters that the English alphabet does. Of course, some of the letters are pronounced differently. Table 3-1 lists the letters and gives you their names in French, which you may find useful if, for example, you have to spell your name on the phone or write down an address.

Table 3-1	The French Alphabet		
Letter	*Pronunciation*	*Letter*	*Pronunciation*
A	ah	N	ehn
B	bey	O	oh
C	sey	P	pey
D	dey	Q	kew
E	uh	R	ehr
F	ehf	S	ehs
G	zhey	T	tey
H	ahsh	U	ew
I	ee	V	vey
J	zhee	W	dooh-bluh-vey
K	kah	X	eeks
L	ehl	Y	ee-grehk
M	ehm	Z	zehd

Uttering Vowel and Consonant Sounds

French is a romance language. Romance languages – which also include Spanish, Italian, Romanian, and Portuguese – share the same origin and thus the same characteristics. One of the most important characteristics of the romance languages is that their sound is mostly based on vowels, unlike the Anglo-Saxon languages – English and German – which are based on consonants. The emphasis on vowels gives French its soft, smooth, even, and musical character. French words certainly contain consonants, but compared to the consonants in English, French consonants are much softer. Read on to find out how to pronounce French vowels and consonants.

The tables in the following sections help you with the pronunciation of French sounds, and they include English words where the French and English pronunciation is the same. However, French also includes sounds that don't exist in the English language. In those cases, we give you tips on how you can pronounce that particular sound.

The vowel sounds

Vowel sounds, listed in Table 3-2, are the most difficult to pronounce in French. They are shorter than in English and usually end a syllable. Almost all of them have an equivalent in English.

Table 3-2		French Vowel Sounds	
French	*Symbol*	*As in English*	*French Word*
a â à	ah	c<u>a</u>rd	**la tasse** (lah tahs) (*cup*); **la pâtisserie** (lah pah-tees-ree) (*pastry shop*); **là-bas** (lah-bah) (*over there*)
e eu	uh	d<u>u</u>ll (approximate)	**le petit** (luh puh-tee) (*little one*); **la fleur** (lah fluhr) (*flower*)
é ez er	ey	m<u>ay</u>	**les cafés** (ley kah-fey) (*coffee houses*); **le nez** (luh ney) (*nose*); **parler** (pahr-ley) (*to speak*)
è ê ai ei et	eh	s<u>e</u>t	**la mère** (lah mehr) (*mother*); **la fenêtre** (lah fuh-neh-truh) (*window*); **clair** (klehr) (*clean, light-colored*); **la neige** (lah nehzh) (*snow*); **le secret** (luh suh-kreh) (*secret*)
i î y	ee	f<u>ee</u>t	**vite** (veet) (*quickly*); **la gîte** (lah zheet) (*shelter*); **le/les pays** (luh/ley pey-ee) (*country/countries*)

(continued)

Table 3-2 *(continued)*

French	Symbol	As in English	French Word
o ô au eau	oh	b<u>oa</u>t	**le mot** (luh moh) (*word*); **les côtes** (ley koht) (*ribs*); **aujourd'hui** (oh-zhoohr-dwee) (*today*); **l'eau** (f) (loh) (*water*)
o	ohh	l<u>o</u>ve	**la pomme** (lah pohhm) (*apple*); **les bottes** (ley bohht) (*boots*)
ou où	ooh	y<u>ou</u>	**l'amour** (m) (lah-moohr) (*love*); **où** (ooh) (*where*)
oi oy	wah	w<u>a</u>tch	**la soie** (lah swah) (*silk*); **moyen** (mwah-yaN (*average*)
u	ew	No English equivalent	**salut** (sah-lew) (*hello*)

Represented in French by the letter **u,** the *ew* sound does not exist in English, and it takes a little practice to get it right. Here is a little trick to help you: Say *ee* with the tip of your tongue against your front bottom teeth; then keeping your tongue against your bottom teeth, round your lips. The sound coming out of your mouth is . . . the French *ew.*

The mute e

When the letter **e** appears at the end of a word or between two consonants, it is usually not pronounced; it is *mute.* For example, you don't pronounce the **e** at the end of **grande** (grahNd) (*tall*) or in the middle of **samedi** (sahm-dee) (*Saturday*).

The nasal sounds

The nasal sound, which is very common in French but does not exist in English, is fairly easy to pronounce. Imagine you have a cold and pronounce the sounds *ah, oh,* and *un* (without the *n*) through your nose. They come out nasalized. Here's a phrase that contains all the nasal sounds in French: **un bon vin blanc** (uhN bohN vaN blahN) (*a good white wine*).

Table 3-3 lists the nasal sounds. Although English has no true equivalent for the French nasal sounds, we include some words in English that come close. When you read these 'equivalents,' don't focus on the word itself: focus on how the vowel sound changes ever so slightly as your mouth prepares to make the *n* or *ng* sound that follows.

Table 3-3		French Nasal Sounds	
French	*Symbol*	*Approximate English Equivalent*	*French Word*
an **am** **en** **em**	ahN	f<u>o</u>nd	**grand** (grahN) (*big, large*); **ambitieux** (ahN-bee-syuh) (*ambitious*); **l'enfant** (m/f) (lahN-fahN) (*child*); **l'employé/e** (m/f)(lahN-plwah-yey) (*employee*)
un	uhN	<u>u</u>ncle	**brun** (bruhN) (*brown*)
ain **in** **aim** **im**	aN	sl<u>a</u>ng	**le pain** (luh paN) (*bread*); **le matin** (luh mah-taN) (*morning*); **la faim** (lah faN) (*hunger*); **impossible** (aN-poh-see-bluh) (*impossible*)
oin	waN	<u>w</u>ang	**loin** (lwaN) (*far*)
ien	yaN	<u>Y</u>ankee	**le chien** (luh shyaN) (*dog*)
on **om**	ohN	wr<u>o</u>ng	**bon** (bohN) (*good*); **le nom** (luh nohN) (*name*)

Consonants

French consonants are pronounced almost like in English, except that you don't linger on them; let them explode and move on to the vowel that follows. Because the consonants are said so quickly, it's important that you articulate them clearly; otherwise, they get lost, and the word is hard to understand.

The French **r** often scares foreigners. No need to be scared. You just have to pronounce it with your throat. Imagine that you've got something stuck in your throat and you're trying to get it out, but make the sound as soft and gentle as you can.

Another thing you need to know about French consonants is that the consonants at the end of a word are not usually pronounced. Consider these examples: **l'argent** (m)(lahr-zhahN) (*money*), **vingt** (vaN) (*twenty*), and **les fruits** (ley frwee) (*fruit*). Of course, this rule has some exceptions. The consonants **c, r, f,** or **l** (think of the consonants in the word *careful* to help you remember) at the end of a word *are* usually pronounced. Here are some examples of these consonants: **chic** (sheek) (*chic, stylish*), **neuf** (nuhf) (*nine, new*), **cher** (shehr) (*dear, expensive*), and **avril** (ah-vreel) (*April*).

Table 3-4 lists the consonants whose sounds in French may change depending on the vowel or the consonant that follows. Note that the letter s is pronounced as an s when it starts a word, but when it's within a word, you pronounce it as you do the letter **z**.

Table 3-4		Tricky French Consonants	
French Letter	*Symbol*	*As in English*	*French Word*
c (in front of **a, o, u**)	k	<u>c</u>ollege	**le collège** (luh koh-lehzh) (*middle school*)
ç (in front of **a, o, u**)	s	<u>s</u>ole	**le garçon** (luh gahr-sohN) (*boy*)
c (in front of **e** and **i**)	s	<u>s</u>ole	**le ciel** (luh syehl) (*sky*)
ch	sh	<u>sh</u>ip	**le chapeau** (luh shah-poh) (*hat*)
g (in front of **a, o, u**)	g	<u>g</u>reed	**le gâteau** (luh gah-toh) (*cake*)
gn	ny	ca<u>ny</u>on	**la montagne** (lah mohN-tah-nyuh) (*mountain*)
gu (in front of **e** and **i**)	g	<u>g</u>reed	**la guerre** (lah gehr) (*war*); **la guitare** (lah gee-tahr) (*guitar*)
j, g (in front of **e** and **i**)	zh	lei<u>s</u>ure	**le jour** (luh zhoohr) (*day*), **le genou** (luh zhuh-nooh) (*knee*)

French Letter	Symbol	As in English	French Word
s (at the beginning of word)	s	<u>s</u>ole	**le soleil** (luh soh-lehy) (*sun*)
s (between two vowels)	z	civili<u>z</u>ation	**la civilisation** (lah see-vee-lee-zah-syohN) (*civilization*)
ss (between two vowels)	s	<u>s</u>ole	**le poisson** (luh pwah-sohN) (*fish*)

The mute h and the aspirate h

French has two different *h*'s: the *mute h* and the *aspirate h* – neither of which you pronounce. So why know the difference? For the following reasons:

- ✔ With the mute h, you drop the vowel of the definite singular article, **le** or **la,** and add an apostrophe before the mute h. For example, to say *the man* in French, you say **l'homme** (m) (lohhm), essentially turning two words into one.

- ✔ With the aspirate h, you don't drop the vowel of the definite article. The words remain separate. Here's an example: **le hockey** (luh oh-keh (*hockey*).

In the plural, a liaison (check out the later section on the liaison) appears between the articles and the mute h. For example, to say *the men,* you say **les hommes** (ley-zohhm) as though it were one word. However, no liaison appears between the article and words that begin with an aspirate h, like in the word **les héros** (ley ey-roh) (*the heroes*). If the liaison were permitted here, the word would have been **les zéros** (ley-zey-roh) (*the zeros*) – not *the heroes.*

Here is a list of some common words, besides **le hockey** and **le héros,** that begin with an aspirate h in French: **le homard** (luh oh-marh) (*lobster*), **le handicapé/la handicapée** (lah ahn-dee-kah-pey) (*handicapped*), **les haricots** (ley ah-ree-koh) (*beans*), **les hors-d'oeuvre** (ley orh-duh-vruh) (*hors d'oeuvres, appetizers*).

With a mute h, there is elision and liaison. With an aspirate h, there is no elision or liaison.

Don't stress; intone instead

In French, every syllable is of equal importance in volume and stress (hence, the absence of stressed syllables in the pronunciations in this book). The emphasis in French words of two or more syllables is on the last one, but it is one of duration rather than intensity. For example, in the English word *photography*, the stress is on the second syllable. In the French word **la photographie** (lah foh-toh-grah-fee) (*photography*), you don't stress any one particular syllable. Instead, French speakers use intonation: they raise or lower their voices in multi-syllable words, phrases, and sentences. For example, to ask a question, the French speakers raise their voices at the end of a statement.

Remembering to 'unstress' the syllable you're used to pronouncing in those words that have similar spellings in French and in English may take quite a bit of practice. It's like ironing the stubborn pleat out of a pair of trousers!

Getting Clear on Accents, Liaisons, and Elisions

French has five accents, or *diacritical marks,* as grammarians like to call them. It is important to note that the accent over a vowel in French does not indicate that that syllable is stressed. The accent only affects the letter on which it stands, and even then, it doesn't change the pronunciation of that letter unless the letter is an **e** or a **c** (refer to Table 3-2). In addition to recognizing the five French accents, you also need to know how liaisons and elisions work. The following sections have the details.

The five French accents

The accent can either change the pronunciation of the letter or distinguish one word from another. In both cases, omitting an accent is like misspelling a word. The following list explains each of the five accents:

✔ **l'accent aigu** (lah-ksahN-tey-gew) (*the sharp accent*). This accent appears only over the **e** (**é**), and its sound closely resembles the *a* in the word *take*: **le café** (luh kah-fey) (*coffee, café*).

✔ **l'accent grave** (lah-ksahN grahv) (*the grave accent*). This accent appears over the letters **e** (**è**), **a** (**à**), and **u** (**ù**), but it only affects the sound of the letter **e**. The **è** is an open *eh* sound, as in the English word *set* or in the French word **la mère** (lah mehr) (*mother*). Over the letters **a** and **u**, this accent distinguishes between two words otherwise spelled the same. With **l'accent grave**, for example, **à** is a preposition meaning *to*, *in*, or *at*. Without the accent, **a** is the third person singular present tense of the verb **avoir** (ah-vwahr), which means *has*. The same goes for the letter **u**. The word **où** (ooh) means *where*, but the word **ou** (ooh) means *or*.

✔ **l'accent circonflexe** (lah-ksahN seehr-kohN-flehks) (*circumflex accent*). When this accent (ˆ) appears over the vowels **a**, **e**, **i**, **o**, and **u**, it represents a letter (usually an **s**) that was dropped from the French word centuries ago but that may still remain in the related English word. Here are some examples: **l'hôpital** (m) (loh-pee-tahl) (*hospital*), **le château** (luh shah-toh) (*castle, chateau*), **la forêt** (lah foh-reh) (*forest*), and **l'arrêt** (m) (lah-reh) (*arrest*).

✔ **la cédille** (lah sey-deey) (*the cedilla*) or **c cédille** (sey sey-deey) (*c cedilla*).This accent appears only under the letter **c** (**ç**). The cedilla indicates that you pronounce the **c** as an **s**. If the letter **c** does not have the cedilla under it and it is followed by **a**, **o**, or **u**, then you pronounce it as you would the letter **k**, as in the English words *can* or *kite*. Check out this French command: **Commençons** (koh-mahN-sohN) (*Let's begin*).

✔ **le tréma** (luh trey-mah) (*dieresis*). This accent (¨) indicates that each vowel in a word is pronounced separately. Check out the following words: **naïf** (nah-eef) (*naïve*), **Noël** (noh-ehl) (*Christmas*).

The liaison

Have you ever thought, when listening to a French conversation, that it sounded like a great big, long word? Probably. That's because of a French phenomenon called the *liaison*. **Faire la liaison** (fehr lah lyey-zohN) (*to make a liaison*) means that the last consonant of a word is linked with the vowel that begins the following word. A liaison affects any final consonant when linked with the vowel of the following word. Check out these examples.

> **C'est un petit appartement.** (seh-tuhN puh-tee-tah-pahr-tuh-mahN.) (*It's a small apartment.*)

> **Vous êtes mon ami depuis six ans.** (vooh-zeht moh-nah-mee duh-pwee see-zahN.) (*You have been my friend for six years.*)

Besides the aspirate h (explained in the earlier section), a liaison never appears with the conjunction **et** (ey) (*and*): **un livre et un crayon** (uhN lee-vruh ey uhN kreh-yohN) (*a book and a pencil*), for example.

The elision

When a word ending with an **e** or an **a** (usually an article or a pronoun) is followed by a word starting with a vowel or a mute h, the first **e** or **a** disappears and is replaced by an apostrophe. This rule, like the liaison, contributes to the easy flow of the French language. Here are some examples:

> **la** + **école** = **l'école** (ley-kohl) (*the school*)

> **je** + **aime** = **j'aime** (zhehm) (*I like*)

> **le** or **la** + **enfant** = **l'enfant** (lahN-fahN) (*the child*)

> **la** + **histoire** = **l'histoire** (lee-stwarh) (*the story, history*)

Note that the elision does not occur with the aspirate h: **le homard** (luh oh-mahr) (*lobster*), for example.

Greetings: Formal and Friendly

Greetings are the first steps in establishing contact with someone, whatever the language. In many cases, a smile does the job, and you just have to wait for the other person to greet you and repeat what he or she just said. However, this section presents plenty of very simple French greetings that you may use on different occasions to help you meet people.

Addressing someone formally or informally

In French, you can vary the level of formality in your speech by how you say the word *you*. Depending on whom you are addressing, you can use the informal **tu** (tew) or the more formal **vous** (vooh). It's important to know when one or the other is appropriate because if you say the wrong thing, at best, you sound a little funny; at worst, you offend someone.

In general, use the formal **vous** when you address somebody you have never met, a superior, or an older person. As you get to know that person better, you may both switch to **tu.** Use the less formal **tu** when you speak to a friend, a child, or an animal. In addition, members of the same family, whatever their age, use the **tu** form.

The environment in which you find yourself also determines the correct form of address. For example, if you're a young person traveling on the train in France and you meet other young people, you would address one another as **tu**. On the other hand, if you're in a store, you'd address the clerk with **vous**, even if she looks a lot younger than you. Also keep in mind that the **vous** form is used to address one person on a formal level, but it is also a plural form used to address any number of people formally or informally.

If you are not sure what to do, use the **vous** form until the person you are addressing asks you to use the **tu** form. Then you avoid any **faux pas** (foh pah) (*social blunder* [literally, *false step*]).

In French, in a formal situation, it is more polite to add **monsieur** (muh-syuh) (*mister, sir*) to address a man, **madame** (mah-dahm) (*ma'am, missus*) to address a married woman, and **mademoiselle** (mahd-mwah-zehl) (*miss*) to address an unmarried woman, after even the simplest of expressions like **bonjour** (bohN-zhoohr) (*good day, hello*) and **merci** (mehr-see) (*thank you*). (The English Ms. has no equivalent in French.) If you don't know whether a woman is married or not, to be on the safe side, use **madame**. Remember also that **monsieur**, **madame**, and **mademoiselle** can be used on their own and are, most of the time.

Saying hello and good-bye

Nothing is easier than saying hello in a foreign language. Actually, the French language has a saying, when referring to something that is really a cinch: **C'est simple comme bonjour** (seh saN-pluh kohm bohN-zhoohr) (*It's as easy as saying hello*). So go ahead and practice these greetings and farewells:

- ✔ **Bonjour!** (bohN-zhoohr!) literally means *Good day!*, but you can use it when first greeting someone in the morning or afternoon, as long as the sun is shining.

  In Québec, people also say **Bonjour** when leaving, giving it the true meaning of *good day*.

- ✔ **Bonsoir!** (bohN-swahr!*)* (*Good evening!*).You use this greeting in the late afternoon and the evening to say hello or good-bye.

- ✔ **Salut!** (sah-lew!) (*Hi! Bye!*). This is the most informal of all hellos and is also a way of saying good-bye. Although you can use it at any time of day, you can't use it with just anybody. Use this word only with children and people you're familiar with.

- ✔ **Au revoir!** (ohr-vwahr!) (*Good-bye!*). Like its English counterpart, you can use this term any time of day or night.

- ✔ **Bonne nuit!** (bohhn nwee!) (*Good night!*). Say this only when you're retiring for the night or when you're putting a child to bed. It essentially means *sleep well*.

- ✔ **A bientôt!** (ah byaN-toh!) (*See you soon!*). Say this when you expect to see the person again in the near future.

- ✔ **A tout à l'heure!** (ah tooh-tah luhr!) (*See you later!*). Use this phrase only when you'll see the person the same day.

- ✔ **A demain!** (ah duh-maN!) (*See you tomorrow!*)

- ✔ **Bonne journée!** (bohhn zhoohr-ney!) (*Have a nice day!*)

Introducing yourself and others

It is not enough to greet people and ask how they are; you also need to introduce yourself and find out what their names are. The purpose of this section is to help you do just that.

In French, when you want to say *My name is. . .*, you use a reflexive form of the verb **appeler** (ahp-ley) (*to call*). Thus, **je m'appelle** (zhuh mah-pehl) literally means *I call myself*. The following table shows all the forms of **appeler** in the present tense. (Refer to Chapter 2 for general information on French verbs.)

Conjugation	*Pronunciation*
je m'appelle	zhuh mah-pehl
tu t'appelles	tew tah-pehl
il/elle/on s'appelle	eel/ehl/ohN sah-pehl
nous nous appelons	nooh nooh-zah-plohN
vous vous appelez	vooh vooh-zah-pley
ils/elles s'appellent	eel/ehl sah-pehl

You may use either of these phrases:

✔ **Je m'appelle . . . .** (zhuh mah-pehl. . . .) (*My name is . . . .*)

✔ **Je suis . . . .** (zhuh swee. . . .) (*I am . . . .*)

If you want to know who that person over there is, you ask **Qui est-ce?** (kee ehs?) (*Who is that?*). And you receive the answer **C'est . . .** (seh. . .) (*That is . . .*). To introduce someone, you say any of the following:

✔ **Je vous présente . . . .** (zhuh vooh prey-zahNt. . . .) (*Let me introduce . . . to you.*) (formal)

✔ **Je te présente . . . .** (zhuh tuh prey-zahNt. . . .) (*Let me introduce . . . to you.*) (informal)

✔ **Voici . . . ./Voilà . . . .** (vwah-see. . . ./vwah-lah. . . .) (*Here is . . . ./There is . . . .*)

After you introduce yourself or someone else, the other person, if a man, typically says **Enchanté!** (ahN-shahN-tey!) or, if a woman, **Enchantée!** (pronounced the same). In either case, the meaning is the same: *Delighted!* Of course, on the playground or at a gathering of young people, you may hear these expressions instead:

Comment tu t'appelles?/Comment t'appelles-tu? (koh-mahN tew-tah-pehl?/koh-mahN tah-pehl-tew?) (*What's your name?*)

Et lui, qui est-ce? (ey lwee kee ehs?) (*And who is he?*), or **Et elle, qui est-ce?** (ey ehl kee ehs?) (*And who is she?*)

Asking Questions to Get to Know People

One of the ways to get information is by asking questions. You may want to ask, for example, whether the bistro around the corner is good, whether the banks are open on Mondays, or whether the train is running on schedule. And what about asking how someone is? Well, you can ask all these questions simply by following the guidelines explained in the following sections.

Informal and formal ways to ask questions

You can form a yes or no question in French in four ways. The first three are very informal, and the last is more formal.

Using intonation

To ask a question using intonation, simply raise your voice at the end of a statement: **Vous parlez français?** (vooh parh-ley frahN-seh?) (*Do you speak French?*)

Using 'n'est-ce pas'

One way to form a question is to add **n'est-ce pas** (nehs pah) to the end of the sentence. This expression takes on the translation of whatever the question is. It could mean *isn't it, don't you, doesn't she,* and so on.) This type of question anticipates a yes answer: **Vous parlez français, n'est-ce pas?** (vooh parh-ley frahN-seh, nehs pah?) (*You speak French, don't you?*)

Using 'est-ce que'

You can form a question by adding **est-ce que** (ehs-kuh) to the front of the statement. The statement **Paris est une** grande ville (pah-ree eht-ewn grahNd veel) (*Paris is a big city*) becomes **Est-ce que Paris est une grande ville?** (ehs-kuh pah-ree eht-ewn grahNd veel?) (*Is Paris a big city?*). Note that the final **e** in **Est-ce que** is dropped when it comes before a vowel: **Est-ce qu'il parle français?** (ehs-keel parhl frahN-seh?) (*Does he speak French?*)

Using inversion

In this method, you switch the places of the verb and the subject pronoun and add a hyphen between them. Consider these examples:

> **Vous parlez français** (vooh parh-ley frahN-seh) (*You speak French*) becomes **Parlez-vous français?** (parh-ley vooh frahN-seh?) (*Do you speak French?*)

> **Tu aimes la musique** (tew ehm lah mew-zeek) (*You like music*) becomes **Aimes-tu la musique?** (ehm-tew lah mew-zeek?) (*Do you like music?*)

To use inversion correctly, when the verb ends in a vowel and the subject pronoun begins with a vowel – mainly **il** (eel) (*he, it*), **elle** (ehl) (*she, it*), **on** (ohN) (*one*) – you add the letter *t* in between them and place hyphens on both sides: **Il parle français** (eel parhl frahN-seh (*He speaks French*) becomes **Parle-t-il français?** (parhl-teel frahN-seh?) (*Does he speak French?*)

Asking and replying to 'How are you?'

Most of the time, when you meet someone, especially someone you already know, your greeting is followed by the question 'How are you?' French has several different ways of asking the question, depending on the level of formality between the two speakers:

> Formal: **Comment allez-vous?** (koh-mahN-tah-ley-vooh?) (*How are you?*) and **Vous allez bien?** (vooh-zah-ley byaN?) (*Are you well?*)

> Informal: **Comment vas-tu?** (koh-mahN vah-tew?) (*How are you?*), **Comment ça va?** (koh-mahN sah vah?) (*How is it going?*), and **Ça va?** (sah vah?) (*Is it going?*, meaning *Are you okay?*).

Of course, others may well want to know how you are. In those cases, they naturally expect you to reply, albeit without going into lengthy details about your health, your work, or your private life. A short phrase will do, such as the following:

- ✔ **Ça va!** (sah vah!) (*I'm okay!*)

- ✔ **Ça va bien!/Ça va très bien!** (sah vah byaN!/sah vah treh byaN!) (*I'm fine!/I'm very well!*)

- ✔ **Bien, merci!/Très bien, merci!** (byaN, mehr-see!/treh byaN, mehr-see!) (*Fine, thank you!/Very well, thank you!*)

- ✔ **Je vais bien, merci.** (zhuh veh byaN, mehr-see.) (*I am well, thank you.*) This is a more formal response.

- ✔ **Pas mal!** (pah mahl!) (*Not bad!*)

Of course, you can also answer negatively. You can say, for example, **Je ne vais pas très bien aujourd'hui** (zhuhn veh pah treh byaN oh-zhoohr-dwee) (*I am not very well today*).

The negative in French has two parts: **ne** (nuh) which you place in front of the conjugated verb and **pas** (pah) (*not*), which you place after the conjugated verb. If the verb begins with a vowel or a mute h, then you drop the **e** from **ne** and you add an apostrophe: **n'**. For example, **Il n'est pas fatigué** (eel neh pah fah-tee-gey) (*He is not tired*).

Whenever you answer a 'How are you?' question, you probably want to follow it up with an inquiry about the well-being of the other person. To do so, you simply follow your answer with either the formal **Et vous?** (ey vooh?) or the informal **Et toi?** (ey twah?). Both mean *And you?*

Revisiting the verb 'aller'

Aller (ah-ley) (*to go*) is a very useful and multifunctional verb in French. As Chapter 2 explains, **aller** is an irregular verb, which means that the stem is different throughout its conjugation:

CULTURAL WISDOM

Friendly greetings

The French touch a lot more than the Anglo-Saxons do in greeting others. The handshake is not restricted to the first meeting between two persons, for example. Instead, most people in an office shake hands every morning when they get to work and every evening when they leave the office. On a more informal level, women friends kiss lightly on each cheek when they greet each other or say good-bye. A man and a woman meeting or saying good-bye do the same. Male family members may kiss one another, too. If you travel to different parts of France, you may be surprised to discover that in some areas people kiss not twice but three times, and sometimes up to four times! You even see a large amount of cheek-pecking between high school students arriving at school in the morning!

Say you're invited to a dinner party by a French family with children and the parents introduce their children to you before they are sent to bed. They may tell the children **Dites bonsoir à tout le monde** (deet bohN-swahr ah tooh luh mohNd) *(Say good evening to everyone)*. Immediately, the little ones might go around the dinner table giving a kiss to all the guests and expecting a kiss back.

Conjugation	*Pronunciation*
je vais	zhuh veh
tu vas	tew vah
Il/elle/on va	eel/ehl/ohN vah
nous allons	nooh-zah-lohN
vous allez	vooh-zah-ley
ils/elles vont	eel/ehl vohN

You use the verb **aller** when you want to say you're going to the store or to the movies, but you also use this verb when you want to talk about how you or someone else is, which makes it a vital verb when you're making introductions and want to ask *How are you?* in French. To do so, you use the interrogative adverb **comment** (koh-mahN) (*how*) in the following ways:

> **Comment est-ce que vous allez?/Comment est-ce que tu vas?** (koh-mahN ehs-kuh vooh-zah-ley?/koh-mahN ehs-kuh tew vah?) (*How are you?*)

> **Comment allez-vous?/Comment vas-tu**? (koh-mahN-tah-ley-vooh?/koh-mahN vah-tew?) (*How are you?*) – This construction is more common.

Chapter 4

Getting Your Numbers, Dates, and Times Straight

- -

In This Chapter

▶ Discovering cardinal and ordinal numbers

▶ Using the calendar and dates

▶ Telling time

- -

*C*ounting and being able to express and understand numbers is an indispensable part of everyday life. You need numbers when you reveal your age, when you are making the perfect soufflé, or when you're trying to find your favorite TV program. One of the most important uses of numbers is to tell time. How else can you keep track of appointments or plan trips? In this chapter, we show you how to do all of that – use numbers, dates, and time – one step at a time.

Counting Your Lucky Stars: Numbers

You don't need to juggle numbers like a mathematician: Most of the time, you can use plain old cardinal numbers from 0 to around 100 to express the number of units of anything: how much money you have in your wallet, how many sheep you have to count before you fall asleep, how many hours you have to wait before your plane takes off, and so on. Fortunately, French numbers follow a pattern, much like numbers in English.

Counting up to 20

The following list shows the numbers **un** (uhN) (*one*) through **vingt** (vaN) (*twenty*):

- ✔ 1 **un** (uhN)
- ✔ 2 **deux** (duh)
- ✔ 3 **trois** (trwah)
- ✔ 4 **quatre** (kah-truh)
- ✔ 5 **cinq** (saNk)
- ✔ 6 **six** (sees)
- ✔ 7 **sept** (seht)
- ✔ 8 **huit** (weet)
- ✔ 9 **neuf** (nuhf)
- ✔ 10 **dix** (dees)
- ✔ 11 **onze** (ohNz)
- ✔ 12 **douze** (doohz)
- ✔ 13 **treize** (trehz)
- ✔ 14 **quatorze** (kah-tohrz)
- ✔ 15 **quinze** (kaNz)
- ✔ 16 **seize** (sehz)
- ✔ 17 **dix-sept** (dee-seht)
- ✔ 18 **dix-huit** (deez-weet)
- ✔ 19 **dix-neuf** (deez-nuhf)
- ✔ 20 **vingt** (vaN)

The pronunciation of some numbers changes when the number is followed by a vowel, a mute h (check out the mute h in Chapter 3), or a consonant. The following list explains:

- ✔ When a number ending in –s or –x is followed by a vowel: In these instances, the final **s** and **x** make a *z* sound: **deux enfants** (duhz-ahN-fahN) (*two children*) and **trois enfants** (trwahz-ahN-fahN) (*three children*), for example.

✔ When the numbers **neuf** (nuhf) (*nine*) and **dix-neuf** (dees-nuhf) (*nineteen*) are followed by a vowel: In these cases, the final **f** makes the *v* sound: **neuf artistes** (nuhv arh-teest) (*nine artists*), for example.

✔ When the numbers **six** (sees) (*six*), **huit** (weet) (*eight*), **dix** (dees) (*ten*) are followed by a consonant: The final consonants of these numbers are not pronounced: **six livres** (see lee-vruh) (*six books*), **huit personnes** (wee pehr-sohhn) (*eight people*), and **dix films** (dee feelm) (*ten films*), for example.

Counting higher

After you count to **vingt**, you're ready to go higher. After all, if you want to make a special purchase like an exceptional bottle of wine, for example, it will surely cost more than 20 euros! With what follows, you can handle almost everything number-related.

For numbers 20 through 69

You form the numbers 20 through 69 in French much as you do in English, counting up from each tens number, until you hit the next tens number and then starting over.

✔ 21 **vingt et un** (vaN-tey-uhN)

✔ 22 **vingt-deux** (vahNt-duh)

✔ 23 **vingt-trois** (vahNt-trwah)

  and so on

✔ 30 **trente** (trahNt)

✔ 31 **trente et un** (trahN-tey-uhN)

✔ 32 **trente-deux** (trahN-duh)

  and so on

✔ 40 **quarante** (kah-rahNt)

✔ 41 **quarante et un** (kah-rahN-tey uhN)

✔ 42 **quarante-deux** (kah-rahN-duh)

  and so on

✔ 50 **cinquante** (saN-kahNt)

- ✔ 51 **cinquante et un** (saN-kahN-tey uhN)
- ✔ 52 **cinquante-deux** (saN-kahNt-duh)

  and so on

- ✔ 60 **soixante** (swah-sahNt)
- ✔ 61 **soixante et un** (swah-sahN-tey uhN)
- ✔ 62 **soixante-deux** (swah-sahNt-duh)

  and so on

For numbers 70 through 99

The number 70 in French is 60 + 10. The number 71 is 60 + 11, 72 is 60 + 12, and so on until you get to 80. For example:

- ✔ 70 **soixante-dix** (swah-sahNt-dees)
- ✔ 71 **soixante et onze** (swah-sahN-tey ohNz)
- ✔ 72 **soixante- douze** (swah-sahNt-doohz)

  and so on

The number 80 is 4 × 20, although the word 'times' isn't used. The number 81 is 4 × 20 + 1, 82 is 4 × 20 + 2 and so on, until you get to 90, which is 4 × 20 + 10. The number 91 is 4 × 20 + 11. (Notice that you don't use the conjunction **et** in the number 81 and higher. Also when another number follows 80, the **s** in **vingt** is dropped.) Here are some examples:

- ✔ 80 **quatre-vingts (**kah-truh-vaN)
- ✔ 81 **quatre-vingt-un** (kah-truh-vaN-uhN)
- ✔ 82 **quatre-vingt-deux** (kah-truh-vaN-duh)

  and so on

- ✔ 90 **quatre-vingt-dix** (kah-truh-vaN-dees)
- ✔ 91 **quatre-vingt-onze** (kah-truh-vaNt-ohNz)
- ✔ 92 **quatre-vingt-douze** (kah-truh-vaN-doohz)

  and so on

If you travel to Switzerland or to Belgium, you may be happy to know that the old – and easier – forms of **septante** (sehp-tahNt) (70) and **nonante** (noh-naNt) (90) are commonly used instead of the French **soixante-dix** and **quatre-vingt-dix**. Some parts of Switzerland use the forms **huitante** (wee-tahNt) or **octante** (ohk-tahNt) for 80.

For the numbers 100 and up

After you hit 100, counting to a thousand or even hundreds of thousands is a breeze. Just indicate the number of hundreds or thousands and count up as you do in English. For example:

- 100 **cent** (sahN)
- 101 **cent-un** (sahN-uhN)
- 102 **cent-deux** (sahN-duh)

  and so on

- 200 **deux cents** (duh sahN)
- 201 **deux cent un** (duh sahN uhN)
- 202 **deux cent deux** (duh sahN duh)

  and so on

- 1,000 **mille** (meel)
- 2,000 **deux mille** (duh meel)
- 3,000 **trois mille** (trwah meel)

  and so on

- 1,000,000 **un million** (uhN mee-lyohN)
- 1,000,000,000 **un milliard** (uhN mee-lyahr)

In the preceding list, notice that you drop the **s** in **cents** when another number follows it. Also, the number **mille** doesn't use an **s**, even when it refers to several thousands. Finally, **un** does not precede **cent** or **mille** when you say *one hundred* or *one thousand*.

Discovering ordinal numbers

Ordinal numbers are important when you need to give or follow directions. (Go to Chapter 7 for info on giving and getting directions in French.) To recognize ordinal numbers, remember that, except for **premiere** (pruh-myey) (*first*), they all have **–ième** (ee-ehm) after the number (just like the *-th* ending in English). Also, whereas English uses the superscript *th* (or *st* or *rd*) to indicate ordinal numbers (5th, for example), in French, the superscript is the letter **e**: 9e, 4e, and so on. Table 4-1 lists the ordinal numbers from first through twentieth, but you can go as high as you like. Here are the rules for forming ordinal numbers:

- ✔ If the cardinal number ends in an **–e,** the **–e** is dropped: For example, **quatre** (kah-truh) (*four*) becomes **quatrième** (kah-tree-ehm) (*fourth*), **seize** (sehz) (*sixteen*) becomes **seizième** (seh-zee-ehm) (*sixteenth*).

- ✔ For the number **cinq** (saNk) (*five*), add a **u** before **–ième: cinquième** (sahN-kee-ehm) (*fifth*).

- ✔ For the number 9, **neuf** (nuhf), the **f** changes to **v: neuvième** (nuh-vee-ehm) (*ninth*).

Table 4-1   Ordinal Numbers, from 1er through 20^e

Abbrev.	French	Pronunciation	Abbrev.	French	Pronunciation
1e	**premiere**	(pruh-myey)	11e	**onzième**	(ohN-zee-ehm)
2e	**deuxième**	(duh-zee-ehm)	12e	**douzième**	(dooh-zee-ehm)
3e	**troisième**	(trwah-zee-ehm)	13e	**treizième**	(treh-zee-ehm)
4e	**quatrième**	(kah-tree-ehm)	14e	**quatorzième**	(kah-tohr-zee-ehm)
5e	**cinquième**	(sahN-kee-ehm)	15e	**quinzième**	(kahN-zee-ehm)
6e	**sixième**	(see-zee-ehm)	16e	**seizième**	(seh-zee-ehm)
7e	**septième**	(seh-tee-ehm)	17e	**dix-septième**	(dee-seh-tee-ehm)
8e	**huitième**	(wee-tee-ehm)	18e	**dix-huitième**	(dee-zwee-tee-ehm)
9e	**neuvième**	(nuh-vee-ehm)	19e	**dix-neuvième**	(deez-nuh-vee-ehm)
10^e	**dixième**	(dee-zee-ehm)	20^e	**vingtième**	(vaN-tee-ehm)

Approximating quantities

Sometimes you want to approximate the numbers instead of being very exact. If you were speculating on someone's age, for example, you may say in English that she is or looks about 40. You can do the same in French by adding the suffix **–aine** (ehn) to the cardinal numbers. Here are some examples:

- ✔ **une dizaine** (ewn deez-ehn) (*about 10*)
- ✔ **une vingtaine** (ewn vaN-tehn) (*about 20*)

If a noun follows the approximate quantity, then add the preposition **de** (duh) or **d'** if the noun begins with a vowel or a mute h, as these examples show:

> **Je voudrais une dizaine de croissants.** (zhuh vooh-dreh ewn deez-ehn duh krwah-sahN.) (*I would like about 10 croissants.*)

> **Il y a une vingtaine d'étudiants dans la classe.** (eel ee ah ewn vahN-tehn dey-tew-dyahN dahN lah klahs.) (*There are about 20 students in the class.*)

You can refer to approximate numbers by using the words **à peu près** (ah puh preh) or **environ** (ahN-vee-rohN), both of which mean *approximately.* For example, **J'ai environ quatre-vingts livres dans mon bureau** (zhey ahN-vee-rohN kah-truh-vaN lee-vruh dahN mohN bew-roh) (*I have approximately 80 books in my office*).

Using the Calendar and Dates

Countries differ in how the date is presented. In French, the day of the month comes first, followed by the month, followed by the year. For example: **le 8 mai, 2011** (luh wee meh duh-meel-ohNz), and it's written 8-5-2011.

Even though a week has seven days, the French refer to a week as **huit jours** (wee zhoohr) (*8 days*) and to two weeks as **quinze jours** (kaNz zhoohr) (*15 days*). The reason is that if you count from Monday to Monday and you include both Mondays, then you have 8 days, and if you continue counting to the following Monday (the third Monday), you have 15 days.

Recounting the days of the week

The French calendar begins on a Monday as the first day of the week. Unlike English, the days of the week are not capitalized in French:

- **lundi** (luhN-dee) (*Monday*)
- **mardi** (mahr-dee) (*Tuesday*)
- **mercredi** (mehr-kruh-dee) (*Wednesday*)
- **jeudi** (zhuh-dee) (*Thursday*)
- **vendredi** (vahN-druh-dee) (*Friday*)
- **samedi** (sahm-dee) (*Saturday*)
- **dimanche** (dee-mahNnsh) (*Sunday*)

When referring to a particular day, state the day without an article: **je travaille samedi** (zhuh trah-vahy sahm-dee) (*I work [on] Saturday*). But if you want to say *I work on Saturdays*, you have to place the definite article **le** (luh) (*the*) in front of the day of the week, like this: **je travaille le samedi** (zhuh trah-vahy luh sahm-dee) (*I work on Saturdays*). Placing the definite article **le** in front of the day(s) of the week is like adding an *s* to the day(s) of the week in English.

Knowing the names of the months

Just like the days of the week, the months of the year are not capitalized in French. Here are the months in French:

- **janvier** (zhahN-vyey) (*January*)
- **février** (fey-vryey) (*February*)
- **mars** (mahrs) (*March*)
- **avril** (ah-vreel) (*April*)
- **mai** (meh) (*May*)
- **juin** (zhwaN) (*June*)
- **juillet** (zhwee-yeh) (*July*)
- **août** (ooht) (*August*)
- **septembre** (sehp-tahN-bruh) (*September*)

✔ **octobre** (ohk-toh-bruh) (*October*)

✔ **novembre** (noh-vahN-bruh) (*November*)

✔ **décembre** (dey-sahN-bruh) (*December*)

To say that something is happening in a certain month, you use the preposition **en** (ahN) (*in*) in front of the month. Here are some examples:

> **Mon anniversaire est en décembre.** (mohN-nah-nee-vehr-sehr eht-ahN dey-sahN-bruh.)(*My birthday is in December.*)

> **En janvier, je pars pour la Martinique.** (ahN zhaN-vyey, zhuh pahr poohr lah mahr-tee-neek.) (*In January, I leave for Martinique.*)

> **Je reviens en avril.** (zhuh ruh-vyaN ahN-nah-vreel). (*I am coming back in April.*)

Setting specific dates

When expressing a specific date, use the following construction:

> **Le** + cardinal number + month + year

You use this formula to express all dates, except for the first of the month, when you use the ordinal number. Here are a couple of examples:

> **C'est le 6 avril 2000.** (seh luh see-zah-vreel duh meel.) (*It's the sixth of April 2000.*)

> **C'est le premier mai.** (seh luh pruh-myey meh.) (*It's the first of May.*)

The following are some important dates in some French-speaking countries:

✔ **le 14 juillet** (luh kah-tohrz zhwee-yeh) (*July14*): The French national holiday

✔ **le premier août** (luh pruh-myey ooht) (*August 1*): The Swiss national holiday

✔ **le 17 juillet** (luh dee-seht zhwee-yeh) (*July 17*): The Belgian national holiday

✔ **le premier juillet** (luh pruh-myey zhwee-yeh) (*July 1*): The Canadian national holiday

Remembering the seasons

The seasons in French are masculine and, unlike in English, require the definite article:

✔ **le printemps** (luh praN-tahN) (*spring*)

✔ **l'été** (ley-tey) (*summer*)

✔ **l'automne** (loh-tohn) (*fall*)

✔ **l'hiver** (lee-vehr) (*winter*)

To express *in the spring*, for example, use **au** (oh) before a consonant sound and use **en** (ahN) before a vowel sound: **au printemps** (oh praN-tahN) (*in the spring*), **en été** (ahN-ney-tey) (*in the summer*), **en automne** (ahN-noh-tohn) (*in the fall*), and **en hiver** (ahN-nee-vehr) (*in the winter*).

Telling Time in French

One of the most important and frequent uses of numbers is, of course, to tell time. The French use both the familiar 12-hour clock and the official 24-hour clock to tell time.

Using the 12-hour clock

To express the time in French using the 12-hour system, you begin with **il est** (eel eh) (*it is*) and add a number representing the hour and then the word **heure(s)** (uhr) (*time, o'clock*). Use the singular **heure** when it's 1:00; use the plural **heures** for all other hours. Here are some examples:

> **Il est huit heures.** (eel eh weet-uhr.) (*It's 8 o'clock.*)

> **Il est neuf heures.** (eel eh nuhv-uhr.) (*It's 9 o'clock.*)

> **Il est une heure.** (eel eh ewn-uhr.) (*It's 1 o'clock.*)

Of course, the time isn't always exactly on the hour. Therefore, you need a way to indicate time past and before the hour, too. To indicate time past the hour, you can simply follow the phrase **il est. . .heure(s)** with the number of minutes it is past the hour. To express time before the hour (10 minutes to 2:00, for example), you add the word **moins** (mwaN), which means *minus.* Consider these examples:

> **Il est huit heures dix.** (eel eh weet-uhr dees.) (*It's 8:10* or *It's 10 past 8.*)

> **Il est huit heures moins dix.** (eel eh weet-uhr mwaN dees.) (*It's 7:50.* [Literally: *It's 8:00 minus 10.*])

> **Il est dix heures moins vingt-cinq.** (eel eh deez-uhr mwaN vahN-saNk.) (*It's 9:35* or *It's 25 to 10:00.* [Literally: *It's 10:00 minus 25 minutes.*])

Alternatively, you can use these French phrases:

- ✔ **et quart** (ey kahr) (*quarter after*). For example: **Il est neuf heures et quart.** (eel eh nuh-vuhr ey kahr.) (*It's 9:15* or *It's quarter past nine.*)

- ✔ **et demi** (e) (ey duh-mee) (*half-past*). For example: **Il est huit heures et demie.** (eel eh weet-uhr ey duh-mee.) (*It's half past 8:00.*)

- ✔ **moins le quart** (mwaN luh kahr) (*quarter till*). For example: **Il est neuf heures moins le quart.** (eel eh nuhv-uhr mwaN luh kahr.) (*It's quarter to 9:00.*)

To distinguish between a.m. and p.m. in the 12-hour clock, use these phrases after the time:

- ✔ **du matin** (dew mah-taN) (*in the morning*)

- ✔ **de l'après-midi** (duh lah-preh-mee-dee) (*in the afternoon*)

- ✔ **du soir** (dew swahr) (*in the evening*)

- ✔ **midi** (mee-dee) (*noon*)

- ✔ **minuit** (mee-nwee) (*midnight*)

Here are a couple of examples:

> **Il est 10 heures du matin.** (eel eh deez-uhr dew mah-taN.) (*It is 10:00 in the morning* [*a.m.*])

> **Il est 10 heures du soir.** (eel eh deez-uhr dew swahr.) (*It is 10:00 in the evening* [*p.m.*])

Both **midi** and **minuit** are masculine, so when you say *half past noon* or *half past midnight*, you don't add an **e** to the word **demi**: **Il est midi et demi** (eel eh mee-dee ey duh-mee) (*It's half past noon*).

In North America, we abbreviate time in the *hour:minute* format: 12:15 for example, or 3:35. In France, time is abbreviated differently. Instead of using a colon to separate the hour from the minutes, you use a lowercase *h*. For example, 11:30 becomes 11h30. You abbreviate in the same way whether you're using the 12-hour system or the 24-hour system. For example, 10h30 means 10:30 a.m. and 22h30 means 10:30 p.m.

Using the 24-hour routine

In Europe, as well as French-speaking Canada, the use of the 24-hour clock, or military time, is very common. It's used for all transportation schedules, concert times, store hours, appointment times, and any other scheduled events. When you use the 24-hour clock, you don't need to distinguish between a.m. or p.m.

If you're accustomed to the 12-hour system, telling time by the 24-hour clock may be a little confusing. Here's what you need to know: You count up from 1:00 a.m. to 12:00 noon just as you're used to, but instead of starting over again at 1, you keep counting up: 13:00, 14:00, and so on until you hit 24:00, which is midnight. So 13:00 is 1:00 p.m., 14:00 is 2:00 p.m. and so on.

To say what time it is in the 24-hour system, simply add the number of minutes to the hour. Here are some examples:

> **Il est 11h15 [onze heures quinze].** (eel eh ohNz uhr kaNz.) (*It's 11:15 [a.m.].*)

> **Il est 16h10 [seize heures dix].** (eel eh sehz uhr dees.) (*It's 4:10 [p.m.].*)

Part II
French in Action

"I practice my French with the owner. So far I've learned how to say, 'Leave me alone', 'Not you again?', and 'Buy something or get out.'"

In this part . . .

We present French in the context of daily life. We show you how to ask key questions, keep up in casual conversations, order in a French restaurant, ask for directions, communicate with coworkers, and much, much more. Along the way, you'll discover some key grammatical constructions that enable you to express yourself, share your likes and dislikes, make comparisons, and talk about the weather, your profession, and your hobbies.

Chapter 5

Getting to Know You: Making Small Talk

● ●

In This Chapter

▶ Asking key questions

▶ Recounting your likes and dislikes

▶ Using demonstrative adjectives

▶ Talking about the weather and what you do for a living

● ●

*W*hether you're conversing with someone you just met or chatting with an old acquaintance, small talk is a key part of many conversations. Although it can lead to more serious discussions, small talk generally deals with innocent subjects such as what you do for a living, your likes and dislikes, the weather, and so on. It's a wonderful way to get acquainted with someone and allows you to decide whether you want to pursue a conversation with the stranger next to you on the plane or bus or go back to the book you're reading. After reading this chapter, you'll have the information you need to **parler de tout et de rien** (pahr-ley duh tooh ey duh ryahN) (talk about everything and nothing).

Basic Questions and Polite Expressions

As Chapter 3 explains, you can ask a yes-or-no question in French in numerous ways: make your voice rise at the end of a sentence, place **est-ce que** (ehs-kuh) in front of the sentence, or invert the subject and the verb. When you make small talk, however, you want to ask questions that elicit more than a yes-or-no answer. With the information in the following sections, you'll be able to ask basic questions and use expressions that are an important part of every conversation.

Using key question words

To get specific information, you need to know these key question words:

- ✔ **à quelle heure** (ah kehl uhr) (*at what time*)
- ✔ **combien de** (kohN-byaN duh) (*how many*)
- ✔ **combien** (kohN-byaN) (*how much*)
- ✔ **comment** (koh-mahN) (*how*)
- ✔ **où** (ooh) (*where*)
- ✔ **pourquoi** (poohr-kwah) (*why*)
- ✔ **qu'est-ce que** (kehs-kuh) (*what*)
- ✔ **quand** (kahN) (*when*)
- ✔ **quel(s)/quelle(s)** (kehl) (*which, what*)
- ✔ **qui** (kee) (*who*)

You can use these question words on their own, just as in English, or you can use them in sentences. For example, to find out someone's name or to ask who someone is, you can ask these questions:

> **Qui est-ce?** (kee ehs?) (*Who is it?*)
>
> **Comment vous appelez-vous?** (koh-mahN vooh-zah-pley-vooh?) (*What's your name?*)
>
> **Comment s'appelle . . . ?** (koh-mahN sah-pehl. . . ?) (*What's . . . name?*)
>
> **Quel est son prénom?** (kehl-eh sohN prey-nohN?) (*What's his/her first name?*)

You can also ask about where someone lives and someone's age with these questions:

> **Où habitez-vous?** (ooh ah-bee-tey-vooh?) (*Where do you live?* [formal or plural])

Quel âge avez-vous? (kehl-ahzh ah-vey-vooh?) (*How old are you?* [formal or plural])

The question **Quel âge avez-vous** uses the verb **avoir** (ah-vwahr) (*to have*) instead of **être** (eh-truh) (*to be*), so the literal translation is *What age do you have?* The logical answer uses the verb **avoir**, as well: **J'ai douze ans** (zhey dooh-zahN) (*I am 12* [Literally: *I have 12 years*]).

Saying the magic words: Polite expressions

Your mother was right: A kind word goes a long way. Saying *please*, *thank you*, and *excuse me*, as well as a few other universal phrases, mark you as a considerate person and one worth getting to know. So use these following expressions liberally:

- ✔ **Pardon/Excusez-moi.** (pahr-dohN/eks-kew-zey-mwah.) (*Excuse me.*)
- ✔ **Je suis désolé/désolée.** (zhuh swee dey-zoh-ley.) (*I am sorry.*)
- ✔ **Ce n'est pas grave!** (suh neh pah grahv!) (*That's okay!*)
- ✔ **De rien.** (duh ryahN.) (*You're welcome.* [Literally: *It's nothing.*])
- ✔ **Je vous en prie.** (zhuh vooh-zahN pree.) (*You are welcome.*)
- ✔ **S'il vous plaît.** (seel vooh pleh.) (*Please.*)

When you're just learning a foreign language, you may need to let the person speaking to you know that you're having a little difficulty understanding or responding. Instead of saying 'Huh?' try out these expressions:

Je ne comprends pas. (zhuhn kohN-prahN pah.) (*I don't understand.*)

Je ne sais pas. (zhuhn seh pah.) (*I don't know.*)

Pouvez-vous parler plus lentement, s'il vous plaît? (pooh-vey-vooh pahr-ley plew lahNt-mahN, seel vooh pleh?) (*Can you speak more slowly, please?*)

> **Pouvez-vous répéter, s'il vous plaît?** (pooh-vey-vooh rey-pey-tey seel vooh pleh?) (*Can you repeat, please?*)

> **Un moment, s'il vous plaît.** (uhN moh-mahN, seel vooh pleh.) (*One moment, please.*)

Pay attention to two little words that you see over and over again in French: **et** (ey) (*and*) and **dans** (dahN) (*in*). To use them correctly, remember these rules:

 ✔ **et:** Never link **et** with the next word (in other words, don't make the liaison, explained in Chapter 3). For example, to say *He is handsome and intelligent,* say **Il est beau et intélligent** (ee-leh boh ey aN-tey-lee-zhahN).

 ✔ **dans:** Use **dans** for time and space (location). Notice that it can have slightly different meanings depending on the context. Here are some examples: **dans un mois** (dahN-zuhN mwah) (*in a month*) and **dans l'avion** (dahN lah-vyohN) (*on/in the plane*).

Stating Your Preferences

One of the ways in which you get to know someone or they get to know you is by expressing likes and dislikes. When you say in French that you like to travel, that you hate waiting in line, or even that you love a certain film, you use *verbs of preference*. These verbs include

 ✔ **aimer** (eh-mey) (*to like, to love*)

 ✔ **aimer mieux** (eh-mey myuh) (*to like better, to prefer*)

 ✔ **adorer** (ah-doh-rey) (*to adore*)

 ✔ **préférer** (prey-fey-rey) (*to prefer*)

 ✔ **détester** (dey-teh-stey) (*to hate*)

Aimer, adorer, and **détester** are all regular –er verbs; go to Chapter 2 for information on conjugating regular verbs. The verb **préférer,** however, has a stem change: The accent on the second **e** changes from an **aigu** (**é**) to a **grave** (**è**), except for the **nous** and **vous** forms. Check out the conjugation of **préférer:**

Conjugation	*Pronunciation*
je préfère	zhuh prey-fehr
tu préfères	tew prey-fehr
il/elle/on préfère	eel/ehl/ohN prey-fehr
nous préférons	nooh prey-fey-rohN
vous préférez	vooh prey-fey-rey
ils/elles préfèrent	eel/ehl prey-fehr

To say that you like or hate something in French, you use the definite article *the* – **le** (luh), **la** (lah), and **les** (ley) – even though the article may not be necessary in English. Check out these examples:

> **J'aime le café au lait.** (zhehm luh kah-fey oh leh.) (*I like coffee with milk.*)

> **Nous préférons les films étrangers.** (nooh prey-fey-rohN ley feelm ey-trahN-zhey.) (*We prefer foreign films.*)

> **Ils détestent le bruit.** (eel dey-tehst luh brwee.) (*They hate noise.*)

Talking about Your Livelihood

In French, when you state your profession, you just say **Je suis. . .** (zhuh swee) (*I am. . .*) and then name the profession. For example, **Je suis professeur** (zhuh swee proh-feh-suhr) means *I am a teacher, professor.* To identify someone else's profession, use the construction **Il/Elle est. . .** (eel/ehl eh) (*He/She is. . .*). **Il est ingénieur** (ee-leh-tahN-zhey-nyuhr), for example, means *He is an engineer.* Notice that in these constructions, you don't use the article **un** (uhN) (*a, an*), as you do in English (I am *a* teacher, for example, or he is *an* engineer).

You use the same construction to describe yourself or someone else: **Je suis optimiste** (zhuh swee-zohp-tee-meest) (*I am optimistic*), for example, or **Il est intelligent** (ee-leh-taN-teh-lee-zhahN) (*He is intelligent*).

Although not exhaustive by any means, this list includes many common occupations.

- **professeur** (proh-feh-suhr) (*high school teacher, college professor*)

- **informaticien/informaticienne** (aN-fohr-mah-tee-syaN/aN-fohr-mah-tee-syehn) (*computer scientist*)

- **secrétaire** (suh-krey-tehr) (*secretary*)

- **médecin** (meyd-saN) (*physician*)

- **infirmier/infirmière** (aN-feer-myey/aN-feer-myehr) (*nurse*)

- **avocat/avocate** (ah-voh-kah/ah-voh-kaht) (*lawyer*)

- **ingénieur** (aN-zhey-nyuhr) (*engineer*)

- **serveur/serveuse** (sehr-vuhr/sehr-vuhz) (*waiter/waitress*)

- **dentiste** (dahN-teest) (*dentist*)

- **retraité/retraitée** (ruh-treh-tey) (*retired*)

- **homme d'affaires/femme d'affaires** (ohhm dah-fehr/fahm dah-fehr) (b*usiness man/business woman*)

- **architecte** (ahr-shee-tehkt) (*architect*)

- **PDG** (pey dey zhey) (*CEO* [**Note:** This acronym stands for **Président Directeur Général**])

Notice that some professions have only one form for the masculine and the feminine. As a rule, nouns and adjectives that end with an *e*, for example – **dentiste** – are the same regardless of gender. (Check out Chapter 2 for more on the transformation of nouns and adjectives.) Some professions on the preceding list do not have a feminine form because the gender designation is a remnant of the (sexist) days when certain professions were mostly filled by men, which is no longer the case in the 21st century.

The following are some useful job-related expressions:

> **Quel est votre métier?** (kehl eh vohh-truh mey-tyey?) (*What is your profession?*)

> **Qu'est-ce que vous faites dans la vie?** (kehs-kuh vooh feht dahN lah vee?) (*What do you do for a living?*)

> **Pour quelle entreprise/compagnie travaillez-vous?** (poohr kehl ahN-truh-preez/kohN-pah-nyee trah-vah-yey-vooh?) (*What company do you work for?*)

> **Voyagez-vous souvent pour votre travail?** (voh-yah-zhey-vooh sooh-vahN poohr vohh-truh trah-vahy?) (*Do you travel often for your job/work?*)

> **Votre métier est intéressant.** (vohh-truh mey-tyey eh-taN-tey-reh-sahN.) (*Your profession is interesting.*)

Chatting about the Weather

Another great topic for small talk is, of course, **le temps** (luh tahN) (*the weather*). As a matter of fact, one way to designate small talk in French is with the phrase **parler de la pluie et du beau temps** (pahr-ley duh lah plwee ey dew boh tahN) (Literally: *to talk about the rain and the nice weather*). In countries of great weather contrasts, like Canada, weather is a constant topic of conversation. Under more temperate climates, like that of France, the weather is still a favorite topic, especially if you want to complain about it.

Of course, you cannot talk about the weather without knowing the names of the seasons; **le printemps** (luh praN-tahN) (*spring*), **l'été (m)** (ley-tey) (*summer*), **l'automne (m)** (loh-tohn) (*fall*), and **l'hiver (m)** (lee-vehr) (*winter*). Check out Chapter 4 for more details on the seasons. You can also ask about the weather with the question **Quel temps fait-il?** (kehl tahN feh-teel) (*What is the weather like?*). To answer this question, you use **Il fait. . . .** (eel feh . . .) (*It's. . . .*) and plug in any of the following phrases:

- ✔ **chaud** (shoh) (*warm, hot*)
- ✔ **froid** (frwah) (*cold*)
- ✔ **frais** (freh) (*cool*)
- ✔ **doux** (dooh) (*mild*)
- ✔ **beau** (boh) (*nice*)
- ✔ **mauvais** (moh-veh) (*bad*)
- ✔ **du vent** (dew vahN) (*windy*)
- ✔ **du soleil** (dew soh-lehy) (*sunny*)

To indicate that it's raining or snowing, you say **Il pleut** (eel pluh) (*It's raining*) or **Il neige** (eel nehzh) (*It's snowing*).

You can also say what the temperature is: **La température est de 20 degrés** (lah tahN-pey-rah-tewr eh duh vaN duh-grey) *(It is 20 degrees [Celsius])*; just substitute the current temperature for the 20.

Throughout the world, the temperature is not stated in Fahrenheit but in Celsius (centigrades). So when you hear **La température est de 25 degrés** (lah tahN-pey-rah-tewr eh duh vaN saNk duh-grey) *(The temperature is 25 degrees)*, it means 25 degrees Celcius.

Notice that all the weather phrases start with **il**. While you may be familiar with **il** as the masculine singular pronoun – **il s'appelle** (eel sah-pehl) *(his name is)* or **il habite** (eel ah-beet) *(he lives)*, for example – this **il** doesn't refer to a male person or a masculine object. Instead, it's impersonal, like the English *it*. Using **il** in this context isn't difficult: As far as conjugation and verb agreement go, the verb form that follows is third person singular (just as it is for any **il** and **elle**).

In every language, the weather is the source of many proverbs. Here is one of those French proverbs: **Une hirondelle ne fait pas le printemps** (ew-nee-rohN-dehl nuh feh pah luh praN-tahN) *(One swallow does not make the spring)*. In France, you can expect cold weather soon when the swallows start gathering on the electric wires, ready to take off to warmer climates; when you see them coming back, you know that spring is close, but it hasn't quite arrived.

Deciding to Keep in Touch

As you get to know your new acquaintances better, you may want to exchange addresses or phone numbers. To trade contact information, you can use these phrases:

- ✔ **Où habitez-vous?** (ooh ah-bee-tey-vooh?) *(Where do you live?)*

- ✔ **Quelle est votre adresse?** (kehl eh vohh-trah-drehs?) *(What is your address?)*

- ✔ **Donnez-moi votre numéro de téléphone.** (dohh-ney-mwah vohh-truh new-mey-roh duh tey-ley-fohhn.) *(Give me your phone number.)*

In this day and age, you are likely to want and give an e-mail address. The French language has a word for it: **l'adresse électronique** (lah-dreh-sey-lehk-troh-neek), but saying **e-mail** (ee-mehl) is so much more convenient; it's even been frenchified as **le mél** (luh meyl)! Of course, French also has a word for the @ sign: **arobas** (ah-roh-bah) or, more commonly, **à** (ah) (*at*); the dot is **point** (pwaN), which means, among many other things, the period at the end of a sentence.

Canada has a local area code – **l'indicatif** (m) (laN-dee-kah-teef) – followed by the seven digits of a personal phone number. In France, each time you make a call, even locally, you have to dial the two-digit area code (which begins with a zero, like 01 or 02) followed by eight numbers that are stated in groups of two (04 94 37 08 56, for example). To call a French number from the United States, dial 011, the code for France (33) and then the number directly, skipping the 0 of the area code (011 33 4 94 37 08 56, for example).

Chapter 6

Asking Directions and Finding Your Way

*W*hen you set out for a trip, you probably have a pretty good idea of all the things you want to do and the places you want to see. You figure out beforehand how you'll manage to get there, what type of transportation you need, and how to arrange for it. After you arrive, however, you'll probably discover that you don't quite know where the nearest bus stop or bank is or how to find the restroom or telephone. And if your plans change, all your previous preparation won't be enough to get you where you want to go. In those situations, you need to know how to ask for directions. Where do you go for the phrases and questions that let you get to where you want to be? Right here.

Asking and Answering 'Where?' Questions

The most common question when you are traveling is probably *Where is. . . ?* You make *where* questions the same way in French as you do in English: You follow the question word **où** (ooh) (*where*) with the verb **être** (eh-truh) (*to be*) or the verb **se trouver** (suh trooh-vey) (*to be located*).

Asking questions with 'où,' plus the verbs 'être' and 'se trouver'

The verb **être** is the verb most often connected with **où**, as these examples show (check out Chapter 2 for the complete conjugation of the verb **être**):

> **Où est le Louvre?** (ooh eh luh looh-vruh?) (*Where is the Louvre?*)
>
> **Où est la place Victor Hugo?** (ooh eh lah plahs veek-tohr ew-goh?) (*Where is the Victor Hugo Square?*)
>
> **Où sont les toilettes?** (ooh sohN ley twah-leht?) (*Where is the bathroom?*)

But, as mentioned previously, another verb, **se trouver**, is also very frequently used to ask *where* questions:

> **Où se trouve le Louvre?** (ooh suh troohv luh looh-vruh?) (*Where is the Louvre [located]?*)
>
> **Où se trouve la place Victor Hugo?** (ooh suh troohv lah plahs veek-tohr ew-goh?) (*Where is the Victor Hugo Square?*)
>
> **Où se trouvent les toilettes?** (ooh suh troohv ley twah-leht?) (*Where is the bathroom?*)

As all the preceding examples show, *where* questions follow this construction:

> **où** + verb + subject

In fact, you use this sentence structure for all other verbs you choose to connect with **où**:

> **Où va ce bus?** (ooh vah suh bews?) (*Where is this bus going?*)
>
> **Où mène cette rue?** (ooh mehn seht rew?) (*Where does this road lead?*)

Answering questions with 'à'

Prepositions are (often) little words, like *to, in,* and *at,* that indicate a relationship between one thing and another in a sentence. They're also a key element in answering *where* questions: Where are you going? To the zoo. Where is the concert? In the park. Where's Alice? At the museum.

Fortunately, rather than remember three French prepositions, you only have to remember one, **à** (ah), which means *to, in,* or *at* (consider it a three-fer). How you use **à**, though, depends on the context of the answer.

As a rule, you use the preposition **à** when you want to say that you are going to or staying in a city or town. For example:

> **Je vais à Lille.** (zhuh veh-zah leel.) (*I am going to Lille.*)
>
> **Ils sont à Montréal.** (eel sohN-tah mohN-rey-ahl.) (*They are in Montreal.*)

However, when you want to talk about going to or staying at places in general, such as museums, cathedrals, or churches, you need to add the definite article – **le** (luh), **la** (lah), or **les** (ley), all of which mean *the* – after **à**. Note that **à** contracts with the masculine, singular **le** and the plural **les**. The following list shows these combinations and provides a sample sentence using that construction:

- ✔ **à** + **le** = **au** – Example: **Sylvie va au musée.** (seel-vee vah oh mew-zey.) (*Sylvie is going to the museum.*)

- ✔ **à** + **la** = **à la** – Example: **Guy veut aller à la cathédrale.** (gee vuh-tah-ley ah lah kah-tey-drahl.) (*Guy wants to go to the cathedral.*)

- ✔ **à** + **l'** = **à l'** – Example: **Les Martin vont à l'église St. Paul.** (ley mahr-taN vohN-tah ley-gleez saN pohl.) (*The Martins go to St. Paul's church.*)

- ✔ **à** + **les** = **aux** – Example: **Allez aux feux!** (ah-ley oh fuh!) (*Go to the traffic lights!*)

Using 'voici' and 'voilà'

Occasionally, the place you're looking for (or being asked about) is right in front of you (or close enough to point to). After all, if you've never been to a particular location before, you may not know quite what you're looking for or you may not recognize that you've already arrived! Similarly, if you're giving directions to your companion as you go along, you'll very likely announce your arrival with *Here is the. . .* or a similar expression. To create these expressions, you use the words **voici** (vwah-see) (*here*) and **voilà** (vwah-lah) (*there*):

> **Voici la poste/le musée/l'université!** (vwah-see lah pohst/luh mew-zey/lew-nee-vehr-see-tey!) (*Here is the post office/the museum/the university!*)

> **Voilà les bureaux!** (vwah-lah ley bew-roh!) (*There are the offices!*)

The difference between **voici** and **voilà** is that **voici** refers to something very close to you (here), and **voilà** refers to something farther away from you (there).

Of course, people are always using expressions that convey the same meaning but with fewer words. To do that with these answers, you simply eliminate the noun (**le musée, l'université,** and so on) and use a pronoun in its place (**le, la,** or **les**) in front of **voici** or **voilà**, as shown in the following answers:

Question	*Answer*
Où est le musée?	**Le voici!**
(ooh eh luh mew-zey?)	(luh vwah-see!)
(*Where is the museum?*)	(*Here* it *is!*)
Où est l'université?	**La voilà!**
(ooh eh lew-nee-vehr-see-tey?)	(lah vwah-lah!)
(*Where is the university?*)	(*There it is!*)
Où sont les bureaux?	**Les voilà!**
(ooh sohN ley bew-roh?)	(ley vwah-lah!)
(*Where are the offices?*)	(*There they are!*)

Getting specific with prepositions

French has many more prepositions than **à**. And you need to know these other prepositions when someone is giving you directions or when you want to give more specific directions to others. With the prepositions in the following list, you'll know, for example, whether the restaurant you are looking for is next to the cathedral, across from the mall, or in front of the square:

- **à côté de** (ah koh-tey duh) (*next to*)

- **à gauche de** (ah gohsh duh) (*to the left of*)

- **à droite de** (ah drwaht duh) (*to the right of*)

- **en face de** (ahN fahs-duh) (*across from, in front of*)

- **près (de)** (preh [duh]) (*near* [*to*], *close* [to])

- **loin (de)** (lwaN [duh]) (*far* [*from*])

- **devant** (duh-vaḥN) (*in front of*)

- **derrière** (deh-ryehr) (*behind*)

- **entre** (ahN-truh) (*between*)

- **dans** (dahN) (*in, inside*)

- **sur** (sewr) (*on, on top of*)

- **sous** (sooh) (*under, underneath*)

Here are some example sentences using these prepositions:

> **Le restaurant est entre la poste et l'hôtel de ville.**
> (luh reh-stoh-rahN eh-tahN-truh lah pohst ey loh-tehl duh veel.) (*The restaurant is between the post office and town hall.*)

> **Le cinéma est en face de l'hôtel.** (luh see-ney-mah eh-tahN fahs duh loh-tehl.) (*The movie theater is across from the hotel.*)

> **La boulangerie se trouve à côté du musée.** (lah booh-lahN-zhree suh troohv ah koh-tey dew mew-zey.) (*The bakery is next to the museum.*)

Getting Direction about Directions

Whenever and wherever you travel, you are bound to need directions at some point. Understanding a few basic expressions can enable you to get the general idea or direction of where to go. The following sections have the details. You can also find information that tells you what to do if you find yourself having difficulty catching everything you're told.

Using direct commands to give directions

When someone directs you to a location, that person is giving you a command. In a command, it's understood that you're being addressed, but French has two ways to say *you* – the familiar **tu** (tew) and the polite **vous** (vooh).

As discussed in Chapter 5, to form the command, you just omit the **tu, nous** (nooh) (*we*), or **vous** in front of the verb (just as you drop the *you* and *we* in English):

> **Va au centre.** (vah oh sahN-truh.) (*Go to the center.*)

> **Allez tout droit.** (ah-ley tooh drwah.) (*Go straight ahead.*)

> **Traversons le pont.** (trah-vehr-sohN luh pohN.) (*Let's cross the bridge.*)

For **–er** verbs only, drop the final **–s** from the **tu** form in all commands, as in these examples:

Infinitive (-er)	Tu Form	Command Form
aller	tu vas	va!
(ah-ley)	(tew vah)	(vah)
(to go)	(you go)	(go!)
continuer	tu continues	continue!
(kohN-tee-new-ey)	(tew kohN-tee-new)	(kohN-tee- new!)
(to continue)	(you continue)	(continue!)

However, when you ask directions from people you don't know or don't know well, you'll probably find that they address you with the polite **vous**. In such a case, remember that the ending of most verbs in the **vous** form is **–ez**. Here are some verbs in the **vous** form that will come in very handy:

✔ **Tournez. . . .** (toohr-ney. . . .) (*turn. . . .*) as in **Tournez à droite/à gauche/à la rue....** (toohr-ney ah drwaht/ah gohsh/ah lah rew. . . .) (*Turn right/left/on. . . street.*)

✔ **Prenez. . . .** (pruh-ney. . . .) (*take. . . .*) as in **Prenez la deuxième rue à droite/à gauche.** (pruh-ney lah duh-zee-ehm rew ah drwaht/ah gohsh.) (*Take the second street on the right/on the left.*)

✔ **Montez. . . .** (mohN-tey. . . .) (*go up. . . .*) as in **Montez la rue. . . /le boulevard. . . /l'avenue. . . .** (mohN-tey lah rew. . . /luh boohl-vahr. . ./lahv-new. . . .) (*Go up. . . street/. . . boulevard/. . . avenue.*)

✔ **Descendez. . . .** (dey-sahN-dey. . . .) (*go down. . . .*) as in **Descendez la rue. . . ./le boulevard. . . ./l'avenue. . . .** (dey-sahN-dey lah rew. . . ./luh boohl-vahr. . . ./lahv-new. . . .) (*Go down. . . street/. . . boulevard/. . . avenue.*)

✔ **Suivez. . . .** (swee-vey) (*follow. . . .*) as in **Suivez la rue. . . ./ le boulevard. . . ./ l'avenue. . . .** (swee-vey lah rew. . . ./ luh boohl-vahr. . . ./lahv-new. . . .) (*Follow. . . street/. . . boulevard/. . . avenue.*)

✔ **Continuez à. . . .** (kohN-tee-new-ey ah. . . .) (*continue on. . . .*) as in **Continuez à la rue. . . ./au boulevard. . . ./ à l'avenue. . . .** (kohN-tee-new-ey ah lah rew. . . ./oh boohl-vahr. . . ./ah lahv-new. . . .) (*Continue on. . . street/. . . boulevard/. . . avenue.*)

✔ **Allez tout droit.** (ah-ley tooh drwah.) (*Go straight.*)

✔ **Traversez. . . .** (trah-vehr-sey. . . .) (*cross. . . .*) as in **Traversez la rue. . . ./le boulevard. . . ./l'avenue. . . ./ le pont.** (trah-vehr-sey lah rew. . . ./luh boohl-vahr. . . ./ lahv-new. . . ./luh pohN.) (*Cross. . . street/. . .boulevard/. . . avenue/the bridge.*)

Softening commands with 'il faut'

Commands tend to sound a bit bossy. So in French, you have a way out of this. You can use just one form for everybody – **il faut** (eel foh) (*one has to*). This impersonal form exists only in the **il** (eel) (*it*) form. When you use **il faut** in commands, the form **il faut** never changes. Simply put the infinitive of any verb after it, as these examples show. Whether the sentence is translated with *I*, *you*, or *we* depends on the context:

- ✔ **Il faut retourner à l'hôtel.** (eel foh ruh-toohr-ney ah loh-tehl.) (*I/you/we have to go back to the hotel.*)

- ✔ **Il faut aller au centre-ville.** (eel foh-tah-ley oh sahNn-truh veel.) (*I/you/we have to go downtown.*)

- ✔ **Il faut prendre un taxi.** (eel foh prahN-druhN tah-ksee.) (*I/you/we have to take a cab.*)

Expressing distances in time and space

As Chapter 3 explains, you can use the preposition **à** for time expressions such as **à demain** (ah duh-mahN) (*see you tomorrow*), **à bientôt** (ah byaN-toh) (*see you soon*), and even **à la semaine prochaine** (ah lah suh-mehn proh-shehn) (*see you next week*), but you can also use **à** for distance away from you, as in the following:

À deux minutes. (ah duh mee-newt.) (*It takes only two minutes, It's two minutes away.*)

À cent mètres. (ah sahN meh-truh.) (*Only 100 meters farther, It's in about 100 meters.*)

C'est à cent mètres (d'ici). (seh-tah sahN meh-truh [dee-see].) (*It's 100 meters [from here].*)

C'est à deux kilomètres. (seh-tah duh kee-loh-meh-truh.) (*It's 2 kilometers away, It's 2 kilometers from here.*)

Paris has 20 districts called **arrondissements** (ah-rohN-dees-mahN), numbered in a clockwise spiral pattern. The first district is in the heart of Paris and includes the Louvre. The higher the number, the farther from the center the district is; the smaller the number, the closer to the center it is. When you speak with people who live in Paris, you often hear them use ordinal numbers to indicate what section of the city a particular location is. For example, if someone says **Dans quel arrondissement est le restaurant?** (dahN kehl ah-rohN-dees-mahN eh luh reh-stoh-rahN?) *(In which district is the restaurant?)*, the response may be **Il est dans le deuxième** (eel eh dahN luh duh-zee-ehm) *(It is in the second [district]).*

If you're going to give or follow directions, you need to know your ordinal numbers so that you know where to turn: at the first, second, or third street or traffic light, for example. Check out the ordinal numbers in Chapter 4.

Going north, south, east, and west

If you're unfamiliar with a place, the directions that use local landmarks (which may only be known by the locals!) aren't going to do you much good. And when the person giving you directions doesn't know *your* exact location (if you're asking for directions over the phone, for example), he or she can't very well tell whether you need to turn right or left to get to your destination. In those cases, it's easier to use cardinal points: north, south, east, and west. What's an added bonus of using cardinal directions? It makes taking unplanned side trips – exploring the French countryside, for example – that much easier.

- ✔ **nord** (nohr) *(north)*, **nord-est** (nohr-ehst) *(northeast)*, and **nord-ouest** (nohr-wehst) *(northwest)*
- ✔ **sud** (sewd) *(south)*, **sud-est** (sew-dehst) *(southeast)*, and **sud-ouest** (sew-dwehst) *(southwest)*
- ✔ **est** (ehst) *(east)*
- ✔ **ouest** (wehst) *(west)*

When you ask for or give directions by using cardinal points, always place **au** (oh) (*to the*) in front of a cardinal point that begins with a consonant and **à l'** (ahl) (*to the*) in front of a cardinal point that begins with a vowel. Here are some examples:

> **Paris est au nord de Nice.** (pah-ree eh-toh nohr duh nees.) (*Paris is north of Nice.*)
>
> **La Suisse est à l'est de la France.** (lah swees eh-tah lehst duh lah frahNs.) (*Switzerland is east of France.*)

Checking directions or your location

What if you get lost on your way to Versailles? Or maybe you just want to make sure that you're on the right track, wherever you may be going. Here are some helpful questions that you can ask:

> **Est-ce que c'est la bonne route pour. . . ?** (ehs-kuh seh lah bohn rooht poohr. . . ?) (*Is this the right way to. . . ?*)
>
> **Où va cette rue?** (ooh vah seht rew?) (*Where does this street go?*)
>
> **Comment s'appelle cette ville?** (koh-mahN sah-pehl seht veel?) (*What's the name of this town?*)
>
> **Pourriez-vous m'indiquer comment aller. . . ?** (pooh-ree-ey-vooh maN-dee-key koh-mahN-tah-ley. . . ?) (*Could you indicate, point out [to me] how to get to. . . ?*)

What to do when you don't understand

What do you do if you don't understand the directions just because the person to whom you are speaking is talking too fast, mumbling, or has a pronounced accent? Well, don't give up! Instead, say that you don't understand and ask the person to repeat the information more slowly. That's when the following phrases can help you:

- ✔ **Pardon. Je ne comprends pas.** (pahr-dohN. zhuh nuh kohN-prahN pah.) (*Pardon. I don't understand.*)

- ✔ **Excusez-moi! Est-ce que vous pouvez répéter, s'il vous plaît?** (ehks-kew-zey-mwah! ehs-kuh vooh pooh-vey rey-pey-tey, seel vooh pleh?) (*Excuse me. Can you repeat that, please?*)

- ✔ **(Parlez) plus lentement.** ([pahr-ley] plew lahNt-mahN.) ([*Speak*] *more slowly.*)

- ✔ **Qu'est-ce que vous avez dit?** (kehs-kuh vooh-zah-vey dee?) (*What did you say?*)

Of course, it's always handy to know how to say *thank you*, or *thank you very much*, which in French is **merci** (mehr-see) or **merci beaucoup** (mehr-see boh-kooh). In reply, you may hear **De rien** (duh ryaN) (*It's nothing*) or **Je vous en prie** (zhuh vooh-zahN pree) (*You are welcome*).

Chapter 7

Bon Appétit! Dining Out and Going to the Market

● ●

In This Chapter

▶ Making restaurant reservations, ordering, and paying the check

▶ Using the conditional tense of **vouloir** and **pouvoir**

▶ Going to the market with the verbs **acheter** and **vendre**

● ●

*E*xploring the food and eating habits of people in another country is one of the most pleasant ways to discover their culture. When the subject is French food and restaurants, the exploration is especially enjoyable. This chapter is undoubtedly the most appetizing and probably one of the most useful if you are planning to visit a French-speaking country or if you just want to impress your date by ordering in French at the hot, new bistro in your town. Whether you want to eat in a fancy two- or three-star restaurant or eat bread and cheese sitting on a park bench, you need to know how to select, order, and then enjoy (which we promise will be easy)! Of course, not every meal is eaten out, so this chapter also explains what kinds of items you can find at the local outdoor markets and the specialty shops.

Dining Out

What better way to enjoy what you're eating than to start with an empty stomach? Then you can say **J'ai faim** (zhey faN) (*I'm hungry*) or **J'ai soif** (zhey swahf) (*I'm thirsty*), and the glorious world of French gastronomy is yours!

French-speaking people like to emphasize the way they feel. So instead of simply saying *I am very hungry* or *I am very thirsty*, a French person tells you **Je meurs de faim** (zhuh muhr duh faN) (*I am dying of hunger*) or **Je meurs de soif** (zhuh muhr duh swahf) (*I am dying of thirst*).

French food is probably one of the most famous and the most praised in the world. And you don't have to go to Paris to enjoy it. You can find French restaurants and specialty food shops in many of the larger metropolitan areas in the United States, although they are often expensive. But just across the border, you can find total satisfaction at reasonable prices in Montreal, Québec's largest city.

French law requires that all restaurants post their menus – with prices – outside, so you won't have any costly surprises when you get in. Some restaurants provide **un menu à prix fixe** (uhN muh-new ah pree feeks) (*a fixed price menu*) that includes an entrée, main dish, and dessert for a reasonable price.

To find a restaurant in Paris, you can consult the **Guide Michelin** (geed meesh-laN) (*The Michelin Guide*). This guide is the restaurant lover's bible. A new edition of this internationally known red book – the one with stars for food quality and forks for the level of formality – is published annually and can make or break a restaurant overnight.

Making a restaurant reservation

In most big cities like Paris or Montreal, many popular or well-known restaurants require a reservation – as much as two months in advance in some cases! For that reason, whenever you plan to dine out casually with friends or go to a fancy restaurant, phone ahead and reserve a table. To do so politely, you have to use the conditional conjugation of verbs. These verbs express a wish, possibility, and supposition. Best of all, the conditional is used to make polite requests, such as *I would like some water, please* or *Could you please pass the salt?*

One verb you use quite often in the conditional is **vouloir** (vooh-lwahr) (*to want*). In its conditional form, its translation is *would like*. You use this verb to make a reservation, for example: **Je voudrais faire une réservation** (zhuh vooh-dreh fehr ewn rey-zehr-vah-syohN) (*I would like to make a reserva-tion*) or **Je voudrais réserver une table** (zhuh vooh-dreh rey-zehr-vey ewn tah-bluh) (*I would like to reserve a table*). The following table shows how to conjugate the conditional tense for **vouloir**:

Conjugation	*Pronunciation*
je voudrais	zhuh vooh-dreh
tu voudrais	tew vooh-dreh
il/elle/on voudrait	eel/ehl/ohN vooh-dreh
nous voudrions	nooh vooh-dree-ohN
vous voudriez	vooh vooh-dree-ey
ils/elles voudraient	eel/ehl vooh-dreh

Pouvoir (pooh-vwahr) (*to be able to*) is another very important verb you use to make polite requests. In its conditional tense, this verb means *may* or *could*, as in *Could you please recommend a good restaurant?* For example, you would say **Pourriez-vous (me/nous) recommander un bon restaurant, s'il vous plaît?** (pooh-ree-ey vooh [muh/nooh] ruh-kohh-mahN-dey uhN bohN reh-stoh-rahN, seel vooh pleh?) (*Could you recommend a good restaurant [to me/to us], please?*). The following table shows the conditional tense for the verb **pouvoir**:

Conjugation	*Pronunciation*
je pourrais	zhuh pooh-reh
tu pourrais	tew pooh-reh
il/elle/on pourrait	eel/ehl/ohN pooh-reh
nous pourrions	nooh pooh-ree-ohN
vous pourriez	vooh pooh-ree-ey
ils/elles pourraient	eel/ehl pooh-reh

You may be asked to spell your name when you make any kind of reservation, so be sure to check the letters of the alphabet and their pronunciations in Chapter 3.

Perusing the menu

In most restaurants in France, you can order from a **menu à prix fixe** (muh-new ah pree feeks) (*set-price menu*). The **prix fixe** menu generally costs less and often offers several set menus, each with a selection of an appetizer, a main dish, and cheese and/or dessert. Alternatively, you can order **à la carte** (ah lah kahrt) (*a la carte*), with a stated price for each dish. When you order **à la carte**, you can choose anything on the menu. Following is a sample of some of the menu items you may find in a French restaurant. Remember, different restaurants may give these things different names, so if you're unsure, ask the waiter or waitress.

Appetizers to get the meal started

Here are **les entrées** (ley-zahN-trey) (*appetizers*) you may find on a French menu:

- ✔ **le pâté/la terrine** (luh pah-tey/lah teh-reen) (*pâtés, meat paste*)

- ✔ **le saumon fumé** (luh soh-mohN few-mey*) (*smoked salmon*)

- ✔ **la salade verte** (lah sah-lahd vehrt) (Literally: *green salad, salad with lettuce only*)

- ✔ **les crudités** (ley krew-dee-tey) (*mixed raw vegetables, crudités*)

The French word **entrée** (ahN-trey) (*entrance, way in*) is a false friend (refer to Chapter 1). Because it leads in to the meal, the **entrée** of a French meal is the first course, not the main course, as it is in the United States. What Americans call the entree, the French call **le plat principal** (luh plah praN-see-pahl) (*the main course*).

Meat and poultry

The French menu may contain any – or all – of these varieties of **les viandes** (ley vyahNd) (*meats*) and **volaille** (voh-lahy) (*poultry*):

- ✔ **le boeuf** (luh buhf) (*beef*). You can order your steak **saignant** (seh-nyahN) (*rare*), **à point** (ah pwaN) (*medium*), or **bien cuit** (byaN kwee) (*well done*).

- ✔ **le veau** (luh voh) (*veal*). **La côte de veau** (lah koht duh voh) is a *veal chop.*

- ✔ **l'agneau** (m) (lah-nyoh) (*lamb*). Selections often include **la côte d'agneau** (lah koht dah-nyoh) (*lamb chop*) or **un gigot** (uhN zhee-goh) (*leg of lamb*).

✔ **le porc** (luh pohr) (*pork*). **La côte de porc** (lah koht duh pohr) (*pork chop*) and **le jambon** (luh zhahN-bohN) (*ham*) are popular items.

✔ **la volaille** (lah voh-lahy) (*poultry*). Your poultry selections can include **le poulet** (luh pooh-leh) (*chicken*)*,* **la dinde** (lah daNd) (*turkey*), and **le canard** (luh kah-nahr) (*duck*).

What a difference an accent can make! **Le pâté** (luh pah-tey) is a meat paste, usually made from pork meat and spices, which is eaten as an appetizer with bread. Of course, there is also the famous **pâté de foie gras d'oie** (pah-tey duh fwah grah dwah) (*goose liver pâté*), which is more expensive. On the other hand, **les pâtes** (ley paht) are the familiar pastas. So watch out for that accent when you order, or you may be surprised by what you receive!

Seafood

Following are a variety of **les fruits de mer** (ley frwee duh mehr) (*seafood*) selections that commonly appear on French menus:

✔ **les poissons** (ley pwah-sohN*)* (*fish*), such as **le saumon** (luh soh-mohN) (*salmon*), **le thon** (luh tohN) (*tuna*), **l'espadon** (m) (leh-spah-dohN) (*swordfish*), and **la truite** (lah trweet) (*trout*)

✔ **les crevettes** (ley kruh-veht) (*shrimp*)

✔ **les huitres** (ley wee-truh) (*oysters*)

✔ **le homard** (luh oh-mahr) (*lobster*)

✔ **les coquilles Saint-Jacques** (ley koh-keey saN zhahk) (*scallops*)

Le riz (luh ree) (*rice*), **les pâtes** (ley paht) (*pasta*)*,* or **les pommes de terre** (ley pohhm duh tehr) (*potatoes*) are often served with all of the above.

Vegetables

Your mother always said, 'Eat your vegetables!' With the selection you find on French menus, doing so isn't a problem at all:

✔ **les légumes** (ley ley-gewm) (*vegetables*)

✔ **les pommes de terre** (ley pohhm duh tehr) (*potatoes*)

✔ **les haricots verts** (ley ah-ree-koh vehr) (*green beans*)

✔ **les petits pois** (ley puh-tee pwah) (*peas*)

✔ **les épinards** (ley-zey-pee-nahr) (*spinach*)

✔ **les asperges** (ley-zah-spehrzh) (*asparagus*)

✔ **le chou** (luh shooh) (*cabbage*)

✔ **le chou-fleur** (luh shooh-fluhr) (*cauliflower*)

✔ **les choux de Bruxelles** (ley shooh duh brewk-sehl)
(*Brussels sprouts*)

✔ **les poireaux** (ley pwah-roh) (*leaks*)

✔ **les champignons** (ley shahN-pee-nyohN) (*mushrooms*)

Cheeses

France is known for its wonderfully delicious **fromages**
(froh-mahzh) (*cheeses*), and most French people eat **le fromage**
with every meal. France is said to have a different cheese for
each day of the year. In fact, France has many sayings about
the importance of cheese, such as this one: **Un repas sans
fromage est comme une journée sans soleil** (uhN ruh-pah
sahN froh-mahzh eh kohhm ewn zhoohr-ney sahN soh-lehy)
(*A meal without cheese is like a day without sun*).

Cheeses you commonly see on a French menu may include **le
chèvre** (luh shehv-ruh) (*goat cheese*), **le camembert** (luh
kah-mahN-behr) (*Camembert*), and **le brie** (luh bree) (*brie*).

Desserts

Here are **les desserts** (ley deh-sehr) (*desserts*) you often see
on French menus.

✔ **la glace** (lah glahs) (*ice cream*)

✔ **la crème** (lah krehm) (*pudding*)

✔ **la crème brulée** (lah krehm brew-ley) (*crème brulée*)

✔ **le gâteau au chocolat** (luh gah-toh oh shoh-koh-lah)
(*chocolate cake*)

✔ **la tarte aux pommes** (lah tahr-toh-pohhm) (*apple tart*)

The French eat ice cream and apple pie, but they don't eat them together, which is funny, considering that the phrase **à la mode** (ah lah mohhd) (*in fashion*), which is often used in the U.S. to indicate pie with a scoop of ice cream, is a French phrase! French apple pies are also very different from their American counterpart. They are very thin and do not have a top crust. They look more like what Americans would call a tart.

Beverages

You surely want to compliment your delicious meal with a drink. Of course, the drink of choice in France is **le vin** (luh vaN) (*wine*). If you are in **une brasserie** (ewn brah-sree) (*a pub*), you may even want to try **une bière à la pression** (ewn byehr ah lah preh-syohN) (*a draught beer*). Of course, not all drinks have to be alcoholic. Here is a list of possible drinks that you can order at the local café or at any restaurant:

- ✔ **le jus d'orange** (luh zhew doh-rahNzh) (*orange juice*)
- ✔ **le jus de pomme** (luh zhew duh pohhm) (*apple juice*)
- ✔ **le jus de fruit** (luh zhew duh frwee) (*fruit juice*)
- ✔ **le lait** (luh leh) (*milk*)
- ✔ **l'eau minérale/gazeuse** (loh mee-ney-rahl/gah-zuhz) (*mineral, sparkling water*)
- ✔ **la boisson gazeuse** (lah bwah-sohN gah-zuhz) (*soda*)
- ✔ **le thé** (luh tey) (*tea*)
- ✔ **le café** (luh kah-fey) (*coffee*)
- ✔ **le chocolat chaud** (luh shoh-koh-lah shoh) (*hot chocolate*)

Un apéritif (uhN-nah-pey-ree-teef) (*an aperitif*) is not just any drink, but more specifically a drink before the meal. Its purpose is to open the meal and the appetite. As an **apéritif**, the French like fairly mild alcoholic drinks like **kir** (keer), which consists of white wine or champagne with **crème de cassis** (krehm duh kah-sees) (*blackcurrant liqueur*); sweet wines like sherry or port, and so on; and they drink regular wine during the meal. **Un digestif** (uhN dee-zheh-steef) is an *after-dinner drink*, usually cognac or brandy, which, as the name indicates, is supposed to aid digestion. In general, **un apéritif** and **un digestif** are reserved for special occasions like family gatherings or dinner parties.

When you want to order specific quantities of a beverage, use these phrases:

- **un verre de. . .** (uhN vehr duh. . .) *(a glass of. . .)*
- **une bouteille de. . .** (ewn booh-tehy duh . . .) *(a bottle of. . .)*
- **une carafe de . . .** (ewn kah-rahf duh . . .) *(a carafe of . . .)*
- **une tasse de** (ewn tahs duh . . .) *(a cup of . . .)*

People seldom order wine by the glass in France. More often they order wine as **un quart** (uhN kahr*)* *(a quarter of a liter)*, **une demi-bouteille** (ewn duh-mee-booh-tehy*)* *(a half a bottle)*, or **une bouteille** (ewn booh-tehy) *(a bottle)*. They order the house wine in **une carafe** (ewn kah-rahf) *(a carafe)* or **un pichet** (uhN pee-sheh) *(a jug)*. In addition, you usually don't have water on the table unless you say **une carafe d'eau, s'il vous plaît** (ewn kah-rahf doh, seel vooh pleh) *(a pitcher of water, please)*.

Coffee break

When you order coffee from a café or a restaurant in France, you get **un express** (uhN-nehk-sprehs) *(an espresso)* in a small cup. Only at breakfast do you get a medium-size pot of *coffee with hot milk* on the side, **un café au lait** (uhN kah-fey oh leh). At home, the French drink **café au lait** in a large bowl in the morning rather than in a cup. If you want milk in your coffee at any other time of the day, you have to order **un café crème** (uhN kah-fey krehm) *(coffee with milk)*. Of course, you can also order one of the following:

- **un double express** (uhN dooh-blehk-sprehs) *(a double espresso)*

- **un grand crème** (uhN grahN krehm) *(a large coffee with milk)*

  Note: Large doesn't mean large in the American sense, but more exactly double, which is the equivalent of two small espresso cups.

- **un déca/un décaféiné** (uhN dey-kah/uhN dey-kaf-fey-ee-ney) *(a decaf coffee)*

If you're really desperate for those gallons of weak coffee, many large hotels in Paris do offer **un café américain** (uhN kah-fey ah-mey-ree-kaN) *(American coffee)*. You can also ask anywhere for **de l'eau chaude** (duh loh shohd) *(hot water)* and carry your instant coffee powder with you.

Placing your order

You may want to ask the waiter a few questions about the dishes on the menu. Actually, the more sophisticated the restaurant, the less likely you are to understand its menu! The art of giving unusual names to dishes is almost as elaborate as the art of actually preparing them. And don't think that you're the only one who doesn't understand. The average French restaurant-goer doesn't either. Your best bet is to ask the waiter. You can also ask for the waiter's recommendation by saying **Qu'est-ce que vous recommandez/suggérez?** (kehs-kuh vooh ruh-kohh-mahN-dey/sewg-zhey-rey?) (*What do you recommend/suggest?*)

When it's time to order, the waiter will ask you these kinds of questions:

> **Qu'est-ce que vous voulez boire?** (kehs-kuh vooh vooh-ley bwahr?) (*What do you want to drink?*). Or you may hear **Qu'est-ce que vous voulez comme boisson?** (kehs-kuh vooh vooh-ley kohhm bwah-sohN?), which more literally translates *What do you want as a drink?*

> **Avez-vous choisi?** (ah-vey-vooh shwah-zee?) (*Have you decided?*)

> **Qu'est-ce que vous voulez prendre?** (kehs-kuh vooh vooh-ley prahN-druh?) (*What do you want to have [to eat/ to drink]?*)

> **Que prenez-vous comme plat principal?** (kuh pruh-ney-vooh kohhm plah praN-see-pahl?) or **Qu'est-ce que vous prenez comme plat principal?** (kehs-kuh vooh pruh-ney kohhm plah praN-see-pahl?), both of which mean *What will you have as a main course?*

The phrase consisting of **comme** (kohhm) (*as*) followed by a noun is very commonly used in French, not only for food and drink items, but also each time you are asked to express a preference. For example, you may ask a friend **Qu'est-ce que vous aimez comme films?** (kehs-kuh vooh-zehm-ey kohhm feelm?) (*What kind of movies do you like?*)

If you want to ask the waiter what kinds of selections are available, you use the question **Qu'est-ce que vous avez comme. . . ?** (kehs-kuh vooh-zah-vey kohhm . . . ?) (*What do you have as. . .?*). Take a look at these examples:

Qu'est-ce que vous avez comme boisson? (kehs-kuh vooh-zah-vey kohhm bwah-sohN?) (*What do you have as a drink?*). Alternatively, you can say **Qu'est-ce qu'il y a comme boisson?** (kehs-keel ee ah kohhm bwah-sohN?) (*What is there as a drink?*)

Qu'est-ce que vous avez comme vin? (kehs-kuh vooh-zah-vey kohhm vaN?) (Literally: *What do you have as wine?* or *What kind of wine do you have?*)

Qu'est-ce que vous avez comme entrée? (kehs-kuh vooh-zah-vey kohhm ahN-trey?) (*What do you have as an appetizer?*)

Qu'est-ce que vous avez comme fromage? (kehs-kuh vooh-zah-vey kohhm froh-mahzh?) (*What do you have as cheese?*)

When you're all set and ready to order, you need to have these phrases handy:

- ✔ **Comme entrée, je prends. . . .** (kohhm-ahN-trey, zhuh prahN. . . .) (*For the first course [appetizer], I'll have. . . .*)

- ✔ **Je voudrais . . . .** (zhuh vooh-dreh. . . .) (*I would like. . . .*)

- ✔ **Pour moi. . . .** (poohr mwah. . . .) (Literally: *For me. . . .*)

- ✔ **Et ensuite. . . .** (ey ahN-sweet. . . .) (*And then. . . .*)

- ✔ **Et comme boisson. . . .** (ey kohhm bwah-sohN. . . .) (*And to drink. . . .*)

- ✔ **Et comme dessert. . . .** (ey kohhm deh-sehr. . . .) (*And for dessert. . . .*)

You no longer address the waiter as **garçon** (gahr-sohN), which is considered condescending because it means *boy.* Use **monsieur** (muh-syuh) (*sir*), instead. In case your server is **une serveuse** (ewn sehr-vuhz) (*a waitress*), you say **madame** (mah-dahm) (*ma'am*) or, if she is very young, **mademoiselle** (mahd-mwah-zehl) (*miss*).

Paying the bill

After you finish your lovely meal, it's time to pay the bill. But don't expect a waiter in France to bring you the check before you ask for it. (That's considered pushy and impolite.) To get your check, call the waiter and say **L'addition, s'il vous plaît** (lah-dee-syohN, seel vooh pleh) (*Check, please*).

In France, the tax and a 15 percent tip are included in the price list: **le pourboire est compris** (luh poohr-bwahr eh kohN-pree) or **le service est compris** (luh sehr-vees eh kohN-pree) (*the tip is included*). What you see is what you get. Of course, you may tip extra if you so desire, especially in a very good restaurant, but in cafés and ordinary restaurants, you don't have to. In Canada, a tax is added to your check, and the waiter expects to be tipped in addition (about 15 percent).

Le pourboire (luh poohr-bwahr) (*the tip*) is a funny word in French. It literally means *in order to drink.* This very old word dates back to the 17th century when it was customary to give a tip so the recipient could go and buy himself a drink (alcoholic supposedly). The name has remained, but its function has changed; today many waiters and theater ushers are paid only with tips.

Finding the restrooms

Before leaving the restaurant, you may want to visit the restroom, in which case you ask **Où sont les toilettes, s'il vous plaît?** (ooh sohN ley twah-leht, seel vooh pleh?) (*Where are the restrooms?*). In French restaurants, the restrooms are usually located **en bas** (ahN bah) (*downstairs*). Don't forget to take some change along with you; you often have to pay to get in! In most places, the pictogram is self-explanatory, but you may also see **Dames** (dahm) (*women*) or **Hommes** (ohhm) (*men*) written on the door.

Going to the Market

Outdoor markets are a delight. They're especially nice in small, country villages, where you can enjoy the local fare and delight in the noises, smells, and accents. But big cities have wonderful markets, too. Certain Paris districts have a market most days of the week in the morning, rain or shine. Montréal is famous for its outdoor all-day markets during the summer months. The largest places and many small town squares also have **les halles** (ley ahl) (*an indoor market*). What better way to try out your French? After all, you can point to what you want and maybe learn the right word from a friendly vendor. Vendors in an outdoor market sell almost everything. In many of them, you can even find clothes, shoes, kitchen utensils, and, of course, flowers.

Making purchases with the verbs 'acheter' and 'vendre'

It is just too tempting to go to **le marché** (luh mahr-shey) (*outdoor market*) and not buy anything. These markets are great places to buy the freshest and most deliciously ripe fruit for your next snack, or some cheese and bread for your picnic. Whatever your purchases, you make them with the use of the verbs **acheter** (ahsh-tey) (*to buy*), and venders sell items with the verb **vendre** (vahN-druh) (*to sell*). **Vendre** is a regular **–re** verb (check out Chapter 2 for the conjugation of regular verbs) and **acheter** is a stem changing verb just like the verb **préférer** (prey-fey-rey) (*to prefer*), discussed in Chapter 6. Here are the conjugations of **vendre** and **acheter.**

Conjugation	*Pronunciation*
je vends	zhuh vahN
tu vends	tew vahN
il/elle/on vend	eel/ehl/ohN vahN
nous vendons	nooh vahN-dohN
vous vendez	vooh vahN-dey
ils/elles vendent	eel/ehl vahNd

Conjugation	*Pronunciation*
j'achète	zhah-sheht
tu achètes	tew ah-sheht
il/elle/on achète	eel/ehl/ohN ah-sheht
nous achetons	nooh-zah-shtohN
vous achetez	vooh-zah-shtey
ils/elles achètent	eel-/ehl-zah-sheht

Often, you use **acheter** in its infinitive form. For example, you may say **Je voudrais acheter des cerises** (zhuh vooh-dreh-zahsh-tey dey suh-reez) (*I would like to buy some cherries*). With so much variety at the fruit stands, you don't have to limit yourself. Here is a list of **fruits** (frwee) (*fruit*) you may find at **le marché** (for a list of meats, seafood, and vegetables available at these markets, refer to the lists in the earlier section 'Perusing the menu'):

- ✓ **la pomme** (lah pohhm) (*apple*)
- ✓ **la banane** (lah bah-nahn) (*banana*)
- ✓ **la poire** (lah pwahr) (*pear*)
- ✓ **la pêche** (lah pehsh) (*peach*)
- ✓ **l'abricot** (m) (lah-bree-koh) (*apricot*)
- ✓ **la cerise** (lah suh-reez) (*cherry*)
- ✓ **la figue** (lah feeg) (*fig*)
- ✓ **le raisin** (luh reh-zaN) (*grape*)
- ✓ **l'ananas** (m) (lah-nah-nah) (*pineapple*)
- ✓ **la prune** (lah prewn) (*plum*)
- ✓ **la framboise** (lah frahN-bwahz) (*raspberry*)
- ✓ **l'orange** (f.) (lohr-ahNzh) (*orange*)
- ✓ **la fraise** (lah frehz) (*strawberry*)
- ✓ **la pastèque** (lah pahs-tehk) (*watermelon*)

Of course, you can't have only one grape or one raspberry, right? To make any of these fruit plural, just make the articles plural **(les)** (ley) (*the*) or ask for some by using the indefinite article **des** (dey) (*some*): for example, **Je voudrais des abricots** (zhuh vooh-dreh deyz-ah-bree-koh) (*I would like some apricots*). Also check out the following section on the metric system to buy a specific quantity.

Specifying how much you want

The metric system was adapted by the French in the 18th century and is used in the majority of countries around the world. If you travel to France or to any other country for that matter, being familiar with the metric system is very handy, especially when you want to buy something scrumptious at the market.

The basic metric unit of weight is the gram, and you usually buy fruit, vegetables, or meat in multiples of the basic gram. Table 8-1 lists the values for the gram.

Table 8-1	Measuring Amounts in Grams		
French	*Pronunciation*	*Translation*	*Conversion*
un gramme	uhN grahm	*1 gram (g)*	1 lb. = 453.60 (g)
un kilogramme/ **un kilo**	uhN kee-loh-grahm/ uhN kee-loh	*1 kilogram (kg)*	1kg = 1000 g, about 2.2 lbs.
un demi-kilo/ **une livre**	uhN duh-mee-kee-loh/ ewn lee-vruh	*half a kilogram/* *a pound*	½ kg = 500 g, = about 1.1 lb.

If you want a pound of cherries, for example, make sure you ask for **une livre de cerises** (ewn lee-vruh duh suh-reez) (*a pound of cherries*) because if you ask for **un kilo de cerises** (uhN kee-loh duh suh-reez), you'll definitely get much more than you can eat!

Metric units are also important when you're traveling, especially when you have to determine distances (meters) or fill up your gas tank (liters). For information on the metric conversions for those units, head to Chapter 12.

Shopping at neighborhood food shops

When you don't have time to go to the outdoor market, or you can't find what you need at the little store, the supermarket comes in handy. France has some huge supermarkets that line the highways as you enter a city. Some of them are so large that they are called **hypermarchés** (ee-pehr-mahr-shey) (*hypermarkets*) instead of **supermarchés** (sew-pehr-mahr-shey) (*supermarkets*). Here, you can find absolutely everything: food, clothes, computers, large appliances, and sometimes even cars! They're certainly convenient, but if you visit France and have some time on your hands, go discover the little neighborhood food stores. You're sure to enjoy them.

Because supermarkets are often rather far from the inner city, the French do their daily shopping in the neighborhood stores. They can buy their bread, meat, and vegetables daily because the stores are so conveniently close to each other.

Following are some of **les petits magasins** (ley puh-tee mah-gah-zaN) (*the little [food] stores*) that you would find in most neighborhoods throughout France:

- **la boulangerie** (lah booh-lahN-zhree) (*the bakery*). **La boulangerie** sells bread and bread products, like **des croissants** (dey krwah-sahN) (*croissants*), and **du pain aux raisins** (dew paN oh reh-zaN) (*raisin bread*).

- **la pâtisserie** (lah pah-tees-ree) (*the confectioner's shop*). These shops specialize in cakes and pastries, usually of a higher quality. They don't sell bread.

- **la boucherie** (lah booh-shree) (*the butcher shop*). Here you can find fresh cuts of all sorts of meats like beef, veal, lamb, goat, and chicken.

- **la charcuterie** (lah shahr-kew-tree) (*deli, butcher shop*). These shops specialize in pork and prepared foods.

- **la poissonnerie** (lah pwah-sohn-ree) (*the fish store*).

- **l'épicerie** (f) (ley-pees-ree) (*the grocery store*). **L'épicerie** is more like a general store.

- **la crèmerie** (lah krehm-ree) (*the dairy shop*). This is where you can buy dairy products and cheese.

- **le marchand de fruits et légumes** (luh mahr-shahN duh frwee ey ley-gewm) (*the produce vendor*). These stores have all kinds of fresh vegetables.

A fairly large number of people – mostly older – still go shopping for food every morning in France. They walk from store to store buying everything they need for the day's meals. It's also not unusual for the French, especially in big cities, to buy bread twice a day. French bread is made without preservatives and doesn't keep well, so buying in small quantities more often makes better sense. Plus, French bread tastes so good when it's freshly baked!

Part III
French on the Go

The 5th Wave — By Rich Tennant

I know <u>how</u> to ask for directions to a McDonald's in French, I'm just afraid to.

In this part . . .

*A*t some point, you may very well find yourself traveling to a country in which French is spoken, and that's what this part is all about. We cover all aspects of travel, from planning a trip and going through customs, to handling emergencies and seeking medical assistance. Furthermore, this part covers exchanging money, using public transportation, and reserving a hotel room.

Chapter 8

Planning a Trip

. . . .

In This Chapter

▶ Planning ahead for your trip

▶ Using geographical prepositions

▶ Using the future tense

▶ Dealing with passports, visas, and other travel necessities

. . . .

*T*raveling is a way to get away, relax, and perhaps seek a new adventure. Planning your travels in advance is the first step to a rewarding, fulfilling time. Whatever you're looking for– adventure, history, natural wonders, or cultural enlightenment – France and other French-speaking countries have it all. In this chapter, we help you decide where you want to go, show you how to make the appropriate travel plans, and get you ready to take that trip you always dreamed of.

Where Do You Want to Go?

When planning a trip to France – or any French-speaking country – one of the first things to do is to decide where you want to go and what you'd like to see. A trip to France, for example, offers these delights: the ocean and beaches, olive trees and vineyards, rolling green meadows bounded by straggling hedgerows, dazzling expanses of naked rock and arid ruddy soil, former homes or playgrounds of kings, counts, and feudal lords, Romanesque village churches and spectacular Gothic cathedrals, and ruins of Roman architecture and medieval monasteries. Here's a sampling of the wonderful places you can go:

✔ **Les Alpes** (ley-zahlp) (*the Alps*), in the southeast

✔ **Les Pyrénées** (ley pee-rey-ney) (*the Pyrenees*) in the southwest

✔ **La Côte d'Azur** (lah koht dah-zewhr) (*the Riviera*), along the Mediterranean coast, **la Méditerranée** (lah mey-dee-teh-rah-ney)

✔ **Le Jura** (luh zhew-rah) mountains in the east

✔ **Les Vosges** (ley vohzh) mountains in the east

✔ **Le Massif Central** (luh mah-seef sahN-trahl), the rugged, dry mountains in central France.

✔ **La Bretagne** (lah bruh-tah-nyuh) (*Brittany*), in the northwest

You can even tour the country by water, by way of France's four major rivers – **la Seine** (lah sehn) (the Seine also runs through Paris), **la Loire** (lah lwahr), **la Garonne** (lah gah-rohn), **le Rhône** (luh rohn) – and many others that crisscross the entire country.

If you want your trip to be more exotic, you can choose to visit an *overseas department of France,* **Départements et Régions d'outre-mer (DROM)** (dey-pahrt-mahN ey rey-zhyohN dooh-truh-mehr [drohm]), such as **la Martinique** (lah mahr-tee-neek) in the French West Indies, or an *overseas collectivity,* **Collectivité d'outre-mer (COM)** (koh-leh-ktee-vee-tey dooh-truh-mehr [kohm]), such as **Tahiti** (tah-ee-tee) in French Polynesia.

If you prefer to visit a French-speaking region closer to home, **Québec** (key-behk) and **Montréal** (mohN-rey-ahl) are all you can ask for. You can wander around the old city, visit the botanical gardens and the Basilica of Notre Dame. What about catching a hockey game at the Olympic stadium or attending the biggest winter festival in the world? If summer concerts are more your style, Québec is the place to be in July.

Using geographical prepositions

Wherever you're going, you have to use the verb **aller** (ah-ley) (*to go*) – see Chapter 2 for the conjugation of this verb – followed by a preposition. Which preposition you use depends on whether the place is a city, province, state, or country.

To indicate that you're from a certain place, you use the verb **être** (eh-truh) (*to be*) or the verb **venir** (vuh-neer) (*to come*), followed by a preposition that means *from*. Here's the present tense conjugation of the verb **venir** (head to Chapter 2 for the conjugation of **être**).

Conjugation	*Pronunciation*
je viens	zhuh vyaN
tu viens	tew vyaN
il/elle/on vient	eel/ehl/ohN vyaN
nous venons	nooh vuh-nohN
vous venez	vooh vuh-ney
ils/elles viennent	eel/ehl vyehn

Saying what city you're from

In French, as in English, you can say *I come from* as well as *I am from*. Use **être** when you want to simply say that you *are from* some place; use the verb **venir** when you want to say that you *come from* some place. Consider these examples:

> **Je suis de New York.** (zhuh swee duh New York.) (*I am from New York.*)

> **Nous sommes de Paris.** (nooh sohm duh pah-ree.) (*We are from Paris.*)

> **Je viens de Montréal.** (zhuh vyaN duh mohN-rey-ahl.) (*I come from Montreal.*)

> **Il vient de Boston.** (eel vyaN duh Boston.) (*He comes from Boston.*)

In French, the question *Where are you from?* is actually *From where are you?* In an interrogative sentence that has a preposition, the preposition is always placed at the beginning of the question. To say *from* in French, you use the preposition **de** (duh). Check out the following examples (notice that **de** becomes **d'** in front of a vowel):

> **D'où êtes-vous?/D'où es-tu?** (dooh eht-vooh?/dooh eh-tew?) (*Where are you from?* [formal/informal])

> **D'où venez-vous?/D'où viens-tu?** (dooh vuh-ney-vooh?/dooh vyaN-tew?) (*Where do you come from?* [formal/informal])

Sounds easy, doesn't it? But notice that the places mentioned in the preceding examples (New York, Paris, Montreal, and Boston) are cities. It gets a little more complicated when you start talking about the state, province, country, or continent you come from, as the next section explains.

Saying what state, province, country, or continent you're from

In French, states, provinces, countries, and continents can be masculine or feminine: **la France** (lah frahNs) and **le Canada** (luh kah-nah-dah), for example. (The state, province, country, and continent names that end in **e** are usually feminine.) Table 8-1 presents a sample list of countries with their genders.

Table 8-1	Genders of Countries
Feminine	*Masculine*
L'Algérie (lahl-zhey-ree) (*Algeria*)	**Le Canada** (luh kah-nah-dah) (*Canada*)
L'Allemagne (lahl-mah-nyuh) (*Germany*)	**Les États-Unis*** (ley-zey-tah-zew-nee) (*the United States*)
L'Angleterre (lahN-gluh-tehr) (*England*)	**Le Portugal** (luh pohr-tew-gahl) (*Portugal*)
La Belgique (lah behl-zheek) (*Belgium*)	**Le Japon** (luh zhah-pohN) (*Japan*)
L'Espagne (lehs-pah-nyuh) (*Spain*)	**Le Sénégal** (luh sey-ney-gahl) (*Senegal*)
La France (lah frahNs) (*France*)	**Le Maroc** (luh mah-rohk) (*Morocco*)
La Grèce (lah grehs) (*Greece*)	**Le Danemark** (luh dahn-mahrk) (*Denmark*)
L'Inde (laNd) (*India*)	**Les Pays-Bas*** (ley pey-ee-bah) (the Netherlands)
L'Italie (lee-tah-lee) (*Italy*)	**Le Liban** (luh lee-bahN) (*Lebanon*)
La Suisse (lah swees) (*Switzerland*)	**Le Mexique** (luh mehk-seek) (*Mexico*)

* *Both **Les États-Unis** and **Les Pays-Bas** are masculine, plural.*

Notice that all feminine countries end with the letter **e**. One exception is **le Mexique** (luh mehk-seek) (Mexico), which is masculine, even though it ends in **e**.

Table 8-2 shows you how to indicate going to or coming from different types of places. Keep in mind that these are general rules; some exceptions do exist.

Table 8-2   Geographical Prepositions

City or Island

Preposition	Example
à (ah) (*to go to or be in*)	**Je vais à Rennes.** (zhuh veh-zah rehn.) (*I am going to Rennes.*)
	Il va à Tahiti. (eel vah ah tah-ee-tee.) (*He is going to Tahiti.*)
de (d') (duh) (*to be from or come from*)	**Je viens de Rennes.** (zhuh vyaN duh rehn.) (*I come from Rennes.*)
	Il vient de Tahiti. (eel vyaN duh tah-ee-tee.) (*He comes from Tahiti.*)

Feminine States, Provinces, Countries (or Masculine Beginning with a Vowel)

Preposition	Example
en (ahN) (*to go to or be in*)	**Nous allons en Californie/en Normandie/en Espagne/en Iran.** (nooh-zah-lohN ahN kah-lee-fohr-nee/ahN nohr-mahN-dee/ahN-neh-spah-nyuh/ahN ee-rahN.) (*We are going to California/to Normandy/to Spain/to Iran.*)
de (d') (duh) (*to be from or come from*)	**Nous sommes de Californie/de Normandie/d'Espagne/d'Iran.** (nooh sohm duh kah-lee-fohr-nee/duh nohr-mahN-dee/deh-spah-nyuh/dee-rahN.) (*We are from California/Normandy/Spain/Iran.*)

(continued)

Table 8-2 (continued)

Masculine States, Provinces, Countries

Preposition	Example
au (oh) (*to go to or be in*)	**Ils vont au Canada/au Portugal/au Maroc.** (eel vohN-toh kah-nah-dah/oh pohr-tew-gahl/oh mah-rohk.) (*They are going to Canada/to Portugal/to Morocco.*)
du (dew) (*to be from or come from*)	**Ils viennent du Canada/du Portugal/du Maroc.** (eel vyehn dew kah-nah-dah/dew pohr-tew-gahl/dew mah-rohk.) (*They come from Canada/from Portugal/from Morocco.*)

Masculine Plural Countries

Preposition	Example
aux (oh) (*to go to or be in*)	**Elle va aux Etats-Unis/aux Pays-Bas.** (ehl vah oh-zey-tah-zew-nee/oh pey-ee-bah.) (*She is going to the United States/to the Netherlands.*)
des (dey) (*to be from or come from*)	**Elle est des Etats-Unis/des Pays-Bas.** (ehl eh deh-zey-tah-zew-nee/dey pey-ee-bah.) (*She is from the United States/from the Netherlands.*)

Because the verb **être** means *to be,* you can use it to mean being *in* a city or country, as well as being *from* a city or country.

Making plans with the future tense

When you plan a trip, you are looking ahead to the future. French has two main future tenses: the immediate or near future and the simple future. As Chapter 2 explains, you form the immediate future by conjugating the verb **aller** in the present followed by an infinitive. The immediate future means *to be going to do something*. The other form of the future tense in French is the simple future. In English, the simple future uses the word *will* plus the verb, as in *I will travel this summer*. In French, you use only the verb but conjugate it in the future tense, which implies *will*.

To form the simple future with **–er, –ir, –re** verbs, take the infinitive (drop the **e** of **–re** verbs because the future stem ends in an **r**) and add the following endings: **–ai, –as, –a, –ons, –ez,** and **–ont.** These endings come from the verb **avoir** (ah-vwahr) (*to have*), except that you drop the **av–** in front of the **nous** (nooh) (*we*) and **vous** (vooh) (*you*) verb forms. To see what we mean, take a look at the conjugation of three verbs – **arriver** (ah-ree-vey) (*to arrive*), **finir** (fee-neer) (*to finish*), and **attendre** (ah-tahN-druh) (*to wait [for]*) – which represent the three main verb categories: **–er, –ir, –re.**

Conjugation	Pronunciation
j'arriverai	zhah-reev-rey
tu arriveras	tew ah-reev-rah
il/elle/on arrivera	eel/ehl/ohN ah-reev-rah
nous arriverons	nooh-zah-reev-rohN
vous arriverez	vooh-zah-reev-rey
ils/elles arriveront	eel-/ehl-zah-reev-rohN

Conjugation	Pronunciation
je finirai	zhuh fee-nee-rah
tu finiras	tew fee-nee-rah
il/elle/on finira	eel/ehl/ohN fee-nee-rah
nous finirons	nooh fee-nee-rohN
vous finirez	vooh fee-nee-rey
ils/elles finiront	eel/ehl fee-nee-rohN

Conjugation	Pronunciation
j'attendrai	zhah-tahN-drey
tu attendras	tew ah-tahN-drah
il/elle/on attendra	eel/ehl/ohN ah-tahN-drah
nous attendrons	nooh-zah-tahN-drohN
vous attendrez	vooh-zah-tahN-drey
ils/elles attendront	eel-/ehl-zah-tahN-drohN

There are also many verbs that have irregular stems but regular endings. To conjugate these verbs in the future tense, you follow the same pattern noted earlier but change the stem as appropriate for the particular verb being conjugated. **Aller** is one of these verbs. The stem of **aller** in the future is **ir**. Here's the conjugation of **aller** in the simple future tense:

Conjugation	*Pronunciation*
j'irai	zhee-rey
tu iras	tew ee-rah
il/elle/on ira	eel/ehl/ohN ee-rah
nous irons	nooh-zee-rohN
vous irez	vooh-zee-rey
ils/elles iront	eel-/ehl-zee-rohN

Table 8-3 shows these types of verbs and their stems.

Table 8-3	Verbs with Irregular Stems but Regular Endings
Verb	**Stem**
aller (ah-ley) (*to go*)	**ir** (eer)
avoir (ah-vwahr) (*to have*)	**aur** (ohr)
courir (kooh-reer) (*to run*)	**courr** (koohr)
devoir (duh-vwahr) (*to owe, to have to*)	**devr** (duh-vruh)
envoyer (ahN-vwah-yey) (*to send*)	**enverr** (ahN-vehr)
être (eh-truh) (*to be*)	**ser** (suhr)
faire (fehr) (*to do, to make*)	**fer** (fuhr)
mourir (mooh-reer) (*to die*)	**mourr** (moohr)
pouvoir (pooh-vwahr) (*to be able to*)	**pourr** (poohr)
recevoir (ruh-suh-vwahr) (*to receive*)	**recevr** (ruh-suh-vruh)
savoir (sah-vwahr) (*to know*)	**saur** (sohr)
venir (vuh-neer) (*to come*)	**viendr** (vyehn-druh)
voir (vwahr) (*to see*)	**verr** (vehr)
vouloir (vooh-lwahr) (*to want*)	**voudr** (vooh-druh)

Here are some sentences that use the future tense with these irregular verbs:

> **Je serai prêt/prête.** (zhuh suh-rey preh/preht.) (*I will be ready.*)

> **Nous recevrons les passeports.** (nooh ruh-suh-vrohN ley pahs-pohr.) (*We will receive the passports.*)

Getting Ready for Your Trip

When you plan your trip, you're likely to hear the questions **Où voulez-vous aller?** (ooh vooh-ley-vooh-zah-ley?) (*Where do you want to go?*). To answer this question, you simply say **Je voudrais aller à. . . .** (zhuh vooh-dreh-zah-ley ah. . . .) (*I would like to go to. . . .*). If you're working with a travel agent, you may also hear **Quand voulez-vous partir?** (kahN vooh-ley-vooh pahr-teer?) (*When do you want to leave?*) and **Quand voulez-vous revenir?** (kahN vooh-ley-vooh ruh-vuh-neer?) (*When do you want to come back?*) Refer to Chapter 4 for information on making date references. If you're reserving seats, you will be asked **Pour combien de personnes?** (poohr kohN-byaN duh pehr-sohhn?) (*For how many people?*) To answer, simply say **Pour. . . personnes** (poohr. . . pehr-sohhn) (*For. . . people*).

Introducing the indirect object pronouns

The preceding dialogue uses the phrase **Ça vous convient?** (sah vooh kohN-vyaN?), which translates as *Does that suit you?* or *Is that convenient for or suitable to you?* The **vous** in this sentence is the indirect object pronoun. The indirect object pronoun replaces the indirect object (the noun) that follows the preposition **à** in the sentence). For example, in the sentence **Je parle à Pierre** (zhuh pahrl ah pyehr) (*I am speaking to Pierre*), **Pierre** is the indirect object. You can replace **à Pierre** with the indirect object pronoun **lui** (lwee) (*to him*) to form the sentence **Je lui parle** (zhuh lwee pahrl) (*I am speaking to him*). Table 8-4 shows the French indirect object pronouns.

Note that sometimes in English, the indirect object pronoun is translated as (*for*) instead of (*to*) as in the earlier example **Ça vous convient?**

Table 8-4	French Indirect Object Pronouns
Pronoun	*Example*
me (muh) (*to me*)	**Ça me convient.** (sah muh kohN-vyaN.) (*That suits me.*)
te (tuh) (*to you*)	**Ça te convient.** (sah tuh kohN-vyaN.) (*That suits you.*)
lui (lwee) (*to him, to her*)	**Ça lui convient.** (sah lwee kohN-vyaN.) (*That suits him/her.*)
nous (nooh) (*to us*)	**Ça nous convient.** (sah nooh kohN-vyaN.) (*That suits us.*)
vous (vooh) (*to you*)	**Ça vous convient.** (sah vooh kohN-vyaN.) (*That suits you.*)
leur (luhr) (*to them*)	**Ça leur convient.** (sah luhr kohN-vyaN.) (*That suits them.*)

By the way, only **lui** and **leur** differ from the direct object pronouns, which are **le, la, les**; the others coincide. (See Chapter 13 for more information on direct object pronouns.)

In the following sentence, you can see how an indirect object pronoun replaces an indirect object noun with **à**: **Ça convient à M. (**or **à Mme) Paulet** (sah kohN-vyaN ah muh-syuh [*or* ah mah-dahm] poh-leh) (*It suits Mr.* [*or Mrs.*] *Paulet*) becomes **Ça lui convient** (sah lwee kohN-vyaN)(*It suits him* [*or* *her*]).

Securing passports and visas

The requirements to enter different countries can vary. Here are some terms and phrases that can get you the information you need:

✔ **le consulat français** (luh kohN-sew-lah frahN-seh) (*the French consulate*)

✔ **voyager** (voh-yah-zhey) (*to travel*)

✔ **un passeport valide** (uhN pahs-pohr vah-leed) (*a valid passport*)

✔ **Est-ce qu'il faut un visa pour aller en/au/aux. . . ?** (ehs-keel foh-tuhN vee-zah pooh-rah-ley ahN/oh/oh. . . ?) (*Do you need a visa to go to. . .?*)

✔ **Je veux rester. . . jours/semaines en/au/aux. . . .** (zhuh vuh rehs-tey. . . zhoohr/suh-mehn ahN/oh/oh. . . .) (*I want to stay. . . days/weeks in . . . .*)

Be sure to check the expiration date on your passport early because getting it renewed can take weeks. Don't even dream that you can get it renewed overnight! If you need a brand new passport because you've never had one, make sure you start procedures at least six weeks before you want to leave. If you're traveling to Europe, once you're there, you can hop from country to country to your heart's desire. In most cases, you won't even be asked to show your passport.

Packing your suitcases with your belongings: Using possessive adjectives

Regardless of when you're going or what you plan to do, when you pack for your trip, you want to bring along some of your most comfortable clothes and shoes. You may also want to bring your sunglasses, your hat, your suntan lotion, and so on – all of which you can do with possessive adjectives.

Possessive adjectives in English are *my, your, his, her, our,* and *their.* In French, because every noun has a gender, the possessive adjectives must agree in gender and in number with the object that is possessed, not with the person possessing the object. That is the reason that, in French, there is no difference, for example, between *his* sunglasses or *her* sunglasses. Table 8-5 lists the possessive adjectives.

Table 8-5	French Possessive Adjectives	
Masculine Singular	*Feminine Singular*	*Masculine/ FemininePlural*
mon (mohN) (*my*)	**ma** (mah) (*my*)	**mes** (mey) (*my*)
ton (tohN) (*your*)	**ta** (tah) (*your*)	**tes** (tey) (*your*)
son (sohN) (*his, her*)	**sa** (sah) (*his, her*)	**ses** (sey) (*his, her*)
notre (nohh-truh) (*our*)	**notre** (nohh-truh) (*our*)	**nos** (noh) (*our*)
votre (vohh-truh) (*your*)	**votre** (vohh-truh) (*your*)	**vos** (voh) (*your*)
leur (luhr) (*their*)	**leur** (luhr) (*their*)	**leurs** (luhr) (*their*)

Here are some examples of the possessive adjectives:

> **Elle a un sac. C'est son sac.** (ehl ah uhN sahk. seh sohN sahk.) (*She has a bag. It's her bag.*) – In this example, notice that the possessive adjective **son** does not agree with the feminine subject, **elle**, but with the masculine, singular noun **sac**.

> **Il porte une chemise. C'est sa chemise.** (eel pohrt ewn shuh-meez. seh sah shuh-meez.) (*He is wearing a shirt. It's his shirt.*) – Here, the possessive adjective **sa** agrees with **chemise**, which is feminine singular, not with the masculine subject **il**.

Keep in mind the local expectations regarding appropriate attire. When you visit historical monuments in France, such as cathedrals and churches, for example, you don't see locals wearing clothing that is too revealing (very short shorts or skirts, for example, or very low-cut tops), and you shouldn't either.

Chapter 9

Dealing with Money in a Foreign Land

● ●

In This Chapter

▶ Understanding French currency

▶ Changing money and cashing checks

▶ Using an ATM and credit cards

● ●

*M*oney, l'argent (lahr-zhahN), makes the world go around, they say, and you need money to go around the world. If you have the opportunity – and pleasure – of traveling to a French-speaking country, you need to know what the currency is and how to complete numerous monetary transactions, like exchanging currency, cashing traveler's checks, using bank machines, and more. In this chapter, we give you the information and phrases you need to express your needs clearly through several kinds of money transactions.

Getting Current with Currency

Unified Europe – the block of countries that are part of the European Union – has made it easier to cross the borders within the EU without the hassle of going through border check points. Furthermore, many countries within the EU have a common currency, the euro (€), which has been legal currency since January 1, 1999. As of January 1, 2011, 17 out of 27 European Union countries, including France, use the euro. Here is a list of French-speaking regions and countries around the world that use the euro:

✔ **In Europe**: France, Monaco, Belgium, Luxemburg, Corsica

✔ **In the Americas:** French Guiana, St. Pierre, and Miquelon

✔ **In the Caribbean:** Martinique, Guadeloupe, St. Barthélemy, and St. Martin

✔ **In the Indian Ocean:** Mayotte and La Réunion

Of course, not all French-speaking countries are part of the European Union, nor do they all use euros. If you travel to any of these countries, you'll want to know the currency used there. The following sections tell you what you need to know.

Getting familiar with euros and cents

The euro, like all other monetary units, comes in the form of coins and bills in several denominations. There are seven different denominations of euro notes, or bills, and each has a distinct color and size. These notes are the same for all countries in the Euro zone, that is, the 17 countries that have adopted the euro. The coins, however, have a common front side, but the designs on the back of the coins are specific to each country. The following sections have the details.

Getting the bills straight

There are seven different denominations of the euro: €5, €10, €20, €50, €100, €200, €500. Unlike U.S. dollar bills, which all have the same size and color, the euro bills increase in size with the denomination and are very colorful. The notes, which are the same for all countries in the Euro zone, denote European symbols such as European architecture, a map of Europe, the name 'Euro' in Greek and Latin, the 12 stars of the European flag, and so on. The front features windows and gateways, and the back depicts European bridges.

Looking at the coins

Euro coins come in denominations ranging from 1 **centime** (sahN-teem) (*cent*) to 50 **centimes** (sahN-teem) (*cents*): There are also €1 and €2 coins. There are eight coins in all: € 0.01, € 0.02, € 0.05, € 0.10, € 0.20, € 0.50, €1, and € 2.

The coins have a common front side, but the backside of the coins differs by country, and they can be used interchangeably throughout the various countries that use the euro. The French coins include these three symbols:

- ✔ **La Marianne** (lah mah-ree-ahn), representing the French Republic of **Liberté, Egalité, Fraternité** (lee-behr-tey, ey-gah-lee-tey, frah-tehr-nee-tey) (_Liberty, Equality, Fraternity_), is on €0.01, €0.02, and €0.05 cent coins.

- ✔ **La Semeuse** (lah seh-muhz) (_the Sower_), a theme carried over from the French Franc, is on €0.10, €0.20, and €0.50 cent coins.

- ✔ **L'Arbre** (lahr-bruh) (_the Tree_) surrounded by a hexagon is on €1 and €2 coins. The tree symbolizes life, continuity, and growth, and the hexagon symbolizes France, which is also called **l'Hexagone** (leh-ksah-gohn) (_the Hexagon_) because of its six-sided shape.

The coins vary in size, but they don't necessarily grow in proportion to the denomination.

When you do your banking or shopping, keep in mind that the French separate euros and **centimes** with a comma, not with a period. For example, 100,00 in French euros is written in English as 100.00.

Beyond Europe and the euro: Currency in other French-speaking countries

As mentioned previously, not all French-speaking countries use the euro. Table 9-1 lists the currencies of several countries where French is either the official language or one of the official languages. (French is also spoken in many more places, such as many regions of Africa, although it is not the official language; this list doesn't include those countries):

Table 9-1	Currency in Other Countries Where French Is Spoken	
Country/Region	*Currency (in English)*	*Currency (in French)*
Switzerland	*Swiss franc* (CHF)	**le franc suisse** (luh frahN swees)
Québec, Canada	*Canadian dollar* (CAD)	**le dollar canadien** (luh doh-lahr kah-nah-dyaN)
Haiti	*Haitian gourdes* (HTG)	**la gourde haïtienne** (lah goohrd ah-ee-syehn)
Madagascar	*Malagasy ariary* (MGA)	**L'ariary malgache** (lah-ree-ah-ree mahl-gahsh)
Tahiti	*CFP* franc* (XPF)	**Le franc pacifique** (luh frahN pah-see-feek)
New Caledonia	*CFP* franc* (XPF)	**Le franc pacifique** (luh frahN pah-see-feek)
Vanuatu	*Vanuatu vatu* (VUV)	**Le Vanuatu vatu** (luh vah-new-ah-tew vah-tew)
Wallis-et-Futuna	*CFP* franc* (XPF)	*Le franc pacifique* (luh frahN pah-see-feek)

* CFP stands for Cour de Franc Pacifique, translated as the Pacific Franc.

Going to the Bank

When you travel to another country, one of the first places you probably need to go is to **la banque** (lah bahNk) (*the bank*), where you can exchange currency, cash a traveler's check, or change large bills into smaller denominations. The following vocabulary terms can help you navigate your way to the right people and areas of a bank and request what you need:

- ✔ **la caisse** (lah kehs) (*cash register*)
- ✔ **le caissier/la caissière** (luh key-syey/lah key-syehr) (*teller*)
- ✔ **le client/la cliente** (luh klee-yahN/lah klee-yahNt) (*customer*)

✔ **le guichet de change** (luh gee-sheh duh shahNzh) (*cashier's window*)

✔ **en argent liquide** (ahN nahr-zahN lee-keed) (*in cash*)

✔ **le reçu** (luh ruh-sew) (*receipt*)

✔ **la signature** (lah see-nyah-tewr) (*signature*)

Banking hours, **heures d'ouverture et de fermeture** (uhr dooh-vehr-tewr ey duh fehr-muh-tewr), can range between **8h** (wee-tuhr) (*8:00 a.m.*) and **10h** (dee-zuhr) (*10:00 a.m.*), and **14h** (kah-tohrz uhr) (*2:00 p.m.*) and **17h** (dee-seht uhr) (*5:00 p.m.*); refer to Chapter 4 for telling time in French. Some banks close during lunch break, which can last up to two hours.

Getting – and requesting – assistance

When you enter a bank, someone there may ask you how he or she can help you. You may hear one of these phrases, both of which mean *Can I help you?*

✔ **Vous désirez?** (vooh dey-zee-rey?)

✔ **Je peux vous aider?** (zhuh puh vooh-zey-dey?)

Instead of waiting to be offered help, you can also just walk up to an employee and state what you want. Start your request with **Je voudrais . . .** (zhuh vooh-dreh. . .) (*I would like . . .*) and then add the specifics, for example, **changer des dollars en euros** (shahN-zhey dey doh-lahr ahN uh-roh) (*to change dollars into euros*) or **encaisser un chèque** (ahN-key-sey uhN shehk) (*to cash a check*).

To say *I need something* in French, you express it as *I have need of something.* You pick the appropriate form of the verb **avoir** (ah-vwahr) (*to have*) – head to Chapter 2 for the conjugation of **avoir** – add **besoin de** (buh-zwaN duh) (*need of*), and then follow it with whatever you need. All together, it looks like this: **J'ai besoin de. . . .** (zhey buh-zwaN duh. . . .) (*I need. . . .*) + a noun or a verb in the infinitive form. Here are some examples:

J'ai besoin d'une pièce d'identité. (zhey buh-zwaN dewn pyehs dee-dahN-tee-tey.) (*I need identification.*)

Christine a besoin d'argent. (krees-teen ah buh-zwaN dahr-zhahN.) (*Christine needs money.*)

Avez-vous besoin de changer des dollars? (ah-vey-vooh buh-zwaN duh shahN-zhey dey doh-lahr?) (*Do you need to change dollars?*)

Exchanging money

Because the majority member states of the European Union use the euro as the shared currency, you have only one exchange rate to deal with for most European countries. Wonderful, right? And perfect for travelers. When you have **une devise (étrangère)** (ewn duh-veez [ey-trahN-zhehr]) (*foreign currency*), you can go to any of the following three convenient places to exchange money at a reasonable rate:

✓ **les banques** (ley bahNk) (*banks*). Especially in smaller towns, banks are often the most convenient place to exchange currency because small towns are less likely to have a specific currency exchange office. Banks charge an additional fee (which may vary from bank to bank) to exchange currency.

✓ **un bureau de change** (uhN bew-roh duh shahNzh) (*a currency exchange office*). These businesses are everywhere in big cities. However, check the rates and commissions first because they can vary greatly. A bank is often a good alternative when no currency exchange office is available.

✓ **la poste** (lah pohst) (*the post office*). In France, you can change money in many post offices. They open at 8:00 a.m. (**8h**) and close at around 7:00 p.m. (**19h**). If you happen to walk into a post office that doesn't offer currency exchange, the postal clerks can direct you to the nearest place that does offer this service.

Other places, such as hotel lobbies, may exchange currency, but their rates are usually less favorable. Likewise, although you may have to change a few dollars at the money exchange counter of the airport upon your arrival, you can usually get a better deal if you wait until you are in town to change money at a bank.

As a general guide, the U.S. dollar is worth less than the euro and slightly more than the Canadian dollar. To find more precise, current exchange rates go to www.finance.yahoo.com. Alternatively, you can simply ask for the current exchange rate with this question: **Quel est votre taux de change?** (kehl eh vohh-truh toh duh shahNzh?) (*What is your exchange rate?*). Here are some other phrases that may come in handy:

> **Est-ce qu'on peut changer de l'argent ici?** (ehs-kohN puh shahN-zhey duh lahr-zhahN ee-see?) (*Can one exchange money here?*)

> **Je voudrais changer des dollars américains pour. . . .** (zhuh vooh-dreh shahN-zhey dey doh-lahr ah-mey-ree-kaN poohr. . . .) (*I would like to change U.S. dollars for. . . .*)

> **Quels sont vos frais de change?** (kehl sohN voh freh duh shahNzh?) (*How much do you charge to change money?*)

Cashing checks and checking your cash

Cashing **un chèque de voyage** (uhN shehk duh voh-yahzh) (a *traveler's check*) is another task you can take care of in **la banque**. When you go to cash your checks, you can say **Je voudrais encaisser. . . .** (zhuh vooh-dreh ahN-key-sey. . . .) (*I would like to cash. . . .*). You'll be asked to provide **une pièce d'identité** (ewn pyehs dee-dahN-tee-tey) (*an I.D.*) and **votre signature** (vohh-truh see-nyah-tewr) (*your signature*).

You can save yourself a lot of trouble by getting these checks in your destination's local currency. Cashing local checks is **gratuit** (grah-twee) (*free of charge*). If it isn't, go to another bank. If your traveler's checks aren't in the local currency, you have to pay a fee to get them exchanged into local money. Another benefit is that many stores accept local checks just as they would cash.

Making change

Large bills can be inconvenient. Pulling out a very large bill to pay for a very inexpensive item can make you feel conspicuous. In addition, some businesses may not accept bills over a certain amount, and you may be asked **Avez-vous de la (petite) monnaie?** (ah-vey-vooh duh lah [puh-teet] moh-neh?) (*Do you have [small] change?*). The same question in Quebec is **Avez-vous du p'tit change?** (ah-vey-vooh dew ptee shahNzh?). Plus, having a variety of small bills makes it a little easier to keep track of how much you're spending and how much change you should get back, which is particularly helpful when you're still learning to count out a new and unfamiliar currency. So when you want to get some change, you can use these phrases:

> **J'ai besoin de monnaie.** (zhey buh-zwaN duh moh-neh.) (*I need change [coins].*)

> **Je voudrais faire du change.** (zhuh vooh-dreh fehr dew shahNzh.) (*I would like to get some change.*) – Quebec

> **Je voudrais faire de la monnaie.** (zhuh vooh-dreh fehr duh lah moh-neh.) (*I would like to get some change.*) – France

Be careful not to accidentally translate the English word *money* to **monnaie.** Although *money* and **monnaie** look and sound so much alike, the word French word for *money* is actually **argent** (ahr-zhahN*).*

Using Credit Cards and ATMs

Sometimes a store may not accept your local traveler's check. In that event, you'll want to have some extra cash when you go shopping. Another option is to use **une carte de crédit** (ewn kahrt duh krey-dee) (*a credit card*) or **un distributeur (de billets)** (uhN dees-tree-bew-tuhr [duh bee-yeh]) (*an automated teller machine, ATM*).

You can find ATMs in big and small towns, usually at a bank, in a shopping area, at train stations, at post offices, and all sorts of other places. You can access them all day and night . . . unless, of course, they are temporarily out of order. But nothing is perfect, right?

Credit cards are widely accepted in French-speaking countries, but some stores have a minimum purchase requirement. For example, they may not accept credit cards if you spend under 20 euros.

If you use your ATM card to exchange money, the exchange rate you get is definitely the most favorable because you're making a direct bank exchange between the ATM's bank and your bank. The fee is slightly more if you use your credit card to access cash at an ATM because most credit cards charge a fee for cash advances.

Usually you can choose your ATM prompts to be in English, but just in case the machine doesn't give you a language choice, here are the French phrases and instructions you need to know to use an ATM:

- ✔ **Insérez votre carte svp.** (aN-sey-rey vohh-truh kahrt seel vooh pleh.) (*Insert your card, please.*)

- ✔ **Tapez votre code svp.** (tah-pey vohh-truh kohhd seel vooh pleh.) (*Type your PIN, please.*)

- ✔ **Retrait d'espèces.** (ruh-treh deh-spehs.) (*Cash withdrawal.*)

- ✔ **Voulez-vous un reçu?** (vooh-ley-vooh uhN ruh-sew?) (*Would you like a receipt?*)

- ✔ **Carte en cours de vérification.** (kahrt ahN koohr duh vey-ree-fee-kah-syohN.) (*Checking your balance.*)

- ✔ **Patientez svp.** (pah-syaN-tey seel vooh pleh.) (*Wait, please.*)

- ✔ **Reprenez votre carte svp.** (ruh-pruh-ney vohh-truh kahrt, seel vooh pleh.) (*Take your card, please.*)

- ✔ **Prenez votre argent svp.** (pruh-ney vohh-truh ahr-zhahN seel vooh pleh.) (*Take your money, please.*)

- ✔ **N'oubliez pas votre reçu.** (nooh-blee-yey pah vohh-truh ruh-sew.) (*Don't forget your receipt.*)

Saying that you can, want, or have to do something

Verbs such as **pouvoir** (pooh-vwahr) (*to be able to*), **vouloir** (vooh-lwahr) (*to want*), or **devoir** (duh-vwahr) (*to have to, to must*) require a verb after them in the infinitive form to express what you can, want, and must do or have to do. Here are some examples:

✔ **Tu peux aller au distributeur.** (tew puh ah-ley oh dees-tree-bew-tuhr.) (*You can go to the ATM.*)

✔ **Vous pouvez insérer votre carte.** (vooh pooh-vey aN-sey-rey vohh-truh kahrt.) (*You can insert your card.*)

✔ **Pouvez-vous signer ici?** (pooh-vey vooh see-nyey ee-see?) (*Can you sign here?*)

✔ **Je veux changer de l'argent.** (zhuh vuh shahN-zhey duh lahr-zhahN.) (*I want to change money.*)

✔ **Il doit aller à la banque.** (eel dwah-tah-ley ah lah bahNk.) (*He has to go to the bank.*)

✔ **Vous devez taper votre code.** (vooh duh-vey tah-pey vohh-truh kohhd.) (*You have to type in your PIN.*)

For the conditional form and usage of the verbs **pouvoir** and **vouloir,** refer to Chapter 8.

Using disjunctive pronouns

After prepositions such as **pour** (poohr) (*for*), **avec** (ah-vehk) (*with*), **sans** (sahN) (*without*), and so on, the French use *disjunctive,* or *stress,* pronouns to refer to people. Table 9-2 lists the disjunctive pronouns.

Table 9-2	French Disjunctive Pronouns
Pronoun	*Example*
moi (mwah) (*me*)	**pour moi** (poohr mwah) (*for me*)
toi (twah) (*you* [singular])	**avec toi** (ah-vehk twah) (*with you*)
lui/elle (lwee/ehl) (*him/her*)	**sans lui** (sahN lwee) (*without him*); **pour elle** (poohr ehl) (*for her*)
nous (nooh) (*us*)	**avec nous** (ah-vehk nooh) (*with us*)
vous (vooh) (*you* [singular formal or plural])	**sans vous** (sahN vooh) (*without you*)
eux/elles (uh/ehl) (*them* [masc. plural/fem. plural])	**pour eux** (poohr uh) (*for them*); **avec elles** (ah-vehk ehl) (*with them*)

Here are some sentences using these disjunctive pronouns:

> **Pouvez-vous traduire pour moi?** (pooh-vey-vooh trah-dweer poohr mwah?) (*Can you translate for me?*)

> **Avez-vous votre carte de crédit avec vous?** (ah-vey-vooh vohh-truh kahrt duh krey-dee ah-vehk vooh?) (*Do you have your credit card with you?*)

> **Il a une pièce d'identité avec lui.** (eel ah ewn pyehs dee-dahN-tee-tey ah-vehk lwee.) (*He has an ID with him.*)

When you are conducting any type of transaction, instead of always using **je** (zhuh) (*I*) or **nous** (nooh) (*we*), you can use the impersonal **on** (ohN) (*one*) in French. For example, you can ask **On peut payer ici?** (ohN puh pey-yey ee-see?) (*Can we can pay here?* [Literally, *Can one pay here?*]) **On peut** sounds a lot better to French ears than the good old **je peux** (zhuh puh) (*I can*) or **nous pouvons** (nooh pooh-vohN) (*we can*) form. **On** (ohN) (*one*, in the impersonal meaning) is what you usually hear. Sometimes **on** also replaces the *they* form, maybe just to be more casual: **Ah, ils ouvrent!** (ah, eel-zooh-vruh!) becomes **Ah, on ouvre!** (ah, ohN-nooh-vruh!), both of which mean *Ah, they are opening!* For more on **on**, check out Chapter 2.

Chapter 10

Getting Around: Planes, Trains, Taxis, and More

*W*hen you travel, your first concern may be getting to your destination country, but as soon as you are there, you want to get around. After all, that's why you came in the first place, right? This chapter can help you navigate your way through the airport, train station, or subway system, as well as rent a car or flag down a taxi to get where you're going.

Getting through the Airport

On the day of your departure, try to arrive at **l'aéroport** (lah-ey-roh-pohr) (*the airport*) early, usually two to two-and-a-half hours before your departure. Remember that, if you are in the front of the line when you check in, you get to choose where you sit on **l'avion** (lah-vyohN) (*the plane*). Have **votre passeport** (vohh-truh pahs-pohr) (*your passport*) and other important documents handy, and in no time, you'll be all set to proceed to the boarding gate.

Before the day of your flight, make sure to check your airline carrier to see how many pieces of luggage you're entitled to bring with you and the maximum allotted weight of each. By adhering to the airline's regulations, you can avoid unpleasant surprises like being charged extra for your luggage.

Finding your way around the airport

Because of their size and the number of people who go through them every day, airports can be overwhelming places, especially when you're unfamiliar with the layout and the language. This section helps you identity some important areas in the airport, such as

- ✔ **départs** (dey-pahr) (*departures*)
- ✔ **arrivées** (ah-ree-vey) (*arrivals*)
- ✔ **enregistrement des bagages** (ahN-reh-zhee-struh-mahN dey bah-gahzh) (*baggage check*)

Your first task when you go to the airport is to find **l'aérogare** (lah-ey-roh-gahr) (*the terminal*) for **la ligne aérienne** (lah lee-nyuh ah-ey-ree-ehn) (*the airline*) you are flying. Then look for **le numéro du vol** (luh new-mey-roh dew vohl) (*the flight number*). After you arrive at **le comptoir** (luh kohN-twahr) (*the airline ticket counter*), you **enregistrer les bagages/les valises** (ahN-reh-zhee-strey ley bah-gahzh/ley vah-leez) (*check your bags/suitcases*). At that time, you'll be given **une carte d'embarquement** (ewn kahrt dahN-bahr-kuh-mahN) (*a boarding pass*). Then you can go to **la porte** (lah pohrt) (*the gate*) and wait until called to board your plane.

Up, up, and away — On the plane

Before landing, you'll be asked to fill out a custom's form which pertains to the purpose and the length of your stay. You'll also be asked if you have anything to declare. If you are traveling with your family, only one form is necessary for all of you.

Once on the plane, sit back and relax. **Un steward/une hôtesse de l'air** (uhN stee-wahr/ewn oh-tehs duh lehr) (*flight attendant*) will be around to see to your comfort, offering reading material, pillows, beverages, and so on.

At different points during the flight, you may hear the following:

- ✔ **Attachez votre ceinture** (ah-tah-shey vohh-truh saN-tewr) (*Fasten your seatbelt*)

- ✔ **Restez assis** (reh-stey ah-see) (*Remain seated*)

- ✔ **Ne fumez pas/Interdiction de fumer** (nuh few-mey pah/ aN-tehr-dee-ksyohN duh few-mey) (*Don't smoke/No smoking*)

- ✔ **Éteignez tout appareil électronique** (ey-taN-nyey tooh-tah-pah-rehy ey-leh-ktroh-neek) (*Turn off all electronic devises*)

The pilot will also share information with you when the plane is going **décoller** (dey-koh-ley) (*to take off*), **atterrir** (ah-teh-reer) (*to land*), or **faire une escale** (fehr ewn eh-skahl) (*to stop over*).

Going through customs

When you arrive in any French-speaking country, you're instantly surrounded by a flood of French language: The porter, the taxi driver, and the customs people all address you in French. Your first hurdle is making it through customs.

Look for signs directing you to **la douane** (lah dooh-ahn) (*customs*). Have your passport(s) and custom form handy, as well as any other documents that may apply, like student or work permits or an extended visa. (A visa is not needed for most of the European countries if you are planning to stay for less than 3 months.) One at a time, you (or your family if you're traveling together) will be called for questioning. Common questions include

- ✔ **Quelle est la raison de votre voyage?** (kehl eh lah reh-zohN duh vohh-truh voh-yahzh?) (*What is the reason for your trip?*)

✔ **Combien de temps restez-vous à/en/au/aux. . . ?** (kohN-byaN duh tahN reh-stey-vooh ah/ahN/oh/oh. . .?) (*How much time are you staying in. . . . ?*) (For more on the geographical prepositions, refer to Chapter 10.)

Most likely, you will only need to show your passport and custom form to the custom's officer; occasionally, you may be picked out for further questioning. In this case, you may hear the following questions:

✔ **Avez-vous quelque chose à déclarer?** (ah-vey-vooh kehl-kuh shoh-zah dey-klah-rey?) (*Do you have something to declare?*)

✔ **Pouvez-vous ouvrir votre sac?** (pooh-vey-vooh-zooh-vreer vohh-truh sahk?) (*Can you open your bag?*)

After you answer the questions, **le douanier/la douanière** (luh dooh-ah-nyey/lah dooh-ah-nyehr) (*the custom officer*) will then stamp your passport, and you'll be on your way.

It's best not to joke around with an immigration or customs officer. He also has to control his sense of humor. He's there for serious business.

Navigating Buses, Trains, and Subways

The public transportation system in most major cities of Europe and Canada is excellent. This section gives general information so you can research some fun and economical ways of getting to your favorite destinations. Check out the following list for ideas on the range of choices available for getting around in various cities:

✔ **Montreal:** Bus, subway, STCUM (urban train system), Amtrak, and VIA Rail (national train system)

✔ **Brussels:** Subway, bus, tramway, and SNCB (national train system)

✔ **Geneva:** Tramway, bus, trolleybus, and CFF (national train system)

> ✔ **Paris:** Subway and RER (express trains between Paris and its suburbs), bus, SNCF (national train system), and tourist boats

When you get on the bus, or before you get on the train or subway, be sure to validate your ticket in a machine installed for that purpose. It gets awfully expensive when **le contrôleur** (luh kohN-troh-luhr) (*the conductor, the ticket inspector*) gets on and checks everybody. And they do!

Boarding the bus

If you have time, **le bus** (luh bews) (*the bus*) is probably the most wonderful way to get not only an impression of the different **quartiers** (kahr-tyey) (neighborhoods) of a city but also to experience that city's people a bit. Buses are clean and pleasant and usually run on 15 to 30 minute intervals. The majority of bus stops in major cities are equipped with an electronic device, which shows when the next bus is expected. Also displayed in the bus stops are **les lignes de bus** (ley lee-nyuh duh bews) (*bus routes*) and neighborhood maps. Major cities have **des excursions en bus** (dey-zehk-skewr-zyohN ahN bews) (*bus tours*), which are a great and inexpensive way to see the city.

You can usually buy **un billet** (uhN bee-yeh) (*a ticket*) from **le conducteur de bus** (luh kohN-dew-ktuhr duh bews) (*the bus driver*), but remember that large bills are not welcome; it's best to have the correct change (Chapter 11 covers money). Generally, buying tickets in a book of ten, **un carnet** (uhN kahr-neh), is cheaper. You can purchase these at metro stations or at any **distributeur automatique** (dees-tree-bew-tuhr oh-toh-mah-teek) (*automated ticket vending machine*). You may also purchase tickets at **le guichet** (luh gee-shey) (*the ticket window*). In many cities, the subway system is connected with the bus system, so you can use the same tickets.

Using the subway

The **métro** (mey-troh) (*subway*) is an economical and fast way to get around the city. Paris, Brussels, Lille, and Lyon, as well as Montreal, all have very efficient subway systems. Big maps in each station make the systems easy to use, and the hours of operation (usually from 5:30 a.m. to 1:00 a.m.) make it very convenient. In these cities, the fare is standard, no matter how far you travel. Here are some words that may come in handy when you're at the métro:

- ✔ **la correspondance** (lah koh-reh-spohN-dahNs) (*transfer point, connection*)

- ✔ **le guichet** (luh gee-sheh) (*ticket window*)

- ✔ **la ligne** (lah lee-nyuh) ([*métro*] *line*)

- ✔ **la place/le siège** (lah plahs/luh syehzh) (*seat*)

- ✔ **le plan** (luh plahN) (*map*)

- ✔ **le quai** (luh key) (*platform*)

- ✔ **la sortie** (lah sohr-tee) (*the exit*)

- ✔ **la station de métro** (lah stah-syohN duh mey-troh) (*métro station*)

- ✔ **la voiture** (lah vwah-tewr) (*métro, car, train car*)

Looking for ticket packages

A number of packages are available for tourists, which can include day or multiple-day passes, as well as weekly passes (you can read about these options in an upcoming list). If you are visiting Paris, for example, you should explore one of the several options available:

- ✔ The **Paris Visite** (pah-ree vee-zeet) (*a Paris visit pass*), which you can use for unlimited trips on the métro, the bus, and the **RER (Réseau Express Régional)** (ehr uh ehr [rey-zoh ehk-sprehs rey-zhee-oh-nahl]), or the **Montmartre Funiculaire** (mohN-mahr-truh few-nee-kew-lehr), which saves you from climbing all those stairs when visiting **Montmartre** in the 18th district. This pass lets you choose the zones in which you'd like to travel, as well as the number of days. For more information, go to www.parispass.com.

- ✔ The **Navigo Découverte** (nah-vee-goh dey-kooh-vehrt) (*Navigo discover pass*), which is valid from Monday through Sunday, can be purchased to include unlimited use of the métro, RER, busses, transportation to the two airports, **Charles de Gaulle** (shahrl duh gohl) and **Orly** (ohr-lee), as well as **le Château de Versailles** (luh shah-toh duh vehr-sahy) (*the palace of Versailles*) and Disney Park. For more information on the **Navigo Découverte**, check out www.transilien.com or http://paris bytrain.com/paris-train-metro-week-pass-navigo-decouverte.

✔ **Un carnet** (uhN kahr-neh) (*a book of 10 tickets*), which you can share with others traveling with you.

You can purchase any of these passes at ticket windows or ticket vending machines at métro, RER, or train stations. Some passes are also available at the Paris tourist office.

Buying your ticket

Most employees in the métro speak enough English to sell tickets and answer your questions. But just in case, here are some helpful phrases:

Un billet, s'il vous plaît. (uhN bee-yeh, seel vooh pleh.) (*One ticket, please.*)

Un carnet, s'il vous plaît. (uhN kahr-neh, seel vooh pleh.) (*A book of [ten]) tickets, please.*)

Comment aller à. . . ? (koh-mahN-tah-ley ah. . . ?) (*How do I get to. . . ?*)

Quelle est la ligne pour. . . ? (kehl eh lah lee-nyuh poohr. . . ?) (*Which line is it for. . .?*)

Est-ce le bon sens pour aller à. . . ? (ehs luh bohN sahNs poohr ah-ley ah. . . ?) (*Is this the right direction to go to. . . ?*)

Est-ce qu'il faut prendre une correspondance? (ehs-keel foh prahN- drewn koh-reh-spohN-dahNs?) (*Do I need to transfer?*)

Où est la sortie, s'il vous plaît? (ooh eh lah sohr-tee, seel vooh pleh?) (*Where is the exit, please?*)

Getting around by train

If you'd like to travel through Europe, there is no better way than by rail. Trains in Europe are modern, clean, fast, and efficient. For long distance travel through Europe, trains are equipped with restaurants or café cars, as well as **des**

couchettes (dey kooh-sheht) (*berths*) if you choose this option. A number of rail passes allow you to travel to the countries of your choice, but remember to purchase them ahead of time. Student and age discounts are also available, so don't forget to ask for those. For more information on these rail passes, go to www.raileurope.com.

In addition, for long-distance traveling between France, Belgium, and the Netherlands, you may want to try the **Train à Grande Vitesse (TGV)** (traN ah grahNd vee-tehs [tey zhey vey]), an extra-high-speed train that you can use only with reservations. It is very fast and efficient, can take you across France in no time, and is truly worth the experience. The **TGV Thalys** (tey-zhey-vey tah-lee) runs Paris to Brussels to Amsterdam and back.

Also convenient, **l'Eurostar/Le Shuttle** (luh-roh stahr/luh shuh-tuhl) is a passenger Channel Tunnel link from London's Waterloo train station to Paris and Brussels with no reservations necessary. The **SNCF (Société Nationale des Chemins de Fer Français)** (ehs ehn sey ehf [soh-see-ey-tey nah-syoh-nahl dey shuh-maN duh fehr frahN-seh]) is the French National Railroad System. There are six major **gares** (gahr) (*train stations*) in Paris alone.

Here are some useful words and phrases that can come in handy when you're traveling by train:

- ✔ **le guichet** (luh gee-sheh) (*ticket window*)

- ✔ **le quai** (luh key) (*platform*)

- ✔ **les renseignements** (ley rahN-seh-nyuh-mahN) (*the information desk*)

- ✔ **la consigne** (lah kohN-see-nyuh) (*baggage room*)

- ✔ **la salle d'attente** (lah sahl dah-tahNt) (*waiting room*)

- ✔ **le bureau des objets trouvés** (leh bew-roh dey-zohb-zheh trooh-vey) (*lost-and-found*)

- ✔ **un [billet] aller-simple** (uhN bee-yeh ah-ley-saN-pluh) (*a one way [ticket]*)

- ✔ **un [billet] aller-retour** (uhN bee-yeh ah-ley-ruh-toohr) (*a round trip [ticket]*)

✔ **le compartiment** (luh kohN-pahr-tee-mahN) (*compartment*)

✔ **composter** (kohN-poh-stey) (*to validate* [*a ticket*])

✔ **la gare** (lah gahr) (*train station*)

✔ **les heures de pointe** (ley-zuhr duh pwaNt) (*rush hour, peak*)

✔ **la période creuse** (lah pey-ree-ohd kruhz) (*off peak*)

✔ **l'horaire** (loh-rehr) (*the schedule*)

✔ **l'indicateur (automatique)** (laN-dee-kah-tuhr [oh-toh-mah-teek]) (*automated train schedule*)

✔ **un tarif réduit** (uhN tah-reef rey-dwee) (*reduced fare*)

✔ **la voie** (lah vwah) (*track*)

✔ **à bord** (ah bohr) (*on board*)

✔ **à destination de** (ah deh-stee-nah-syohN duh) (*bound for*)

✔ **direct(e)** (dee-rehkt) (*direct, non-stop*)

Getting help at the train station

Train stations around the world are always busy, noisy, and confusing, but you can usually find helpful people around, such as the police and station employees, that you can turn to for direction.

You can use these questions to find what you're looking for:

✔ **Pardon, où sont. . . ?** (pahr-dohN, ooh sohN. . . ?) (*Pardon, where are . . .?*)

✔ **Excusez-moi, où est. . . ?** (ehk-skew-zey-mwah, ooh eh. . . ?) (*Excuse me, where is . . . ?*)

Consider these examples:

Pardon, où sont les guichets? (pahr-dohN, ooh sohN ley gee-sheh?) (*Pardon, where are the ticket windows?*)

Excusez-moi, où est la salle d'attente? (ehk-skew-zey-mwah, ooh eh lah sahl dah-tahNt?) (*Excuse me, where is the waiting room?*)

When asking questions involving the words *which* or *what*, you use **quel(s)/ quelle(s)** (kehl), depending on whether the noun referred to is masculine or feminine and singular or plural. **Quel** and its other forms are adjectives and must be either followed by a noun with which they agree or separated from the noun by the verb **être** (eh-truh) (*to be*). Here are some examples:

- ✔ **Il arrive par quel train?** (eel ah-reev pahr kehl traN?) (*Which train is he arriving on?*)

- ✔ **De quelle ville es-tu?** (duh kehl veel eh-tew?) (*Which city are you from?*)

- ✔ **Quelles places avez-vous?** (kehl plahs ah-vey-vooh?) (*Which seats do you have?*)

- ✔ **Quel est le nom de la gare?** (kehl eh luh nohN duh lah gahr?) (*What is the name of the train station?*)

- ✔ **Quelles sont les heures de pointe?** (kehl sohN ley-zuhr duh pwaNt?) (*What are the peak hours?*)

Buying tickets and checking the schedule

When you are traveling, you undoubtedly need to ask questions about plane and train schedules. Here are a few questions and answers that may come in handy.

- ✔ **Quand voulez-vous partir?** (kahN vooh-ley-vooh pahr-teer?) (*When do you want to leave?*)

- ✔ **Où voulez-vous aller?** (ooh vooh-ley-vooh-zah-ley?) (*Where do you want to go?*)

- ✔ **Voulez-vous un aller-retour ou un aller-simple?** (vooh-ley-vooh-zuhN ah-ley-ruh-toohr ooh uhN ah-ley-saN-pluh?) (*Do you want a round trip or a one way?*)

- ✔ **Pour combien de personnes?** (poohr kohN-byaN duh pehr-sohhn?) (*For how many people?*)

Similarly, you may have some questions of your own:

- ✔ **A quelle heure y a-t-il un train pour. . . ?** (ah kehl uhr ee ah-teel uhN traN poohr. . . ?) (*What time is there a train for. . . ?*)

- ✔ **Est-ce que le train est à l'heure?** (ehs-kuh luh traN eh-tah luhr?) (*Is the train on schedule/time?*)

To this last question, you may get any of the following answers:

- ✔ **Le train est à l'heure.** (luh traN eh-tah luhr.) (*The train is on time.*)

- ✔ **Le train est en avance.** (luh traN eh-tahN-nah-vahNs.) (*The train is early.*)

- ✔ **Le train est en retard.** (luh traN eh-tahN ruh-tahr.) (*The train is late.*)

Getting Around by Car

If convenience and fast service are more important to you than paying the fare, then taking a taxi is a good way to get around. Or, if you're more adventurous and like driving, you may want to rent a car. This way, you can stop wherever you want, visit local towns, meander through the **marchés** (mahr-shey) (*outdoor markets*), and change plans according to the weather or your mood. The following sections tell you what you need to know.

Hailing a taxi

Taxis are readily available at all airports and train stations, as well as all over major cities. Although taxis come in all colors, depending on the country you are visiting, they are easily recognizable because of the international word on them: Taxi. (Keep in mind though, that taxis have a passenger as well as a luggage limit.)

Although many taxi drivers in large international cities have a basic knowledge of English, have your destination address printed out to avoid any misunderstandings. Be prepared to pay in cash because some taxis do not take credit or debit cards.

The following terms and phrases are ones you'll use when you take a taxi:

- ✔ **le chauffeur de taxi** (luh shoh-fuhr duh tah-ksee) (*cab driver*)

- ✔ **le tarif** (luh tah-reef) (*fare*)

> ✔ **la station de taxi** (lah stah-syohN duh tah-ksee) (*taxi stand*)
>
> ✔ **Où voulez-vous aller?** (ooh vooh-ley-vooh-zah-ley?) (*Where do you want to go?*)
>
> ✔ **Je voudrais aller à. . . .** (zhuh vooh-dreh-zah-ley ah....) (*I would like to go to. . . .*)

Tipping is optional in Belgium, although it is customary to round up to the nearest euro, but in other European countries, expect to leave about a 10 percent tip.

Driving in a foreign land

Louer une voiture (looh-ey ewn vwah-tewr) (*renting a car*) in Europe may be a little expensive. However, if you share the car with two or three others, this option may be less expensive than purchasing individual rail passes. If you decide to rent a car and drive yourself, it is always best to do your research and to talk to your rental agency about your travel plans. Keep these points in mind:

✔ The minimum driving age for car rentals in Europe is between 21 and 25, and the maximum age is usually 70. If you are a younger or older driver, you may be asked to pay additional insurance against collision damage. Purchasing additional insurance anyway just for your peace of mind may be a good idea, but that is totally up to you. Check with your credit card company to see whether they cover the insurance on rental cars.

✔ When you are renting a car, make sure you tell the agency about your travel plans because some agencies may have border restrictions or limits and you may need to pay extra insurance fees for this. Also if you are renting a car in one country and would like to drop it off in another, you may be required to pay drop-off fees.

✔ In most countries all you need is your normal, valid driver's license. In others, they may ask you for your International Drivers' Permit, or IDP, which is basically a translation of your license in many different languages. It is a good idea to get an IDP anyway, especially if you are not certain where your car travels may take you or if you are stopped by the police.

✔ Many French **autoroutes** (oh-toh-rooht) (*highways*) require **des péages** (dey pey-ahzh) (*tolls*), and they are not cheap. Always have coins handy, although most of the time you pick up a ticket at the point of entry and pay at the exit. In France, tollbooths usually accept credit cards: Just insert your ticket into a machine at the tollbooth, then your credit card, wait, get your receipt, and make sure you pull your card out again.

Here are some words and phrases related to driving and **la circulation** (lah seer-kew-lah-syohN) (*traffic*):

✔ **le rond-point** (luh rohN-pwaN) (*roundabout*)

✔ **le stationnement/le stationnement interdit** (luh stah-syohNn-mahN/ luh stah-syohNn-mahN aN-tehr-dee) (*parking/no parking*)

✔ **le piéton/la piétonne** (luh pyey-tohN/lah pyey-tohhn) (*pedestrian*)

✔ **le trottoir** (luh troh-twahr) (*sidewalk*)

✔ **la sortie** (lah sohr-tee) (*exit*)

✔ **le carrefour** (luh kahr-foohr) (*intersection*)

✔ **l'embouteillage** (lahN-booh-teh-yahzh) (*traffic jam*)

✔ **le sens unique** (luh sahNs ew-neek) (*one way*)

✔ **le pont** (luh pohN) (*bridge*)

✔ **ralentir** (rah-lahN-teer) (*to slow down*)

✔ **rouler vite** (rooh-ley veet) (*to drive fast*)

✔ **demi-tour** (duh-mee-toohr) (*U turn*)

Filling up at the gas station

As you probably are aware, **faire le plein** (fehr luh plaN) (*to fill the gas tank*) in Europe, or in France specifically, costs a lot. Don't get too excited when you see postings at the **station-service** (stah-syohN-sehr-vees) (*gas station*) for 1.55; that's in euros and per liter, not per gallon. A gallon of **essence** (eh-sahNs) (*gas*) is 3.78 liters. Although gas prices fluctuate, gas is usually cheaper at supermarkets and hypermarkets than it is on major highways.

In France you have a choice of **sans-plomb** (sahN-plohN) (*unleaded*), **ordinaire** (ohr-dee-nehr) (*regular unleaded*), **super** (sew-pehr) (*super unleaded*), and **gazole/diesel** (gah-zohl/dyey-zehl) (*diesel*).

If you travel to Europe, make sure you're familiar with the metric system and its three most common units: the meter, the gram, and the liter. One kilometer equals 0.621 of a mile. For example, from the center of Paris to Versailles is about 21 kilometers, or approximately 13 miles. For more information on weights, check out Chapter 8.

Gas stations on the major highways do have **des pompistes** (dey pohN-peest) (*gas station attendants*), but others may not. Generally, you pump your gas first and then pay. Although you can pay a cashier with a credit card, a credit card may not work in the automated machines. Some European countries, including France, have adapted "chip-and-pin cards," which are the only ones accepted at self-serve pay at the pump stations.

The following little phrases can help you out when you are looking to fill up the tank:

> **Où est-ce qu'il y a une station-service?** (ooh ehs-keel ee ah ewn stah-syohN-sehr-vees?) (*Where is there a gas station?*)

> **Est-ce qu'il y a une station-service près d'ici?** (ehs-keel ee ah ewn stah-syohN sehr-vees preh dee-see?) (*Is there a gas station near here?*)

> **Le plein, s'il vous plaît.** (luh plaN, seel vooh pleh.) (*Fill it up, please.*)

When talking about unspecified quantities, French uses an article called the **partitif** (pahr-tee-teef) (*partitive*) because it describes a 'part' of a quantity. You construct it by combining the preposition **de** (*of*) and the definite article **le, la, les:**

- **de + le = du** (dew)
- **de + la = de la** (duh lah)
- **de + les = des** (dey)
- **de + l' = de l'** (duhl)

You can translate these constructions as *some*, as in this
example: **Je voudrais du carburant** (zhuh vooh-dreh dew
kahr-bew-rahN) (*I would like some fuel.*) Check out Chapter 2
for more on the partitive.

Here's a little advice: Fill up during the day at a manned
station and keep some cash on hand in case the automated
machines don't accept your credit card. Also be aware that
gas stations in town may be closed on Sundays. This is not
the case on the highways.

Getting help when you have car trouble

Hopefully, your journey will be smooth and trouble-free,
but in the event you have car trouble or see **un avertisseur
lumineux** (uhN ah-vehr-tee-suhr lew-mee-nuh) (a *warning
light*), you may need to talk to **un mécanicien** (uhN mey-kah-
nee-syaN) (*a mechanic*). Here are some words and phrases
that can help you identify what the trouble is:

- **la batterie** (lah bah-tree) (*battery*)
- **le capot** (luh kah-poh) (*the hood*)
- **l'essuie-glace** (ley-swee-glahs) (*windshield wiper*)
- **les freins** (ley fraN) (*the brakes*)
- **le pare-brise** (luh pahr-breez) (*windshield*)
- **les phares** (ley fahr) (*headlights*)
- **le pneu/le pneu crevé** (luh pnuh/luh pnuh kruh-vey)
  (*tire/flat tire*)
- **tomber (être) en panne** (tohN-bey [eh-truh] ahN pahn)
  (*to break down [car]*)
- **vérifier (les niveaux)** (vey-ree-fyey [ley nee-voh]) (*check
  [the levels]*)
- **la vidange** (lah vee-dahNzh) (*oil change*)

Deciphering road signs

You can't travel safely on your own without being able to
understand **les panneaux routiers** (ley pah-noh rooh-tyey)
(*road signs*). Although many signs are easily recognizable —
like the stop and yield signs — others have less obvious

meanings. You must review these before you get behind the wheel. The following information is a good start.

To avoid **une contravention** (ewn kohN-trah-vahN-syohN) (*a ticket*), keep in mind that **les limitations de vitesse** (ley lee-mee-tah-syohN duh vee-tehs) (*speed limits*) in France (indicated by a round sign with a red border) are approximately 80 mph or 130 km/h on the highways, 55 mph or 90 km/h on open roads, and 30 mph or 50 km/h in the city. Speed limits are strictly enforced, and you pay a fine on the spot. Also the traffic arriving on the right always has **la priorité à droite** (lah pree-oh-ree-tey ah dwaht) (*the right of way*; Literally: *priority to the right*).

Here are some important signs that you have to be aware of:

- ✔ **arrêt** (ah-reh) (*stop*)
- ✔ **cédez le passage** (sey-dey luh pah-sahzh) (*yield*)
- ✔ **chaussée rétrécie** (shoh-sey rey-trey-see) (*road narrows*)
- ✔ **chaussée glissante** (shoh-sey glee-sahNt) (*slippery road*)
- ✔ **interdiction de faire demi-tour** (aN-tehr-dee-ksyohN duh fehr duh-mee-toohr) (*no U Turn*)
- ✔ **passage interdit** (pah-sahzh aN-tehr-dee) (*no entry*)
- ✔ **passage piéton** (pah-sahzh pyey-tohN) (*pedestrian crossing*)
- ✔ **risque de chutes de pierre** (reesk duh shewt duh pyehr) (*falling rocks*)
- ✔ **sens unique** (sahNs ew-neek) (*one way*)
- ✔ **travaux** (trah-voh) (*road work*)
- ✔ **virage à droite/virage à gauche** (vee-rahzh ah dwaht/ vee-rahzh ah gohsh) (*bend to the right/bend to the left*)

Road signs are distinguishable by shape, color, and by graphics. Here are a few you should become familiar with:

- ✔ Triangles with a red border indicate a warning or a danger. Example: **Chaussée glissante**.
- ✔ Round signs with a thick red border indicate restrictions. Example: **Interdiction de faire demi-tour.**

- ✔ Round signs with blue background indicate what you are required to do. Example: **obligation de tourner à gauche.**

- ✔ Square and rectangular signs guide you. Example: **Autoroute** (oh-toh-rooht) (*highway*), which always begins with a capital **A** (for **Autoroute)** followed by the highway number.

Chapter 11

Finding a Place to Stay

• •

In This Chapter

▶ Choosing accommodations and amenities

▶ Checking in to and out of a hotel

• •

*N*ot everybody is so lucky as to have good friends abroad with whom they can stay when they're traveling. Most likely, you'll need to book a hotel room as part of your trip planning, right along with composing an itinerary of the sights you want to see. Even if you're traveling on business and your choice of hotel is limited to those selected by your company, you may still have questions about the accommodations.

In this chapter, you get the information you need to find accommodations, make reservations, and check in and check out of your hotel.

Finding Accommodation

Hotels are your home away from home – even if you just consider it a place to lay your head after a day on the go – so it's good to know how to secure the kind of lodging you prefer. When thinking about what you want in a hotel, price is a consideration, but price alone does not determine whether a place is a wonderful one to stay in. Each type of accommodation – whether you want **un hôtel une étoile** (uhN-noh-tehl ewn ey-twahl) (*a one-star hotel*) or **un hôtel cinq étoiles** (uhN-noh-tehl saNk ey-twahl) (*a five-star hotel*) – offers advantages that may be just what you're looking for.

Les hôtels (ley-zoh-tehl) (*hotels*) range from basic one-star accommodations to luxury five-star establishments. Room prices vary according to amenities, size, rating, and location.

Most hotels offer breakfast (usually a continental breakfast, which includes either a croissant or a roll with butter and jam, and coffee or tea), but not all have a restaurant. The names for different types of hotels may vary a little throughout the French-speaking countries.

Hôtel garni (oh-tehl gahr-nee) means *bed and breakfast,* and **maison de logement** (meh-zohN duh lohzh-mahN) in French-speaking Canada refers to a smaller hotel or tourist home, which in other countries is sometimes also called **une pension (de famille)** (ewn pahN-syohN [duh fah-meey]) (*a boarding house*) or **une auberge** (ewn oh-behrzh) (*inn*).

And then, in France, there are also those exquisite **châteaux** (shah-toh) (*castles*), which have been refurbished into hotels. Sure, they tend to be on the more expensive side, but the ambiance and the high-quality service are hard to surpass if you're looking for something special.

In recent years, alternatives to traditional hotels have become increasingly popular, such as **les gîtes ruraux** (ley zheet rew-roh) in France, which are furnished holiday cottages or flats, farmhouse arrangements in Belgium, chalets in Switzerland, or even former monasteries.

Finally, for the young and young at heart, France alone has about 200 **auberges de jeunesse** (oh-behrzh duh zhuh-nehs) (*youth hostels*), well scattered throughout the country, with varying facilities. Your national youth hostel association can give you details, or you can go online. For information about Canadian youth hostels, for example, go to www.hostel lingmontreal.com and for hostels in other parts of the world, check out www.hostels.com.

The closer your hotel is to the center of the city, the more expensive it is likely to be. Also remember to figure in the city tax of about one euro per day per person, which is typically not included in the hotel rate.

Choosing your amenities

After you do your research and know exactly what kind of hotel you want to stay in, you should think about the kinds of amenities that you may be looking for. Here is a list of expressions that will tell you more about your accommodations:

✔ **la climatisation** (lah klee-mah-tee-zah-syohN) (*air conditioning*)

✔ **la piscine** (lah pee-seen) (*swimming pool*)

✔ **la salle de gym** (lah sahl duh zheem) (*fitness room*)

✔ **le site historique** (luh seet ee-stoh-reek) (*historic site*)

✔ **la blanchisserie** (lah blahN-shee-sree) (*laundry service*)

✔ **la navette d'aéroport** (lah nah-veht dah-ey-roh-pohr) (*airport shuttle*)

✔ **une connexion Wi-Fi** (ewn kohN-neh-ksyohN wee-fee) (a *Wi-Fi connection*)

In many countries, **un lavabo** (uhN lah-vah-boh) (*a bathroom sink*) and **une baignoire** (ewn beh-nywahr) (*a bathtub*) and/or **une douche** (ewn doohsh) (*a shower*) are separate from the toilet and the bidet, an arrangement which is wonderful, of course. However, some showers are hand-held in the bathtub with no curtain around it, and that method takes a bit getting used to, but works fine, too.

Many hotels and other types of lodgings have Internet access, which is pretty affordable and reliable. Often you find computers in the hotel lobby, which you may be able to use free of charge or for a small fee. If your hotel doesn't provide this service, don't worry: Numerous Internet cafés and **cybercafés** (see-behr kah-fey) (*cybercafés)* are located throughout major cities. Most hotels also provide Internet jacks into which you can plug your Ethernet cable.

The voltage in Europe is 220 volts as opposed to 110 volts used in the U.S. and Canada. If you're bringing any type of electronic equipment (hair dryer, electric shaver, laptop, and so on), you'll want to buy an adapter to bring with you. You can purchase these at any electronics store. In case you forget your adapter, you may buy one in an electronics store or any hypermarket in the country you are visiting.

Making reservations

You usually book a room online or through a travel agent, but just in case you call in person, you need to know what to say. This section includes some questions and phrases that can get you started.

When you call a hotel, you will probably first be connected to **le/la standardiste** (luh/lah stahN-dahr-deest) (*the switchboard operator*). You need to tell that person why you're calling. You can say something like the following:

> **Je voudrais retenir/réserver une chambre, s'il vous plaît.** (zhuh vooh-dreh ruh-tuh-neer/rey-zehr-vey ewn shahN-bruh, seel vooh pleh.) (*I would like to reserve a room please.*)

> **Avez-vous une chambre libre?** (ah-vey-vooh ewn shahN-bruh lee-bruh?) (*Do you have a room available?*)

You also need to say how long you'll be staying. To tell the operator or hotel clerk that you are staying from a certain date to a certain date, you use **du** (dew) (*from*) and **au** (oh) (*to*). For example, if you are staying *from June 4 to June 9*, you say **du quatre juin au neuf juin** (dew kah-truh zhwaN oh nuhf zhwaN). Alternatively, you can say **du 4 au 9 juin** (dew kaht-ruh oh nuhf zhwaN), which means the same thing. If you are staying from the first of the month or to the first of the month, then say **du premier** (dew pruh-myey) (*from the first*) and **au premier** (oh pruh-myey) (*to the first*). For example, **du premier au sept juillet** (dew pruh-myey oh seht zhwee-yeh) (*from the first to the seventh of July* [or *from July 1 to July 7*]). Chapter 4 has more on setting specific dates.

Specifying the kind of room you want

When you call to reserve a room, you have to tell them what type of room you're interested in. For example, do you want a single or a double room? Do you want one bed or two beds? Do you want the room to be facing the garden, the beach, or the court yard? To state the type of room you want, place any of these terms after the phrase **une chambre...** (ewn shahN-bruh...).

- ✔ **simple** (sahN-pluh) (*single*)

- ✔ **double** (dooh-bluh) (*double*)

- ✔ **pour deux/trois/quatre personnes** (poohr duh/trwah/kaht-ruh pehr-sohhn) (*for two/three/four people*)

✔ **à un lit/à deux lits** (ah uhN lee/ah duh lee) (*with one bed/with two beds*)

✔ **à deux lits jumeaux** (ah duh lee zhew-moh) (*with two twin beds*)

Do you want a room that faces or looks onto somewhere beautiful or romantic? Then you use the expression **donner sur** (dohh-ney sewr) (*facing, overlooking*). The verb **donner** (dohh-ney), whose literal meaning is *to give,* is a regular –er verb, which you conjugate the same way you conjugate the verb **parler** (pahr-ley) (*to speak*). (For the conjugation of regular verbs, refer to Chapter 2.) You would say **Je voudrais une chambre qui donne sur. . . .** (zhuh vooh-dreh ewn shahN-bruh kee dohhn sewr. . . .) (*I would like a room that faces. . . .*) and then specify any of the following:

✔ **le jardin** (luh zhahr-daN) (*the garden*)

✔ **la piscine** (lah pee-seen) (*the swimming pool*)

✔ **la montagne** (lah mohN-tah-nyuh) (*the mountain*)

✔ **la cour** (lah koohr) (*the court yard*)

✔ **la plage** (lah plahzh) (*the beach*)

✔ **la mer** (lah mehr) (*the sea*)

✔ **le lac** (luh lahk) (*the lake*)

Asking about the price

An important consideration before booking a room is the price. When you ask about room prices, also consider asking about whether a deposit is needed and whether the establishment accepts credit cards. The following sequence of questions and answers may help you:

> **Quel est le prix de la chambre?** (kehl eh luh pree duh lah shahN-bruh?) (*What is the price of the room?*)

> **Le prix est 250 euros par jour.** (luh pree eh duh-sahN saN-kahNt uh-roh par jour.) (*The price is 250 euros per day.*)

> **Est-ce qu'il faut un acompte/des arrhes?** (ehs-keel foh uhN-nah-kohNt/dey-zahr?) (*Do you need a deposit?*)

Il faut un acompte/des arrhes de 20 pour cent. (eel foh uhN-nah-kohNt/dey-zahr duh vaN poohr sahN.) (*You need a 20 percent deposit.*)

Acceptez-vous des cartes de crédit? (ah-kseh-ptey-vooh dey kahrt duh krey-dee?) (*Do you accept credit cards?*)

Oui, bien sûr. (wee, byahN sewr.) (*Yes, of course.*)

Checking In to a Hotel

After a long trip, arriving at a hotel is probably your first highlight . . . and perhaps your first interaction with French. You may wonder how to address the hotel staff, especially when you arrive to inquire about a room. The titles **Monsieur** (muh-syuh) (*Sir, Mister* [*Mr.*]), **Madame** (mah-dahm) (*Ma'am, Misses* [*Mrs.*]), and **Mademoiselle** (mahd-mwah-zehl) (*Miss*) are used in French much more than in English and do not sound as formal. In fact, it is polite to add them after **bonjour** (bohN-zhoohr) (*hello, good morning*), especially when addressing someone you don't know.

Using direct object pronouns

In a conversation, you wouldn't sound very natural if you kept repeating the same words: 'I would like a room. Can I see the room? Let's go and see the room.' Instead, you'd say, 'I would like a room. Can I see it? Let's go and see it,' which sounds a lot better. So drop the direct object and replace it with one of the following direct object pronouns:

- ✔ **me** (muh) (*me*)
- ✔ **te** (tuh) (*you* [singular informal])
- ✔ **le** (luh) (*him, it*)
- ✔ **la** (lah) (*her, it*)
- ✔ **nous** (nooh) (*us*)
- ✔ **vous** (vooh) (*you* [singular formal or plural])
- ✔ **les** (ley) (*them*)

Just remember that the pronoun you choose depends on whether the noun it replaces is feminine or masculine, singular or plural. The placement of the pronoun is also important. You must put the direct object pronoun in front of the conjugated verb.

The object pronouns **me**, **te**, **nous**, and **vous** are easy to remember because each has only one form for both masculine and feminine. For example,

> **Est-ce que tu me vois?** (ehs-kuh tew muh vwah?) (*Do you see me?*)

> **Oui, je te vois.** (wee, zhuh tuh vwah.) (*Yes, I see you.*)

> **Est-ce qu'il nous appelle?** (ehs-keel nooh-zah-pehl?) (*Is he calling us?*)

> **Oui, il vous appelle.** (wee, eel vooh-zah-pehl.) (*Yes, he is calling you.*)

Things are a little trickier with the direct object pronouns in the third person, **le**, **la**, and **les**. The French forms of these pronouns change based on the gender and number of the noun they replace. Follow these rules:

- ✔ Use **le** when the noun being replaced is masculine singular. For example, the sentence **Il voit l'hôtel** (eel vwah loh -tehl) (*He sees the hotel*) changes to **Il le voit** (eel luh vwah) (*He sees it*).

- ✔ Use **la** when the noun being replaced is feminine singular. For example, the sentence **Nous suivons la réceptionniste** (nooh swee-vohN lah rey-sehp-syohN-neest) (*We are following the receptionist*) becomes **Nous la suivons** (nooh lah swee-vohN) (*We are following her*).

- ✔ In the third person plural, there is only one pronoun that replaces both a masculine and a feminine plural noun: **les**. For example, the sentence **Elle vérifie les dates** (ehl vey-ree-fee ley daht) (*She is checking the dates*) becomes **Elle les vérifie** (ehl ley vey-ree-fee) (*She's checking them*).

Naturally, there is an exception to the rule that the direct object pronoun must appear in front of the conjugated verb: When you have a helping verb plus an infinitive in your sentence, you need to put the object pronoun in front of the infinitive form, as in the following examples:

Il veut voir la chambre. (eel vuh vwahr lah shahN-bruh.) (*He wants to see the room.*) – direct object

Il veut la voir. (eel vuh lah vwahr.) (*He wants to see it.*) – direct object pronoun

Je dois vérifier les prix. (zhuh dwah vey-ree-fyey ley pree.) (*I must check out the prices.*) – direct object

Je dois les vérifier. (zhuh dwah ley vey-ree-fyey.) (*I must check them out.*) – direct object pronoun

Filling out a registration form

When you arrive at a hotel, chances are, you have to fill out **une fiche** (ewn feesh) (*a registration form*). This form may ask you for these items:

- ✔ **nom/prénom** (nohN/prey-nohN) ([*last*] *name/first name*)
- ✔ **lieu de résidence/adresse** (lyuh duh rey-zee-dahNs/ahd-rehs) (*address*)
- ✔ **rue/numéro** (rew/new-mey-roh) (*street/number*)
- ✔ **ville/code postal** (veel/kohhd poh-stahl) (*city/zip code*)
- ✔ **état/pays** (ey-tah/pey-ee) (*state/country*)
- ✔ **numéro de téléphone** (new-mey-roh duh tey-ley-fohhn) (*telephone number*)
- ✔ **nationalité** (nah-syoh-nah-lee-tey) (*nationality*)
- ✔ **date/lieu de naissance** (daht/lyuh duh neh-sahNs) (*date/place of birth*)
- ✔ **numéro de passeport** (new-mey-roh duh pahs-pohr) (*passport number*)
- ✔ **signature** (see-nyah-tewr) (*signature*)
- ✔ **numéro d'immatriculation de la voiture** (new-mey-roh dee-mah-tree-kew-lah-syohN duh lah vwah-tewr) (*license plate number*)
- ✔ **date de l'arrivée** (daht duh lah-ree-vey) (*date of arrival*)
- ✔ **date du départ** (daht dew dey-pahr) (*date of departure*)

Should you tip hotel staff such as bellboys and maids? A service charge is generally included in hotel and restaurant bills. However, if the service has been particularly good, you may want to leave an extra tip.

Asking for towels and other essentials

Okay, you're settling in to your hotel room, but you discover you need more towels, blankets, and pillows. Or maybe you discover that the light bulb is out, or there's no more toilet paper. If you need any of these items, you would call down to the desk and say **Il nous faut. . . .** (eel nooh foh. . . .) (*We need. . . .*) and add the articles from the following list, as appropriate:

- ✔ **une/des couverture(s)** (ewn/dey kooh-vehr-tewr) (a *blanket/blankets*)
- ✔ **un/des oreiller(s)** (uhN/dey-zoh-reh-yey) (a *pillow/pillows*)
- ✔ **une/des serviette(s)** (ewn/dey sehr-vee-eht) (a *towel/towels*)
- ✔ **des cintres** (dey sahN-truh) (*hangers*)
- ✔ **une/des ampoule(s)** (ewn/dey-zahN-poohl) (a *light bulb/light bulbs*)
- ✔ **du savon** (dew sah-vohN) (*soap*)
- ✔ **du papier hygiénique/de toilette** (dew pah-pyey ee-zhee-ey-neek/duh twah-leht) (*toilet paper*)

In Chapter 7, we discuss the impersonal expression **il faut** (eel foh) (*it is necessary*) followed by the infinitive. However, you can personalize this construction by adding an indirect object pronoun of your choice in front of the verb: **me** (muh) (*to me*), **te** (tuh) (*to you*), **lui** (lwee) (*to him/to her*), **nous** (nooh) (*to us*), **vous** (vooh) (*to you*), and **leur** (luhr) (*to them*). (Check out the indirect object pronouns in Chapter 10.) Look at the following examples but note that you cannot translate these examples literally:

Il me faut des serviettes. (eel muh foh dey sehr-vee-eht.) (*I need towels.*)

Il nous faut du savon. (eel nooh foh dew sah-vohN.) (*We need soap.*)

Checking Out of a Hotel

For whatever reason, the checkout time is hardly ever convenient, but you probably realize that rooms have to be cleaned before the next guest arrives. Of course, before leaving, you have to pay your bill or at least verify it to see whether you have accrued any additional charges during your stay. The following phrases can come in handy when it's time to check out:

- ✔ **À quelle heure faut-il libérer la chambre?** (ah kehl uhr foh-teel lee-bey-rey lah shahN-bruh?) (*At what time do I/ we have to check out?*)

- ✔ **Ces frais supplémentaires sont corrects/incorrects.** (sey freh sew-pley-mahN-tehr sohN koh-rehkt/aN-koh-rehkt.) (*These additional charges are correct/incorrect.*)

- ✔ **J'ai une question en ce qui concerne la note.** (zhey ewn kehs-tyohN ahN skee kohN-sehrn lah nohht.) (*I have a question regarding the bill.*)

- ✔ **Je voudrais un reçu.** (zhuh vooh-dreh uhN ruh-sew.) (*I'd like a receipt.*)

You may have to remove your belongings from your room before you're ready to depart from your location. Fortunately, many hotels allow you to leave your luggage in the lobby or some other place until you leave. To find out whether your hotel offers this service, ask **Je peux laisser mes bagages ici jusqu'à . . . .?** (zhuh puh ley-sey mey bah-gahzh ee-see zhews-kah. . .?) (*Can I leave my luggage here until. . . ?*)

Chapter 12

Handling Emergencies

· ·

In This Chapter

▶ Getting medical help

▶ Asking for help from the police

· ·

*I*t goes without saying that emergencies are no fun. They're bad enough when you're on home turf, but they're even worse when you're in a foreign environment. Hopefully, the only help you'll ever need to ask for when you're traveling is where the nearest bus terminal is or what local cuisine your hosts would recommend. But if you do find yourself in an emergency situation, you can use the information and vocabulary in this chapter to get the help you need.

We've divided this chapter into two main sections: The first half deals with health problems, and the second half deals with legal matters.

Getting Help Fast

If you're ever in an accident or have an emergency, the following key French phrases will alert those nearby and get you help right away:

    ✔ **À l'aide! Vite!** (ah lehd! veet!) (*Help! Fast!*)

    ✔ **Au secours!** (oh skoohr!) (*Help!*)

    ✔ **Au feu!** (oh fuh!) (*Fire!*)

    ✔ **Arrêtez-le/la!** (ah-reh-tey-luh/lah!) (*Stop him/her!*)

    ✔ **Au voleur!** (oh voh-luhr!) (*Catch the thief!*)

    ✔ **Police!** (poh-lees!) (*Police!*)

The emergency number for the entire European Union is 112. When you call this number, it connects you to the local first responders. Be sure you give them your location, the type of emergency, and your telephone number.

The French are required by law to provide assistance in an emergency. At the very least, they will stop, ask you what the problem is (if it's not evident), and call or tell you which number to call for the particular type of emergency.

Chances are that one of the first responders will speak enough English to communicate with you directly or will call someone who does. Just in case, you can always ask for someone who speaks English by saying **Est-ce qu'il y a quelqu'un qui parle anglais?** (ehs-keel ee ah kehl-kuhN kee pahrl ahN-gleh?) (*Is there someone who speaks English?*)

Getting Medical Help

If you have a medical concern – you have **une maladie** (ewn mah-lah-dee) (*an illness*), for example – you may simply need to go **chez le médecin** (shey luh meyd-saN) (*to the doctor's office*) or **au cabinet médical** (oh kah-bee-neh mey-dee-kahl) (*to the medical office*). To do this, you'll want to **prendre rendez-vous** (prahN-druh rahN-dey-vooh) (*make an appointment*). Although doctors usually have consultation hours for patients who don't have appointments, you may have to wait a long time. (If you are too ill to go to the doctor, don't worry. They can come to your hotel room or wherever you're staying.)

Your hotel can provide the addresses and phone numbers of local doctors or specialists. You can also get this information from a pharmacist. On Sundays, holidays, or after-hours, the local **gendarmerie** (zhahN-dahr-muh-ree) (*police station*) can also provide the number of **le médecin de garde** (luh meyd-saN duh gahrd) (*the doctor on duty*) or **la pharmacie de garde** (lah fahr-mah-see duh gahrd) (*the 24-hour pharmacy*).

If you have been involved in an accident, you may need to go to **un hôpital** (uhN-noh-pee-tahl) (*a hospital*) or **les urgences** (f) (ley-zewr-zhahNs) (*the emergency room*). In such an emergency, you can use either of the following phrases:

✔ **Il me faut un docteur.** (eel muh foh tuhN dohk-tuhr.)
(*I need a doctor.*)

✔ **Il lui faut une ambulance.** (eel lwee foh-tewn ahN-bew-lahNs.) (*He/She needs an ambulance.*)

Before leaving home, check with your insurance provider to see whether your policy covers emergencies or doctor visits abroad. If emergencies or medical treatments abroad aren't covered, you may need to purchase coverage for the dates you're traveling. If you need any sort of medical services while abroad, simply show your providers proof of your insurance. Also be sure to call your insurance company back home to explain what's happening. Usually you'll have to pay your bill (with your credit card) when you receive medical care, but your insurance company will reimburse you when you present the detailed bill back home. Remember to keep all your receipts and any **feuilles de soins** (fuhy duh swaN) (*medical claim forms*) that you sign.

Talking with doctors when you're ill or injured

France has one of the best healthcare systems in the world. Rest assured that, whether you're simply not feeling well and want to discuss your symptoms with **un médecin/un docteur** (uhN meyd-saN/uhN dohk-tuhr) (*a doctor*) or have been hurt in an accident, you'll receive world-class care.

Describing what body part hurts

To describe what's bothering you, you need to be able to convey to the doctor what body part hurts or feels uncomfortable:

✔ **la bouche** (lah boohsh) (*mouth*)

✔ **le bras** (luh brah) (*arm*)

✔ **la cheville** (lah shuh-veey) (*ankle*)

✔ **les côtes** (f.) (ley koht) (*ribs*)

✔ **le cou** (luh kooh) (*neck*)

✔ **le doigt** (luh dwah) (*finger*)

- ✔ **le dos** (luh doh) (*back*)

- ✔ **l'épaule** (ley-pohl) (*shoulder*)

- ✔ **l'estomac/le ventre** (leh-stoh-mah/luh vahN-truh) (*stomach*)

- ✔ **la figure** (lah fee-gewr) (*face*)

- ✔ **le genou** (luh zhuh-nooh) (*knee*)

- ✔ **la gorge** (lah gohrzh) (*throat*)

- ✔ **la jambe** (lah zhahNb) (*leg*)

- ✔ **la main** (lah maN) (*hand*)

- ✔ **le nez** (luh ney) (*nose*)

- ✔ **le pied** (luh pyey) (*foot*)

- ✔ **la poitrine** (lah pwah-treen) (*chest*)

- ✔ **l'oeil/les yeux** (luhy/ley-zyuh) (*eye/eyes*)

- ✔ **l'oreille** (loh-rehy) (*ear*)

- ✔ **l'orteil** (lohr-tehy) (*toe*)

- ✔ **la tête** (lah teht) (*head*)

To tell the doctor that something hurts, simply use the expression **J'ai mal à (à la/au/aux). . . .** (zhey mahl ah (ah lah/oh/oh. . . .) (*My . . . hurts*) and follow this with the body part. This construction uses the verb **avoir** (ah-vwahr) (*to have*) conjugated in the present (refer to Chapter 2 for the conjugation of this verb) plus the preposition **à** (ah). Whether you use **à la/au/aux** before the body part depends on the gender and number of the body part: If the body part is masculine singular, use **au;** if it is feminine singular, use **à la,** and if it's masculine or feminine plural, use **aux.** Here are some examples:

> **J'ai mal au bras.** (zhey mahl oh brah.) (*My arm hurts.*)

> **J'ai mal à la poitrine.** (zhey mahl ah lah pwah-treen.) (*My chest hurts.*)

> **J'ai mal aux pieds.** (zhey mahl oh pyeh.) (*My feet hurt.*)

You can also indicate what hurts on someone else by changing the subject pronoun at the beginning and conjugating the verb **avoir** appropriately, as shown in these examples:

Il a mal au dos. (eel ah mahl oh doh.) (*His back hurts.*)

Nous avons mal à la tete. (nooh-zah-vohN mahl ah lah teht.) (*We have a headache.*)

Describing other symptoms

If you don't feel well – you have a fever or feel nauseous or faint, for example – you'll want to explain those symptoms to the doctor. In this case, you want to be able to tell the doctor *I have a fever* or *I am nauseous.* To create many of these expressions, you use the verb **avoir**, as explained in the preceding sections, but without the preposition **à.** You say, for example, **j'ai** (zhey) (*I have*) and follow it with the appropriate symptom. Following are some symptoms:

- ✔ **de la fièvre** (duh lah fyeh-vruh) (*a fever*)

- ✔ **de la température** (duh lah tahN-pey-rah-tuhr) (*a temperature*)

- ✔ **des problèmes à respirer** (dey proh-blehm ah reh-spee-rey) (*problems breathing*)

- ✔ **de l'asthme** (duh lah-smuh) (*asthma*)

- ✔ **une migraine** (ewn mee-grehn) (*a migraine*)

- ✔ **un (gros) rhume** (uhN [groh] rewm) (*an [awful] cold*)

- ✔ **la grippe** (lah greep) (*the flu*)

- ✔ **le nez bouché** (luh ney booh-shey) (*a stuffy nose*)

- ✔ **une toux** (ewn tooh) (*a cough*)

- ✔ **une eruption/des taches rouges** (ewn ey-rewp-syohN/ dey tahsh roohzh) (*a rash/red spots*)

- ✔ **la diarrhée** (lah dyah-rey) (*diarrhea*)

- ✔ **une coupure** (ewn kooh-pewr) (*a cut*)

Keep in mind that the English translation may not actually include the verb *to have,* as these examples show:

J'ai de la nausée/J'ai mal au coeur. (zhey duh lah noh-zey/zhey mahl oh kuhr.) (*I am nauseous.*)

J'ai des vertiges. (zhey dey vehr-teezh.) (*I am dizzy.*)

Saying that you broke, sprained, twisted, or cut something

In French, to express that you have broken your arm, sprained or twisted your ankle, or cut a part of your body, you use reflexive verbs. (Check out the explanation and conjugation of such verbs in the present in Chapter 5. For more on the past tense, refer to Chapter 9.) To form the past tense of reflexive verbs, take the present tense conjugation of the auxiliary **être** (eh-truh) (*to be*) and follow it with a past participle. Here is an example of the verb **se casser** (suh kah-sey) (*to break*) in the **passé composé** (pah-sey kohN-poh-zey) (*the past tense [compound past]*):

> **Je me suis cassé la jambe.** (zhuh muh swee kah-sey lah zhahNb.) (*I broke my leg.*)

> **Tu t'es cassé la cheville.** (tew teh kah-sey lah shuh-veey.) (*You broke your ankle.*)

> **Il/Elle s'est cassé la bras.** (eel/ehl seh kah-sey lah brah.) (*He/She broke his/her arm.*)

> **Nous nous sommes cassé les orteils.** (nooh nooh sohm kah-sey ley-zohr-tehy.) (*We broke our toes.*)

> **Vous vous êtes cassé les doigts.** (vooh vooh-zeht kah-sey ley dwah.) (*You broke your fingers.*)

> **Ils/Elles se sont cassé les côtes.** (eel/ehl suh sohN kah-sey ley koht.) (*They broke their ribs.*)

Follow this pattern with other verbs and then add the part of the body that is affected. Here are examples using other verbs:

- ✔ **Je me suis foulé. . . .** (zhuh muh swee fooh-ley. . . .) (*I sprained. . . .*)

- ✔ **Je me suis tordu. . . .** (zhuh muh swee tohr-dew. . . .) (*I twisted. . . .*)

- ✔ **Je me suis coupé. . . .** (zhuh muh swee kooh-pey. . . .) (*I cut. . . .*)

English uses the possessive adjectives with the parts of the body, but French uses the definite articles. For example, in English, you say *I broke my foot.* In French, **je me suis cassé le pied** (zhuh muh swee kah-sey luh pyey), which means *I broke my foot* but translates literally as *I broke the foot to me.*

Undergoing a medical examination

When you go to the doctor, he or she will undoubtedly ask you a few questions, such as **Où avez-vous mal?** (ooh ah-vey-vooh mahl?) (*Where does it hurt?*) or **Quels sont vos symptômes?** (kehl sohN voh saN-ptohm?) (*What are your symptoms?*). To answer these questions, use the terms and phrases provided in the preceding sections. Unless the problem is very obvious and easy-to-treat, other questions and procedures may be required, as the following sections explain.

If you've been involved in an accident and hurt yourself, a frequently used idiomatic expression is the question **Qu'est-ce qui s'est passé?** (kehs-kee seh pah-sey?) (*What happened?*). Another common expression is **Ça fait mal!** (sah feh mahl!) (*That hurts!*) You'll want to memorize both of these.

Sharing information about existing conditions

The doctor may ask you questions, such as the following, to determine whether you have other conditions he or she needs to know about:

> **Êtes-vous cardiaque?** (eht-vooh kahr-dyahk?) (*Do you have a heart condition?*)

> **Êtes-vous diabétique?** (eht-vooh dee-ah-bey-teek?) (*Are you a diabetic?*)

> **Avez-vous de l'hypertension?** (ah-vey-vooh duh lee-pehr-tahN- syohN?) (*Do you have high-blood pressure?*)

> **Êtes-vous allergique à. . .?** (eht-vooh-zah-lehr-zheek ah . . .?) (*Are you allergic to. . .?*)

> **Prenez-vous des médicaments?** (pruh-ney-vooh dey mey-dee-kah-mahN?) (*Are you taking any medications?*)

Of course, you can also offer this information before you're asked, by using these phrases:

> ✔ **Je suis cardiaque.** (zhuh swee kahr-dyahk.) (*I have a heart condition.*)

> ✔ **J'ai de l'hypertension.** (zhey duh lee-pehr-tahN-syohN.) (*I have high blood pressure.*)

> ✔ **Je suis diabétique/allergique à . . . .** (zhuh swee
> dee-ah-bey-teek/ah-lehr-zheek ah. . . .) (*I am diabetic/
> allergic to . . . .*)

Talking about tests

After you tell the doctor what your concern is, he or she will
examine you and may want to **prendre votre pouls** (prahN-
druh vohh-truh poohl) (*take your pulse*) and **ausculter votre
coeur** (oh-skewl-tey vohh-truh kuhr) (*listen to your heart*) or
even do the following, as warranted:

> ✔ **prendre votre tension artérielle** (prahN-druh vohh-truh
> tahN-syohN ahr-tey-ree-ehl) (*to take your blood pressure*)
>
> ✔ **faire une prise de sang** (fehr ewn preez duh sahN) (*to
> take, draw blood*)
>
> ✔ **faire une radiographie** (fehr ewn rah-dyoh-grah-fee) (*to
> do an x-ray*)

When the exam is complete, the doctor will tell you what
you need to do. The doctor may **prescrire des médicaments**
(preh-skreer dey mey-dee-kah-mahN) (*prescribe medication*),
which you can get at a pharmacy.

Going to a pharmacy for minor ailments and medications

The pharmacy is often the first place you go in France for
minor medical concerns. In addition to filling **des ordonnances**
(dey-zohr-doh-nahNs) (*prescriptions*), the highly trained
pharmacien/pharmacienne (fahr-mah-syaN/fahr-mah-syehn)
(*pharmacist*) can dress wounds; give advice on how to remedy
a bad cold, migraines, sunburn, and so on; and give nutritional
advice as well. French pharmacies are easily recognizable by
the big green cross on them.

When you go to a pharmacist for medical care, you can ask
Pourriez-vous me donner un conseil? (pooh-ree-ey-vooh muh
dohh-ney uhN kohN-sehy) (*Could you give me some advice?*).
If the problem is more serious and requires further medical
attention, the pharmacist will refer you to the doctors in the
area.

In addition, **les médicaments** (ley mey-dee-kah-mahN) (*medication*) in France is sold only in pharmacies, not in supermarkets or anywhere else. The following vocabulary can help you request the medication you need:

- ✔ **les antibiotiques** (ley-zahN-tee-bee-oh-teek) (*antibiotics*)
- ✔ **l'aspirine** (lah-spee-reen) (*aspirin*)
- ✔ **les pastilles** (ley pah-steey) (*lozenges*)
- ✔ **le sirop (pour la toux)** (luh see-roh [poohr lah tooh]) (*syrup* [*cough syrup*])
- ✔ **les vitamines** (ley vee-tah-meen) (*vitamins*)

If you need medication, provide the generic name of the medication to the pharmacist because the name brand may not exist in the country where you are traveling. For example, you can say **acétaminophène** (ah-sey-tah-mee-noh-fehn) (*acetaminophen*) or **ibuprofène** (ee-bew-proh-fehn) (*ibuprophen*).

Even though you probably won't need a fully stocked **trousse de secours** (troohs duh skoohr) (*first-aid kit*), you can also get some basic items like **de l'alcool** (duh lahl-kohhl) ([*rubbing*] *alcohol*) and **des pensements** (dey pahN-suh-mahN) (*bandages*) at pharmacies, too.

Pharmacy hours are usually Monday to Saturday 9:00 a.m. to 7:00 p.m. and closed on Sundays. For night and Sunday hours, there is always **une pharmacie de garde** (ewn fahr-mah-see duh gahrd) (*a 24-hour pharmacy* [Literally: *a pharmacy on duty*]) nearby.

Braving the dentist

Anything can happen while traveling. You may get **une rage de dents** (ewn razh duh dahN) (*a violent toothache*) or lose a filling. If this happens, you can ask for the name of a local **dentiste** (dahN-teest) (*dentist*) at your hotel or inquire at the nearest pharmacy. Here's some vocabulary pertaining to common ailments involving your teeth:

- ✔ **un abcès** (uhN-nahp-seh) (*an abscess*)

- ✔ **une couronne cassée** (ewn kooh-rohn kah-sey) (*a broken crown*)

- ✔ **la dent (sensible)** (lah dahN [sahN-see-bluh]) (*[sensitive] tooth*)

- ✔ **les gencives saignantes** (ley zhahN-seev seh-nyahNt) (*bleeding gums*)

- ✔ **le plombage est tombé** (luh plohN-bahzh eh tohN-bey) (*the filling fell out*)

Handling Legal Matters

Most vacations and trips take place without any sort of issues that would require you to talk to the police or need help from your consulate. But occasionally, you may find yourself in a situation where such conversations are necessary. Perhaps your wallet or purse has been stolen, you've been involved in or have witnessed an accident, or you've lost your passport. This section provides you with the information you need to deal with such incidents if they should occur.

Talking to the police

You should report any accident, emergency, theft, and so on to **le commissariat de police** (luh koh-mee-sah-ree-aht duh poh-lees) (*the police station*) in major cities or to **la gendarmerie** (lah zhahN-dahr-muh-ree) in smaller towns. (See the earlier section 'Getting Help Fast' for emergency numbers.) To find the nearest police station, you can say **Où est le commissariat de police le plus proche?** (ooh eh luh koh-mee-sah-ree-aht duh poh-lees luh plew prohsh?) (*Where is the closest police station?*). Once there, you can explain your purpose by saying **Je veux signaler . . .** (zhuh vuh see-nyah-ley) (*I want to report . . .*) and filling in with the following phrases:

- ✔ **un accident** (uhN-nah-ksee-dahN) (*an accident*)

- ✔ **une agression** (ew-nah-greh-syohN) (*a mugging*)

- ✔ **un cambriolage** (uhN kahN-bree-oh-lahzh) (*a burglary*)

- ✔ **un vol** (uhN vohl) (*a theft*)

At this point, the conversation is likely to go beyond the French you know. In that case, you can say **Est-ce qu'il y a quelqu'un qui parle anglais?** (ehs-keel ee ah kehl-kuhN kee pahrl ahN-gleh?) (*Is there anyone who speaks English?*)

Reporting an accident

In the event of an accident, report the accident to **un agent de police** (uhN- nah-zhahN duh poh-lees) (*a police officer*) to make a report of major accidents in towns, or to **un gendarme** (uhN zhahN-dahrm) (*a police officer*) for accidents on country roads. You can say **Il y a eu un accident. . . .** (eel ee ah ew uhN-nah-ksee-dahN. . . .) (*There has been an accident. . . .*) and then follow this with these phrases:

- ✔ **sur l'autoroute** (sewr loh-toh-rooht) (*on the highway*)

- ✔ **sur la route** (sewr lah rooht) (*on the road*)

- ✔ **près de....** (preh duh...) (*near. . . .*)

When the police arrive, they usually ask a great many questions, such as the following:

- ✔ **Est-ce que je peux voir votre . . . ?** (ehs-kuh zhuh puh vwahr vohh-truh) (*Can I see your . . . ?*)

    permis de conduire (pehr-mee duh kohN-dweer) (*driver's license*)

    carte d'assurance (kahrt dah-sew-rahNs) (*insurance card*)

    carte grise (kahrt greez) (*vehicle registration document*)

- ✔ **Quel est votre nom et adresse?** (kehl eh vohh-truh nohN ey ah-drehs?) (*What is your name and address?*)

- ✔ **À quelle heure est-ce que ça s'est passé?** (ah kehl uhr ehs-kuh sah seh pah-sey?) (*At what time did this happen?*)

- ✔ **Est-ce qu'il y a des témoins?** (ehs-keel ee ah dey tey-mwaN?) (*Are there any witnesses?*)

They may also say **Vous devez venir au commissariat pour faire une déposition** (vooh duh-vey vuh-neer oh koh-mee-sah-ree-ah poohr fehr ewn dey-poh-zee-syohN) (*You have to come to the station to make a statement*) or **Vous devez payer une amende** (vooh duh-vey pey-yey ewn ah-mahNd) (*You have to pay a fine*).

The following phrases may help you explain what happened:

> **Il m'est rentré dedans.** (eel meh rahN-trey duh-dahN.) (*He ran into me.*)

> **Elle a conduit trop vite/près.** (ehl ah kohN-dwee troh veet/preh.) (*She drove too fast/close.*)

> **Je faisais . . . kilomètres à l'heure.** (zhuh fuh-zeh . . . kee-loh-meh-truh ah luhr) (*I was doing . . . kilometers per hour.*)

At any time, feel free to say **Je voudrais un interprète/un avocat.** (zhuh vooh-dreh–zuhN-naN-tehr-preht/uhN-nah-voh-kah.) (*I would like an interpreter/a lawyer.*)

Describing what was stolen

If things have been stolen from you, a police officer will ask **Qu'est-ce qui vous manque?** (kehs-kee vooh mahNk?) (*What is missing?*). You can say **On m'a volé . . . .** (ohN mah voh-ley. . . .) (*They stole. . . .*) and add the item stolen. Here are some items that are commonly stolen:

- ✔ **mon appareil-photo** (mohN-nah-pah-rehy foh-toh) (*my camera*)

- ✔ **mes cartes de crédit** (mey kahrt duh krey-dee) (*my credit cards*)

- ✔ **mon sac** (mohN sahk) (*my bag*)

- ✔ **mon argent** (mohN-nahr-zhahN) (*my money*)

- ✔ **mon passeport** (mohN pahs-pohr) (*my passport*)

- ✔ **mon porte-monnaie** (mohN pohrt-moh-neh) (*my wallet*)

The officer may also ask **Pouvez-vous décrire la personne?** (pooh-vey-vooh dey-kreer lah pehr-sohhn?) (*Can you describe the person?*). If you happened to see the culprit, you can say **C'était quelqu'un . . . .** (sey-teh kehl-kuhN. . . .) (*It was someone . . . .*) and then fill in the following descriptors:

- ✔ **aux cheveux blonds/bruns/roux/gris** (oh shuh-vuh blohN/bruhN/rooh/gree) (*with blond/brown/red/gray hair*)

- ✔ **un peu chauve** (uhN puh shohv) (*balding*)

✔ **grand/petit/mince/gros** (grahN/puh-tee/maNs/groh) (*tall/short/skinny/fat*)

✔ **d' environ . . . ans** (dahN-vee-rohN . . . ahN) (*of about . . . years* [*of age*])

Getting legal help

As a foreigner, you may feel overwhelmed and welcome some help. You can ask to do one of the following things:

J'ai besoin d'un avocat qui parle anglais. (zhey buh-zwaN duhN-nah-voh-kah kee pahrl ahN-gleh.) (*I need a lawyer who speaks English.*)

Je voudrais téléphoner à un/e ami/e en ville. (zhuh vooh-dreh tey-ley-fohh-ney ah uhN/ewn ah-mee ahN veel.) (*I would like to call a friend in town.*)

Je dois contacter le consulat. (zhuh dwah kohN-tah-ktey luh kohN-sew-lah.) (*I have to contact the consulate.*)

While you're in a foreign country, the laws of that country override the laws of your own. In an emergency, your consul is the most appropriate person to help you. He or she is on your side, more so than any local lawyer or police.

Part IV
The Part of Tens

Obviously you're pronouncing the phrase "Throw us a...," correctly in French, but the word for "lifesaver" just isn't coming out right.

Amis de la Mer

In this part . . .

Every *For Dummies* book includes top-ten lists, and this book has some good ones. Here, we provide you with favorite French expressions and phrases that will make you sound French.

Chapter 13

Ten Favorite French Expressions

After you get tuned into French a little, you may suddenly hear people use very French expressions that seem to just sort of slip out at any given occasion. You may even have heard some of these already; now it's time to casually use them yourself.

'À mon avis'

If you want to express your opinion in French, you use this handy phrase. **À mon avis** (ah mohN-nah-vee) means *in my opinion.* You can use the expression before or after you state your opinion.

'C'est pas vrai'

If you hear something that is hard to believe, you say **C'est pas vrai** (seh pah vreh) (*No way!, You don't say!*) This expression's literal meaning is *It is not true.* Note that, grammatically, this expression should be **Ce n'est pas vrai** (suh neh pah vreh); however, in oral French, the **ne** is often omitted, and you only hear the **pas.**

'Avec plaisir'

Avec plaisir (ah-vehk pleh-zeer) means *with pleasure,* and it's a great way to accept an invitation to lunch or to see a film, for example. You can also use this expression to show that you are willing and happy to do a favor for someone.

'Bon appétit!'

Bon appétit! (bohN-nah-pey-tee!) literally means *Good appetite!* However, it certainly is not commenting on anyone's good or bad appetite. You use this phrase when you begin to eat or when you see someone eating and want to express your desire that that person enjoy the meal. **Bon appétit!** is much like the English *Enjoy!* except that the French say **Bon appétit!** much more freely.

'C'est génial'

Use **C'est génial** (seh zhey-nyahl) to convey excitement about something. It means *It's fantastic!* or *It's great!* It can also suggest that something is really clever or, *It's brilliant.*

'À votre santé'

When the French raise their glasses, they say **À votre santé** (ah vohh-truh sahN-tey) in the singular formal or plural, or **À ta santé** (ah tah sahN-tey) in the familiar form. These phrases literally mean *to your health,* but their general meaning is the same as their English counterpart: *Cheers!*

'À vos souhaits'

When someone sneezes, in English you say *Bless you.* In French, you say **À vos souhaits** (ah voh sweh) (*to your wishes*), which is more formal, or **À tes souhaits** (ah tey sweh), which is more familiar or informal. Both expressions mean that you hope the sneezer's wishes come true.

'Quelle horreur!'

Quelle horreur! (kehl oh-ruhr!) means *What a horror!* You use it not only for real horrors but also to express any kind of disgust, as in these expressions: *What a terrible thought! How nasty!* and *I can't believe it!* You also use this expression when something looks, sounds, or smells terrible.

'À bientôt'

The literal translation of **À bientôt** (ah byaN-toh) is *Until soon*. You use this expression when you expect to see the departing person within a reasonable time frame.

'Pas mal'

Use **pas mal** (pah mahl) (*not bad*) when you want to express that something isn't great, but it's not terrible either; instead it's in-between. Generally, you use this phrase in response to someone asking you how you are feeling or how things are going.

Chapter 14

Ten Phrases That Make You Sound French

C hapter 13 provides you with some typically French expressions that almost everyone who speaks a little French knows and uses. The phrases in this chapter go a few steps beyond those common ones: These expressions are so very French that you may even pass for a native French speaker when you use them!

'Passez-moi un coup de fil!'

Passez-moi un coup de fil! (pah-sey mwah uhN kooht feel!) means *Give me a call!* You could say, of course, **Appelez-moi!** (ah-pley-mwah) or **Téléphonez-moi!** (tey-ley-fohh-ney-mwah!) (*Call me!*), both of which mean the same thing, but those phrases don't sound as sophisticated! You can also use the **tu** (tew) (*you* [singular]) form with these expressions: **Passe-moi un coup de fil** (pahs-mwah uhN kooht feel!), **appelle-moi** (ah-pehl-mwah), and **téléphone-moi** (tey-ley-fohhn-mwah).

'On y va!' or 'Allons-y!'

On y va! (oh-nee vah!) or **Allons-y!** (ah-lohN-zee!) both mean *Let's go [there]!* You can also send someone off somewhere with the imperative **Allez-y!** (ah-ley-zee!) (*Go ahead!*) – or **Vas-y!** (vah-zee!) for the familiar form — if you want to get a little insistent about it.

'Je n'en sais rien'

To indicate you're in the dark about something, say **Je n'en sais rien** (zhuh nahN seh ryaN) (*I don't know anything about it*). In casual speech, you can also say (and this is what you hear most of the time) **J'en sais rien** (zhahN seh ryaN) to indicate the same thing. Technically, **J'en sais rien** is grammatically incorrect because it is missing the **ne** (nuh) before the pronoun, but in spoken French, the **ne** is often dropped.

'Je n'en reviens pas'

If you hear something surprising or unbelievable, you can say **Je n'en reviens pas** (zhuh nahN ruh-vyaN pah) or you can omit the **n'** and say **J'en reviens pas** (zhahN ruh-vyaN pah). Both mean *I can't get over it* or *I'm amazed*. If you were to translate this expression literally, it wouldn't make sense: *I am not coming back from it.*

'Ça vaut la peine'

To express that something is worth the trouble, you can say **Ça vaut la peine** (sah voh lah pehn) or even **Ça vaut le coup** (sah voh luh kooh), which both mean *It's worth it*. The literal translations of theses expressions are *It's worth the pain* and *It's worth the effort*. You can also use these expressions in the negative: **Ça ne vaut pas la peine** (sah nuh voh pah lah pehn) or even **Ça ne vaut pas le coup** (sah nuh voh pas luh kooh), which mean *It's not worth it*. As with the expressions in the preceding sections, the **ne** is often dropped in spoken French, and you may hear **Ça vaut pas la peine** (sah voh pah lah pehn) or even **Ça vaut pas le coup** (sah voh pah luh kooh).

'C'est pas grave'

Literally, **C'est pas grave** (seh pah grahv) means *It isn't serious* (*grave*), but the colloquial translation is *It's no big deal*. The full expression is **Ce n'est pas grave** (suh neh pah grahv), but the **ne** is eliminated when speaking, and the emphasis is on **pas**.

'Ça m'est égal'

If you don't mind one way or another about something, then use the expression **Ça m'est égal** (sah meh-tey-gahl), which means *I don't mind* or *I don't care*. The literal translation is *It's equal to me*.

'N'importe'

N'importe (naN-pohrt) is a very common and versatile expression because it can be followed by so many interrogative adverbs, pronouns, or adjectives. By itself, the phrase means *no matter*, and when you tack on an interrogative expression, such as **qui** (kee) (*who*), **où** (ooh) (*where*), **quand** (kahN) (*when*), **comment** (koh-mahN) (*how*), **quoi** (kwah) (*what*), and so on, it means *No matter who, where, when, how, or what,* respectively.

'Tu cherches midi à 14h'

Tu cherches midi à 14h (tew shehrsh mee-dee ah kah-tohrz uhr) has to be the best one of all. Try to translate this literally and what you come up with is *You are looking for noon at 2 p.m.* Not sure what that means? Well, the meaning is fairly complex, but this phrase is so neat and so heavily used that you're very likely to hear it, and if you want to sound French, you'll want to say it, too. So here goes: **Tu cherches midi à 14h** means that so-and-so is making things more difficult than necessary, that he or she is sort of off the mark, has lost perspective, and is complicating the issue. You can also practice saying **Il ne faut pas chercher midi à 14h!** (eel nuh foh pah shehr-shey mee-dee ah kah-tohrz uhr!) (*You shouldn't get so obsessive about it!*)

Use **Tu cherches midi à 14h** when you're talking to the person who is making things unnecessarily difficult; use **Il/Elle cherche midi à 14h** (eel/ehl shehrsh mee-dee ah kah-tohrz uhr) when you're describing someone else.

'Prenons un pot!'

Use **Prenons un pot** (pruh-nohN-zuhN poh) when you want
to say. . . *Let's take a pot?* No, that can't be it, or can it? Well,
if you stretch your imagination a bit, you can see that the
phrase actually means *Let's have a drink!* (Not a whole potful
maybe, but . . . .) You can also use the expression **Prenons un
verre** (pruh-nohN-zuhN vehr), which means *Let's have a drink*
(it's literal translation is *Let's have a glass*).

Part V
Appendixes

The 5th Wave · By Rich Tennant

It's amazing what happens when you learn a little of their language.

In this part . . .

*L*ast but not least, we give you the appendixes, which you will no doubt find quite useful. In addition to a pretty comprehensive mini-dictionary, we also provide verb tables that show you how to conjugate regular and irregular verbs.

French-English Mini-Dictionary

A

à bientôt (ah byaN-toh): see you soon

à côté de (ah koh-tey duh): next to

à demain (ah duh-mahN): see you tomorrow

à droite (ah drwaht): on the right

à gauche (ah gohsh): on the left

à l'heure (ah luhr): on time

abricot (ah-bree-koh) m: apricot

absolument (ahb-soh-lew-mahN): absolutely

accepter (ah-kseh-ptey): to accept

acheter (ahsh-tey): to buy

addition (ah-dee-syohN) f: check

adorer (ah-doh-rey): to love, to adore

adresse (ah-drehs) f: address

adresse électronique (ah-dreh-sey-lehk-troh-neek) f: e-mail address

aérogare (ah-ey-roh-gahr) f: airport terminal

affaires (ah-fehr) fpl: business

affranchissement (ah-frahN-shee-smahN) m: postage

agneau (ah-nyoh) m: lamb

agrafe (ah-grahf) f: staple

agrafeuse (ah-grah-fuhz) f: stapler

agréable (ah-grey-ah-bluh): pleasant

aider (ey-dey): to help

aimer (eh-mey): to like, to love

aller (ah-ley): to go

aller-retour (ah-ley-ruh-toohr) m: round trip

aller-simple (ah-ley-saN-pluh) m: one-way (ticket)

allumette (ah-lew-meht) f: match

ami/amie (ah-mee) m/f: friend

ananas (ah-nah-nah) m: pineapple

aneth (ah-neht) m: dill

antibiotique (ahN-tee-bee-oh-teek) m: antibiotic

août (ooht) m: August

appareil-photo (ah-pah-rehy foh-toh) m: camera

appeler/s'appeler (ah-pley/sah-pley): to call/to call oneself, to be named

architecte (ahr-shee-tehkt) m/f: architect

argent (ahr-zhahN) m: money

armoire (ahr-mwahr) f: armoire

arrêt (ah-reh) m: stop

arrivée (ah-ree-vey) f: arrival

arriver (ah-ree-vey): to arrive

arroser (ah-roh-zey): to water

ascenseur (ah-sahN-suhr) m: elevator

asperge (ah-spehrzh) f: asparagus

assiette (ah-syeht) f: plate

attendre (ah-tahN-druh): to wait

attrapper (ah-trah-pey): to catch

au fond (oh fohN): in the back

au revoir (ohr-vwahr): good-bye

aubaine (oh-behn) f: sales [Quebec]

aujourd'hui (oh-zhoohr-dwee): today

aussi (oh-see): also

auteur (oh-tuhr) m: author

automne (oh-tohn) m: fall

avion (ah-vyohN) m: plane

avocat/avocate (ah-voh-kah/ah-voh-kaht) m/f: lawyer

avoir (ah-vwahr): to have

avoir faim (ah-vwahr faN): to be hungry

avoir soif (ah-vwahr swahf): to be thirsty

avril (ah-vreel) m: April

B

baignoire (beh-nywahr) f: bathtub

balance (bah-lahNs) f: scale

banane (bah-nahn) f: banana

bande dessinée (bahNd deh-see-ney) f: comic strip

banque (bahNk) f: bank

basilic (bah-zee-leek) m: basil

basket (bahs-keht) m: basketball

baskets (bahs-keht) fpl: sneakers

beau/belle (boh/behl) m/f: nice, beautiful, handsome

beurre (buhr) m: butter

bicyclette (bee-see-kleht) f: bicycle

bien sûr (byaN sewr): of course

bière (byehr) f: beer

bifteck (beef-tehk) m: steak

bijouterie (bee-zhooh-tree) f: jewelry store

billet (bee-yeh) m: ticket

bizarre (beez-ahr): weird, bizarre

blanc/blanche (blahN/blahNsh) m/f: white

blazer (blah-zehr) m: blazer

bleu/bleue (bluh) m/f: blue

boeuf (buhf) m: beef

boire (bwahr): to drink

boîte aux lettres (bwaht oh leh-truh) f: mailbox

bon/bonne (bohN/bohhn) m/f: good

bonheur (boh-nuhr) m: happiness

bonjour (bohN-zhoohr): hello, good day

bonne nuit (bohhn nwee) f: good night (when going to bed)

bonsoir (bohN-swahr) m: good evening, good night

bottes (bohht) fpl: boots

bouche (boohsh) f: mouth

boucherie (booh-shree)
f: butcher shop

boulangerie (booh-lahN-zhree)
f: bakery

bras (brah) m: arm

bronzer (brohN-zey): to tan

brosse (brohs) f: brush

bruyant/bruyante (brwee-ahN/
brwee-ahNt) m/f: noisy

bureau (bew-roh) m: office, desk

bureau de change (bew-roh duh
shahNzh) m: currency
exchange office

C

ça va (sah vah): okay

cabine d'essayage (kah-been
dey-sey-ahzh) f: fitting room

café (kah-fey) m: coffee, café

caisse (kehs) f: cash register

caissier/caissière (key-syey/
key-syehr) m/f: cashier

calendrier (kah-lahN-dree-yey)
m: calendar

cambriolage (kahN-bree-oh-
lahzh) m: burglary

campagne (kahN-pah-nyuh)
f: countryside

canapé (kah-nah-pey) m: sofa

canard (kah-nahr) m: duck

canne à pêche (kahn ah pehsh)
f: fishing pole

capot (kah-poh) m: hood
(of a car)

carotte (kah-roht) f: carrot

carrefour (kahr-foohr)
m: intersection

carte d'embarquement (kahrt
dahN-bahr-kuh-mahN)
f: boarding pass

carte de crédit (kahrt duh
krey-dee) f: credit card

casse-croûte (kahs-krooht)
m: snack

ceinture (saN-tewr) f: belt

celui-ci/celle-ci (suh-lwee-see/
sehl-see) m/f: this one

celui-là/celle-là (suh-lwee-lah/
sehl-lah) m/f: that one

centre commercial (sahN-truh
koh-mehr-syahl) m: mall

cerfeuil (sehr-fuhy) m: chervil

cerise (suh-reez) f: cherry

champignon (shahN-pee-nyohN)
m: mushroom

chanter (shahN-tey): to sing

chapeau (shah-poh) m: hat

charmant/charmante (shahr-
mahN/shahr-mahNt)
m/f: charming

château (shah-toh) m: castle

chaud/chaude (shoh/shohd)
m/f: warm, hot

chaussettes (shoh-seht) fpl: socks

chaussons (shoh-sohN) mpl:
slippers

chaussures (shoh-sewr)
f pl: shoes

chemise (shuh-meez) f: shirt

chemisier (shuh-mee-zyey)
m: blouse

cher/chère (shehr) m/f: expensive,
dear

cheville (shuh-veey) f: ankle

choisir (shwah-zeer): to choose

chou (shooh) m: cabbage

chou-fleur (shooh-fluhr)
m: cauliflower

choux de Bruxelles (shooh duh brewk-sehl) mpl: Brussels sprouts

cinéaste (see-ney-ahst)
m/f: filmmaker

cinéma (see-ney-mah) m: movies

cinq (saNk): five

ciseaux (see-zoh) mpl: scissors

clair/claire (klehr)
m/f: light-colored

classeur à tiroirs (klah-suhr ah tee-rwahr) m: file cabinet

clavier (klah-vyey) m: keyboard

climatisation (klee-mah-tee-zah-syohN) f: air conditioning

code postal (kohhd poh-stahl)
m: zip code

coffre (koh-fruh) m: trunk

colis (koh-lee) m: package

collègue (koh-lehg) m/f:
colleague, coworker

combien (kohN-byaN): how much

comment (koh-mahN): how

commode (koh-mohhd) f: dresser

compagnie (kohN-pah-nyee)
f: company

complet (kohN-pleh) m: suit
[France]

composter (kohN-poh-stey):
to validate a ticket

comptoir (kohN-twahr) m:
counter

conduire (kohN-dweer): to drive

confiture (kohN-fee-tewr) f: jam

consigne (kohN-see-nyuh)
f: baggage room

conte de fée (kohNt duh fey)
m: fairy tale

contravention (kohN-trah-vahN-syohN) f: traffic ticket

coquilles Saint-Jacques (koh-keey saN zhahk) fpl: scallops

corbeille à papiers (kohr-behy ah pah-pyey) m: wastepaper basket

coriandre (koh-ree-ahN-druh)
m: coriander

costume de bains (kohs-tewm duh baN) m: bathing suit [Québec]

côtes (koht) f: coast

côtes (koht) fpl: ribs

cou (kooh) m: neck

couleur (kooh-luhr) f: color

cour (koohr) f: courtyard

courir (kooh-reer): to run

couteau (kooh-toh) m: knife

couverts (kooh-vehr) mpl:
silverware

couverture (kooh-vehr-tewr)
f: blanket

cravate (krah-vaht) f: tie

crayon (krey-ohN) m: pencil

crème (krehm) f: cream

crémerie (kreym-ree) f: dairy product and cheese store

crevettes (kruh-veht) fpl: shrimp

crudités (krew-dee-tey) fpl: mixed greens, raw vegetables

cuillère (kwee-yehr) f: spoon, teaspoon

cuir (kweer) m: leather

cuisinière (kwee-zee-nyehr)
f: stove

D

d'accord (dah-kohr): all right, okay

dans (dahN): in, inside

danser (dahN-sey): to dance

décembre (dey-sahN-bruh) m: December

dehors (duh-ohr): outside

déjeuner (dey-zhuh-ney) m: lunch (as a verb: to have lunch)

demi-tour (duh-mee-toohr) m: U turn

dent (dahN) f: tooth

dentifrice (dahN-tee-frees) m: toothpaste

dentiste (dahN-teest) m/f: dentist

départ (dey-pahr) m: departure

derrière (deh-ryehr): behind

descendre (dey-sahN-druh): to go down, to get off

désolé/désolée (dey-zoh-ley) m/f: sorry

dessert (deh-sehr) m: dessert

dessin animé (deh-sahN ah-nee-mey) m: cartoon

détester (dey-teh-stey): to hate

deux (duh): two

devant (duh-vahN): in front of

devenir (duh-vuh-neer): to become

devoir (duh-vwahr): to have to

dinde (daNd) f: turkey

directeur/directrice (dee-rehk-tuhr/dee-rehk-trees) m/f: manager (of a company, business)

distributeur (de billets) (dees-tree-bew-tuhr [duh bee-yey]) m: ATM

dix (dees): ten

dix-huit (deez-weet): eighteen

dix-neuf (deez-nuhf): nineteen

dix-sept (dee-seht): seventeen

docteur (dohk-tuhr) m: doctor

documentaire (doh-kew-mahN-tehr) m: documentary

doigt (dwah) m: finger

donner (dohh-ney): to give

donner sur (dohh-ney sewr): facing, overlooking

dormir (dohr-meer): to sleep

dos (doh) m: back

doux/douce (dooh/doohs) m/f: mild, sweet

douze (doohz): twelve

draps (drah) mpl: sheets

E

échecs (ey-shehk) mpl: chess

éclairage (ey-kleh-rahzh) m: lighting

eau (oh) f: water

effets spéciaux (ey-feh spey-syoh) mpl: special effects

égalité (ey-gah-lee-tey) f: equality

élastique (ey-lah-steek) m: rubber band

elle (ehl) f: she

elles (ehl) fpl: they

embouteillage (ahN-booh-teh-yahzh) m: traffic jam

employé/employée (ahN-plwah-yey) m/f: employee

en face de (ahN fahs duh): across from, in front of

en retard (ahN ruh-tahr): late

enchanté/enchantée (ahN-shahN-tey) m/f: delighted

enfant (ahN-fahN) m/f: child

ennuyeux/ennuyeuse (ahN-nwee-uh/ahN-nwee-uhz): m/f: boring

entre (ahN-truh): between

entrée (ahN-trey) f: appetizer, entrance

entrer (ahN-trey): to enter

enveloppe (ahN-vlohhp) f: envelope

envoyer (ahN-vwah-yey): to send

épaule (ey-pohl) f: shoulder

épicerie (ey-pees-ree) f: grocery store, general store

épinards (ey-pee-nahr) mpl: spinach

époux/épouse (ey-pooh/ey-poohz) m/f: spouse

escalier roulant (ehs-kah-lyey rooh-lahN) m: escalator

essence (ey-sahNs) f: gas

essuie-glace (ey-swee-glahs) m: windshield wiper

est (ehst): east

estragon (ehs-trah-gohN) m: tarragon

été (ey-tey) m: summer

être (eh-truh): to be

étroit/étroite (ey-trwah/ey-trwaht) m/f: narrow

évier (ey-vyey) m: kitchen sink

F

facile (fah-seel): easy

faire (fehr): to do, to make

faire du jardinage (fehr dew zhahr-dee-nahzh): to garden

faire le plein (fehr luh plaN): to fill the gas tank

fatigué/fatiguée (fah-tee-gey) m/f: tired

femme (fahm) f: woman, wife

fenêtre (fuh-neh-truh) f: window

fêtes (feht) fpl: holidays

février (fey-vryey) m: February

fichier (fee-shyey) m: file

fier/fière (fyehr) m/f: proud

figue (feeg) f: fig

figure (fee-gewr) f: face

fille (feey) f: daughter or girl

film d'amour (feelm dah-moohr) m: romance film

film d'aventures (feelm dah-vahN-tewr) m: adventure film

film d'épouvante/d'horreur (feelm dey-pooh-vahNt/doh-ruhr) m: horror film

film d'espionnage (feelm deh-spee-oh-nahzh) m: spy film

film de science-fiction (feelm duh syahNs fee-ksyohN) m: science-fiction film

film policier (feelm poh-lee-syey) m: a detective film

fils (fees) m: son

fin (fahN) f: end

finir (fee-neer): to finish

flanelle (flah-nehl) f: flannel

fleur (fluhr) f: flower

foncé/foncée (fohN-sey) m/f: dark

football/soccer (fooht-bohl/soh-kehr) m: soccer

football américain (fooht-bohl ah-mey-ree-kaN) m: (American) football

foulard (fooh-lahr) m: scarf

four à micro-ondes (foohr ah mee-kroh-ohNd) m: microwave

fourchette (foohr-sheht) f: fork

fraise (frehz) f: strawberry

framboise (frahN-bwahz) f: raspberry

freins (fraN) mpl: brakes (of a car)

frère (frehr) m: brother

froid (frwah): cold

fromage (froh-mahzh) m: cheese

fruits (frwee) mpl: fruit

G

gagner (gah-nyey): to win

garçon (gahr-sohN) m: boy

gare (gahr) f: train station

gâteau (gah-toh) m: cake

générique (zhey-ney-reek) m: credits

genou (zhuh-nooh) m: knee

gérant/gérante (zhey-rahN/ zhey-rahNt) m/f: manager (restaurant, hotel, shop)

gigot d'agneau (zhee-goh dah-nyoh) m: leg of lamb

glace (glahs) f: ice cream

gomme (gohm) f: eraser

goûter (gooh-tey) m: snack (as a verb: to taste)

graine (grehn) f: seed

grand/grande (grahN/grahNd) m/f: big, tall, large

grand magasin (grahN mah-gah-zaN) m: department store

grippe (greep) f: flu

gros/grosse (groh/grohs) m/f: large, fat, thick

guichet (gee-shey) m: ticket window

guitare (gee-tahr) f: guitar

H

habit (ah-bee) m: suit [Québec]

habiter (ah-bee-tey): to live

haricots verts (ah-ree-koh vehr) mpl: green beans

heure de pointe (uhr duh pwaNt) f: rush hour, peak

heureux/heureuse (uh-ruh/ uh-ruhz) m/f: happy

hiver (ee-vehr) m: winter

homard (oh-mahr) m: lobster

horaire (oh-rehr) m: schedule

horloge (ohr-lohzh) f: clock

hortensia (ohr-tahN-syah) m: hydrangea

hôtel (oh-tehl) m: hotel

hôtesse de l'air (oh-tehs duh lehr) f: flight attendant

huit (weet): eight

huitres (wee-truh) fpl: oysters

I

icône (ee-kohn) f: icon

idée (ee-dey) f: idea

il (eel) m: he

il y a (eel ee ah): there is, there are

ils (eel) mpl: they

imperméable (aN-pehr-mey-ah-bluh) m: raincoat (n); rain-proof (adj)

imprimante (aN-pree-mahnt) f: printer

infirmier/infirmière (aN-feer-myey/aN-feer-myehr) m/f: nurse

informaticien/informaticienne (aN-fohr-mah-tee-syaN/ aN-fohr-mah-tee-syehn) m/f: computer scientist

ingénieur (aN-zhey-nyuhr) m: engineer

J

jambe (zhahNb) f: leg

jambon (zhahN-bohN) m: ham

janvier (zhahN-vyey) m: January

jardin (zhahr-daN) m: yard, garden

jardin d'agrément (zhahr-daN dah-grey-mahN) m: flower garden

jaune (zhohn): yellow

je (zhuh): I

jean (jeen) m: jeans

joindre (zhwaN-druh): to attach

joli/jolie (zhoh-lee) m/f: pretty

jonquille (zhohN-keey) f: daffodil

jouer (zhooh-ey): to play

jour (zhoohr) m: day

journal (zhoohr-nahl) m: newspaper

juillet (zhwee-yeh) m: July

juin (zhwaN) m: June

jupe (zhewp) f: skirt

jusqu'à (zhews-kah): until

L

là-bas (lah-bah): over there

lac (lahk) m: lake

laine (lehn) f: wool

lait (leh) m: milk

laitue (ley-tew) f: lettuce

lancer (lahN-sey): to launch, to throw

large (lahrzh): large, wide

lavabo (lah-vah-boh) m: bathroom sink

lave-vaisselle (lahv veh-sehl) m: dishwasher

lecteur de CD/de DVD (lehk-tuhr duh sey dey/duh dey vey dey) m: CD, DVD player

légumes (ley-gewm) mpl: vegetables

lendemain (lahN-duh-mahN) m: next day

liberté (lee-behr-tey) f: freedom

librairie (lee-brey-ree) f: bookstore

limonade (lee-moh-nahd) f: lemonade

lin (laN) m: linen

lire (leer): to read

lit (lee) m: bed

livre (lee-vruh) f: pound = 500 g, about 1.1lb.; m: book

logiciel (loh-zhee-syehl) m: software

long-métrage (lohN mey-trahzh) m: feature film

lui (lwee) m: him

lunettes de soleil (lew-neht duh soh-lehy) fpl: sunglasses

M

madame (mah-dahm) f: ma'am, missus

mademoiselle (mahd-mwah-zehl) f: miss

magasin (mah-gah-zaN) m: store

mai (meh) m: May

maillot de bains (mah-yoh duh baN) m: bathing suit

main (maN) f: hand

maintenant (maN-tuh-nahN): now

mais (meh): but

maison (meh-zohN) f: house

maladie (mah-lah-dee) f: illness

manger (mahN-zhey): to eat

manquer (mahN-key): to miss

manteau (mahN-toh) m: coat

marchand/marchande (mahr-shahN/mahr-shahNd) m/f: vendor

margarine (mahr-gah-reen) f: margarine

marguerite (mahr-gah-reet) f: daisy

mari (mah-ree) m: husband

marron (mah-rohN): brown

mars (mahrs) m: March

matériel (mah-tey-ryehl) m: equipment, material

mauvais/mauvaise (moh-veh/moh-vehz) m/f: bad

médecin (meyd-saN) m: physician

mél (mehl) m: e-mail

même (mehm): even, same

mémoire (mey-mwahr) f: memory

menthe (mahNt) f: mint

mentir (mahN-teer): to lie

mer (mehr) f: ocean

merci (mehr-see): thank you

mère (mehr) f: mother

messagerie (mey-sah-zhree) f: e-mail account

metteur-en-scène (meh-tuhr-ahN-sehn) m: film director

mettre (meh-truh): to put, to place

mille (meel) m: thousand

miroir (mee-rwahr) m: mirror

mobile (moh-beel) m: cell phone

moderne (moh-dehrn) m/f: modern

moi (mwah): me

moniteur (moh-nee-tuhr) m: monitor

monsieur (muh-syuh) m: mister

montagne (mohN-tah-nyuh) f: mountain

monter (mohN-tey): to go up, to climb, to get on

montre (mohN-truh) f: watch

montrer (mohN-trey): to show

moquette (moh-keht) f: carpet

mot de passe (moh duh pahs) m: password

mourir (mooh-reer): to die

moyen/moyenne (mwah-yaN/mwah-yehn) m/f: average

N

naissance (neh-sahNs) f: birth

naître (neh-truh): to be born

natation (nah-tah-syohN)
f: swimming

navigateur (nah-vee-gah-tuhr)
m: web browser

neige (nehzh) f: snow

nettoyer (neh-twah-yey): to clean

neuf (nuhf): nine

neuf/neuve (nuhf/nuhv)
m/f: brand new

nez (ney) m: nose

noir/noire (nwahr) m/f: black

nom (nohN) m: last name

nord (nohr) m: north

nous (nooh): we

nouveau/nouvelle (nooh-voh/
nooh-vehl) m/f: new

novembre (noh-vahN-bruh)
m: November

nuage (new-ahzh) m: cloud

numéro de téléphone (new-mey-
roh duh tey-ley-fohhn) m:
phone number

O

octobre (ohk-toh-bruh)
m: October

oeil/yeux (uhy/yuh) m: eye/eyes

oeillet (uh-yeh) m: carnation

oignon (ohh-nyohN) m: onion

oiseau (wah-zoh) m: bird

oncle (ohN-kluh) m: uncle

onze (ohNz) eleven

orange (oh-rahNzh) f: orange

ordinateur (ohr-dee-nah-tuhr)
m: computer

oreille (oh-rehy) f: ear

oreiller (oh-rehy-ey) m: pillow

orteil (ohr-tehy) m: toe

oseille (oh-zehy) f: sorrel

où (ooh): where

ou (ooh): or

ouest (ooh-wehst) m: west

P

page d'accueil (pahzh dah-kuhy)
f: home page

pain (paN) m: bread

pantalon (pahN-tah-lohN)
m: pants, slacks

pantoufles (pahN-tooh-fluh)
fpl: slippers

pardessus (pahr-duh-sew)
m: overcoat

pare-brise (pahr-breez)
m: windshield

parfait/parfaite (pahr-feh/
pahr-feht) m/f: perfect

parler (pahr-ley): to speak, to talk

partir (pahr-teer): to leave

pas du tout (pah dew tooh):
not at all

passeport (pahs-pohr) m: passport

passer (pah-sey): to pass [by]

pastèque (pahs-tehk)
f: watermelon

pastille (pah-steey) f: lozenge

pâtes (paht) fpl: pasta

pâtisserie (pah-tees-ree) f: pastry
shop

pays (pey-ee) m: country

PDG (pey dey zhey): CEO

pêche (pehsh) f: peach

pêcher (pehsh-ey): to go fishing

peigne (peh-nyuh) m: comb

pensée (pahN-sey) f: thought

pensement (pahN-suh-mahN) m: bandage

penser (pahN-sey): to think

père (pehr) m: father

période creuse (pey-ree-ohd kruhz) f: off peak

permis de conduire (pehr-mee duh kohN-dweer) m: driver's license

persil (pehr-see) m: parsley

personnes (pehr-sohhn) fpl: people

peser (puh-zey): to weigh

petit/petite (puh-tee/puh-teet) m/f: small, short

petit déjeuner (puh-tee dey-zhuh-ney) m: breakfast

petite-fille (puh-teet feey) f: granddaughter

petit-fils (puh-tee fees) m: grandson

petits pois (puh-tee pwah) mpl: peas

petits-enfants (puh-tee-zahN-fahN) mpl: grandchildren

photo (foh-toh) f: picture

photocopieuse (foh-toh-koh-pyuhz) f: copy machine

piano (pyah-noh) m: piano

pièce (pyehs) f: room, theatrical play

pièce jointe (pyehs zhwaNt) f: attachment

pied (pyey) m: foot

piéton/piétonne (pyey-tohN/pyey-tohhn) m/f: pedestrian

piscine (pee-seen) f: swimming pool

place (plahs) f: seat, city or town square

plage (plahzh) f: beach

plan (plahN) m: map

planche à voile (plahNsh ah vwahl) f: windsurfing

plate-bande (plaht-bahNd) f: flowerbed

pneu (pnuh) m: tire

pointure (pwaN-tewr) f: shoe size

poire (pwahr) f: pear

poireau (pwah-roh) m: leak

poisson (pwah-sohN) m: fish

poissonnerie (pwah-sohn-ree) f: fish store

poitrine (pwah-treen) f: chest

poivre (pwah-vruh) m: pepper

police (poh-lees) f: police

pomme (pohhm) f: apple

pommes de terre (pohhm duh tehr) fpl: potatoes

pont (pohN) m: bridge

porc (pohr) m: pork

portable (pohr-tah-bluh) m: laptop

porte (pohrt) f: door

portefeuille (pohrt-fuhy) m: wallet

porter (pohr-tey): to wear, to carry

poste (pohst) f: post office

potager (poh-tah-zhey) m: vegatable garden, vegetable

poulet (pooh-leh) m: chicken

pourboire (poohr-bwahr) m: tip

pourquoi (poohr-kwah): why

pouvoir (pooh-vwahr): to be able to

préférer (prey-fey-rey): to prefer

prendre (prahN-druh): to take

prénom (prey-nohN) m: first name

présenter (prey-zahN-tey): to introduce

printemps (praN-tahN) m: spring

professeur (proh-feh-suhr) m: high school teacher, college professor

promenade (prohm-nahd) f: walk

propriétaire (proh-pree-ey-tehr) m/f: owner

prune (prewn) f: plum

pseudo (psooh-doh) m: username

publicité (pew-blee-see-tey) f: advertisement

puis (pwee): then

pull (pewl) m: sweater

Q

quai (key) m: platform

quand (kahN): when

quatorze (kah-tohrz): fourteen

quatre (kah-truh): four

quel/quelle (kehl) m/f: which

quelque chose (kehl-kuh shohz): something

qu'est-ce que/quoi (kehs-kuh/ kwah): what

qui (kee): who

quinze (kaNz): fifteen

R

raisin (reh-zaN) m: grape

ralentir (rah-lahN-teer): to slow down

randonnée (rahN-doh-ney) f: hike

rasoir (rah-zwahr) m: razor

réalisateur/réalisatrice (rey-ah- lee-zah-tuhr/rey-ah-lee-zah- trees) m/f: director

recevoir (ruh-suh-vwahr): to receive

reçu (ruh-sew) m: receipt

réfrigérateur (rey-free-zhey-rah- tuhr) m: refrigerator

regarder (ruh-gahr-dey): to watch

rendez-vous (rahN-dey-vooh) m: appointment

rendre (rahN-druh): to return (something)

rendre visite à (rahN-druh vee- zeet ah): to visit a person

renseignement (rahN-seh-nyuh- mahN) m: information

rentrer (rahN-trey): to return, to go home

repas (ruh-pah) m: meal

répondre (rey-pohN-druh): to answer

représentation (ruh-prey-zahN- tah-syohN) f: performance

réseau (rey-zoh) m: network

rester (rehs-tey): to stay

retraité/retraitée (ruh-treh-tey) m/f: retiree

réveil (rey-vehy) m: alarm clock

rez-de-chaussée (reyd shoh-sey) m: ground [first] floor

rhume (rewm) m: a cold

rideau (ree-doh) m: curtain

riz (ree) m: rice

robe (rohhb) f: dress

roman (roh-mahN) m: novel

romarin (roh-mah-raN) m: rosemary

rouge (roohzh): red

ruban adhésif (rew-bahN ahd-ey-zeef) m: tape

rue (rew) f: street

S

s'abonner (sah-boh-ney): to subscribe

s'amuser (sah-mew-zey): to have fun

s'en aller (sahN-nah-ley): to leave

s'habiller (sah-bee-yey): to get dressed

sable (sah-bluh) m: sand

sac (sahk) m: bag

sac de couchage (sahk duh kooh-shahzh) m: sleeping bag

saison (seh-zohN) f: season

salade verte (sah-lahd vehrt) f: green salad, salad with lettuce only

salle d'attente (sahl dah-tahNt) f: waiting room

salon de chat (sah-lohN duh chaht) m: chat room

salut (sah-lew): hi

sandales (sahN-dahl) fpl: sandals

sauge (sohzh) f: sage

saumon (soh-mohN) m: salmon

savoir (sah-vwahr): to know

savon (sah-vohN) m: soap

se doucher (suh dooh-shey): to shower

se laver (suh lah-vey): to wash

se lever (suh-luh-vey): to get up

se réveiller (suh rey-vey-yey): to wake up

séance (sey-ahNs) f: (a movie) showing

secrétaire (suh-krey-tehr) m/f: secretary

seize (sehz): sixteen

séjour (sey-zhoohr) m: stay

sel (sehl) m: salt

semaine (suh-mehn) f: week

sens unique (sahNs ew-neek) m: one way

sept (seht): seven

septembre (sehp-tahN-bruh) m: September

serveur/serveuse (sehr-vuhr/sehr-vuhz) m/f: waiter/waitress

serviette (sehr-vyeht) f: napkin, towel

seulement (suhl-mahN): only

siège (syehzh) m: seat

siffler (see-fley): to whistle

six (sees): six

slip (sleep) m: underpants, briefs

soeur (suhr) f: sister

soie (swah) f: silk

soirée (swah-rey) f: evening, party

sol (sohl) m: soil

soldes (sohld) mpl: sales [France]

soleil (soh-lehy) m: sun

sortie (sohr-tee) f: exit

sortir (sohr-teer): to exit, to go out

soucoupe (sooh-koohp) f: saucer

souris (sooh-ree) f: mouse

sous (sooh): under, underneath

sous-vêtements (sooh-veht-mahN) m: underwear

souvent (sooh-vahN): often

sportif/sportive (spohr-teef/spohr-teev) m/f: athletic

stationnement (stah-syohn-mahN) m: parking

station-service (stah-syohN-sehr-vees) f: gas station

steward/hôtesse de l'air (stee-wahr/oh-tehs duh lehr) m/f: flight attendant

stylo (stee-loh) m: pen

sucre (sew-kruh) m: sugar

sud (sewd) m: south

supermarché (sew-pehr-mahr-shey) m: supermarket

sur (sewr): on, on top of

surveillant/surveillante de plage, de baignade (sewr-vehy-ahN/sewr-vehy-ahNt duh plahzh, duh beh-nyahd) m/f: lifeguard

sweat (sweht) m: sweatshirt

T

tableau d'affichage (tah-bloh dah-fee-shahzh) m: bulletin board

tailleur (tahy-uhr) m: women's suit

tant pis (tahN pee): too bad

tante (tahNt) f: aunt

tapis (tah-pee) m: rug

tarif réduit (tah-reef rey-dwee) m: reduced fare

tarte aux pommes (tahr-toh-pohhm) f: apple tart

tasse (tahs) f: cup

taux de change (toh duh shahNzh) m: exchange rate

télécharger (tey-ley-shahr-zhey): to download

télécopie (tey-ley-koh-pee) f: fax

télécopieur (tey-ley-koh-pyuhr) m: fax machine

téléphoner (tey-ley-fohh-ney): to telephone or call

tennis (tey-nees) m: tennis

tête (teht) f: head

thé (tey) m: tea

thon (tohN) m: tuna

thym (taN) m: thyme

timbre (taN-bruh) m: stamp

toi (twah): you

tomate (toh-maht) f: tomato

tomber (tohN-bey): to fall

tondeuse à gazon (tohN-duhz ah gah-zohN) f: lawn mower

tondre la pelouse/le gazon (tohN-druh lah puh-loohz/luh gah-zohN): to mow the lawn

toujours (tooh-zhoohr): always

tous (toohs): all

tout le monde (tooh luh mohNd): everyone, everybody

toux (tooh) f: a cough

train (traN) m: train

travailler (trah-vah-yey): to work

travailleur/travailleuse (trah-vah-yuhr/trah-vah-yuhz) m/f: hardworking

treize (trehz): thirteen

trois (twah): three

trop (troh): too much

trottoir (troh-twahr) m: sidewalk

trucages (trew-kahzh) mpl: special effects

truite (trweet) f: trout

tu (tew): you, informal, singular

tuyau d'arrosage (tewy-oh dah-roh-zahzh) m: garden hose

U

un/une (uhN/ewn) m/f: one

V

vague (vahg) f: wave

valise (vah-leez) f: suitcase

veau (voh) m: veal, calf

vedette (veh-deht) f: [movie] star

vendre (vahN-druh): to sell

venir (vuh-neer): to come

verre (vehr) m: glass

vert/verte (vehr/vehrt) m/f: green

veste (vehst) f: jacket (for men and women)

veston (vehs-tohN) m: man's suit jacket

viande (vyahNd) f: meat

victoire (veek-twahr) f: victory

vidange (vee-dahNzh) f: oil change

vieux/vieille (vyuh/vyehy) m/f: old

ville (veel) f: city/town

vin (vaN) m: wine

vingt (vaN): twenty

violon (vyoh-lohN) m: violin

visiter (vee-zee-tey): to visit (a place)

vitrine (vee-treen) f: store window

voie (vwah) f: track

voile (vwahl) f: sailing

voir (vwahr): to see

voiture (vwah-tewr) f: car

vol (vohl) m: flight, theft

vouloir (vooh-lwahr): to want

vous (vooh): you, singular formal or plural

voyage d'affaires (voh-yahzh dah-fehr) m: business trip

voyager (voh-yah-zhey): to travel

English-French Mini-Dictionary

A

absolutely: **absolument** (ahb-soh-lew-mahN)

(to) accept: **accepter** (ah-kseh-ptey)

across from, in front of: **en face de** (ahN fahs-duh)

address: **adresse** (ah-drehs) f

adventure film: **film d'aventures** (feelm dah-vahN-tewr) m

advertisement: **publicité** (pew-blee-see-tey) f

air conditioning: **climatisation** (klee-mah-tee-zah-syohN) f

airport terminal: **aérogare** (ah-ey-roh-gahr) f

alarm clock: **réveil** (rey-vehy) m

all right, okay: **d'accord** (dah-kohr)

all: **tous** (toohs)

also: **aussi** (oh-see)

always: **toujours** (tooh-zhoohr)

American football: **foot(ball) américain** (fooht[bohl] ah-mey-ree-kaN) m

ankle: **cheville** (shuh-veey) f

(to) answer: **répondre** (rey-pohN-druh)

antibiotic: **antibiotique** (ahN-tee-bee-oh-teek) m

appetizer, entrance: **entrée** (ahN-trey) f

apple tart: **tarte aux pommes** (tahr-toh-pohhm) fpl

apple: **pomme** (pohhm) f

appointment: **rendez-vous** (rahN-dey-vooh) m

apricot: **abricot** (ah-bree-koh) m

April: **avril** (ah-vreel) m

architect: **architecte** (ahr-shee-tehkt) m/f

arm: **bras** (brah) m

armoire: **armoire** (ahr-mwahr) f

arrival: **arrivée** (ah-ree-vey) f

(to) arrive: **arriver** (ah-ree-vey)

asparagus: **asperge** (ah-spehrzh) f

athletic: **sportif/sportive** (spohr-teef/spohr-teev) m/f

ATM: **distributeur (de billets)** (dees-tree-bew-tuhr [duh bee-yey]) m

attach: **joindre** (zhwaN-druh)

attachment: **pièce jointe** (pyehs zhwaNt) f

August: **août** (ooht) m

aunt: **tante** (tahNt) f

author: **auteur** (oh-tuhr) m

average: **moyen/moyenne** (mwah-yaN/mwah-yehn) m/f

B

back: **dos** (doh) m

bad: **mauvais/mauvaise** (moh-veh/moh-vehz) m/f

bag: **sac** (sahk) m

baggage room: **consigne** (kohN-see-nyuh) f

bakery: **boulangerie** (booh-lahN-zhree) f

banana: **banane** (bah-nahn) f

bandage: **pensement** (pahN-suh-mahN) m

bank: **banque** (bahNk) f

basil: **basilic** (bah-zee-leek) m

basketball: **basket** (bahs-keht) m

bathing suit: **maillot de bain/cos-tume de bains** (Québec) (mah-yoh duh baN/kohs-tewm duh baN) m

bathroom sink: **lavabo** (lah-vah-boh) m

bathtub: **baignoire** (beh-nywahr) f

(to) be: **être** (eh-truh)

beach: **plage** (plahzh) f

(to) be able to: **pouvoir** (pooh-vwahr)

(to) be born: **naître** (neh-truh)

(to) become: **devenir** (duh-vuh-neer)

bed: **lit** (lee) m

beef: **boeuf** (buhf) m

beer: **bière** (byehr) f

behind: **derrière** (deh-ryehr)

belt: **ceinture** (saN-tewr) f

between: **entre** (ahN-truh)

bicycle: **bicyclette** (bee-see-kleht) f

big, tall, large: **grand/grande** (grahN/grahNd) m/f

bird: **oiseau** (wah-zoh) m

birth: **naissance** (neh-sahNs) f

black: **noir/noire** (nwahr) m/f

blanket: **couverture** (kooh-vehr-tewr) f

blazer: **blazer** (blah-zehr) m

blouse: **chemisier** (shuh-mee-zyey) m

blue: **bleu/bleue** (bluh) m/f

boarding pass: **carte d'embarquement** (kahrt dahN-bahr-kuh-mahN) f

bookstore: **librairie** (lee-brey-ree) f

boots: **bottes** (bohht) fpl

boring: **ennuyeux/ennuyeuse** (ahN-nwee-uh/ahN-nwee-euhz) m/f

boy: **garçon** (gahr-sohN) m

brakes (of a car): **freins** (fraN) mpl:

bread: **pain** (paN) m

breakfast: **petit déjeuner** (puh-tee dey-zhuh-ney) m

bridge: **pont** (pohN) m

brother: **frère** (frehr) m

brown: **marron** (mah-rohN)

brush: **brosse** (brohs) f

Brussels sprouts: **choux de Bruxelles** (shooh duh brewk-sehl) mpl

bulletin board: **tableau d'affichage** (tah-bloh dah-fee-shahzh) m burglary: **cambriolage** (kahN-bree-oh-lahzh) m

business trip: **voyage d'affaires** (voh-yahzh dah-fehr) m

business: **affaires** (ah-fehr) f pl

but: **mais** (meh)

butcher shop: **boucherie** (booh-shree) f

butter: **beurre** (buhr) m

(to) buy: **acheter** (ahsh-tey)

C

cabbage: **chou** (shooh) m

cake: **gâteau** (gah-toh) m

calendar: **calendrier** (kah-lahN-dree-yey) m

(to) call/to call oneself, to be named: **appeler/s'appeler** (ah-pley/sah-pley)

camera: **appareil-photo** (ah-pah-rehy foh-toh) m

car: **voiture** (vwah-tewr) f

carnation: **oeillet** (uh-yeh) m

carpet: **moquette** (moh-keht) f

carrot: **carotte** (kah-roht) f

cartoon: **dessin animé** (deh-sahN ah-nee-mey) m

cashier: **caissier/caissière** (key-syeh/key-syehr) m/f

cash register: **caisse** (kehs) f

castle: **château** (shah-toh) m

(to) catch: **attraper** (ah-trah-pey)

cauliflower: **chou-fleur** (shooh-fluhr) m

CD, DVD player: **lecteur de CD/de DVD** (lehk-tuhr duh sey dey/ duh dey vey dey) m

cell phone: **mobile** (moh-beel) m

CEO: **PDG** (pey dey zhey)

charming: **charmant/charmante** (shahr-mahN/shahr-mahNt) m/f

chat room: **salon de chat** (sah-lohN duh chaht) m

check: **addition** (ah-dee-syohN) f

cheese: **fromage** (froh-mahzh) m

cherry: **cerise** (suh-reez) f

chervil: **cerfeuil** (sehr-fuhy) m

chess: **échecs** (ey-shehk) mpl

chest: **poitrine** (pwah-treen) f

chicken: **poulet** (pooh-leh) m

child: **enfant** (ahN-fahN) m/f

(to) choose: **choisir** (shwah-zeer)

city/town: **ville** (veel) f

(to) clean: **nettoyer** (neh-twah-yey)

clock: **horloge** (ohr-lohzh) f

cloud: **nuage** (new-ahzh) m

coast: **côtes** (koht) f

coat: **manteau** (mahN-toh) m

coffee, café: **café** (kah-fey) m

cold (noun): **rhume** (rewm) m

cold: **froid/froide** (frwah/ frwahd) m/f

colleague, coworker: **collègue** (koh-lehg) m/f

color: **couleur** (kooh-luhr) f

comb: **peigne** (peh-nyuh) m

(to) come: **venir** (vuh-neer)

comic strip: **bande dessinée** (bahNd deh-see-ney) f

company: **compagnie** (kohN-pah-nyee) f

computer scientist: **informaticien/ informaticienne**

(aN-fohr-mah-tee-syaN/aN-fohr-mah-tee-syehn) m/f

computer: **ordinateur** (ohr-dee-nah-tuhr) m

copy machine: **photocopieuse** (foh-toh-koh-pyuhz) f

coriander: **coriandre** (koh-ree-ahN-druh) m

cough (noun): **toux** (tooh) f

counter: **comptoir** (kohN-twahr) m

country: **pays** (pey-ee) m

countryside: **campagne** (kahN-pah-nyuh) f

courtyard: **cour** (koohr) f

cream: **crème** (krehm) f

credit card: **carte de crédit** (kahrt duh krey-dee) f

credits: **générique** (zhey-ney-reek) m

cup: **tasse** (tahs) f

currency exchange office: **bureau de change** (bew-roh duh shahNzh) m

curtain: **rideau** (ree-doh) m

D

daffodil: **jonquille** (zhohN-keey) f

dairy product and cheese store: **crémerie** (kreym-ree) f

daisy: **marguerite** (mahr-gah-reet) f

(to) dance: **danser** (dahN-sey)

dark: **foncé/foncée** (fohN-sey) m/f

daughter, girl: **fille** (feey) f

day: **jour** (zhoohr) m

dear, expensive: **cher/chère** (shehr) m/f

December: **décembre** (dey-sahN-bruh) m

delighted: **enchanté/enchantée** (ahN-shahN-tey) m/f

dentist: **dentiste** (dahN-teest) m/f

department store: **grand magasin** (grahN mah-gah-zaN) m

departure: **départ** (dey-pahr) m

dessert: **dessert** (deh-sehr) m

detective film: **film policier** (feelm poh-lee-syey) m

(to) die: **mourir** (mooh-reer)

dill: **aneth** (ah-neht) m

director (film): **metteur-en-scène/réalisateur/réalisatrice** (meh-tuhr-ahN-sehn/rey-ah-lee-zah-tuhr/rey-ah-lee-zah-trees) m/f

director/manager (of a company or business): **directeur/directrice** (dee-rehk-tuhr/dee-rehk-trees) m/f

dishwasher: **lave-vaisselle** (lahv veh-sehl) m

(to) do, to make: **faire** (fehr)

doctor: **docteur** (dohk-tuhr) m

documentary: **documentaire** (doh-kew-mahN-tehr) m

door: **porte** (pohrt) f

(to) download: **télécharger** (tey-ley-shahr-zhey)

dress: **robe** (rohhb) f

dresser: **commode** (koh-mohhd) f

(to) drink: **boire** (bwahr)

(to) drive: **conduire** (kohN-dweer)

driver's license: **permis de conduire** (pehr-mee duh kohN-dweer) m

duck: **canard** (kah-nahr) m

E

ear: **oreille** (oh-rehy) f

easy: **facile** (fah-seel)

(to) eat: **manger** (mahN-zhey)

eight: **huit** (weet)

eighteen: **dix-huit** (deez-weet)

elevator: **ascenseur** (ah-sahN-suhr) m

eleven: **onze** (ohNz)

e-mail account: **messagerie** (mey-sah-zhree) f

e-mail address: **adresse électronique** (ah-dreh-sey-lehk-troh-neek) f

e-mail: **mél** (mehl) m

employee: **employé/employée** (ahN-plwah-yey) m/f

end: **fin** (fahN) f

engineer: **ingénieur** (aN-zhey-nyuhr) m

(to) enter: **entrer** (ahN-trey)

envelope: **enveloppe** (ahN-vlohhp) f

equality: **égalité** (ey-gah-lee-tey) f

equipment, material: **matériel** (mah-tey-ryehl) m

eraser: **gomme** (gohm) f

escalator: **escalier roulant** (ehs-kah-lyey rooh-lahN) m

even, same: **même** (mehm)

evening party: **soirée** (swah-rey) f

everyone, everybody: **tout le monde** (tooh luh mohNd)

exchange rate: **taux de change** (toh duh shahNzh) m

exit: **sortie** (sohr-tee) f

(to) exit, to go out: **sortir** (sohr-teer)

expensive: **cher/chère** (shehr) m/f

eye/eyes: **oeil /yeux** (uhy/yuh) m

F

face: **figure** (fee-gewr) f

facing, overlooking: **donner sur** (dohh-ney sewr)

fairy tale: **conte de fée** (kohNt duh fey) m

fall: **automne** (oh-tohn) m

(to) fall: **tomber** (tohN-bey)

fat, large: **gros/grosse** (groh/grohs) m/f

father: **père** (pehr) m

fax machine: **télécopieur** (tey-ley-koh-pyuhr) m

fax: **télécopie** (tey-ley-koh-pee) f

feature film: **long-métrage** (lohN mey-trahzh) m

February: **février** (fey-vryey) m

fifteen: **quinze** (kaNz)

fig: **figue** (feeg) f

file cabinet: **classeur à tiroirs** (klah-suhr ah tee-rwahr) m

file: **fichier** (fee-shyey) m

(to) fill the gas tank: **faire le plein** (fehr luh plaN)

filmmaker: **cinéaste** (see-ney-ahst) m/f

finger: **doigt** (dwah) m

(to) finish: **finir** (fee-neer)

first name: **prénom** (prey-nohN) m

fish store: **poissonnerie** (pwah-sohn-ree) f

fish: **poisson** (pwah-sohN) m

fishing pole: **canne à pêche** (kahn ah pehsh) f

fitting room: **cabine d'essayage** (kah-been dey-sey-ahzh) f

five: **cinq** (saNk)

flannel: **flanelle** (flah-nehl) f

flight attendant: **steward/hôtesse de l'air** (stee-wahr/oh-tehs duh lehr) m/f

flight: **vol** (vohl) m

flower garden: **jardin d'agrément** (zhahr-daN dah-grey-mahN) m

flower: **fleur** (fluhr) f

flowerbed: **plate-bande** (plaht-bahNd) f

flu: **grippe** (greep) f

foot: **pied** (pyey) m

fork: **fourchette** (foohr-sheht) f

four: **quatre** (kah-truh)

fourteen: **quatorze** (kah-tohrz)

freedom: **liberté** (lee-behr-tey) f

friend: **ami/amie** (ah-mee) m/f

fruit: **fruits** (frwee) mpl

G

(to) garden: **faire du jardinage** (fehr dew zhahr-dee-nahzh)

garden hose: **tuyau d'arrosage** (tewy-oh dah-roh-zahzh) m

gas station: **station-service** (stah-syohN-sehr-vees) f

gas: **essence** (ey-sahNs) f

glass: **verre** (vehr) m

(to) get dressed: **s'habiller** (sah-bee-yey)

(to) get up: **se lever** (suh-luh-vey)

(to) give: **donner** (dohh-ney)

(to) go: **aller** (ah-ley)

(to) go down, to get off: **descendre** (dey-sahN-druh)

(to) go fishing: **pêcher** (pehsh-ey)

(to) go up, to climb, to get on: **monter** (mohN-tey)

good: **bon/bonne** (bohN/ bohhn) m/f

good-bye: **au revoir** (ohr-vwahr)

good day, hello: **bonjour** (bohN-zhoohr)

good evening, good night: **bonsoir** (bohN-swahr) m

good night (when going to bed): **bonne nuit** (bohhn nwee) f

grandchildren: **petits-enfants** (puh-tee-zahN-fahN) mpl

granddaughter: **petite-fille** (puh-teet feey) f

grandson: **petit-fils** (puh-tee fees) m

grape: **raisin** (reh-zaN) m

green beans: **haricots verts** (ah-ree-koh vehr) mpl

green salad, salad with lettuce only: **salade verte** (sah-lahd vehrt) f

green: **vert/verte** (vehr/vehrt) m/f

grocery store, general store: **épicerie** (ey-pees-ree) f

ground [first] floor: **rez-de-chaussée** (reyd shoh-sey) m

guitar: **guitare** (gee-tahr) f

H

ham: **jambon** (zhahN-bohN) m

hand: **main** (maN) f

happiness: **bonheur** (boh-nuhr) m

happy: **heureux/heureuse** (uh-ruh/uh-ruhz) m/f

hardworking: **travailleur/ travailleuse** (trah-vah-yuhr/ trah-vah-yuhz) m/f

hardware: **matériel** (mah-tey-ree-ehl) m

hat: **chapeau** (shah-poh) m

(to) hate: **détester** (dey-teh-stey)

(to) have: **avoir** (ah-vwahr)

(to) have fun: **s'amuser** (sah-mew-zey)

(to) have to: **devoir** (duh-vwahr)

he: **il** (eel) m

head: **tête** (teht) f

(to) help: **aider** (ey-dey)

hi: **salut** (sah-lew)

high school teacher, college professor: **professeur** (proh-feh-suhr) m

hike: **randonnée** (rahN-doh-ney) f

him: **lui** (lwee) m

holidays: **fêtes** (feht) fpl

home page: **page d'accueil** (pahzh dah-kuhy) f

hood (of a car): **capot** (kah-poh) m

horror film: **film d'épouvante/ d'horreur** (feelm dey-pooh-vahnt/doh-ruhr) m

hotel: **hôtel** (oh-tehl) m

house: **maison** (meh-zohN) f

how much: **combien** (kohN-byaN)

how: **comment** (koh-mahN)

(to be) hungry: **avoir faim** (ah-vwahr faN)

husband: **mari** (mah-ree) m

hydrangea: **hortensia** (ohr-tahN-syah) m

I

I: **je** (zhuh)

ice cream: **glace** (glahs) f

icon: **icône** (ee-kohn) f

idea: **idée** (ee-dey) f

illness: **maladie** (mah-lah-dee) f

in front of: **devant** (duh-vahN)

in the back: **au fond** (oh fohN)

in, inside: **dans** (dahN)

information: **renseignement** (rahN-sehn-yuh-mahN) m

intersection: **carrefour** (kahr-foohr) m

(to) introduce: **présenter** (prey-zahN-tey)

J

jacket (for men and women): **veste** (vehst) f

jam: **confiture** (kohN-fee-tewr) f

January: **janvier** (zhahN-vyey) m

jeans: **jean** (jeen) m

jewelry store: **bijouterie** (bee-zhooh-tree) f

July: **juillet** (zhwee-yeh) m

June: **juin** (zhwaN) m

K

keyboard: **clavier** (klah-vyey) m

kitchen sink: **évier** (ey-vyey) m

knee: **genou** (zhuh-nooh) m

knife: **couteau** (kooh-toh) m

(to) know: **savoir** (sah-vwahr)

L

lake: **lac** (lahk) m

lamb: **agneau** (ah-nyoh) m

laptop: **portable** (pohr-tah-bluh) m

large, wide: **large** (lahrzh) m/f

last name: **nom** (nohN) m

late: **en retard** (ahN ruh-tahr)

(to) launch, to throw: **lancer** (lahN-sey)

lawn mower: **tondeuse à gazon** (tohN-duhz ah gah-zohN) f

lawyer: **avocat/avocate** (ah-voh-kah/ah-voh-kaht) m/f

leak: **poireau** (pwah-roh) m

leather: **cuir** (kweer) m

(to) leave: **partir/s'en aller** (pahr-teer/sahN-nah-ley)

leg of lamb: **gigot d'agneau** (zhee-goh dah-nyoh) m

leg: **jambe** (zhahNb) f

lemonade: **limonade** (lee-moh-nahd) f

lettuce: **laitue** (ley-tew) f

(to) lie: **mentir** (mahN-teer)

lifeguard: **surveillant/surveillante de plage, de baignade** (sewr-vehy-ahN/sewr-vehy-ahNt duh plahzh, duh beh-nyahd) m/f

light-colored: **clair/claire** (klehr) m/f

lighting: **éclairage** (ey-kleh-rahzh) m

(to) like, to love: **aimer** (eh-mey)

linen: **lin** (laN) m

(to) live: **habiter** (ah-bee-tey)

lobster: **homard** (oh-mahr) m

(to) love, to adore: **adorer** (ah-doh-rey)

lozenge: **pastille** (pah-steey) f

lunch (as a verb: to have lunch): **déjeuner** (dey-zhuh-ney) m

M

ma'am, missus: **madame** (mah-dahm) f

mailbox: **boîte aux lettres** (bwaht oh leh-truh) f

(to) make, to do: **faire** (fehr)

mall: **centre commercial** (sahN-truh koh-mehr-syahl) m

man's suit jacket: **veston** (vehs-tohN) m

manager (of a company, business): **directeur/directrice** (dee-rehk-tuhr/dee-rehk-trees) m/f

manager (restaurant, hotel, shop): **gérant/gérante** (zhey-rahN/zhey-rahNt) m/f

map: **plan** (plahN) m

March: **mars** (mahrs) m

margarine: **margarine** (mahr-gah-reen) f

match: **allumette** (ah-lew-meht) f

May: **mai** (meh) m

me: **moi** (mwah)

meal: **repas** (ruh-pah) m

meat: **viande** (vyahNd) f

memory: **mémoire** (mey-mwahr) f

microwave: **four à micro-ondes** (foohr ah mee-kroh-ohNd) m

mild, sweet: **doux/douce** (dooh/doohs) m/f

milk: **lait** (leh) m

mint: **menthe** (mahNt) f

mirror: **miroir** (mee-rwahr) m

miss (title): **mademoiselle** (mahd-mwah-zehl) f

(to) miss: **manquer** (mahN-key)

mister: **monsieur** (muh-syuh) m

mixed greens, raw vegetables: **crudités** (krew-dee-tey) fpl

modern: **moderne** (moh-dehrn) m/f

money: **argent** (ahr-zhahN) m

monitor: **moniteur** (moh-nee-tuhr) m

mother: **mère** (mehr) f

mountain: **montagne** (mohN-tah-nyuh) f

mouse: **souris** (sooh-ree) f

mouth: **bouche** (boohsh) f

movie star: **vedette** (veh-deht) f

movies: **cinéma** (see-ney-mah) m

(to) mow the lawn: **tondre la pelouse/le gazon** (tohN-druh lah puh-loohz/luh gah-zohN)

mushroom: **champignon** (shahN-pee-nyohN) m

N

napkin, towel: **serviette** (sehr-vyeht) f

narrow: **étroit/étroite** (ey-trwah/ey-trwaht) m/f

neck: **cou** (kooh) m

network: **réseau** (rey-zoh) m

new, brand new: **neuf/neuve** (nuhf/nuhv) m/f

new: **nouveau/nouvelle** (nooh-voh/nooh-vehl) m/f

newspaper: **journal** (zhoohr-nahl) m

next day: **lendemain** (lahN-duh-mahN) m

next to: **à côté de** (ah koh-tey duh)

nice, beautiful, handsome: **beau/belle** (boh/behl) m/f

nine: **neuf** (nuhf)

nineteen: **dix-neuf** (deez-nuhf)

noisy: **bruyant/bruyante** (brwee-ahN/brwee-ahNt) m/f

north: **nord** (nohr) m

nose: **nez** (ney) m

not at all: **pas du tout** (pah dew tooh)

novel: **roman** (roh-mahN) m

November: **novembre** (noh-vahN-bruh) m

now: **maintenant** (maN-tuh-nahN)

nurse: **infirmier/infirmière** (aN-feer-myey/aN-feer-myehr) m/f

O

ocean: **mer** (mehr) f

October: **octobre** (ohk-toh-bruh) m

of course: **bien sûr** (byaN sewr)

off peak: **période creuse** (pey-ree-ohd kruhz) f

office, desk: **bureau** (bew-roh) m

often: **souvent** (sooh-vahN)

oil change: **vidange** (vee-dahNzh) f

okay: **ça va** (sah vah)

old: **vieux/vieille** (vyuh/vyehy) m/f

on the left: **à gauche** (ah gohsh)

on the right: **à droite** (ah drwaht)

on time: **à l'heure** (ah luhr)

on, on top of: **sur** (sewr)

one way: **sens unique** (sahNs ew-neek) m

one: **un/une** (uhN/ewn) m/f

one-way ticket: **aller-simple** (ah-ley saN-pluh) m

onion: **oignon** (ohh-nyohN) m

only: **seulement** (suhl-mahN)

or: **ou** (ooh)

orange: **orange** (oh-rahNzh) f

outside: **dehors** (duh-ohr)

over there: **là-bas** (lah-bah)

overcoat: **pardessus** (pahr-duh-sew) m

owner: **propriétaire** (proh-pree-ey-tehr) m/f

oysters: **huitres** (wee-truh) fpl

P

package: **colis** (koh-lee) m

parking: **stationnement** (stah-syohn- mahN) m

parsley: **persil** (pehr-see) m

(to) pass (by): **passer** (pah-sey)

passport: **passeport** (pahs-pohr) m

password: **mot de passe** (moh duh pahs) m

pasta: **pâtes** (paht) fpl

pastry shop: **pâtisserie** (pah-tees-ree) f

peach: **pêche** (pehsh) f

pear: **poire** (pwahr) f

peas: **petits pois** (puh-tee pwah) mpl

pedestrian: **piéton/piétonne** (pyey-tohN/pyey-tohhn) m/f

pen: **stylo** (stee-loh) m

pencil: **crayon** (krey-ohN) m

people: **personnes** (pehr-sohhn) fpl

pepper: **poivre** (pwah-vruh) m

perfect: **parfait/parfaite** (pahr-feh/pahr-feht) m/f)

performance: **représentation** (ruh-prey-zahN-tah-syohN) f

phone number: **numéro de télé-phone** (new-mey-roh duh tey-ley-fohhn) m

physician: **médecin** (meyd-saN) m

piano: **piano** (pyah-noh) m

picture: **photo** (foh-toh) f

pillow: **oreiller** (oh-rehy-ey) m

pineapple: **ananas** (ah-nah-nah) m

plane: **avion** (ah-vyohN) m

plate: **assiette** (ah-syeht) f

platform: **quai** (key) m

(to) play: **jouer** (zhooh-ey)

pleasant: **agréable** (ah-grey-ah-bluh)

plum: **prune** (prewn) f

police: **police** (poh-lees) f

pork: **porc** (pohr) m

post office: **poste** (pohst) f

postage: **affranchissement** (ah-frahN-shee-smahN) m

potatoes: **pommes de terre** (pohhm duh tehr) fpl

pound (f) (500 g, about 1.1 lb), book(m): **livre** (lee-vruh)

(to) prefer: **préférer** (prey-fey-rey)

pretty: **joli/jolie** (zhoh-lee) m/f

printer: **imprimante** (aN-pree-mahnt) f

proud: **fier/fière** (fyehr) m/f

(to) put, to place: **mettre** (meh-truh)

R

raincoat (n), rainproof (adj): **imperméable** (aN-pehr-mey-ah-bluh) m

raspberry: **framboise** (frahN-bwahz) f

razor: **rasoir** (rah-zwahr) m

(to) read: **lire** (leer)

receipt: **reçu** (ruh-sew) m

(to) receive: **recevoir** (ruh-suh-vwahr)

red: **rouge** (roohzh)

reduced fare: **tarif réduit** (tah-reef rey-dwee) m

refrigerator: **réfrigérateur** (rey-free-zhey-rah-tuhr) m

retiree: **retraité/retraitée** (ruh-treh-tey) m/f

(to) return (something): **rendre** (rahN-druh)

(to) return, to go home: **rentrer** (rahN-trey)

ribs: **côtes** (koht) fpl

rice: **riz** (ree) m

romance film: **film d'amour** (feelm dah-moohr) m

room, theatrical play: **pièce** (pyehs) f

rosemary: **romarin** (roh-mah-raN) m

round trip: **aller-retour** (ah-ley ruh-toohr) m

rubber band: **élastique** (ey-lah-steek) m

rug: **tapis** (tah-pee) m

(to) run: **courir** (kooh-reer)

rush hour, peak: **heure de pointe** (uhr duh pwaNt) f

S

sage: **sauge** (sohzh) f

sailing: **voile** (vwahl) f

sales [France]: **soldes** (sohld) mpl

sales [Quebec]: **aubaine** (oh-behn) f

salmon: **saumon** (soh-mohN) m

salt: **sel** (sehl) m

sand: **sable** (sah-bluh) m

sandals: **sandales** (sahN-dahl) fpl

saucer: **soucoupe** (sooh-koohp) f

scale: **balance** (bah-lahNs) f

scallops: **coquilles Saint-Jacques** (koh-keey saN zhahk) fpl

scarf: **foulard** (fooh-lahr) m

schedule: **horaire** (oh-rehr) m

science-fiction film: **film de science-fiction** (feelm duh syahNs fee-ksyohN) m

scissors: **ciseaux** (see-zoh) mpl

season: **saison** (seh-zohN) f

seat, city or town square: **place** (plahs) f

seat: **siège** (syehzh) m

secretary: **secrétaire** (suh-krey-tehr) m/f

(to) see: **voir** (vwahr)

see you soon: **à bientôt** (ah byaN-toh)

see you tomorrow: **à demain** (ah duh-mahN)

seed: **graine** (grehn) f

(to) sell: **vendre** (vahN-druh)

September: **septembre** (sehp-tahN-bruh) m

(to) send: **envoyer** (ahN-vwah-yey)

seven: **sept** (seht)

seventeen: **dix-sept** (dee-seht)

she: **elle** (ehl) f

sheets: **draps** (drah) mpl

shirt: **chemise** (shuh-meez) f

shoe size: **pointure** (pwaN-tewr) f

shoes: **chaussures** (shoh-sewr) f pl:

shoulder: **épaule** (ey-pohl) f

(to) show: **montrer** (mohN-trey)

(to) shower: **se doucher** (suh dooh-shey)

showing (a movie): **séance** (sey-ahNs) f

shrimp: **crevettes** (kruh-veht) fpl

sidewalk: **trottoir** (troh-twahr) m

silk: **soie** (swah) f

silverware: **couverts** (kooh-vehr) mpl:

sister: **soeur** (suhr) f

six: **six** (sees)

sixteen: **seize** (sehz)

skirt: **jupe** (zhewp) f

slacks, pants: **pantalon** (pahN-tah-lohN) m

(to) sleep: **dormir** (dohr-meer)

sleeping bag: **sac de couchage** (sahk duh kooh-shahzh) m

(to) sing: **chanter** (shahN-tey)

slippers: **chaussons/pantoufles** (shoh-sohN/ pahN-tooh-fluh) mpl/fpl

(to) slow down: **ralentir** (rah-lahN-teer)

small, short: **petit/petite** (puh-tee/ puh-teet) m/f

snack (as a verb: to taste): **goûter** (gooh-tey) m

snack: **casse-croûte** (kahs-krooht) m

sneakers: **baskets** (bahs-keht) fpl

snow: **neige** (nehzh) f

soap: **savon** (sah-vohN) m

soccer: **football** (fooht-bohl [France]), **soccer** (soh-kehr [Canada]) m

socks: **chaussettes** (shoh-seht) fpl

sofa: **canapé** (kah-nah-pey) m

software: **logiciel** (loh-zhee-syehl) m

soil: **sol** (sohl) m

something: **quelque chose** (kehl-kuh shohz)

son: **fils** (fees) m

sorrel: **oseille** (oh-zehy) f

sorry: **désolé/désolée** (dey-zoh-ley) m/f

south: **sud** (sewd) m

(to) speak/to talk: **parler** (pahr-ley)

special effects: **effets spéciaux** (ey-feh spey-syoh) mpl

special effects: **trucages** (trew-kahzh) mpl

spinach: **épinards** (ey-pee-nahr) mpl

spoon, teaspoon: **cuillère** (kwee-yehr) f

spouse: **époux/épouse** (ey-pooh/ ey-poohz) m/f

spring: **printemps** (praN-tahN) m

spy film: **film d'espionnage** (feelm deh-spee-oh-nahzh) m

stamp: **timbre** (taN-bruh) m

staple: **agrafe** (ah-grahf) f

stapler: **agrafeuse** (ah-grah-fuhz) f

stay: **séjour** (sey-zhoohr) m

(to) stay: **rester** (rehs-tey)

steak: **bifteck** (beef-tehk) m

stop: **arrêt** (ah-reh) m

store window: **vitrine** (vee-treen) f

store: **magasin** (mah-gah-zaN) m

stove: **cuisinière** (kwee-zee-nyehr) f

strawberry: **fraise** (frehz) f

street: **rue** (rew) f

(to) subscribe: **s'abonner** (sah-boh-ney)

sugar: **sucre** (sew-kruh) m

suit: **complet** (kohN-pleh [France]) m

suit: **habit** (ah-bee [Québec]) m

suitcase: **valise** (vah-leez) f

summer: **été** (ey-tey) m

sun: **soleil** (soh-lehy) m

sunglasses: **lunettes de soleil** (lew-neht duh soh-lehy) f pl

supermarket: **supermarché** (sew-pehr-mahr-shey) m

sweatshirt: **sweat** (sweht) m

sweater: **pull** (pewl) m

swimming pool: **piscine** (pee-seen) f

swimming: **natation** (nah-tah-syohN) f

T

(to) take: **prendre** (prahN-druh)

(to) tan: **bronzer** (brohN-zey)

tape: **ruban adhésif** (rew-bahN ahd-ey-zeef) m

tarragon: **estragon** (ehs-trah-gohN) m

tea: **thé** (tey) m

(to) telephone, to call: **téléphoner** (tey-ley-fohh-ney)

ten: **dix** (dees)

tennis: **tennis** (tey-nees) m

thank you: **merci** (mehr-see)

that one: **celui-là/celle-là** (suh-lwee-lah/sehl-lah) m/f

theft: **vol** (vohl) m

then: **puis** (pwee)

there is, there are: **il y a** (eel ee ah)

they: **elles** (ehl) fpl

they: **ils** (eel) mpl

(to) think: **penser** (pahN-sey)

(to be) thirsty: **avoir soif** (ah-vwahr swahf)

thirteen: **treize** (trehz)

this one: **celui-ci/celle-ci** (suh-lwee-see/sehl-see) m/f

thought: **pensée** (pahN-sey) f

thousand: **mille** (meel) m

three: **trois** (twah)

thyme: **thym** (taN) m

ticket window: **guichet** (gee-shey) m

ticket (traffic): **contravention** (kohN-trah-vahN-syohN) f

ticket: **billet** (bee-yeh) m

tie: **cravate** (krah-vaht) f

tip: **pourboire** (poohr-bwahr) m

tire: **pneu** (pnuh) m

tired: **fatigué/fatiguée** (fah-tee-gey) m/f

today: **aujourd'hui** (oh-zhoohr-dwee)

toe: **orteil** (ohr-tehy) m

tomato: **tomate** (toh-maht) f

too bad: **tant pis** (tahN pee)

too much: **trop** (troh)

tooth: **dent** (dahN) f

toothpaste: **dentifrice** (dahN-tee-frees) m

track: **voie** (vwah) f

traffic jam: **embouteillage** (ahN-booh-teh-yahzh) m

train station: **gare** (gahr) f

train: **train** (traN) m

(to) travel: **voyager** (voh-yah-zhey)

trout: **truite** (trweet) f

trunk: **coffre** (koh-fruh) m

tuna: **thon** (tohN) m

turkey: **dinde** (daNd) f

twelve: **douze** (doohz)

twenty: **vingt** (vaN)

two: **deux** (duh)

U

U turn: **demi-tour** (duh-mee-toohr) m

uncle: **oncle** (ohN-kluh) m

under, underneath: **sous** (sooh)

underpants, briefs: **slip** (sleep) m

underwear: **sous-vêtements** (sooh-veht-mahN) m

until: **jusqu'à** (zhews-kah)

username: **pseudo** (psooh-doh) m

V

to validate a ticket: **composter** (kohN-poh-stey)

veal, calf: **veau** (voh) m

vegatable garden: **potager** (poh-tah-zhey) m

vegetables: **légumes** (ley-gewm) mpl

vendor: **marchand/marchande** (mahr-shahN/mahr-shahNd) m/f

victory: **victoire** (veek-twahr) f

violin: **violon** (vyoh-lohN) m

to visit (a place): **visiter** (vee-zee-tey)

to visit (a person): **rendre visite à** (rahN-druh vee-zeet ah)

W

(to) wait: **attendre** (ah-tahN-druh)

waiter, waitress: **serveur/serveuse** (sehr-vuhr/sehr-vuhz) m/f

waiting room: **salle d'attente** (sahl dah-tahNt) f

(to) wake up: **se réveiller** (suh rey-vey-yey)

walk: **promenade** (prohm-nahd) f

wallet: **portefeuille** (pohrt-fuhy) m

(to) want: **vouloir** (vooh-lwahr)

warm/hot: **chaud/chaude** (shoh/shohd) m/f

(to) wash: **laver/se laver** (lah-vey/suh lah-vey)

wastepaper basket: **corbeille à papiers** (kohr-behy ah pah-pyey) m

watch: **montre** (mohN-truh) f

(to) watch: **regarder** (ruh-gahr-dey)

water: **eau** (oh) f

(to) water: **arroser** (ah-roh-zey)

watermelon: **pastèque** (pahs-tehk) f

wave: **vague** (vahg) f

we: **nous** (nooh)

(to) wear, to carry: **porter** (pohr-tey)

web browser: **navigateur** (nah-vee-gah-tuhr) m

week: **semaine** (suh-mehn) f

(to) weigh: **peser** (puh-zey)

weird, bizarre: **bizarre** (beez-ahr)

west: **ouest** (ooh-wehst) m

what: **qu'est-ce que/quoi** (kehs-kuh/kwah)

when: **quand** (kahN)

where: **où** (ooh)

which: **quel/quelle** (kehl) m/f

(to) whistle: **siffler** (see-fley)

white: **blanc/blanche** (blahN/blahNsh) m/f

who: **qui** (kee)

why: **pourquoi** (poohr-kwah)

(to) win: **gagner** (gah-nyey)

window: **fenêtre** (fuh-neh-truh) f

windshield wiper: **essuie-glace** (ey-swee-glahs) m

windshield: **pare-brise** (pahr-breez) m

windsurfing: **planche à voile** (plahNsh ah vwahl) f

wine: **vin** (vaN) m

winter: **hiver** (ee-vehr) m

woman, wife: **femme** (fahm) f

women's suit: **tailleur** (tahy-uhr) m

wool: **laine** (lehn) f

(to) work: **travailler** (trah-vah-yey)

Y

yard, garden: **jardin** (zhahr-daN) m

yellow: **jaune** (zhohn)

you (singular formal, plural): **vous** (vooh)

you (singular informal): **tu** (tew)

you: **toi** (twah)

Z

zip code: **code postal** (kohhd poh-stahl) m

Appendix B
Verb Tables

● ●

*N*ote: This appendix shows the conjugation of the present indicative, passé composé (past), and simple future tenses. For more on the conjugation of these tenses, refer to Chapter 2.

Regular French Verbs

Regular Verbs Ending with –er
For example: parler (to speak)
Past Participle: parlé (spoken); Present participle: parlant (speaking)

	Present	Past	Future
je/j' (I)	parle	ai parlé	parlerai
tu (you, inf.)	parles	as parlé	parleras
il/elle/on (he/she/it/one)	parle	a parlé	parlera
nous (we)	parlons	avons parlé	parlerons
vous (you, form., pl.)	parlez	avez parlé	parlerez
ils/elles (they)	parlent	ont parlé	parleront

Regular Verbs Ending with –ir
For example: finir (to finish)
Past Participle: fini (finished); Present Participle: finissant (finishing)

	Present	Past	Future
je/j' (I)	finis	ai fini	finirai
tu (you, inf.)	finis	as fini	finiras
il/elle/on (he/she/it/one)	finit	a fini	finira
nous (we)	finissons	avons fini	finirons
vous (you, form., pl.)	finissez	avez fini	finirez
ils/elles (they)	finissent	ont fini	finiront

Regular Verbs Ending with –re

For example: vendre (to sell)

Past Participle: vendu (sold); Present Participle: vendant (selling)

	Present	Past	Future
je/j' (I)	vends	ai vendu	vendrai
tu (you, inf.)	vends	as vendu	vendras
il/elle/on (he/she/it/one)	vend	a vendu	vendra
nous (we)	vendons	avons vendu	vendrons
vous (you, form., pl.)	vendez	avez vendu	vendrez
ils/elles (they)	vendent	ont vendu	vendront

Reflexive Verbs

For example: se laver (to wash oneself)

Past Participle: lavé (washed); Present participle: me/te/se/nous/vous/ lavant (washing)

	Present	Past	Future
je/j' (I)	me lave	me suis lavé/e	me laverai
tu (you, inf.)	te laves	t'es lavé/e	te laveras
il/elle/on (he/she/it/one)	se lave	s'est lavé/e	se lavera
nous (we)	nous lavons	nous sommes lavés/es	nous laverons
vous (you, form., pl.)	vous lavez	vous êtes lavé/e/s/es	vous laverez
ils/elles (they)	se lavent	se sont lavés/es	se laveront

Auxiliary French Verbs

Avoir (ah-vwahr) (*to have*) and **être** (eh-truh) (*to be*) are the two auxiliary verbs used to form all compound past tenses in French.

avoir (to have)
Past Participle: eu (had); Present Participle: ayant (having)

	Present	Past	Future
je/j' (I)	ai	ai eu	aurai
tu (you, inf.)	as	as eu	auras
il/elle/on (he/she/it/one)	a	a eu	aura
nous (we)	avons	avons eu	aurons
vous (you, form., pl.)	avez	avez eu	aurez
ils/elles (they)	ont	ont eu	auront

être (to be)
Past Participle: été (been); Present Participle: étant (being)

	Present	Past	Future
je/j' (I)	suis	ai été	serai
tu (you, inf.)	es	as été	seras
il/elle/on (he/she/it/one)	est	a été	sera
nous (we)	sommes	avons été	serons
vous (you, form., pl.)	êtes	avez été	serez
ils/elles (they)	sont	ont été	seront

Irregular and Stem-Changing French Verbs

		Present	Past	Future
acheter				
to buy	*j'*	achète	ai acheté	achèterai
Past participle:	*tu*	achètes	as acheté	achèteras
acheté (bought)	*il/elle/on*	achète	a acheté	achètera
Present participle:	*nous*	achetons	avons acheté	achèterons
achetant (buying)	*vous*	achetez	avez acheté	achèterez
	ils/elles	achètent	ont acheté	achèteront

		Present	**Past**	**Future**
aller				
to go	je/j'	vais	suis allé/e	irai
Past participle: allé	tu	vas	es allé/e	iras
(went)	il/elle/on	va	est allé/e	ira
Present participle:	nous	allons	sommes allés/es	irons
allant (going)	vous	allez	êtes allé/e/s/es	irez
	ils/elles	vont	sont allés/es	iront

		Present	**Past**	**Future**
appeler				
to call	j'	appelle	ai appelé	appellerai
Past participle:	tu	appelles	as appelé	appelleras
appelé (called)	il/elle/on	appelle	a appelé	appellera
Present participle:	nous	appelons	avons appelé	appellerons
appelant (calling)	vous	appelez	avez appelé	appellerez
	ils/elles	appellent	ont appelé	appelleront

		Present	**Past**	**Future**
boire				
to drink	je/j'	bois	ai bu	boirai
Past participle: bu	tu	bois	as bu	boiras
(drank)	il/elle/on	boit	a bu	boira
Present participle:	nous	buvons	avons bu	boirons
buvant (drinking)	vous	buvez	avez bu	boirez
	ils/elles	boivent	ont bu	boiront

	Present	Past	Future
commencer			
to begin	*je/j'* commence	ai commencé	commencerai
Past participle:	*tu* commences	as commencé	commenceras
commencé (began)	*il/elle/on* commence	a commencé	commencera
Present participle:	*nous* commençons	avons commencé	commencerons
commençant	*vous* commencez	avez commencé	commencerez
(beginning)	*ils/elles* commencent	ont commencé	commenceront

	Present	Past	Future
comprendre			
to understand	*je/j'* comprends	ai compris	comprendrai
Past participle:	*tu* comprends	as compris	comprendras
compris (understood)	*il/elle/on* comprend	a compris	comprendra
Present participle:	*nous* comprenons	avons compris	comprendrons
comprenant	*vous* comprenez	avez compris	comprendrez
(understanding)	*ils/elles* comprennent	ont compris	comprendront

	Present	Past	Future
conduire			
to drive	*je/j'* conduis	ai conduit	conduirai
Past participle:	*tu* conduis	as conduit	conduiras
conduit (drove)	*il/elle/on* conduit	a conduit	conduira
Present participle:	*nous* conduisons	avons conduit	conduirons
conduisant	*vous* conduisez	avez conduit	conduirez
(driving)	*ils/elles* conduisent	ont conduit	conduiront

		Present	**Past**	**Future**
connaître				
to know (people and places)	*je/j'*	connais	ai connu	connaîtrai
	tu	connais	as connu	connaîtras
Past participle:	*il/elle/on*	connaît	a connu	connaîtra
connu (knew)	*nous*	connaissons	avons connu	connaîtrons
Present participle:	*vous*	connaissez	avez connu	connaîtrez
connaissant (knowing)	*ils/elles*	connaissent	ont connu	connaîtront

		Present	**Past**	**Future**
devoir				
to have to	*je/j'*	dois	ai dû	devrai
Past participle: dû (had to)	*tu*	dois	as dû	devras
	il/elle/on	doit	a dû	devra
Present participle:	*nous*	devons	avons dû	devrons
devant (having to)	*vous*	devez	avez dû	devrez
	ils/elles	doivent	ont dû	devront

		Present	**Past**	**Future**
dire				
to say	*je/j'*	dis	ai dit	dirai
Past participle: dit (said)	*tu*	dis	as dit	diras
	il/elle/on	dit	a dit	dira
Present participle:	*nous*	disons	avons dit	dirons
disant (saying)	*vous*	dites	avez dit	direz
	ils/elles	disent	ont dit	diront

	Present	**Past**	**Future**
écrire			
to write	*j'* écris	ai écrit	écrirai
Past participle:	*tu* écris	as écrit	écriras
écrit (wrote)	*il/elle/on* écrit	a écrit	écrira
Present participle:	*nous* écrivons	avons écrit	écrirons
écrivant (writing)	*vous* écrivez	avez écrit	écrirez
	ils/elles écrivent	ont écrit	écriront

	Present	**Past**	**Future**
entendre			
to hear	*j'* entends	ai entendu	entendrai
Past participle:	*tu* entends	as entendu	entendras
entendu (heard)	*il/elle/on* entend	a entendu	entendra
Present participle:	*nous* entendons	avons entendu	entendrons
entendant (hearing)	*vous* entendez	avez entendu	entendrez
	ils/elles entendent	ont entendu	entendront

	Present	**Past**	**Future**
envoyer			
to send	*j'* envoie	ai envoyé	enverrai
Past participle:	*tu* envoies	as envoyé	enverras
envoyé (sent)	*il/elle/on* envoie	a envoyé	enverra
Present participle:	*nous* envoyons	avons envoyé	enverrons
envoyant (sending)	*vous* envoyez	avez envoyé	enverrez
	ils/elles envoient	ont envoyé	enverront

		Present	Past	Future
espérer				
to hope	*j'*	espère	ai espéré	espérerai
Past participle:	*tu*	espères	as espéré	espéreras
espéré (hoped)	*il/elle/on*	espère	a espéré	espérera
Present participle:	*nous*	espérons	avons espéré	espérerons
espérant (hoping)	*vous*	espérez	avez espéré	espérerez
	ils/elles	espèrent	ont espéré	espéreront

		Present	Past	Future
faire				
to do, to make	*je/j'*	fais	ai fait	ferai
Past participle:	*tu*	fais	as fait	feras
fait (did, made)	*il/elle/on*	fait	a fait	fera
Present participle:	*nous*	faisons	avons fait	ferons
faisant (doing,	*vous*	faites	avez fait	ferez
making)	*ils/elles*	font	ont fait	feront

		Present	Past	Future
lire				
to read	*je/j'*	lis	ai lu	lirai
Past participle:	*tu*	lis	as lu	liras
lu (read)	*il/elle/on*	lit	a lu	lira
Present participle:	*nous*	lisons	avons lu	lirons
lisant (reading)	*vous*	lisez	avez lu	lirez
	ils/elles	lisent	ont lu	liront

		Present	Past	Future
manger				
to eat	*je/j'*	mange	ai mangé	mangerai
Past participle:	*tu*	manges	as mangé	mangeras
mangé (ate)	*il/elle/on*	mange	a mangé	mangera
Present participle:	*nous*	mangeons	avons mangé	mangerons
mangeant (eating)	*vous*	mangez	avez mangé	mangerez
	ils/elles	mangent	ont mangé	mangeront

		Present	Past	Future
mettre				
to put, to put on	*je/j'*	mets	ai mis	mettrai
(as with clothes), to place	*tu*	mets	as mis	mettras
Past participle:	*il/elle/on*	met	a mis	mettra
mis (put, put on, placed)	*nous*	mettons	avons mis	mettrons
Present participle:	*vous*	mettez	avez mis	mettrez
mettant (putting, putting on, placing)	*ils/elles*	mettent	ont mis	mettront

		Present	Past	Future
offrir				
to offer	*j'*	offre	ai offert	offrirai
Past participle:	*tu*	offres	as offert	offriras
offert (offered)	*il/elle/on*	offre	a offert	offrira
Present participle:	*nous*	offrons	avons offert	offrirons
offrant (offering)	*vous*	offrez	avez offert	offrirez
	ils/elles	offrent	ont offert	offriront

	Present	Past	Future
partir			
to leave	*je* pars	suis parti/e	partirai
Past participle:	*tu* pars	es parti/e	partiras
parti (left)	*il/elle/on* part	est parti/e	partira
Present participle:	*nous* partons	sommes partis/es	partirons
partant (leaving)	*vous* partez	êtes parti/e/s/es	partirez
	ils/elles partent	sont partis/es	partiront

	Present	Past	Future
payer			
to pay	*je/j'* paie	ai payé	paierai
Past participle:	*tu* paies	as payé	paieras
payé (paid)	*il/elle/on* paie	a payé	paiera
Present participle:	*nous* payons	avons payé	paierons
payant (paying)	*vous* payez	avez payé	paierez
	ils/elles paient	ont payé	paieront

	Present	Past	Future
préférer			
to prefer	*je/j'* préfère	ai préféré	préférerai
Past participle:	*tu* préfères	as préféré	préféreras
préféré (preferred)	*il/elle/on* préfère	a préféré	préférera
Present participle:	*nous* préférons	avons préféré	préférerons
préférant (prefering)	*vous* préférez	avez préféré	préférerez
	ils/elles préfèrent	ont préféré	préféreront

		Present	Past	Future
pouvoir				
to be able to (can)	*je/j'*	peux	ai pu	pourrai
Past participle: pu	*tu*	peux	as pu	pourras
(could)	*il/elle/on*	peut	a pu	pourra
Present participle:	*nous*	pouvons	avons pu	pourrons
pouvant (being able	*vous*	pouvez	avez pu	pourrez
to)	*ils/elles*	peuvent	ont pu	pourront

		Present	Past	Future
prendre				
to take (*to have*	*je/j'*	prends	ai pris	prendrai
[with food and drink]	*tu*	prends	as pris	prendras
or *to have a meal*)	*il/elle/on*	prend	a pris	prendra
Past participle: pris	*nous*	prenons	avons pris	prendrons
(took)	*vous*	prenez	avez pris	prendrez
Present participle:	*ils/elles*	prennent	ont pris	prendront
prenant (taking)				

		Present	Past	Future
recevoir				
to receive	*je/j'*	reçois	ai reçu	recevrai
Past participle: reçu	*tu*	reçois	as reçu	recevras
(received)	*il/elle/on*	reçoit	a reçu	recevra
Present participle:	*nous*	recevons	avons reçu	recevrons
recevant (receiving)	*vous*	recevez	avez reçu	recevrez
	ils/elles	reçoivent	ont reçu	recevront

		Present	Past	Future
rendre				
to give back	je/j'	rends	ai rendu	rendrai
Past participle: rendu	tu	rends	as rendu	rendras
(gave back)	il/elle/on	rend	a rendu	rendra
Present participle:	nous	rendons	avons rendu	rendrons
rendant (giving back)	vous	rendez	avez rendu	rendrez
	ils/elles	rendent	ont rendu	rendront

		Present	Past	Future
rire				
to laugh	je/j'	ris	ai ri	rirai
Past participle: ri	tu	ris	as ri	riras
(laughed)	il/elle/on	rit	a ri	rira
Present participle:	nous	rions	avons ri	rirons
riant (laughing)	vous	riez	avez ri	rirez
	ils/elles	rient	ont ri	riront

		Present	Past	Future
savoir				
to know (facts,	je/j'	sais	ai su	saurai
information)	tu	sais	as su	sauras
Past participle: su	il/elle/on	sait	a su	saura
(knew, discovered,				
found out)	nous	savons	avons su	saurons
Present participle:	vous	savez	avez su	saurez
sachant (knowing)	ils/elles	savent	ont su	sauront

		Present	Past	Future
servir				
to serve	*je/j'*	sers	ai servi	servirai
Past participle: servi	*tu*	sers	as servi	serviras
(served)	*il/elle/on*	sert	a servi	servira
Present participle:	*nous*	servons	avons servi	servirons
servant (serving)	*vous*	servez	avez servi	servirez
	ils/elles	servent	ont servi	serviront

		Present	Past	Future
sortir				
to go out	*je*	sors	suis sorti/e	sortirai
Past participle: sorti	*tu*	sors	es sorti/e	sortiras
(went out)	*il/elle/on*	sort	est sorti/e	sortira
Present participle:	*nous*	sortons	sommes sortis/es	sortirons
sortant (going out)	*vous*	sortez	êtes sorti/e/s/es	sortirez
	ils/elles	sortent	sont sortis/es	sortiront

		Present	Past	Future
tenir				
to hold	*je/j'*	tiens	ai tenu	tiendrai
Past participle: tenu	*tu*	tiens	as tenu	tiendras
(held)	*il/elle/on*	tient	a tenu	tiendra
Present participle:	*nous*	tenons	avons tenu	tiendrons
tenant (holding)	*vous*	tenez	avez tenu	tiendrez
	ils/elles	tiennent	ont tenu	tiendront

		Present	**Past**	**Future**
venir				
to come	*je*	viens	suis venu/e	viendrai
Past participle:	*tu*	viens	es venu/e	viendras
venu (came)	*il/elle/on*	vient	est venu/e	viendra
Present participle:	*nous*	venons	sommes venus/es	viendrons
venant (coming)	*vous*	venez	êtes venu/e/s/es	viendrez
	ils/elles	viennent	sont venus/es	viendront

		Present	**Past**	**Future**
vivre				
to live	*je/j'*	vis	ai vécu	vivrai
Past participle:	*tu*	vis	as vécu	vivras
vécu (lived)	*il/elle/on*	vit	a vécu	vivra
Present participle:	*nous*	vivons	avons vécu	vivrons
vivant (living)	*vous*	vivez	avez vécu	vivrez
	ils/elles	vivent	ont vécu	vivront

		Present	**Past**	**Future**
voir				
to see	*je/j'*	vois	ai vu	verrai
Past participle:	*tu*	vois	as vu	verras
vu (saw)	*il/elle/on*	voit	a vu	verra
Present participle:	*nous*	voyons	avons vu	verrons
voyant (seeing)	*vous*	voyez	avez vu	verrez
	ils/elles	voient	ont vu	verront

		Present	Past	Future
vouloir				
to want	*je/j'*	veux	ai voulu	voudrai
Past participle:	*tu*	veux	as voulu	voudras
voulu (wanted)	*il/elle/on*	veut	a voulu	voudra
Present participle:	*nous*	voulons	avons voulu	voudrons
voulant (wanting)	*vous*	voulez	avez voulu	voudrez
	ils/elles	veulent	ont voulu	voudront

Index

FOR DUMMIES®

Making Everything Easier! ™

UK editions

BUSINESS

Bookkeeping For Dummies
978-0-470-97626-5

Leadership For Dummies
978-0-470-97211-3

Starting & Running a Business All-in-One For Dummies
978-1-119-97527-4

REFERENCE

British Politics For Dummies
978-0-470-68637-9

DIY For Dummies
978-0-470-97450-6

Researching Your Family History Online For Dummies
978-0-470-74535-9

HOBBIES

Growing Your Own Fruit & Veg For Dummies
978-0-470-69960-7

Allotment Gardening For Dummies
978-0-470-68641-6

Electronics For Dummies
978-0-470-68178-7

Asperger's Syndrome For Dummies
978-0-470-66087-4

Basic Maths For Dummies
978-1-119-97452-9

Boosting Self-Esteem For Dummies
978-0-470-74193-1

British Sign Language For Dummies
978-0-470-69477-0

Cricket For Dummies
978-0-470-03454-5

Diabetes For Dummies, 3rd Edition
978-0-470-97711-8

English Grammar For Dummies
978-0-470-05752-0

Flirting For Dummies
978-0-470-74259-4

IBS For Dummies
978-0-470-51737-6

Improving Your Relationship For Dummies
978-0-470-68472-6

Keeping Chickens For Dummies
978-1-119-99417-6

Lean Six Sigma For Dummies
978-0-470-75626-3

Management For Dummies, 2nd Edition
978-0-470-97769-9

Neuro-linguistic Programming For Dummies, 2nd Edition
978-0-470-66543-5

Nutrition For Dummies, 2nd Edition
978-0-470-97276-2

Available wherever books are sold. For more information or to order direct go to www.wiley.com or call +44 (0) 1243 843291

FOR DUMMIES®

A world of resources to help you grow

UK editions

SELF–HELP

Cognitive Behavioural Therapy FOR DUMMIES
Rhena Branch
Rob Willson
978-0-470-66541-1

Creative Visualization FOR DUMMIES
Robin Nixon
978-1-119-99264-6

Mindfulness FOR DUMMIES
Shamash Alidina
978-0-470-66086-7

STUDENTS

Philosophy FOR DUMMIES
Martin Cohen
978-0-470-68820-5

Student Cookbook FOR DUMMIES
Oliver Harrison
978-0-470-74711-7

Sociology FOR DUMMIES
Nasar Meer, PhD
Jay Gabler, PhD
978-1-119-99134-2

HISTORY

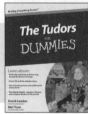
The Tudors FOR DUMMIES
David Loades
Mel Tiviw
978-0-470-68792-5

Medieval History FOR DUMMIES
Stephen Batchelor
978-0-470-74783-4

British History FOR DUMMIES
Dr. Seán Lang
978-0-470-97819-1

Origami Kit For Dummies
978-0-470-75857-1

Overcoming Depression For Dummies
978-0-470-69430-5

Positive Psychology For Dummies
978-0-470-72136-0

PRINCE2 For Dummies, 2009 Edition
978-0-470-71025-8

Project Management For Dummies
978-0-470-71119-4

Psychometric Tests For Dummies
978-0-470-75366-8

Reading the Financial Pages
For Dummies
978-0-470-71432-4

Rugby Union For Dummies, 3rd Edition
978-1-119-99092-5

Sage 50 Accounts For Dummies
978-0-470-71558-1

Self-Hypnosis For Dummies
978-0-470-66073-7

Study Skills For Dummies
978-0-470-74047-7

Teaching English as a Foreign Language
For Dummies
978-0-470-74576-2

Time Management For Dummies
978-0-470-77765-7

Training Your Brain For Dummies
978-0-470-97449-0

Work-Life Balance For Dummies
978-0-470-71380-8

Writing a Dissertation For Dummies
978-0-470-74270-9

**Available wherever books are sold. For more information or to order direct go to
www.wiley.com or call +44 (0) 1243 843291**

FOR DUMMIES®

The easy way to get more done and have more fun

LANGUAGES

Spanish FOR DUMMIES

978-0-470-68815-1
UK Edition

French FOR DUMMIES

978-1-118-00464-7

German FOR DUMMIES

978-0-470-90101-4

MUSIC

Ukulele FOR DUMMIES

978-0-470-97799-6
UK Edition

Guitar Chords FOR DUMMIES

978-0-470-66603-6
Lay-flat, UK Edition

DJing FOR DUMMIES

978-0-470-66372-1
UK Edition

SCIENCE & MATHS

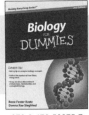

Biology FOR DUMMIES

978-0-470-59875-7

Algebra I FOR DUMMIES

978-0-470-55964-2

Genetics FOR DUMMIES

978-0-470-55174-5

Art For Dummies
978-0-7645-5104-8

Bass Guitar For Dummies, 2nd Edition
978-0-470-53961-3

Criminology For Dummies
978-0-470-39696-4

Currency Trading For Dummies,
2nd Edition
978-1-118-01851-4

Drawing For Dummies, 2nd Edition
978-0-470-61842-4

Forensics For Dummies
978-0-7645-5580-0

Guitar For Dummies, 2nd Edition
978-0-7645-9904-0

Hinduism For Dummies
978-0-470-87858-3

Index Investing For Dummies
978-0-470-29406-2

Knitting For Dummies, 2nd Edition
978-0-470-28747-7

Music Theory For Dummies, 2nd Edition
978-1-118-09550-8

Piano For Dummies, 2nd Edition
978-0-470-49644-2

Physics For Dummies, 2nd Edition
978-0-470-90324-7

Schizophrenia For Dummies
978-0-470-25927-6

Sex For Dummies, 3rd Edition
978-0-470-04523-7

Sherlock Holmes For Dummies
978-0-470-48444-9

Solar Power Your Home
For Dummies, 2nd Edition
978-0-470-59678-4

**Available wherever books are sold. For more information or to order direct go to
www.wiley.com or call +44 (0) 1243 843291**

FOR DUMMIES®

Helping you expand your horizons and achieve your potential

COMPUTER BASICS

Laptops FOR DUMMIES

978-0-470-57829-2

PCs ALL-IN-ONE FOR DUMMIES

978-0-470-61454-9

Windows 7 FOR DUMMIES

978-0-470-49743-2

DIGITAL PHOTOGRAPHY

Digital Photography FOR DUMMIES

978-0-470-25074-7

Digital SLR Photography ALL-IN-ONE FOR DUMMIES

978-0-470-76878-5

Nikon D3100 FOR DUMMIES

978-1-118-00472-2

MICROSOFT OFFICE 2010

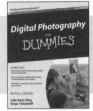

Office 2010 FOR DUMMIES

978-0-470-48998-7

Office 2010 For Seniors FOR DUMMIES

978-0-470-58302-9

Excel 2010 FOR DUMMIES

978-0-470-48953-6

Access 2010 For Dummies
978-0-470-49747-0

Android Application Development
For Dummies
978-0-470-77018-4

AutoCAD 2011 For Dummies
978-0-470-59539-8

C++ For Dummies, 6th Edition
978-0-470-31726-6

Computers For Seniors For Dummies,
2nd Edition
978-0-470-53483-0

Dreamweaver CS5 For Dummies
978-0-470-61076-3

iPad For Dummies 2nd Edition
978-1-118-02444-7

Macs For Dummies, 11th Edition
978-0-470-87868-2

Mac OS X Snow Leopard For Dummies
978-0-470-43543-4

Photoshop CS5 For Dummies
978-0-470-61078-7

Photoshop Elements 9 For Dummies
978-0-470-87872-9

Search Engine Optimization
For Dummies, 4th Edition
978-0-470-88104-0

The Internet For Dummies,
12th Edition
978-0-470-56095-2

Visual Studio 2010 All-In-One
For Dummies
978-0-470-53943-9

Web Analytics For Dummies
978-0-470-09824-0

Word 2010 For Dummies
978-0-470-48772-3

WordPress For Dummies, 4th Edition
978-1-118-07342-1

Beyond the

Psychoanalytic Dyad

Beyond the

Psychoanalytic Dyad

Developmental Semiotics
in Freud, Peirce, and Lacan

John P. Muller

 Routledge
Taylor & Francis Group

NEW YORK AND HOVE

First published 1996 by Routledge

711 Third Avenue, New York, NY 10017
27 Church Road, Hove, East Sussex, BN3 2FA

Routledge is an imprint of the Taylor & Francis Group, an informa business

The publisher greatfully acknowledges the following sources:

China Men, by Maxine Hong Kingston, © by Maxine Hong Kingston, reprinted with permission of Alfred A. Knopf Inc. 1980, and Picador, London. *The Sheltering Sky* by Paul Bowles. © 1949 by Paul Bowles. First published by the Ecco Press in 1978. Joyce Carol Oates "Old Budapest" © by Joyce Carol Oates, originally published in the *Kenyon Review*, v.5, n.4, pp. 8–36. Reprinted with permission of Scribner, an imprint of Simon & Schuster, Inc. from *Still Life* by A.S. Byatt. Copyright © 1985 A.S. Byatt, and with permsission from The Peters Fraser & Dunlap Group Ltd., London.

Parts of the author's own work have been previously published in the following:

"Language, Psychosis, and Spirit," by John P. Muller, in: *Attachment and the Therapeutic Process*, Sacksteder, ed., 1987, pp. 99–116. "A Re-reading of *Studies on Hysteria:* The Freud-Breuer Break Revisited" in *Psychoanalytic Psychology*, v. 9, n. 2, Spring 1992, pp. 129–56. "The Mirror; Psychoanalytic Perspectives" in *Psychoanalytic Inquiry*, v. 5, n. 2, 1985, pp. 233–52, by the Analytic Press. "Lacan and Kohut: From Imaginary to Symbolic Identification in the case of Mr. Z" in *Self-Psychology: Comparisons and Contrasts,* Detrick and Detrick, eds., published in 1989 by the Analytic Press.

Library of Congress Cataloging-in-Publication Data

Muller, John P., 1940–
   Beyond the psychoanalytic dyad : developmental semiotics in Freud, Peirce, and Lacan / John P. Muller
      p.   cm.
   Includes bibliographical references and index.
   ISBN 0–415–91068–4 (hb) — ISBN 0–415–91069–2 (pb)
   1. Psychoanalysis and culture. 2. Symbolism (Psychology) 3. Semiotics. 4. Lacan, Jacques, 1901–1981. 5. Peirce, Charles S. (Charles Sanders), 1839–1914. 6. Freud, Sigmund, 1856–1939. I. Title.
   BF175.4.C84M85   1995
   150.19'5—dc20   95-14600
                                                                              CIP

To: William J. Richardson, S.J., Ph.D.,
teacher, colleague, friend

Contents

Acknowledgments

This book spans more than a decade of writing; the first half was written while I was the Erik Erikson scholar in residence at the Austen Riggs Center, 1992–1993. I am warmly grateful to Edward Shapiro, M.D., and M. Gerard Fromm, Ph.D., for making available to me an extraordinarily tranquil year among deeply reflective clinicians. Chapter 5 was chosen as the co-winner of the 1995 Deutsch Prize of the Boston Psychoanalytic Society Institute and was the Erikson Scholar lecture presented in May, 1993, at Riggs. Several of the later chapters appeared in earlier forms elsewhere. Chapter 6 was previously published as "Language, Psychosis, and Spirit" in *Attachment and the Therapeutic Process: Essays in Honor of Otto Allen Will, Jr., M.D.*, edited by J. Sacksteder, D. Schwartz, and Y. Akabane. (New York: International Universities Press, 1987, pp. 99–116). Chapter 8 appeared as "Lacan's Mirror Stage" in a 1985 issue on mirroring of *Psychoanalytic Inquiry*, volume 5, pp. 233–252. Chapter 9 was published in *Self Psychology: Comparisons and Contrasts*, edited by D. Detrick and S. Detrick. (Hillsdale, NJ: The Analytic Press, 1989, pp. 363-394). Chapter 10 was presented to the Chicago Psychoanalytic Society and was previously published as "A Re-reading of *Studies on Hysteria*: The Freud-Breuer Break Revisited," in *Psychoanalytic Psychology*, 1992, volume 9, pp. 129–156.

I am grateful to all those who have generously read various chapters, made numerous suggestions, and helped to set high standards for this kind of inquiry.

Introduction

In *The Songlines*, a remarkable view of native Australian culture, the late Bruce Chatwin wrote:

> Aboriginal Creation myths tell of the legendary totemic beings who had wandered over the continent in the Dreamtime, singing out the name of everything that crossed their path—birds, animals, plants, rocks, water-holes—and so singing the world into existence. (1988, p. 2)

In the traditional "Walkabout" ritual, one retraced this ancestral path, singing the names of these beings in order to keep them and oneself in existence. The formative power of signs, their causal impact on mind, brain, body, and subjectivity, is the overarching theme of this book, which examines the broad field of semiotics. My interest in semiotics and its application in the practice of psychoanalysis is shaped by my reading of Lacan and my psychoanalytic work, much of it with hospitalized patients. I have also participated in textual studies in which a psychoanalytic perspective informs the reading of literature. It is this weighing of words which, in turn, moves us toward a more differentiated reading of Freud.

My interest in culture is both personal and conceptual. My mother tongue is Hungarian. I learned to speak English as I approached my fifth birthday, and I have gone out of my way to make it possible to speak and hear Hungarian in my own analysis. I also worked and lived for three years on the Rosebud Sioux Reservation assisting in the development of a Psychology department at a new community college. The experience that endures beyond such intercultural contact is not simply that cultures are different, but that one's own culture is now different, experienced as different from itself.

In his recent book, the eminent psychologist Jerome Bruner urges us to consider why culture must be a central concept for psychology. "Begin with the concept of culture itself—particularly its constitutive role," he tells us (1990, p. 11). The constitutive role of culture, what Northrop Frye has called "a semi-transparent envelope" through which we view nature (1981, p. 129), has been neglected by the individualistic orientation of American psychology as well as by ego psychology and the more recent dyadic focus of psychoanalysis. We are coming to realize, however, that a third is required to frame the dyad, to provide an orienting structure, and this third may be understood as the semiotic framework and context of culture.

For Bruner, human evolution crossed a divide "when culture became the major factor in giving form to the minds of those living under its sway" (1990, p. 12). Bruner emphatically agrees with Clifford Geertz, who writes, "there is no such thing as human nature independent of culture" (1973, p. 49). In arguing for a cultural psychology, Bruner takes issue with a major nineteenth-century legacy, the prioritization of biology in our attempts to understand human behavior:

> The causes of human behavior were assumed to lie in that biological substrate. What I want to argue instead is that culture and the quest for meaning within culture are the proper causes of human action. The biological substrate, the so-called universals of human nature, is not a cause of action but, at most, a constraint upon it or a condition for it. (1990, pp. 20–21)

Bruner reverses the traditional relation of biology and culture with respect to human nature:

> it is culture, not biology, that shapes human life and the human mind, that gives meaning to action by situating its underlying intentional states in an interpretive system. It does this by imposing the patterns inherent in the culture's symbolic systems—its language and discourse modes, the forms of logical and narrative explication, and the patterns of mutually dependent communal life. (1990, p. 34)

As others have emphasized (Sacks, 1989; Levin, 1991; Harré and Gillett, 1994), the human brain is especially plastic in response to the discursive environment whose structures of narrativity govern what is preserved in memory. Narrativity, in turn, "relies upon the power of tropes—upon metaphor, metonymy, synecdoche, implicature, and the rest" (Bruner, 1990, p. 59). We shall also see that this process of narrativity, whereby the human infant becomes an active participant in what Bruner calls a "protolinguistic system," is inaugurated soon after birth (1990, p. 69).

In the following chapters I will argue that the framework of culture anchors the development as well as the psychoanalytic investigation of the individual, for subjectivity emerges first of all as intersubjectivity. The transmission of culture operates through the semiotic codes governing the rhythm of touching, gazing, and vocalizing of both mother and infant. The individual emerges in dialogue with another sign-using subject, through a process of mutual recognition and generalization. As Bruner writes, "Is not Self a transactional relationship between a speaker and an Other, indeed, a Generalized Other?"(1990, p. 101). This Other is indispensable for understanding the Self.

The psychoanalytic features of such a self and its transactions, the complexities of human development and of psychological structure, are discerned in a new way in the work of the French psychoanalyst Jacques Lacan (1901–1981). Lacan's chief contribution, in my view, consists in opening up experience into three registers or dimensions which he called the Real, the imaginary, and the symbolic. I take these three registers as constituting, in a broad way, Lacan's semiotic code for interpreting experience, his code that specifies what is a signifier, what is a representation, what is unsignable, and what rules govern the dynamics of each. This way of discerning experience has been quite useful for thinking about cultural phenomena as well as the complexities of another realm, the treatment of psychotic patients and the understanding of treatment impasses. From a Lacanian perspective, for example, the structural difficulty giving rise to psychotic states consists in the absence of marked boundaries between the human subject and the dimension of the Real. Because of early developmental failures to create a stable edge for the self, the risk of dissolution and merger with the Other remains high. There is no firm line drawn on this side of which is the predictable, consensually validated realm of shared experience, and on the other side of which lies the field of the uncanny, the traumatic, the unnameable. This perspective, of course, is not unique to Lacan, for we can find it from Sullivan (1953) to Ogden (1989).

What I find distinctive in Lacan is how he attempts to call our attention to the fragile but necessary boundaries that circumscribe reality. These boundaries are effects of language that create stable relations by naming objects as well as subjects. This signifying function of language enables us to have perspective on experience and provides a zone of mediation so that we are not wholly captivated by the immediate. But this taming and liberating function of language is limited. Beyond its limits lies the undifferentiated Real. Lacan calls it the Real to distinguish it from reality, which is a differentiated social construction, a collage built of images and language. Oliver Sacks (1990) is forthright about this:

"The world does not have a predetermined structure: our structuring of the world is our own—our brains create structures in the light of our experiences" (1990, p. 48), and they do so continuously.

Although Lacan pointed to the Real as "what resists symbolization absolutely" (1953–54, p. 66), we can come close to it in Buddhist texts, in the writings of Christian mystics, and in literature. Usually we go through our day without attending to the limits of our consensually validated reality, but now and then we encounter the Real in the form of danger, catastrophe, death. Psychotic loss of boundaries, the breakdown of stable categories of thought, the effects of trauma, all bring the experience of the Real to the forefront. We see how sexual abuse victims struggle to reclaim their bodies and their histories by gradually fitting images and then names to their traumatic unintegrated experience. Kohut describes a specific type of dream, the "self-state" dream, as an attempt to cover "frightening nameless processes with nameable visual imagery" (1977, p. 109).

Visual images are the stuff of the register of the imaginary, the narcissistic field of self-presentation. The essential feature of Lacan's imaginary register lies in the one-to-one correspondence between features of an object and its image, unlike the arbitrary and pluralistic relations between signs, meanings, and objects. Despite the acquisition of speech, the Lacanian ego, formed by its image in a mirroring object, remains caught in the allure of external representations of itself. The ego is narcissistically sustained in its cohesion by reflections of itself such as photographs, automobiles, monuments, and, in the interpersonal field, admiration, imitation, and especially the glow that comes from being found desirable as glimpsed in the eyes of an other. Joyce Carol Oates, in her short story "Old Budapest," presents the imaginary register with precision:

> Or was it, Marianne sometimes wondered, the first significant *gaze* that passed between her and a man, heavy with erotic meaning, almost intolerably exciting in all that it promised, or hinted at, or threatened?—This gaze, this exchange of looks, that constituted the pinnacle of romance: for she had experienced looks from men that penetrated her to the very marrow of her being, and left her dazed, and baffled, and weak, and, in a sense, obliterated. And stricken by the realization that no physical gesture, following such promise, could be equal to it. (1983, p. 24)

We can approach the interrelationships among the registers of the Real, the imaginary, and the symbolic by examining the status of the deaf as described by Oliver Sacks in *Seeing Voices* (1989). According to Sacks, only recently (Stokoe, 1960) has American Sign Language (ASL, or Sign) been recognized as a language, as satisfying "every linguistic criterion of a genuine language, in its lexicon and syntax, its capacity to generate an infinite number of propositions" (1989, p. 77). The symbolic capacity of this language and of most deaf people had been underestimated or ignored, for signing was seen as merely "a species of picture writing in the air" (Encyclopedia Britannica, 14th Edition, 1960), for, as Sacks put it, it was the common notion "that 'the sign language' of the deaf is no more than a sort of pantomime, or pictorial language" (1989, p. 76). The signs of the deaf were thereby reduced to iconic units, functioning mainly in the imaginary register, governed in form by a one-to-one correspondence between the sign and its referent. The deaf were therefore judged incapable of more than a type of concrete cognitive activity, unless they went on to learn how to sign English or to lip read. This stereotype of the deaf is itself the type of thinking fostered by the imaginary register, as we shall see when we examine the Lacanian ego in later chapters.

Contrary to the stereotype, Stokoe, according to Sacks, was the first to analyze the structural features of signs, for he "was convinced that signs were not pictures, but complex abstract symbols with a complex inner structure" (1989, p. 77). What is distinctive, moreover, about Sign is its complex use of space:

> We see then, in Sign, at every level—lexical, grammatical, syntactic—a linguistic use of space: a use that is amazingly complex, for much of what occurs linearly, sequentially, temporally in speech, becomes simultaneous, concurrent, multileveled in Sign. The 'surface' of Sign may appear simple to the eye, like that of gesture or mime, but one soon finds that this is an illusion, and what looks so simple is extraordinarily complex and consists of innumerable spatial patterns nested, three-dimensionally, in each other. (1989, p. 87)

Sacks therefore concludes that the use of "picturing, pictorial power, goes with the use of Sign—even though Sign is not in the least a 'picture-language' itself" (1989, p. 107).

Sacks provides additional data for the symbolic status of Sign, data that supports Lacan's distinction between the symbolic and the imaginary registers. Sacks writes:

> Though unconscious, learning language is a prodigious task—but despite the differences in modality, the acquisition of ASL by deaf children bears remarkable similarities to the acquisition of spoken language by a hearing child. Specifically, the acquisition of grammar seems identical, and this occurs relatively suddenly, as a reorganization, a discontinuity in thought and development, as the child moves from gesture to language, from prelinguistic pointing or gesture to a fully-grammaticized linguistic system: this

occurs at the same age (roughly twenty-one to twenty-four months) and in the same way, whether the child is speaking or signing. (1989, p. 90)

As a language, Sign "is processed by the left hemisphere of the brain, which is biologically specialized for just this function" (Sacks 1989, p. 95), as in the case of speech. But since Sign is so spatial, this means the brain must distinguish between two kinds of space, space encompassed by the symbolic register and space functioning in point-to-point correspondence: "The fact that Sign is based here in the left hemisphere, despite its spatial organization, suggests that there is a representation of 'linguistic' space in the brain completely different from that of ordinary, 'topographic' space" (Sacks, 1989, p. 95).

Additional evidence for this distinction between the symbolic and the imaginary registers comes from the specific dysfunctions found in deaf people with aphasia. In such "Sign aphasias" the dysfunction can appear in various ways, in the patient's lexicon or grammar or in the capacity to make propositional statements:

> But aphasic signers are not impaired in other, nonlinguistic visual-spatial abilities. Gesture, for example—the non-grammatical expressive movements we all make (shrugging the shoulders, waving goodbye, brandishing a fist, etc.)—is preserved in aphasia, even though Sign is lost, emphasizing the absolute distinction between the two. (Sacks, 1989, p. 94)

In these cases the use of symbolic space is impaired, but not the use of routine gestures in their one-to-one correspondences. In other cases the reverse is true:

> Signers with right hemisphere strokes, in contrast, may have severe spatial disorganization, an inability to appreciate perspective, and sometimes neglect of the left side of space—but are not aphasic and retain perfect signing ability despite their severe visual-spatial deficits. (Sacks, 1989, p. 94)

In these patients the routine, fixed use of space is impaired, but the richly ambiguous use of symbolic space is not. In addition, signers use the face in a distinct manner, linguistically, in addition to the routine, affective use of the face, and once again the neurological findings corroborate the distinction between the symbolic and the imaginary registers:

> The few cases studied of the effects of brain lesions in deaf signers upon facial recognition show a similar dissociation between the perception of affective and linguistic facial expressions. Thus, with left hemisphere lesions in signing subjects, the linguistic "propositions" of the face may become unintelligible (as part and parcel of an overall Sign aphasia), but its expressiveness, in the ordinary sense, is fully preserved. With right hemisphere lesions, conversely, there may be an inability to recognize faces or their

ordinary expressions (a so-called prosopognosia), even though they are still perceived as "propositionizing," fluently, in Sign. (Sacks, 1989, p. 100)

Signing, therefore, is an elaborate symbolic activity utilizing visual thought patterns not simply as images but as symbols, not based on iconic resemblance any more than words are. This fundamental, systematic difference between iconic resemblance and symbolic convention, sometimes referred to as analog versus digital coding (Wilden, 1972), in which the former is hierarchically integrated into the latter, appears to have determined how the brain organizes spatial relationships.

This revolution in our understanding of Sign as a language has dislodged our stereotype and allowed us to see deaf people as having their own culture. Having a culture means that deaf people have a symbolically-mediated world, a socially constructed field of intersubjectivity. Without such linguistic engagement, through speech or Sign, the dominant register of experience would be the Real. Deaf signers do not live in the Real but in socially constructed reality, as Sacks again tells us: "It is certain that we are not 'given' reality, but have to construct it for ourselves, in our own way, and that in doing so we are conditioned by the cultures and worlds we live in" (1989, p. 73).

The construction of reality requires the use of names, the symbolic delineation of the surrounding environment. The passage from the imaginary register to the opening up of reality through the symbol is presented by Sacks as he describes pioneering work with a deaf pupil who had no language until almost age 14:

> Then, to introduce Massieu to language, Sicard wrote the names of the objects on their pictures. At first, his pupil "was utterly mystified. He had no idea how lines that did not appear to picture anything could function as an image for objects and represent them with such accuracy and speed." Then, very suddenly, Massieu got it, got the idea of an abstract and symbolic repesentation: "at that moment [he] learned the whole advantage and difficulty of writing . . . [and] from that moment on, the drawing was banished, we replaced it with writing."(1989, p. 47)

With this change, when Massieu "perceived that an object, or an image, might be represented by a name, he developed a tremendous, violent hunger for names" (1989, p. 47). Names create "a region of order in the chaos" of the Real (1989, p. 55), the undifferentiated register in which one without language appears to be fixed "like an animal, or an infant, to be stuck in the present, to be confined to literal and immediate perception, though made aware of this by a consciousness that no infant could have" (1989, p. 44). Sacks describes such a consciousness as he could perceive it in an eleven-year-old with no language at all:

> It was not only language that was missing: there was not, it was evident, a clear sense of the past, of "a day ago" as distinct from "a year ago." There was a strange lack of historical sense, the feeling of a life that lacked auto-biographical and historical dimension, the feeling of a life that only existed in the moment, in the present . . . [with] an intelligence largely confined to the visual . . . He seemed completely literal—unable to juggle images or hypotheses or possibilities, unable to enter an imaginative or figurative realm. (1989, p. 40)

In a word, he had not been acculturated, culture did not hold him, he existed in the register of the Real.

Being deprived of language means not only being incapable of symboli-cally differentiating experience; it also means that the development of the brain is altered: "Early language acquisition, whether speech or Sign, seems to kindle the linguistic powers of the left hemisphere; and deprivation of language, par-tial or absolute, seems to retard development and growth in the left hemi-sphere" (Sacks, 1989, p. 105). Sacks warns of the neurological hazards of congenital deafness, for if language experience is severely deficient, or other-wise aberrant, it may delay the maturation of the brain: "Neither language nor the higher forms of cerebral development occur 'spontaneously'; they depend on exposure to language, communication, and proper language use" (1989, p. 110). Becoming a human subject is an effect of language, and this is what I take to be Lacan's essential legacy for psychoanalysis.

In both teaching and writing I begin from the position that the Lacanian perspective may be unfamiliar to readers; for this reason the notions of imagi-nary, symbolic, and Real will unfold gradually and be presented as distinctive approaches to data from a variety of sources such as cognitive, social, and devel-opmental psychology, literature, history, art, and psychoanalytic treatment. Because the notion of the Real is especially difficult to approach, it is com-monly omitted from discussion. As Brett stated: "Like many others who discuss Lacan's work I will bracket the Real and talk only about the Imaginary and Symbolic" (1981, p. 193). But to omit the Real, or to designate it with a "capi-tal X," as some do (e.g., Weber, 1982, p. 140), skews the meaning of the other registers. I have found it helpful to approach the Real through literature, not as a means of interpreting the work but rather in an attempt to explore how the work interprets us, how it sets up effects in us by providing contact with the Real. In this exploration I will try to use the triadic structure of the sign as elaborated by Charles Sanders Peirce, as well as his three categories of logical relations, which appear to have much in common with Lacan's three registers. I hope by the end of the book the reader will come to know and to evaluate how these registers, as a semiotic code of experience, can contribute to psy-choanalytic understanding.

Readers who want an introduction to the ideas of Lacan may find useful the books by Felman (1987), Clark (1988), Boothby (1991), and Muller and Richardson (1982, 1988). The book in hand is an attempt at integration rather than exposition; I don't mean thereby to justify lack of clarity, but to alert the reader. I do not take part in the current debate pitting hermeneutics against natural science, since there seems to me no quarreling with the position that it is helpful to bring findings into an argument and that findings are only found and interpreted through a point of view, as so cogently argued by Phillips (1991) in his definitive survey of the philosophical issues.

The book's first four chapters present my reading of selected data from child development research, psychology, and linguistics, and approximate a semiotic model of "normal" development. The following three chapters examine in a Lacanian framework the structural basis of psychotic states as indicative of massive semiotic failure in development. The final three chapters on human narcissism suggest why "normal" development may be impossible. I conclude with an attempt to integrate hierarchical models in semiotics and psychoanalysis.

Part One

Developmental Semiotics

1

Mother–Infant Mutual Gazing

The contemporary emphasis in psychoanalytic theory on the dyad is often presented as an advance over individualistic, intrapsychic, defense/drive models of human functioning. The relation to "objects" is conceptualized as a separate developmental line, progressing cognitively from partial to whole perceptions or affectively from split to integrated relationships (Kernberg, 1980). Kohut (1971, 1977, 1984) elaborated a developmental line of narcissistic integration in which the notion of a "selfobject" is offered to account for how one person may be used by another to carry out one's own psychological functions, the most important of which is the maintenance of a sense of cohesiveness.

A chief function of the selfobject is to "mirror" the infantile, grandiose self, whose developmentally appropriate exhibitionistic behavior is ideally met in childhood by an approving, admiring, mirroring adult. If this process does not occur, the ensuing narcissistic pathology signifies a developmental arrest. The appropriate treatment, according to self-psychologists (e.g., Wolf, 1976; Ornstein, 1990; Fosshage, 1990), is for the therapist to "mirror" the patient by sustaining an intersubjective congruence, meeting demands for admiration, maintaining affective attunement. They invoke recent research on mother-infant face-to-face interaction (e.g., Beebe and Lachmann, 1988) as evidence for the positive impact of empathic resonance.

I will try to re-formulate the results of these infant studies in terms of developmental semiotics, with semiotics as defined by Charles Morris:

Semiotic has for its goal a general theory of signs in all their forms and manifestations, whether in animals or men, whether normal or pathological, whether linguistic or nonlinguistic, whether personal or social. Semiotic is thus an interdisciplinary enterprise. (1964, p. 1)

By examining infant studies in the light of semiotics (Deely, 1990; Colapietro, 1993), we may be in a position to elaborate a distinctive developmental line (A. Freud, 1963). This developmental line, I will suggest, spans a movement from coerced mirroring to recognition, or, in semiotic terms, from enacted iconicity to index to symbol. From this perspective, mirroring appears to be an early constraint on the infant's behavior whereby the mother's emotional presentation induces a mirroring response in the infant. This dynamic is what I take Lacan to mean by the imaginary register, whose dynamics govern dyadic relations. Recognition, in contrast, does not coerce sameness but posits difference, and appears in the mother's utilization of a semiotic code which the infant begins to use in mutual interaction with the mother. Understood in this way, the code, situated in the symbolic register, functions as a third to the dyad from the earliest period of development, with decisive consequences for our understanding of the analytic relationship and the relationship between psychoanalysis and culture.

Before I attempt to establish the semiotic status of such a code in the following chapters, I would like to emphasize Bruner's reference to a protolinguistic framework. Bruner conceptualizes the child's entry into meaning as a process of cultural transmission in which specific communicative functions are developed before the child has mastered formal linguistic expression, and these functions include "indicating, labelling, requesting, and misleading" (1990, p. 71). Such a "protolinguistic system" (1990, p. 69) provides knowledge of context, cuing, and ostensive reference and is organized by a narrative format with four major constituents: goal-directed action, a segmented order, a sensitivity to what is normative and what is deviant in human interaction, and a narratorial perspective (1990, p. 77).

I think we can find evidence for most, if not all, of the features of Bruner's protolinguistic system in some observations of early infant-mother interaction made a generation ago. Brazelton, Koslowski, and Main (1974) analyzed the behavior of five mother-infant pairs by coding films of short periods of intense interaction involving attention and withdrawal. The infants were from two to twenty weeks old and were judged to be normal. By three weeks of age two distinct systems of infant behavior had emerged, one for objects and one for mother. The difference was striking: "We felt that we could look at any segment of the infant's body and detect whether he was watching an object or interacting with his mother—so different was his attention, vocalizing, smiling, and motor behavior with the inanimate stimulus as opposed to the mother" (1974, p. 53).

By four weeks, sitting tensely before the inanimate object, with shoulders hunched as if to "pounce," fixating on the object (by six weeks) for as long as two minutes, the infant would suddenly look away, flail, cry out, and then look at something else. Brazelton and his colleagues write:

> The period of disruption was followed by a turning back to the object and a resumption of the "hooked" state of attention.
>
> Striking in all of this was the intent prolonged state of attention, during which tension gradually built up in all segments of his body until abrupt disruption seemed the inevitable and necessary relief for him. This behavior was most striking by twelve to sixteen weeks. (1974, p. 54)

The authors affirm: "Of course the expectancy engendered in an interaction with a static object, as opposed to a responsive person, must be very different" (1974, p. 55). Such expectancy is generated in response to the mother's desire and they describe the ensuing interaction with a wealth of semiotic detail.

The typical unit of observed behavior begins with the infant looking back at the mother, with brightening eyes and face, extremities extended toward her. As mother responds to his looking at her, "the infant assumes a state of attention in which he alternately sends and receives cues" (1974, p. 56). His smiling is reinforced by her contingent smiling, he becomes more active, and his excitement peaks, leading to a gradual deceleration with a dull expression that is quite different from the sudden drop in activity before an inanimate object. The infant then appears to withdraw from his mother, looking away but keeping her in his peripheral vision. He then turns back toward his mother, signalling he is ready for another period of interaction. These "time outs" may be more than simply self-soothing maneuvers, attempts to reduce arousal that has become noxious; they may be the infant's efforts to process information, to "digest what he has taken in during the interaction" (1974, p. 59). During these moments the infant may be learning the basic rule of the interaction, to know when "to turn her off, to decrease his receptivity to information from her" in order to develop his "capacity to attend to messages in a communication system" (1974, p. 60).

On the mother's side, the "most important rule for maintaining an interaction seemed to be that a mother develop a sensitivity to her infant's capacity for attention and his need for withdrawal—partial or complete—after a period of attention to her" (1974, p. 59). This rule for the mother and the infant's basic rule about when to withdraw conjoin to form "the first rule each must learn from the other" (1974, p. 60). This rule is superordinate because it governs the learning of all other rules, cues, and codes. With the learning of this superordinate rule, the mother goes beyond the eliciting of smiling by smiling: by recognizing the infant as requiring and capable of taking a time out, she therefore also recognizes him or her as capable of sending signals as signs. This opens the field of communication to symbolic resonance and a responsiveness vastly broader than the one-to-one smiling response.

Although they do not build upon an explicit semiotic framework, Brazelton and his colleagues describe the mother-infant interaction in terms that seem to require it. The mother's recognition serves to reinforce the infant's semiotic capacity, and she does this by "adjusting her rhythm to his, following his cues for attention and withdrawal, and adding her cues when he demonstrates his receptiveness" (1974, p. 64). She increases his capacity "to receive and send messages" by "[a]llowing for reciprocity with sensitivity to his signals" (1974, p. 64). Moreover, she appears "to teach the infant how to suppress and channel his own behavior into a communication system" by learning the conditions "for containing her infant," through restraint or "with her face, her gestures, or her voice" (1974, pp. 64–65). In all of this she "attempts to elicit a signal from the infant confirming that he is in touch with her" (1974, p. 65), and thereby confirming that in some way she has been recognized by him. Her gestures, her holding and smiling, her emphasis on speech rhythms, "[t]hese behaviors were all designed to heighten the information-giving aspect of this interaction sequence" (1974, p. 66). Even when the infant's observable response is minimal, she will "endow the smallest movements with highly personal meaning and react to them affectively" (1974, p. 68). In her status as a desiring subject, not as an object, she recognizes in her anticipatory action, and therefore makes possible, the semiotic status of the infant.

The authors refer to the then unpublished research of Tronick, which demonstrated "reactions to violation of expectancy, which are seen as early as four weeks" (1974, p. 70). This research, subsequently published by Tronick, Als, Adamson, Wise, and Brazelton, invokes a semiotic dimension from its first sentence: "In face-to-face interactions young infants begin to learn and define the rules of social interaction," for they learn "cognitive and affective information which allows them to fit into their culture, to identify with their caregivers, and to identify themselves" (1978, p. 1). For these infants aged two to twenty weeks, this culturally-specific "communication system" consists of "phases of an interaction" that includes "initiation of the interaction, mutual orientation of the partners, greetings, cyclical exchange of affective information as in play dialogues and games, and mutual disengagement" (1978, p. 1). This rule-governed behavior is an enormous achievement, one that "requires that the system be mutually regulated, that is, that both participants reciprocally modify their actions based on the feedback they receive from their partner" (1978, p. 2).

The semiotic weight of this achievement, its social gravity, becomes evident when the experimenters instruct the mother to break the learned rules, to violate the infant's learned expectations by remaining unresponsive to the infant, by maintaining an expressionless face. Tronick, Brazelton, and Als describe this phenomenon as follows:

> For example, if the mother remains still faced and immobile in front of an infant, the infant attempts to get the interaction back on track with a specific set of a sequence of behaviors. Initially the infant orients to the adult and smiles, but when the mother fails to respond, the infant sobers. His facial expression is serious and he stills. He stares at the adult and smiles again, but briefly. Then he looks away. He repeatedly looks toward and away from the adult, smiling briefly in conjunction with the look toward, and sobering with the look away. Eventually he slumps in his seat with his chin tucked, his head and eyes oriented away from the adult. (1978, p. 10)

In 1982, Cohn and Tronick videotaped the responses of twelve male and twelve female three-month-old infants in their laboratory setting. Mothers were instructed to show normal or simulated depressed expressions in two face-to-face interaction periods with their infants. They attempted to test prevailing hypotheses regarding infant motivation and response. Stimulation-regulation theories (as found in Stern, 1985) would argue that simulated maternal depression would not provide sufficient stimulation to arouse interest and so the infant would look away more and episodes of upset would be unlikely. Schema-discrepancy theories (such as found in Kagan, 1974) would argue that the change in mothers' expressions would lead to positive interest in the infants or, in extreme discrepancy, some degree of upset followed by positive interest. The results argue against both of these views and favor a rule violation hypothesis, as Cohn and Tronick conclude:

> The rule violation hypothesis predicts that infants will respond to simulated maternal depression with increased frequencies of positive elicitations (brief positive) and increased proportions of negative displays. It predicts that the structure of infant behavior will clearly differ between conditions and that differences in negativity may continue into the next period of normal interaction. These predictions were confirmed. Infants in the simulated depressed condition had significantly and markedly higher proportions of protest and wary [ratings of behavior]. . . . Normal condition infants, conversely, spent a minimal proportion of their time in negative states (13 percent) and about 40 percent of their time in positive or monitor [states]. (1982, p. 75–76)

In short, the infants "structured their behavior in a radically different manner" in each condition (1982, p. 76). The effect on the infant of the still face, furthermore, occured only with people, not with objects. Ellsworth, Muir, and Hains (1993), in studies of three- and six-month-olds, found that interactive objects such as a cloth hand puppet whose movements were accompanied by a synthesizer voice pattern did not elicit the effect.

The infants' status as semiotic agents was quite apparent to their mothers. In the study reported by Tronick, Als, Adamson, Wise, and Brazelton, mothers reported that

> they found it very difficult to sit still-faced in front of the infant and resist his powerful sallies and bids to interaction. They found it at the same time very reassuring that the infant trusted his own powers to engage them in interaction. They well understood the infant's anger at reunion and were flattered by his demonstration of their importance to him. (1978, p. 10)

The authors conclude that the "infant's recognition of the mother's violation of reciprocity in the still-face condition begins very early," with anecdotal evidence for it as early as two to three weeks, while the pattern described above "is clearly established by four weeks" (1978, p. 12).

These results not only favor a semiotic perspective, but they also argue for a significant memory capacity in the three-week- to three-month-old infant. This means that, under these conditions of rule violation, the infant is not simply responding to the immediately preceding maternal cue, but to a more extended interactive sequence as measured against a learned semiotic code which has become an integral feature of the interactional context (Lewis and Lee-Painter, 1974). Infants are much more capable of long-term memory than has generally been assumed. In an intitial study, infants averaging six-and-a-half months old reached in the dark for an object that made sounds; when the study was repeated one or two years later, the infants showed that they had retained a memory of this one-time experience (Perris, Myers, and Clifton, 1990).

Tronick and his colleagues conceptualize the observed mother–infant interaction "as a goal-oriented, reciprocal system in which the infant plays a major active role, constantly modifying his own communicative displays in response to the feedback provided by his partner" (1978, p. 10). The "rule-governed" interaction consists of "emotional displays of the infant and adult as message-carrying displays" with a clear semiotic import: "Language is not yet a part of the interaction, but there appears to be a lexicon of expression that conveys information to each about their partner's inner emotional state and serves to regulate the interaction" (1978, p. 11). The interaction seems to be regulated by the reciprocal cuing. Such cues, however, may not convey information about "inner" emotional states, but rather may signal quite overt conditions of recognition: "The regulatory aspect of a signal contains information about a communicant's acceptance, rejection, or modification of the current state of the interaction" (1978, p. 11). In other words, the participants signal their mutual recognition, or the refusal of such recognition, in the very act of communicating, as a meta-communication.

As we shall see in subsequent chapters, such mutual recognition in the act of communicating is bound up in the use of the personal pronouns "I" and "you" (Benveniste, 1956). Tronick's study, furthermore, appears to agree with Bruner's notion of a protolinguistic framework that sets the stage for saying "I" and "you" when it concludes that "prior to the incorporation of language into the interaction, the infant has developed and practiced the ability to regulate the pragmatic aspects of an interchange" (1978, p. 11). The experience of recognition is intimately tied to such learning, for "the seriousness of the infant's reaction when the mother remains unresponsive despite his efforts demonstrates how critical reciprocity is to him" (1978, p. 12). To equate such reciprocity with its affective components overlooks how the interaction is ordered, sustained, and rendered significant through its semiotic dimension, and it is precisely the semiotic violation, as a refusal of recognition, that brings about the negative affective response.

Unlike their responses to such refusal of recognition, infants react quite differently to interactive errors or simple miscuing. Tronick and Cohn (1989) examined the role of synchrony and miscoordination in their sample of fifty-four three-, six-, and nine-month-old infants and their mothers. They found that mother-son dyads were more likely than mother-daughter dyads to be in synchronous states, although overall matching occurred less than 30 percent of the time. The authors speculate that the 70 percent of the time spent in miscoordination is crucial to "the learning of the rules of interaction" (1989, p. 90). In such learning the interactive errors are identified and repaired; in an earlier study, Tronick and Gianino (1986) found that "during normal face-to-face interactions at six months of age about one-third of the interactive errors are repaired in the next step of the interaction" and that in Tronick and Cohn's study "the repair rate ranges from about once every 3 seconds to once every 5 seconds" (1989, p. 90).

Cohn and Tronick observed eighteen mother-infant pairs each at three, six, and nine months of age (1988). They looked for evidence of periodic cycling of behavior (as reported earlier by Lester, Hoffman, and Brazelton, 1985), as well as the direction of influence in the mother-infant face-to-face interaction. Their results challenged the view that the infant's behavior is biologically impelled, manifested in blind periodic cycles which the infant gradually synchronizes with the mother's behavior. Cohn and Tronick found a significant periodic component in only five of eighteen infants in the three-month-old group, in one of eighteen at six months, and none at nine months, with the observed periodicity accounting for less than 3 percent of the variation in subsequent behavior. Instead of showing periodicity, roughly a third of the interactive behavior of the infant as well as the mother was observed to be correlated with the immediately preceding behavior: "Babies were more likely to respond to changes in their mother's behavior if the mother were responsive to changes in their behavior" (1988, p. 388). Except at six months, when mothers were more likely to follow their infants' leads, "infants and mothers were equally influential in influencing the direction of the interaction," leading the authors to conclude: "We found strong support for the belief that face-to-face interactions are a product of bidirectional influence" (1988, p. 388). The meaning of these findings can be simply put: "Early mother–infant face-to-face interactions have a conversation-like pattern in which each partner appears to be responsive to the other" (1988, p. 386).

This conversation-like pattern has been found to show cross-cultural variability, further arguing against blind biological periodicity. In 1988, Fogel, Toda, and Kawai videotaped thirty-six Japanese and thirty-six American three-month-old infant-mother dyads in a standardized laboratory setting in their own countries. Mothers, all urban, middle-income, and over twenty-one, were instructed to play with their babies as they would at home. Observations were primarily directed toward the facial, gaze, and vocal features of the interaction.

Although there were no differences in the rate and proportion of maternal expressiveness while the infant gazed at them, American mothers combined facial expressiveness with vocalization, whereas Japanese mothers combined facial expressiveness with leaning close. In particular, Japanese mothers significantly increased their leaning close as well as their touching when the infant shifted from gazing away to gazing at their mothers. Infants in both cultures smiled overall about the same proportion of time, but the American infants smiled three times as often as the Japanese infants, while the Japanese infants smiled for longer average durations. During the nine seconds following the onset of infant smiling, mothers in both cultures significantly reduced their frequency of facial and vocal expressiveness, but the Japanese mothers, as they did with infant gazing, increased the frequency of leaning close and touching in response to infant smiling.

Both culture and sex affected vocalization. Just as they did with smiling, Japanese infants vocalized less often but for more extended periods than the American infants, while girls in both cultures vocalized a greater proportion of time and less frequently than boys. American mothers were more expressive than Japanese mothers while their infants were vocalizing, and only the American mothers co-vocalized with their infants. For the Japanese mothers, no significant co-occurrences were observed between their behavior and infant vocalization. In contrast to the American mothers, moreover, the Japanese mothers signalled more with their hands, by clapping, waving, and making intricate hand displays several times in a session. There were no differences, however, in global measures of maternal behavior: mothers in both cultures showed facial expressiveness 70 percent of the time, touched their babies about 50 percent of the time, and vocalized about 80 percent of the time to their babies. This global similarity highlights the specificity of the findings, those cultural variations evidenced in timing and targeting of maternal cues. The authors conclude that in "both cultures, by three months of age a complex system of interpersonal communication of affect was well established" (1988, p. 405) and they speculate that the observed variations are consistent with the greater nonverbal features of the Japanese, whereas American mothers rely heavily on speech to communicate about and indicate a response to affective states.

Specific differences have also been observed with variations in social class. In 1972, Lewis and Wilson observed infants and mothers from middle-class and working-class backgrounds and found no differences in frequency of maternal vocalization in the presence of the infant. Middle-class mothers, however, were more likely than working-class mothers to respond to their infants' vocalization with a vocalization.

At this point we may tentatively conclude that these infant studies support the following semiotic claims:

1. The mother-infant interaction is governed by an exchange of cues structured by a code.
2. This code has the essential features of a semiotic code insofar as it specifies cues as signs, indicates their legitimate substitution and combination, and organizes the pragmatics of turn-taking for the positions of sender and receiver of these cues.
3. The infant learns to use and respond to such cues.
4. The mother recognizes the infant as actively cuing.
5. The infant's role as semiotic partner impacts the mother's semiotic behavior.
6. The mother's violation of the semiotic code is disruptive to the infant and this indicates that the infant has learned the basic rudiments of the code.
7. The semiotic rules for the interaction are culturally distinct.
8. The code that structures the interaction stands as a third term to the dyad, as the holding environment for both mother and infant.
9. The mother's distinctive responsivity, what distinguishes her from other objects in the infant's environment, is not as a desired object but rather as a desiring subject.
10. The process of mutual semiotic recognition leads to the emergence of subjectivity in the infant, eventually effected in the use of "I" and "you."

Among psychoanalysts, two distinct biases have led away from conclusions of this sort. The first lies in the narcissism of consciousness, which insists that the use of signs requires a conscious ego. But to insist on this is to dismiss or overlook the essential Freudian discovery regarding meaningful unconscious activity, the unconscious play of signifiers in the dreams and parapraxes of adults. The second bias equates the preverbal with the prelinguistic and invokes a prelinguistic stage of development in which the use of signs is impossible. But, as Bruner has shown, the verbal does not emerge from the preverbal, but rather from the protolinguistic, the semiotic code. Child development specialists have concluded that "there is no such thing as a 'prelinguistic' child" (Osofsky and Connors, 1979, p. 528). My own integrative wish is to embrace each of these phases through Lacan's semiotic registers. If we can discern the "conversation-like" components of the face-to-face interaction as opening onto the dimension of the symbolic register, then perhaps we may likewise examine the observed affective components, especially when synchrony is present, as the operation of the imaginary register in that broad intersubjective arena that we call empathy.

In order to examine the early developmental structure of empathy, three hypotheses embedded in the observations of Brazelton and his colleagues were tested by Cohn and Tronick:

> (1) Interactions begin with the mother's positively eliciting her infant's attention; (2) maternal positive expression precedes the onset of infant's positive expression; and (3) when the infant becomes positive, the mother will remain positive until the infant again becomes disengaged. (1987, p. 68)

These hypotheses were tested on three groups of 18 mother-infant pairs at three, six, and nine months of age, and all three were confirmed. The evidence suggests just how powerful the influence of a mother's emotional state is in producing a mirroring effect in the infant.

Their "dyadic-states model of mother-infant face-to-face interaction" proposes that "maternal positive affective expression (e.g., smile, exaggerated 'play face,' or animated vocal expression) frames the infant's positive affective expression (e.g., bright face, smile, or soft vocalization) as the infant cycles from attention to and away from the mother" (1987, p. 68). In their study the mother almost always became positive before the infant at three and six months; at nine months "there was a significant increase in the probability of the infant's becoming positive before the mother" (1987, p. 73). Observations of interactions (Beebe and Gerstman, 1980; Fafouti-Milenkovic and Uzgiris, 1979; Kaye and Fogel, 1980) as well as experimental studies (Cohn and Tronick, 1983; Tronick, Als, Adamson, Wise, and Brazelton, 1978) support the hypothesis that "the change from a neutral expression to a positive expression follows the mother's becoming positive" (1987, p. 69). Infants are more likely to vocalize once the mother vocalizes than when she remains silent (Anderson, Vietze, and Dolecki, 1977; Penman, Friedman, and Meares, 1986; Stern, Jaffe, Beebe, and Bennett, 1975). Vocalization, however, may not be as constrained as vision in mirroring the other; one study showed that what is most effective in producing infant vocalizations are not maternal vocalizations but specific maternal turn-taking signals (Kozak-Mayer and Tronick, 1985).

The responses of ten-week-old infants (six boys and six girls) were studied in response to mothers' presentations of happy, sad, and angry faces and vocalizations (Haviland and Lelwica, 1987). The authors hypothesized that "even an infant younger than three months might respond with an emotion that mirrored the emotion stimulus," based on the assumption "that the emotion presentation, itself, is a stimulus for the infant's emotion" (1987, p. 97). They refer to the work of Tomkins, who wrote: "All affects . . . are specific activators of themselves—the principle of contagion. This is true whether the affect is initially a response of the self, or the response of the other" (1962, p. 296).

In the study by Haviland and Lelwica, mothers made four 15-second presentations of joy, sadness, and anger. To qualify as a mirroring response, the infant's response had to follow the mother's presentation by no more than one second. The authors summarize as follows:

> The results of this study support three major conclusions: First, by ten weeks of age, infants respond differently to three maternal affect expressions when the presentation is simultaneously facial and vocal—joy, anger, and sadness. Second, these infants can match or mirror joy and anger expressions. Third, the infants' matching responses to the maternal affects are only part of complex but predictable behavioral patterns that seem to indicate meaningful affect states and possibly self-regulation in the infants. (1987, p. 102)

Specifically, the infants showed significant mirroring of mothers' joy expressions on the first presentation and a significant increase in interest on later presentations of joy; significant matching of anger responses occurred on all but the second anger presentation, while infant movement and interest decreased; in response to the sad presentations, infants tended to gaze down and engaged in significantly more "mouthing" behavior: lip and tongue sucking, pushing the lips in and out. The authors comment: "This behavior did not occur frequently under the other conditions. The infants' mouthing behaviors in response to the sad expressions could be seen as self-soothing" (1987, p. 103). The self-soothing would follow the state of coerced empathy, an iconic identification with the mother's sad presentation. The authors conclude:

In our opinion the induced-affect hypothesis provides the most reasonable explanation for infant matching of adult facial expressions of emotion. The mothers' expressions seem to have caused an emotional experience in the infants corresponding to the expression presented. (1987, p. 103)

This mirroring effect, or what semioticians have called "enacted iconicity" (Johansen, 1993), as evidenced in the above studies of infants under six months, appears to sharply decrease after six months of age. Wolff notes how "the quasi-obligatory facial response of six-week-old waking infants to faces and voices" gives way at four months to a semiotic selectivity: "The four-month-old infant seems to be making 'choices' of whether or not to smile, and in which way to acknowledge the encounter" (1987, p. 239), a shift which Wolff calls "the infant's apparent release from 'stimulus-boundedness'" (1987, p. 124). Cohn and Tronick found that from "3 to 9 months there was a steady decrease in the strength of association, or sequential constraint, among dyadic states" (1987, p. 73). Maccoby and Martin (1983) and Schaffer (1984) "theorized that during the second half-year of life there is a trend toward a more symmetrical relationship in which both mothers and infants initiate positive dyadic states." Cohn and Tronick conclude: "The implication for the dyadic states model is that it may need to be modified to reflect an (hypothesized) increase in the probability of joint positive engagement being initiated by the infant" (1987, p. 69). That is to say, as the semiotic structuring of the infant develops, the infant becomes less vulnerable to the mirroring constraints and more capable of initiating semiotic interactions.

This brief examination of research on early mirroring responses suggests an important distinction between empathy and recognition. As presented above, the earliest empathic responses, as well as the affective component of later responses, are automatic, almost coerced in constraining one's subjective state and behavior to match that of a model. The affective presentation is contagious, captivating, and produces a replica in the other. Recognition, on the contrary, is an action that posits difference from self, acknowledging the specific state of the other as other, not as an extension or repetition of oneself. Gedo cautions the analyst to refrain from assuming "that the analysand is nothing but an alter ego" (1981, p. 184) and states: "From this perspective, it may be no exaggeration to state that the most difficult self-denial is the necessity to curb our natural human propensity to take the measure of others by means of empathy, that is, to delay closures until the analysand finds his voice and is able to speak for himself" (1981, p. 178).

The distinction between mirroring and recognition has serious implications for the theory and practice of psychoanalysis insofar as therapists are encouraged to mirror, by way of empathy, the affective state of patients, especially in response to patients who insist on it. It may be more helpful to such patients to respond by recognizing that perhaps they demand to be mirrored because they experienced inadequate recognition. Such recognition, in analysis, is often best achieved in an accurate interpretation, for "an accurately detailed, well-timed, vivid, and tactful interpretation carries arguably as much caring, authenticity, and gratification as anything a psychoanalyst may do" (Schwartz, 1990, p. 563). Even Schwartz, a neurobiological psychiatrist, who takes the position "that associative, representational, and affective processes are all biological phenomena" (1990, p. 554), states that "after all, what deeper and more meaningful pleasure can a suffering human being receive than precise emotional understanding and unqualified acceptance delivered with a verbal and prosodic tact that in itself conveys a profound comprehension and concern?" (1990, p. 563).

Recognition requires not objects but subjects—recognition of a subject by a subject, as not the same, but precisely as other, with whom one is joined by a code as Third. In such joining, as opposed to merger or fusion, dyadic states are contextualized by the defined shared task and relativized by the code (Shapiro and Carr, 1991). One shares with another this affective state in rule with the code so that the state can be held: that is to say, the affective state can be bound, be meaningful, and become predictable through its signs. It is quite otherwise in the state of induced affective resonance, or enacted iconicity, for such resonance is coercive, fixed solely by the affective state of the other, and eclipses any Third.

The semiotic initiation of protolinguistic behavior appears to move from iconic mirroring to symbolic recognition and promotes a movement that eventuates, with speech, in the saying of "I" and "you" by a human subject. The subjectivity of self, ownership of desire, and action in history are opened up in what semioticians call the deixis of here-now/there-then articulation. This movement toward assuming one's status as subject takes place as we learn to sign ourselves. Psychoanalytic treatment aims at engendering semiotic empowerment, the capacity to sign oneself and to recognize others, as a step toward the assumption of semiotic responsibility, the ability to say what one wants and means and also to reflect on the conditions that prevent the keeping of one's word. Psychoanalytic treatment, by taking behavior as communication, affirms the operational presence of a semiotic code for interpretation, and essential to this code is the recognition of interacting subjects. For some hospitalized patients who have not been initiated into the semiotic code, who quite precisely come from another culture, the articulation of subjective states is simply impossible at first. For them the notion that behavior is communication addressed to an other comes as a shock to their protective isolation and may seem absurd. When the therapeutic community insists on taking their behavior as signifying something, as something other than conscious actions, these patients may, for the first time, begin to experience the opening up of their own subjectivity.

2

Semiotic Perspectives on the Dyad

In her comprehensive integration of psychoanalytic perspectives with data from developmental psychology, Urwin emphasized the role of the semiotic regulation of the contexts in which children learn; such an emphasis sharply contrasts with what have been called "desert-island" or "bell-jar" views of mother-infant interaction that isolate the dyad (1984). When the semiotic aspects of such learning contexts are explicitly acknowledged, studies of mother-infant interaction are enriched and become more comprehensible. In his examination of pathological mother-infant interaction, for example, Massie stated:

> It is not just what a mother or child does in the presence of the other and the intensity with which they act that is significant, but also in response to what cues, with what rhythm, and in what sequence. Functionally, these elements underlie and become incorporated into the structure of language, as Bruner [1978] has pointed out. Likewise, they characterize the regulation of behavior between two people in the nonverbal as well as the verbal realm. (1982, p. 161–162)

If cues are taken as signs, rhythm as marking the act of signifying, and sequence as denoting ordered, syntactic relations among signs, then the above paragraph refers to the domains of semiotics as specified by Morris in 1938: pragmatics defines the rules for interaction (such as turn-taking and timing), semantics indicates the meanings of signs, and syntactics specifies the grammar for sequencing signs.

While not named as such, a semiotic perspective appears to be present in the reflections of Tronick, Brazelton, and Als who state three initial capacities required in order to achieve skillful reciprocity or intersubjectivity, namely "organized units of behavior that convey the messages of the infant," "the arousal of an intention or a goal," and "a syntax or set of rules . . . that orders the sequence of constituent expressive behaviors"; they go on to state that both communicators "have to share the meaning of the constituent expressive behaviors" (1978, p. 1), but the last capacity is not required by a broad spectrum of semiotic theory and some would doubt that the infant has this capacity from birth. The infant does appear to possess the capacity to organize segments of behavior, to make appropriate substitutions among these units, and to combine them in orderly sequence in interaction with the mother's sequence. The authors stress that a "syntax, or set of ordering rules", is operative in both the gesture of reaching and the behavioral displays of face-to-face interaction, and such a syntax makes it possible for joint regulation to occur. The syntax, or semiotic code, makes joint regulation possible: "Mutual regulation requires that the syntax be shared" (1978, p. 8). Such a syntax of action presupposes that "infants activate different behavioral constituents in the presence of different stimuli" (1978, p. 10).

For example, two studies (Yogman et al., 1976; Dixon et al., 1976) found that infants acted conjointly with both mothers and fathers, but that the sequence of their actions was different with each. With fathers infants vocalized less but had longer play sequences than with mothers; with strangers, however, infants were more disjointed than with their parents and spent more time monitoring and averting gaze.

In contrast to how the Brazelton group acknowledges the structuring influence of a semiotic code, a semiotic perspective appears to be absent in Stern's work of 1985 and 1990, leading at times to a sort of atheoretical muddle, although many of his observations are congruent with how Lacan presents the imaginary register. For example, Stern states that the neonate is captivated in specific ways by visual images. Referring to this as "obligatory attention" (1990, p. 20), Stern writes of the six-week-old infant: "At this age, babies often stare at things as if their gaze has indeed been captured and they are obliged to stare at one spot" (1990, p. 19). There appear to be inborn visual preferences for curves, light–dark contrasts, acute angles, vertical symmetry, and movement within a frame, all of which predispose the infant toward the visual presentation of the mother's face (1990, p. 48).

Stern emphasizes the dynamic, stimulating aspects of eye contact ("mutual gaze is extremely arousing" [1990, p. 50]), and notes the either/or quality of this dimension of experience: "In humans, mutual gaze seems to elicit either strong positive or negative feeling depending on the context" (1990, p. 50).

Stern views such arousal in terms of the infant's "need for stimulation," and, as we saw in the previous chapter, he emphasizes the absence of such stimulation as the main variable in the maternal still-face experimental condition. He describes the four-month-old in this condition as constrained by what I am calling coerced mirroring: "He not only reacts to the lack of expected stimulation, but may also identify with his mother; he may even imitate her and follow her into her state ... In identifying with her, he feels her emotional dullness creeping into himself" (1990, p. 61). Stern's psychoanalytic training alerts him to the importance of identification, but he acknowledges its obscurity: "The process of identification ... though little understood, ... is of great clinical importance" (1990, p. 61). He notes in the infant what he calls "two capacities essential for identification":

> First, he imitates, almost automatically, the facial expressions and gestures of others. In fact, he has been performing parts and pieces of these imitations almost since birth. Second, he, like an adult, is susceptible to emotional contagion.... This contagion goes beyond mere imitation. The other person's emotional state invades you, so to speak, to set up a responsive feeling within you. (1990, p. 62)

Stern's description of "emotional contagion" recalls the experimental studies of induced affective response as well as Lacan's notion of the imaginary register; Lacan quotes Freud "that suggestion (or more correctly suggestibility) is actually an irreducible, primitive phenomenon, a fundamental fact in the mental life of man" (1953–54, p. 56; Freud, 1921a, p. 89).

Stern sees in this dimension, as he imagines the infant gazing into the mother's eyes, the fuel for mutual recognition: "I stare down into their depths. And there I feel running strong the invisible currents of her excitement. They churn up from those depths and tug at me" (1990, p. 58). But the four-month-old cannot yet use "I," despite Stern's claim that "three major kinds of human events are now forming: events of the self; events of others; and events of the self-with-another. It is for this reason that I can now use I, we, and her when speaking in [the infant's] voice" (1990, p. 55). This particular kind of anthropomorphizing is unsupportable from a semiotic perspective, for pronouns such as "I" are not in the four-month-old's repertoire since they do not function as routine signs, but, as we shall see in Chapter 4, they have special status as "shifters" or "indexes" indicating the subjective presence of the speaker in the act of speaking (Benveniste, 1956).

Stern's formulations omit the formative role of the semiotic framework as a Third to the mother-infant dyad. He writes, for example, of their gazing interactions as if no code were operative: "They invent it as they go along" (1990, p. 51). Such alleged inventiveness, however, is tempered by the obvious influence of rules in interactive smiling and vocalizing play: "It is the baby's first and principal lesson in turn taking, the cardinal rule for all later discourse between two people" (1990, p. 65). When Stern describes nose-touching, he writes: "There are a host of such international baby games . . . and they follow an intricate and interesting pattern. While the idea is simply to have fun, it is achieved by conforming to certain rules" (1990, p. 68). Stern does not state that such rules are culturally specific, or that the transmission of a culture's rules is an immense semiotic achievement precisely because an infant's "mother does these things without thinking, as part of 'intuitive' parental behavior" (1990, p. 68). Because culture as a factor is elided, Stern can only say it "is astounding how many things an average parent knows to do intuitively"; culture is perhaps overlooked precisely in order to favor biology: "Evolution has apparently shaped parental behavior to complement babies' auditory preferences" (1990, p. 69). But as the Japanese mothers have indicated, the situation is far too complex for such a theory of evolution to encompass usefully, and "theory is the deciding factor as to what we can observe, because it determines the type of observation" (T. von Uexküll, 1986. p. 122).

Semiotic theory addresses this complexity by distinguishing hierarchical levels of communicative organization, each with its own proper semiotic domain and codes. Sebeok broadly states that the "subject matter of semiotics—ultimately a mode of extending our perception of the world—is the exchange of any messages whatever and of the systems of signs which underlie them" (1976, p. 1). Within the broad domain of semiotics Sebeok distinguishes three areas: anthroposemiotics deals with species-specific human sign systems, zoosemiotics embraces the study of animal communication in the broadest sense, and endosemiotics studies cybernetic systems within the body. The latter has become the dominant paradigm in the life sciences, as seen, for example, in a recent issue of *Science Times*: "One mechanism whose universalism has only recently become clear is a vital signaling system in which cells respond to messages controlling their fate. The system works essentially the same way in determining the development of certain biological functions in worms, mice, and humans. And in each case, the molecules that respond to the signals are also molecules known to cause cancer when they go awry" (Kolata, 1993, p. C1).

In considering infant-mother interaction, we might avoid reductionism by conceiving the process as one in which the mother's anthroposemiotic system quickly transforms the infant's zoosemiotic system into an anthroposemiotic one, with decisive consequences for the endosemiotic system of the developing brain. We can understand developmental semiotics as an attempt to give an account of this transition, this movement from neonatal reflexes to an intersubjective position of semiotic empowerment.

From time to time Lacan refers in his seminars to the work of Charles Sanders Peirce (1839-1914), whose influence on Lacan seems undeniable (Balat, 1992a,b), leading him at one point to wonder if some of his audience will accuse him of fishing in Peircean waters (see the seminar of May 23, 1962 [1961-1962, vol. II, p. 449]). He may indeed have found in Peirce the source of what he called "my categorical registers of the imaginary, the symbolic, and the real" (1974, p. 559). In his seminar on Joyce, *Le Sinthome*, speaking of our tendency to drift into dualistic thinking, Lacan noted that

> every object depends on a relation. What is annoying is that there is language, and that relations are expressed in it with epithets. Epithets push toward yes or no. Someone named Charles Sanders Peirce built on this his logic, which, because of his emphasis on relation, leads him to construct a trinitarian logic.
>
> This is exactly the same path I follow, except that I call things by their names—symbolic, imaginary, and real. (1976, p. 33, my translation)

In his seminar, *The Ethics of Psychoanalysis*, after stating that human libido is "subjugated by the structure of the world of signs," Lacan notes: "And the sign, as Peirce put it, is that which is in the place of something else for someone" (1959–60b, p. 91; see also 1966, p. 840; 1977, p. 222).

Trained as a chemist, astronomer, and mathematician, Peirce is often cited as the most creative American philosopher and the founder of American pragmatism (Gregory, 1987, p. 596). In an attempt to develop a logic of scientific discovery and communication, he spent forty years elaborating the rules of the production, classification, and meaning of signs (see Brent, 1993, for an excellent biography). Staking out a philosophical position he called "fallibilism," he made contributions to probability theory and developed procedures for estimating measurement error. In addition to the standard modes of logical inference known traditionally as deduction and induction, he added a third mode of inference which he called "abduction," a disciplined form of guessing from the odd detail (Eco and Sebeok, 1983; Ginzburg, 1983). Also referred to as "the play of musement," it resembles closely what Freud called "evenly hovering attention" and what Sherlock Holmes referred to as his "method" (Sebeok, 1981); we may also compare it to what Poe's detective Dupin refers to as "analysis" (Muller and Richardson, 1988).

A triadic approach governs Peirce's thinking, specified in terms of three conceptions "so very broad and consequently indefinite that they are hard to seize and may be easily overlooked." Peirce calls these "the conceptions of First, Second, Third," and defines them as follows:

First is the conception of being or existing independent of anything else. Second is the conception of being relative to, the conception of reaction with, something else. Third is the conception of mediation, whereby a first and second are brought into relation. (1891, p. 296)

In the field of psychology, Peirce finds that "the elementary phenomena of mind fall into three categories," which he elaborates as follows:

First, we have Feelings, comprising all that is immediately present, such as pain, blue, cheerfulness . . . A feeling is a state of mind having its own living quality, independent of any other state of mind. Or, a feeling is an element of consciousness which might conceivably override every other state until it monopolised the mind, although such a rudimentary state cannot actually be realized, and would not properly be consciousness . . .

Besides Feelings, we have Sensations of reaction; as when a person blindfold suddenly runs against a post, when we make a muscular effort, or when any feeling gives way to a new feeling . . .

Very different both from feelings and from reaction-sensations or disturbances of feeling are general conceptions. When we think, we are conscious that a connection between feelings is determined by a general rule, we are aware of being governed by a habit. (1891, pp. 290–91)

Feelings, not as discrete affects but as unlabelled, in themselves undifferentiated states, have their status in Lacan's register of the Real, corresponding to Peirce's category of Firstness whose members, Peirce wrote, "need not be subject to any law, not even to the principle of contradiction" (1966, p. 404). When such feelings are experienced as reactions to an other, they belong to Peirce's category of Secondness and are governed by the dynamics of the imaginary register. Accordingly, Hervey states that the "appropriate mode of representation for 'Secondness,' and for things that belong to the category of 'seconds,' is as pairs: that is to say as *dyads*" (1982, p. 24). When feelings are perceived as related, as predictable by rule or conception of behavior, they become organized according to the laws of the symbolic register. Of this register of Thirdness, Hervey states: "We may say, therefore, that the keyword of this hierarchically highest level of existence is mediation. A given thing is a 'third' if its nature (in fact its overriding purpose . . .) is to mediate a particular, otherwise non-existent, relationship between two further things" (1982, p. 24). Peirce emphasized that Thirdness is required for thinking: "In its genuine form, Thirdness is the triadic relation existing between a sign, its object, and its interpreting thought, itself a sign, considered as constituting the mode of being of a sign. A sign mediates between the *interpretant* sign and its object" (1966, p. 389).

Signs themselves have a triadic structure and are "triadic mediators that exemplify 'Thirdness' *par excellence*" (Hervey, 1982, p. 26). For Peirce a sign does not simply refer to an object; in place of such an unmediated dual relation, Peirce introduces the notion of the "interpretant" which is roughly equivalent to the sign's meaning as distinct from its referent. Peirce succinctly defined a sign as follows:

> A sign stands *for* something *to* the idea which it produces, or modifies . . . That for which it stands is called its *object*; that which it conveys, its *meaning*; and the idea to which it gives rise, its *interpretant*. (quoted in Eco, 1976, p. 69)

The interpretant cannnot be equated with the object or with the interpreter; it functions itself as another sign, to be in turn interpreted. Furthermore, "the interpretant can be a response, a behavioral habit determined by a sign, and many other things" (Eco, 1976, p. 70). This great variability and apparently endless interpretability of the sign in feeling, action, and thought constitute the rich process of semiosis. Eco writes: "The idea of the interpretant makes a theory of signification a rigorous science of cultural phenomena, while detaching it from the metaphysics of the referent" (1976, p. 70). Feminist theory, for example, has found in Peirce's notion of habit as the active by defining interpretant of a sign a tool for analyzing oppressive practices (deLauretis, 1984). Thus Hervey states that Peirce's "general theory of signs presumably embraces every field where the 'signification' of something can in some way or other be 'interpreted'" (1982, p. 36). Peirce's semiosis is thus the American forerunner of French deconstructionism; Pettigrew (1995) writes that Derrida spent one year at Harvard studying Peirce's manuscripts prior to his 1967 publications on the sign. French structuralism, moreover, inaugurated by Saussure (1916) and elaborated by Barthes (1964), with its pairing of signifier-signified domains, is a more restricted framework than contemporary semiotics as shaped by Peirce. This broader conception of the field of semiotics (Sebeok, 1971), present in the work of Jakobson (1974) and in Lacan, may be termed the Peircean effect: it includes a reference to the object as well as the actions of speakers.

Peirce distinguished three types of signs: the icon, the index, and the symbol, although he emphasized that most signs include features of all three. Tursman defines these features as follows:

> Iconic semiosis or sign-action is the representing of the object of the sign by resembling the object. Indexical semiosis is representation by actual connection with the object, as, for example, by being the physical effect of the object. Symbolic semiosis is representation or signification by virtue of being so understood, and that by nature or by convention. (1987, p. 47)

With the major exception of the work of Piaget (1947), whose formulations regarding signs and representations rely on the distinctions drawn initially by Peirce and Saussure, we find that "the ontogenetic development of signs, which ought to be of central interest in semiotics, has been neglected as a special field of semiotic inquiry" (Krampen, 1986, p. 153).

Despite our uncertainty, we can tentatively consider how the field of developmental semiotics suggests a movement from enacted iconicity to the index to the symbol. This progression may appear to be at odds with a standard presentation in which the child's active use of signs develops from the index to the icon (as internal representation) to the symbol. As Johansen (1993) shows, however, the very earliest semiotic participation is through enacted iconicity, the induced affective mirroring response examined in Chapter 1.

At the earliest stage the infant may be described as already retaining visual and auditory associations that differentiate sectors of experience, and so the utterly simple, undifferentiated status of the Real, of Peirce's Firstness, is a mythic original state, not an actual origin but rather a level of later regression from a more differentiated state. As Demos cogently argues, evidence from developmental psychology "clearly supports the hypothesis that the capacity for psychic experience exists at the beginning of extrauterine life, and may even exist before" (1992, p.207). Initially the infant's interactive movement, voice, and gaze are iconically stimulated and structured by the mother's movement, voice, and gaze which gradually come to function as indices of the mother's caretaking presence. Associations based on contiguity, the basis for subsequent part-whole metonymic relations, develop predictability so that by four weeks the functioning code of mother-infant face-to-face interaction can be violated, as we saw in Chapter 1.

The standard test for the presence of mental icons has been whether "the child begins actively seeking objects which have disappeared" (T. von Uexküll, 1986, p. 136). In her detailed integration of psychoanalytic perspectives and developmental data, Urwin claims that children "refer to absent objects and events far earlier than the object permanence model presumes" (1984, p. 312). The results of Tronick's studies with the maternal still-face paradigm suggest that such active seeking of what is lost begins much earlier than Piaget proposed. By four weeks the infant shows the ability to seek the interactive gaze of the mother when it is withdrawn. The infant's gaze appears to enact iconically what the infant has come to expect from the mother, implying the use of a rudimentary icon of the mother's gaze. The infant's own act of gazing aims at the mother's corresponding gaze, and when it is not found in the withdrawn face of the mother, visible and corresponding withdrawal on the part of the infant occurs; the mother's gaze and vocalizing, moreover, through emotional induction or "contagion," creates its icon in the mirroring response of the infant. In time the automatic mirroring response decreases as the infant gains semiotic autonomy in the interaction.

The responsive gaze functions not only as an icon of the other's gaze or as an index of contiguous presence; it also emerges as a *symbol* with a distinctive *interpretant*—in this case, I suggest, the interpretant of the responsive gaze (the gaze of either the mother or the infant) is initially the responsive gaze of the other. As Peraldi states, "The child has always produced signs, long before he uses such signs as signs of something else" (1981, p. 174). To conceive of the infant as semiotically engaged is not preposterous; Peirce himself encouraged us to think of the infant in this way. While noting, with Kant, that children's relatively late use of the personal pronoun "I" "indicates an imperfect self-consciousness in them," Peirce emphasized that "children manifest powers of thought much earlier" than their use of personal pronouns:

> Indeed, it is almost impossible to assign a period at which children do not already exhibit decided intellectual activity in directions in which thought is indispensable to their well-being. The complicated trigonometry of vision, and the delicate adjustments of coordinated movement, are plainly mastered very early. There is no reason to question a similar degree of thought in reference to themselves. (1992, pp. 18–19)

Peirce's vision of the perceiving, thinking, intending infant is quite congruent with contemporary infant research (e.g., Demos, 1992), as I will report in the next chapter.

There is no exclusion of affect as sign from the semiotic field, for Peirce includes it in his notion of the sign's interpretant: "But we may take a sign in so broad a sense that the interpretant of it is not a thought, but an action or experience, or we may even so enlarge the meaning of sign that its interpretant is a mere quality of feeling" (1966, p. 389). Such "feeling," as a response produced by the sign, as an interpretant of the sign, is itself another sign that must receive its own interpretant. This ongoing process of signing is almost instantaneous, largely unconscious, and seems to lie at the heart of the "talking cure" and of all dialogue.

This is not a matter of constructing a subjective, or even an intersubjective, phenomenology of perception, but of delineating, if possible, the effective structure of the sign whose status is not reducible to its position in consciousness. This, I believe, has fundamental implications for psychoanalysis: the sign is not dependent on consciousness for its effects, and the enactive response it produces opens up the dimension of the repetition compulsion.

If the sign can be taken not in its subjective but rather in its objective mode, what is its function? Peirce states:

> It appears to me that the essential function of a sign is to render inefficient relations efficient—not to set them into action, but to establish a habit or general rule whereby they will act on occasion. According to the physical

doctrine, nothing ever happens but the continued rectilinear velocities with the accelerations that accompany different relative positions of the particles. All other relations, of which we know so many, are inefficient. Knowledge in some way renders them efficient; and a sign is something by knowing which we know something more. (1966, p. 390)

In our example of the responsive gaze as sign, the object or referent is determined by how the sign functions. Taken as an icon, its object is the partner's responsive gaze; taken as an index, as "a type of sign causally connected with its object" (Eco, 1976, p. 115), its object is the individual's contiguous presence; as a symbol, its object is recognition. The interpretant of the responsive gaze, I am proposing, is initially the responsive gaze of the other, the emotional arousal produced by the gaze, and eventually the experience of mutual recognition.

What I am suggesting is that by using Peirce's notions of the sign we can situate the infant as an active semiotic participant, prior to the ability to speak and perhaps prior to the ability to represent (although, as we saw in the work of Tronick and associates, the ability to represent what is absent may develop before one month of age). Our manner of so conceiving the infant is greatly facilitated by the notion of the interpretant as variable, as existing on a developmental line: "Peirce distinguishes between interpretants which are feelings, those which are actions, and those which are kinds of ideas or recurring patterns of idea clustering. These three kinds of interpretants are called *emotional, energetic,* and *logical,* respectively" (Tursman, 1987, p. 53).

If we can say that the logical interpretant of the responsive gaze taken as a symbol is the practice of mutual recognition, then we have within the framework of semiotics the potential tools for a psychoanalytic understanding of the emergence of the human subject. In this framework the earliest unconscious basis for the repetition compulsion would not lie in "instinct" or "need" but in coerced, iconic, and enactive mirroring, structured by signs, including most importantly the affect state of the other, whose logical interpretants are not available to the subject's consciousness. Demos, much like the early Freud (as we shall see in Chapter 10), puts it in terms of the infant's psyche "protecting itself from disorganization and creating defensive strategies, whenever necessary, that can result in keeping some meanings and contents out of awareness or in an unconscious mode" (1992, p. 202). The outcome of this defensive process, from a Lacanian point of view, is the unconscious "structured in the most radical way like a language" (Lacan, 1977, p. 234), i.e., semiotically.

To restrict the field of the emerging subject to the dyad cuts off the field from the primary structures of semiosis that make the dyad possible and effective. The notion of the emotional and active interpretant, furthermore, provides a way of conceptualizing early development not as a preformed biological unfolding but as a cultural transmission. The excellent integrative summary by Demos of her own and others' research on infancy, while acknowledging the importance of culture, is a good example of how the dyadic framework calls for a semiotic grounding. Drawing on the ideas of Tomkins (1962, 1963, 1981) and the research of Ekman and his colleagues (1983), Demos emphasizes the primacy of affect states in the developing psyche. She endorses Sander's epithet, contrary to Freud, that the ego begins as a "state ego, rather than a body ego" (Sander, 1985, p. 20; Demos, 1992, p. 206); she argues for the primacy of nonverbal communication over language, which she circumscribes as "a symbolic form of representation, but only one of several such possible forms. . . and one that has gone through several steps of translation from direct experience" (1992, p. 209); and she claims that in the affective, nonverbal infant, before language, "the distance between experience and expression is much shorter" than in the adult (1992, p. 209). This recalls Stern's claims that the infant, prior to using linguistic symbols, is "confined to reflect the impress of reality" (1985, p. 182), that "infants from the beginning mainly experience reality" (1985, p. 255), for the infant is "a relatively faithful recorder of reality and all deviations from the normal are close to the accurate reflections of the impress of interpersonal reality" (1985, p. 230). As we saw earlier, this "impress" model may have some merit in the very earliest phase of coerced mirroring, characterized by the induced affective response, but such enacted iconicity quickly gives way to indexical learning as semiotic autonomy increases. This is learning mediated by signs much before the use of linguistic symbols, making possible the lifelong process Demos emphasizes as disembedding knowledge from specific contexts and applying it to broader contexts (1993, p. 11).

The pre-eminent semiotics scholar Thomas Sebeok[1] (1994) takes the position that the self is "bio-semiotic," by which he means there is a double envelope to the self. The core self is body-based and consists of the immune system. All living beings have such a self insofar as they have a system for recognizing the difference between self and not-self. The second envelope consists of the field of signs that constitutes a social space (the *Umvelt*, as J. von Uexküll [1934] referred to it). Animals have such a field whose signs (icons and indices) have mostly fixed objects and interpretants; for humans, the signs include symbols and enter syntactic combinations in novel, intersubjectively determined ways that impact on the immune system. For human beings the boundaries of the *Umvelt* are not simply given but must be constructed and maintained in a cultural context. Freud was well-grounded, then, in claiming that the ego is "first and foremost a bodily ego" (1923, p. 26). The "state"

---

1. Sebeok was a student of Charles Morris at the University of Chicago; Morris was a student of John Dewey; Peirce taught Dewey during his brief tenure at Hopkins.

aspect of such ego-emergence, as Lacan argued, is of decisive importance, but not as a state but rather as a "cut" in a state, as the discontinuous shift from a prior state of helplessness to a post-mirroring state of illusory coherence.

To valorize the nonverbal over the verbal may be an attempt to redress a perceived cognitive bias favoring later stages of development. What may be more helpful, however, is to pursue a hierarchical model by considering Sebeok's distinctions among communication, language, and speech. Communication occurs in all living systems according to semiotic principles. Animals communicate but do not use language (Sebeok, 1981). Language, furthermore, did not emerge for communication (which carries on quite well without it), but for model-building. Language provides a system for making complex differentiations, especially among types of relationships, and a syntax for making complex substitutions, combinations, and reconfigurations, especially of our pasts and futures. Language does not require speech but speech requires language. Speech, in turn, through forms of address and deixis promotes recognition (as we shall examine in Chapter 4). For Lacan, "Speech is essentially the means of gaining recognition" (1953–54, p. 240), and such recognition constitutes intersubjectivity: "Finally, it is by the intersubjectivity of the 'we' that it assumes that the value of a language as speech is measured" (Lacan, 1977, p. 86).

The communication systems of living organisms, which include, in mammals, nonverbal affect states, do not have a syntax because their signifying relations are fixed, each system using a certain number of signs. Demos notes "that the infant possesses perceptual biases ["stimulus characteristics"] inherent in possessing a human nervous system, brain and body. Thus, the infant can hear sounds only within certain frequencies, can see colors only in certain wave lengths, can perceive motion only at certain rates, and visually prefers light-dark contrasts and contours" (1993, p. 9). Living systems therefore perceive reality according to such "stimulus characteristics" which are the limited sign systems proper to them and their *Umvelt*. There is no direct experience available because all perception is governed by signs (Peirce, 1868), a position taken by Freud in his letter to Fliess dated December 6, 1896 (Masson, 1985, p. 208).

Because human experience has been shaped by language in all cultures, we inhabit a "languaged" world and do not readily experience language as salient, as other, since it is as much in us as we are in it. Language, then, is not just one of several possible forms of representation, it is a unique system proper to humans that alone enables us to conceive of other forms of representation; by eliciting new connections, furthermore, language shapes both culture and the human brain. Levin (1991) reports some remarkable research by Tsunoda (1987) showing that Japanese, unlike Westerners, hear vowels, affect-signs such as laughter, crying, and humming, as well as sounds of nature such as crickets, with the left hemisphere; other Asian groups such as Polynesians and Koreans lateralize, as Westerners do, to the right hemisphere. Westerners, however, who are fluent in Japanese also lateralize such listening activities to the left hemisphere. Levin concludes from this research "that one's natural language is capable of serving as a vehicle for altering the brain's operating instructions"; if a natural language can so affect the brain, it may do so because it has some commonality with "the language-based determinants of the brain's hierarchical rules of operation" (1991, p. 115). Levin helps us to see how limiting it is to restrict the role of language to communication: "For the function of language," wrote Lacan, "is not to inform but to evoke" (1977, p. 86).

But Lacan further added, given the narcissism of the human ego, that he agrees with those who say that "speech was given to man to hide his thoughts" (1951, p. 12). That language, especially writing, facilitates dissimulation (Todorov, 1982, argues that it made possible the Spanish conquest of America) does not mean that the preverbal is somehow unmediated and provides direct experience. Experience is always mediated. In addition to its mediating function, however, what language also seems to provide is the vehicle for the uniquely human propensity for self-deception. While deception occurs among all living things, self-deception does not appear to exist in animals and may not be possible without language. The salient role of self-deception in human behavior is perhaps the chief enduring legacy of Freud: the human subject is split, "the ego is not master in its own house" (Freud, 1917, p. 139).

Psychoanalysis has recognized two prevalent forms of self-deception: repression and disavowal. Levin examines data suggesting that these processes can be understood "in the form of functional disconnections of the two cerebral hemispheres" (1991, pp. 37–38), as previously formulated by Basch:

> The consciousness of self that we call "I" requires that the right-brain self-experience, the episodic memory, be translated into verbal or other forms of discursive language. In repression it is the path from episodic to semantic memory, from right to left, that is blocked. The self-experience can no longer be articulated and, therefore, cannot be either thought about or made conscious. Disavowal works to block communication in the opposite direction, from left to right. That is, what is apprehended on the semantic, left-brain level in terms of language and logical categories cannot be translated into right-brain, episodic, self-experience. (1983, p. 151)

Self-deception appears to require a hierarchical model of the self in which language structures both brain and psyche.

Freud appeared to say as much when he called repression a failure in translation in the 1896 letter to Fliess previously cited:

As you know, I am working on the assumption that our psychical mechanism has come into being by a process of stratification: the material present in the form of memory traces being subjected from time to time to a rearrangement in accordance with fresh circumstances—to a retranscription [*eine Umschrift*, 1986, p. 217]. Thus what is essentially new about my theory is the thesis that memory is present not once but several times over, that it is laid down in various kinds of indications. [*Zeichen*, 1986, p. 217; "signs" is the better word in this semiotic context]

Freud goes on to consider various registrations, "arranged according to associations by simultaneity," "other, perhaps causal relations," and "the third transcription, attached to word presentations and corresponding to our official ego." He continues:

I should like to emphasize the fact that the successive registrations [*Niederschriften*, 1986, p. 218] represent the psychic achievement of successive epochs of life. At the boundary between two such epochs a translation [*Übersetzung*, 1986, p. 218] of the psychic material must take place. I explain the peculiarities of the psychoneuroses by supposing that this translation has not taken place in the case of some of the material, which has certain consequences.

These consequences are epigenetic and speak to a hierarchical model:

If a later transcript [*Überschrift*, 1986, p. 219] is lacking, the excitation is dealt with in accordance with the psychological laws in force in the earlier psychic period and along the paths open at that time. Thus an anachronism persists . . .

At this point Freud gives his semiotic definition of repression:

A failure of translation—this is what is known clinically as "repression" ["Die Versagung der Übersetzung, das ist das, was klinisch 'Verdrängung' heist," 1986, p. 219]. The motive for it is always a release of the unpleasure that would be generated by a translation; it is as though this unpleasure provokes a disturbance of thought that does not permit the work of translation. (Masson, 1985, pp. 207–208, 215)

Translation involves a syntax, a code that governs the lawful substitution and combination of signs. Such a code appears necessary for the operation of what Freud called repression, and such an operation, or the one we call disavowal, seems to require language for successful self-deception to occur. Such self-deception may operate through the distinction Lacan draws between the level of the enunciation and the level of the enunciated (1964, p. 138). In any act of speaking the enunciating subject "fades" as the chain of signifiers emerges.

This yields a double limitation: what is enunciated can never adequately express the subject, and, moreover, the subject is not in complete control over what is said, with the result that "slips" occur in the substitution and combination of signs that reveal the subject's unconscious desire.

Levin (1991) proposes that a code governs processes in the brain in a manner congruent with semiotic theory, specifically with Jakobson's model of the two axes governing all significant human activity. In examining aphasic deficits, Jakobson (1956) concluded that the use of signs is subject to deterioration in two distinct ways. Some aphasics can string words together according to lawful combinations, but cannot substitute one word for another; other aphasics can provide substitutes for words based on a principle of similarity but cannot combine them in any lawful sequence. The axis of substitution, also referred to as the paradigmatic domain, regulates the classification and interchange of signs—"one word for another," as Lacan put it, referring to metaphor (1977, p. 157). For, as Jakobson indicated, the structure of metaphor is that of a substitution based on some kind of similarity in the objects of the signs. The axis of combination, also referred to as the syntagmatic domain, regulates the placing of one sign after another—"the word-to-word connexion," which Lacan (1977, p. 156) saw, following Jakobson, as the basis of metonymy, since the element of contiguity was essential in the objects of the signs.

Levin joins the axis of combination, based on contiguity, to the sensory modality of touch, and the axis of substitution, based on similarity, to vision and, based on the work of Hermann (1936) and Fonagy (1983; see Muller, 1989b), he adds to these a third axis, that of sonority (hearing), in order to delineate how the brain integrates information. He attempts to ground the neurological aspects of intersensory integration and abstraction in the following way:

> Those readers familiar with the mapping of the central parietal cortex will appreciate especially the beauty of this, since this parietal sensory integration zone is placed equidistant from the primary cortical sensory areas for the perception of touch, vision, and hearing. And it is within this parietal integration area that the perceptual equalities of experience become "abstracted" into memories that are no longer coded according to any sensory tag. In fact, this lack of attachment to immediate sensory experience is the essence of abstraction. (1991, p. 160)

Like many analysts, I am unequipped to judge the accuracy of Levin's proposal, but I can share the wonder of his anticipation as additional findings further map the brain-language link (e.g., Jackendoff, 1994). I would also add that, according to Peirce, what Levin delineates is the essence of Thirdness, of mediation, of lawful regularity, which is required for any systemic organization of experience to develop. As noted earlier, in humans such organization is the product of acculturation and is transmitted through signs, semiotically, in a framework that holds the dyad in a defined relationship. As we shall see in the following chapter, this process begins at or before birth.

3

Developmental Foundations of Infant Semiotics

Chapter 1 examined a specific paradigm of infancy research, mother-infant mutual gazing, in order to address its rich semiotic components. Chapter 2 elaborated a semiotic perspective based on my understanding of some ideas of Peirce as they relate to dyadic interaction as well as to Lacan's registers of experience. I will now review additional data from infancy research in order to spell out more cogently and concretely a semiotic model of development.

If we attempt to use a semiotic model in understanding research on infant-mother interaction, we must examine in what ways the infant can be said to be semiotically competent. I think we can usefully proceed by continuing to take developmental psychology from a Peircean perspective. The linguist Roman Jakobson emphasized the great breadth of Peirce's semiotic perspective: "Peirce's semiotic edifice encloses the whole multiplicity of significative phenomena, whether a knock at the door, a footprint, a spontaneous cry, a painting or a musical score, a conversation, a silent meditation, a piece of writing, a syllogism, an algebraic equation, a geometric diagram, a weather vane, or a simple bookmark" (1974, p. 442).

As we began to examine in Chapter 2, instead of using a dual model of sign and referent or signifier and signified, Peirce emphasized the triadic character of the process of semiosis, the process whereby signs have such pervasive influence:

> It is important to understand what I mean by *semiosis*. All dynamical action, or action of brute force, physical or psychical, either takes place between

two subjects ... or at any rate is a resultant of such actions between pairs. But by "semiosis" I mean, on the contrary, an action, or influence which is, or involves, a cooperation of three subjects, such as a sign, its object, and its interpretant, this tri-relative influence not being in any way resolvable into actions between pairs. (1940, p. 282)

As the cultural variations indicate, the interactive behavior of mother and infant is not intelligible unless the code is taken into account, nor can we make sense of the behavior of each in relation to the code unless we include the behavior of the other. In our specific example from early development, the mother's smiling gaze functions for the infant as a sign, an icon of the infant's smiling gaze as well as an index whose contiguous object is her recognizing presence and whose dynamic interpretant is the infant's smiling gaze in response. It must be emphasized that for Peirce the interpretant is not defined as a state of consciousness: "For the proper significate outcome of a sign, I propose the name, the *interpretant* of the sign ... it need not be of a mental mode of being" (1940, p. 275). For Charles Morris, the heir of the pragmatism of Dewey and Mead at the University of Chicago, the interpretant was conceived in behaviorist terms: "[T]he interpretant, as a disposition to react in a certain way because of the sign (food-seeking behavior or site-probing behavior in the case of bees), has no necessarily 'subjective' connotation" (1964, p. 3).

Interpretants may be conceived as the effects of the sign, "the proper significate effects" of signs (Peirce, 1940, p. 276), effects that operate in the interpreter in an ongoing way on many levels and are productive of further signs:

> The first proper significate effect of a sign is a feeling produced by it. There is almost always a feeling which we come to interpret as evidence that we comprehend the proper effect of the sign, although the foundation of truth in this is frequently very slight. This "emotional interpretant," as I call it, may amount to much more than that feeling of recognition; and in some cases, it is the only proper significate effect that the sign produces. (1940, p. 277)

This first feeling-effect usually leads to action, which Peirce conceives as a necessary feature of any further elaboration of the interpretant:

> If a sign produces any further proper significate effect, it will do so through the mediation of the emotional interpretant, and such further effect will always involve an effort. I call it the energetic interpretant. The effort may be a muscular one, as it is in the case of the command to ground arms; but it is much more usually an exertion upon the Inner World, a mental effort. (1940, p. 277)

In our example, the infant's responsive smiling gaze is the energetic or action interpretant of the mother's smiling gaze, as sign, and, in turn, functions as a sign to the mother, eliciting another feeling and action interpretant on her part. A later stage of elaboration of the interpretant, assuming the cognitive capacity, is what Peirce called the "logical interpretant" (1940, p. 277), or a concept. In our case of infant-mother interaction, the concept of "mutual recognition" (present perhaps to the adult) would then be the logical interpretant of their smiling gazes, produced and brought into actuality by the preceding feeling and action interpretants, that is, by the affect and interaction of the smiling and gazing.

For Peirce, this process of semiosis is dynamic, for "the logical interpretant is an effect of the energetic interpretant, in the sense in which the latter is an effect of the emotional interpretant" (1940, p. 283). Semiosis is incessant; we may wonder how it drives development at all levels in an intrinsically social way. In our example, the concept as well as the state of mutual recognition are determined by the actions taken to produce them, and these actions, in turn, are the consequences of the feelings elicited by the smiling gaze as sign. Such feelings are in themselves variable, possess for Peirce only "slight" reliability in themselves, and are easily changed by their interpretants, especially as influenced by the narcissistic rationalizations of the ego, as Peirce wrote: "Men many times fancy that they act from reason when, in point of fact, the reasons they attribute to themselves are nothing but excuses which unconscious instinct invents to satisfy the teasing 'whys' of the ego. The extent of this self-delusion is such as to render philosophical rationalism a farce" (quoted in Colapietro, 1989, p. 40).

I am emphasizing two main points in all of this: the infant cannot be excluded from semiotic participation on the grounds of cognitive immaturity, and the experience of mutual recognition, the foundation for the experience of human subjectivity, is an effect of semiosis.

The foundations of semiotic capacity in the infant are well documented in the research and writing of Colwyn Trevarthen and his associates. Spanning more than two decades, this body of research constitutes a significant turn in the field of infancy research, although, perhaps because he is not American, his work is not widely cited by American psychoanalysts. Trevarthen acknowledges the influence on him of the philosopher Macmurray (1957, 1961), whose Gifford Lectures of 1953-1954 grounded the self as an agent in relationships, and the psychoanalyst Fairbairn (1941, 1952), whose object-relations approach, together with Klein and Winnicott, marked psychoanalysis with an interactional perspective on infancy.

Trevarthen, Murray, and Hubley review the history of infancy research to point out how "a mistrust of mentalism and of inner explanations of human consciousness" led to "the hypothesis that, at birth, and for the first few months at least, a human being has little consciousness and no independent volition" (1981, p. 211). This hypothesis was a bias that hampered research:

> Whereas preceding scientific accounts stated the newborn to possess only simple, unconscious, reflex brain functions, and expected the process of psychological development to lag behind acquisition of autonomous motor control and of communication by speech, now there is abundant evidence that infants have elaborate consciousness even in early weeks. Increasingly, psychologists are led to revise and greatly expand their assessment of the innate potentialities of human beings for conscious, voluntary and interpersonal aspects of life. (1981, p. 211)

Microanalytic research techniques made possible by video recordings have yielded sufficient data to conclude that "there is powerful competence in infants for communication with other people. Indeed, it is now seen that infants actively engage in interpersonal relationships with their caretakers in the first weeks after birth, and that newborns establish remarkably effective control over the mental process of those who seek communication with them" (1981, p. 212). We have a striking convergence of data regarding gestures, facial expression, gazing, grasping, vocalization, and representation that shows the foundations of the infant's early semiotic capacity.

I will attempt to summarize Trevarthen's findings by focusing on his paper, "Signs Before Speech" (1989), whose main purpose "is to describe *infant semiotics*—the beginnings and early development of symbolic communication" (1989, p. 689). Trevarthen takes a broad view of the domain of human semiotics, distinguishing it from animal semiotics which, beyond its role in cooperative animal behavior, may even convey ideas and assist other animals to change their consciousness of surroundings. This is well documented in the case of bees by Benveniste who views their communication not as a language but as a signal code: "All the characteristics of a [signal] code are present: the fixity of the subject matter, the invariability of the message, the relation to a single set of circumstances, the impossibility of separating the components of the message, and its unilateral transmission" (1952, p. 54). Trevarthen writes: "But human beings live uniquely in a world where everything perceived and all related thoughts and actions that may be important in their life together are known in a symbolic form of consciousness—a consciousness shared by means of signs that are arbitrary both in their perceived form and in their produced uses, and independent of the 'here and now' in any one individual's experience" (1989, p. 689–90). This human world is not simply the product of social cooperation as, for example, we find in the social structure of baboons, ants, or bees; Trevarthen stresses that human meaning is the product of a unique mental tradition, not reducible to the signal code of animals, and requires the distinctive quality of intersubjectivity.

The period of what Trevarthen calls "primary intersubjectivity," from birth to nine months, has specific innate foundations in the child's anticipatory seeking for meaningful sharing. The semiotic process "requires that minds will meet in mutual, mirroring consciousness, that they will negotiate and make some measure of agreement about how to represent the factual but imaginary story they want to share" (1989, p. 690). Such agreement, such acts of cooperation in getting at meaning "require relationships of trust, admiration, respect, or obedience. In a word, they require varieties of *empathy*" (1989, p. 690). From his review of infancy research, Modell concurs "that mother and infant unconsciously replicate within themselves the affective experience of the other" (1993, p. 120).

Such replicative empathy, insofar as from the start it involves a mirroring consciousness, rests on an iconic process. This process, a feature of Lacan's register of the imaginary that he calls "homeomorphic identification" (1977, p. 3), is found in animals. Trevarthen writes: "Many species of animal have a level of intersubjectivity, but only humans have evolved an interest in sharing, both imitatively and expressively, a symbolic world of historically generated meaning" (1989, p. 692). This early, iconic, automatic form of intersubjectivity develops into what Trevarthen calls "secondary intersubjectivity" not found in animals. This developmental advance requires that a specifically semiotic structure be operative from or even before birth:

> A seemingly inescapable conclusion from the evidence of the efficiency of infant communication behavior. . . . is that the intersubjective mind has to be built in development by self-organization of a starting state that is *dual*—that is, it has to have a distinct *self* and a different *other* virtually functional in it from the first time it communicates. (1989, p. 692)

This "other" in the infant's mind I would interpret as equivalent to Lacan's notion of the counterpart, an iconic structure that enables mirroring and empathy to constitute the earliest moments of consciousness. For Trevarthen, such otherness appears to be a built-in feature of semiotic capacity, perhaps intrinsic to the act of signing.

Trevarthen seems to be saying that some sort of psychological self-other distinction must be present at birth in order to account for the rapid semiotic learning that takes place in the infant. The infant's reactions to the still-face mother, for example, also "give revealing evidence as to the emotional and other equipment with which the child is endowed to repair or escape from a communication that threatens to fall apart" (1989, p. 693). The evidence he goes on to present "for the thesis of 'innate intersubjectivity'" (1989, p. 694) comes from observations of the interacting infant's gestures, facial expressions, gazing, and rhythm.

Within a few hours of birth, the human infant shows a selective preference for his or her mother's specific characteristics of speech or voicing, a familiarity that must have been learned in utero, as well as selective orientation to a mother's individual odor. The infant's orientation to the mother, so unlike the autistic state some psychoanalysts claimed for the infant, was well known to Lacan, for in 1951 he had written of the neonate: "His lack of sensory and motor coordination does not prevent the new-born baby from being fascinated by the human face, almost as soon as he opens his eyes to the light of day, nor from showing in the clearest possible way that from all the people around him he singles out his mother" (1951, p. 15). At one or two days infants will suck to produce their mother's voice, prefer speech sounds to other sounds, and prefer female to male voices; by five months of age infants can identify which silent visual image of lips articulating a sound matches a previously heard vowel sound (Kuhl and Meltzoff, 1982), a set of findings about the salience of the human voice that leads Murray and Trevarthen to conclude: "Evidence is accumulating that the quality of emotion is transmitted with particular precision and refinement in the human voice, by pitch and intonation characteristics and quality of the voice, and that these aspects have high salience in infant perception" (1985, p. 180). Terhune (1979) has also noted, from his twenty-five years of pediatric practice, the infant's sensitivity to the human voice, as well as the relative scarcity of psychoanalytic references to the ear and hearing.

Some newborns, a few minutes old, can mimic a variety of things like facial expressions of emotion, mouth openings, simple hand movements, and tongue protrusions (Field, 1985; Field et al., 1982; Maratos, 1982; Meltzoff, 1985; Meltzoff and Moore, 1977, 1983). Although some of these observations were initially challenged (Jacobson and Kagan, 1979), the findings have remained robust, lending support to the developmental primacy of the icon in coerced empathy. Expressive gestures are especially reactive to the flow of the mother's vocalizations and facial expressions (Trevarthen, 1986). Regarding these neonatal observations, Trevarthen (1989) concludes that "the uniformity of the basic features of *timing* (kinematics), anatomic *form* (physiognomy) and *energy* of expressions, and their transitions in close engagements is sure evidence that autonomous, self-organizing principles of brain development create matching capacities for intersubjective engagement between infant and caretaker" (1989, p. 698). He then examines how the infant progresses from the intensely intimate matching behaviors to "the kind of open communication that leads to the making of what a semiotician would call a sign" and states that this change "to genuine, reciprocal exchange of messages with informative and referential potential comes very early" (1989, p. 698). By three or four weeks of age some infants will stop crying at the sight or sound of the mother's approach (Demos, 1992), suggesting that the indices of her presence are being used to alter states of upset.

Around six weeks of age there is noticeable improvement in the infant's ability to perform selective visual orientations; the eyes are focused more quickly and fixed more definitely on the eyes of a person leaning toward the baby and speaking softly. The infant's response to voice and gaze "gives a strong signal" (1989, p. 698) to the mother whose intonations are paced in alternation with the infant's to create a turn-taking form of vocalization that is tightly regulated. But this mutually controlled process not only controls sound: it also coordinates head movements, facial expressions, and hand gestures with such precision that this form of expressive interaction has been called a "protoconversation" (Bateson, 1975). Indeed, at two months of age infants can discern phonetic changes, such as from "ba" to "ga", in less than one-half second, as determined by studies of brain electrical currents (Dehaene-Lambertz and Dehaene, 1994).

From six to twelve weeks of age such protoconversations are "intensely and directly interpersonal, and exclusive of other kinds of interest" (Trevarthen, 1989, p. 701). But infants are capable of interrupting and withdrawing from these interactions and may even turn away to focus on something else, indicating that when interaction does occur it is a mutual engagement:

> Protoconversation between infants and their caretakers has, then, invariant features which reflect (a) coordination between the various channels of expression and modalities of awareness of the infant, who behaves as a coherent subject; and (b) a mutual comprehension or empathy by means of which infant and partner assist each other to create an integrated and patterned engagement. Different qualities of engagement are determined by a common or shared *spectrum of emotions* which gain organization between them by their mutual influence on each other in the communications. (1989, p. 702)

Infant communications are better coordinated and more elaborate in response to a partner showing appropriate empathy, acting according to "matching emotional and cooperative rules," implying that "the infant is prepared to participate in a certain way" (1989 pp. 702–703). Contrary to other widely held views, Trevarthen concludes that such semiotic preparation is not reducible to a search for recurrent stimulation, an interest in novelty, or the production of contingent events, for "the peculiar regularities of emotions are evidence for a motivation that defines persons as having additional, special conversational and empathic properties" (1989, p. 703).

This specifically human motivation, what Lacan called "the subject's fundamental need, which is to gain recognition" (1953–54, p. 247), is salient, as we
saw earlier, in the distinctive way infants relate to persons versus inanimate
objects as well as in the unmistakable response to the still-face interaction:

> If the mother holds herself still and unreactive, this causes the baby to
> become unhappy and watchful, then withdrawn and distressed . . . The
> behavior of the infant is sad or angry, depressed or protesting; it is not
> chaotic or uninterpretable. . . . Movements of the body, face, eyes, and vocal
> system are coordinated to make clear and distinct messages that elicit strong
> feelings of concern, unhappiness, and anxiety in the mother. (Trevarthen,
> 1989, p. 703)

Such distress in view of the still-face mother is highly specific, for the infant is
not distressed by the distracting entrance of the experimenter (Murray and
Trevarthen, 1985), perhaps because the 30-second interruption is not experienced by the infant as the mother's refusal to recognize but as a mutual state of
interruption caused by a third.[1] Distress does occur, however, when the infant,
engaging in live interaction by means of video screens, is unexpectedly presented with a video replay (a 30 second delay) of the mother in a previous
happy and lively interaction with the infant which, of course, is now inappropriate to the ongoing moment of the protoconversation. What is missing in this
delayed video condition is not the mother's gaze or positive affect but rather her
meaningful, organized behavior, her responsive recognition of the infant's specific semiotic gestures: "The test proves that it is the precise interplay of address
and reply in time that keeps the happy engagement going" (Trevarthen, 1989, p.
703). From their data Murray and Trevarthen conclude: "The more complex
motivations attributed to infants by psychoanalytic and ethological theorists
are substantiated by the distinctive quality of response evoked in the infant by
each of the different kinds of perturbation" (1985, p. 192).

When the test is reversed and the mother, during live video interaction, is
presented, without being informed, with a delayed video replay of the infant,
she feels something is wrong: in her anxious response she becomes more

---

1. In his Seminar Lacan refers to a paper by Susan Isaacs which mentions "that very
    early on, at an infants age still, between eight and twelve months, the child simply
    does not react in the same way to an accidental knock, to a fall, a brutal mechani-
    cal act related to a piece of clumsiness, and, on the other hand, to a slap with a
    punitive intention" (1953–54, p. 179). Lacan had already alluded to this finding in
    his 1948 paper, "Aggressivity in Psychoanalysis," where he wrote: "Only Melanie
    Klein, working on the child at the very limit of the appearance of language, dared
    to project subjective experience back to the earlier period when observation
    enables us nevertheless to affirm its dimension, in the simple fact for example that a
    child who does not [yet] speak reacts differently to punishment or brutality" (1977,
    p. 20).

directive, corrective, and negative toward the infant, similar to the communicative attempts made by those who work with autistic children (Murray and Trevarthen, 1986). From a Peircean perspective, we can say that the basic disruption is in the process of semiosis, the ongoing interplay between sign and interpretant, with the feeling and action interpretants no longer functioning as signs eliciting responses from the other partner despite repeated productions of signs. When the other's responses to the signing process fall out of timing, the structure of intersubjective recognition collapses. Such disrupted semiosis, furthermore, may provide some of the necessary conditions for projective identification to occur whereby the feeling and action interpretants of one's signs are disavowed and enacted by the other member of the dyad.

Around three months of age the infant shows greater exploration of the environment and manipulation of objects. He or she can now locate and track distant objects and events by sight and hearing, and the attempts to touch objects by hand become better controlled. The beginning of deictic activity, namely pointing, has been reliably observed to occur before three months, in conjunction with arm extension, vocalization, and mouthing (Turkington, 1992). Such pointing behavior may indicate the infant's growing semiotic competence to shift from iconic coercion to a more directive and ostensive use of the index. As we shall see later, this shift from enacted iconicity to active use of the index and deixis may function as the semiotic fulcrum of reality testing.

By three and one-half months infants behave in ways that indicate they understand something about object permanence. Demos (1992) reviews the work of Baillargeon (1990) who demonstrated that infants understand that objects go on existing even when hidden, that they cannot traverse space occupied by objects, and that space is continuous. The infant's experiences of concern at failure and joy in mastery are also evident at this time. The inherent motivation for exploring and performing actions, as so cogently presented by White (1960), assists in the learning of representations and opens up the "consciousness of an integrated 'behavior space' centered on the body" (Trevarthen, 1989, p. 707). More elaborate "person-person" games develop, including the singing of four-line musical stanzas, used by mothers across varying cultures, which last about 12 seconds. The rhythm is quickly learned by the infant and the song's introduction, build-up, climax, and resolution provide the infant with a proto-narrative structure (1989, p. 709).

By four and a half months infants recognize their own names, prefer to listen to their own names in a prosodically similar series, and therefore appear to have a differentiated representation of the sound patterns of their own names (Mandel, Jusczyk, and Pisoni, 1994). By six months, as reported by Kuhl and her associates, the exposure to a specific language alters phonetic perception, resulting in "language-specific phonetic prototypes that assist infants in organizing speech sounds into categories" (1992, p. 608).

After five months Trevarthen notes the appearance of what he calls "a quality of pretense" as the infant displays "*self-regard, self-imitation,* and, later, *posing for self-appreciation in a mirror*" (1989, p. 711). Lacan (1977), as we shall examine in later chapters, had noted the infant's fascination with his or her mirror image as starting around six months; Trevarthen observed infants at four months staring at their mirror images in a one-way mirror: "Attention to the mirror is evidently a side effect of self-consciousness in response to the attention of others (i.e., part of a self-other consciousness), because at the same time he or she discovers the fun of watching the mirror self, the baby is becoming more expert at *sharing jokes and showing off,* with precisely and appropriately regulated eye contact, with the familiar and appreciative partner" (1989, p. 716). In this way the infant has begun to "play with the intentions of others" (1989, p. 716), tuning in to their desires, engaging desire with desire.

At six months of age the infant's play with mother is full of "metacommunications" in the form of teasing, learned vocal performances, using habitual grimaces or gestures, challenging one another's expressions: "The infant *imitates* more deliberately and with more discrimination, and uses the imitated acts as signs which can be offered or withheld to control the partner" (1989, p. 716), thereby showing greater ability to orient behavior to her interests and intentions. In the maternal still-face experiment, infants now will often repeat a learned trick or funny expression "with insistence and looking hard at the mother to excite some response, thereby making it very difficult for the mother to keep sober and unresponsive" as she "averts her gaze and struggles not to laugh" (1989, p. 717):

> The very wide range of mannerisms, expressions, actions, and ritual performances that are "shown off" as "jokes" or "tricks" by infants between six and twelve months of age gives us a broad scope for interpretation of "infant semiotics." . . . All these "displays" increase in subtlety and complexity in the second year, but they start in the first. It should be emphasized that such acts of communication are not simply framed or "scaffolded" by the partner, although they are learned at first by imitation in interaction. They are recreated by the child out of this favorable intersubjective learning situation. (1989, p. 731)

At seven to eight months of age the infant, when confronted by a stranger, will make a brief show of friendliness, of learned tricks, along with indicating suspicious fear and sensitivity to incomprehension or ridicule by a stranger to whom such displays are unfamiliar. Trevarthen describes these "offerings" of learned fragments of behavior as "protosigns," family conventions:

Their use with strangers, while inappropriate, is particularly interesting because it demonstrates that these acts are, for the baby, something to be exchanged socially . . . Unlike a sign stimulus in animal communication, it does not stimulate any particular innate pattern of response; it has an inherent arbitrariness of form or application carried in phatic communication. (1989, p. 720)

Over the second six months of age the infant learns to more carefully coordinate with the mother's orientation: "'Checking' behavior, by which the baby directs attention to the eyes, face, voice, or hands of the partner (or to various combinations of these) shows how the infants' growing awareness of how to coordinate with the other person's mind is coupled to a need for specific information on expressed details of their feelings, interests, and intentions" (1989, p. 724). From the earliest months the infant has regulated such direct interpersonal contacts, but the checking-back behavior shows remarkable development over the first year:

After six months they are increasingly aware of the possibility that what they are about to do can be qualified by how their mothers will feel about it, and they systematically start to orient to gain *emotional referencing* from their mothers' faces and voices . . .

All these interactions of subjectivities (intersubjectivities) lay the groundwork for joint appreciation of reality and for communication by symbols and language. (1989, pp. 724–25).

All of this I have quoted at length because it has enormous importance for a psychoanalytic understanding of identification and desire. The infant as a communicative and dissimulating semiotic partner appears to be intent on knowing how his or her actions please or displease mother; intent, we might say, on being found desirable.

After nine months of age the infant moves on to what Trevarthen calls "secondary intersubjectivity," as marked by performance on an experimental procedure in which mothers were asked to get their infants to put three wooden dolls in a toy truck. Before the age of nine months, infants play with the toys but do not attend to the instructions. After nine months, however, they are able and willing to attend and comply with the mother's instructions. Infants can now assist and comment on another person's interest through gesture and voice; such a two-channel system can be codified protolinguistically for deaf as well as hearing infants: "Thus at the age when a normal hearing child is mastering how to perform illocutionary acts by vocalizing in a speech-like way with the help of gestures, a deaf child in a signing family starts to pay attention to and imitate hand signs, using them appropriately to indicate wishes, interests, and purposes to companions" (1989, p. 728).

Referentiality is now explicit and inclusive of what lies beyond the dyad, for the "nine- to twelve-month-old's awareness of a shared reality and its signifi- cance" means the infant can now learn about things from observing how others treat them (1989, p. 731). A similar timetable for triadic interaction is reported by Bakeman and Adamson wherein by thirteen months infants can "enter read- ily into nonverbal referential communication with a person about a present object" (1984, p. 1279). In the first study to demonstrate such results, fourteen- month-olds were observed to imitate a peer who was previously trained to produce specific effects with a set of objects; the imitation was observed across different contexts (from lab to home, from day care center to home), and took place even with a delay of two days (Hanna and Meltzoff, 1993).

Toddlers comprehend what is said in specific pragmatic and interpersonal contexts even though they have little or no production of speech. Although their attempts at speech may be poorly articulated, they can control "a range of protolanguage vocalizations with subtle and appropriate intonation" (Trevarthen, 1989, p. 734) and gestural communication is also well-developed. Handedness now emerges, indicating hemispheric differentiation of semiotic functioning, echoing our earlier discussion of how the brain distinguishes semi- otic space from sensory-motor space in deaf signers:

> An interesting feature is that, as children's manipulation of objects becomes ruled by shared conventions and semantic principles, a majority of them show an increasingly clear *handedness*. Most are right-handed for manipu- lative acts of meaning, for using implements, signs, etc., either in commu- nication or for their private imaginative play . . . Ordinary "sensory-motor" or exploratory play, unqualified by interpretations or recognitions that function in communication, does not show such clear asymmetry. (Trevarthen, 1989, p. 734–35)

A fundamental change in self-awareness appears near the end of the second year with the appearance, as Kagan (1981) reported, of "a *heightened anxiety* about broken or defective things, about naughty (punishable) acts, and about potential criticism—especially from a stranger—about inability to understand something or do a prescribed task" (Trevarthen, 1989, p. 735). The experience of self-cohesion, of a bounded self, now appears dependent on the meeting of standards, on the embrace of an ideal, on being found pleasing (the role imita- tion plays in this will be examined in Chapter 8). Congruent with the consol- idation of a Lacanian ego, some authors stress how the second year is marked by the infant's exercise of power in relationships, self-assertion, and attempts to control others, fostering an illusion of omnipotence which, when challenged, leads to crying (Urwin, 1984).

Imaginative play in this period is more discriminating and has more structure when done with mother than when done alone. Play with peers, described as "parallel" or in "clusters," tends not to be complementary but replicative and iconic. Lacan (1977) wrote of the "transitivism" of the toddler who tends to confuse his or her self-image with the visual presentation of another as counterpart, so that a child will cry or even fall when watching another child being struck or pushed.

By three years of age the child has become more self-possessed and articulate and can speak to others about non-present events; there is a great deal of evidence "for the entry of a child of this age into a symbolic and cultural world" (Trevarthen, 1989, p. 737), into what Lacan called the symbolic order or what Peirce termed "Thirdness."

For Trevarthen, the semiotic child grows out of the semiotic infant, engaged in communication from the start, open to the other and to the semiotic field. He cites Vygotsky (1962) in affirming the priority of intermental processes over intramental ones: "We think and remember symbolically because we communicate symbolically," because there is "motivation for inter-subjective relatedness and mixing of thoughts with an 'other'" (Trevarthen, 1989, p. 738), contrary to "the Piagetian theoretical system [in which] the toddler is described as 'preoperational' and 'egocentric,' as if incapable of engaging with another person's thoughts or noticing their differing point of view" (Trevarthen, 1989, p. 742; see also Gibson, 1987). For Trevarthen, the foundation for the infant's semiotic capacity is "a general expressive mechanism in the brain that links oral, auditory, manual, and visual sensory and motor channels in such a way that they are complementary and equivalent for making ideas expressive in language" (Trevarthen, 1986, p. 154). In Peircean terms, all of these channels participate in semiosis, are governed by a common semiotic code, and are elaborated in a developmental line from enacted iconicity (coerced mirroring) to indexicality (pointing) to symbolization (conventional gestures and words), engaging a range of signs whose "feeling interpretants" are more commonly referred to as affects or emotions. In this framework "emotions are, if nothing else, semiotic mediators linking the body, the subject, and the social" (G. White, 1994, p. 220). Framed by a semiotic code that is culturally determined, "emotions can be viewed as a set of socially shared scripts composed of various processes—physiological, subjective, and behavioral—that develop as individuals actively (personally and collectively) adapt and adjust to their immediate sociocultural, semiotic environment" (Markus and Kitayama, 1994, pp. 339–40).

In demonstrating the iconic capacity of neonates, just thirty-six hours after birth, to discriminate and mimic three different facial expressions (happy, sad, and surprised), Field and her associates conclude that there is an innate ability to compare the sensory information of a visually perceived expression (as evidenced in this study by their ability to discriminate the facial expressions) with the proprioceptive feedback of the movements involved in matching that expression (as manifested by their differential responses to the facial expressions). (1982, p. 181)

This is remarkably similar to the way Freud in his "Project for a scientific psychology" described how we learn to know others (1895, pp. 393–94).

Iconic resemblance powerfully fosters knowledge and solidarity across all natural domains. Peirce insisted the icon was essential to all forms of knowledge: "The only way of directly communicating an idea is by means of an icon; and every indirect method of communicating an idea must depend for its establishment upon the use of an icon" (1940, p. 105). The contemporary examination of layered resemblance known as "fractals" (Kellert, 1993), may have great methodological importance in future psychoanalytic research. We are familiar with the layered ways that repetition occurs. For example, in supervision a therapist reports that a patient speaks of taking on some responsibility and thereby feeling "ahead" of the therapist's other patients; the therapist responds by pointing out how this is similar to the patient's rivalry with a sibling. The patient experiences this remark as hurtful and becomes angry. The supervisor points out how the therapist's remark appears to have narcissistically injured the patient, placing the therapist "ahead" of the patient. When the therapist in turn looks injured by the supervisor's comment, the supervisor notes that perhaps the therapist now experiences a narcissistic injury because the supervisor is now "ahead." The repetition appears to have a fractal structure, like a coastline whose broad outlines are repeated no matter how small and detailed is the piece of littoral we examine. Such resemblances have mathematical and topological implications for complexity, chaos, and catastrophe theories (see also Moran, 1991).

The infant's iconic response or, insofar as it is automatic, this coerced mirroring of the facial expression of the other, is but one of a set of profoundly isomorphic natural processes elucidated by René Thom (1973) in his pioneer paper on catastrophe theory. Thom, who participated for a time in Lacan's seminars, noted how a number of images appear naturally, according to physical processes, such as the sun casting a man's shadow on the ground, or a foot leaving an impression on the sand. He states that both an image and its model are extended in space, and that their correspondence may be formulated according to a geometrical transformation.

An additional feature determining the image's longevity is the plasticity of the imaging medium or receptor system, its "competence": the dynamic of life, even at the molecular level of DNA, has evolved remarkable competence in creating reproductive icons with homeostatic systems. Processes of perception are also remarkable for their capacity to receive sensorial impressions, store them in memory, and remain plastic for new ones. In this iconic proliferation, the signifier (the image) is engendered by the signified (the model), but the off-spring in turn will engender its own image. Lacan had called attention to the engendering power of the icon as he reviewed data from ethological studies: "These data showed that the sexual maturation of the female pigeon depends entirely on its seeing a member of its own species, male or female, to such an extent that while the maturation of the bird can be indefinitely postponed by the lack of such perception, conversely the mere sight of its own reflection in a mirror is enough to cause it to mature almost as quickly as if it had seen a real pigeon" (1951, p. 14).

For a living being to survive, certain actions are indispensable, especially with regard to its prey and its predators. The effects of such actions are signs, what Peirce specified as indices. Unlike icons, which impact through what Jakobson calls a "factual similarity," indices operate "by a factual, existential contiguity" (1965, p. 415). To prevent or gain the biological "catastrophes" of eating or being eaten, such indices (tracks, odors, shadows) must be precisely interpreted and soon enough.

In distinction from the icon and the index, the symbol stands for its object through learned convention, or, as Jakobson states, "through imputed, learned contiguity" (1965, p. 415). Human language consists of a system of symbols which vastly increases our capacity to represent and to anticipate, if not always to forestall, catastrophe, including the ultimate catastrophe of death. Among humans, as among animals, semiotic activity originates in regulation, the home-ostatic regulation of the living organism, as well as the stability of the social body. Semiotics at first has an imperative value, which endures unconsciously, linked, Thom stated, to the experience of the sacred.

The symbol and the culture it makes possible have so altered experience that humans now differ from animals in three distinct ways. First, the psychic life of animals appears captured in automatic reactions to the perception of biologically important objects such as prey or predators. At the sight of prey there is a "catastrophe" of perception in which the predator psychically "becomes" its prey, it identifies with it, and does so only when an index of actual prey has been apprehended, not imagined or remembered. The index, perceived and interpreted, triggers a fixed set of motor actions that run their course toward capture. Second, because of such "fascinations" (just the word Lacan used with reference to "imaginary captivations"), the "ego" of the animal is not permanent but is re-formed in each sensory-motor pursuit. The animal, moreover, does not seem to have an ongoing consciousness of its body as the center of its activities, as Trevarthen ascribes to the infant. Third, the animal does not seem to have a continuous notion of space, a Euclidean geometry, but rather a set of unintegrated maps for actions taken by distinct "egos" in pursuit, escape, feeding, and courtship, maps, in other words, for specific "physiological callings" (Thom, 1973, p. 103).

Humans, in contrast, are liberated from the fascination of things by giving them a name and thereby inhabiting a "semantic space" structured by concepts, roles, relationships, and codes (this recalls the symbolic use of space, as Sacks noted, in left-brain activity). This liberation from the immediacy of things enables humans to establish more permanent egos based on the representation of the body in space, a space conceived as a universal continuum, a subset of which is enclosed by the reflective surface of the mirror, whose captivating quality is thereby relativized. Such a mental construction of space, in turn, provides a structure for founding the identity of things on their spatial localization. One can consider, Thom stated, that the infant evolves from a state of fascination by things as the use of symbols develops and the grip of the "here-and-now" is loosened. We recall Wolff's comment about the apparent release of the infant from "stimulus-boundedness," an example of how "ontogenesis comprises a sequence of discontinuous 'catastrophes'" (Wolff, 1987, p. 266; see also Kagan, 1979). Such a sequence is not controlled by either intrinsic or extrinsic executives, but brought about through small variations in the self-organizing dynamics of the infant interacting with small differences (such as the phonetic differentiations that begin to take hold by six months) in environmental input (see also Fogel and Thelen, 1987; Thelen and Smith, 1994; Thelen, 1995).

Thom ends his paper by considering how, before ten months of age, the infant's vocalizations include all the phonemes (the phonetic inclusiveness of babbling is parallelled by the gestural inclusiveness of the "sign-babbling" of deaf infants, as reported by Petitto and Marentette [1991]). As parents discourse in their own language, the child retains only those phonemes he or she hears (or, in the case of gestures, sees) as the language is learned. In a closing metaphor, Thom describes how the mathematician (Thom, referring to himself) likewise babbles before nature; but only those who can hear Mother Nature's response will open a dialogue with her and go on to learn a new language. And where, Thom asks, can the mathematician hear the response of nature? "The voice of reality is in the sense [le sens] of the symbol" (Thom, 1973, p. 106).

I take symbol here in the broadest sense, to mean sign, and therefore inclusive of the icon and the index. This is crucial, for the problem of referentiality, of what Freud called reality testing and the perception of "signs" of reality ("Realitätszeichen," 1950, p. 417; 1985, p. 395) as well as scientific investigation, requires a consideration of the index. In Lacan's terms, how is it that psychoanalysis can impact on the Real? How can speech alter physical processes? The system of language is vast, and semiosis is an open-ended hierarchical process, as summarized by Dewey (1946) who stated

that Peirce uniformly holds (1) that there is no such thing as a sign in isolation, every sign being a constituent of a sequential set of signs, so that
apart from membership in this set, a thing has no meaning—or is not a
sign; and (2) that in the sequential movement of signs thus ordered, the
meaning of the earlier ones in the series is provided by or is constituted by
the later ones as their interpretants, until a conclusion (logical as a matter of
course) is reached. Indeed, signs, . . . as such, form an infinite series, so that
no conclusion of reasoning is forever final, being inherently open to
having its meaning modified by further signs. (1946, p. 88)

This endless dissemination of meaning would lead to madness if we could not
anchor the process. Dewey at this point invoked the role of the index:

> Linguistic signs, constituting thought and conferring generality, continuity,
> law, are cases of Thirdness. They have of themselves no reference to
> "things." Such connection as they can have is, accordingly, dependent upon
> the intervention of another factor. This factor (called Secondness by
> Peirce) is of a radically different sort from Thirdness. It is particularity as
> against generality; brute interruption as against continuity; contingency as
> against law. (1946, p. 90)

Any "reference of linguistic signs to things is accomplished," according to
Dewey, "through their getting into connection with indexical signs" (1946, p.
90) so that, I take it, contiguous "facts" and "effects" become anchors for
thought; but the index brings us into connection with "things" (with the
actions of persons, more to the point) because, Dewey writes,

> there is a conjunction of the "Secondness" of an indexical sign with the
> movement of linguistic signs, or "Thirdness," thereby bringing the latter to
> a close in a way which links it to the former, and thereby also conferring
> generality, reasonableness, upon what in itself is like a sheer bumping of
> things into one another. (1946, p. 91)

The movement of signs, the process of semiosis, must be under way for the
index to be apprehended as an index with general import, not simply as a signal
triggering a fixed response as in animals. But the semiotic process, and psychoanalysis itself as the talking cure, would be an irrelevant or maddening drift of
verbiage without the action of indices to impact on the Real and on the verbal
process.

In early infancy iconic relations are enacted. The mother's smiling gaze
brings about its replica in the infant; the infant's smiling gaze, in turn, produces
a mirroring response in the mother. While these are indices of contiguous presence, their immediate impact comes from their function as icons, replicating
what is at first missing in the other. The relationship between these iconic

enactments is reversible in direction of causality and representability: either smiling gaze can bring about the other. In the case of the index, however, Dewey states that we find a "principle of irreversibility" which anchors the semiotic process in reality.[2] Iconic relations are the support of fantasy and hallucination; indexical relations with their irreversible conditions are required for reality testing to develop, and for causal relations to be apprehended, for no amount of staring at the footprint of a departed person will cause the person to return. The descriptive power of iconic relations supports the illusion that one can reproduce what is missing, but the index is required to confirm what is present. Peirce wrote:

> The actual world cannot be distinguished from a world of imagination by any description. Hence the need of pronouns and indices, and the more complicated the subject the greater the need of them (1992, p. 227)
>
> The index asserts nothing; it only says "There!" It takes hold of our eyes, as it were, and forcibly directs them to a particular object, and there it stops. (1992, p. 226)

The index is an affront to infantile grandiosity; we must learn to follow the index if we are to survive, rather than imagine reality as we wish it to be. Such bowing to necessity, as Freud emphasizes, constrains us in a number of ways. We must learn to take the index *as an index,* not simply as an object; this requires that what we perceive is also inscribed in another register, that of signs. The sign, the index, refers to an object; we cannot simply imagine the object as we wish it to be, but as we learn of it from the index. We cannot simply retrieve the lost object by imagining its index: the index must strike us, we are not in control of it. In its irreversibility, the index teaches us that we must suffer the loss, make memorials to the past, and make do with substitutes.

---

2. Jakobson makes the same point when he states: "Indices, which the physicist extracts from the external world, are not reversible" (1985, p. 31).

4

Intersubjectivity through Semiotics

In attempting to show that psychoanalysis must go beyond the psychoanalytic dyad, I have emphasized the place of the Third as inclusive of the semiotic code that positions speakers, determines deixis, and governs semiosis. Brickman conceptualizes the Third as the use of inference in conjunction with "a working model of a dynamic unconscious," whose effect is to stabilize the dyad and "prevent a drift toward symbiosis" (1993, p. 905). I take him to mean by this what I have been calling coerced mirroring: "A major effect of the deliberate and undisavowed use of inference is the prevention of therapeutic tautology and symbiosis, as exists in the phenomenon of 'tracking'" (1993, p. 911). An emphasis on tracking and attunement, "on mutual understanding at the expense of interpretation of conflictual material in the transference," may evoke "merger anxiety" (1993, p. 912). The Third is required to frame the dyad and thereby enable the partners to relate without merging.

In this chapter I will try to show that the contemporary paradigm shift in psychoanalysis, a dyadic framework referred to as "intersubjectivity" (see, for example, Stolorow and Atwood, 1992), requires and rests on a broader foundation than self-psychology can provide and has a two-hundred-year-old history in continental philosophy. The complexity of intersubjectivity, many have argued (Williams, 1992; Theunissen, 1977), can best be understood when the dyadic processes of empathy and recognition are taken as operating in a triadic context in which a semiotic code frames and holds the dyad. It is the determining presence of such a code, shaping culture, communication, and context, that makes possible the saying of "I" and "you" whereby the human horizon is opened to the reach of intimacy, both personal and perhaps also transcendent.

The complexity of the reach is perhaps most clearly seen in the case of autistic children, who have a well-documented difficulty in the use of "I" and "you" (Fay, 1979). In a remarkable interview with an autistic adult, Temple Grandin, a farm-science Ph.D. whose publications, animal-handling methods, and cattle-pen designs are widely known among agriculturalists, Oliver Sacks writes:

> I was struck by the enormous difference, the gulf, between Temple's immediate, intuitive recognition of animal moods and signs and her extraordinary difficulties understanding human beings, their codes and signals, the way they conducted themselves. One could not say that she was devoid of feeling or had a fundamental lack of empathy. On the contrary, her sense of animals' moods and feelings was so strong that these almost took possession of her, overwhelmed her at times. She feels she can have sympathy for what is physical or physiological—for an animal's pain or terror—but lacks empathy for people's states of mind and perspectives. (1993–94, p. 116)

From the model we have been examining, we would say that a severe impasse occurred on the semiotic developmental line from iconic mirroring to index to symbol; she is gifted in using icons and indices but has ongoing difficulty with culturally determined symbols. In Lacanian terms, the transition from imaginary to symbolic registers was severely disrupted: "At the level of the sensorimotor, the concrete, the unmediated, Temple is enormously sensitive," writes Sacks (1993–94, p. 116), but she does not have "an implicit knowledge of social conventions and codes, of cultural presuppositions of every sort," and as a child "she mixed all her pronouns up, not able to grasp the different meanings of 'you' and 'I,' depending on context" (1993–94, p. 116). She looks back on a childhood marked by confusion and social alienation:

> Something was going on between the other kids, something swift, subtle, constantly changing—an exchange of meanings, a negotiation, a swiftness of understanding so remarkable that sometimes she wondered if they were all telepathic. She is now aware of the existence of these social signals. She can infer them, she says, but she herself cannot perceive them, cannot participate in this magical communication directly, or conceive the many-levelled, kaleidoscopic states of mind behind it. (1993–94, p. 116)

If we keep Peirce's perspective in mind, I think we can hear this as a precise and poignant description of the process of semiosis in human beings, a process that is intrinsically intersubjective for Peirce, and what happens to this process when the sign's interpretant becomes fixed or the movement from sign to interpretant to sign-for-another becomes blocked. There is a frozen quality to Temple's narrations, evident in her manner of repeating stories in virtually the same words. Sacks writes:

> I was struck both by the vividness of the reexperience, the memory for her—it seemed to play itself in her mind with extraordinary detail—and by its unwavering quality. It was as if the original scene, its perception (with all its attendant feelings), was reproduced, replayed, with virtually no modification. This quality of memory . . . seemed to me both prodigious and pathological—prodigious in its detail and pathological in its fixity, more akin to a computer record than to anything else. (1993–94, p. 121)

Temple does not alter her narrative in response to cues from her listener, and therefore does not seem to be including the subjective perspective of her listener in her account. But semiosis is intrinsically dialogic, the interpretants of our signs (the feeling, action, and logical interpretants) circulate through the feelings, actions, and thoughts of others and return to us, transformed by the subjectivity of the other, as new signs. This process seems impeded for Temple, her interpretants seem fixed, perhaps because they are constituted non-dialogically and hence not open to their role as signs for another and thereby open to influence by another mind. If this is the case, we can understand why, as Sacks writes, "achieving genuine friendship, appreciating other people for their otherness, for their own minds, may be the most difficult of all achievements for an autistic person" (1993–94, p. 117).

The question of how we can appreciate other minds, other people in their otherness, has been a major philosophical question at least since Kant. If, as Kant concluded, we cannot know "things in themselves" but only the appearances of things as structured by the categories of perception and understanding, then how can we affirm the knowledge of independently existing others? More than a century later, Husserl grappled with the same question as he explored the consequences of his phenomenological method. I state this only to suggest the dimensions of the problem, not to dwell on it; readers who wish to pursue this are encouraged to examine the work of Theunissen (1977), who surveys how sociality is handled in the work of Husserl, Heidegger, Sartre, and Buber, and concludes that dialogic considerations must play a central role in accounting for the knowledge of the other as other. The emergence of such knowledge of the other, moreover, is correlative with the emergence of self-consciousness and is the result of the active process of mutual recognition. This is essentially the position of Hegel, as presented by Williams (1992).

The relevance of Hegel (1807) for an understanding of intersubjectivity was emphasized by Lacan (1977) and has been noted subsequently (Muller, 1982a; Benjamin, 1990; Kirshner, 1992). In his most recent book, Modell states: "I doubt whether our present psychology of intersubjectivity could have developed without Hegel ... Hegel can justifiably be termed the first inter-subjective or relational psychologist" (1993, pp. 98–99). Although he has been stereotyped as an Idealist, dealing in abstractions, Hegel saw the complexity of intersubjective processes in their impact on desire, knowledge, and action. For Hegel, intersubjectivity rests on more than intuition or feeling, for it requires a broader base in a cultural and linguistic determination of a "we."

Notions of the human subject as a multilevelled process came prominently into Western philosophy through Hegel, in whose work both Lacan and Peirce found an emphasis on the self not as substance but as subject, not as isolated subject but as a subject in the intersubjective matrix of culture, not as a fixed entity but a subject understood as process, and not as a process that gradually unfolds positively but, rather, a process that operates through the dialectic of negation, suffering, division, and the shared memorialization of loss.

Williams states that "whenever the problem of the other is taken seriously, Hegel sooner or later becomes a topic of discussion" (1992, p. 12). Williams begins his own discussion of Hegel by noting what Hegel took from his predecessor, J.G. Fichte (1794): the notion of recognition as an action, a prior action by an other who summons me to a free response. For Fichte, Williams writes, "Human existence, as distinct from bare existence, is possible only as an inter-subjectively mediated social reality" (1992, p. 59) or, as Fichte put it, "Kein Du, Kein Ich," (1992, p. 53). What is crucial in constituting an "I" is not a perception or knowledge of the other but rather an act on my part whereby I recognize the other recognizing me. Williams writes: "This transposition of the problem of the other from epistemology to action is perhaps Fichte's most original contribution" (1992, p. 62).

Fichte's emphasis on action is of decisive importance to Hegel, for Hegel's effort to give an account of intersubjectivity is part of his effort as a social reformer to re-think the place of history, religion, law, and community. Hegel affirmed that we cannot adequately conceptualize the individual apart from a community, and, even further, the individual does not have an immediate relation to the self but relates to self only as mediated by the other. Since such mediation is never conflict-free, what Hegel adds to Fichte's notion of recognition is the dimension of domination, alienation, and struggle. Conflict becomes a moment in the process of achieving mutual recognition in the case of love or in the more widely cited example of the struggle between master and slave.

In the master-slave episode of Hegel's *Phenomenology of Spirit*, we have the classic example of how by forcing it one loses what is most desired. Initially one human consciousness is confronted by another in a primordial mirroring. Each first finds itself outside of itself, in another, in a moment of self-alienation. In order to overcome the sense of alienation and to confirm its unique status, each seeks then to impose itself on the other as the object of the other's desire, as the uniquely human object of desire. Each proclaims its human privilege by declaring its own biological existence worth risking in a struggle to the death to obtain the other's recognition. In this mythical encounter one must yield to the other, otherwise both would be dead and the process of history would go no further. The one who yields in fear of death becomes the slave, recognizing the other as master. The slave's products are consumed by the master, who thereby confers recognition on them as human products. In the master's case, however, the recognition for which he struggled is nullified, for its source is the slave whom the master will not recognize as human. While Hegel continues the process in its subsequent evolution through stoicism, skepticism, Christianity, and Western capitalism, for our purposes we stop with the master-slave episode as arguing for the importance of mutual recognition in the resolution of impasse.

Williams criticizes the "mistaken identification of master and slave with Hegel's entire account of intersubjectivity" (1992, p. 143), for Hegel's concern is to delineate a more general paradigm of intersubjectivity as a process in which: 1) the original, naive, and parochial consciousness is unable to recognize the other as other but finds only itself in the other; 2) this "self-othering" is experienced not as an elaboration but as an alienation from the self, as a reduction from an all-inclusive status to a relativized, particular one, what we might call a narcissistic affront to the grandiose, infantile self; 3) this loss of self must be overcome, particularity must be cancelled by the cancellation of the opposing other, the other as opposing; 4) in the ensuing struggle to gain the other's recognition, the necessity for the other's mediation becomes established; 5) such mediation is achievable only by letting the other go free, to freely provide recognition. In this process the self is returned to itself, not as it was immediately taken to be, but as enriched by the actions of mutual recognition. Williams writes: "This situation of mutual recognition is one of communicative freedom, which Hegel describes as being at home with self in another . . . The road to interiority passes through the other" (1992, pp. 149, 151).

I want to try, as clearly as I can, to elaborate the complexity of this process. What Hegel is saying, as Williams emphasizes (or at least as I understand it), is that intersubjectivity involves a relation of relations, a complex doubling that is not a reflection of sameness. In this process the immediate consciousness of singularity of identity becomes mediated through another subjectivity to yield a permanently altered sense of "we" along with an inner relation to oneself. It is the self's relation to itself, in both parties, that must be active and transformed in the act of mutual recognition. The dual structure of a "being-for-self" and a "being-for-other" are enhanced in both parties. Therefore Hegel can write:

"Self-consciousness is in and for itself in and through the fact that it exists in and for itself for an other. That is, it exists only as recognized or acknowledged" (1807, p. 111). I must do to the other what I desire the other to do to me, that is, to act as a self-consciousness freely recognizing the other as a self-consciousness different from me.

The psychological genesis of such a dual structure—a being-for-self as a subject and a being-for-other as intersubjective—is most clearly realized through love, as Williams writes: "In love, there is risk, but no loss of self; rather love involves a finding of self in the recognition given by the other. Love renounces coercion and allows the other to be" (1992, p. 184).

In originary love, whose effects may be observable in the descriptions of mother-infant mutual gazing, one is summoned to be, addressed as a "you" in a clearing opened up by deixis through the semiotic code that structures I-you-here-now positions. To the extent that the unconscious resonates with recognition and is capable of addressing and being addressed, we can speak of a semiotic subject not limited to the conscious ego. In the process of mutual recognition through which I becomes I in being addressed as a "you," we experience a "you" as the source and process of a calling-to. Such a calling-to or summoning, often most eloquent in silence (Dauenhauer, 1980), can be transformative (Buber, 1970). Some religious traditions find in the potentiality for such an unpredictable and unwarranted address by a "you," the arena for the signs and operations of what has been called grace. In any case, the status of "you" cannot be reduced to a projection of the ego or a replication of the self.

A. S. Byatt, in her novel *Still Life*, presents a mother and her newly-born son:

> She had not expected ecstasy. She noted that he was both much more solid, and, in the feebleness of his fluttering movements of lip and cheek muscle, the dangerous lolling of his uncontrolled head, more fragile, than she had expected. . . . She put out a finger and touched [his] fist; he obeyed a primitive instinct and curled the tiny fingers round her own, where they clutched, loosened, tightened again. "There," she said to him, and he looked, and the light poured through the window, brighter and brighter, and his eyes saw it, and hers, and she was aware of bliss, a word she didn't like, but the only one. There was her body, quiet, used, resting; there was her mind, free, clear, shining; there was the boy and his eyes, seeing what? And ecstasy. Things would hurt when this light dimmed. The boy would change. But now in the sun she recognized him, and recognized that she did not know, and had never seen him, and loved him, in the bright new air with a simplicity she had never expected to know. "You," she said to him, skin for the first time on skin in the outside air, which was warm and shining, "you." (1985, pp. 100–101)

Such a saying of "you" opens the dimension of intersubjectivity, not in what Kohut termed a self-selfobject relation but rather in what I would call a self-selfsubject relation made possible by the semiotics of dialogic exchange. I do not think the infancy research, as we saw in the last chapter, can be adequately comprehended by referring to the mother's role as a selfobject function, as carrying out for the infant a function necessary to the structuring of a cohesive self and thereby experienced by the infant as part of the self. What I believe Trevarthen (1989) shows is how an infant engages a mother, already known by voice and smell and tactile contiguity, not as an object but as a subject. The mother is not needed or sought as an object of desire or to carry out functions for the infant; the mother is sought as a subject, precisely with her own horizon of desire and intention, in order to carry out functions with the infant in acts of mutual recognition. Mutual recognition, as Benjamin reminds us, "is not a passion but a relational category" (1993, p. 448).

Such acts of mutual recognition are possible because the infant's rudimentary semiotic competence is engaged by the mother's deictic framework, concretized by her use of pronouns. The French linguist, Emile Benveniste, to whose work Lacan often refers (1955–56, 1966), wrote several papers on pronouns and subjectivity that have great relevance for psychoanalysis. In "The Nature of Pronouns" he notes that all languages have pronouns in order to carry out a set of complex functions. Pronouns are peculiar signs in utterances that are pragmatic, acts that include the one using the signs. These signs, the pronouns "I" and "you," are "shifters," they have no fixed content, but instead refer to a unique being each time they are used. In fact, what they refer to is not an object but a highly specific moment: *I* is "the individual who utters the present instance of discourse containing the linguistic instance *I*" (1956, p. 218). The same kind of reference is governed by "you" as the individual spoken to in the actual situation of an address. These pronouns, unlike other words, do not refer to a concept, do not assert anything, do not stand alone. "I" and "you" are reciprocally, dialectically held in distinction. They mark out positions in the dialogic space.

Consciousness of self can develop because this dialogic field is anchored by the personal pronouns. Benveniste writes:

> Consciousness of self is only possible if it is experienced by contrast. I use *I* only when I am speaking to someone who will be a *you* in my address. It is this condition of dialogue that is constitutive of *person*, for it implies that reciprocally *I* becomes *you* in the address of the one who in his turn designates himself as *I*. (1956, pp. 224–25).

Because of their intrinsic reference to the present moment of discourse, "I" and "you" are linked to a series of indices of the here-now-this sort that "delimit the spatial and temporal instance coextensive and contemporary with the present instance of discourse containing *I*" (1956, p. 219). In Peirce's terms, these are indexical signs, contiguously related to their objects, as in a finger pointing to an object, the smoke that indicates the presence of fire, or, in the case of "I" and "you," as products of the same act of speech. Such deictic terms direct the listener to the speaker's temporal and spatial coordinates, as Lyons states: "the basic function of deixis is to relate the entities and situations, to which reference is made in language, to the spatio-temporal zero-point—the here-and-now—of the context of utterance" (1982, p. 121). Deixis is required to establish context, an interweaving knotted at one pole by the speaker's spoken "I" as an index in contiguity with his or her act of speaking, and at the other pole by "you," spoken as pointing to the intended listener, who is also indicated by gazing. The psychologist Karl Bühler noted that (in Western culture, at least) "the most common form of indicating the addressee is through turning to the person and fixing him with one's eyes" (Innis, 1982, p. 21). It is the indexical structure of deixis that makes intersubjectivity possible and that gives it a sustaining structure. Unfortunately, as Mahony has written, "The important linguistic notion of deixis has been woefully neglected in Anglo-American psychoanalytic literature" (1989, p. 45).

Benveniste states of the pronouns: "The importance of their function will be measured by the nature of the problem they serve to solve, which is none other than that of intersubjective communication" (1956, p. 219). Pronouns achieve this by converting language, a general abstract system, into discourse, a particular concrete act of giving voice: "It is by identifying himself as a unique person pronouncing *I* that each speaker sets himself up in turn as the 'subject'" (1956, p. 220). I become I by using "I" in relation to "you" each time I refer to the instance of my own discourse. I become a subject, with a subjective dimension, by being addressed as "you" by a "you" whom I address, and this by subjecting my voice to the structure of language and thereby becoming capable of performing unique acts of discourse, of developing my unique voice.

In his paper, "Subjectivity in Language," Benveniste emphasizes that language is not a tool taken up by a human subject. On the contrary, language "is in the nature of man, and he did not fabricate it . . . It is in and through language that man constitutes himself as a *subject*" (1958, p. 224). Language alone establishes the voice of the self in its actuality, as actually saying "I": "The 'subjectivity' we are discussing here is the capacity of the speaker to posit himself as 'subject'" (1958, p. 224), and such self-positing is possible only in a reciprocal relation to a "you." Such a reciprocity of persons is "the fundamental condition in language" which makes discourse possible and is "the linguistic basis of subjectivity" (1958, p. 225). Because the use of "I" "refers to the act of individual discourse in which it is pronounced, and by this it designates the speaker," Benveniste can claim: "It is in the instance of discourse in which *I* designates the speaker that the speaker proclaims himself as the 'subject'" (1958, p. 226).

Such a self-positing has bearing on other central features of language. The indicators of deixis depend on the pronouns, for they organize spatial and temporal relationships around the "subject" taken as referent. The expression of temporality, its linguistic organization into tenses (whether governed by verbs, adverbs, or other particles), always involves a reference to the present. But the "present," writes Benveniste, is never a determination apart from the subject:

> Now this "present" in its turn has only a linguistic fact as temporal reference: the coincidence of the event described with the instance of discourse that describes it. The temporal referent of the present can only be internal to the discourse . . . Linguistic time is self-referential. (1958, p. 227)

To indicate the present requires an act of speech whose spatial-temporal coordinates of past and future are anchored by the spoken "I" of the speaker speaking in the present moment. The semiotic knot tied by this "I," its stable anchoring of an entire epistemological framework, is what Barratt (1993) insists Freud has overturned with his discovery of unconscious processes. I hope to address this in the final chapter.

Benveniste concludes his paper with a discussion of that special class of utterances that are called "performatives," speech acts that do not simply describe or refer to a state of affairs but that bind the speaker insofar as the speaker speaks them: "The utterance *I swear* is the very act which pledges me, not the description of the act that I am performing" (1958, p. 229). The utterance is the act that binds, but this is not given in the meaning of the verb, for "it is the 'subjectivity' of discourse which makes it possible" (1958, p. 229), as can be seen when we substitute "he swears" for "I swear" and thereby retain merely a description of the behavior. A similar subjective dimension distinguishes saying to someone "I forgive you," or its reciprocal, "I am sorry," from the statement, "He is sorry," or even, "I am the type of person who is sorry. . . ."

The main points of these papers by Benveniste are taken up by Ana-Maria Rizzuto in a remarkable paper that joins them to her psychoanalytic practice. She concurs with him when she writes that "the experience of being oneself in an act of subjective and intersubjective self-recognition results from the use of personal pronouns" (1993, p. 535). The pronouns "I," "me," "myself," and "you" "are the indispensable mediators of all affective experiences," while "I" is "the indispensable mediator of all intrapsychic knowledge" (1993, p. 536). Because "I" and "you" anchor the poles of dialogue, they thereby give a firm place from which to address an other, to express needs and desires, to direct

anger and love, to focus empathy and forgiveness. Without pronouns, the entire
range of human resonance would remain in obscure undifferentiation. Rizzuto
endorses Benveniste's claim regarding the sense of subjectivity developing from
the use of pronouns:

> The factual, concrete speech act is the only manner of knowing that there
> is an ego, a private reality to speak about. (1993, p. 540)
>
>   We need the mediation of the pronouns I, me, and you in dialogual
> exchange, even in internal speech, for any act of conscious awareness and
> self-awareness. There is no self-perception without them. (1993, p. 545)

Pronouns enable us to contain, elaborate, and refer to what Rizzuto calls so
well "the exquisite particularity" of our experiences of being loved and recognized (1993, p. 541). The pronouns are the signs that *claim* the territory of affective experience. They are not the signs that indicate some presumed, prior,
pre-semiotic claim; they *do* the claiming. The entire process of long-term treatment may be understood as a process of gradual semiotic empowerment, of
developing a voice, of claiming one's experience.

The "exquisite particularity" of experience begins to be structured semiotically, as we have seen, very early in infancy, perhaps even in utero. I have
emphasized that the infant-mother dyadic interaction is framed from the start
by the structuring Third of the semiotic code, organizing cultural and linguistic forms of child care and communication, including the mother's use of
pronouns and other forms of deixis. Infancy research is often used at the
present time to support dyadic theories of interaction, as if what goes on could
be understood in terms of a two-person system, apart from a larger context.
For example, Stolorow and Atwood write: "An impressive body of research
evidence has been amassed documenting that the developing organization of
the child's experience must be seen as the property of the child-caregiver
system of mutual regulation" (1992, p. 23). I would change that to read, "must
be seen as the property of the triadic child-caregiver-cultural system whose
code structures response-predictability within which mutual regulation
becomes possible." Atwood and Stolorow likewise use infancy research to
support a dyadic view of the analytic process when they write: "Patient and
analyst together form an indissoluble psychological system, and it is this system
that constitutes the empirical domain of psychoanalytic inquiry" (1984, p. 64).
Again, this is much too limited, for the domain of psychoanalytic inquiry must
include the frame, the cultural limits and borders and how they do or do not
hold the participants.

This notable effort to hammer down intersubjectivity as a psychoanalytic
conception does not go far enough if it fails to include the structuring role of
culture, semiotics, and linguistics, for a psychology of the self based on self-

object functions or on a psychobiology is unable to give an account of the dialogic process. Dialogue is made possible not simply through empathic resonance but through the work of clearing and marking positions carried out by personal pronouns as well as the work of anchoring reference carried out by deixis and the pronoun as index. The deictic function of pronouns is not grounded in conceptual reference nor in intersubjective feelings and is not a property of either member of the dyad, but is part of the Third that structures the dialogue, the Third of culture and semiotics that grounds the positions of each member of the dyad and makes possible a relationship between them. A systematic understanding of the dyadic process is not possible without taking this Third into account.

For Lacan dyadic process, *as dyadic,* operates in the imaginary register: "the imaginary economy has meaning, we gain some purchase on it, only in so far as it is transcribed into the symbolic order, where a ternary relation is imposed" (1954–55, p. 255). But this does not mean that for Lacan the symbolic register makes a late appearance; on the contrary, it is present from early infancy:

> Anyone who's observed a child has seen that the same blow, the same knock, the same slap, isn't received in the same fashion, depending on whether it is punitive or accidental. The symbolic relation is constituted as early as possible, even prior to the fixation of the self image of the subject, prior to the structuring image of the ego, introducing the dimension of the subject into the world, a dimension capable of creating a reality other than that experienced as brute reality, as the encounter of two masses, the collision of two balls. (1954–55, p. 257)

The complexity and distinctiveness of our work is at present under threat from two directions: by some aspects of contemporary theory and by the management of contemporary practice. Shapiro (1994) calls attention to how both management and interpretation are required for analysis to be effective. Interpretation without management of the frame fosters a fusion with the patient, while management without interpretation of the unconscious repetition of transference means we direct patients as objects. Neither of these, in my view, is the kind of analytic relationship in which one can speak of a "real" relationship. The "real" relationship can, I think, be specified as the impact on the patient of the interpreting analyst's management of the frame, according to the analyst's character. The effective relationship is the history of the impact of the analyst's unconscious (feeling and action) interpretants as well as conscious, logical notions on the setting or re-establishment of the frame, especially when the patient acts to transgress the boundaries of the frame.

A two-person model may be used to simplify the interactional field, making it easier to reduce psychopathology to victimization, as damage done by one to another, as the encounter of two masses, limiting it to Peirce's category of Secondness. Patients themselves pressure us to think of them as victims. Such one-way thinking sees the patient as developmentally arrested by trauma and such thinking lends itself to one-way solutions: young, non-analytically trained therapists, cheaper to enroll in "preferred provider" organizations, readily take to the assignment of doing something to or for the patient to compensate for the developmental deficit, the traumatization of the patient by someone else. Their practice is supported by the sort of contemporary theory that Morris Eagle has called "the deficiency-compensation model" (1984, p. 135). Such non-analytic practice deletes the "I" of the patient, the patient as distinctive subject, brackets the meaning of unconscious repetition, and manages the treatment in the ways one might manage a business.

If the contemporary rush toward the dyad in our theories has served to eclipse the place we give the Third, one possible outcome is to leave the field vacant for an unwelcome intruder. The place of the Third, I think, has been seized by the "managed care" effort: the managers now structure the dyadic process from first phase to last, they determine its semiotic conditions, influence what is to be said or not said, dictate what shall be taken as meaningful and what shall be desired as an outcome of the dialogical process. They do this in the so-called "best interests" of the patient who requires expedient and effective repair for debilitating symptoms. They orient new providers—I was told by a senior colleague in Connecticut—by telling them to avoid developing relationships with patients because it prolongs the treatment. The *New York Times* reported that Sterling Winthrop, a pharmaceutical company, reduced its employee psychotherapy bills by 47 percent by "using the Integra system" of standardizing symptoms, treatment, and outcome, so that "the number of therapy visits averaged 3.5 per patient, down from 5.5 visits two years ago" (Freudenheim, 1994, p. D2). Those of us with experience, who have functioned as supervisors and mentors to those less experienced, as in most other fields that involve a practice, have now in our own field become suspect, especially if we teach the complexity of our work. We are guilty of engaging in long-term treatment.

We do so because our more seriously troubled patients suffer from a profound dis-culturation or radical failure in acculturation. They do not read cues predictably, in a consensually validated manner. They experience their participation in social groups as if they were foreigners, or as infiltrators. While medicine can mitigate the anxiety they experience, no medicine can enculture them. They need us for that and that takes time. If we don't acknowledge the ongoing presence of a semiotic code as instilling a culture that holds both of us to our tasks, patients will believe that we simply impose our wills on them or, worse, that we can fabricate together whatever code is expedient.

Part Two

Registers of Experience

5

The Real and Boundaries
Walking or Falling into the Wild

A recent *New Yorker* article (Brown, Feb. 8, 1993) presented the fatal life course of Chris McCandless, a 24-year-old college graduate who wandered for two years and was found dead of starvation in Alaska. I believe his desperate wandering, an aberrant version of the Australian Walkabout, exemplifies at the extreme what Erik Erikson (1959) called a "life crisis" whose solution required a "moratorium" on routine activities. Chris's moratorium, insofar as it may be viewed as a compulsive effort to attain the Real, Lacan's register of undifferentiation, failed because there was no structure available to keep him on this side of the boundary of life. Such compulsive movement toward the edge contrasts with the effort others make to avoid collapsing into the Real; they often do this by cutting themselves, as if to place a secure mark at the boundary of the Real.

The "Real" is a notion to be distinguished from reality as its epistemological frontier; if reality is a system of images, logical categories, and labels, yielding a differentiated, usually predictable sequence of experience, then the Real is what lies beyond as the unimaginable, nameless, undifferentiated otherness in experience. Lacan stated: "In other words, behind what is named, there is the unnameable. It is in fact because it is unnameable, with all the resonances you can give to this name, that it is akin to the quintessential unnameable, that is to say to death" (1954–55, p. 211). To make contact with the Real usually causes great anxiety, which may be thrilling for some, fragmenting for others. We receive hints of the Real in the details of Chris's death: when his decomposing body was discovered in the shelter of an old bus in the Denali wilderness, the presence of a horrific odor stopped the hunter who found him. When the writer Brown visited the site five weeks later he was told, "The smell's gone," but his guide said, referring to the cot where the body had been, "I might have to put a tarp down before I sleep there again" (1993, p. 37). Smells have permeable boundaries; the tarp will provide a barrier against the Real for the next sleeper.

Boundary Loss in Conrad's *Heart of Darkness*

It may be difficult to experience the progressive loss of boundaries as the Real is approached; it has, however, been powerfully conveyed in certain literary works and I think it gives Conrad's *Heart of Darkness* (1899) its persisting appeal. The loss of boundaries begins almost immediately, in the second paragraph: "The sea-reach of the Thames stretched before us like the beginning of an interminable waterway. In the offing the sea and the sky were welded together without a joint" (1899, p. 3).

The waterway is "interminable" because it has no defined end: the journey's end up-river in Africa will be in the undefinable Real. The absence of the horizon line, what the late Francois Peraldi used to point to as the basic differentiation in Chinese ideographs, suggests the absence of a fundamental orienting structure, the division between heaven and earth.

After an inland trek Conrad's protagonist, Marlow, finds his boat has sunk; as he waits for repairs and learns of Kurtz, the station chief at his destination, he observes the "'smell of mud, of primeval mud . . . the high stillness of primeval forest . . . great, expectant, mute . . . I wondered whether the stillness on the face of the immensity looking at us . . . were meant as an appeal or as a menace'" (1899, p. 27). Marlow has encountered the edge of his civilized reality, and as he steams up-river he joins a cosmic regression toward massive dedifferentiation:

> Going up that river was like travelling back to the earliest beginnings of the world, when vegetation rioted on the earth and the big trees were kings. An empty stream, a great silence, an impenetrable forest. The air was warm, thick, heavy, sluggish. There was no joy in the brilliance of sunshine. The long stretches of the waterway ran on, deserted, into the gloom of overshadowed distances. . . . The broadening waters flowed through a mob of wooded islands; you lost your way on that river as you would in a desert, and butted all day long against shoals, trying to find the channel, till you thought yourself bewitched and cut off for ever from everything you had known once—somewhere—far away—in another existence perhaps. (1899, p. 34)

As one moves toward the Real, the usual categories of experience, that is, the logic of space, time, and causality, no longer afford the stability of differentiated structures. The loss of familiar signs leads to a pervasive sense of alienation:

> We penetrated deeper and deeper into the heart of darkness. . . . We were wanderers on a prehistoric earth, on an earth that wore the aspect of an unknown planet. (1899, p. 35–36)

The loss of signification, the breakdown of the process of semiosis, of signs eliciting interpretations, is complete:

> We could not understand because we were too far and could not remember, because we were travelling in the night of first ages, of those ages that are gone, leaving hardly a sign—and no memories. (1899, p. 36)

As they continue up-river, the inevitable dedifferentiation occurs:

> It was not sleep—it seemed unnatural, like a state of trance. Not the faintest sound of any kind could be heard. You looked on amazed, and began to suspect yourself of being deaf—then the night came suddenly, and struck you blind as well. (1899, p. 40)

Nothing can be differentiated in this dark stillness: there are no gaps, no separations, no absences, as if we had entered Peirce's category of Firstness, of immediacy and indeterminateness. The coming of daylight, ordinarily reassuring by highlighting differences and boundaries, fails in this primeval place:

> When the sun rose there was a white fog, very warm and clammy, and more blinding than the night. It did not shift or drive; it was just there, standing all round you like something solid. . . What we could see was just the steamer we were on, her outlines blurred as though she had been on the point of dissolving, and a misty strip of water, perhaps two feet broad, around her—and that was all. The rest of the world was nowhere, as far as our eyes and ears were concerned. Just nowhere. Gone, disappeared; swept off without leaving a whisper or a shadow behind. (1899, pp. 40–41)

Neither the symbolic register (no whisper) nor the imaginary register (no shadow) can gain a hold on the undifferentiated Real.

The Russian sailor, explaining how he became Kurtz's assistant, tells Marlow, in words that could have been spoken by Chris McCandless,

> "I went a little farther," he said, "then still a little farther—till I had gone so far that I don't know how I'll ever get back. Never mind. Plenty time. I can manage." (1899, p. 55)

The loss of boundaries is not just perceptual and logical but also moral, for the Russian says of Kurtz that "there was nothing on earth to prevent him killing whom he jolly well pleased" (1899, p. 57), and on the riverbank of his station Kurtz made of his killing a perverse sign of the Real, as Marlow describes:

> You remember I told you I had been struck at the distance by certain attempts at ornamentation, rather remarkable in the ruinous aspect of the place. Now I had suddenly a nearer view, and its first result was to make me throw my head back as if before a blow. Then I went carefully from post to post with my glass, and I saw my mistake. These round knobs were not ornamental but symbolic; they were expressive and puzzling, striking and disturbing—food for thought and also for vultures if there had been any looking down from the sky. . . . I had expected to see a knob of wood there, you know. I returned deliberately to the first I had seen—and there it was, black, dried, sunken, with closed eyelids—a head that seemed to sleep at the top of that pole, and, with the shrunken dry lips showing a narrow white line of the teeth, was smiling too, smiling continuously at some endless and jocose dream of that eternal slumber. (1899, p. 58)

Marlow is not so much frightened by death itself as by Kurtz's being beyond limits. As Marlow pursues the ailing Kurtz in the jungle, he realizes:

> don't you see, the terror of the position was not in being knocked on the head—though I had a very lively sense of that danger too—but in this, that I had to deal with a being to whom I could not appeal in the name of anything high or low . . . There was nothing either above or below him, and I knew it. He had kicked himself loose of the earth. Confound the man! he had kicked the very earth to pieces. He was alone, and before him I did not know whether I stood on the ground or floated in the air." (1899, p. 67)

But the dissolution of horizons, the perceptual, logical, and moral loss of boundaries, eventually leads to the darkness of death, the Real as the place of death; Marlow tells us:

> I had turned to the wilderness really, not to Mr. Kurtz, who, I was ready to admit, was as good as buried. And for a moment it seemed to me as if I also were buried in a vast grave full of unspeakable secrets. I felt an intolerable weight oppressing my breast, the smell of the damp earth, the unseen presence of victorious corruption, the darkness of an impenetrable night . . . (1899, p. 63)

Walking into the Wild: The Negation of Boundaries

Chris McCandless seemed compulsively drawn to this frontier of the Real, drawn by its unboundedness. Most of us can probably acknowledge fantasizing about negating some boundaries; a recent advertisement appealed to such a desire. In a sepia photograph, a man was shown riding a horse in beach water, against a fading horizon line between ocean and sky, with the words, "The essence of living without boundaries: Safari for men by Ralph Lauren." Unlike most of us, however, Chris seemed intent on actively erasing all boundaries, all conventional categories and limits. While hitchhiking in Alaska, his driver asked him if he had a hunting license, and Chris said he did not: "Why should the government tell us what we can hunt? Fuck all those rules," he responded (Brown, 1993, p. 42). On a W-4 form he wrote in capital letters: "EXEMPT EXEMPT EXEMPT" (1993, p. 38). He began to use a different name, one he created: "Alexander Supertramp." When asked if he had a compass, he said: "I don't want a compass . . . I don't have to know where I am," and when asked about a map, he responded: "I don't want to know where I'm going" (1993, P. 42). When his driver asked why he would give away his watch, he stated: "I'm just going to throw it away. I don't want to know what day it is, or what time it is" (1993, p. 42). He seemed desperate to erase all conventional markers, all semiotic indicators not of his making, as if to reach some non-arbitrary, ultimate limit from where he might begin to be. Such repudiation of semiotic limits stamps Beckett's *The Unnamable* (1959):

> At the most obvious level the refusal of the speaker in *The Unnamable* to enter into language as code, is very specifically linked to the assumption of identity since what he finds intolerable is the confraternity implied in adopting the shared language of humanity.

> At a deeper level however . . . a much more radical refusal becomes evident. The factitious demarcations by which language structures the universe are by turns derided and dissolved. (Cox, 1994, p. 88–89)

Without the bond between names and things, reference points dissolve, the subject becomes lost in "the unthinkable unspeakable" (Cox, 1994, p. 89).

Perhaps, in Winnicott's phrase, Chris had an "urgent need not to be found" (1963, p. 185). Brown writes: "He craved blank spots on the map, at a time when his father was designing radar that could produce maps from space—maps that could practically show the beaver in the pond. Chris wanted to take nature unfiltered, unscreened, alone, and he found a characteristic solution to the problem of maps without blank spots: he threw the maps away" (1993, p. 40). Chris's desperate attempt to throw away all signs, to erase all markers, even to the point of getting lost in the Real, may have been a response to being objectified, severely constrained, negated by the signifiers others placed on him. As Winnicott put it:

> At the centre of each person is an incommunicado element, and this is sacred and most worthy of preservation. (1963, p. 187)

This preservation of personal isolation is part of the search for identity, and for the establishment of a personal technique for communicating which does not lead to violation of the central self. (1963, p. 190).

We do not have much information, but we are told that Chris's father said, "I misread him" (Brown, 1993, p. 39), and Chris himself scratched onto a plywood-covered window of his deathbed shelter:

Two Years He Walks The Earth. No Phone, No Pool, No Pets, No Cigarettes. Ultimate Freedom. An Extremist. An Aesthetic Voyager Whose Home is *The Road*. Escaped from Atlanta. (1993, p.44)

He had graduated from college in Atlanta and last saw his parents there two years earlier. Since then he had been wandering; his favorite song was "King of the Road." During his final weeks in Alaska he read Tolstoy's *The Death of Ivan Ilyich* and wrote in the margins: "Civilization—Falsity—A Big Lie" (1993, p. 45). He had also scratched on the plywood in the shelter:

And Now After Two Rambling Years Comes the Final and Greatest Adventure. The Climactic Battle To Kill The False Being Within And Victoriously Conclude the Spiritual Revolution! Ten Days and Nights of Freight Trains and Hitching Bring Him to the Great White North No Longer to Be Poisoned By Civilization He Flees, and Walks Alone Upon the Land To Become *Lost* in the *Wild*. (1993, p. 44)

The poison of civilization may have been, in extreme form, the constraints every adolescent must struggle against in order to find a way to be more than just the object of someone else's semiotic code and desire. Winnicott states:

At adolescence when the individual is undergoing pubertal changes and is not quite ready to become one of the adult community there is a strengthening of the defences against being found, that is to say being found before being there to be found. That which is truly personal and which feels real must be defended at all cost, and even if this means a temporary blindness to the value of compromise. (1963, p. 190)

The compulsion to erase boundaries, without compromise, had a tragic and ironic outcome in Chris's case, for without a map he could not find a way to cross the Teklanika River, now a swollen boundary, to reach help, and so he starved to death; on August 5, two weeks before he died, he wrote in his journal:

Day 100! Made it! But in weakest condition of life. Death looms as serious threat, too weak to walk out, have literally become trapped in the wild—no game. (Brown, 1993, p. 46)

The grandiose capital letters, which earlier called attention to their author, have here dropped out, in conformity to some acknowledgment of limits, both semiotic as well as physical.

Chris's "life crisis" indicates that the issues of boundaries and identity are, as Erikson describes it, life and death matters:

> On the other hand, should a young person feel that the environment tries to deprive him too radically of all the forms of expression which permit him to develop and integrate the next step, he may resist with the wild strength encountered in animals who are suddenly forced to defend their lives. For, indeed, in the social jungle of human existence there is no feeling of being alive without a sense of identity. (1968, p. 130)

What Erikson perhaps believed, but did not state, is that developing a sense of identity is a semiotic process, involving an exchange of signs, in mutual recognition with an other, according to a code as a stable Third. Because semiotic processes define relationships from before birth, they define identity as rooted in kinship and cultural forms of address in specific social settings. Semiotic breakdown results in loss of identity, if we affirm, as the anthropologist Milton Singer states, "the conception of the self as a semiotic structure and process of communication" (1989, p. 233).

When the social jungle of adolescence becomes impassable, when the transition to manhood or womanhood has no meaningful path, then what Erikson called a "psychosocial moratorium" becomes urgent:

> A MORATORIUM is a period of delay granted to somebody who is not ready to meet an obligation or forced on somebody who should give himself time. By psychosocial moratorium, then, we mean a delay of adult commitments, and yet it is not only a delay. It is a period that is characterized by a selective permissiveness on the part of society and of provocative playfulness on the part of youth, and yet it often leads to deep, if often transitory, commitment on the part of youth, and ends in a more or less ceremonial confirmation of commitment on the part of society. (1968, p. 157)

In referring to Shaw's moratorium, Erikson (1968) describes Chris McCandless: "Potentially creative men like Shaw build the personal fundament of their work during a self-decreed moratorium, during which they often starve themselves, socially, erotically, and, last but not least, nutritionally, in order to let the grosser weeds die out, and make way for the growth of their inner garden. Often when the weeds are dead, so is the garden" (1968, p. 41–42). For Chris the process of semiosis, the ground and matrix of significance, had become paralyzed, fixated, rigidified. In order to survive at all as a human subject, Chris compulsively sought to negate all imposed meaning and erase all conventional distinctions, the gross weeds choking his life; he desperately declared himself to be exempt from all conventional limits, and placed himself beyond human contact. He represents an extreme type, unclaimable and unaccountable, as if exempt from context and constraint.

Dissolution at the Edge of the Real

The psychological effects of such a compulsion toward the Real are portrayed by Paul Bowles in *The Sheltering Sky*, in his character Port, a troubled young composer, in whom we find an obsession with going to the edge to test the limits of Western ways of anchoring reality. The novel is marked by a mounting dread of what lies beyond the edge. For example, Port and his wife, Kit, sit on a cliff gazing at the vast North African desert below:

> "You know," said Port, and his voice sounded unreal, as voices are likely to do after a long pause in an utterly silent spot, "the sky here's very strange. I often have the sensation when I look at it that it's a solid thing up there, protecting us from what's behind . . . "
>
> "From what's behind?"
>
> "Yes."
>
> "But what is behind? . . . "
>
> "Nothing, I suppose. Just darkness. Absolute night." (1949, pp. 100–101).

When the sky is experienced as a protective covering against the undifferentiated Real, the vision of what may lie "behind" opens upon the vision of death and of those silent infinite spaces that so terrified Pascal (1670). As Port becomes deathly ill, he begins to experience the breakdown of his symbolic system and struggles to maintain an imagistic hold on the consequent destructuring of reality:

> He did not look up because he knew how senseless the landscape would appear. It takes energy to invest life with meaning, and at present this energy was lacking. He knew how things could stand bare, their essence having retreated on all sides to beyond the horizon, as if impelled by a sinister centrifugal force. (1949, p. 165)

Later, near death, as semiosis shuts down, his mind struggles to avoid collapsing into a dedifferentiated mass:

> He opened his eyes. The room was malignant. It was empty. "Now, at last, I must fight against this room." But later he had a moment of vertiginous clarity. He was at the edge of a realm where each thought, each image, had an arbitrary existence, where the connection between each thing and the

next had been cut. As he labored to seize the essence of that kind of consciousness, he began to slip back into its precinct without suspecting that he was no longer wholly outside in the open, no longer able to consider the idea at a distance. It seemed to him that here was an untried variety of thinking, in which there was no necessity for a relationship with life. (1949, p. 236)

Port's thinking has disintegrated, without mediation, without relationship, almost without structure:

> "The thought in itself," he said . . . They were coming again, they began to flash by. He tried to hold one, believed he had it. "But a thought of what? What is it?" Even then it was pushed out of the way by the others crowding behind it. While he succombed, struggling, he opened his eyes for help. "The room! The room! Still here!!" . . . He looked at the line made by the joining of the wall and the floor, endeavored to fix it in his mind, [that he might have something to hang on to when his eyes should shut.] There was a terrible disparity between the speed at which he was moving and the quiet immobility of that line, but he insisted. So as not to go. To stay behind. To overflow, take root in what would stay here. A centipede can, cut into pieces. Each part can walk by itself. Still more, each leg flexes, lying alone on the floor. There was screaming in each ear . . . (pp. 236–37).

It is Port who is screaming in the horror of disintegration, and we are led to wonder what the dying hours of Chris McCandless were like.

Falling into the Wild: Fear of Breakdown

These walkers into the wild seem compelled to erase boundaries in order to achieve, if they can survive, a semiotic reconstruction through some sort of contact with the Real. They seem to be, in Winnicott's terms, in "the stage of *I am* with the inherent implication *I repudiate everything that is not me*" (1974, p. 107). Only by going to the edge, to the limit, can they be sure that the repudiation is complete. I think we can distinguish them from those who are terrified of losing their boundaries, always on the verge of falling into the wild, into the Real, into a regressive dedifferentiation and merger, or what Winnicott called "a breakdown of the establishment of the unit self" (1974, p. 103)—a state of fragmentation that becomes possible only after the ego has been constellated. Ogden refers to this state as the "autistic-contiguous position" which "involves the experience of impending disintegration of one's sensory surface . . . resulting in the feeling of leaking, dissolving, disappearing, or falling into shapeless unbounded space" (1989, p. 133). What is at stake in regression, therefore, is not a return to infancy (Weston, 1990), but rather a loss of structure developed in infancy, the structure of Thirdness, of mediated relationships between persons and things. The body as sign fragments into a scrambled message and there is a collapse of symbolic perspectives, a verging on the Real.

Patients whose daily efforts go toward maintaining a barrier between themselves and the Real have often suffered severe trauma. The post-traumatic development may lack the usual semiotic markers that make possible stable and predictable relations, a ravaged state akin to what Bion called the destruction of alpha-elements, elements that are "indispensable to the experience that enables the individual to know something" (1992, p. 183), whose destruction leads to "starvation of the psyche in its supply of reality" (1992, p. 96) because experience remains undigested. Bion writes: "But we must now consider another consequence of the destruction of alpha. Since its destruction makes it impossible to store experience, retaining only undigested 'facts,' the patient feels he contains not visual images of things but things themselves" (1992, p. 97). In such a state the patient is "unable to transform the experience so that he can store it mentally," it remains unmediated, devoid of relationships. He continues: "the experience (and his sense impressions of it) remains a foreign body; it is felt as a "thing" lacking any of the quality we usually attribute to thought or its verbal expression (1992, p. 180). I think Bion is here describing what it is like to be in contact with Lacan's register of the Real which, although we grope for words and concepts to place it at an epistemological frontier, must remain nameless. Bion states: "I could try to put it this way: the fundamental reality is "infinity," the unknown, the situation for which there is no language—not even that borrowed from the artist or the religious—which gets anywhere near to describing it" (1992, p. 372).

Most of us are spared the task of avoiding or describing "it," but now and then we brush against the precariousness of existence with sudden terror, as William James described:

> While in this state of philosophic pessimism and general depression of spirits about my prospects, I went one evening into a dressing-room in the twilight, to procure some article that was there; when suddenly there fell upon me without any warning, just as if it came out of the darkness, a horrible fear of my own existence . . . It was like a revelation; and although the immediate feelings passed away, the experience has made me sympathetic with the morbid feelings of others ever since . . . I dreaded to be left alone. I remember wondering how other people could live, how I myself had ever lived, so unconscious of that pit of insecurity beneath the surface of life. (quoted in Erikson, 1968, p. 152)

The protective barrier that prevented James from falling into that pit, that marked its edge as a fence, was scripture, the repetition of specific signifiers:

I have always thought that this experience of melancholia of mine had a religious bearing . . . I mean that the fear was so invasive and powerful, that, if I had not clung to scripture-texts like "The eternal God is my refuge, etc. Come unto me all ye that labor and are heavy-laden, etc., I am the Resurrection and the Life, etc." I think I should have grown really insane. (quoted in Erikson, 1968, pp. 152–53)

Cutting as Marking Boundaries

When signifiers fail, when the threat of dissolution into the Real becomes overwhelming, patients struggle desperately to place a stable boundary-marker at the edge of the self and they often begin with their own skin, by marking or cutting into it.

While we can agree that all cutting is a form of communication (Anzieu, 1985; Bick, 1967), I try to attend to the specific semiotic import of mutilating the skin. In attempting to establish the self's boundaries with reliable markers, patients who cut often trace figures, even letters, that are based on a system of signs. Often the meaning is obvious. For example, a young schizophrenic woman frequently yielded to the commands of auditory hallucinations to insert and clip safety pins through the skin of her arms, leaving them over several days to become infected. She attempted to stop these commands by writing "em pleh" on her wrist, read as "help me" as though written from the inside on her skin as a transparent membrane. Another patient, with a history of masochistic perversion and prone to psychotic agitation, scratched into her wrist, in an act she labelled as "recreational cutting," the gang name of a biker boyfriend, oriented so that the name faced the viewer as if it were a tag claiming ownership of her body and its pleasures, an identity tag for her self as the object of someone else's desire.

Patients who engage in superficial or moderate repetitive cutting report "relief from a variety of unpleasant symptoms such as heightened anxiety and tension, intense anger and rage, racing thoughts, depersonalization, depression, and feelings of loneliness"; the subsequent scars "impart a sense of security and uniqueness that is difficult to give up" (Favazza and Rosenthal, 1993, p. 137). Such a self-inflicted scar functions as an index; Peirce comments, "Anything which startles us is an index, in so far as it marks the junction between two portions of experience" (1940, pp. 108–109). The scar as index functions as a Third, a sign of a boundary, providing a bounded experience of self by mediating inside and outside. As Davoine (1989) reminds us, people are never more aware of the exact location of national boundaries than when an invading army crosses them. Patients who cut are attempting to set a marker at the edge of the self so that they can experience a limit and not become fragmented in a diffuse unnamable scatter.

Cutting is often viewed as a regulatory action, but what does cutting regulate?

Cutting soothes, I think, not because it provides a release but because it prevents one. That is, the imperative and transgressive marking of the skin signifies that there is a boundary between the subject and the Real, it prevents merging into a dedifferentiated existence. Such merger would bring not only dissolution of the self but also of the world of experience, as Fast states:

> Every boundary loss, then, is a dedifferentiation of self and nonself, and a loss in self structure and in the individual's subjective structure of the world. No boundary loss can occur without loss in the other. In the massive dedifferentiations of psychotic breakdown, the individual's experience is of utter disintegration of self and total dissolution of the world around. (1985, p. 63)

Fast stresses that "in self-other dedifferentiation both self and the nonself world are unarticulated" (1985, p. 64), that is, radically bereft of the guiding discriminations provided by either words or images. A recent study of inpatient self-injuries found that more than twice as many occur on the evening shift as on the day shift, congruent "with patients' reports that episodes of derealization, despair, or general tension increase during the evening hours and that the patients feel compelled to hurt themselves to provide some kind of relief" (Hemkendreis, 1992, p. 394). I would suggest, again, that the relief is in the form of the marking of a boundary in order to manage the dread of dedifferentiation before sleep. In such moments object relations also have a boundary-defining function: it is especially at night that others are sought to provide reassuring feedback that boundaries endure, that the self's cohesion is stable, that the regression of sleep is temporary.

Two Modes of Semiotic Breakdown

I would now like to suggest that these two desperate actions taken at the edge of the Real, either by erasing boundaries or by marking boundaries on the skin, are the result of two different kinds of semiotic breakdown. Peirce, a contemporary of William James, defined the self as a living sign for others and unconsciously responsive to the evocativeness of others as signs (Colapietro, 1989). As may have been the case with Chris McCandless, whose father said "I misread him," when signs so overdetermine a human being, rigidly assigning an objectified status and congealing a meaning for others, the only path to a possible survival as a subject may lie in a compulsion to erase boundaries, to tear off a suffocating semiotic skin. Such individuals often carry the burden of a parent's or grandparent's trauma, a contact with the Real that was contained by displacing it through some signifying chain onto the patient. For example, when a child is named after a deceased grandparent or sibling and that death was problematic, as in the case of a disappearance or a violent accident, murder, or suicide (Davoine, 1992), the one bearing the name of, or a named likeness to, the deceased, inevitably produces in the family the resonances, significances, and echoes of meaning that the original member produced in life and in death.

The weight of such signifying baggage, of an unconscious script, can be suffocating, leading to semiotic breakdown because the individual is blocked from producing in action his or her own signs and thereby creating in others his or her own significance. Such an identity crisis may then lead one to defy all conventional limits, to strip away the displaced signifiers in order to bump up against the Real so that the original trauma can be named, or to find an ultimate limit that can hold from where the subject, surviving this encounter with the unimaginable and unnamable, can then proceed, with a somewhat fresh semiotic slate, to collaborate in the acknowledgment and definition of limits. For such a patient, however, the grandiosity, entitlement, and contempt for the rest of us who do not go this far may make human relationships almost impossible and leave the individual with a deep sense of being culturally displaced.

In the case of those who mark their skin to prevent dissolution, the parental trauma has often been directly repeated on them in the form of a cycle of family violence. Rather than being named as the container of the trauma, they suffer the trauma on their skin at the hands of those who should most protect them. The inherent contradiction between parental protection and parental abuse perverts the symbolic dimension of their experience. Semiotic breakdown occurs not because signs have become too rigid but rather too confusing and unstable, signs have no consensual validation. When parental desire becomes omnipotent whimsy, when through parental madness, hypocrisy, or perversion words have lost their power to bind, there is radical failure in the boundary-setting function of language. For such patients the code remains mysterious, anything can mean anything. Sounds and smells produce unpredictable and disturbing resonances, leading to a basic chaos in communication and an ongoing apprehension about what meaning others find in one's speech and actions.

In examining these two extreme maneuvers at the edge of the Real, to radically erase or push beyond a boundary or to mark one, I began to see them as exaggerations of two interactive tendencies present in all of us and operative in a parallel series of dual processes. One thinks of Balint's philobat and ocnophil (1959), Hermann's drive to go in search and drive to cling (1936), Bakan's agency and communion (1966), Blatt's introjective and anaclitic personalities (1990), and even the two semiotic axes of Roman Jakobson (1956), substitution and contiguity.

But I remained uneasy about this way of bringing this chapter to a close, putting a boundary around it by invoking a series of parallel conceptions, my own efforts to tame the Real. As Peirce might say, there were unwelcome feeling interpretants from this narrative that I found disturbing. I went back to Chris's last weeks and his marginal notes to *The Death of Ivan Ilyich*: "Civilization— Falsity—A Big Lie."

Tolstoy's powerful work presents the illness and death of a successful 45-year-old magistrate who had always acted to please those with money and power in order to gain prestige and comfort. The story begins with his death notice, in response to which each of his associates thinks, "Well, he's dead but I'm alive!" This common reaction is something like Woody Allen's: "It's not that I'm afraid to die, I just don't want to be there when it happens." But Tolstoy's story does make it happen as he presents Ivan Ilyich's horribly painful act of dying, and we see the major social institutions of that time, education, law, medicine, marriage, family, religion, exposed for their rigid conformity to social pressure, intolerance of individuality, disavowal of death, and a false and fragile sense of meaning.

Tolstoy brings home the unexpectedness of physical illness:

> They were all in good health. It could not be called ill health if Ivan Ilyich sometimes said that he had a queer taste in his mouth and felt some discomfort in his left side. (1886, p. 120)

As his medical symptoms increase, however, he is aghast:

> There was no deceiving himself: something terrible, new, and more important than anything before in his life, was taking place within him of which he alone was aware. Those about him did not understand or would not understand it, but thought everything in the world was going on as usual. (1886, p. 125)

He tried to go back to work in order to distract himself from the edge:

> But suddenly in the midst of those proceedings the pain in his side . . . would begin its own gnawing work. . . . It would come and stand before him and look at him, and he would be petrified and the light would die out of his eyes, and he would again begin asking himself whether It alone was true. . . . And what was worst of all was that It drew his attention to itself not in order to make him take some action but only that he should look at It, look it straight in the face: look at it and without doing anything, suffer inexpressibly. (1886, p. 133)

In consequence, he begins to assess his life:

> It occurred to him that what had appeared perfectly impossible before, namely that he had not spent his life as he should have done, might after all be true. It occurred to him that his scarcely perceptible attempts to struggle against what was considered good by the most highly placed people, those

scarcely noticeable impulses which he had immediately suppressed, might have been the real thing, and all the rest false. (1886, p. 152)

So this story that occupied Chris McCandless's final weeks is a story that makes one think about death, not in the abstract, but one's own death, one's own precarious existence, and one's own desire, how one should live. Death is the ultimate boundary and limit, of one's body, of one's culture. It tests any culture's ability to establish standards, to provide meaning, to sustain life. When it works, culture gives us a shared security, a common purpose, and a framework for forgiveness, based on a process of mutual recognition, including the recognition of our mortality. But Tolstoy's words and Chris's aberrant behavior show us that, from the perspective of our own death, many of the things we do and invest in and worry about seem wasteful, vain, misdirected. They may even seem ridiculous. It does not seem ridiculous, however, to attempt to answer a young person's questions about the meaning of life, about the real boundary of death. It may be impossible, but not ridiculous. We could do worse than to say with Rilke:

> We're not at one. We've no instinctive knowledge
> like migratory birds. Outstripped and late,
> we force ourselves on winds and find no welcome
> from ponds where we alight. We comprehend
> flowering and fading simultaneously.
> And somewhere lions still roam, all unaware
> while yet their splendor lasts of any weakness.
> (quoted in Auden and Kronenberger, 1962, pp. 3–4)

6

Language, Psychosis, and Culture

During a flagrant psychotic episode, a patient described his auditory, verbal hallucinations as "an internal tape recorder that goes on and off," frightening, and not in his control. I want to compare this example to statements made by a French Canadian with whom I shared an afternoon fishing in Northern Lake Huron. Ray was in his forties, married, with two grown children, and ran a small restaurant in Ontario. He spoke of how he and his wife took part in a weekly, church-sponsored Bible reading group and of how much the charismatic movement had changed their lives, in quite concrete ways. For example, when he was considering going into the restaurant business, after selling a small lumber mill, he debated whether he should buy a downtown restaurant and take on a large debt, or whether he should purchase a small diner in a suburban mall. One day while he was stopped for a red light, the Spirit told him: "Don't go into debt!" He promptly bought the small diner. He gave additional examples of how the Spirit, he said, communicates with him. This man did not seem to be psychotic and, based on the evidence of one fine breakfast, at least, he seemed to know his work.

Is there a difference between these two linguistic moments? I would like to suggest that they are very different, that words uttered by the "internal tape recorder" exemplify the status of words that have passed into what Lacan calls the Real, while the words uttered to Ray by "the Spirit" may represent the process whereby what is just at the border of the Real passes into words. But to go further we can step back for a moment and try to find some additional ways of talking about the Real and what Lacan seems to mean by it, as well as what he means by the "imaginary" and the "symbolic" registers of experience. I'd like to begin by sharing some excerpts from a marvelous book called *China Men* by Maxine Hong Kingston.

The *New York Times* book reviewer, John Leonard, wrote in 1980: "Fiction, memoir, dream, epic, or elegy—whatever Maxine Hong Kingston is writing, it is certainly art. Four years ago in the same space I said: *The Woman Warrior* [her first book] was the best book I've read in years. *China Men* is, at the least, the best book I've read in the four years since." *China Men* (a Chinese-American's account of the migration of her ancestors to the U.S., where they helped build the railroads, among other things) is for me the best concrete introduction to Lacan in English, precisely because of the author's ability to move smoothly among the three dimensions or registers of the imaginary, the Real, and the symbolic—"these three registers which," Lacan tells us, "are indeed the essential registers of human reality" (1953a, p. 2).

The imaginary, as we have seen, is defined by the image, where the image is taken to function in a structure governed by point-to-point correspondences, as when an object is placed before a mirror or when an image is projected on a screen (Lacan, 1964, p. 86). When Kingston exposes the imaginary, she makes note of mirrors, movies, reflections, racial stereotypes, and narcissistic preening, this last highlighted in images of flying. These cues denote the arena of visual captivation by a lure that is often erotic. Fantastic scope is given to desire, ferocious images of bodily fragmentation shape hatred. The alluring power of the image has its origin, for Lacan, in the mirror stage of child development. Sometime during the period from six to eighteen months (or even earlier, as we saw in Chapter 3), the human infant, still neurologically incomplete, becomes capable of recognizing its reflection in a mirror, identifies itself with the exterior, erect, whole form of the human body, becomes narcissistically invested in this visible, external form and thereby alienated from itself, and this identification with its reflected image constitutes the ego. Henceforth the ego will be concerned not with objectivity and adaptation to "reality," as ego psychologists have proposed, but rather with demands for recognition and with defensive maneuvers to protect self-esteem. Images of oneself and of others dominate this register, images that distort, that promise an illusory happiness, that camouflage basic human longing.

An example from *China Men*: With some earned money, the father buys an expensive suit: "In the three-way mirror, he looked like Fred Astaire. He wore the suit out of the store" (1980, p. 61). He and his friend "strolled down Fifth Avenue and caught sight of themselves in windows and hubcaps" (1980, p. 61). There follow, in the subsequent four pages, references to posing, to photographs (nine times), two more references to movies, and another reference to mirrors.

At the end of this episode, the three other partners cheat the father out of his share in the laundry business and the "perfectly legal" theft sends the author's disillusioned parents to search for a new life in California.

Kingston also structures the imaginary register by using cross-racial iconic symmetries that undercut racial stereotypes. For example, the father's difficulties in China in teaching Chinese children "who were more bestial than animals" (1980, p. 35) are mirrored later in the book by the teacher brother's "surprise at how dumb the students were" in his class in America (1980, p. 277). There are at least eight such symmetrical, corresponding episodes involving birth, death, migration, and longing, and Kingston seems to be telling us that stereotypes on both sides are in a mirror-relationship, that they are reflections from the same source; this source, in a Lacanian framework, is the imaginary order, the register of narcissistic images that lure and captivate our gaze and shape what we call reality.

In distinction from "reality," the register of the Real has not been easy to comprehend in the work of Lacanians, who variously refer to it as "always in the same place" and "already there" (Faladé, 1974, p. 33), as that "which lacks nothing" (1974, p. 30), brute, undifferentiated experience that invades us from time to time but to which we usually have a relationship mediated by language. Such mediation transforms our contact with the Real into reality, something very different from the Real, for reality is "a montage of the symbolic and the imaginary" (1974, p. 36). When there is "loss of reality," as in psychosis, then contact with the real can be horrifying and maddening. The Real, then, must be somehow filtered or shielded from experience. There is a kind of "struggle against the Real" (M.-L. Lauth, 1982, p. 62). There is a tearing-out or "uprooting from the Real by the symbolic" (1982, p. 61), the Real must be "made to draw back" (1982, p. 63). This "struggle against the Real" is precisely what Kingston provides a metaphor of in the labor of the China men cutting away jungle to establish sugar cane on Hawaii. And the Real is even more forbidding as the China men cut through mountains building a railroad:

> Beneath the soil, they hit granite. Ah Goong struck it with his pickax, and it jarred his bones, shattered his teeth. He swung his sledgehammer against it, and the impact rang in the dome of his skull. The mountain that was millions of years old was locked against them and was not to be broken into. . . . He hit at the same spot over and over again, the same rock. Some chips and flakes broke off. The granite looked everywhere the same. It had no softer or weaker spots anywhere, the same hard gray. . . . The rock is what is real, he thought. This rock is what real is, not clouds or mist, which make mysterious promises, and when you go through them are nothing. When the foreman measured at the end of twenty-four hours of pounding, the rock had given a foot. (1980, p. 132)

We touch the Real in the violent deaths of the men blown up by explosives, men falling thousands of feet. The unburied corpse was an unbearable intrusion of the Real: "After a fall, the buzzards circled the spot and reminded the workers for days that a man was dead down there. The men threw piles of rocks and branches to cover bodies from sight" (1980, p. 130). The horror of unburied corpses—corpses denied a place in the symbolic order—haunted the living as they began to learn to use dynamite:

> The men who died slowly enough to say last words said, "Don't leave me frozen under the snow. Send my body home. Burn it and put the ashes in a tin can. . . ." "Shut up," scolded the hearty men. "We don't want to hear about bone jars and dying." "You're lucky to have a body to bury, not blown to smithereens. . . ." "Aiya. To be buried here, nowhere." "But this is somewhere," Ah Goong promised. "This is the Gold Mountain. We're marking the land now. The track sections are numbered, and your family will know where we leave you." But he was a crazy man, and they didn't listen to him. (1980, p. 136)

But this "crazy man" clearly realized that the only way to overcome the Real is by marking it, cutting into its mass with signifier, transforming its undifferentiated fullness through a kind of negation so that divisions appear and mediated relationships become possible. Frontiers can then be established making repression possible, graves can and must have markers so that the dead can be forgotten and not haunt the living. And the railroad was a budding symbolic network making such markings possible.

When the Kingston storybook character Lo Bun Sun shipwrecks against an unknown shore he manages to retrieve many useful items over several days, however: "One morning, he awoke and the ship was gone. No man-made hulk served as a marker against all that sea" (1980, p. 226). Totally alone, he immediately orders his life by putting marks on the Real: he marks the days with notches on a board, he writes in his diary, he fires clay pots and decorates them, he teaches a parrot to say his name, "so that he would hear a voice other than his own, a voice calling him by name" (1980, p. 229). This socialization of the Real so that it becomes reality is, Lacan tells us, the effect of the signifier, marking the Real, the effect of the symbolic order.

The symbolic register is the network of language and ritual. The decisive feature of this register, or order of symbols, is that it consists of a relatively closed system of reciprocally differentiated units, each of which has no meaning in itself but is differentiable solely with reference to all the other units in the system. This system is language, structurally understood as a system of phonemes or signifiers related by convention to what they signify but only in the context of the ensemble. Unlike the imaginary register, there are no one-to-one correspondences in the symbolic order. The symbolic order, with its polyphonic and polysemic structure, is the source of meaning; it roots, it sustains subjects, it even contains ghosts. Kingston introduces the register of the symbolic by calling attention to words, syllables, phonemes, names, and a variety of speech acts such as cursing, blessing, chanting, singing, screaming, as well as speaking, writing, and the force of silence. In Kingston's text more than one out of two pages deals explicitly with these signifying elements, and they occur in clusters, more frequent serially when the register of the symbolic is in play, absent when the imaginary takes over. Even the book's title—*China Men*—is used in the text to emphasize the symbolic network of culture, as distinct from what Kingston calls "the slurred-together word" chinamen, reflecting the stereotypic image the whites have for the Chinese.

It is the act of speech that affords us a barrier against the Real and sustains us, and Kingston provides numerous examples of this. While crossing the ocean with a stowaway in a crate, the smuggler periodically comes and knocks "a code on the wood, and the stowaway father signalled back. This exchange of greetings kept him from falling into the trance that overtakes animals about to die" (1980, p. 49). Forbidden to speak while clearing Hawaii for sugar cane, the great-grandfather coughed out his cursing syllables in the dust: "He felt better after having his say. He did not even mind the despair which dispelled upon speaking it. The suicides who walked into the ocean or jumped off the mountains were not his kindred" (1980, p. 102). Later, another grandfather enables the author to name an aspect of the Real in an example that shows how the three registers articulate:

> Say Goong took my hand and led me into a cavernous shed black from the sun in my eyes. He pointed into the dark, which dark seemed solid and alive, heavy, moving, breathing. There were waves of dark skin over a hot and massive something that was snorting and stomping—the living night. In the day, here was where night lived. Say Goong pointed up at a wide brown eye as high as the roof. I was ready to be terrified but for his delight. "Horse," he said. "Horse." He contained the thing in a word—*horse*, magical and earthly sound. A horse was a black creature so immense I could not see the outlines. (1980, p. 165)

This is a good example of how the Real, initially undifferentiated as the living night, opens up in a look, a seeing and being seen that is compelling and frightening when the child's eye meets the horse's look, unleashing the captivating power of the image, and then the experience is knotted together and given a boundary, a frontier, once it is contained in the word *horse*, so that a mediated relation is now established.

The author does not hide her admiration for the China men, but the true hero of the book is language, for language alone sustains these men and women (as well as writer and reader). As she narrates the psychotic episodes of six of her relatives, she shows us that what is central to psychosis has to do with slippage in the symbolic order, failures in ritual, social upheavals, and cultural displacements, and how ritual itself is restorative.

In her first example, a grandfather goes in and out of madness while blasting the American railroad out of rock, far away from home: "When he stumbled out" of the tunnel, writes Kingston, "he tried to talk about time. 'I felt time,' he said, 'I saw time. I saw world'" (1980, p. 132). The second relative, a great-grandfather, begins to see visions and hear ghosts on Hawaii and wonders: "Now that he was in a new land, who could tell what normal was?" (1980, pp. 107–109). The third relative, a cousin with a home and family in California, receives letters of horror from his starving mother in China, imploring him to sell his daughters and return to China. When she dies, she haunts him day and night, accusing him of letting her starve to death. Finally, he buys a boat ticket and returns, talking with her all the while, to her grave:

> "Here you are mother," he said, and the villagers heard him say it. "You're home now. I've brought you home. I spent passage fare on you. It equals more than the food money I might have sent. . . . Rest, Mother. Eat." He heaped food on her grave. . . . He poured wine into the thirsty earth. He planted the blue shrub of longevity, where white carrier pigeons would rest. He bowed his forehead to the ground, knocking it hard in repentance. "You're home, mother. I'm home, too. I brought you home." He set off firecrackers near her grave, not neglecting *one* Chinese thing. "Rest now, heh, Mother. Be happy now." He sat by the grave and drank and ate for the first time since she had made her appearance. . . . He boarded the very same ship sailing back. . . . to America, where he acted normal again, continuing his American life, and nothing like that ever happened to him again. (1980, pp. 178–79)

A fourth relative, an older cousin in America, gets caught up in the great postwar upheavals in China and becomes delusional about wheat germ and communism: "When he connected his two big ideas [wheat germ and communism], he touched wrong wires to each other, shot off sparks, and shorted out. He had become a paranoiac. 'They are trying to poison me,' he said, running into the laundry . . . " (1980, p. 195). He calms down when he decides to return to Communist China. The fifth relative, an uncle by marriage, was torn between remaining in Hong Kong with his shoe factory, or coming to the U.S., where his wife was living. After a brief visit to the U.S., he persuaded his wife to return with him, despite fears of a Communist takeover. One day he became sensitive to light and sounds: "He explained later how he understood the stopping quality of red light and the go of green. . . . He passed a book store. Jets of colored light jumped along the books' spines; he wanted to stop and see whether *Red Chamber Dream* and Communist books were red . . . " (1980, p. 213). He went to a bank, withdrew all his money and left it with strangers. Twice he did this, recovered, and then returned once again with his wife to the U.S., having "said goodbye properly, goodbye forever" (1980, p. 216). The sixth relative, the author's father, became severely depressed after the police closed down the Chinese gambling house and social hall he had managed in Stockton. He stopped shaving, sat and stared, drank whiskey, no longer went out, and screamed in his sleep (1980, p. 246ff). In her seventh example, a "wild man" is found living alone in a Florida swamp. When the police have him speak with a Chinese interpreter, he tells how he left Taiwan and his seven children to sail on a Liberian freighter to earn money; how, becoming homesick and screaming and weeping as they tried to return him on a plane, he was hospitalized and then later escaped into the swamp. After being recaptured, he hangs himself in jail (1980, pp. 222–24).

All of Kingston's examples of psychotic states involve the link between madness and some catastrophe in the social order, and we shall return to this. To recapitulate: what we do as humans is structured by reflected images that lure our desire and reinforce our egos, but we remain grounded in a symbolic network that pervasively supports our speech, ritual, and even our perception of the world, and we from time to time come to the edge and touch upon the nameless, the Real that is always there but usually mediated by language. Now what if language does not function as such a recourse against the Real? What if the Real is experienced without the mediation of language? What if words themselves lose their referential context and are experienced as *in* the Real? To say that words are in the Real is to say that words have become like things: whether they come from the therapist or the titles of books or the "internal tape recorder," they can strike the patient's ears, eyes, forehead, chest, like objects. They do not mediate and refer to objects. Mediation involves a distancing whereby the person has a status as distinct from surroundings, precisely through having a relationship to words, which themselves comport relationships with other words. The word, the name, is taken as a substitute for the object, not identified with it, and correlatively the object itself is taken as distinct from oneself, its name, and its interpretant. But in psychotic states the mediation language gives us is problematic, and I would like to approach a discussion of psychosis by moving from Kingston to Canada and drawing upon a meeting held in August 1982 on an island in Georgian Bay.

This five-day meeting was sponsored by the Niobrara Institute, under the leadership of Gerald Mohatt, in order to bring together American therapists, Lacanian analysts, and native people, including medicine men, all of whom had an interest in the nonpharmaceutical treatment of psychosis—that is, whose practice relied essentially on the use of words. We met in a native setting (the Whitefish River Ojibwa Reserve) in order to question our accustomed modes of thinking, and we all shared the experience that working with psychotic patients challenges notions about reality. Otto Will (who had a long-standing interest in Plains and Southwest Indians) could not be there, but much of his work exemplified our concerns. We read, for example, in one of his papers that "the psychotic process, bizarre as it may be, reflects conflict, is problem-solving, and is goal-directed" (1972, p. 35). He wrote of "dissociated representations of experience" as "processes that lack the refinement (in terms of time, logical sequences, cause and effect, space, and identity of self and object) of the ordinary day-by-day forms of thought," and "are not to be approximated in language" (1972, pp. 37–38). From this point of view, he wrote: "schizophrenia is not looked upon as a disease, but as a reaction to, and an expression of, the social scenes in which an organism with certain biological endowments—usually adequate, so far as I know, to the task of becoming fully human—has its being" (Will, 1959, p. 218). This view was supported by what emerged as we discussed the nature of psychotic experience, and the remarks made at that meeting may clarify our two examples of the tape recorder speaking and the Spirit speaking.

The French Lacanian analysts Françoise Davoine and Jean-Max Gaudillière stressed through case presentations that psychosis is not a function of the individual personality but rather always involves a relationship of a special kind. The patient in psychosis relates by putting death between himself or herself and the other. If this other is the analyst, the patient will attempt to force the analyst to that special place in the transference where the death can be interposed. What death is this? It has to do with a catastrophe, personal as well as social. This catastrophe occurred originally in the presence of another who simply registered it without responding, without naming it. The patient in turn registered it in an unsymbolized mode, akin to Bollas's "unthought known" (1987), on his or her own body—that is to say, in the Real. Unable to name it, the patient attempts to interpose it so that it can be named in the analysis. Many patients have suffered a catastrophe of gigantic social proportions: the horrors of war, massacres, the genocide of native peoples, the radical changing of national boundaries, the disappearance of entire nations. On the level of personal proportions there is the disappearance, death, suicide, mutilation, or prolonged depression of a parent or other close relation. For the psychotic patient the experience has no name and no image. The experience remains foreclosed from the imaginary and symbolic registers. The experience remains in the Real, in Peirce's category of Firstness, and it is to this place the patient leads the analyst, who tries to resist by a variety of secondary process activities—theory-building, fine interpretations, encouragement to get on with life—failing to see that the patient is embarked on a way of knowing, on a path where the terrain does not become intelligible through ordinary concepts of time, space, identity, and causality. The exploration of this field exists in a different time, a sort of time-lessness, and in a space without the usual boundaries.

Lacan (1953, p. 104), following Hegel, insists that there is an intimate link between death and naming, for the act of naming a thing amounts to a kind of "murder of the thing." How is this so? Because in the name, or the concept of the thing, the object is contained independent of its immediacy and its phys-icality. The philosopher Sokolowski, in his book, *Presence and Absence*, writes:

> A vocal response can become a name when I not only have the object before me, but appreciate it as present. I recognize that the object here does not have to be here; it could have been absent instead. I appreciate its pres-ence as contrasted to its absence. I not only enjoy the object, I enjoy the object as present. Then I can name it; I am no longer limited to making a voiced response to it. I am said to have acquired some distance towards the object. But the distance in question is not spatial, it involves only the intru-sion of the "as present" between the object and me. This is what makes the object nameable.
>
> I now can "have" the object in mind as something to be spoken about; I no longer merely have it to be consumed, fondled, or provoked. Things can be said about an object only when it is so held by a name. (1978, p. 4)

To so hold or contain something or someone by a name transforms its imme-diacy; that is, the name, functioning as a sign, introduces Thirdness by giving us a mediated relation to the person or thing. Recall Kingston's example of the horse whose fearsome image becomes instantly transformed into a part of her world: "He contained the thing in a word—*horse*, magical and earthly sound. A horse was a black creature so immense I could not see the outlines" (1980, p. 165). Even though the child could not see the outlines, she now, given the name, knew they existed, and she could, furthermore, go on to name the horse in its absence (1980, p. 167). Sokolowski stresses that such naming is not simply a matter of images or representations:

> When we name something absent, we do name what is absent. We do not name a copy, an image, a phantasm, or some other present representative of it. Names stretch into what is not here. . . . Even when they name what is present, they do so with a sense of its capacity to be not present. (1978, pp. 28–29)

Lacan put it succinctly: "Nomination is invocation of presence, and sustaining of presence in absence" (1954–55, p. 255). Such naming, furthermore, is not solipsistic: "Naming constitutes a pact whereby two subjects in the same moment agree to recognize the same object" (1954–55, p. 202).

In the psychoanalytic treatment of psychosis the heart of the problem is the struggle to kill, to destroy the catastrophe as imprinted on the body by naming it, by the creation of a signifier for what has remained unnameable because it remains embedded in the Real. What is in the Real is neither present nor absent: it is immediate, that is, unmediated. "There is no absence in the real," Lacan stated (1954–55, p. 359). To render a thing present or absent requires negating it through naming it: presence and absence are a function of the symbolic register. This is not a matter of lifting a repression, as with an experience that is forgotten because it has been inscribed in memory. On the contrary, the task is to create boundaries that make it possible to have repression. Psychotic patients are conscious of the catastrophe; they are, in fact, haunted by the thing (Davoine, 1992). What must be done in naming is to make an inscription of it so that it *can* be forgotten. "Otherwise," Davoine writes:

> this thing without a name will return through hallucination to persecute the living by asking for rest and oblivion. So that when, for any reason, it has been impossible to accomplish this naming of the thing, to accomplish the inscription of its disappearance in order to change it into a signifier, one will necessarily have to make it disappear a second time in order to stop the return of its ghost, which Lacan calls the return of the real. Well, the only way to make it disappear is to kill it, to destroy it. . . . The exploration of the psychotic search consists in the creation and destruction of limits in this space of the real, even if these limits should be those of the body itself. . . . This lasts until something is definitely destroyed and gives place to a new signifier. (1981)

The therapeutic frame must hold on long enough so that the patient's body survives and the catastrophe can be truly forgotten, that is, inscribed in the unconscious. Davoine continues: "Freud defines the unconscious as a compromise between oblivion and memory. It is the only place where the paradox of memory comes to a resolution, the paradox being that nothing is more present than an unspeakable disappearance. On the other hand, the only way to let it go is to have it written somewhere in order to forget it through memory." She gives the name on a tombstone as an example of the function of such inscription: "Not so much that one will forever remind somebody because it is written, but rather that we will forget thanks to this inscription." (For a résumé of the many texts in Freud dealing with inscription, see Derrida, 1966.)

In summary, the psychotic patient's report of being dead, decayed, or empty, the negativism, thought disorder, and disturbed family communication patterns that are well identified (e.g., Karon, 1992; Karon and Widener, 1994) have as their context a specific field in a relationship where the representation of an unnamed catastrophe has to be killed: better for this killing to be symbolic rather than real, and the symbolic killing occurs through naming. Such naming can be done in words or ritual, even by gesture or by the use of transitional objects. When we met in Canada we all witnessed another kind of naming, as enacted by a practicing medicine man. The late Joe Eagle Elk, a Lakota Sioux then in his fifties, from Rosebud, South Dakota, described how he had become a medicine man, how he experienced his relationship to what are called "spirits," and how he practiced.

Joe described how the same dream recurred to him four times, beginning when he was twelve years old, when his father scolded him for having such dangerous dreams, until his thirties, when he finally brought it to a medicine man for interpretation. The medicine man prepared Joe to make a vision quest, whose outcome made clear that Joe had to become a medicine man, and he began his rigorous training. He was thereafter very respected and very busy. In describing his work with patients, he said, quite simply, that he has no power of his own. The spirits tell him what is the nature of the problem and what has to be done about it. Often they do not tell him the cause. When he conducts a ceremony, he calls the spirits into the room, by name, for they are his friends. That is the general name for them: friends. Each spirit is called by its own individual name, and when they enter the room they speak to him. He in turn articulates what they have to say about the patient and what the patient has to do. We witnessed his healing ceremony for an allegedly hexed Ojibwa woman who, by her own report, had suffered from multiple somatic symptoms, including diabetes, liver dysfunction, vision problems, and severe headaches that had been ascribed by physicians to cerebral tumors. At one point in the ceremony Joe put on the light and asked the woman to stand in a special place while holding the ceremonial pipe. He asked her to tell the thirty-five or so of us what her problem was. Then, in total darkness, we each voiced our concerns for this woman, ourselves, and others. Then there was further chanting while the spirits spoke to Joe (the manifestation of the spirits' presence in the darkness consisted of small movements of phosphorescent-like light.) Then he again turned on a light and asked the woman to stand as before and told her, through a translator, that the spirits said: "There is nothing wrong with you. You have just been confused by what others have told you." In subsequent discussion with Joe about the actual Lakota words spoken, he said the spirits told him her problem was in her *wowacin*: the Lakota word means confidence as a combination of thought and desire (Buechel, 1970). It is the word used in the phrase "to lose one's mind," but this was not her condition. The spirits said, through Joe, that her problem is what she allowed herself to assume from others, namely the thoughts and desires of others about her; she accepted their labels into her *wowacin*, and she took these labels and exaggerated them into her symptoms. She was to leave her fears and worries in the spot where she was standing, and the spirits instructed Joe to prepare an herbal medicine, for which she was to return the next day. She did, and at a follow-up report, one year later, she was said to be fine.

Numerous psychoanalytic authors have described such an event in terms of projection and introjection, or even paranoia (Ducey, 1976); others have invoked notions of group dynamics, suggestion, and non-verbal communication (Erikson, 1950, pp. 174–75); some call it outright trickery or magic, where the medicine man is no more than a master illusionist or conjuror who takes advantage of the so-called "primitive" beliefs of the people (Boyer, 1964, pp. 403–404). Such approaches fundamentally assume "reality" as given and do not adequately take into account what Lacan draws our attention to as "the Real," and how language shapes "reality." In contrast to these psychoanalysts, Bruner and his associate write that speakers "come into a world already constituted by language" and that the child cannot learn to speak "until the child is inducted into a social world where language has already made a deep impression in shaping and even constituting the reality to which speech will refer" (Bruner and Feldman, 1982, p. 36). In his introduction to his thoughtful and richly detailed overview of South American religions, Sullivan cautions us: "Suppositions about prelogical mentality, infantilism, and primitivism are revealing poses of modern thought and deserve no depiction here. They mirror back to us the illusory self-definitions that flaunt a fragile, even wistful, hope for a privileged place in human history" (1988, p. 2).

We can attempt to conceptualize the medicine man's practice in perhaps another way. The medicine man, after rigorous discipline, is enabled to stand at the edge of the Real in highly specific, community-based rituals. Standing at the edge without being terrified, he is at the point where, through him and the ritualized space, the Real passes into language. In his culture and in those carefully defined moments, this passage of the Real into language takes the form of spirits who become articulated through his voice. In this way the patient, who addresses her demands to the Real, the Real of part of her body, the Real of death, destruction, and cultural catastrophe, receives a response, through the medicine man, from this Real. The response is framed by the entire symbolic structure that includes, in this place and time, what are called spirits. They are part of the group's reality once their presence is named. Standing at the edge of the Real, the medicine man *names*: he exercises what Sokolowski calls the mastery of presence and absence; his articulation establishes for himself, the patient, and the community a mediated relation with the Real.

In this context what we do in the analytic moment of the psychotic transference is similar: with whatever disciplined ways we possess, we stand at the edge of the Real to which our patients have led us. This may well be experienced as the patient's attempt to drive us crazy, and our discipline will often fail us as we resist. But eventually we do stand at the edge, and now and then we name: we name the death the patient brings between us, we find, usually without forethought, some signifier, gesture, or object that overcomes the immediacy of the Real, that frees the patient from a fusion with us and the surroundings, that renews perspective on his or her body, that eventually leads to an unconscious inscription that allows the catastrophe to begin to be repressed, that puts a stop to "the internal tape recorder."

What now can be said of the two examples with which we began? For the patient in the psychotic state, words no longer function in the symbolic order: they have passed into the Real, and the patient is left with only the fantastic quality of images with which to grab hold of their import. These images alternately terrify or seduce, promising destruction or paradise. The community no longer has a mediating role; the sense of isolation is extreme. For Ray, in his community of charismatics, it appears quite different. He remains firmly embedded in a structure of ritual in which standing at the edge of the Real has its own discipline and safeguards. Native religion itself can be viewed as the universal human effort to find ways to stand at the edge so that the Real can pass into language, can receive an articulation that is fresh and that challenges the complacent notions of reality to which we all too readily become adapted. The voice of the Spirit, then, may be the particular manifestation of this semiotic process, particular to Ray's community (a rather large and growing one) with its specific rituals.

To speak in this way may perhaps remind some of Carlos Casteneda and Don Juan's exploits of seeing and flying: but it has nothing to do with Casteneda, for the pervasive absence in his work of community ritual undercuts his whole fictional enterprise. As Mohatt, a psychologist who spent twenty years working on the Rosebud Sioux Reservation, cautions us:

> The medicine man does not expect that we common people are confronted with spirits only for idiosyncratic reasons. This experience says something about us in relationship to our community. Was a ritual of grieving not accomplished? Was the group in jeopardy because of disharmony and unrepaired rips in family relationships? In addition, common people aren't expected to interpret and meet spirit phenomena in everyday life. Ritual is the proper place, the medicine man the proper person. Too often current literature has encouraged a romantic idea that spirit experience can free a person or is the stuff of mystical experience. To the medicine man, the solitary spirit experience for the common man is dangerous. (1982, p. 14)

Spirits, then, may be conceptualized as the mode of passage of the Real into language in a specific context of culture and ritual. To name them is to engage them as present, in the way names allow things to be present, in the way they were presented to us by Ray, Maxine Hong Kingston, and Joe Eagle Elk. Spirits need not be thought of as substances but rather as processes, perhaps an aspect of the incomplete process of the Real as Being coming into presence through language in a particular way, particular to a cultural setting of place and a ritual moment of time. Such coming into language recalls the Heideggerean notion of Being as "perpetually under way to language" (Heidegger, 1947, p. 239). But such coming into language, as Heidegger shows, is problematic, for he writes: "But if man is to find his way once again into the nearness of Being he must first learn to exist in the nameless" (1947, p. 199). Even if Heidegger, in what we can take as a confession, can claim to have done this, few of us can exist in the nameless: perhaps the most we can do in our clinical work is to acknowledge with our patients that there *is* a nameless and from time to time stand at its edge as a witness (Felman and Laub, 1992).

In any case, to pronounce that spirits are impossible within our narrow day-to-day conceptual framework or to reduce them to projections is to pretend to know the Real. We do not and cannot know the Real. In our usual frames of reference we know about reality, this necessary construction that allows us to maintain what we call sanity, on this side of the Real, and it is language that makes this possible, as the Mexican poet Octavio Paz writes:

> The reality that poetry reveals and that appears behind language—is literally intolerable and maddening. At the same time, without the vision of this reality, man is not man, and language is not language. Poetry is the necessarily momentary perception (which is all that we can bear) of the incommensurable world which we one day abandon and to which we return when we die. Language sinks its roots into this world but transforms its juices and reactions into signs and symbols. Language is the consequence (or the cause) of our exile from the universe, signifying the distance between things and ourselves. At the same time it is our recourse against this distance. (1974, p. 132)

7

A Semiotic Correlate of Psychotic States

The breakdown that occurs in psychotic states leads us to once again question the adequacy of the dyadic paradigm for psychoanalysis, for psychosis is characterized by the structural inadequacy of the Third in both limiting and mediating the human subject. This chapter deals with the analytic Third, as recently emphasized by Shapiro and Carr (1991), Brickman (1993), Ogden (1994), Schoenhals (1995), and others who conceptualize the Third in terms of task and function, but I will explicitly refer to the foundational status of the Third as the semiotic code. As formulated by Crapanzano, it is this Third that holds the dyad: "The signifying chain, the Symbolic order, culture, and grammar we might say, serves to stabilize the relations between self and other by functioning as a Third" (1982, p. 197).

In 1946 Lacan told Henri Ey: "Not only can man's being not be understood without madness [la folie], it would not be man's being if it did not bear madness within itself as the limit of his freedom" (1966, p. 176). He repeated this in 1958 and added: "What I am saying here is that it is the business of reason to recognize the drama of madness, . . . because it is in man's relation to the signifier that this drama is situated" (1977, p. 214).

This drama was presented by a nineteen-year-old patient first hospitalized in a psychotic state. Because other patients had disturbed him, he was in the Quiet Room on the afternoon when I met him (this was not at the Austen Riggs Center). After a nurse introduced us and left, I closed the door and stood there as William sat on his mattress writing on a pad of paper. When I told him I would be his therapist, he looked up at me and then continued writing. I waited, observing that he was a fragile-looking young man, thin, very alert, intense. When William paused, I said I expected to see him in my office and that if he wanted to work today I would be there.

Ten minutes later William came, carrying the same pencil and pad of paper. I closed the door and said, "You seem very serious about what you are doing." He responded, "Write that down." I looked at him, unsure about how to take that, and asked, "You want me to write down what I say—is that what you are doing?" "Write that down, write that down," he repeated. I decided to do this, but at the cost of not knowing what it might mean: what was I for him? Was I reinforcing his sense of omnipotence? Or acting like an imaginary counterpart? I got up, found on my desk a pad of paper and a pen, and sat down, asking what were his reasons for coming into the hospital. He responded, "The experience must take its toll, the experience must take its course." The words sounded like a tape-recorded message. I then asked, while writing, "Have you had this experience before?" This may indeed have sounded to him like a tape-recorded question. He then looked up and I said, "Words can be such slippery things." He just looked at me and I repeated, "Have you had this experience before?" "My whole life," he answered. "I believe you," I said. After a pause during which his breathing was audible and he began almost to gasp, he said: "People always say to me 'Are you mad at me?' Leave me alone. It's ten to twelve."

I asked, "Would you like me to write these words down too?" He nodded yes, saying, "I can't write." I again asked, "Do you know why you came to this hospital?" He answered, "To let the experience take its toll, its course." "Do you know how long it will take?" He responded, "I know enough to know the experience must be done now. You can't think you know it all, you have all the answers." He was breathing hard. I did not tell him I was worried about his death and had to ask questions for the hospital to assess his suicidal potential.

He then said, "Come up for air." I responded, "Sometimes it feels like you're drowning." "Write that down!" he insisted, and then he went on: "I could never swim. As hard as I tried." "Something prevented you from learning?" I asked. "Write that down!" he responded and fell silent. I then said, "You strike me as the kind of person who, as your t-shirt says, makes a 100 percent effort" (his t-shirt, in red, white, and blue colors, said: "How much effort do you give?" with "100 percent" beneath the words). I went on, "You don't take things lightly or in a sloppy way." He answered immediately, "Right. I would have affirmations, like from Robert, the guy from machinery systems, the guy from professional services—asking—him questions. A question—the response—it was such a good question that it would take a whole semester to answer. I don't know if I can answer it all here." "You don't have to," I responded, not knowing the time, person, or place he was referring to but encouraged that he seemed more willing to speak, even if in a grandiose way.

He responded, "But I'll try to. You're right, I don't have to." I said: "I think you came here with some deep questions. It will take some time to ask them and to begin to answer." He responded, "I know enough not to know. The experience must take its course, its toll." I then said, "I think you came to a good place to ask questions," pressing to have some limit, some lack in him acknowledged. He responded, "I can't ask questions. I can only entrust gracefully through God. Silence in trusting you." I responded, "It may take time for you to trust me and I understand that." He then said, "Everything happens gradually—" "Yes," I almost clapped in agreement—but he continued, "—through the subconscious," and he went on: "God entrusted me to write the torus—take its toll." He paused, then added, "He always knows the truth." I said, "Which is sometimes hard for us to see," attempting to mark the difference between us and God. But he corrected me, saying about the truth, "It can only be heard. For us to see is questioned—in question—in questioning." I was struck by his attentiveness to language and wondered about his hearing voices.

I now attempted to focus on some smaller, nearby truth that I had heard and I said, "So you were in the Quiet Room because it was the most comfortable place for you?" He responded, "He has entrusted—write that down first (I had continued to write throughout the session)—he has entrusted me to let the truth be known." He paused, then went on, "He has given me profound harmony and peace, gracefully and clear—spirit of experiences." I attempted again to limit his grandiosity by saying, "We have to be patient for the truth to emerge." He gestured with his finger for me to write that down, then said, "O.K." and added, "Write *that* down." He then said, "I know enough not to know—it happens for a reason." "I agree with you," I said, and I added: "We hope to keep you safe while the experience goes on." He responded, "Write this down: I entrust you it should be written down. I know enough not to know that I must recall experiences, must be entrusted upon a person's real life experience. They only know their experience. I cannot tell you what I think they don't know." I then told him, thinking of his self-assured claim not to know, "What you say reminds me of what Socrates the philosopher taught." I then said we had to stop for today, gave him an appointment for the next day, and stood up and opened my door as I continued to write.

He remained seated and said something that sounded like "we are two noted spetshirt—nothing is possible in a state of metaphysical forgetfulness. Philosophy is a way that helps us recall what we sometimes forget. The spiritual—any spiritual experience can only be in relation to the experience. We know that people can't say two opposites at the same time. They can't say, 'I like myself' and say 'I hate myself.' Rejection moves us to the ultimate power of acceptance in the present tense."

I finished writing and told him, "I am ending the session now," and I gestured for him to leave. He got up and as we walked down the corridor he put out his hand for me to shake, I did, and then he put his arm around my shoulder, saying "Thanks." I reminded him about our next appointment time and he began to write that down as I handed him over to the head nurse who said hello to him. He did not look at her but continued writing. She looked annoyed and said, "So you don't feel like talking?" and I tried to explain that he finds words to be slippery so he writes them down.

If we reflect on this brief drama of madness, what can we say about William's relation to the signifier? What is odd about William's speech? In general, William makes sense when he speaks. Despite a few grammatical aberrations and perhaps a few neologisms, his chief problem is not with the selection and combination of signifiers, the two axes of language as presented by Roman Jakobson (1956). What, then, is his problem? Rosenbaum and Sonne (1986) examined 100 samples of psychotic discourse and concluded the aberration is in the structure of the enunciation, the ways in which the speaker as first person anchors the text in a consistent pattern of deixis, or "I-you-here-now" references (Innis, 1982; Benveniste, 1958). Jakobson and Lubbe-Grothues, in their analysis of the late poems of the nineteenth-century German poet Hölderlin, which he composed while entrenched in his extended psychotic state, called attention to the fact that "these poems have no deictic language signs or any references to the actual speech situation" (1985, p. 138), they note "the abandonment of deixis" in these poems, "the suppression of any allusion both to the speech act and its time as well as to the actual participants" (1985, p. 139). In contrast to the earlier poems, the dialogic competence of his later poems "is more or less destroyed," and the authors quote Peirce to indicate the essential role played by indices of time, place, and person in any discourse:

> It was Charles Sanders Peirce who particularly stressed the vital importance of the various "indices" for daily speech: "If, for example a man remarks, 'Why, it is raining!' it is only by some such circumstances as that he is now standing here looking out a window as he speaks, which would serve as an Index (not, however, as a Symbol) that he is speaking of this place at this time, whereby we can be assured that he cannot be speaking of the weather on the satellite Procyon, fifty centuries ago." (1985, p. 138)

Sass also notes the failure in deictic aspects of the speech of schizophrenic patients (1992, p. 177). Such deictic references are often absent in William's speech; his use of first-person references, moreover, appeared only after I repeatedly addressed questions to him as "you." As we saw in Chapter 4, this "you," spoken by an "I" as its necessary correlative, not only designates the other in dialogue: the saying of "you" is performative, it opens an intersubjective space that makes possible the emergence of the subjectivity of the other.

We may place William's grandiosity not in a linguistic context but in the larger framework of semiotics (Deely, 1982). In a semiotic framework, taken as the structure that makes possible the use of signs, I think his problem consists of an identification with the Other, with a capital O, understood as Lacan conceives it, as "le lieu où se constitue le je qui parle avec celui qui entend" (1966, p. 431), "The locus in which is constituted the I who speaks to him who hears" (1977, p. 141), "the Other qua locus of the code" (1957–58, December 11, p. 1). The Other is that which opens the signifying dimension as such, antecedent to the individuals who are speaking. The implicit premise when I speak to you who listen is that we are both subordinated to the context and code governing our exchange. Or, as someone at the Austen Riggs Center once said, "Two people cannot, without being psychotic, have a dialogue unless they are aware of the Other saying 'no'" and thereby setting limits on the generalizability and grandiosity of their speech (Ess A. White, M.D., quoted in Muller and Richardson, 1988, p. 366). The Other, Lacan tells us, is "the guarantor of good faith" (1977, p. 173), for "the signifier requires another locus—the locus of the Other, the Other witness, the witness Other than any of the partners" (1977, p, 305). The Other is "a third locus which is neither my speech nor my interlocutor"; Lacan goes on: "This locus is none other than the locus of signifying convention" (1977, p. 173). The Other is not simply the collection of words, as in a dictionary, nor is it an abstract underlying grammar, but rather we must invoke, Lacan writes, "the notion of the Other with a capital O as being the locus of the deployment of speech" (1977, p. 264). This locus includes all the complexity of culture and context in which humans exchange signs.

In terms of Peirce's architectonic theory, William, by identifying with the Other, has collapsed Thirdness onto Firstness: the category of law and mediation has been aggrandized by him in a posture of exaggerated control and mono-relatedness, thereby eliminating a place for Secondness, for the dyad, dialogue, deixis, and negation. Dewey quotes Peirce: "The idea of other, of not, becomes a very pivot of thought" (1946, p. 90), and it is precisely this which is structurally problematic in psychotic states.

William's grandiosity is distinguished from infantile grandiosity, whose exhibitionism and idealizations are addressed to others, whereas his psychotic grandiosity, as an identification with the Other, dismisses others, we others with small o's. The tragic element in William's case has to do with the fragility of this identification. His young age, his newness to treatment, his changeability in the course of our session, suggest he has not consolidated a delusional identification. At first, in the Quiet Room, he wrote what he heard, as if he is the

Other who inscribes all, the witness and record of the truth. In our initial encounter, when I invited him to join me in some work, he insisted I write down what I say, retaining his omnipotent position. When I offered to write down what he said also, he stated, "I can't write," giving up his identification with the Other, no longer in control of the code, the signifying convention, and I became with him a co-participant in the Other—until the limit of time put an end to our joint work. He then rejoined the Other as special agent, the suffering servant of God, the one with access to the whole truth based on what he hears that no one else can hear: "God entrusted me to write. . . . He always knows the truth. . . . He has entrusted me to let the truth be known. . . . Write this down: I entrust you it should be written down."

How may we understand structurally the semiotic problem here? If one says, in a Lacanian framework, that symbolic castration, the affirmation of limit, has been foreclosed in the psychotic patient, this means that difference as such is repudiated, refused, not recognized. As Francois Peraldi stated, the notion of difference "prevents us from thinking we are God, or talking black into white, . . . or to confuse the sign with the signified" (1981, p. 171). The most basic difference is between oneself and the Other. William has not established a firm boundary here and therefore his grandiosity, his delusion of omniscience, is inevitable. The inability to claim that one is incomplete is correlative with the delusional omnipotence of the Other. For such a patient there is no constraint on the Other as delusional totality and therefore no place for what Lacan calls the Barred Other, the Other as finite, as the limited field of signifying convention. If the Other can do anything or mean anything, then one must be prepared to be terrorized, to be the object of the Other's unlimited pleasure, or else one must *be* the Other and thereby find salvation.

During that first night of his hospitalization, William tried to leave the unlocked lodge several times, until finally the security staff was called. They simply stood in his way and he returned to his room. The next day, and in subsequent sessions, William did not insist that I write, so I am now using my summary notes. He was late for his session. I waited ten minutes and then went to find him. He was again sitting in the Quiet Room but came with me to my office. He began by saying he had learned to "trust" the night before when "ten security guards had to be called twice." He stated he felt more relaxed now, and I saw that he was breathing calmly.

I made some reference to his Slavic name and he said he is not Slavic. His father was adopted and he took their name. His mother, he thinks, has an English name. He went on to speak of his mother's aunt who took care of him at age three when his mother was frequently hospitalized for psychosis. He spoke warmly of this aunt.

In his next session he was again late. I once again went to find him. When we sat down in my office I brought up an earlier patient community meeting in which patients had spoken about his violations of boundaries: his walking into others' rooms, lying on others' beds, bumping into people, and opening their food in the patient refrigerator, taking a bite, even rubbing his snot on the food, and returning it to the refrigerator. When asked at the meeting to explain his behavior, he had said that it had to do with sexual feelings. I now asked him what he meant and he said, "Sexual feelings means elation." I encouraged him to say more about this, but I got nowhere and then reminded him that he had to observe the community's boundaries in order to live here.

Then I asked him how he understood his reasons for being here. He said he was here so that others could experience and grow from what God has entrusted to him. I then asked how long he thought he would be here. He said until he invents an automobile engine without exhaust. I said that may take some time and asked how much insurance coverage he had. He said he didn't know but had requested the telephone number of the Chairman of the Board of the insurance company and that "God will provide out of his great abundance." I said that would be great, but I had to know how much time we had to work together, and so I would inquire. When I asked him if he would like to know what I found out, he said "No."

For our fourth session he was again late and after ten minutes I went to find him. He had told me the previous day that he remembers everything and did not need my appointment card (which I had given to him anyway). I pointedly asked him why he was late—did he forget after telling me he remembered everything? He said he forgot. We again spoke of that morning's patient community meeting when patients again spoke to him about his ongoing assault on their boundaries and their culture. I said I hoped he could learn from what they had said to him. He said he would and had already learned. I said it was important that we acknowledge that he was here for help for himself and not just for the sake of others.

I then told him what I had learned of his medical history: that he had been born with cerebral palsy, was in no way retarded cognitively, but had a slight limp and his speech was marked by a mild dysarthria and intermittent stutter. I asked him how he had managed all these years to deal with his vulnerabilities. He said they were obstacles given by God to be overcome. "What obstacles?" I asked. He said not walking until age three and believing for a time that he had a speech problem because his father would insist that he pronounce words correctly. He said his father rejected him. I did not say that I heard that his chronically angry parents married because his mother was pregnant with him, and that he was born two months prematurely a few days after his mother became very drunk in a half-conscious attempt to abort him, and that she had periods of psychiatric hospitalization during his childhood. William went on to say he notices how some people use words of four syllables in order to get attention or show off that they had wealth—he had difficulty saying the word "wealth." I asked if he felt I would criticize his speech, that I would be like his father. He said he told his father, "I cannot satisfy your needs and I'm not willing to do so." "What were my needs in the transference?" I wondered to myself. He then went on to speak of how his mother had called his aunt to tell her, "William is afraid you are going to die—can't you tell him something?"

I had read in his record that one week before his hospitalization he became alarmed when he heard that his aging aunt, actually his mother's aunt, had breast cancer and was to have surgery. He had stayed up all night, insisted on visiting her, and had to be escorted from her hospital bedside. He had also threatened to run in front of a truck if his parents did not take him to his favorite restaurant. I did not say this to him, and William went on to tell me that in the previous year as part of his "neuro-linguistic programming" course he had "walked on fire," on hot coals, and did not feel pain or get hurt.

That night he again tried to push his way out of the lodge and had to be restrained physically by staff for several minutes. He came on time for his fifth session and said he felt relieved, that during the night he was "trying to test force with force to find the force." I told him I had been informed of another limit, namely that his insurance covered sixty days of hospitalization and that maybe we could work out a treatment plan for continuing outpatient treatment after that. He became very quiet. I waited and then asked him what he was thinking. He said he was thinking about medication. Up to that point he had refused all medication from the psychiatrist and I now urged him to take medication so that he would not feel so agitated.

Before our next, and last, session I learned there had been a mistake, that he had only thirty days of coverage, or just two weeks more. When I told him this he looked momentarily stunned and then declared that he did not need to be here anymore and wanted to leave. I explained the legal procedures of his signing a five-day notice and then a psychiatrist would assess him regarding his safety which would probably lead to a court-ordered transfer to a notoriously bad state hospital. He said he knew all of that and was eager to fight with the judge for his freedom and that if God decided he should go to a state hospital then it would be so that he could help other patients there. I urged him to stay with us so that we could perhaps make other plans, although at the moment I had no better alternative. He decided to leave and then was transferred to the state hospital. I have heard nothing of him since then.

William's problem with the Other has evident roots in his precarious, undesired existence and in the frequent breakdowns of, as Lacan puts it, "the subject who is actually led to occupy the place of the Other, namely, the Mother" (1977, p. 311). A kind of substitute mother was available in the aunt, but her recent illness exposed William's precarious existence and the radical failure of what has been called "the holding environment."

I will attempt to translate Lacan's Other into the notion of the "holding environment" in order to elaborate the semiotic framework of treatment. The notion of the holding environment was presented by Winnicott in 1954 when he wrote about the earliest period of infancy: "In primary narcissism the environment is holding the individual, and *at the same time* the individual knows of no environment and is at one with it" (1975, p. 283). Prior to the differentiation of subject and object, a process which, Freud stressed (1925a), requires the act of negation, and which, in the developmental model I am proposing, requires shifting away from enacted iconicity, there is only the Other. In an earlier paper, Winnicott (1945) did not use the notion of "holding environment" directly but foreshadowed it by describing how the early months of infancy are marked by unintegration and that the process of integration is promoted by "the technique of infant care whereby an infant is kept warm, handled and bathed and rocked and named" (1975, p. 150), thereby combining physical holding with the containing function of the name as sign. This paper was discussed by Lacan in his Seminar, *The Formations of the Unconscious* (1957–58, February 5). He stated that corresponding to the role of instincts in mapping the world of animals, the signifying dimension maps the human world before the use of speech:

> . . . even before language-learning is elaborated on the motor plane, and on the auditory plane, and on the plane that understands what he is being told, there is already from the beginning, from his first relationships with the object, from his first relationship with the maternal object, in so far as it is the primordial, primitive object, the one on which depends his first survival, subsistence in the world, this object is already introduced as such into the process of symbolization, it already plays a role that introduces into the world the existence of the signifier, this at an ultra-precocious stage. (1957–58, p. 9)

The maternal holding is structured by and as a semiotic field.

Modell takes up the notion of "holding environment" in analysis as a "frame" with "constraints" (1990, p. 39), functioning as an "illusion" (1990, p. 88), not a literal repetition of physical holding but a symbolic one. In this frame, levels of experience are transformed in terms of time, meaning, and memory. Modell makes an explicit reference to Lacan when he writes:

> The experience of the analytic setting as a holding environment is not uncommonly elaborated further into the illusion that this setting functions as a protective alternative environment that stands between the patient and a dangerous world. This is truly a transformation into another level of

reality that is not the "real" world, nor is it the world of imagination and pure fantasy. Perhaps this is what Lacan (1978 [1964]) meant when he distinguished the real, the symbolic, and the imaginary. (1990, p. 47)

The Real aspects include the element of time as a movement toward death, aspects of the body, and some destructive actions taken as attacks on the frame of treatment (what the French call "passage à l'act"). The imaginary aspects include all forms of mirroring (as we shall see in the next two chapters), while the symbolic aspects include the semiotic code governing substitutions and combinations, the unconscious as dynamic system, and enactments as conjoining both partners in displaced semiosis.

Such analytic transformation, we might say, reiterates an original transformation in which the effect of the Other is to initiate semiosis, to articulate the infant's body through signs as a set of needs. Such signing eventually transforms the experience of need-satisfaction into the desiring subject, probing and responsive to the desire of the mother. Likewise the analytic framework transforms the patient into the transference subject, probing and desiring the analyst's response, keen to know and respond to the analyst's desire. Understood in this way, the holding environment is precisely what socializes the infant, transforming the level of brute need into a culturally-based ritual of nurturing that involves an exchange of cues. The semiotic fault in psychosis appears to be due to a failure in this process.

The radical failure of the holding environment to serve as a limited field of signifying convention and thus contain grandiosity is typically seen in the psychotic patient's conviction that radio, television, and other signs are self-referential and mutually implicated: the patient's ego totally overlaps the field of the Other, so that the patient resonates with all signifying possibilities. When there is a failure in treatment to articulate clear and firm boundaries, the psychotic patient's grandiosity swells to fill the available space. Such responsivity to variations in boundary-defining acts of others suggests that some degree of differentiation has occurred and this is our basis of hope that such patients can change.

William's responsivity appeared in his readiness to enter into the relations defined by "I" and "you" once I indicated my willingness to share in his illusion of the holding environment as inscription. Neither of us challenged the basic function of the Quiet Room as holding him, but I presumed and expected him to be capable of doing work according to the code of my office, to be held by the symbolic order, as I was. I seduced him into an imaginary role with me as my patient just as he seduced me into being his scribe. My participation in these illusions, through my writing, my questions, my comments about how he "seemed" to me, was an attempt to create an alternative imaginary register, one that was not, however, purely personal, for I had not left my place in the symbolic framework of the hospital and the culture, and I deliberately introduced into our sessions the culture and boundaries of the therapeutic community. Building these shared illusions with such patients can provide an alternate frame for eventually transforming their delusional identifications by establishing a transitional space as a wider boundary outside of their imaginary domains. By building such illusions we attempt to work with the imaginary register as a necessary transitional moment. In this regard we can quote Winnicott again:

> Ought we not to say that by fitting in with the infant's impulse the mother allows the baby the *illusion* that what is there is the thing created by the baby: as a result there is not only the physical experience of instinctual satisfaction, but also an emotional union, and the beginning of a belief in reality as something about which one can have illusions. (1975, p. 163)

We have already noted an unfortunate prejudice among psychoanalysts who work with severely disturbed patients and among those who engage in infancy research—namely, a kind of preverbal bias. The phenomena they examine occur before the child can speak, and so they conclude that such phenomena are pre-linguistic, pre-symbolic, and primarily biological. What we must not overlook, as psychoanalysts, is the pervasive role of the Other, as Dore emphatically reminds us:

> We all readily believe that children acquire language in some sense. We are less ready to believe that "language acquires children...." We need a theory of what happens between speakers, and especially a theory of the interaction between how the child acquires language cognitively and how a society acquires a child functionally. (1989, p. 256)

Wilson and Weinstein attempt to introduce psychoanalytic readers to the ideas of Lev Vygotsky who died in 1934 and in whose work we can also find the place of the Other: "To Vygotsky, all higher mental functions first appear as social ("interpsychological") processes...which are interiorized ("privatized"), and transformed under the aegis of language" (1992, p. 362). In a similar manner, Wertsch and Tulviste present Vygotsky's ideas in terms of their relevance to developmental psychologists:

> Instead of beginning with the assumption that mental functioning occurs first and foremost, if not only within the individual, [Vygotsky] assumes that one can speak equally appropriately of mental processes as occurring *between* people on the intermental plane. Indeed [he] gives analytic priority to such intermental functioning in that intramental functioning is viewed as being derivative. (1992, p. 548)

The development of "interiorized," "privatized," "intramental" processes is facilitated by the appearance, around age three, of what Vygotsky terms "egocentric speech," the child's self-speech, whose dialogic features, however, as Lacan noted, mark it as inclusive of the Other and not truly egocentric (see also Wertsch, 1991). Such self-speech appears to be crucial in the child's learning to separate his or her thoughts from those of others and thereby learn to control one's behavior as one's own. "What we find once again here," Lacan states, "is the constitution of the subject in the field of the Other" (1964, p. 208). Such a subject is not only intersubjective but is in subjection to the semiotic frame as holding environment, as Third, as the limited basis for predictability. But identification with the Other, with the unbarred Other, negates intersubjectivity because it negates the place of the Third, thereby removing limits on grandiosity and omnipotence.

Some clinical implications follow from this semiotic correlate of psychotic states. A point of view, a perspective that includes the Third, the Other, this is the most important aspect of working with psychotic patients, and the most difficult to maintain in the face of transference pressures. As Rosenbaum and Sonne (1986) emphasized, these patients make you feel as if your position and your point of view don't exist. This refusal of recognition results from the profound disturbance at the level of the enunciation wherein the second person of the address is eliminated or converted into the Other with a capital O. They address the Other, not you. You are trivial, incommensurate with their grandiose aims. As transference develops, however, you can become identified with the Other, the unbarred Other, all-powerful to the patient. Such moments of psychotic transference may be dangerous, for the patient may attack you in order to destroy such pretensions in the Other, may interpret your responses as a command to attack someone else, or may attempt suicide in order to eliminate the felt difference and separation from the Other.

If I perceive such a psychotic transference developing, I try to emphasize the limits of my knowledge and power by clearly admitting my ignorance as well as by declaring that the framework of treatment, the rules of the Other, apply to me equally, and precede me, and are not the product of my whimsy. I try to indicate that each of us, singly and as a dyad, are bound by and secured in the Third. It is crucial at times for the analyst to speak *for* the Other, but not *as* the Other.

It is only after the patient and I begin to mark the boundaries that limit us that I attempt to address symbolic derivatives, such as William's messing with food or concern about exhaust, as possible signifiers. I think it is important to hear these elements, but not to interpret them in speech, for their signifying function, their generativity in producing associated signifiers will, I think, most likely be overwhelmed by the patient's narcissism. If our own narcissism compels us to show how smart we are in hearing these clues, we will likely generate hostility.

When the patient's identification with the Other is challenged, the patient often reacts by attacking limits and boundaries. Such behavior includes coming late, wanting to meet in the patient's room, not washing, threatening to injure somebody, throwing things in the office, and the various ways William showed he was not subject to the culture of the therapeutic community. Such boundary violations must be addressed directly, calmly, and repeatedly, and in a hospital setting it is important to explain to other staff and patients, who have to endure the unpleasantness, and sometimes destructiveness, of such behavior, that the patient is ambivalently struggling to put an acceptable marker at the edge of his or her being and requires feedback from others to succeed in containing his or her inflated ego.

Such repeated boundary violations, when addressed in this way, usually expose in the patient a powerful contempt for the symbolization of limits. This contempt often takes the form of seeing the other patients as inferior because they have swallowed the staff's ideology that symbolization can provide stable references, that cultural norms can contain behavior, that there is any weight to forms of human influence beyond brutal force. Such patients eventually say quite clearly that words are useless. They put to the test Peirce's claim that semiosis produces effects at least equal to those of mechanical forces.

Because words are indeed slippery things, because they can mean anything or nothing, they are often useless to such patients. Instead of attempting verbal interpretations, I have sometimes found that asking the patient to draw has proved stabilizing during psychotic episodes in order to perform a kind of reverse sublimation, a transformation whereby the edge of the Real becomes an object (Muller, 1987b). I have also attempted to take an explicit semiotic stance with patients who periodically become speechless and then deliberately cut themselves. I ask what they cut and more often than not, as noted earlier, such cutting appears to be a form of writing, of inscription on the skin, as if the patient is attempting to put a marker at the edge of the self, to mark the frontier by transgressing it (Davoine, 1989). The challenge for our treatment of these kinds of patients is to articulate and sustain the holding environment, the Other, long enough so that they do not destroy themselves or the therapeutic community.

As William's case sadly illustrates, however, such a holding environment, where we can conduct the kind of necessary treatment, is not available in most of the United States because of the economic politics of health care. This is not only detrimental to the patient but also to us, for we must continue to learn from such work what makes us human beings, and to understand what Bataille meant when he wrote, "no longer to wish oneself to be everything is for a human being the highest ambition, it is to *want* to be human" (1954, p. 25).

8

The Ego and Mirroring in the Dyad

For Lacan, the grandiosity of the psychotic ego, the narcissistic rejection of limits, has its structural basis in the ego itself. Lacan endorses that side of Freud's critique of human self-awareness that sees the ego as narcissistic, as when Freud wrote: "The desire for a powerful, uninhibited ego may seem to us intelligible; but, as we are taught by the times we live in, it is in the profoundest sense hostile to civilization" (1938, p. 185).

In this chapter I will review data that supports Lacan's critique of the ego. This data suggests that the limited capacity of the subject to say "I" in any but a self-serving manner casts doubt on the "I-you" relation itself. I am inclined to think (owning at least some of my own self-serving biases) that the ego's narcissistic domination of the "I-you" relation is in part illusory and dislodged by the unpredictability of "you" speaking from the position of the Other. For this reason, I believe, Lacan stated: "The I is essentially fleeting in nature and never entirely sustains the thou" (1955–56, p. 287).

But there may be more to the ego than Lacan grants: Smith (1991) has cogently argued that in Freud and even within Lacan's own framework we have to grant to the ego a non-defensive function that seeks to face danger and to integrate rather than disavow data. Lacan's critique of the ego, however, is in part a reaction to its elevation in American ego psychology to the position of arbiter of reality, a role especially reserved in that tradition to the ego of the analyst. His critique may be useful to engage now as we see in the ascendancy of the dyad the elevation of the function of mirroring.

As mirror phenomena have received increased attention, we have found a diffusion of meaning. Dervin sees mirroring as perhaps "a quite natural phenomenon that contributes to both self and object representations" (1980, p. 138). On the other hand, C. Goldberg (1984) views the double as a second self but, at the same time, also a counter-self and a mirror of unacknowledged, even unattainable aspects of oneself. Thus, what is mirrored can include what is visible at the surface as well as what is not visible, that which is disavowed, and even impossible. In this usage, the mirror becomes not a reflector but a kind of magical window. While Goldberg stresses how mirror phenomena cast doubt on the self's unity and identity, Pines claims the opposite. Pines emphasizes that the mother's selective responses to the child's behaviors reinforce certain behaviors and thereby promote an identity: "basically the same invariant personal theme of identity has been laid down in a mirroring relationship to mother" (1984, p. 32). But under a category of mirroring response, Pines includes a wide variety of responses and in the process seems to equate feedback and responsiveness of any sort with a mirroring response. Feedback about one's actions or presentations, however, is not necessarily mirroring; feedback may convey a recognition of difference and otherness precisely by refusing to mirror.

Lacan provides a framework for understanding this distinction between mirroring and recognition in the way he specifies the structure of mirroring phenomena. He locates mirroring in the register of the imaginary, that sensuous, perceptible aspect of experience that has point-to-point correspondence as its essential feature (Lacan, 1954–55, p. 65; 1964, p. 86). The imaginary register is structured by a field of spatial (and usually visual) representations whose chief visual property is fixed but illusory correspondence. For example, between a slide or image in an overhead projector and its reflected image on a screen, a series of straight lines can be drawn, passing through lenses that create virtual images so that the pattern of relationships of their points of origin is duplicated by the pattern on the screen. This illusory point-to-point correspondence is the essential feature of mirroring, the chief and most salient process in the register of the imaginary. Thus, mirroring reflects back the illusion of sameness and is almost always found in a dyadic relationship wherein one seeks to be affirmed as idealized by the other, to be found iconically in the consciousness of the other just as one is found in one's own narcissistic consciousness. When the other does not hold this view, one may then seek to impose it, often in aggressive coercion.

Given this structure of illusory correspondences, conveying differences is beyond the capacity of mirroring. In order to convey difference there must be a structure that does more than merely represent iconically, for it must have the capacity to symbolize opposition, and such a structure is provided only by language (Fodor, 1981). Thus, for Lacan, difference is a function of the symbolic register, that aspect of experience whereby signification is introduced as distinct from representation. Representation, understood as Peirce's icon, requires resemblance, whereas signification rests on difference, the difference between the index and its cause, the difference between the symbol, its interpretant, and its object. At its most basic level, signification rests on the absence of the object named, on the difference between word and thing, and on the differences among words: "in language there are only differences," wrote Saussure (1916, p. 120). Jakobson and Halle followed with: "All phonemes denote nothing but mere otherness" (1956, p. 11). Words have salience, not through any positive substance or value each is assumed to contain (and certainly not because they resemble things), but rather through the reciprocal differentiations enabling phonetic distinctiveness to occur: "Phonemes are characterized not, as one might think, by their own positive quality but simply by the fact that they are distinct. Phonemes are above all else opposing, relative, and negative entities" (Saussure, 1916, p. 119). For differences to be conveyed, therefore, there must be some form of articulation (making use of words, gestures, even images taken as signifiers) that mirroring, as such, cannot provide. When a group provides such articulation in the form of feedback about an individual's behavior, it would seem inappropriate to call this mirroring rather than recognition and feedback. Therefore, I will use the notion of interpersonal mirroring to mean that kind of iconic relationship in which one images another, reflecting back an identity of thoughts, feelings, or behavior, implying an identification of desires, a positive agreement, an admiration that provides narcissistic support.

In 1936 Lacan delivered at the 14th International Psychoanalytic Congress in Marienbad an unpublished paper on the origins of the ego in the "mirror phase" of child development, whose basic themes then appeared in an encyclopedia article on "The Family" (1938). His later published paper, "The Mirror Stage as Formative of the Function of the I as Revealed in Psychoanalytic Experience," was delivered at the 16th International Congress of Psychoanalysis in Zurich in 1949. This paper provided Lacan's basic formulations about the mirror phase, together with "Aggressivity in Psychoanalysis," delivered in 1948, and, in 1951, "Some Reflections on the Ego." The first two were published in his collection of papers titled *Ecrits* (1966) and were selected by Lacan for translation into English (1977).

Lacan, drawing on the work of the French child psychologist Henri Wallon (1931), presented a basic observation which "consists simply in the jubilant interest shown by the infant over eight months at the sight of his own image in a mirror . . . [and] in games in which the child seems to be in endless ecstasy when it sees that movements in the mirror correspond to its own movements" (1951, p. 14). Lacan presented this paper, in English, to the British Psychoanalytic Society; Winnicott later responded by emphasizing "the child's seeing the self in the mother's face" (1967, p. 117). Although Lacan recognized (1938, pp. 45, 48) that the whole human form with whose image the child is likely to identify is that of another's body, and specifically the mother's (Richardson, 1978–79), he took as his basic paradigm for the origin of the ego the infant's positive response to its image in a mirror.

From the work of W. Köhler (1925) Lacan knew that chimpanzees are also capable of responding to their mirror reflections as images of themselves, but they soon lose interest, whereas the infant sustains a "jubilant" response to his or her own image (1977, p. 2). Research by Gallup (1977) later found that chimpanzees and orangutans are the only animals thus far showing this capability.[1] The research of Lewis and Brooks-Gunn (1979) moreover, provided ample experimental verification for Lacan's description of the infant before the mirror (Muller, 1982b).

Lewis and Brooks-Gunn reported that most infants indicate they perceive the image in the mirror as their own by eighteen months of age, and at equivalent mental ages similar indications are given by mentally retarded children (Mans et al., 1978; Hill and Tomlin, 1981). This period from eight to eighteen months wherein Lacan located the mirror phase (at times he dated its onset at six months) also includes the consolidation of object permanence required if the infant is capable of identifying its own image as persisting and distinct from others (Baer and Wright, 1974, pp. 37–38; Lewis and Brooks-Gunn, 1979, p. 224). Moreover, this is also when the capacity for long-term memory appears, as evidenced in delayed visual recognition of previously presented complex forms (Cohen, 1979; Rose, 1981), although, as we have seen earlier, some capacity for long-term memory is evident by one month.

Lacan attributed the infant's positive response to the whole form of the human body with which it identifies to the universal human condition of prematurity at birth, a condition noted by Freud (1926, p. 154) and argued by Gould as necessary if the infant's head (only one-quarter of its eventual size) is not to exceed the limits of the maternal pelvic cavity. Gould cited evidence that led him to conclude: "Human babies are born as embryos, and embryos they remain for about the first nine months of life" (1976, p. 22)—that is, they are "ready" to be born during the period at which Lacan located the mirror phase, the period of readiness to perceive and identify with the *Gestalt* of the human form. The infant's jubilance at this moment is due to the imaginary anticipation of the form's coherence, mastery, stature, and unity, a *Gestalt* that

---

1.   Epstein and colleagues have attempted a Skinnerian demonstration of this capability in pigeons (1981) and have presented it in a film which has been criticized sharply (Gallup, 1984). Gallup, in turn, has been criticized for claiming that mirror self-recognition is linked to the cognitive capacity to attribute mental states to others (Bard, 1994).

sharply contrasts with the concomitant features of prematurity, namely, a pervasive neuromuscular discoordination and experience of helplessness. To identify with the whole human form in this narcissistic way has a defensive function of concealing helplessness and discoordination under the cover of perceived coherence, unity, and mastery, and this defensive function is one of the central roles the ego will come to play in development, for the body in humans is never simply a given in experience, but must be constructed through the elaboration of the body image (Ver Eecke, 1983).

A further consequence of the mirror phase is what Lacan, following C. Bühler (1927) and E. Köhler (1926), called "transitivism."[2] During the period from six months to two-and-a-half years the child is subject to a captivation by the image of another child of roughly the same age (Lacan, 1977, p. 19). In dual play each is observed to alternate between the positions of pursuer/pursued, seducer/seduced, master/slave. One cries at seeing the other fall. What one desires the other wants. This confusion of identities argues for the powerful effect of the visual form of the counterpart as well as the luring aspect of being seen by another.

The vision of the human form as a *Gestalt* that the infant takes to be oneself, this mirror-reflection of the human body, is for Lacan distinct from "the self" or "the subject." In calling it the ego, Lacan emphasized its structure as the foundational, narcissistic identification and basis for all subsequent identifications; in this sense it is precisely the ego defined by Freud as "the precipitate of abandoned object-cathexes" (1923, p. 29) and is consistent with his view of the ego as "first and foremost a bodily ego" (1923, p. 26), responsible for resistance, self-protective, and the first love object (1914a, p. 75). The structure of reflected identity that gives rise to the ego necessarily situates the ego in an inevitable distortion proper to all mirrors (Thomas, 1980) and in an alienation from the individual taken as subject. Reflected identity is an object for the subject, an other for the subject, for its origin grounds it as an exterior representation. Consciousness thereby becomes prone to viewing itself as "correct" when it reflects reality, and this iconic notion of the mind being a "mirror" of nature has been a major obstacle to genuine inquiry (Rorty, 1979). Not only is an intrusive alienation thus established at the center of consciousness, but the ego as reflection is a rigid representation functioning as "the armour of an alienating identity, which will mark with its rigid structure the subject's entire mental development" (Lacan, 1977, p. 4). The ego resists flexible change, exerts a repressive effect on the unconscious desire of the subject (Freud, 1918, pp.

---

2. Henri Wallon, whose influence Lacan acknowledged (1977, p. 18) referred this notion to Wernicke (1900, p. 226): "The attribution to another of what is proper to us results from an illusion signalled by Wernicke under the name of transitivism" (1921, p. 53).

110–12), and shapes reality to suit its own requirements—namely, the maintenance of its own attributes of permanence, identity, and substantiality (Lacan, 1977, p. 17). The mirror phase, moreover, establishes the framework for intersubjective illusion insofar as it enables the child now to mirror the mother's desire, to be what the mother wants so as to please her.

An early, persistent, and perhaps more common way of pleasing others is by imitating them. The self-serving role of imitation as mirroring appears, for example, in the effect that imitation generally has of making the imitator more attractive to the one being imitated (Yando et al., 1978). Thelen and Kirkland (1976) summarized research indicating that being imitated increases one's attraction toward the imitator and leads to increased allocation of rewards and to reciprocal imitation. They also found that schoolchildren like and imitate those *older* children who imitate them, but this was not the case when imitated by younger children (presumably, because the younger children were viewed as of lower status and less masterful). The same children also judged their own performances to be better when they were imitated by an older child than when imitated by a younger child, whose imitation was actually found to be unwanted.

While the research tradition in the area of imitation is vast, previous naturalistic observation as well as controlled studies tended to date the capacity for imitation at "around the end of the first year, roughly between nine and thirteen months" (Abravanel and Sigafoos, 1984, p. 381). These researchers attempted to produce imitation in younger infants, but generally no well-formed copies of adult modeling appeared in infants aged one to five months (tongue protrusion, they suggested, appeared as a released response, not a genuine imitation). An earlier study reported that imitative behavior was observed during the first weeks of life (Meltzoff and Moore, 1977), but this report was severely criticized on methodological grounds (Anisfeld, 1979; Masters, 1979) and an attempt to replicate it (Jacobson and Kagan, 1979) failed to obtain results showing that one- to two-month-old infants can selectively imitate a model. As we have seen, however, the more recent research of Field and her associates (1982) as well as Trevarthen (1989) confirm that very young infants can indeed be brought into a resonantial, iconic facial mirroring response to adults. The degree of active control that imitation requires may be unavailable at this early age, and this variable of control may usefully distinguish imitation from the involuntary, empathic, and less conscious processes of identification based on emotional contagion and enacted iconicity.

We have additional data congruent with the Lacanian model of the mirror-phase infant. Asendorpf and Baudonniere (1993) observed 112 pairs of nineteen-month-olds in dyadic play. Sustained synchronic imitation occurred only in those dyads in which both partners showed, on another measure, the capacity for explicit self-recognition. This suggests that overt imitation of another peer requires discrete self-awareness. Kagan found that infants begin to imitate an adult's behavior around nine or ten months of age, but thereafter peer imitation increased with age, especially after two years. This period (after one year) includes the appearance of "mastery smiles" occurring while pursuing or having attained a goal in solitary play. At eighteen to twenty-four months Kagan observed the emergence of evaluative standards, as indicated by attention to broken toys, missing upholstery buttons, and other *Gestalt* violations, which, in a psychoanalytic context, can also be viewed as cues suggesting the possibility of bodily fragmentation and, therefore, a violation of the basic evaluative standard of body integrity. Kagan also observed distress following an adult model's performance, indicating apprehension "because of a self-imposed obligation to perform actions that [the child] is not sure she can implement" (1981, p. 54). Such "obligation," we can further surmise, is imposed by the ego's pursuit of mastery in imitation of masterful models or in an attempt to maintain desirability in the eyes of the masterful model.

A review of more than 80 studies on imitation in children yielded an account of imitation as a cognitive tool enhancing competence and strengthening attachments (Yando et al., 1978). One would expect, therefore, that children will prefer to imitate parents, and this is precisely what Rothbaum (1976) reported in his study of children aged seven, ten, and fourteen years, who were found to imitate parents over strangers, and especially parents who agreed with each other. Children are also more likely to imitate a model's behavior if they are rewarded for doing so (that is, imitation gets them what they want); some characteristics of the model, such as prestige, competence, or dominance, can signal to the child that imitation of these models will get them what they want (Bandura, 1971).

Children may also know that through imitation they can manipulate adults, for the self-enhancing effects of being mirrored through imitation extend to adults. Bates (1975) found that adult models were more sensitive to children who imitated them than toward those who did not; that is, adults displayed in the presence of the imitating child more nonverbal cues of positiveness and responsiveness, talked more, remained in closer proximity, looked at the child's face more, showed fewer negative expressions, and, further, they rated the imitating child higher on intellectual and social characteristics. The effects of mirroring and being mirrored even appear to influence punitiveness. Berkowitz and Dunand (1981) found that subjects in a hot room gave the most severe punishment to a peer when she appeared not to be bothered by the heat and were least punitive when she seemed to share in the suffering: "In sum, we come to like those who (we believe) have the same emotional feelings we do when they are exposed to the same unpleasant condition" (Berkowitz, 1983, p. 114).

Evidence for such narcissistic influences on judgment extend well beyond research on imitation. Consistent and repeated experimental findings show a pervasive self-serving bias in one's judgments (Greenwald, 1980; see also Muller, 1986). This bias takes the form of exaggerating one's role in effecting desired outcomes while minimizing one's role in bringing about undesired outcomes. For example, in a study by Johnston (1967), subjects were told that each had a partner with whom they had to perform a task of skill; "feedback" was subsequently given to each "team" (there was, in fact, no partner). Afterward, in cases of designated "above average" performance, subjects took credit for the success, while the assumed partner was blamed when the performance was labeled "below average." Even when the performance was called "average," subjects believed that their own above-average performance was lowered by the below-average performance of the fictive partner, and this resulted in the "average" designation. There are many experiments of this sort that yield a consistent pattern of results (Zuckerman [1979] reviewed more than 75 such attribution studies; see also Greenberg and Pyszczynski [1985]) in which the self-serving bias appears when subjects engage in direct competition with one another or when one's own performance is the focus of the evaluation, but not when another is the focus. It is in the domain of oneself that we find the ego's self-enhancing activity to be predictably prominent. A recent study by Jussim (reported in Bower, 1994) once again found that college students claimed more responsibility for their performance outcomes when they were given positive feedback than when they were criticized, but this finding held only for those with high self-esteem and was reversed in the case of those with low self-esteem.

Additional findings (Abramson and Alloy, 1981) indicate that depressed subjects, when compared to "normal" subjects, do not show this self-serving bias; that is, nondepressed subjects exaggerate others' positive views of them (Lewisohn et al., 1980); they claim to be able to control uncontrollable events (Alloy et al., 1981); they underestimate the amount of negative feedback others give them (Nelson and Craighead, 1977); they overreward their own performances (Rozensky et al., 1977); and they make internal attributions for their successes while blaming their failures on external factors (Abramson and Alloy, 1981). On the other hand, those who make such self-serving, distorted attributions have better cancer outcomes. Taylor (1983) examined the treatment course and beliefs of women with breast cancer and found that patients who do best make exaggerated and illusory attributions that they or their physicians can control the illness, and they make self-enhancing social comparisons (no matter how severe their illness, they claim to be better off than others). If idealization can be termed a form of "mirroring up," then these self-enhancing social comparisons can be viewed as a type of "mirroring down" wherein the reflection of the other contains one's misfortune, but worse. In subsequent research (reported in Bower, 1994) Taylor found that people are realistic when assessing and making plans to resolve personal problems, but manifest positive illusions about themselves when implementing their plans.

The joining of this experimental data with Lacan's model of ego formation in the mirror phase can be interpreted in light of a constraints model of the ego. Keil (1981) suggests a paradigm that we can use to conceptualize the ego as a set of constraints restricting and distorting knowledge of the domain of oneself. Such a set of constraints limits how this domain is viewed, accounts for the effortless and rapid acquisition of distorted knowledge of this domain, makes such knowledge less accessible to conscious introspection and change, is associated with felt anomalous neurotic symptoms, and leads to specific structural features.

If we view the arena of imitation, social comparison, and self-evaluation in this way, namely, as the field wherein the ego attempts to buttress its position of mastery and coherence through mirroring illusions, then these empirical findings appear to confirm some psychoanalytic observations. For example, Freud describes "the metamorphosis of the parental relationship into the super-ego" in the following terms:

> The basis of the process is what is called an "identification"—that is to say, the assimilation [*eine Angleichung,* a likening or approximation] of one ego to another [*ein fremdes,* a foreign, even unfamiliar] one, as a result of which the first ego behaves like the second in certain respects, imitates it and in a sense takes it up into itself. (1933, p. 63)

The first ego, confronted with the overwhelming (and strange) superior authority of the parent, does its best to resemble by imitation that parent, and thereby placates him or her by mirroring. Just three years later Anna Freud went on to describe identification as "one of the ego's most potent weapons in its dealings with external objects which arouse its anxiety" (1936, p. 110). She explicates "one of the most natural and widespread modes of behavior on the part of the primitive ego" as "the physical imitation of an antagonist" (1936, p. 111): "By impersonating the aggressor, assuming his attributes or imitating his aggression, the child transforms himself from the person threatened into the person who makes the threat" (1936, p. 113). We can wonder how much this mirroring procedure of the ego accounts for children's aggressive behavior (Hall and Cairns, 1984) as well as for the influence of televised aggression (Huesmann et al., 1984), especially if the growing child appears to learn that in our society aggression is a sanctioned way to assert mastery.

Given the defensive, self-protective, and distorting effects of imitation and identification, what valence do we give such processes when they do occur in treatment, when, for example, the patient begins to dress, act, speak, or think like the analyst, adopting the analyst's attitudes and opinions, and inquiring silently what the analyst would do in a given situation? Meissner views such forms of imitation as problematic:

> A difficult question for the analyst to assess is whether these imitations serve the purposes of the analysis or whether they represent resistances. When these imitative patterns are motivated by the need to please, placate, or attach oneself to an idealized or feared object, they must be recognized as defensive. (1981, p.12)

If the Lacanian ego is at work here, such imitation would seem to be intrinsically defensive. Is this not precisely how the ego, with its iconic structure, necessarily functions? Meissner distinguishes imitation (which he views as an external behavior) from identification (which he calls an internal process) and then reserves a positive place for "the ego's inherent tendency toward identification" because the "patient's imitative use of analytic attitudes, especially in the context of a positive therapeutic alliance, can have a powerful inductive impact on the development of meaningful, constructive identifications with the analyst" (1981, p. 15). Such iconic processes may be required to prevent fragmentation, to establish cohesion and boundaries for the self in the most regressed modes of a hierarchical framework (Gedo and Goldberg, 1973; Gedo, 1993), but they may be a source of resistance when assumed as a goal of treatment.

This goal of analysis, formulated in terms of some kind of internalization of or identification with the analyst, appears to be widely accepted. Loewald states that identification between patient and analyst "is, as is always claimed, a necessary requirement for a successful analysis" (1960, p. 19). Schafer writes of "a kind of internalization of the analyst as analyst into the analysand's ego and ego ideal organization that has much to do with his or her subsequent capacity for, and interest in, benignly influential self-analysis" (1976, p. 47). Kohut addresses how the analytic process, through "optimal frustrations" and "timely interpretations," leads to "the transmuting internalization of the selfobject analyst and his functions and thus to the acquisition of psychic structure" (1984, p. 172). Atwood and Stolorow also underscore "the patient's gradual internalization of the analyst's observational stance" (1984, p. 61). The patient becomes able to tolerate separation by using "an image of the analyst's empathic responsiveness," and gradually "the concrete images of the analyst" are no longer necessary "once the internalization of the analyst's empathic qualities becomes fully integrated into the subjective self" (1984, p. 62). This contemporary formulation can be read as essentially re-presenting earlier ones; for example, Strachey emphasized that the chief curative mechanism in altering the status of introjected and projected "bad objects" lies in the way the patient's super-ego is modified by "the repeated process of introjection of imagos of the analyst" which functions as the patient's "auxiliary super-ego" through mutative interpretations whose aim is "to cause the introjection of the analyst" (1934, p. 157n).

Simultaneous with Strachey's paper appeared a paper by Sterba (1934) and, although Bergmann and Hartman view the two as "poles apart in what they consider crucial for the process of psychoanalytic treatment" (1976, p. 361). Sterba also stressed the curative value of interpretation in the context of "a certain amount of positive transference, on the basis of which a transitory strengthening of the ego takes place through identification with the analyst. This identification is induced by the analyst" (1934, p. 121). This focus on identification with the analyst is neither old-fashioned nor a "deviance" due to self-psychology; Solomon, in her presidential address to the American Psychoanalytic Association, stated:

> Thus self- and object representations are modified as a result of analysis. The modification of the self-representation is based in part on the identification with the analyst. The effective identification is . . . with the "realness" demonstrated by the consideration and respect for the patient. . . (1982, p. 341).

Blum, endorsing Loewald's position, states that the "analyst is an extraordinary new object with whom the patient identifies and who offers the patient the awareness of the patient's developmental potential" (1981, p. 59); Blum goes on to endorse the views of Strachey and Sterba on the patient's identification with the analyst (1981, p. 61). One finds similar views voiced elsewhere (e.g., Greenson, 1967; Zetzel, 1970).

Since I have not been able to find a citation of Freud advancing the curative role of identification with the analyst, I wonder if Freud ever promoted this notion. Clearly Lacan does not (1954–55, p. 88), and he criticizes this "terminal identification" of the patient's ego with the analyst's ego because it leads to a "reinforced alienation" (1977, p. 274) of the original alienation of the mirror phase. That is, the patient enters analysis precisely because he suffers from symptoms due to the splitting off of his unconscious desire by an ego rigidly maintaining the faltering illusion of coherence and mastery. How then can analysis assist if it serves to reinforce and strengthen the ego's illusory position? There is no doubt that the patient's ego will aim at an identification with the analyst, and it may be true that Lacan's own analysands suffered such a fate (Silverman, 1983), but what can justify giving this process a central curative role in the theory of psychoanalysis?

Althusser offers one way to understand the promotion of the goal of identification with the analyst when he analyzes the concept of ideology in terms of mirroring. He argues from a Marxist position that the repressive State apparatus achieves its goal of maintaining control by means of ideology, whose main effect is to create the illusion of individual subjectivity, whose fictive autonomy mirrors, as a reflection, the autonomy, in turn, of an absolute Subject. In his concrete example, he analyzes the tradition of Judaeo-Christian religious teaching and practice in terms of the way it "*subjects* the subjects to the Subject, while giving them in the Subject in which each subject can contemplate its own image (present and future) the *guarantee* that this really concerns them and Him" (1971, p. 180). Althusser's analysis captures, I think, the way religion operates when it loses its place in the Third in relation to the State; in other words, when it identifies with political aspirations, thereby colluding with dyadic processes, including the love-hate oscillations that increase the likelihood of violence. Likewise when identification with the analyst becomes the goal of treatment, the analyst has lost the required place in the Third from which dyadic processes can be discerned (as we will see in the next chapter on Kohut's analysis of Mr. Z). Althusser draws on Lacan in utilizing the category of the imaginary for all ideologies insofar as they are inherently structured by mirroring modes. If we utilize this framework regarding the view of psychoanalysis that relies on identification with the analyst as a central curative factor and a goal, then we may wonder how much of the effect of treatment is due to the effects of ideology. The "psychoanalytic ideology" would aim, then, to create the illusion of individual, autonomous subjectivity strengthened as a result of mirroring the presumed autonomous knowing subject who is the analyst (Muller, 1992b).

A relentless suspicion governs Lacan's treatment of the ego: "That the ego is a capacity to fail to recognize [*méconnaissance*] is the very foundation of the technique of analysis" (1953–54, p. 153). But from the ego's defensive position, any regression to an earlier period is associated with anxiety and loss of autonomy: "This illusion of unity, in which a human being is always looking forward to self-mastery, entails a constant danger of sliding back again into the chaos from which he started" (1951, p. 15). Such regression, Lacan notes, typically occurs in dreams that involve body fragmentation, decapitation, ripping open, etc., especially during a phase of analysis dealing with

> the earliest problems of the patient's ego and with the revelation of latent hypochondriacal preoccupations. . . . Their appearance heralds a particular and very archaic phase of the transference, and the value we attributed to them in identifying this phase has always been confirmed by the accompanying marked decrease in the patient's deepest resistances. (1951, p. 13)

Such archaic transference must, of course, be treated with care, for any attempt to dismantle the ego produces aggressivity as an inevitable response (1977, pp.

16–22). All aggression, in fact, can be viewed as a response to insult, challenge to the ego's sense of mastery, or physical violation of the sense of bodily integrity. Guntrip writes that "aggression is a personal meaningful reaction to bad object relations, to a threat to the ego, aroused initially by fear" (1971, p. 37). The ensuing aggression serves to reinforce the ego's illusion of coherence and mastery, and as noted earlier, research evidence suggests that the absence of such illusions is associated with depression.

In paranoia, such illusions remain intact but become expansive to the point that otherness as such becomes intolerable. There are no relative perspectives, there is only one truth (the ego's), and what is attacked in delusions of perse- cution is precisely one's ideal ego projected onto others. DeWaelhens writes: "The paranoiac is one for whom every relation to otherness is structurally a reproduction of the mirror-couple" (1972, p. 74), which is the product of the mirror phase, namely, the libidinal tie between the subject and its image, the ego. In this mirror-couple, "the ego and its other are indefinitely reciprocal and reversible. The subject seeks to find his identity in the image, but this identity with himself is, in some fashion, his other" and this other is the privileged member of the couple "since it will serve as the norm, the *imago*, of that which I must become . . . in order to be." The desire to eliminate "all difference between the members of the couple, and the impossibility of accomplishing it, engenders a destructive aggressivity that, on whichever member of the couple it is set loose, will always be self-destructive" (DeWaelhens, 1972, p. 73). Thus Lacan uses the pun *haine-amouration* (love – hate = enamoration) to describe the affective tie binding dyadic object relations in which ego is related to ego as an "imaginary couple" (1966, pp. 54, 344–45). Such a view of psychoanalytic practice as reduced to a dyadic relation, as a practice in which the symbolic register is suppressed in favor of a "utopian rectification of the imaginary couple" can arouse in "everyone of good faith" only "the sentiment of abjec- tion" (1966, p. 54, my translation).

Lacan acknowledges that mirroring and identification are inevitable ego processes and, therefore, that they will go on in analysis. He charts their place in the course of treatment that begins with a "rectification of the subject's relation with the real"; I take this to include making those interventions that are "beyond interpretation" (Gedo, 1993), in order to assist the patient suffer- ing from fragmentation anxiety, by putting a boundary at the edge of the Real. We move from the Real to the imaginary register as treatment then "proceeds . . . to the development of the transference," wherein the analysand repetitively seeks to lure the analyst into a dyadic hate-love relationship as ego to ego. The observation of such repetitive reconfigurations leads "then to interpretation" (Lacan, 1977, p. 237), whereby the semiotic matrix of the patient's unconscious desire can be recognized and articulated. For Lacan, "there is no two-body psychology without the intervention of a third element. If, as we must, we take speech as the central feature of our perspective, then it is within a three- rather than two-term relation that we have to formulate the analytic experience in its totality" (1953–54, p. 11; see also 1974). The treatment ends not with the patient's identification with the analyst but with the patient finding the analyst to be no longer necessary, since the patient would now have the capability of finding and being held by the Third in future situations and relationships.

If identification with the analyst and thereby strengthening the ego is not the goal of treatment, what then becomes the aim of analysis? Lacan stresses that the aim of analysis is the recognition and articulation of desire. Desire emerges in the gap or lack (*manque*) opened by the separation between the infant's fantasy and the mother's reality. This separation is due to the mother's intermittent absence and the child's realization that the mother has other objects of desire besides the child. The separation is enforced by the law against incest and other societal norms whose delegate is the father, or the paternal function.

Lacan's paradigm for the moment when "desire becomes human" (1977, p. 103) was the *Fort-Da* episode of Freud's grandson (described by Freud, 1920, pp. 14-15) in which the child was observed to throw a spool tied to a string over the edge of his crib uttering "O-O-O-O" (the German *Fort*, "Gone") and, when retrieving it, *Da!* ("there"). The absent and then present spool, conjoined with the reciprocally opposed phonemes, is taken as an enactment in transitional space of both the mother's absence as well as a loss of that aspect of oneself implicated in the former imagined state of being the mother's completion. Thus the symbolization makes a place for absence, as such, whose recognition is henceforth inscribed in language. The want is a want-to-be or lack in being ("*manque-à-être*," 1977, p. xi) that gives rise to desire as an incessant series of displacements of this original want, a series structured by articulated linguistic formations whose conventional structures stand in the way of free associations. Lacan asks:

> What use do we make of language and of speech in the cure? In the analytic relation there are two subjects linked by a pact. This pact is set up on levels which are very diverse, even very confused, at the beginning. It isn't, in essence, any the less a pact. And we do everything, via the preliminary rules, to establish this aspect quite firmly at the beginning. Within this relation, the initial task is to untie the moorings of speech. (1953–54, p. 181)

When desire is repressed by a strong, not a "weak" ego, substitutions appear: these are symptoms, structured as metaphors (Muller and Richardson, 1982, pp. 113–14), whose dissolution is achieved when the repressed signifier is articulated through the process of interpretation. In this paradigm of analysis, the identification of the patient's ego with that of the analyst is a repetition of the original mirror-phase transference onto an idealized image taken as oneself. As a narcissistic and aggressive attempt to shore up a faltering sense of coherence and mastery, clearly it will occur, but just as clearly it is a questionable goal of treatment.

9

From Imaginary to Symbolic Identification in the Case of Mr. Z

Clinical implications of Lacan's critique of human narcissism stand out when we compare the ideas of Lacan and Kohut. Kohut's widely cited paper on his two analyses of Mr. Z (1979), now alleged to be in fact about himself and his self-analysis (Cocks, 1994), helps us to see more clearly, in a clinical context, the differences between Lacan's imaginary and symbolic registers. Although Kohut does not mention Lacan in his paper (he did elsewhere, e.g., 1977), they participated in a common if not shared effort. Not only did their lives overlap, both dying in 1981, but their work, too, shows remarkable correspondences, at least at first glance. Both were practicing analysts who drew upon their own experience to offer a reformist critique of mainstream psychoanalysis, especially of ego psychology. Both criticize making the ego the criterion for truth and reality, Kohut by focusing on a comprehensive notion of "self," and Lacan by elaborating the "subject of the unconscious." Both men emphasize disintegration anxiety and put mirroring phenomena in the forefront of processes of identification that shape subjective experience. Both challenge the accepted notion of the patient's "resistance" and instead stress the clinical importance of recognition. Both criticize the kind of training provided by psychoanalytic institutes and are equally critical of the "therapeutic maturity- or reality-morality" reinforced by such training (Kohut and

1. The reader is referred to the following texts to pursue similarities between Kohut and Lacan.In their criticism of ego psychology, see Kohut (1984, p. 59, 65, 148), Lacan (1977, pp. 1–29, 128–29, 132, 306); in their critique of naive notions of "reality," see

Wolf, 1978, p. 423).[1] In their overall characterization of contemporary existence, both Kohut and Lacan use the figure of "tragic man" (Kohut, 1984,
pp. 45, 207–208; Lacan, 1951, p. 16; 1959–60, p. 361). Finally, although both
openly operated from a reformist position, each stressed his proper orthodoxy.
While Kohut offered "a new definition of the essence of the self and a new
conceptualization of its structural development" (1984, p. 8), he maintained
that his viewpoint "is placed squarely in the center of the analytic tradition,
that it is in the mainstream of the development of psychoanalytic thought"
(1984, p. 95). Lacan, critical of the neo-Freudians, reiterated that his effort
consists in a "return to Freud" and to the foundations of psychoanalysis (1977,
p. 117). Lacan never abandoned this claim, even though he was considered a
renegade by most analysts after he was excluded in 1953 from the
International Psychoanalytic Association (Turkle, 1978).

The Freudian unconscious, according to Lacan, is "structured in the most
radical way like a language" (1977, p. 234): the unconscious, as Other to consciousness, as intruding on rational discourse, is an articulation governed not by
biological instincts but by semiotic patterns. Freud (1900a) describes how the
dream-work follows the two governing principles of condensation and displacement; Lacan (1977, pp. 160, 258), applying the structural linguistics of
Saussure (1916) and Jakobson (1956), reinterprets Freud's data in terms of
metaphoric substitution and metonymic combination. The unconscious articulation, preserved in repression and insistently repeated in symptoms and parapraxes, is inscribed in a manner foreign to the conscious ego. The unconscious,
therefore, is the "discourse of the Other" (Lacan, 1977, p, 172), and human
desire is "the desire of the Other" (1977, pp. 264, 312).

The Other

As we saw in Chapter 7, the Other is not any individual person (although the
Other is often projected onto individuals), nor is it a kind of universal, like
Mead's "the generalized other" (1925, p. 193). For Lacan, the Other is a field,
"the very foundation of intersubjectivity" (1956, p. 35), anchoring the place in
which dialogue can arise and meaning become possible. Lacan illustrates this
with a joke of Freud's: "'Why were you lying to me?', one character shouts
breathlessly. 'Yes, why do you lie to me saying you're going to Cracow so I
should believe you're going to Lemberg, when in reality you *are* going to

---

Kohut (1984, p. 36, 173), Lacan (1977, p. 135, 230); on disintegration anxiety, see Kohut
(1984, p. 16), Lacan (1977, p. 11, 137); on resistance: Kohut (1984, p. 144, 148), Lacan
(1977, p. 78, 101, 143, 169, 235); on training and reform, see Kohut (1984, p. 40, 164),
Lacan (1977, p. 35–37, 76, 144); on "reality-morality," see Kohut (1984, p. 208), Lacan
(1959–60, p. 349; 1966, p. 677).

Cracow?'" (1956, p. 36; Freud, 1905a, p. 115). To make sense of this joke, the listener must go beyond the words themselves, beyond their literal signification, and also beyond the speakers themselves into another dimension or position beyond words and speakers, into the semiotic field. In understanding this joke, we affirm the status of the Other, not an other person in an I-you relation, but the Other as the structural Third, giving perspective on any I-you relation, the Other as a potential place to stand and judge the truth of any two-party contract. The very fact that it is possible to lie, Lacan reminds us, is an affirmation of this third position, for to tell a lie requires that the speaker take into account the perspective of truth, the perspective afforded by the Other. For this reason Lacan refers to the Other as "the guarantor of Good Faith" (1977, p. 173) and "witness to the Truth" (1977, p. 305).

This reference to the Other resonates with Freud's use of Fechner's phrase, *ein anderer Schauplatz* (an other scene), in describing the unconscious staging of dreams and as a general reference to the unconscious (Freud, 1900a, p. 48; 1900b, pp. 50–51). As "the discourse of the Other," which transcends it, the unconscious articulates what is received from elsewhere and what is primarily received is "the desire of the Other." Desire arises in an intersubjective context structured by the Other, by the semiotic fields of language and the unconscious. Lacan wrote that it is "as desire of the Other that man's desire finds form" (1977, p. 311), that is, "it is *qua* Other that he desires" (p. 312). In the matrix of the mother-infant relation, one's desire finds its form, becomes unconsciously structured by, and as, the desire of another, and this identification of one's desire with that of another can never be completely dissolved; is the dynamism expressed in repetition, and persists as structured by signifiers.

Lacan illustrates the Freudian discovery by means of ex-centric circles, circles whose centers do not coincide and that cannot be subsumed and unified by a larger circle with a single center. He cautions that "if we ignore the self's radical ex-centricity to itself with which man is confronted, in other words, the truth discovered by Freud, we shall falsify both the order and methods of psychoanalytic mediation" (1977, p. 171). We cannot mediate this split as analysts by believing the patient can become a "whole person" or a "complete self" (1954–55, p. 243). Lacan objects "to any reference to totality in the individual" (1977, p. 80) because the in-dividuum is not conceivable given the split introduced by "the subject of the unconscious" (1977, pp. 128, 299). Thus, Lacan insists that the "radical heteronomy that Freud's discovery shows gaping within man can never again be covered over without whatever is used to hide it being profoundly dishonest" (1977, p. 172). For this reason Lacan's model of the human subject is not the sphere, connoting wholeness, but the topological figure of the torus, the doughnut with an empty center. For Lacan (as for Wright, 1991) loss is essential to the constitution of the human subject.

Fragmentation and Mirroring

How, then, does consciousness come to experience itself as a unity, as cohesive instead of as fragmented? Lacan claims that the source for such experience of unity lies in the formation of the ego in what he called the "mirror stage" of child development. As noted in the preceding chapter, Lacan's attention was drawn to mirroring phenomena by the French psychologist Henri Wallon. Wallon's early emphasis on the infant's visual precocity and sociality (1921, 1931; see also Voyat, 1984) made it clear that there was no initial primary narcissism or autistic period of infancy. The human infant is born into a linguistically structured social milieu in which its consciousness of self is shaped by what it takes itself to be as the object of the mother's desire. Beginning in utero as the object of the mother's fantasies (Ver Eecke, 1984, p. 76; see also Kohut and Wolf, 1978, p. 416), the visually precocious newborn moves toward psychological differentiation through the process of identification with the image of the whole human body as a *Gestalt*.[2]

Processes of mirroring lead to the cementing of identifications, not just between the ego and its image in others, but also between the ego and objects in the world. The ego takes onto itself from the mirror the attributes of coherence, substantiality, and permanence and in turn projects these attributes of itself onto the objects of its world. The Lacanian ego, as Freud describes it, is "first and foremost a bodily ego" and "the projection of a surface" (1923, p. 26). That is, the ego arises with the image of the body to form a projected plane, the foundational grid of consciousness. This grid establishes consciousness of self as a staging arena in which an "I" coordinates the narrative sequence of experience, a stage on which this "I" creates representations that distort experience but enhance one's sense of mastery and effectiveness by exaggerating one's importance and, as we have seen, by minimizing the positive contributions of others. The perception, furthermore, that someone else has what one wants is intolerable to the ego and breeds envy, resentment, and revenge. In writing of "the drama of primordial jealousy" (1977, p. 5), Lacan acknowledges Klein's contribution in understanding the role of resentment in our culture (1977, p. 20-21). He notes how the envy of the analyst's skill is an affront to the ego as the patient exclaims, "I can't bear the thought of being freed by anyone other than myself" (1977, p. 13). He quotes from Augustine's *Confessions* how he "foreshadowed psychoanalysis" when he observed "the psychical and somatic coordinates of original aggressivity":

---

2.   We can speculate about how the infant's own form is reflected in the pupils of the mother's eyes. Brown and Witkowski found that "slightly over one-third of the languages of the world equate pupil of the eye with a human or humanlike object" (1981, p. 600), including "established figurative expressions translating literally as 'baby of eye,' 'girl of eye,' or 'doll of eye'" (1981, p. 597).

I have seen with my own eyes and known very well an infant in the grip of jealousy: he could not yet speak, and already he observed his foster-brother, pale and with an envenomed stare. (1977, p. 20)

Lacan emphasizes certain consequences of this process of mirror identification. Since left and right are reversed, the reflection is distorted (1961–62, p. 471). Since it takes place before the infant has an active role in making meaning through speech, this reversal process is a compelling one: the infant is iconically captured by its image which lures its narcissistic investment. But because this image comes to it from another and is perceived as being "out there" as an other, some confusion persists about identities. As we saw in Chapter 8, in this confused period the infant, identifying with the image of the body of another, will cry at the sight of another child falling or being struck as if he or she were suffering the injury.

In this stage of ego development the child is learning to manage competitive aggression and to maintain self-esteem. The ego for Lacan plays a dynamic role in structuring a sense of imaginary identity with unity and coherence precisely because without its defensive armoring the child would experience bodily fragmentation, an experience of *corps morcelé*, the body in bits and pieces. To avoid this loss of coherence, the ego will strive to buttress its masterful position against threats from within as well as from others. In identifying with parental and other adult desires, the ego uses denial, disavowal, repression, and projection to evade one's own desire. Contrary to Coen's claim (critical of Kohut) that maintaining cohesion "is not a predominant motivation for behavior" (1981, p. 404), when experiencing an attack on its cohesion or preeminence, the ego mobilizes fantasies of another's fragmented body in its counterattack. For Kohut, aggression is "always motivated by an injury to the self" (1984, p. 116). Likewise for Lacan, aggression is "secondary to identification" (1938, p. 39) and is a structural correlate of the ego; he defined it as "the correlative tendency of a mode of identification that we call narcissistic" (1977, p. 16). The narcissistic investment in one's cohesive image, when threatened by the other, is turned into an effort to fragment the other, in a primitive, iconic reversal of the threat. Aggressiveness, therefore, cannot be controlled by strengthening the ego, by reinforcing the ideal ego, but rather by shifting focus to "the pacifying function of the ego ideal" (1977, p. 22) through "Oedipal identification," which is "that by which the subject transcends the aggressivity that is constitutive of the primary subjective individuation" (1977, p. 23).

Identification and the Ego Ideal

Before we go further with Lacan's thinking about "Oedipal identification," we have to acknowledge that the notion of identification as such poses enormous difficulties. As Widlocher noted, "In psychoanalysis, the concept of identification is a blurred one, and will probably remain so for a long time to come" (1985, p. 31). This confusion is especially prominent with regard to the concept of "primary identification," which "turns out to be anything but clear" (Etchegoyen, 1985, p. 5). In this instance, the psychoanalytic confusion appears to rest on the complexity of the history of the word itself. In the *Compact Edition of the Oxford English Dictionary* (1971) we read that identification is "the action of identifying or fact of being identified." Two definitions follow: 1) "the making, regarding, or treating of a thing as identical with . . . another, or of two or more things as identical with one another. . ."; 2) "the determination of identity; the action or process of determining what a thing is; the recognition of a thing as being what it is."

Identification thus means both being in an iconic relation of identity with or *likeness* to another and also being determined or recognized as being *separate*, as being what one is. The word "identity," which has as an obsolete form the word "idemptitie," derives from the late Latin word *identitas*, which is "peculiarly formed from ident(i)-, for [the Latin] *idem* 'same' + -tas, -tatem." Its meaning is given as the "quality or condition of being the same . . . essential sameness; oneness . . . the condition or fact that a person or thing is itself and not something else." In the dictionary there is explanatory note regarding the origin of the word "identity" from the Latin *idem*: "Various suggestions have been offered as to the formation. Need was evidently felt of a noun of condition or quality from *idem* to express the notion of 'sameness,' side by side with those of 'likeness' and 'oneness,' expressed by *similitas* and *unitas*: hence the form of the suffix." All of the psychological confusion of oneness, sameness, and likeness is packed into the history of the word itself, and Lacan therefore began here in his attempt to make sense of the concept of identification.

He started with the Latin root *idem* and then considered its Indo-European root *em*, as found, for example, in the French word for "same," *même*. He then considered identification from the angle of recognizing someone, of determining that he or she is the "same," the very person one has taken him or her to be. He postulated that such "identity" of the subject rests on a signifier, a name, not on a specific appearance nor on a consciousness of continuity. The "primary identification" is achieved through naming, through the use of a signifier, functioning as an index, contiguously related to the one named as an effect of the act of naming. This form of identification is *symbolic* identification, it is the process whereby one is identified by a sign and in fact is designated as "this one" only through the use of a sign. Such symbolic identification is also operative when one's identity is unconsciously constellated by other signifiers, bestowed by parents in specifically designated ways. We are all subjected to these words in childhood, and they structure a kind of unconscious symbolic map of desire that Lacan termed the ego ideal. It is the ego ideal that enables one to channel desire, and Lacan contrasted it to the ideal ego, which, in striving for competitive mastery, resists the assumption of one's necessarily limited desire. The ideal ego is the product of an imaginary identification, an identification *with* the image held by consciousness as a reflection of the mirror or the mirroring gaze of another. In imaginary identification, a dual, iconic relation is established based on a likeness in which one or both poles are idealized, inflating the ego. Such imaginary identification cannot be primary since it occurs only with the onset of the mirror stage and ordinarily follows upon the decisive consequences of naming, kinship specification, and initiation into the semiotic code.

In Lacan's view, the oedipalization of the subject does not stimulate conflict but, rather, generates structure. If the mother's role in the genesis of the subject is to engage desire, then the father's role is to structure desire and symbolically individuate it through the action of what others have called "early triangulation" (Abelin, 1975, p. 296) and what Lacan called the "paternal metaphor" (1977, p. 199). In metaphor, one signifier is substituted for another, which remains operative but in a repressed state. In the "paternal metaphor" the father's name is the signifier of the symbolic order, a consequence of which is the incest prohibition, the end of mother-infant duality, and the introduction of a third. This structure of symbolization as such substitutes for a fusion of desires associated with what Lacan called the "phallus." The phallus, the image of what is imagined to be lacking in the mother, is what the infant becomes for the mother in an imaginary identification. With the structure of the paternal metaphor, the infant "gives up" being the phallus, the latter then becoming repressed as a generalized signifier of the desire of the Other. In repression it continues to function but now precisely as a another signifier in unconscious associative networks of signifiers that follow the laws of displacement and condensation. As a consequence, the child becomes a subject, not simply of language, but of desire, and no longer just an object of the mother's or father's desire, as identified in an imaginary manner with their desire. The child can now symbolize and experience as a desiring subject the parent's absence. But the very possibility of imaginary identification, of experiencing oneself as complete and the completing object of another's desire, rests on the more fundamental identification by a name as *this one*. To be named is to be placed in a symbolic network that sets one apart precisely as not being someone else. Kinship relations, sex roles, social status, prescribed obligations and opportunities all rest on what Lacan, following Lévi-Strauss, called "the symbolic order" (1954–55, pp. 29, 326).

The Symbolic Order and the Signifier

In this and the previous chapter we have focused primarily on the imaginary register, that aspect of experience structured by dual resemblances, point-to-point correspondences, and mirroring reflections. At the heart of such reflections is the lure of likeness, of being liked or liking because of likeness, of narcissistic preening, ostentatious display, competition, and comparison. The imaginary register includes what is proper to the image, the sensuous play of light and sound that draws our interest and that constitutes much of what we call "reality," to be distinguished from what Lacan calls the Real.

As we have seen in earlier chapters, the register of the Real is what we from time to time encounter in ecstasy or in horror as that which has no name. It appears in that startling moment of the breakdown of technology (as in the explosion of the Challenger or the Bhopal gas leak) as the intrusion of loss of meaning, sudden catastrophe, death. The Real is what remains when images and symbols carve out objects in experience; it is a margin of not just what is "undecidable" but what is impossible to symbolize or imagine. We are brought to the edge of the unspeakable Real in a piece by the German painter Anselm Kiefer, titled *Ausbrennen des Landkreises Buchen, Cauterization of the Rural District of Buchen* (Rosenthal, 1987, p. 65). As I view this work, the atrocity of Buchenwald, and the retroactive effort to place it in a semiotic framework (to put it in a "book"), is presented in the form of a series of large open "books" constructed of bound burlap sheets whose "pages" are covered with black oil and charcoal. The eye searches desperately for a text or an image by which to grasp the horror, but there is no word and no image: the "book" brings us to the very edge of signification and, by this very negation of word and image, the horror of the unspeakable and unimaginable is conveyed to us.

If we manage to live without going mad, it is because we construct and maintain a boundary at the edge of the Real; this line, this lining of our daily lives, provides the essential, primal boundary for the human subject. Ordinarily, the images and words provided by our culture shield us from contact with the Real, but in severely traumatized or psychotic states patients are often at the edge of the Real; and the experience of being driven slightly crazy by psychotic patients is a response to their attempt to bring the treatment to that edge so that they can draw some kind of boundary there, to place some marker at that frontier.

The marker that sets off the Real, that "introduces difference as such in the Real" (Lacan, 1961–62, p. 78) is the signifier, a semiotic term Lacan took from Ferdinand de Saussure, the Swiss founder of modern structural linguistics. Saussure made a basic distinction between speech and language, insisting that speech is an individual psychomotor act whereas language is a system of signs that makes speech possible. The linguistic sign is composed of the junction of a signifier and a signified, a signifier being a phonetic sound-image, a concept being the signified. Saussure stressed that signifier and signified are related solely by convention, that is arbitrarily, without intrinsic connection. He also emphasized that each, in itself, is without positive substance but consists, rather, solely in its difference from the other units in the linguistic system:

Everything that has been said up to this point boils down to this: in language there are only differences. Even more important: a difference generally implies positive terms between which the difference is set up; but in language there are only differences *without positive terms*. Whether we take the signified or the signifier, language has neither ideas nor sounds that existed before the linguistic system, but only conceptual and phonic differences that have issued from the system. The idea or phonic substance that a sign contains is of less importance than the other signs that surround it. (Saussure, 1916, p. 120)

Putting it another way, *language is a form and not a substance.* . . . This truth could not be overstressed, for all the mistakes in our terminology, all our incorrect ways of naming things that pertain to language, stem from the involuntary supposition that the linguistic phenomenon must have substance. (p. 122)

It is this "distinctive feature" of the signifier, the fact that it is established within the system not as an identity but as a difference, that distinguishes the symbolic register from the imaginary register, on one hand, dominated as it is by its mirroring identities, and, on the other hand, from the register of the Real, where there is no differentiation. This notion of the substanceless signifier as identity-in-difference finds its prime expression in music: a single note has no "meaning" in itself, it derives its value solely through its difference from other notes. I once heard a Japanese psychoanalyst describe this even more succinctly when he said that the music rests on the silence between the notes.

The Subject of the Unconscious

We encounter great difficulty with this notion of pure difference when it is used to define the human subject. As we have seen, Lacan sharply distinguishes ego from subject and locates Freud's *Kern unseres Wesens*, what Kohut (1984) likewise calls "the core of our being" (1984, p. 140), not in consciousness but at the level of the subject. But this means that we are dealing not only with what Lacan calls "a subject without a head" (1954–55, p. 167; see also Richardson, 1983) but a subject without positive substance. The subject of the unconscious, the subject of psychoanalysis, is not constituted by positive attributes. Rather, it receives its identity through a process of symbolic identification whereby it is designated as some "one." Such symbolic identification is achieved through signifying differentiation, concretized in the conferral of a proper name. Lacan stated that "to name is first of all something that has to do with a reading of the mark *one* designating the absolute difference" (1961–62, p. 148). Such identification, such "one-ing," is not founded on qualitative differences or representable content. Self and object representations (as used, for example, in object relations theory) are secondary to this more fundamental identification based on the signifying difference, "the inaugural identification of the subject with the radical [or root] signifier" (Lacan, 1961–62, p. 38). What seems to be at stake here is the affirming of a structural basis for uniqueness, and Lacan found it in the signifier: "It is as pure difference that the unit, in its signifying function, is structured, is constituted" (1961–62, p. 58). This unit marks the subject as "one," and this mark, given in one's name, is the least determined by any qualitative, positive characteristic. Being so symbolically marked as "one" is the necessary condition of possibility for the subject to differentiate from others, and specifically from the field of the desire of the mother.

Lacan linked his view of symbolic identification to Freud's second type of identification. Freud wrote that with this type "identification has appeared instead of object-choice, and that object-choice has regressed to identification" (1921a, p. 106–107). In other words, this type of identification occurs in the place of the lost object, and such identification is "the earliest and original form of emotional tie" (1921a, p. 107). It can occur in relation to one who is loved, or one who is not loved, but "in both cases the identification is a partial and extremely limited one and only borrows a single trait [*einen einzigen Zug*] from the person who is its object" (1921a, p. 107; 1921b, p. 117). Lacan zeroed in on Freud's phrase *einen einzigen Zug* as suggestive of a single trace, *une trait unaire* in French, basically just a line or a mark. He explored the origin of this mark, following the linguistic research of Leroi-Gourhan (1964, pp. 262–4), in the cuts or notches made on bones 35,000 years ago, notches made perhaps to indicate a "one" in a series of ones, keeping count, for example, of births or animal kills or astronomical phenomena (see also Harris, 1986). The use of this trace or mark, Lacan speculated, gave rise to the experience of segmented temporality, narrative sequentiality, and firm object boundaries. This trace or mark is a signifier, specifically an index, and as such has its status in the Other, "the locus of the signifier" (Lacan, 1977, p. 310), the semiotic field; and because this mark gives the first, radical structure to the human subject, it is "the foundation, the kernel of the ego ideal" (Lacan, 1964, p. 256), the first intervention of the Third as ordering principle.[3] By being designated "one," one is affirmed as not being something or someone else. Psychotic structure appears to lack this mark, and therefore, as we saw in Chapter 7, we find boundary blurring and fusion with a cosmic Other in psychosis.

---

3.   Ultimately the designation or mark of "one" rests on an act of writing, Lacan claimed, but that would take us too far from our task, although it is of some historical interest to see Lacan grappling in his 1961–1962 seminar with the relation between speech and writing as later would Derrida.

The Analytic Field

The effect of this mark of "one" is not to unify but rather to make unique. Besides insisting that the subject-ego split can never be healed, Lacan rejected a two-person model of analysis: "the field that our experience polarizes in a relation that is only apparently two-way, for any positing of its structure in merely dual terms is as inadequate to it in theory as it is ruinous for its technique" (1977, p. 56). Instead of a dyadic relationship, Lacan offered a four-cornered structure (1977, pp. 139, 193), as presented in Figure A: Position 1, the Subject corner, locates the patient as barred or divided ($) within himself or herself, that is, irremediably split by repression, disavowal, and language, and therefore incapable of full knowledge regarding who he or she is, what he or she is actually saying, why there is this symptom. Position 2, the Ego corner, is the place of the patient's ego as reflecting the so-called objective world but especially reflecting other egos. Position 3 marks the place of other egos, and specifically the place of the analyst's ego, which the patient's ego attempts to lure iconically and maintain in a mirroring reflection with itself. In position 4 Lacan located the Other, from where "the discourse of the Other" can be articulated. Here the analyst as subject resonates with those sonorous and gestural, as well as thematic, aspects of the patient's discourse that are not in his or her or even the analyst's awareness until the analyst speaks. Familiar to seasoned clinicians, this experience includes the use of unintended puns, the spontaneous guessing of a disavowed loss or pleasure, the sudden appearance of a vivid image.

The discourse of the Other is Lacan's way of calling attention to how language, as other than, wider than, not reducible to, the individual consciousness of any speaker, has already structured human experience and therefore has already

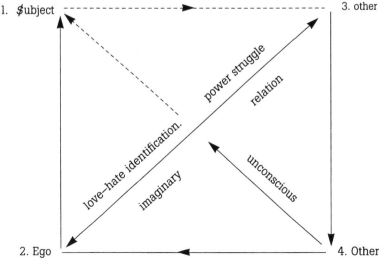

Figure A: Lacan's Schema L (modified)

channelled human desire. As we saw earlier, the discourse of the Other is that semiotic structuring of desire which Freud discovered in his analysis of dreams and symptoms as constitutive of the unconscious. Lacan maintained that because the unconscious is structured like a language, the effects of the unconscious can be understood and interpreted. Position 4 therefore provides perspective on what is happening to the patient's desire in his or her symptoms as well as what is happening between the two individuals when they relate as egos, when the so-called object relation between patient and analyst develops.

This object relation Lacan called an "imaginary relation," marked on both sides by narcissism and illusion, an effect of mirrors. On this axis linking the patient's ego and the analyst's ego we can observe all the emotional variations of that *haine-amouration* we noted earlier, an oscillating love-hate relationship. Competition, coercion, power struggle, seduction, and imaginary identification are pursued on this axis of object relations. According to Lacan, the American emphasis on strengthening the ego, on encouraging the patient's ego to model itself on and identify with the analyst's ego, marks a fundamental betrayal of Freud and of the place of the Other, leading to loss of perspective regarding the subject of the unconscious, the subject as distinct from the ego. As we saw in the preceding chapter, this emphasis on getting the patient to identify with the analyst has a long tradition and is still being maintained as a goal of treatment in mainstream American psychoanalytic writing.

Kohut appeared uneasy with the notion of such identification, referring to "gross identification" when the issue was raised (1984, pp. 101, 169; see also pp. 100, 160). It may be useful to introduce into Kohut's framework Lacan's distinction between symbolic identification *by* the Other and the imaginary identification *with* an other, with an image of the other or with an image of oneself held by the other. Imaginary identification reinforces likeness and constrains the field of desire in a mirroring relation; symbolic identification structures difference and opens desire onto the field of substitution and displacement. The distinction is one that Kohut appeared to make but only by separating "gross identification" from "transmuting internalization." Thus, for example, he described a patient who "at the end of a long analysis during which there had been periods of gross identification with me, . . . said: 'Now I am similar to you only in one respect: I am an independent person just like you'" (1984, p. 169). The patient had gone from modelling himself as a reflection or image of the analyst in imaginary identification to assuming the status of one who is symbolically identified by the Other and so recognized by the analyst.

The Desire of the Other

When recognition is effective it is because the other's desire has been recognized. The most dominant aspect of psychic structure is not the satisfaction or frustration of needs but the phenomenon of desire, and therefore desire is the dominant feature of transference-countertransference.

How does desire arise? In distinguishing the three registers of Real, imaginary, and symbolic, we can follow Lacan and argue for a parallel distinction among need, demand, and desire. Needs are physiological conditions, rooted in the organism's tissues and organs, and they are imperative: food, water, warmth, and air are essential for life, and there are no substitutes for them—we cannot live on their metaphors. These needs in infancy are met by a caretaking other (usually the mother), who nurtures in a cultural, familial, and semiotic system of intersubjective exchanges in which both the infant and the mother learn to associate the infant's expressions of need with organic and psychic states. As we examined in earlier chapters, rhythm, touch, affect, and mutual responsivity quickly establish, in ways specific to the given culture, a semiotic framework of communication in which language is present from the beginning as structuring the mother's world. The child's cries soon become signifiers, with the result that the child's needs are channeled through "the defiles of the structure of the signifier" (Lacan, 1977, pp. 255, 309). One of Lacan's students expressed it in this way:

> When the mother responds to the cries of the infant, she recognizes them in constituting them as a demand, but what is more momentous is that she interprets them on the level of desire: desire of the infant to have the mother next to her, desire that she bring her something, desire to aggress against her, or whatever. What is certain is that by its response the Other is going to give the dimension of desire to the cry of need and that this desire with which the infant is invested is always initially the result of a subjective interpretation, a function of just the mother's desire, of her own phantasm. (Aulagnier, 1962, p. 401; my translation)

This rapid development means that it becomes impossible to directly express needs or directly respond to them (Muller, 1990). The state of need becomes partially articulated when addressed to an other and in this signifying form functions as a demand. The other can no longer respond only to the state as need but must respond to it as an articulated demand. In this responding, the other will of necessity indicate just how he or she is recognizing the one making the demand (as manipulative, as appropriate, as delightful, as obnoxious). In turn, the child making the demand will obtain from the other's response proofs and disproofs of love and caring, evidence that the relationship affirms the child as desirable or undesirable. The process is one in which semiosis takes over: one's interpretant for an index becomes in turn an index for the other that generates its own interpretant, and so on.

With the constellation of the ego, as discussed earlier, the child seeks to maximize his or her position as the all-fulfilling object of the mother's desire. This will so entangle the child's desire with the mother's desire that we can then speak of an identification of the child's desire with the mother's desire. This identification necessarily takes place at the level of the unconscious, indeed as part of the process whereby the unconscious is structured: "It is through the bias of the unconscious of the Other that the subject makes his entrance into the world of desire, and he will have to initially constitute his desire as a response, as an acceptance or refusal to take the place that the unconscious of the Other designates for him" (Aulagnier, 1962, p. 401; my translation). In an intersubjective matrix there can never be any "natural" desires, since the idiosyncrasies of the other's unconscious responses, what in Peirce's terms we may call disavowed interpretants, will determine how the infant's desires emerge into awareness or are enacted.

Such an identification of desires may be total and supported by the mother's words and behavior and, if so, will absorb the child's desire, consciously and unconsciously, in the absence of any effective intervention by a Third. This Third, for Lacan, is the presence in the mother's life of sociocultural frameworks that contextualize and delimit the role of the child in her life and is usually highlighted by the presence of the father, who sets limits on the grandiose totalization of desire.

Specifically, it is the "symbolic father," or paternal function, that lays the foundation for differentiation by naming the child. As we have seen, such naming marks the child as other than all others, and in being so identified the child has the structural possibility of eventually assuming his or her own desire rather than being merged in the desire of the mother or of the father. This symbolic identification then enables the child to mobilize his or her ego ideal as a "signifying mapping" (Lacan, 1964, p. 272), which then subordinates the ideal ego to the task of limiting and channeling desire according to the constraints of finite existence. This is how Lacan conceived of the Oedipal resolution, whose outcome is "symbolic castration," structuring the subject as pluralistically related (no longer in a dual relation with the mother), as sexed (no longer being the phallus but rather having a penis or having a vagina), and as capable of finding and combining substitute objects of desire (rather than claiming the wholeness of totalized desire and not desiring at all).

The Two Analyses of Mr. Z

In my reading of "The Two Analyses of Mr. Z" (Kohut, 1979; unless otherwise indicated, all subsequent quotations are from this text), a reading informed by how I use Lacan, I find that desire occupied the central place both in Mr. Z's history and in the transference-countertransference relationship with his analyst. In so emphasizing the crucial importance of desire, I am drawing on Lacan's theory of desire in the spirit of A. Goldberg when he quotes Popper in affirming that "facts are interpreted in the light of theories; they are soaked in theory, as it were" (1980, p. 91). In the first analysis of Mr. Z, despite his initial resistance, the analyst (K1) promoted an identification between himself and Mr. Z so that Mr. Z shifted his desire from his mother's desire to K1's desire. In so identifying with his analyst, Mr. Z reinforced K1's position as the one who is supposed to know (Muller, 1992b), thus rendering him desirable, and, in turn, by identifying with his desire, Mr. Z also became more desirable in his analyst's eyes. This identification of desires constituted an imaginary identification: it was based on Mr. Z's becoming like his analyst's model of him. Kohut acknowledged in the second analysis that Mr. Z's changed behavior is rightly called a "transference success" (p. 16). As he did when his desire was merged with his mother's desire, Mr. Z showed "an attitude of compliance and acceptance that he had now reinstated with regard to me and to the seemingly unshakable convictions that I held" (p. 16). Kohut writes:

> The improvement which resulted from the first analysis must therefore be considered in essence as a transference success. Within the analytic setting, the patient complied with my convictions by presenting me with oedipal issues. Outside the analytic setting, he acceded to my expectations by suppressing his symptoms (the masochistic fantasies) and by changing his behavior, which now took on the appearance of normality as defined by the maturity morality to which I then subscribed (he moved from narcissism to object love, i.e. he began to date girls). (p. 16)

But in the second analysis, the analyst (K2) no longer fostered such compliance: he shifted from trying to be recognized to recognizing Mr. Z. After Mr. Z disengaged his desire from his analyst and from his mother, Kohut promoted the process of symbolic identification in which Mr. Z's ego ideal could be affirmed and engaged to delimit his desire as his own.

Kohut emphasizes how he at first viewed the "analytic material entirely from the point of view of classical analysis" (p. 3), whereas the second analysis occurred after his shift to "a new viewpoint, which, to state it briefly, allowed me to perceive meanings, or the significance of meanings, I had formerly not consciously perceived" (p. 3). But what is at stake in this shift is not only a matter of perception, but more profoundly a shift in what Lacan (1959–60b; 1977, p. 252; see also Richardson, 1987) designated as the ethical fulcrum of psychoanalysis, namely a shift in Kohut's *desire*, a shift not so much in how he thinks as in where he desires. This shift in desire has a profound impact on the patient.

Mr. Z's identification with his mother's desire was indicated by his fantasies of being a woman's slave with no will of his own, reinforced in his childhood by his mother's reading aloud to him *Uncle Tom's Cabin*, which opens with the threatened separation of a slave-child from his mother. Indeed, Mr. Z's mother spent much time "reading to him, playing with him, talking with him, and spinning out fantasies with him about what his future would be like" and "in her imagery about him as a grown man, she had always taken totally for granted that, however great his successes in life, their relationship would never be altered, he would never leave her" (p. 14).

As the first analysis drew to a close, Mr. Z appeared to be reluctantly complying with the desire of the analyst. The reluctance is signified in a dream that occurred about a half a year before termination of the first analysis, a dream Kohut saw as the "most significant sign of his advance": "he was in a house, at the inner side of a door which was a crack open. Outside was the father, loaded with giftwrapped packages, wanting to enter. The patient was intensely frightened and attempted to close the door in order to keep the father out" (p. 8).

The patient's associations pointed to the time when the absent father rejoined the family, and he also had "many associations referring to present experiences (including the transference) and to the past. Our conclusion was that it referred to his ambivalent attitude toward the father" (pp. 8–9) and therefore was taken as confirmation of the castration-anxiety theme proposed by Kohut. But what is the ambivalence about? I myself hear the "giftwrapped" in the dream as "gift-trapped": Mr. Z fears being bribed and trapped in the father/analyst's desire as he was in his mother's desire. It does not seem, as Ostow suggests, that "the patient sees the analyst (as well as the father) as an intruder into his attachment to the mother" (1979, p. 532), but rather that he feels Kohut's desire is coercing him, as we can read for ourselves:

> And, in view of the overall image I had formed of the construction of his personality and of his psychopathology, I stressed in my interpretations and reconstructions especially his hostility towards the returning father, the castration fear, vis-à-vis the strong, adult man; and, in addition, I pointed out his tendency to retreat from competitiveness and male assertiveness either to the old pre-oedipal attachment to his mother or to a defensively taken submissive and passive homosexual attitude toward the father.
>
> The logical cohesiveness of these reconstructions seemed impeccable and . . . in line with . . . precepts that were then firmly established in me as almost unquestioned inner guidelines in conducting my therapeutic work. . . . (p. 9)

Kohut's desire here is to get Mr. Z to recognize him as the one who knows, who knows not only Mr. Z's character structure but also what constitutes reality and maturity, and Mr. Z eventually complies by acting in accordance with Kohut's desire.

Initially, Mr. Z struggled to get the analyst to mirror *his* states, but in the end, as his desire became disengaged from his mother's, he identified with Kohut's desire but risked feeling trapped again. Kohut sensed that something was "wrong" with the termination of the first analysis because it was "emotionally shallow and unexciting" (p. 9). But such a state would be congruent if, in fact, Mr. Z did not experience termination. That is to say, there was no cut between them since Mr. Z's desire remained identified now with Kohut's desire. As Lacan put it, "such imaginary identification is merely a pause, a false termination of the analysis which is very frequently confused with its normal termination" (1964, p. 145). This would also account for the lack of zest and "emotional depth," since Mr. Z did not experience the process as his own, as the realization of his own desire (Thompson, 1985). In short, Mr. Z as subject was not recognized in the dual, imaginary relation between positions 2 and 3 of Lacan's Schema L, as presented in Figure A.

Second Analysis

Four and a half years later, Mr. Z contacted Kohut to renew the analysis.[4] At that time he continued to live alone in his own apartment, did not enjoy his work, and had a succession of affairs with women, but he felt his sexual relations with women were unsatisfying and shallow. We can see that he still had not claimed his desire as his own and was beginning to regress to an identification with his mother's desire: he felt increasingly isolated socially, just as his mother had become, one of the signs of her serious personality change, which included a set of circumscribed paranoid delusions. Kohut wondered whether Mr. Z "was being confronted with the loss of a still unrelinquished love object from childhood or with guilt feelings about having abandoned her" (p. 10), as if she were the object of his desire. In fact, as was determined later, Mr. Z felt relief in the face of his mother's growing disability, since it allowed him to disengage from her desire even more freely.

The material for the second analysis can be divided into two phases, "the almost exclusive preoccupation with the mother" and "thoughts concerning his father" (p. 12). As we have seen, material about the mother was also plentiful in the first analysis; and in attempting to articulate what was different about its emergence in the second analysis, Kohut emphasized "that between Mr. Z's first and second analysis my theoretical outlook had shifted" (p. 12). What

---

4. My examination of the second analysis is written as if Kohut were the analyst and not the analysand. If he in fact was both, as Cocks (1995) has argued, we could examine the paradoxes entailed by his conforming to his new paradigm and thereby reinforcing his transference position as the one who is supposed to know. The use I make of the reported data remains as is—although we can only wonder what the "termination" of the analysis might mean in such a case of self-transference.

is this shift about? "I had in the first analysis looked upon the patient in essence as a centre of independent initiative and had therefore expected that he would, with the aid of analytic insights that would enable him to see his path clearly, relinquish his narcissistic demands and grow up" (p. 12).

With this attitude, Kohut believed Mr. Z could choose to orient his desire; he saw "the patient's persistent attachment to the mother as a libidinal tie that he was unwilling to break" (p. 12). He assumed that Mr. Z's desire was his own, thereby presuming the very condition Mr. Z came into treatment to achieve. The shift, therefore, from the first to the second analysis (which to me marks a decisive difference, contrary to the efforts of Wallerstein [1981] to harmonize the two phases) required two changes; first, in Kohut's own desire: "I was now able, more genuinely than before, to set aside any goal-directed therapeutic ambitions. Put differently, I relinquished the health- and maturity-morality that had formerly motivated me" (p. 12). The second change was in his view of the patient. He no longer saw the patient's self as "resisting change or as opposing maturation because it did not want to relinquish its childhood gratifications, but, on the contrary, as desperately—and often hopelessly—struggling to disentangle itself from the noxious selfobject, to delimit itself, to grow, to become independent" (p. 12). The shift in Kohut's own desire enabled him to see the patient's desire differently: "Where we had formerly seen pleasure gain, the sequence of drive demand and drive gratification, we now recognized the depression of a self that, wanting to delimit and assert itself, found itself hopelessly caught within the psychic organization of the selfobject" (p. 17)—caught, in other words, in the mother's desire.

The effort to give an account of this shift held Kohut's attention as more childhood history was reported, having to do with the mother's intense scrutiny of Mr. Z's feces up to the age of six and then her searching his face for blackheads:

> We are again confronted by the puzzling question why this crucial material had not appeared during Mr. Z's first analysis. To be sure, it had indeed appeared, but—what is even more incomprehensible—it had failed to claim our attention. I believe that we come closest to the solution of this puzzle when we say that a crucial aspect of the transference had remained unrecognized in the first analysis. (p. 15)

What was unrecognized in the first analysis? Kohut affirms that it was how his own convictions "had become for the patient a replica of the mother's hidden psychosis" (p. 16), with which the patient complied. But in a Lacanian framework the crucial transference issue that remained unrecognized was how Mr. Z's entanglement in K1's desire replicated his enmeshing with his mother's desire.

What does this perspective add to Kohut's formulation? It clarifies some of Mr. Z's symptoms. We have already seen how the "sexual masochism" was the enactment in fantasy of Mr. Z's position as the object of mother's desire with no desire of his own. Kohut noted, and I would agree, that an object relations approach "fails to do justice" to this symptom as well as to the "chronic despair which could often be felt side by side with the arrogance of his demandingness" (p. 12). I suggest that Mr. Z's demandingness was his mother's demandingness with which he was identified (we are told that she "emotionally enslaved those around her and stifled their independent existence," p. 13), and his despair was precisely over this state of his desire. He could not but act in accordance with the unconscious structure of his desire, formed by his mother's desire. Thus, when he reported with "the most intense shame" that as a young child "he had smelled and even tasted his own feces" (p. 17), he was indicating just how his desire was identified with his mother's desire in taking such intense interest in his feces. When Kohut rationalizes that "he had come to understand for the first time in empathic consonance with another human being, that these childhood activities were neither wicked nor disgusting, but they had been feeble attempts to provide for himself a feeling of aliveness" (p. 17), he does not acknowledge that Mr. Z's shame was over the fact that he was like her, that he desired what she desired.

While the structure of Mr. Z's desire was not explicitly posed, Kohut grasped its obvious import in relation to the mother: "His most significant psychological achievement in analysis was breaking the deep merger ties with his mother" (p. 25). And earlier: "No independent self had gradually formed; what psychological existence he had managed to build was rooted in his attachment to the mother" (p. 23). His very status as a self—in Lacanian terms, as subject of desire—rested on the imaginary identification of desires. His mother's desire provided the psychic scaffolding on which he built an unhappy and fragile sense of himself. Because his experience of cohesion rested on this mirroring, reflective structure, he experienced "the deepest anxiety he had ever experienced" in a dream of "a starkly outlined image of the mother, standing with her back toward him" (p. 19). This occurred as Mr. Z was focusing explicitly in the analysis on his father. An immediate sense of the dream occurred to Mr. Z that as he moved closer to his father, his mother turned her back on him, just as she used to treat him with "icy withdrawal" whenever "he attempted to step toward independent maleness." Her tactic, her "chilling look of disapproval" (p. 15), always brought him back emotionally.

But the "deeper meaning of the dream" concerned "the unseen, the unseeable frontal view of the mother" which, when the patient tried to imagine it, brought intense, nameless anxiety. When Kohut (acting for the moment like K1 did in the first analysis) suggested "the horror of castration, of the sight of the missing external genital, of fantasies of blood and mutilation," in response "the patient brushed these suggestions aside"; while he agreed that "the imagery of mutilation, castration, and blood was related to the unnamed horror, he was sure that this was not the essential source of the fear" (p. 20). Another formulation was offered by Kohut: "When I suggested that the mother may not have lost her penis but her face, he did not object but responded with prolonged silence from which he emerged in a noticeably more relaxed mood" (p. 20).

I will attempt a Lacanian understanding of Kohut's approach: the images of mutilation relate to the experience of bodily fragmentation and ego disintegration and are, as the patient insisted, secondary consequences of a more primary collapse. This primary fall is the loss of status as a desiring subject, being no longer embraced by the mother's gaze or addressed by her voice. The dream-trauma consisted not in what was unseeable but in the fact that the mother was unseeing, no longer holding her son in her desiring gaze and no longer putting his face before her as a reflection—all of this implying, of course, that she never did see him as he was but only as her image. The very structure of Mr. Z's psychic consistency was here declared to be undone, and Kohut pointed to this (by mentioning the loss of her face) and allowed the prolonged silence to register the shift. While we doubt that "the unseen side of the mother in this dream stood for her distorted personality and her pathological outlook" (p. 16), since conscious acknowledgement rather than repression of her pathology had recently brought relief, we can agree that the dream "expressed his anxiety at the realization that his conviction of the mother's strength and power [of her desire]—a conviction on which he had based a sector of his own personality [as subject] in intermeshment with her [desire]—was itself a delusion [as are all such imaginary identifications]" (p. 20, my interpolations). What *is* he, if he is no longer that something he was in his mother's desire?

The disengagement of Mr. Z's desire from his mother's desire now moved ahead differently than in the first analysis: Kohut did not seduce compliance with his own desire but instead, by keeping his desire in the analytic place of the Other, he enabled Mr. Z to engage in a process of retrieving the kernel of his ego ideal by focusing on his father. The issue of the father was posed at the beginning of the second analysis. The night before the beginning of the second analysis, Mr. Z had the following dream without action or words:

> It was the image of a dark-haired man in a rural landscape with hills, mountains, and lakes. Although the man was standing there in quiet relaxation, he seemed to be strong and confidence-inspiring. He was dressed in city clothes, in a complex but harmonious way—the patient saw that he was wearing a ring, that a handkerchief protruded from his breast pocket,

and that he was holding something in each hand—perhaps an umbrella in one hand, and possibly a pair of gloves in the other. The figure of the man was visually very plastic and prominent—as in some photographs in which the object is sharply in focus while the background is blurred. (p. 11)

Mr. Z's associations showed the figure to be a composite of a childhood friend, a camp counselor (based on the landscape features relating to the summer camp), the father (his hair), and the analyst (the umbrella, gloves, handkerchief, and ring). Mr. Z also recalled the dream of his father "loaded with packages," and this "established a link with the terminal phase of the first analysis—announcing as it were that the second analysis was a continuation of the first one" and that "it took off from the very point where the first one had failed most significantly" (p. 11).

If the second analysis took off from this point, then we must consider the dream as occurring just when the patient, feeling he was still the object of K1's desire, was once again going to confront the amorphousness of his own desire. If we can understand the first dream of the father "loaded down with giftwrapped packages" in terms of Mr. Z's asking the question, "What does the other want from me?" then this dream presents the other as desiring nothing from the subject, as holding his gloves and umbrella, rather than gifts, in his hands. There may yet be a space for the subject's own desire to emerge.

Idealization and the Ego Ideal

How does "the second phase of the second analysis" (p. 18) proceed? Having given up the ideal ego fashioned in mirroring response to and identification with his mother's desire, Mr. Z now attempts to recover and articulate the sources of his ego ideal, or, more specifically, what Lacan called "the paternal identification of the ego-ideal" (1977, p. 197). For a time, Mr. Z's mood remained hopeless and despairing, specifically because "his father was weak,. . . The mother dominated and subdued him" (p. 18). He then focused on his counselor friend briefly, and then began "to express intense curiosity about me," about the analyst's past, his early life, his interests, his family, his relationship to his wife and children (p. 18). I hear this as Mr. Z's attempt to find out something about Kohut's desire, where it was, what sustained it, whether Mr. Z would again be seduced into compliance—all attempts to safely anchor his ego ideal. But Kohut initially responded to this as he had earlier: "Whenever I treated his inquiries as a revival of infantile curiosity and pointed out the associative connections with the sex life of his parents, he became depressed and told me I misunderstood him" (p. 18). Gradually Kohut changed his view and "finally ventured the guess that it was his need for a strong father that lay behind his questions, that he wanted to know whether I, too, was weak, subdued in intercourse by my wife, unable to be the idealizable emotional support of a son" (p. 18). As I hear the questions, Mr. Z was addressing Kohut about the following: 1) Am I still the object of your desire? 2) Are you a subject of desire, and do you have any other objects of desire? 3) Do you have something I can pin my ego ideal on and mobilize my desire along signifying lines? In other words, Mr. Z wanted to make contact with the paternal function: did Kohut know how to use his penis, and was he able to set limits. Kohut set limits with "friendly firmness" in denying Mr. Z's requests for information. In response to Kohut's change in approach, Mr. Z dropped his demands and became dramatically less depressed and hopeless. He also "made do with certain bits of information which he had obtained either accidentally or via inference—my interest in art and literature, for example" (p. 18). "Art and literature" served as the verbal bridge between his mother (p. 4), his counselor friend (p. 7), and Kohut, and, we can speculate, formed one kernel of his ego ideal.

At this point "the analysis took a new turn" (p. 19) and focused directly on Mr. Z's father, who until then had remained a shadowy figure. Mr. Z now began to talk about "positive features in his father's personality," and he did so "with a glow of happiness, of satisfaction" (p. 19). For Kohut, this was, "as can be judged in retrospect, the crucial moment in the treatment—the point at which he may be said to have taken the road toward emotional health" (p. 19). However, while on this road Mr. Z had "a number of frightening quasi-psychotic experiences in which he felt himself disintegrating and was beset by intense hypochondriacal concerns. At such times he dreamed of desolate landscapes, burned-out cities, and most deeply upsetting, of heaps of piled-up human bodies . . . he was not sure whether the bodies were those of dead people or of people still barely alive" (p. 19).

This description calls to mind Lacan's earlier comments regarding bodily-fragmentation fantasies:

> What struck me in the first place was the phase of the analysis in which these images came to light: they were always bound up with the elucidation of the earliest problems of the patient's ego. . . . Their appearance heralds a particular and very archaic phase of the transference, and the value we attributed to them in identifying this phase has always been confirmed by the accompanying marked decrease in the patient's deepest resistances. (1951, p. 13)

In Kohut's view,

> Mr. Z was now relinquishing the archaic self (connected with the selfobject mother) that he had always considered his only one, in preparation for the reactivation of a hitherto unknown independent nuclear self (crystallized around an up-to-now unrecognized relationship to his selfobject father). (p. 19)

The moment had arrived for Mr. Z to let go of what had structured him, namely his place in the eyes of his mother. At precisely this point Mr. Z's dream of his mother occurred in which she was "starkly outlined" like the dream of the standing man. In the aftermath of this third dream, which finally freed Mr. Z's desire from his mother's, and the ensuing relaxed mood, Mr. Z recalled positive memories of his father, "preceded and accompanied by his idealization" of Kohut, including a short-lived wish to become an analyst. This "idealization" was nothing like the grandiosity-building idealization of his mother (to which we shall return shortly) but was more properly a bringing into focus of the field of his ego ideal.

The main memory of his father to emerge at this point was of a trip to Colorado he had taken at the age of nine. He spoke "with an increasing glow of joy" of his father's traits; as a "man of the world," he could amuse others with stories, was a good skier, showed "resoluteness, perceptiveness, and skill" in business dealings and, above all, Mr. Z recovered "the intensely experienced awareness that his father was an independent man who had a life independent from the life of the mother" (p. 21)—that is, that father had his own desire independent of his mother's. Then Mr. Z complained about how little he knew about his father, and, after "a brief period of transference fantasies," he suddenly voiced the suspicion "that his father had a woman friend" who had been present during the trip to Colorado and that they met in a bar the night before leaving. Mr. Z never mentioned this episode to his mother when they returned. Although his father did not explicitly request this, "he felt that there was a silent understanding between them that he would be quiet about it" (p. 21). This experience suggests the presence of a number of key factors in the psychic structure of Mr. Z at that time: firstly, he knew that his father had a penis and knew how to use it, and therefore was a subject of desire, not just an object; secondly, the sight of his father with this other woman demonstrated to Mr. Z his inferiority to his father, that his father possessed anterior sexual knowledge; thirdly, he could identify with a paternal prohibition by keeping the secret, but precisely because it was a secret it lent itself to repression; finally, in keeping the secret he won recognition from his father as being his ally. To be sure, this secret identification and identification through the secret must have rested on some earlier foundation of symbolic identification (such as sharing his name with his father), but we can agree that because of its secret status "this material represents, in terms of the structure of Mr. Z's personality, the deepest layer of the repressed" and that "no pathogenic oedipal conflicts still lay in hiding" (p. 22). The aforementioned ingredients of psychic structure suggest that the Colorado trip achieved symbolic castration for Mr. Z, insofar as the paternal function decisively intervened and set limits to the mother-child dual relation.

I question, therefore, Kohut's conceptualization of the outcome of this process as the result of an idealization. There is something amiss in the formulation of Mr. Z's "glow of joy and the invigorating sense of having finally found an image of masculine strength—to merge with temporarily as a means of firming the structure of his self, of becoming himself an independent centre of strength and initiative" (p. 22). The "glow of joy" indicated the mobilization of his own desire, not because of any additional merger (he has, with relief, just ended his merger of desires with his mother) but because he has constellated an ego ideal that delimited and anchored his desire and therefore facilitated his becoming a subject with "strength and initiative." That his recognition and affirmation of the paternal function were repressed and split-off seems likely, but this repression appears to be a product of his grandiose ego, fueled by the idealized mother with whom he was "enmeshed," "submitted to the role of being her phallus" (in Kohut's words) and displaying "a grandiosity that was bestowed upon him by the mother so long as he did not separate himself from her" (p. 24). In terms of the patient's narcissism, it would be inconsistent for his ideal ego to repress another idealization (since another idealization would only inflate his ego further); it is equally unlikely that in the split-off sector required by the narcissism of maternal enmeshment he would have "preserved the idealizations that maintained a bond to his father" (p. 24).

Kohut understandably wanted to go beyond an object relations formulation resting on drive-cathexes of representable objects, but in its place he appeared to make idealization serve the function of establishing ties, not between a drive and an object, but between a needy self and a selfobject. It seems to me, however, that Mr. Z's recovery of the repressed was not the recovery of an idealization but of an identification. That identification was, furthermore, based not on "an image of masculine strength" for him to copy, but on some marking by symbols, including the penis as symbol of masculinity *versus* the phallus as a symbol of the other's desire (see Julien, 1987; Lacan, 1938, p. 59). While I agree that the dream of attempting to slam the door on the gift-laden father "was not motivated by castration anxiety" (Kohut, 1984, p. 86), Mr. Z's reformulation of his dream (with which Ornstein, 1981, concurred), in which the danger of the father's return allegedly consisted in the traumatic state of being suddenly offered "all the psychological gifts, for which he had secretly yearned" (p. 23), seems inadequate. With the father back, there was no reason why "male psychological substance" could not have been gradually handled, provided the father could set limits. The *ad hoc* explanation of "too much, too fast" appears less compelling than one that emphasizes the structural effects of being identified with the desire of the mother, one effect being the kind of grandiose mutual idealization that would split off any delimiting Third and that left the young Mr. Z without an operative ego ideal.

Termination

The termination of the second analysis was different from that of the first one. The idealization of the analyst was short-lived and worked through, with the analyst falling from being identified with the Other and the resulting gap providing a place for Mr. Z's desire. There was no return of earlier symptoms (the underlying structure of desire supporting the sexual masochism fantasies had dissolved); there was no severe anxiety in the face of losing the analyst's presence. For several weeks Mr. Z was sad about losing his analyst and regretted that, with his father dead, he would have no chance to develop a friendly relationship with him. Significantly, "for a few sessions he also expressed considerable anger towards me for having originally failed him, like his father in childhood" (p. 24)—a failure by the father to disengage his desire from his mother's desire, a failure by Kohut in forcing compliance with his own desire. Months were spent reviewing the past and anticipating the future. During the last few weeks, Kohut "was very impressed by his expanded empathy with and tolerant attitude towards the shortcomings of his parents" (p. 24). Such contextualization in a symbolic matrix extended especially to his mother, with her pathology but also with her positive features, which he could see "without a trace of the idealizations with which he had begun his first analysis" (p. 25). The content of his ambitions and ideals, which

> had arisen in the matrix of the now abandoned merger relationship with the mother, [persisted but the] ... working through of his transference relationship to me enabled him to reestablish a link with his father's maleness and independence, and thus the emotional core of his ambitions, ideals, and basic skills and talents was decisively altered, even though their content remained unchanged. But now he experienced these assets of his personality as his own. ... (p. 25)

He had made his desire his own and could pursue its realization according to its own signifying pattern.

Returning to Lacan's Schema L, we can map onto it the two positions of Kohut as we have come to understand them (see Figure B). In the first analysis, Kohut abandoned his analytic stance and coerced the patient's desire to identify with his own; in the second analysis, he successfully achieved symbolic recognition of Mr. Z as subject, not allowing himself to become lured by Mr. Z's grandiose ego into the imaginary collusion of "strengthening the ego." As a result, Mr. Z claimed his desire as his own in his efforts to realize his desire with others; this was made structurally possible by the constellation of an ego ideal that delimited his desire, giving it scope and direction. The ingredients of the ego ideal had their source in the symbolic matrix of the father/analyst—not that he can fill the place of the Other; on the contrary, his very limitations, as

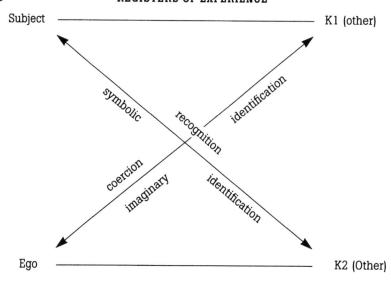

Figure B: Kohut and Schema L

Kohut stressed, are the fulcrum for the shift brought about by "transmuting internalizations." In the end, the analyst becomes *an* other, one among many others whose significance to the patient, like that of his parents, is now contextualized in the symbolic register, no longer captivating him as isolated elements in the imaginary register. Here we see that the positive features of oedipalization and the goals of analysis overlap: to move from duality to plurality, from focus on the ideal ego to the ego ideal, from imaginary identification that represses desire in order to imagine oneself as like another to symbolic identification as being different in one's own desire.

Clearly, in many details Kohut and Lacan reveal a similarity of purpose, and in their assessment of psychoanalysis they said similar things, although the obvious differences have been noted by Lacanians (see, for example, Laurent and Schneiderman, 1977; Harari, 1986; Cottet, 1985; Peraldi, 1987). Despite these differences, Kohut provides us with invaluable documentation of what for Lacan was the essential analytic responsibility: to discern the effects of one's own desire. We are all pressed, at certain moments in every treatment, toward the K1 position: this is an effect of the transference, an effect of the patient's desire that constellates the supposed knowing subject in us and engages our own narcissism in countertransference (Lacan, 1964; Renik, 1993). Our only recourse (and the patient's as well) is to take note of just how we are (or were) being lured out of position. In such moments we learn most about our patients, about ourselves, and about the Freudian discovery.

10

A Re-Reading of *Studies on Hysteria*

When Lacan claims his approach is a "return to Freud," what Freud does he return to? I have attempted to show that in the case of Freud or of Lacan, the return is not to an idealized figure but to a conception of the complexity of human behavior, a semiotic conception. This chapter attempts to take up what Gadamer called "the burden" of historical consciousness, which he defined as "the privilege of modern man to have a full awareness of the historicity of everything present and the relativity of all opinions" (1975, p. 8). It is in this spirit that we can re-read *Studies on Hysteria* (Breuer and Freud, 1895) in order to re-interpret the Freud-Breuer break, not as resulting from differences regarding the role of sexuality, as commonly assumed, but rather from a disagreement about the role of language in the unconscious determination of symptoms. My thesis is that the commonly accepted view, that Freud fearlessly uncovered sexuality whereas Breuer shrank back, is a myth, propounded by Freud and Ernest Jones, which served to eclipse Freud's more disturbing discovery that language structures human experience in ways that are completely out of conscious awareness.

Breuer, I think, could not tolerate such an affront to rationalism, yet for a time Freud persisted in his attempt to convince Breuer of the non-physiological, broadly linguistic determination of symptoms as may be seen throughout the Fliess correspondence (Masson, 1985), in the *Project for a Scientific Psychology* (1895), and in his exposition of his treatment of Dora (1905b). Freud, however, in later years, by so emphasizing sexuality as the content of symbolism and promoting himself as a "conquistador" of sexuality, pushed aside his discovery of how, as Lacan puts it, "the unconscious is structured in the most radical way like a language" (1977, p. 234), as a semiotic system of differential traces (for related views, see Bär, 1975; Basch, 1976).

The commonly accepted view of Breuer's termination of his treatment with Anna O. comes to us from Jones who writes: "Freud has related to me a fuller account than he described in his writings of the peculiar circumstances surrounding the end of this novel treatment. It would seem that Breuer had developed what we should nowadays call a strong countertransference to his interesting patient . . . and he decided to bring the treatment to an end" (1953, p. 224).

According to Jones, Breuer announced the termination to Anna O., who later the same evening summoned him back "in the throes of an hysterical childbirth (pseudocyesis), the logical termination of a phantom pregnancy that had been invisibly developing in response to Breuer's ministrations" (Jones, 1953, pp. 224–25). Jones then presents what has become the stereotype of Breuer:

> Though profoundly shocked, he managed to calm her down by hypnotizing her, and then fled the house in a cold sweat. The next day he and his wife left for Venice to spend a second honeymoon, which resulted in the conception of a daughter; the girl born in these curious circumstances was nearly sixty years later to commit suicide in New York. Confirmation of this account may be found in a contemporary letter Freud wrote to Martha, which contains substantially the same story. (p. 225)

Jones went on to state that the separation between Breuer and Freud "was brought about by Breuer's unwillingness to follow Freud in his investigation of his patients' sexual life, or rather, in the far-reaching conclusions Freud was drawing from it. That disturbances in the sexual life were the *essential* factor in the etiology of both neuroses and psychoneuroses was a doctrine Breuer could not easily stomach. Nor was he alone in that!" (p. 253).

As reported by Gay, Freud wrote to his fiancée Martha in 1882 that Breuer had revealed "some things" about his former patient Anna O. that "I am supposed to repeat only 'once I am married to Martha'" (1988, p. 64). Gay does not tell us what these things were but goes on to endorse, in its essential details, Jones's picture of Breuer, that he was hesitant to publish his case of Anna O. because of reluctance "to admit that the ultimate origins of hysteria, and some of its florid manifestations, were sexual in nature" (1988, p. 66). Curiously, Gay goes on to contradict himself by stating, as Jones himself had done thirty-five years earlier (1953, p. 254), that Breuer did not deny "the influence of sexual conflicts on neurotic suffering" (1988, p. 68). Both Jones and Gay, despite their own contrary evidence, present Breuer, in contrast to Freud, as timorous in the face of sexuality. This view of Breuer is repeated by contemporary psychoanalysts (Person, 1988; Rosenbaum and Muroff, 1984)[1] as well as in a recent edition of Freud's works by Anna Freud who writes: "Even the first surmises that sexual impulses might be at the bottom of hysterical symptoms cost Freud the collaboration and friendship of Josef Breuer" (1986, p. 271). How do we account for the persistence of this stereotype?

Freud himself maintained that his chief discovery had to do with the role of sexuality and that this cost him the good opinion of others. In his Clark University lectures, referring to his colleagues, he said, "they all began by completely disbelieving my assertion that sexual aetiology was of decisive importance" (Freud, 1909, p. 40). In a later essay on the history of psychoanalysis, Freud (1914b) wrote that Breuer "broke off all further investigation" after perceiving the "sexual motivation" of Anna O.'s transference:

He never said this to me in so many words, but he told me enough at different times to justify this reconstruction of what happened. When I later began more and more resolutely to put forward the significance of sexuality in the aetiology of neuroses, he was the first to show the reaction of distaste and repudiation which was later to become so familiar to me, but which at that time I had not yet learnt to recognize as my inevitable fate. (1914b, p. 12)

In Freud's autobiographical paper, which Strachey in the "Editor's Note" misdescribed as "a cool and entirely objective account of the evolution of his scientific views" (1925b, p. 5), Freud stated that his investigation of the sexual life of patients based on his "surprising discovery" of "deriving hysteria from sexuality" cost him his "popularity as a doctor" (1925b, p. 24; see also p. 48). Regarding Breuer, Freud wrote, "it was easy to see that he too shrank from recognizing the sexual aetiology of the neuroses" (1925b, p. 26). He then gave his view of Breuer's termination with Anna O.:

I came to interpret the case correctly and to reconstruct, from some remarks which he had made, the conclusion of his treatment of it. After the work of catharsis had seemed to be completed, the girl had suddenly

---

1. In her widely popular book, Person wrote: "Breuer, who had become increasingly fascinated with Anna O.'s treatment, is thought to have ignored his wife and thereby provoked her jealousy. Belatedly recognizing the nature of his wife's reaction, Breuer terminated Anna O.'s treatment. Shortly afterward, he was called back to find his patient in the throes of a hysterical childbirth. He calmed her down but, the next day, took his wife on a second honeymoon" (1988, p. 245).

developed a condition of 'transference love'; he had not connected this
with her illness, and had therefore retired in dismay. (1925b, p. 26)

As reported by Pollock, Freud also presented his view of Anna O.'s termination in a letter to Stefan Zweig in 1932:

> What really happened with Breuer's patient I was able to guess later on,
> long after the break in our relations, when I suddenly remembered some-
> thing Breuer had once told me in another context before we had begun
> to collaborate and which he never repeated. On the evening of the day
> when all her symptoms had been disposed of, he was summoned to the
> patient again, found her confused and writhing in abdominal cramps.
> Asked what was wrong with her, she replied, "Now Dr. B.'s child is
> coming!" (1976, p. 140)

Freud went on to say:

> I was so convinced of this reconstruction of mine that I published it
> somewhere. Breuer's youngest daughter (born shortly after the above-
> mentioned treatment, not without significance for the deeper connections)
> read my account and asked her father about it (shortly before his death). He
> confirmed my version, and she informed me about it later. (Pollock, 1976,
> p. 140)

Ferenczi also reiterated this view of Breuer as timorous in contrast to Freud:

> Upon the first manifestations of uninhibited instinctual life he [Breuer]
> left not only the patient but the whole method in the lurch ...
> Psychotherapy had to wait for a man of stronger calibre, who would not
> recoil from the instinctual and animal elements in the mental organization
> of civilized man; there is no need for me to name this pioneer. Freud's
> experience forced him relentlessly to the assumption that in every case of
> neurosis a *conditio sine qua non* is a sexual trauma. (1929, pp. 109–110)

Now what position, in print, did Breuer take regarding a sexual etiology for
neurosis? Jones himself quoted from Breuer's "Theoretical" chapter in *Studien
über Hysterie* (cf. Breuer and Freud, 1895, pp. 200, 210, 244, 245) with Breuer's
text translated as follows:

> The sexual instinct is certainly the most powerful source of lasting
> increases in excitation (and, as such, of the neuroses).
>   That such conflict between incompatible ideas has a pathogenic effect
> is a matter of daily experience. It is mostly a matter of ideas and processes
> belonging to the sexual life.

This conclusion (about the disposition to hysteria) implies in itself that sexuality is one of the great components of hysteria. We shall see, however, that the part it plays is still greater by far, and that it cooperates in the most diverse ways in constituting the disease.

The greater number and the most important of the repressed ideas that lead to (hysterical) conversion have a sexual content. (Jones, 1953, p. 254)

In these passages, Breuer clearly endorsed the sexual etiology of neurosis but Freud, together with subsequent psychoanalysts, have somehow persistently denied this. Freud's self-characterization, moreover, as a maligned solitary because he proposed a sexual etiology of neurosis has been disputed by the evidence presented by Ellenberger (1970), Decker (1977), and Sulloway (1979), which shows that Freud's work was not ignored by his medical colleagues.

Breuer's "cold sweat" termination of his treatment with Anna O. has likewise been fabricated. As pointed out by Pollock (1976) and Ellenberger (1970), Breuer's youngest daughter, named Dora, was born on March 11, 1882, well before the termination of Anna O.'s treatment, and, contrary to Jones's statement, she "committed suicide when the Gestapo knocked at her door in 1944" (Pollock, 1976, p. 143). The view of Breuer as weak appears even in what is perhaps the most sympathetic psychoanalytic account of Breuer, which stated that he "did not have enough strength to continue" (Gedo and Pollock, 1976, p. 134). Pollock stated that Breuer was "frightened of the personal countertransference reactions he perceived," leading him "to deny, withdraw, and attempt to isolate himself from what was too threatening" (1976, p. 148). But, according to Ellenberger, in Breuer's original case notes "there is nowhere any mention of a hysterical pregnancy," and "Jones's version of the false pregnancy and hysterical birth throes cannot be confirmed and does not fit into the chronology of the case" (1972, p. 279). Breuer's biographer, Hirschmüller, stated unequivocally: "The Freud–Jones account of the termination of the treatment of Anna O. should be regarded as a myth" (1978, p. 131). According to Reeves, moreover, the finding of "seven other case studies by Breuer, all employing the same cathartic technique, six of which were begun after his treatment of Anna O. . . . effectively disposes of Jones's contention that Breuer was unnerved by his involvement with the case" (1982, p. 210). Hirschmüller (1978), who challenged Freud's account of his appeal to Breuer's daughter as witness, had previously also emphasized the importance of these additional case reports of patients with undisguised sexual symptoms, although Hirschmüller doubted that Breuer used the cathartic method to treat them.

Reeves proposed that we take the phrase attributed to Anna O., "Now Dr. Breuer's baby is coming," as a reference to the anniversary of the conception of Breuer's daughter Dora, whose birth on March 11 would make her conception

approximately between June 4 and June 11, 1881. Because the patient was re-
living each day as it had occurred a year earlier, her alleged remark makes sense
as a recognition of this event in Breuer's life. The termination date of June 7,
1882, moreover, was not a result of Breuer's withdrawing in a cold sweat, but
rather marked the anniversary of Anna O.'s commitment to the sanitorium at
Inzersdorf on June 7, 1881; the termination date was planned by her in
commemoration of that event. Reeves therefore concluded:

> On this hypothesis it is quite credible that some such verbal exchange as
> that reported by Freud did actually occur between Anna O. and Breuer
> and probably on the final day of her treatment. I do not, however, feel that
> there are any grounds for believing in the phantom pregnancy and the
> hysterical childbirth symptoms. It seems more plausible to suppose that this
> reconstruction of what took place was based on Freud's faulty recollection
> of what Breuer had actually reported to him. (1982, p. 210)

Reeves proposed that we take what Freud himself called a "reconstruction" as
a "screen memory" (1982, p. 211) whose distortions were motivated by an
intellectual as well as personal rift between Breuer and Freud. "Breuer's apparent repudiation (or so it appeared to Freud) of all that they had jointly stood
for" was manifested in his criticism of Freud's overgeneralizations: "In essence,
what Breuer was saying about Freud's latest innovation (in his theory of
defence and repression) was that whilst *descriptively* is was full of interest, *scien-
tifically* it was lacking a true basis in hard empirical data (*S.E.* 2, p. 236)"
(Reeves, 1982, p. 213).

What I am proposing, more specifically, is that what Breuer objected to in
Freud's conceptualization was the role he gave language in the unconscious
structuring of symptoms. Breuer's rebuke, furthermore, so wounded Freud that
it remained a major issue in his correspondence with Fliess; it prompted him to
write the *Project* as a defense of his view of the central importance of speech
processes; and it drove him to conduct the treatment of the patient he named
"Dora," who was the same age as Breuer's daughter, Dora, in such a way that he
might obtain proof for his claims about the unconscious linguistic determination of symptoms. The Dora case, as Decker demonstrated (1982, 1991), is
replete with allusions to Breuer and was, I think, the culmination of a long
struggle by Freud to prove himself to Breuer.

The Polemic in the Text

Breuer decisively influenced Freud's thinking in November, 1882, when he
first told Freud details of his treatment of Anna O., the patient most often
named and discussed by Freud (Karpe, 1961). We too can begin by reading
Breuer's account of the case in *Studies on Hysteria*, not in order to update our

assessment of the patient, but rather of the text. Our historical consciousness regarding the origin of psychoanalysis may be already shaped by how we have read or by what others have said about *Studies on Hysteria*. It may be instructive, therefore, to attempt a re-reading, in accord with Freud's own advice in his 1908 preface to the second edition:

> The attentive reader will be able to detect in the present book the germs of all that has since been added to the theory of catharsis: for instance, the part played by psychosexual factors and infantilism, the importance of dreams and of unconscious symbolism. And I can give no better advice to any one interested in the development of catharsis into psycho-analysis than to begin with *Studies on Hysteria* and thus follow the path which I myself have trodden. (p. xxxi)

We attempt to follow the first steps of this path in order to grasp the germs of Freud's discovery of unconscious symbolic activity in the context of his relationship to Breuer.

In his report of the treatment of Anna O., conducted between December, 1880, and June, 1882, Breuer made numerous observations regarding his patient's speech processes. He noted that she had great "poetic" gifts and suffered from "paraphasia" (Breuer and Freud, 1895, pp. 21–22). During episodes of her *absences* she would "stop in the middle of a sentence, repeat her last words and after a short pause go on talking" (1895, p. 24). In the afternoons she would enter a somnolent state until after sunset:

> She would then wake up and complain that something was tormenting her—or rather, she would keep repeating in the impersonal form "tormenting, tormenting." For alongside of the development of the contractures there appeared a deep-going functional disorganization of her speech. It first became noticeable that she was at a loss to find words, and this difficulty gradually increased. Later she lost her command of grammar and syntax; she no longer conjugated verbs, and eventually she used only infinitives, for the most part incorrectly formed from weak past participles; and she omitted both the definite and indefinite article. In the process of time she became almost completely deprived of words. She put them together laboriously out of four or five languages and became almost unintelligible. (1895, p. 25)

This is a remarkably precise description of a patient's speech difficulties, with a wealth of detail perhaps unmatched in psychoanalytic observations of speech phenomena. Breuer's aptitude as an objective observer has been noted by many commentators. Breuer himself wrote in a letter that in his treatment of Anna O., he did not allow "any preconceived opinions to interfere with the simple observation of the important data" (Cranefield, 1958, pp. 319–20). Pollock

wrote: "Breuer, the careful observer and scientist, researcher and experimental-
ist, could report the behavior of his famous patient in great detail" (1976, p.
148). Schlessinger et al. (1976) emphasized that Breuer had an impressive ability
to observe objectively. As far as I know, only Rizzuto (1989) has tied this impressive ability of Breuer's to his observations of speech phenomena.

Breuer continued to describe his patient's course of illness four months into
treatment:

> Her paraphasia receded; but thenceforth she spoke only in English—appar-
> ently, however, without knowing that she was doing so. She had disputes
> with her nurse who was, of course, unable to understand her. It was only
> some months later that I was able to convince her that she was talking
> English. Nevertheless, she herself could still understand the people about
> her who talked German. (Breuer and Freud, 1895, p. 25)

After her father died she became more disturbed:

> She now spoke only English and could not understand what was said to
> her in German. . . . She was, however, able to read French and Italian. If
> she had to read one of these aloud, what she produced, with extraordinary
> fluency, was an admirable extempore English translation. (1895, p. 26)

The psychoanalytic method itself was launched because Breuer repeatedly
noted changes in his patient's condition that correlated with changes in her
speech. She herself noted how she would lose her obstinate mood through
what she called this "talking cure" (1895, p. 30), an approach initiated "to begin
with accidentally but later intentionally" by making use of a few of her
"muttered words":

> someone near her repeated one of these phrases of hers while she was
> complaining about the "tormenting." She at once joined in and began to
> paint some situation or tell some story, hesitatingly at first and in her para-
> phasic jargon; but the longer she went on the more fluent she became, till
> at last she was speaking quite correct German. . . . A few moments after
> she had finished her narrative she would wake up, obviously calmed down,
> or, as she called it, "gehäglich". . . . If for any reason she was unable to tell
> me the story during her evening hypnosis she failed to calm down after-
> wards, and on the following day she had to tell me *two* stories in order for
> this to happen. (1895, p. 29)

By the autumn of that first year of treatment Breuer "was hoping for a
continuous and increasing improvement, provided that the permanent burden-
ing of her mind with fresh stimuli could be prevented by her giving regular
verbal expression to them" (1895, p. 32). (In three pages here [pp. 30–32],

Breuer repeats the phrase "verbal utterance" or "verbal expression"—in German, *Aussprache*—at least seven times.) Breuer then discovered that such utterances not only had a palliative effect, but could also bring about the disappearance of symptoms: "When this happened for the first time—when, as a result of an accidental and spontaneous utterance of this kind, during the evening hypnosis, a disturbance which had persisted for a considerable time vanished—I was greatly surprised" (1895, p. 34). The patient's inability to drink water for six weeks vanished after she angrily recalled how her maid's dog drank from a glass in her room. By so articulating the experiences that gave rise to her symptoms, they were eliminated one by one. The symptoms were "talked away" by following back "the thread of memories" with the result that "finally [even] her disturbances of speech were 'talked away'" (1895, p. 35). These disturbances included "not hearing" when someone spoke to her; Breuer detailed seven types of such inability to hear and gave a separate count of the occurrences in each category (1895, p. 36), although he apologized for the "incompleteness" of his notes (1895, p. 40).

But in his "Theoretical" contribution to *Studies on Hysteria*, "from which," Freud wrote to Fliess on June 22, 1894, "I wholly disassociate myself" (Masson, 1985, p. 83), Breuer minimized the role of speech and language, in almost shocking contrast to the previous wealth of his observations. He discussed the hysterical symptom under the rubric of a "reflex" (1895, p. 208) which is facilitated "according to the general laws of association":

> But sometimes (though, it must be admitted, only in higher degrees of hysteria) true sequences of associated ideas lie between the affect and its reflex. Here we have *determination through symbolism*. What unites the affect and its reflex is often some ridiculous play upon words or associations by sound, but this only happens in dreamlike states when the critical powers are low and lies outside the group of phenomena with which we are here dealing. (1895, p. 209)

In this way Breuer attempted to restrict the role of language to "higher" hysterics and in this case only during inferior states of mind; in any case, he insisted that this phenomena lay beyond our current interests. When he later pressed his claim that "hypnoid states are the cause and necessary condition of many, indeed of most, major and complex hysterias," he again wrote almost contemptuously of the role of language:

> Thus it is almost only in these states that there arises a somewhat complicated irrational "symbolic relation between the precipitating cause and the pathological phenomenon" [p. 5], which, indeed, is often based on the most absurd similarities of sound and verbal associations. (1895, p. 216)

Not only did Breuer once again show disdain for the way language is tied up with symptoms, but he also took the opportunity to distance himself from Freud by quoting their joint "Preliminary Communication," written in 1892 (1895, p. xiv), precisely at the point when that statement addressed the relationship of language to the formation of symptoms. But Breuer did not simply quote the statement: He bracketed it between two negative terms, claiming that the relationship is an "irrational" one based on "the most absurd similarities."

How can we understand this sharp contrast between Breuer's careful, attentive report of the functions of speech in his patient, a report in which he reiterated his surprise and willingness to learn from the patient (1895, p. 46), and, on the other hand, his dismissive approach to the role of language when he offered his theoretical reflections? Breuer himself suggested a partial explanation when he wrote somewhat polemically:

> If it seems to us, as it does to Binet and Janet, that what lies at the centre of hysteria is a splitting off of a portion of psychical activity, it is our duty to be as clear as possible on this subject. It is only too easy to fall into a habit of thought which assumes that every substantive has a substance behind it—which gradually comes to regard "consciousness" as standing for some actual thing; and when we have become accustomed to make use metaphorically of spatial relations, as in the term "sub-consciousness," we find as time goes on that we have actually formed an idea which has lost its metaphorical nature and which we can manipulate easily as though it was real. Our mythology is then complete. (1895, pp. 227–28)

Although Breuer urged us to avoid being "tricked by our own figures of speech" (p. 228), his argument here was not just with language but, I believe, with Freud. Freud had used the term "*le sub-conscient*" in his 1893 French paper on motor paralyses (Breuer and Freud, 1895, p. 45, editor's footnote), which MacMillan (1990) viewed as Freud's elaboration of Janet's thesis that hysterical symptoms are a function of ideas (or, in Peircean terms, of failed semiosis). Freud (1893b, p. 52) distinguished organic lesions from the hysteric's "lesions" in which the conception of a body-part loses its associative linkage: "Le bras se comporte comme s'il n'existait pas pour le jeu des associations" ["The arm behaves as though it did not exist for the play of associations"] (Freud, 1893a, p. 170). But the arm, through its dissociated conception, is engaged in a subconscious association ("est engagé dans une association subconsciente," 1893b, p. 52–53). Any psychic impression becomes traumatic, Freud went on to say, when an individual cannot discharge its affective value in motor reactions or by means of associative psychic work. Such discharge is impossible when the impression remains in the subconscious ("L'impossibilité de l'élimination s'impose quand l'impression reste dans le subconscient," 1893b, p. 54). Freud went on to state that "we" ("Breuer et moi") lay claim to this theory and its corresponding psychotherapeutic method. Breuer, then, with his critical reference to the term "sub-consciousness," appears to have been criticizing Freud and taking his distance from him in a typically positivistic manner, accusing Freud of engaging in mythology by postulating a systemic unconscious with its associative symbolic network.

Freud seems to have been aware of the dispute, for he too made a polemical reference to the statement about symbolization found on page five of the joint "Preliminary Communication," which as Freud earlier wrote to Fliess on December 18, 1892, "has cost enough in battles with my esteemed partner" (Masson, 1985, p. 36). The reference occurs in his final case history (Fraulein Elisabeth Von R.) of *Studies on Hysteria* in which he wrote:

> The patient ended her description of a whole series of episodes by complaining that they had made the fact of her "standing alone" painful to her. In another series of episodes, which comprised her unsuccessful attempts to establish a new life for her family, she was never tired of repeating that what was painful about them had been her feeling of helplessness, the feeling that she could not "take a single step forward. . . ." I could not help thinking that the patient had done nothing more or less than look for a *symbolic* expression of her painful thoughts and that she had found it in the intensification of her sufferings. The fact that somatic symptoms of hysteria can be brought about by symbolization of this kind was already asserted in our "Preliminary Communication" [p. 5]. (Breuer and Freud, 1895, p. 152)

In fact, Freud was now asserting much more, for the "Preliminary Communication" did not state that somatic symptoms of hysteria can be "brought about" by symbolization, but rather that there is a symbolic relation between the precipitating cause and the pathologic phenomenon. Freud here explicitly reaffirmed what Breuer found unpalatable, and he claimed to have proof.

This argument with Breuer about the role of symbolization appears to have been an ongoing one. Freud, in the case report of his encounter with Katharina, stated: "We [Breuer and I] had often compared the symptomatology of hysteria with a pictographic script which has become intelligible after the discovery of a few bilingual inscriptions" (1895, p. 129). Because little, if any, of this semiotic perspective entered Breuer's theoretical formulations, we can only assume that it was Freud who was making the comparisons between symptoms and script and attempting to convince Breuer of their truth.

Freud was obsessed with this truth from the moment he heard the details of Anna O.'s treatment. As Rizzuto put it, "The power of the spoken word had taken over Freud's professional career" (1989, p. 112). Jones reported that hearing about Breuer's treatment of Anna O. made a profound impression on Freud:

> Freud was greatly interested in hearing of the famous case of Anna O., which he did soon after its termination in June 1882; to be exact, on November 18 [unpublished letter from Freud to Martha Bernays, November 19, 1882]. It was so far outside his experience that it made a deep impression on him, and he would discuss the details of it with Breuer over and over again. (1953, p. 226)

Even a cursory chronology bears witness to this impact on Freud.

In November, 1882, Breuer told Freud about his treatment of Anna O. We may assume, because Breuer provided so much detail in his report of her treatment, that he told Freud of her "paraphasias." "He repeatedly read me pieces of the case history," wrote Freud, "and I had an impression that it accomplished more towards an understanding of neuroses than any previous observation" (1925b, p. 19).

In 1885, Freud, still taken with Breuer's report, repeated it to Charcot when he went to Paris, but Charcot appeared uninterested (Jones, 1953, p. 226; see also Freud, 1925b, pp. 19-20). Charcot did accept Freud's offer to translate a new volume of his lectures, three of which were on aphasia, into German. Forty years later, Freud recalled the theme of aphasia in Charcot's letter: "I can still remember a phrase in the letter, to the effect that I suffered only from 'l'aphasie motrice' [motor aphasia, i.e., the inability to speak] and not from 'l'aphasie sensorielle du français' [French sensory aphasia, i.e., the inability to hear and understand French]" (1925b, p. 12).

In 1886, upon Freud's return to Vienna, he "turned once more to Breuer's observation and made him tell me more about it" (1925b, p. 20). Freud concluded: "The state of things which he had discovered seemed to me to be of so fundamental a nature that I could not believe it could fail to be present in any case of hysteria if it had proved to occur in a single one" (p. 21).

In 1888, Freud wrote four unsigned papers for Villaret's medical dictionary, one of which was on aphasia (Kris, 1954, pp. 18, 448).

In 1888 or 1889, Freud used Breuer's cathartic method to treat Emmy von M. and had probably begun his treatment with his "teacher," Frau Caecilie (Breuer and Freud, 1895, pp. xii, 48; see also Masson, 1985, p. 20, note 2; Swales, 1986).

In 1889, Freud visited Liébault and Bernheim in Nancy and later wrote: "I was a spectator of Bernheim's astonishing experiments upon his hospital patients, and I received the profoundest impression of the possibility that there could be powerful mental processes which nevertheless remained hidden from the consciousness of men" (1925b, p. 17).

In 1891 he publicly indicated his interest in the issue of language by publishing his monograph *On Aphasia*, dedicating it to Breuer. As Jones commented, "he had hoped thereby to win Breuer into a better humor and was disappointed that for some obscure reason it had the opposite effect" (1953, p. 213). In this book, which Freud refused to include in the German edition of his complete works "on the grounds that it belonged to his neurological and not to his psycho-analytic works" (Kris, 1954, p. 19, note 1), his remarks about paraphasia are suggestive, for he stated that:

> The paraphasia observed in aphasic patients does not differ from the incorrect use and the distortion of words which the healthy person can observe in himself in states of fatigue or divided attention or under the influence of disturbing affects—the kind of thing that frequently happens to our lecturers and causes the listener painful embarrassment. It is tempting to regard paraphasia in the widest sense as a purely functional system, a sign of reduced efficiency of the apparatus of speech associations. (Freud, 1891, p. 13)

Freud also expressed "doubt about the localization of speech centres" (Kris, 1954, p. 18), as Brun (1936) wrote:

> Moreover he firmly declines to localize ideas in locally circumscribed areas of the brain ("centres") and instead explains the function of speech genetically (on the basis of its gradual acquisition in childhood) as the result of the restimulation of a widespread visual, acoustic, tactile, kinaesthetic, etc., network of association. It was the breaking of this network of association and not the destruction of any special motor, sensory or "understanding" centres which led to "crippling" of the functions of speech and so produced the various forms of aphasia. (quoted in Kris, 1954, p. 18, note 3)

Freud argued for the systemic status of a "zone of language" independent of anatomic localization. Such a "zone," anathema to the prevailing neuropathological theories, would lend support to his developing view of hysteria, according to which symptoms are not a function of anatomical lesions (Forrester, 1980, p. 25) but rather a function of disturbances in the network of symbolization. Indeed, Rizzuto (1989) argued that Freud wrote his book on aphasia precisely in order to give an account of the remarkable speech symptoms of Anna O., Emmy von M., and Frau Caecilie.

From 1888 to 1892, Freud and Breuer actively collaborated in the treatment of Freud's cases (Pollock, 1976) and Freud was intent on collaborating with Breuer with regard to theory as well, although not without disagreement, as Freud later recalled: "There had been differences of opinion between us at an early stage, but they had not been a ground for our separating" (1925b, pp. 22–23). But gradually they did separate, and for years Freud argued with Breuer in his letters to Fliess. For example, on June 28, 1892, Freud wrote to Fliess: "The reason for writing to you is that Breuer has declared his willingness to publish jointly our detailed theory of abreaction, and our other joint witticisms on hysteria. A part of it that I first wanted to write alone is finished, and under different circumstances would certainly have been communicated to you" (Masson, 1985, p.31).

Freud here apparently was referring to the "Preliminary Communication," first published in 1893 (Breuer and Freud, 1895, pp. ix, xiii), in which the issue of the role of "symbolization" is pressed by Freud. His phrase, "our other joint witticisms on hysteria," recalls the symbolic puns of his patients' symptoms as well as Breuer's dismissal of these as "some ridiculous play upon words," as quoted earlier (1895, p. 209).

Freud began his first case history in *Studies on Hysteria*, that of Frau Emmy von M., by stressing that her "symptoms and personality interested me so greatly that I devoted a large part of my time to her" (1895, p. 48). This echoed Breuer's interest in and time-consuming commitment to the treatment of Anna O., and Freud made explicit that Breuer's treatment of Anna O. was his model at this inaugural moment. When he discerned that his patient could be easily hypnotized he decided to "make use of Breuer's technique of investigation under hypnosis, which I had come to know from the account he had given me of the successful treatment of his first patient. This was my first attempt at handling that therapeutic method" (1895, p. 48). Freud's own account of this first treatment emphasizes, as Breuer's account did, the dimension of speech in his patient. After giving us an initial description of Frau Emmy's physical appearance, Freud began his presentation of her symptoms as follows:

> She spoke in a low voice as though with difficulty and her speech was from time to time subject to spastic interruptions amounting to a stammer. . . .
>
> What she told me was perfectly coherent and revealed an unusual degree of education and intelligence. This made it seem all the more strange when every two or three minutes she suddenly broke off, contorted her face into an expression of horror and disgust, stretched out her hand towards me, spreading and crooking her fingers, and exclaimed, in a changed voice, charged with anxiety: "Keep still!—Don't say anything!— Don't touch me!" She was probably under the influence of some recurrent hallucination of a horrifying kind and was keeping the intruding material at bay with this formula. (1895, pp. 48–49)

This dramatic opening up of the dimension of speech marks Freud's inaugural move: He at once placed himself on the side of Breuer, the listener and observer of his patient's speech.

At the conclusion of his final case study, that of Fraulein Elisabeth von R., Freud provided a synopsis of his treatment of his "teacher," Frau Caecilie. In it he emphasized the role of symbolization in the formation of symptoms, and thereby managed to maintain continuity with his initial focus on speech phenomena, as Breuer had done, while engaging in the ongoing polemic with Breuer over the theoretical significance to be given to such observations.

Frau Caecilie provided the "best examples of symbolization that I have seen," wrote Freud, and he described her case as "my most severe and instructive one" (1895, p. 176), enabling him to gain "the most instructive information on the way in which hysterical symptoms are determined" (1895, p. 178). Freud then added, significantly for his polemic with Breuer, that this case was as weighty for him as the case of Anna O. was for Breuer: "Indeed, it was the study of this remarkable case, jointly with Breuer, that led directly to the publication of our 'Preliminary Communication'" (1895, p. 178).

Freud next focused on a series of examples of the symbolic determination of symptoms, for example, her recurrent symptom of facial neuralgia:

> I was curious to discover whether this, too, would turn out to have a psychical cause. When I began to call up the traumatic scene, the patient saw herself back in a period of great mental irritability towards her husband. She described a conversation which she had had with him and a remark of his which she had felt as a bitter insult. Suddenly she put her hand to her cheek, gave a loud cry of pain and said: "It was like a slap in the face." With this her pain and her attack were both at an end.
>
> There is no doubt that what had happened had been a symbolization. She had felt as though she had actually been given a slap in the face. (p. 178)

The skeptics here must include Breuer, to whom Freud deferred when it came to explaining the "first attack of neuralgia, more than fifteen years earlier. Here there was no symbolization but a conversion through simultaneity," stated Freud (1895, p. 178), and then he went on to explain: "The generation of the neuralgia at that moment was only explicable on the assumption that she was suffering at the time from slight toothache or pains in the face, and this was not improbable, since she was just then in the early months of her first pregnancy" (p. 179). This assumption of a somatic, not a symbolic, basis for the symptom appears to be offered in order to placate Breuer's physiological bias.

In his following example, "which demonstrates the action of symbolization under other conditions," Freud explicated how violent pain in his patient's right heel arose when her physician was about to escort her downstairs to the dining room after she had spent a week in bed, and how the pain disappeared "when the patient told me she had been afraid at the time that she might not 'find herself on a right footing' with these strangers" (1895, p. 179). Freud then yielded additional ground to the opposition: "This seems at first to be a striking and even a comic example of the genesis of hysterical symptoms through symbolization by means of a verbal expression. Closer examination of the circumstances, however, favours another view of the case" (1895, p. 179). Freud then indicated that the pains in her feet had been present before the physician's gesture was made, since they were, in fact, the reason why she was in bed in the first place! Because no one could argue with this, Freud concluded: "In these examples the mechanism of symbolization seems to be reduced to secondary importance, as is no doubt the general rule" (1895, p. 179).

Yielding thus, Freud then insisted: "But I have examples at my disposal which seem to prove the genesis of hysterical symptoms through symbolization alone" (1895, p. 179). He then presented "one of the best," involving the same patient, who, at the age of fifteen, felt a penetrating pain in the forehead after her grandmother had given her a "piercing" look; this pain, reproduced in treatment after fifteen years, also disappeared with this narration of origins. Freud went on to give examples of "a regular collection of symbolizations of this kind" found in his patient: "A whole set of physical sensations which would ordinarily be regarded as organically determined were in her case of psychical origin or at least possessed a psychical meaning" (1895, p. 180). There follow examples of stabbing pains in the heart, the sensation of nails being driven into the head, an "aura" in the throat, each with their accompanying articulation. Freud then ended his case presentation and concluded this section of the book with an extended reflection on the role of symbolization, whose mechanism "has its place, in some sense, midway between autosuggestion and conversion" (1895, p. 180). That is to say, symbolization does not operate as a kind of conscious thinking or indirect suggestion (Macalpine, 1950, p. 504), nor is it governed by the physical processes that convert repressed energy into physical symptoms:

> It is my opinion, however, that when a hysteric creates a somatic expression for an emotionally-coloured idea by symbolization, this depends less than one would imagine on personal or voluntary factors. In taking a verbal expression literally and in feeling the "stab in the heart" or the "slap in the face" after some slighting remark as a real event, the hysteric is not taking liberties with words, but is simply reviving once more the sensations to which the verbal expression owes its justification. (Freud, 1895, pp. 180–81)

Freud then suggested that the figure of speech of "swallowing something," used to describe an inability to respond to insult, "did in fact originate from the innervatory sensations which arise in the pharynx when we refrain from speaking and prevent ourselves from reacting to the insult" (1895, p. 181). He then wrote:

> All these sensations and innervations belong to the field of "The Expression of the Emotions," which, as Darwin [1872] has taught us, consists of actions which originally had a meaning and served a purpose. These may now for the most part have become so much weakened that the expression of them in words seems to us only to be a figurative picture of them, whereas in all probability the description was once meant literally; and hysteria is right in restoring the original meaning of the words in depicting its unusually strong innervations. Indeed, it is perhaps wrong to say that hysteria creates these sensations by symbolization. It may be that it does not take linguistic usage as its model at all, but that both hysteria and linguistic usage alike draw their material from a common source. (1895, p. 181)

Although Freud here did not specify what that "common source" might be, it may well be the unconscious semiotic registration of experience as signs, producing feeling and action interpretants.

In the volume's final piece, "The Psychotherapy of Hysteria," written by Freud in 1895, we can observe how he took his distance from Breuer, specifically around the issue of a systemic unconscious "intelligence," which apparently was abhorrent to Breuer. We can observe a clear progression in the extent to which Freud was willing to stake out a position regarding the possibility of unconscious articulation by means of an ordered set of associations functioning as signs.

Freud tells us that in attempting to use Breuer's method with a large number of patients he was forced to make more precise what distinguishes hysteria from other "neuroses" (1895a, p. 256), such as neurasthenia and "anxiety neurosis." The latter, he maintained, "arises from an accumulation of physical tension, which is itself once more of sexual origin. This neurosis, too, has no psychical mechanism" (1895a, p. 258), unlike hysteria, as observed by Freud in twelve cases, "whose analysis provides a confirmation of the psychical mechanism of hysterical phenomena put forward by us" (1895a, p. 260). In reviewing the five cases published in the present volume, Freud was led to affirm that only one (Miss Lucy R.) could "perhaps best be described as a marginal case of pure hysteria" (1895a, p. 260), whereas the others presented hysteria in combination with different neuroses. For example, in the "combination of anxiety neurosis and hysteria" in the case of Katherina, "the former created the symptoms, while the latter repeated them and operated with them" (1895a, p. 260). Freud here was apparently reinforcing the point he had made earlier about the origin of Frau Caecilie's facial neuralgia in a supposed toothache, namely that the symptom results from a physical cause but is propagated by psychical mechanisms, the chief of which is symbolization.

But he quickly warns us not to wrongly think that he does not wish "to allow that hysteria is an independent neurotic affliction" (his use of double negation here suggests that some intellectual contortion is present), or that he views hysteria "merely as a psychical manifestation of anxiety neurosis," or that he attributes only "'ideogenic' symptoms" to hysteria while "transferring the somatic symptoms (such as hysterogenic points and anaesthesias) to anxiety neurosis" (1895a, p. 261). "Nothing of the sort," insists Freud (1895a, p. 261), and we can wonder at this point about the danger of his position becoming transformed, distorted, and partially evaporating in his attempt to accommodate Breuer. Freud now contradicts himself regarding the etiology of hysterical symptoms, as he postulates the following:

1. Hysterical symptoms are maintained by psychical mechanisms, the chief of which is symbolization.
2. Hysterical symptoms, "as a matter of theory," can be eliminated by the articulation of the underlying symbolic associations.
3. Hysteria does not occur independently of other disorders.
4. These other disorders are the result of physical mechanisms.
5. In its origin the hysterical symptom has a physical cause.

At the end of his summary of his views regarding hysteria, Freud notes a problem:

> It remains for me to mention the apparent contradiction between the admission that not all hysterical symptoms are psychogenic and the assertion that they can all be got rid of by a psychotherapeutic procedure. The solution lies in the fact that some of these non-psychogenic symptoms (stigmata, for instance) are, it is true, indications of illness, but cannot be described as ailments; and consequently it is not of practical importance if they persist after the successful treatment of the illness. (1895a, p. 265)

The argument here has a spurious quality. Who, except the patient, is able to say that "stigmata" or other "indications of illness" are not "ailments" and of no practical importance if they persist? But now Freud makes a complete about-face:

> As regards other such [non-psychogenic] symptoms, it seems to be the case that in some roundabout way they are carried off along with the

psychogenic symptoms, just as, perhaps, in some roundabout way they are after all dependent on a psychical causation. (1895a, p. 265)

It is as if Freud, after struggling to give proper ground to Breuer's physicalism, weary from the effort that he realized was convoluted and contradictory, finally gave up accommodating and affirmed the role of psychical, and therefore symbolic, causation.

In the following section of the paper, Freud gradually articulates a consistent position regarding the role of unconscious symbolic articulation in determining hysterical symptoms. With patients who could not be hypnotized, "although their diagnosis was one of hysteria and it seemed probable that the psychical mechanism described by us operated in them" (1895a, p. 267), Freud pressed the patients to recollect how their symptom had begun. In the course of thus working without hypnosis he was led to see that:

> *by means of my psychical work I had to overcome a psychical force in the patients which was opposed to the pathogenic ideas becoming conscious (being remembered).* A new understanding seemed to open before my eyes when it occurred to me that this must no doubt be the same psychical force that had played a part in the generating of the hysterical symptom and had at that time prevented the pathogenic idea from becoming conscious. (1895a, p. 268)

Such distressing pathogenic ideas were "put out of consciousness" by a defensive maneuver on the part of the ego: "The patient's ego had been approached by an idea which proved to be incompatible, which provoked on the part of the ego a repelling force of which the purpose was defence against this incompatible idea" (1895a, p. 269). Although the "psychical trace" of the idea "was apparently lost to view," nevertheless "that trace must be there" (1895a, p. 269):

> If I endeavored to direct the patient's attention to it, I became aware, in the form of *resistance*, of the same force as had shown itself in the form of *repulsion* when the symptom was generated. If, now, I could make it appear probable that the idea had become pathogenic precisely as a result of its expulsion and repression, the chain would seem complete. (1895a, p. 269)

Freud appears to have recovered from the contorted state he was in earlier as he now more clearly approached a conceptualization of unconscious processes as the result of disturbance in semiosis brought about by the disavowal of a sign's interpretants:

> Thus a psychical force, aversion on the part of the ego, had originally driven the pathogenic idea out of association and was now opposing its return to memory. The hysterical patient's "not knowing" was in fact a "not

wanting to know"—a not wanting which might be to a greater or less extent conscious. The task of the therapist, therefore, lies in overcoming by his psychical work this resistance to association. (1895a, pp. 269–70)

In this context resistance is an obstacle to making the unwanted idea part of conscious articulation.

In describing the method he used, pressing the patient's forehead for a few seconds and asking the patient to describe what came to mind, Freud writes that he could "dissociate the patient's attention from his conscious searching and reflecting" and thereby approach the pathogenic idea which is "always lying ready 'close at hand' and can be reached by associations that are easily accessible," usually through an idea "which is an intermediate link in the chain of associations between the idea from which we start and the pathogenic idea which we are in search of" (1895a, p. 271). This concatenation of associations, the ongoing dynamic process of semiosis that bypasses the ego, out of consciousness but verbally retrievable, may be so elaborate that Freud is led to wonder:

All these consequences of the pressure give one a deceptive impression of there being a superior intelligence outside the patient's consciousness which keeps a large amount of psychical material arranged for particular purposes and has fixed a planned order for its return to consciousness. I suspect, however, that this unconscious second intelligence is no more than an appearance. (1895a, p. 272)

We can wonder if precisely this notion of an "unconscious second intelligence" prompted Breuer's stern warning that we not be tricked by "figures of speech" into making substantive what he judged not to be so.

Freud's disclaimer, however, does not remain a firm one, for after providing several pages of clinical vignettes he writes: "The revelations which one obtains through the procedure of pressing occasionally appear in a very remarkable form and in circumstances which make the assumption of there being an unconscious intelligence even more tempting" (1895a, p. 275). But Freud does not want us to shy away from this temptation, for he now provides us with an example of a woman suffering from phobias and obsessions who offered a single word, "Concierge," to his hand pressure, and then another single word, "Night-gown." Freud writes: "I saw now that this was a new sort of method of answering, and by pressing repeatedly I brought out what seemed to be a meaningless series of words: 'Concierge'—'night-gown'—'bed'—'town'—'farm-cart.' 'What does all this mean?' I asked" (p. 276). She then told him "the story" that had just come into her head of how her psychotic sister had to be taken away in a cart when she was a child. Freud reflects on the process:

The peculiarity of this case lay only in the emergence of isolated key-words which we had to work into sentences; for the appearance of discon-nectedness and irrelevance which characterized the words emitted in this oracular fashion applies equally to the complete ideas and scenes which are normally produced under my pressure. When these are followed up, it invariably turns out that the apparently disconnected reminiscences are closely linked in thought and that they lead quite straight to the patho-genic factor we are looking for. (1895a, p. 276)

After providing additional clinical examples, and discounting along the way Breuer's notion of hypnoid states ("Strangely enough, I have never in my own experience met with a genuine hypnoid hysteria," p. 286), Freud no longer hesitates to make his claim:

The first and most powerful impression made upon one during such an analysis is certainly that the pathogenic psychical material which has ostensibly been forgotten, which is not at the ego's disposal and which plays no part in association and memory, nevertheless in some fashion lies ready to hand and in correct and proper order. It is only a question of removing the resistances that bar the way to the material. In other respects this material is known, in the same way in which we are able to know anything; the correct connections between the separate ideas and between them and the non-pathogenic ones, which are frequently remembered, are in existence; they have been completed at some time and are stored up in the memory. The pathogenic psychical material appears to be the prop-erty of an intelligence which is not necessarily inferior to that of the normal ego. (1895a, p. 287)

This "intelligence" structures the psychical material in three different ways: linear dossiers or files of memories are organized by separate themes; each theme is also "stratified concentrically round the pathogenic nucleus"; and there is also linkage of thought-content by a "logical thread which reaches as far as the nucleus and tends to take an irregular and twisting path, different in every case. This arrangement has a dynamic character" (1895a, p. 289), like the way the knight moves in chess. Freud expands:

I must dwell for a moment longer on this last simile in order to empha-size a point in which it does not do justice to the characteristics of the subject of the comparison. The logical chain corresponds not only to a zig-zag, twisted line, but rather to a ramifying system of lines and more particularly to a converging one. It contains nodal points at which two or more threads meet and thereafter proceed as one; and as a rule several threads which run independently, or which are connected at various points by side-paths, debouch into the nucleus. To put this in other words, it is very remarkable how often a symptom is determined in several ways, is "overdetermined." (1895a, p. 290)

Such "overdetermination" of symptoms is made possible by the semiotic complexity of organized unconscious processes. Signs registered as "traces" continue to produce symptoms as their feeling and action interpretants which, in turn, become new signs evident in the unaware speaker's tone and behavior. The semiotic space opened up by the presence of a listener enables the disjointed semiosis to proceed through the listener who can then observe and resonate with the signs' interpretants and return them to the speaker. The complexity of semiosis suggests the operation of an intelligence, a symbolic register, that does not require the ego's awareness, that operates without conscious awareness. This is what I think Breuer found most objectionable in Freud's thinking about hysteria, not his emphasis on sexuality.

Sexuality and Its Contingent Signifiers

Freud's position regarding the complexity of unconscious processes has received contemporary corroboration from beyond the field of psychoanalysis:

> Cognitive science views began to stress the automatic nature of activation of semantic networks [e.g., Collins and Loftus, 1975]. In studies of memory, complex semantic information could be activated without attention ... [and] processes occurring outside the focal awareness of the subject were both lawful and complex. (Posner, Rothbart, and Harmon, 1994, p. 199-200; see also J. Singer, 1990; Epstein, 1994)

Within psychoanalysis, I have attempted to show how dyadic conceptions of child development and of the analytic process generally reduce the semiotic field in a variety of ways. These positions may emphasize the learning of speech as a dyadic phenomenon and as an outgrowth of "pre-linguistic" stages. They may treat language as a derivative communicative process rather than as a structuring system. They may assume an externalist position and claim that psychopathology does not involve any sort of translation but is the direct result of victimization. They may espouse a deficit model in which unconscious dynamics do not require interpretation and are simply an echo of conscious experience. It is still an open debate whether and what kind of symptoms can be determined, structured, and resolved through symbolization.

This debate repeats, regarding sexuality, the very terms of Freud's dispute with Breuer. Do symptoms require a physical predisposition? Can sexual fantasy, either defended against or encouraged, produce symptoms? Is adult psychopathology the consequence of childhood abuse? Do unconscious processes play a role? Do "retrieved" recollections carry weight as fantasy, as re-categorizations, or as historical evidence of past abuse? Does childhood sexuality exist? Do dreams and symptoms have symbolic significance? Can we say what, if anything, is specifically human about human sexuality?

The ease with which sexuality could be made to dominate all of Freud's discoveries, to the extent that his observations about the functioning of language could almost disappear, is perhaps contingent on the nature of language itself and the relationship between language and the body. It is precisely this relationship that Freud addressed in his initial cases and his theoretical formulations in *Studies on Hysteria*: how the hysteric makes the mute body-part speak; how the symptom goes about "joining in the conversation" (Breuer and Freud, 1895, p. 296); how "verbal bridges," "nodal points," and "switchwords" (1895, p. 290) operate in an unconscious system that determines symptoms; and how a doctor must position himself or herself in relation to this Third so as to be able to hear and read and be a participant in the dialogue. The fact that the structuring effect of language as a central Freudian discovery could almost drop out of much subsequent psychoanalytic reflection, is partly a function of what Heidegger (1950) called the "nearness" of language itself. Language, that which enables us to "see" and make sense of our experience of the world, is itself difficult to "see," somewhat like wearing a pair of comfortable, well-functioning eyeglasses that are taken for granted.

Perhaps there is also something about human sexuality, at least in Western culture, that made it relatively easy for Freud to accuse Breuer of faltering and to promote himself as a conquistador of sexuality. Barthes stated:

> In the West, sexuality lends itself only to a language of transgression, and that but poorly; but to make of sexuality a field of transgression is still to keep it imprisoned in a binary logic, a paradigm, a meaning. . . . What is difficult is not to liberate sexuality according to a more or less libertarian plan but to disengage it from meaning, including transgression as meaning. (1981, p. 123)

This suggests that sexuality's "truth" may have something to do with its status as beyond signification, in the Real, as Lacan put it, not fully embraced by the register of images or symbols. Freud's proposition of the sexual etiology of psychoneurosis not only presumed the patient's experience of sexuality as transgressive, but in so exposing sexuality, Freud promoted himself as the solitary investigator whose discoveries transgressed contemporary mores, for which he was punished by rejection. In this myth, Breuer, in contrast, accommodated himself to prevailing views and by not transgressing them did not suffer what Freud did. Sexuality seen primarily as a field of transgression could then become a weapon in the service of the ego; not only was Freud's ego served in relation to the narcissistic injury inflicted by Breuer, but this manner of using sexuality—as a field to be liberated, as a domain to be claimed and mastered and appropriated by the ego—served to buttress the role of the ego in ego psychology and in the history of psychoanalysis. And as we have seen in Chapter 8, there is a good deal of evidence suggesting how human narcissism will distort experience for self-serving purposes, especially by claiming to possess rational objectivity about itself.

But human sexuality persists in defying the ego's rationality and, because of this element of nonsense, passionate love has been viewed, at least since Plato, with great ambivalence (Nussbaum, 1986). This nonsense is presented to us in a particular manner: it is infantile sexuality, sensuality, and bodily delight, and not the ego, that bring some elements of experience into signification. This does not mean that sexuality creates semiotics or the structure of language; on the contrary, the symbolic register provides the opening for there to be any "experience" at all. What sexuality does is to so invest bits and pieces of experience with salience that it generates effects outside of the conscious awareness of the ego. Freud saw these effects and speculated about the role of a "second intelligence." But such "intelligence" is a contradiction to our conscious intellection and its operations contradict our conscious thought, as Barratt states:

> In this way, psychoanalytic method exhibits the two dimensionalities of meaning that compose our lives and demonstrates their inherent *contradictoriness*. It is this discovery of the contradictoriness grounding all experiencing and understanding that is an anathema to metaphysics since Plato and to the prevailing canons of official science. (1988, p. 232)

Barratt goes on to characterize the unconscious dimension of human experience as a "recondite temporality—the temporality of the 'sexual body,' of a subtle 'energy,'" that he, along with Lacan and others, calls "desire" (1988, p. 233). In our conscious thinking and speaking, manifest signs serve to repudiate this other dimension, the unconscious, to deny its contradictoriness and maintain cohesion. As Barratt concludes:

> Thus, it seems that each manifest content of consciousness endlessly repudiates a meaningfulness that is not even "there" semiotically, but is already alienated or estranged "within" the manifest production itself, not as a sign generated by the law and order of the semiotic totality, but rather as the contradictorious being of its recondite temporality. (1988, p. 233)

Because language has reached into the human subject through acculturation, we are given perspective on experience, we have partially overcome its immediacy, its chaos, and its unpredictability. But the opening on experience made possible by signs comes at the cost of an opening, a gap in ourselves. This opening is what Freud referred to as the unconscious, that dimension of ourselves that involuntarily contradicts our conscious selves, that makes use of substitutions and combines them in ways that are bizarre to our conscious minds. The semiotics of conscious discourse are not the same as the semiotics of unconscious inscription.

This recondite dimension of the unconscious, with its infantile pace and insistence, may provide the basis for intense and personally important signifying effects we sometimes produce in one another. Such always surprising transference effects rest on the prior selection and investment of specific cues, cues that become signs invested by sexuality with the salience given by contiguity in a radically contingent and ad hoc manner.

This radical contingency means that where human sexuality is concerned (unlike animal sexuality), anything may serve as an index of anything else. There is no pre-given signifier-signified set of relationships structuring human desire or human symptoms. At best perhaps we can speak of a "semiotic *a priori*" consisting of Roman Jakobson's two axes, combination (touch) and substitution (vision), the structure of language that governs the concatenation of signs. As we saw in Chapter 2, Levin added an axis of sonority (voice) and referred to the use of these semiotic axes as a "major synthesis . . . regarding fundamental principles" and he suggested they are "most likely based on the brain's integration of information along three axes: contiguity (touch), similarity (vision), and sonority (hearing)" (1991, p. 160). These empty semiotic frames are painted in through the arbitrary highlighting of absurd details by a necessarily disjointed infantile sexuality. This disjointedness is not simply due to its "recondite" temporality, its contradictoriness to ego aims; at a more basic level, the disjointedness of human sexuality perhaps arises from its fleshly function to be at the edge of the Real and to mark this edge as the edge of life. The edge of human life, its borders, is marked out in a libidinal way. A special investment is made in the body's openings. Lacan called attention to how drive formations originate at these erogenous zones as on the edge of a rim: the mouth, the anus, the genitals, the ears, the eyes, whose drive objects include the breast, feces, the voice, the gaze. I would add that it is at these openings that an exchange is established, an *in* and *out* movement that itself is the sign of life and that congeals a psychic inside and outside. The Real of death, of the undifferentiated and unimaginable non-existence of my subjectivity, is held back for a while at this border of life.

From this border of the fleshly Real, early sexuality snares, or is snared by, contingent contiguities of sonority, smell, touch, color, movement, in order to establish, within the semiotic frame of combination and substitution, certain anchor points, certain familiar bits, so that repetition can begin. It is as if the sameness of the Real, in itself uninscribable, is preserved in the repetition of sexuality as a way to sustain transitoriness and the burden of mortality. Sexuality would then be somewhat like the "Dionysian" in Nietzsche:

> An urge to unity, a reaching out beyond personality, the everyday, society, reality, across the abyss of transitoriness: a passionate-painful overflowing into darker, fuller, more floating states; an ecstatic affirmation of the total character of life as that which remains the same, just as powerful, just as blissful, through all change; the great pantheistic sharing of joy and sorrow that sanctifies and calls good even the most terrible and questionable qualities of life; the eternal will to procreation, to fruitfulness, to recurrence; the feeling of the necessary unity of creation and destruction. (1901, p. 539)

In the end, what may have disturbed both Breuer and Freud was Freud's vision of an interpenetration of intelligence and sexuality, operating according to a semiotic code completely out of the ego's awareness. I believe this remains as disturbing for us today as it was 100 years ago.

Conclusion

In this book I have tried in various ways to be integrative rather than disjunctive. Writing in an analytic vein for psychologists, reporting psychological research data to analysts, relating infancy research to semiotic models, experiencing literature as I am, I have perhaps lost focus more than the reader would wish. In fact I have not tried to maintain focus through a common practice of taking sides. I have not cast my vote with the empiricists against the hermeneuticists (or the other way around) because I have tried to avoid such dichotomous thinking. By now it may be clear that in my perspective such dichotomous thinking is itself a symptom, a sign of the either/or operation of Lacan's imaginary register, a loss of Peirce's Thirdness.

I would like to leave the reader with some reflections about three implications of this perspective. The first has to do with the way Lacan and Peirce ground the field of free association. If we allow Peirce to mediate between Freud and Lacan, we can then think of Freud's notion of the *Vorstellung,* the representation or idea that gets placed before us, the association, as a sign in a semiotic process. We can likewise think of Lacan's signifier in the way he insisted, that it does not represent something for someone but rather leads to another signifier in a chain of signifiers we can call the process of semiosis. For when Lacan claims that the signifier represents the subject for another signifier, I read him as precisely articulating what Peirce stated when he called the human being a sign for others, a sign whose interpretants are produced in others, even without their awareness. As a subject I am held a certain way by these interpretants produced in others: I am admired or reviled, called upon or abandoned, feared or desired, recognized in one way or another because semiosis works in me, through me, and beyond me for others, always, out of awareness, apart from my conscious intent.

Such semiosis is not a linguistic process, at least not for Peirce and Lacan. In a letter Peirce cautioned his correspondent against abstraction, telling her "that perhaps you are in danger of falling into some error in consequence of limiting your studies so much to Language and among languages to one very peculiar language, as all Aryan languages are; and within that language so much to words" (1966, p. 421). Lacan shows similar misgivings about words; he distinguishes language as studied by linguists from what he calls "lalangue," his neologism (related to the Latin verb *lallare*, to sing "lala" or lullabye) for the discourse of the unconscious:

> If I have said that language is what the unconscious is structured like, that's because language, at first, does not exist. Language is what one tries to know about the function of lalangue. . . . The unconscious is the witness of a knowing insofar as to a large extent it escapes the speaking being. This being provides occasions for perceiving where the effects of lalangue proceed, in that he presents all sorts of affects which remain enigmatic. These affects are what result from the presence of lalangue, in that, as a knowing, it articulates things that go much beyond what the speaking being puts up with in his enunciated knowing. . . .
>
> Lalangue affects us first of all by all that it entails as effects which are affects. If one can say that the unconscious is structured like a language, it is because the effects of lalangue, already there as a knowing, go well beyond everything that the being who speaks is capable of enunciating (1972–73, pp. 126–27, my translation).

Far from privileging a grammar of conscious discourse, Lacan's notion of "lalangue" raises doubts about the very possibility of a semiotic approach. As we saw in the last chapter, Barratt (1988, 1993) argues that the Freudian unconscious subverts not only the rational logic of semiotics, but operates as a "contradictorious being" (1988, p. 233) in any semiotically-organized discourse. This serious claim, challenging much of our integrative, interdisciplinary efforts, may be addressed if we can speak of "lalangue" and its effects as operating in a Peircean framework; "lalangue" would then refer to the earliest forms of semiosis whose unconscious aspects can only be glimpsed in the infancy research we reviewed. With the development of psychic structure in a semiotic surround, we can expect that some form of semiosis governs unconscious processes no less than conscious activities, somewhat the way Freud spelled out repression as a failure to translate, to re-transcribe from an earlier to a later level of experience and functioning. In other words, a semiosis of lalangue is not out of the question if we take Peirce's notion of the interpretant to include, necessarily, the repressed, disavowed, incomplete, and inarticulable aspects of experience.

Intersubjectivity means we incessantly engage in a conjoint process of producing interpretants that become signs generating their own interpretants in feeling, action, and thought. The production of interpretants is not in my control, is wider than my conscious ego, and is enacted in our mutual behavior. Free association in the analysand, with its corresponding evenly hovering attention in the analyst, is Freud's method for bringing into articulation our mutually generated interpretants. Free association is intrinsically dialogic and therefore different from speaking to a mirror or into a tape recorder. The dialogue, furthermore, is not simply dyadic, but passes through the Other, the semiotic field, the field of the unconscious resonances of history and culture.

The second implication I want to address is how triadic structures stretch back from the Oedipal to earlier periods of development. Triadic structures, in a Peircean sense, are present and operative from before birth and generate the semiotic development of the human brain and the human subject. We have learned following Winnicott to say there is no such thing as an infant, but rather an infant-mother dyad. The more common condition, however, is that there is no infant-mother dyad but rather an infant-mother-Other triad. The infant-mother dyad is held by the Third of culture, as Kirshner states: "This symbolic framework, in fact, is the prerequisite for the basic maternal function in human development' (1994, p. 241). When culture does not hold the dyad, when the mother is alienated from her culture or when cultural transmission has broken down, then the infant-mother dyad is in trouble. For this reason I have come to view dyadic processes in treatment as regressive: that is, we can define a good deal of regression in treatment as the patient or analyst reducing the field to dyadic relations. In such regressive moments we see the return of archaic wishes, narcissistic illusions, the early ways in which infant or mother were intent on being found as the all-fulfilling object of the other's desire. The dyad provides a refuge from universality and community. The dyad's members are convinced that only they possess knowledge of particulars, that only they know one another, that no one else sees what they see, that they can keep a promise to provide what is "needed" by the other. Transference will always include elements of such archaic dyadic relations, and the countertransference under such press is to leave one's place in the Third and abandon oneself to dyadic mirroring or, in institutions, to abandon the therapeutic dyad to their own dynamics, to give up functioning as the Third to the dyad.

Peirce's architectonic theory and Lacan's three registers lead toward a hierarchical model for psychoanalysis, such as that proposed by Gedo and Goldberg (1973) and further elaborated by Gedo (1993). In this model archaic modes of functioning require recognition of structural vulnerabilities through analytic responsiveness that is "beyond interpretation" (Gedo, 1993). Having re-discovered this dimension of psychoanalysis (one can make a case that this is what Ferenczi grappled with and for which he was scorned), we are in danger of declaring we have in "intersubjectivity" a new paradigm for our analytic work. If I have argued one thing in this book, it is that the dyad is not a new paradigm but rather a reduction of the field.

The third implication, flowing from the first two, is that we can extend the "linguistic turn" of our epistemic framework back into semiotics as its broader base. The triadic notions of Peirce assist us here as they did Jakobson and, less consistently, Lacan as well. The triadic model of the sign allows us to read the so-called prelinguistic realm of dyadic enactments as an articulated sequence of signs productive of feeling and dynamic interpretants which, in turn, become signs for the other member of the dyad. While it seems reasonable to say that the form of communication or response that we call enactive is preverbal, perhaps even in certain conditions prelinguistic, the sign status of such enactments remains complex.

The enactive, if not sheer random motoricity, if indeed the enactment constitutes a repetition, is iconic of the earlier experience. Such iconic features, present as signs in the dyadic enactment, are observable in the oddities of the behavior or in the reaction of the observer; this reaction is embraced by Peirce's notion of the interpretant of the sign as distinct from the object of the sign. The feeling interpretant brings about a coerced affective mirroring of the past, bearing a resemblance to the past, a resemblance not usually perceived by the other member of the dyad, and rarely by the one acting, who is blind to the action's meaning or to its status as a repetitive icon. Modell singles out such repetitive aspects in the transference as "the iconic transference" (1993, p. 49). Earlier he had written of the transference repetition as "the unconscious attempt to manipulate the secondary object through the affects induced in the countertransference" (1984, p. 35). The iconic features of a repetition are generally available for interpretation only from the position of the Third, by one whose position is distinct from the dyadic poles. This is the position occupied by the analyst who is simultaneously (and this makes the role unique) also a member of the dyad. At times it may also be the position of an astute relative or knowledgeable friend witnessing an interaction but whose voice, unlike that of the analyst, is usually disqualified by the patient precisely because it comes from outside the dyad.

The enactment which can be so interpreted from the position of the Third may be said to be pre-symbolic, surely pre-verbal, but not pre-semiotic, since it consists of signs, is ordered as signs, is structured with reference to signs of the past. The sign-dimension of the enactment is usually not available to the actor, however, because the interpretant of the sign is disavowed by the actor. As

Freud defined disavowal, it pertains not to drives but to unwanted demands from reality, and what is disavowed is specifically "the perceptions which bring to knowledge this demand from reality" (1938, p. 204). We can take Peirce's interpretant as the perception of the sign which brings to knowledge something about the sign's object, in this case as a demand from reality that bears upon the subject. When the interpretant of a given sign is disavowed, it is not the subject but the other who feels or reacts in response to the enactment, through what Peirce called "the Dynamical Interpretant," which consists in direct effects "actually produced by a Sign upon an Interpreter of it" (1966, p. 413). For Peirce, signs were so fundamental that he argued that the interpreter does not produce the sign's significance, its interpretant, but rather the sign in a given context produces an interpretant in a receiver who may thereby become an interpreter.

As we have seen, Peirce's notion of the sign explicitly includes feeling and action as preliminary aspects of the sign's signifying effects. The feeling interpretant is the sign's initial impact on the sign's receiver, an impact that is a form of coerced mirroring. This initial impact may be subliminal and directly lead to action, as when traffic comes to a momentary halt before a street "Stop" sign, or when we shake the hand extended to us for a handshake. Such action constitutes the sign's dynamic interpretant, the sign's actualized, pragmatic meaning. The abstract meaning of the sign, its logical interpretant, a generalization requiring the use of verbal symbols, is a further development of semiosis in a hierarchy of iconic, enactive, and symbolic communication.

Based on these Peircean suggestions, we can view enactment as a dynamic interpretant, or the action-significance of a sign, prompted by an induced affect state and potentially leading to a verbal interpretation. As Boesky (1982) and Gedo (1988) indicate, there is no reason to assume that enactments are intrinsically defensive; in a Peircean framework, they function as interpretants of signs and in turn become signs to be further interpreted. In Johan's reporting of a recent panel on enactments, Jacobs stated: "Because verbal communication is of the greatest importance in analysis, enactments often express what is not yet otherwise expressible . . . they are avant-garde messengers that anticipate and signal what is to come" (1992, p. 836). Of course in psychoanalytic work we often encounter enactments whose semiotic movement is interrupted by developmental disability or defense. The patient may acknowledge the action, but disavow any pertinent affect, thereby cutting the action-significance off from the feeling-significance of a given sign. Or the patient may project the initial interpretant, the feeling-significance, so that the analyst now bears the impact of a sign that is not yet in evidence, and may recognize its presence through an impulse to action, as Chused stated in the same panel: "During analysis a symbolic action that generates a corresponding impulse for action in the analyst can provide substantial information about unconscious forces and affects within a patient" (Johan, 1992, p. 828). Or the patient may acknowledge the feeling and the action, but disavow the logical interpretant as expressed in the analyst's interpretation of the enactment. Or the patient may deny that any of this has to do with the sign or its object, as they may appear, for example, in dreams or in a relationship. Or the patient's failure to connect may be due to a failure to learn, to what Gedo calls an "apraxia" (Gedo and Gehrie, 1993, p. 130).

Looking at enactment in this way, we can view repression and disavowal as bearing on different aspects of the semiotic process. Repression impacts on the sign, it negates the relationship between the sign and its object; as Freud suggests, it fails to provide the equivalent sign in translation. Disavowal bears on the interpretant itself, refusing to give the feeling or action-significance the status of meaning elicited by a particular sign. This is a refusal that, as Morris (1993) suggests, may be a foundational act of a human self-in-the-making, a self that narcissistically claims the right to create meaning and thereby inaugurate a split between the interpreting subject and the interpreted self. As we saw in Chapter 2, such a split may require a degree of hemispheric disjunction that Levin (1991) and Basch (1983) propose as the neurological correlate of repression and disavowal.

The interpreting subject's emergence as a self requires the use of signs. In summarizing Peirce, Short writes: "Our capacity to represent ourselves to ourselves [in a necessarily distorted manner, I would add] transforms the sort of selves we are. However, that capacity is dependent not only on biologically inherited cerebral powers, but also on culturally inherited (i.e., learned) linguistic powers" (1992, p. 122). Cavell emphasizes the narrative form of such self-representations: "A creature that can tell a story about itself, and only such a one, is a self, someone to whom we can attribute subjectivity" (1993, p. 117). Does narrative tend to elicit more enactments than other forms of discourse? If so, then perhaps the structure of narrative has something to do with it. Bruner claims we have a "primitive predisposition to narrative organization" (1990, p. 80), and, as noted earlier, he defines four essential features of narrative: agency, sequence, norms of deviance from social expectations, and narratorial voice or point of view. These features of narrative are evident by three years of age, although narrative structure is inherent much earlier "in the praxis of social interaction before it achieves linguistic expression" (1990, p. 77), in that "protolinguistic" framework I examined in the Introduction. These earliest semiotic traces provide a rich developmental base for the narrativation of the categories of memory. We can speculate that once the narrative act is enjoined, the patient as well as the analyst anticipates, possibly with dread or excitement, the elements implicit in the narrative format: separate or merged active subjects, actions that have consequences, objects that are gained or lost or changed, wishes that are approved or prohibited, conflicting points of view. The narrative structure is full of danger zones for precarious selves without firm boundaries or for conflicted subjects with ambivalent wishes and confused priorities, and in touching any part of the semiotic web of narrative, a string of signs may elicit a variety of feelings and enactments as their disavowed interpretants.

An object relations approach (e.g., Bion, 1992; Ogden, 1986) typically emphasizes the analyst's role (or in the case of the child, the parent's role) as container for the patient's disavowed or projected feelings; by containing them, the analyst or parent de-toxifies the projected feelings and thereby makes possible their re-internalization by the patient or child. This is typically accomplished through the analyst/mother's reverie which creates an inner space for containment. I would conceptualize this as a semiotic process in which the analyst's function is to remove the obstacle to semiosis without imposing one's own interpretant onto the patient. The reverie of free association facilitates the sign's reception in all of its ambiguity and resonance. It counters the fixity of stereotyped responses, as when a child has become a fixed sign to a parent of some narcissistic injury; it interrupts the projection and counterprojection of disavowed feeling interpretants; it challenges the habitual action-interpretants of family members to a child's sign-presence; and it provides an open forum to discuss the skewed, even delusional conceptual interpretants of child and parent as signs for each other.

When we are dealing with a patient without firm boundaries, we intervene in a manner that is "beyond interpretation," even beyond language as such. We introduce by tone, gesture, object, or silent reflection the transitional space for the patient to create a signifying marker at the needed boundary: between patient and therapist, between conscious and repressed, between thought and action, between words and things. Such work goes on with severely disturbed patients in what Kristeva calls the domain of the "semiotic" as distinct from the "symbolic" (1980, pp. 133–35). We use mirroring icons and limit-setting indices rather than symbols in order to prevent further psychotic fragmentation and to establish boundaries. By doing so we do not abandon our position in the Third. We are no less analysts for taking into account the patient's vulnerabilities as well as our own.

References

Abelin, E. 1975. Some further observations and comments on the earliest role of the father. *International Journal of Psycho-Analysis.* 56: 293–302.

Abramson, L., and L. Alloy. 1981. Depression, nondepression, and cognitive illusions: Reply to Schwartz. *Journal of Experimental Psychology: General Psychology.* 110, 436–447.

Abravanel, E., and A. Sigafoos 1984. Exploring the presence of imitation during early infancy. *Child Development.* 55: 381–392.

Alloy, L., L. Abramson, and D. Viscusi. 1981. Induced mood and the illusion of control. *Journal of Personality and Social Psychology,* 41: 1129–1140.

Althusser, L. 1971. *Lenin and Philosophy.* New York: Monthly Review Press.

Anderson, B., R. Vietze, and P. Dolecki. 1977. Reciprocity in vocal interactions of mothers and infants. *Child Development.* 48: 1676–1681.

Anisfeld, M. 1979. Interpreting "imitative" responses in early infancy. *Science.* 205: 215–216.

Anzieu, D. 1985. *The skin ego.* New Haven: Yale University Press, 1989.

Asendorpf, J. and P.-M. Baudonniere. 1993. Self-awareness and other-awareness: Mirror self-recognition and synchronic imitation among unfamiliar peers. *Developmental Psychology.* 29: 88–95.

Atwood, G., and R. Stolorow 1984. *Structures of subjectivity: Explorations in psychoanalytic phenomenology.* Hillsdale, NJ: The Analytic Press.

Auden, W. H. and L. Kronenberger. 1962. *The Viking Book of Aphorisms: A Personal Selection:* New York: Dorset Press, 1981.

Aulagnier, P. 1962. "Angoisse et identification." In *séminaire*, 1961–62, *L'identification*, by J. Lacan. Unpublished manuscript. International Research Center. New York: International General. 396–412.

Baer, D., and J.C. Wright. 1974. Developmental psychology. *Annual Review of Psychology*: 1–82.

Baillargeon, R. 1990. "Young infants' physical knowledge." Paper presented at the 98th annual convention of the American Psychological Association, Boston.

Bakan, D. 1966. *The duality of human existence: An essay on psychology and religion.* Chicago: Rand McNally.

Bakeman, R. and L. Adamson. 1984. Coordinating attention to people and objects in mother-infant and peer-infant interaction. *Child Development.* 55: 1278–1289.

Balat, M. 1992a. *Des fondements sémiotiques de la psychanalyse: Peirce, Freud et Lacan.* Paris: Meridiens-Klincksieck.

———. 1992b. Le musement, de Peirce à Lacan. *Revue Internationale de Philosophie.* no. 180: 101–125.

Balint, M. 1959. *Thrills and regressions.* New York: International Universities Press.

Bandura, A. (ed.) 1971. *Psychological modeling: Conflicting theories.* Chicago: Aldine-Atherton.

Bär, E. 1975. *Semiotic approaches to psychotherapy.* Bloomington: Indiana University Press.

Bard, K. 1994. Developmental issues in the evolution of the mind. *American Psychologist.* 49: 760–761.

Barratt, B. 1988. Why is psychoanalysis so controversial? Notes from left field! *Psychoanalytic Psychology.* 5: 223–239.

———. 1993. *Psychoanalysis and the postmodern impulse: Knowing and being since Freud's psychology.* Baltimore: The Johns Hopkins University Press.

Barthes, R. 1964. *Elements of semiology.* New York: Hill and Wang, 1978.

———. 1981. *The grain of the voice: Interviews, 1962–1980.* New York: Hill and Wang, 1985.

Basch, M. 1976. Psychoanalysis and communication science. *The Annual of Psychoanalysis.* New York: International Universities Press. Vol. IV: 385–421.

———. 1983. The perception of reality and the disavowal of meaning. *The Annual of Psychoanalysis.* Chicago: Chicago Institute for Psychoanalysis. Vol. XI: 125–153.

Bataille, G. 1954. *Inner experience.* Albany: State University of New York Press, 1988.

Bates, J. E. 1975. Effects of a child's imitation versus nonimitation on adults' verbal and nonverbal positivity. *Journal of Personality and Social Psychology.* 31: 840–851.

Bateson, M. 1975. Mother-infant exchanges: The epigenesis of conversational interaction. *Developmental psycholinguistics and communication disorders* (Annals of the New York Academy of Sciences, 263). New York: New York Academy of Sciences.

Beckett, S. 1959. *The Unnamable*. London: Calder and Boyars.

Beebe, B. and L. Gerstman. 1980. The "packaging" of maternal stimulation in relation to infant facial-visual engagement: A case study at four months. *Merrill-Palmer Quarterly*. 4: 321–339.

Beebe, B. and F. Lachmann. 1988. The contribution of mother–infant mutual influence to the origins of self and object representations. *Psychoanalytic Psychology*, 5: 305–337.

Benjamin, J. 1990. An outline of intersubjectivity. *Psychoanalytic Psychology*, 7: Supplement, 33–46.

———. 1993. Reply to Burack. *Psychoanalysis and Contemporary Thought*. 16: 447–454.

Benveniste, E. 1952. Animal communication and human language. *Problems in general linguistics*. Coral Gables: University of Miami Press, 1971. 49–54.

———. 1956. The nature of pronouns. *Problems in general linguistics*. Coral Gables: University of Miami Press, 1971. 217–222.

———. 1958. Subjectivity in language. *Problems in general linguistics*. Coral Gables: University of Miami Press, 1971. 223–230.

Bergmann, M., and F. Hartman. (eds.). 1976. *The evolution of psychoanalytic technique*. New York: Basic Books.

Berkowitz, L. 1983. The experience of anger as a parallel process in the display of impulsive, "angry" aggression. *Aggression: Theoretical and empirical reviews*, R. Geen and E. Donnerstein (eds.). New York: Academic Press. Vol. 1: 103–133.

Berkowitz, L., and M. Dunand. 1981. "Misery wants to share the misery." Unpublished data. Cited in Berkowitz, 1983.

Bick, E. 1967. The experience of the skin in early object-relations. *Melanie Klein Today*. E. Bott Spillius (ed.). London: Routledge, 1988. Vol I: 187–191.

Bion, W. 1992. *Cogitations*. F. Bion (ed.). London: Karnac Books.

Blatt, S. 1990. Interpersonal relatedness and self-definition: Two personality configurations and their implications for psychopathology and psychotherapy. *Repression and dissociation: Implications for personality theory, psychopathology, and health*. J. Singer (ed.). Chicago: University of Chicago Press. 299–335.

Blum, H. 1981. Some current and recurrent problems of psychoanalytic technique. *Journal of the American Psychoanalytic Association*. 29: 47–68.

Boesky, D. 1982. Acting out: A reconsideration of the concept. *International Journal of Psychoanalysis*. 63: 39–55.

Bollas, C. 1987. *The shadow of the object: Psychoanlayis of the unthought known*. New York: Columbia University Press.

Boothby, R. 1991. *Death and desire: Psychoanalytic theory in Lacan's return to Freud*. New York: Routledge.

Bower, B. 1994. Charge of the "right" brigade. *Science News.* 146: 280–282.

Bowles, P. 1949. *The sheltering sky.* New York: Vintage, 1990.

Boyer, L.B. 1964. Folk psychiatry of the Apaches of the Mescalero Indian Reservation. *Magic, faith, and healing: Studies in the primitive psychology today.* A. Kiev (ed.). New York: The Free Press. 384–419.

Brazelton, T., B. Koslowski, and M. Main. 1974. The origins of reciprocity. M. Lewis and L. Rosenblum (eds.). *The effect of the infant on its caregiver.* New York: Wiley. 49–75.

Brent, J. 1993. *Charles Sanders Peirce: A life.* Bloomington: Indiana University Press.

Brett, J. 1981. Self and other in the child's experience of language: Hofmannsthal's "Letter of Lord Chandos". *International Review of Psycho-Analysis.* 8: 191–201.

Breuer, J., and S. Freud. 1895. Studies on hysteria. *S.E.,* 2. London: Hogarth Press, 1955.

Brickman, H. 1993. "Between the devil and the deep blue sea": The dyad and the triad in psychoanalytic thought. *International Journal of Psycho-Analysis.* 74: 905–915.

Brown, C. 1993. Annals of exploration: I now walk into the wild. *The New Yorker,* February 8: 36–47.

Brown, C., and S. Witkowski. 1981. Figurative language in a universalist perspective. *American Ethnology.* 8: 596–615.

Brun, R. 1936. Sigmund Freud's Leistungen auf dem Gebiet der organischen Neurologie. *Schweiz. Arch. of Neur. Psychiat.* 37.

Bruner, J. 1978b. Learning how to do things with words. *Human development. Wolfson Lectures, 1976–1977.* J. Bruner and A. Garton (eds.). Oxford: Oxford University Press.

———. 1990. *Acts of meaning.* Cambridge: Harvard University Press.

Bruner, J., and C. F. Feldman. 1982. Where does language come from? *New York Review of Books.* June 24: 34–36.

Buber, M. 1970. *I and Thou.* New York: Scribner.

Buechel, E., S.J. 1970. *A dictionary of the Teton Dakota Sioux language.* Paul Manhart, S.J. (ed.). Pine Ridge, SD: Red Cloud Indian School.

Bühler, C. 1927. *Soziologische und psychologische Studien über das erste Lebensjahr.* Jena: Fischer.

Byatt, A. S. 1985. *Still life.* New York: Macmillan.

Cavell, M. 1993. *The psychoanalytic mind: From Freud to Philosophy.* Cambridge: Harvard University Press.

Chatwin, B. 1988. *The songlines.* New York: Penguin Books.

Clark, M. 1988. *Jacques Lacan: An annotated bibliography.* Vol. I and II. New York: Garland.

Cocks, G. 1994. Introduction. *The curve of life: Correspondence of Heinz Kohut, 1923–1981.* G. Cocks. (ed.). Chicago: University of Chicago Press.

————. 1995. Reply. *Psychoanalytic Books.* 6: 6–10.

Coen, S. 1981. Notes on the concept of selfobject and preoedipal object. *Journal of the American Psychoanalytic Association.* 29: 395–411.

Cohen, L. B. 1979. Our developing knowledge of infant perception and cognition. *American Psychologist,* 34. 894–899.

Cohn, J., and E. Tronick. 1982. Communicative rules and the sequential structure of infant behavior during normal and depressed interaction. *Social interchange in infancy: Affect, cognition, and communication.* E. Tronick (ed.). Baltimore: University Park Press. 59–78.

————. 1983. Three-month-old infants' reaction to simulated maternal depression. *Child Development.* 54: 185–193.

————. 1987. Mother-infant face-to-face interaction: The sequence of dyadic states at 3, 6, and 9 months. *Developmental Psychology,* 23: 68–77.

————. 1988. Mother-infant face-to-face interaction: Influence is bidirectional and unrelated to periodic cycles in either partner's behavior. *Developmental Psychology.* 24: 386–392.

Colapietro, V. 1989. *Peirce's approach to the self: A semiotic perspective on human subjectivity.* Albany: State University of New York Press.

————. 1993. *Glossary of semiotics.* New York: Paragon House.

Collins, A. and E. Loftus. 1975. A spreading-activation theory of semantic processing. *Psychology Review,* 82: 407–428.

Compact edition of the Oxford English dictionary. 1971. New York: Oxford University Press.

Conrad, J. 1899. *Heart of darkness.* New York: Norton, 1963.

Cottet, S. 1985. Présentation: Le plus novateur des analystes américains. H. Kohut, *Les deux analyses de M. Z.* G. Laurent-Sivry and C. Leger-Paturneau (eds.). Paris: Navarin/Seuil.

Cox, O. 1994. Beckett's *Unnamable:* not I, not mad. *The Letter,* Summer. 82–94.

Cranefield, P. F. 1958. Josef Breuer's evaluation of his contributions to psychoanalysis. *International Journal of Psycho-Analysis.* 39: 319–322.

Crapanzano, V. 1982. The self, the third, and desire. In *Psychosocial theories of the self.* B. Lee (ed.). New York: Plenum Press. 179–206.

Darwin, C. 1872. *The expression of the emotions in man and animals.* London: Murray.

Dauenhauer, B. 1980. *Silence: The phenomenon and its ontological significance.* Bloomington: Indiana University Press.

Davoine, F. 1981. "Freud's death-drive reconsidered." Paper presented at the symposium, Adaptation as Negation, Annual Convention of the American Psychological Association. Los Angeles.

————. 1989. Potential space and the space in between two deaths. *The facilitating environment: Clinical applications of Winnicott's theory.* M. Fromm and B. Smith (eds.). Madison, CT: International Universities Press. 581–603.

————. 1992. *La folie Wittgenstein*. Paris: E.P.E.L.

Decker, H. 1977. *Freud in Germany: Revolution and reaction in science, 1893–1907*. New York: International Universities Press.

————. 1982. The choice of a name: "Dora" and Freud's relationship with Breuer. *Journal of the American Psychoanalytic Association*. 30: 113–136.

————. 1991. *Freud, Dora, and Vienna 1900*. New York: The Free Press.

Deely, J. 1982. *Introducing semiotic: Its history and doctrine*. Bloomington: Indiana University Press.

————. 1990. *Basics of semiotics*. Bloomington: Indiana University Press.

Dehaene-Lambertz, G. and S. Dehaene. 1994. Speed and cerebral correlates of syllable discrimination in infants. *Nature*. 370: 292–295.

de Lauretis, T. 1984. *Alice doesn't: Feminism, semiotics, cinema*. Bloomington: Indiana University Press.

Demos, E.V. 1992. Early organization of the psyche. *Interface of psychoanalysis and psychology*. J. Barron, M. Eagle, and D. Wolitzky (eds.). Washington, D.C.: American Psychological Association. 200–232.

————. 1993. Developmental foundations for the capacity for self-analysis: Parallels in the roles of caregiver and analyst. *Self-analysis: Critical inquiries, personal visions*. J. Barron (ed.). Hillsdale, NJ: Analytic Press. 5–27.

Derrida, J. 1966. Freud and the scene of writing. *Writing and Difference*. Chicago: University of Chicago Press, 1978. 196–231.

Dervin, D. 1980. Lacanian mirrors and literary reflections. *Journal of the Philadelphia Association for Psychoanalysis*. 7: 129–142.

DeWaelhens, A. 1972. *Schizophrenia: A philosophical reflection on Lacan's structuralist interpretation*. Pittsburgh: Duquesne University Press, 1978.

Dewey, J. 1946. Peirce's theory of linguistic signs, thought and meaning. *Journal of Philosophy*. 63: 85–95.

Dixon, S., M. Yogman, E. Tronick, L. Adamson, H. Als, and T. Brazelton. 1976. "Early social interaction of infants with parents and strangers." Paper, American Academy of Pediatrics. Chicago.

Dore, J. 1989. Monologues as reenvoicement of dialogue. *Narratives from the crib*. K. Nelson (ed.). Cambridge: Harvard University Press. 231–260.

Ducey, C. 1976. The life history and creative psychopathology of the shaman: Ethnopsychoanalytic perspectives. *The Psychoanalytic Study of Society*. W. Meunsterberger (ed.). New Haven, CT: Yale University Press. Vol. 7: 173–230.

Eagle, M. 1984. *Recent developments in psychoanalysis: A critical evaluation*. Cambridge: Harvard University Press.

Eco, U. 1976. *A theory of semiotics*. Bloomington: Indiana University Press, 1979.

Eco, U. and T. Sebeok (eds.). 1983. *The sign of three: Dupin, Holmes, Peirce*. Bloomington: Indiana University Press.

Ekman, P., W. Friesen, and R. Levansen. 1983. Autonomic nervous system activity distinguishes among emotions. *Science.* 221: 1208–1210.

Ellenberger, H. 1970. *The discovery of the unconscious: The history and evolution of dynamic psychiatry.* New York: Basic Books.

———. 1972. The story of "Anna O": A critical review with new data. *Journal of the History of the Behavioral Sciences.* 8: 267–279.

Ellsworth, C., D. Muir, , and M. Hains, 1993. Social competence and person-object differentiation: An analysis of the still-face effect. *Developmental Psychology.* 29: 63–73.

Encyclopedia Britannica. 1960. Fourteenth Edition.

Epstein, R., R.P. Lanza, and B.F. Skinner. 1981. "Self-awareness" in the pigeon. *Science.* 212: 695–696.

Epstein, S. 1994. Integration of the cognitive and the psychodynamic unconscious. *American Psychologist.* 49: 709–724.

Erikson, E. 1950. *Childhood and society,* 2nd Ed. New York: Norton, 1963.

———. 1959. Identity and the life cycle. *Psychological Issues,* No. 1. New York: International Universities Press.

———. 1968. Identity: Youth and crisis. *Austen Riggs Monograph,* No. 7. New York: Norton.

Etchegoyen, R. 1985. Identification and its vicissitudes. *International Journal of Psycho-Analysis.* 66: 3–18.

Fafouti-Milenkovic, M. and I. Uzgiris. 1979. The mother-infant communication system. *New Directions for Child Development.* 4: 41–56.

Fairbairn, W. 1941. A revised psychopathology of the psychoses and the psychoneuroses. *International Journal of Psycho-Analysis.* 22: 250–279.

———. 1952. *Psychoanalytic studies of the personality.* London: Tavistock, 1978.

Faladé, S. 1974. Sur le réel. in *Lettres de L'École Freudienne, 16. Bulletin intérieur de L'École Freudienne de Paris.* Proceedings of the 7th Congress of the École Freudienne of Paris, Rome, October 31 – November 3, 1974. Paris, 1975. 30–36.

Fast, I. 1985. *Event theory: A Piaget-Freud integration.* Hillsdale, NJ: Erlbaum.

Favazza, A. and R. Rosenthal. 1993. Diagnostic issues in self-mutilation. *Hospital and Community Psychiatry.* 44: 134–140.

Fay, W. 1979. Personal pronouns and the autistic child. *Journal of Autism and Developmental Disorders.* 9: 247–260.

Felman, S., 1987. *Jacques Lacan and the adventure of insight: Psychoanalysis in contemporary culture.* Cambridge: Harvard University Press.

Felman, S. and D. Laub. 1992. *Testimony: Crises of witnessing in literature, psychoanalysis, and history.* New York: Routledge.

Ferenczi, S. 1929. The principle of relaxation and neocatharsis. *Final contributions to the problems and methods of psycho-analysis.* M. Balint (ed.). New York: Brunner/Mazel, 1980. 108–125.

Fichte, J. 1794. *Science of knowledge.* P. Heath and J. Lachs. (eds.). New York: Appleton Century Crofts, 1970.

Field, T. 1985. Neonatal perception of people: Maturational and individual differences. *Social perception in infants.* T. Field and N. Fox (eds.). Norwood, NJ: Ablex. 31–52.

Field, T., R. Woodson, R. Greenberg, and D. Cohen. 1982. Discrimination and imitation of facial expressions by neonates. *Science.* 218: 179–181.

Fodor, J. 1981. Imagistic representation. *Imagery.* N. Block (ed). Cambridge: A Bradford Book–MIT Press. 63–86.

Fogel, A., S. Toda, and M. Kawai. 1988. Mother-infant face-to-face interaction in Japan and the United States: A laboratory comparison using 3-month-old infants. *Developmental Psychology.* 24: 398–406.

Fogel, A., and E. Thelen. 1987. Development of early expressive and communicative action: Reinterpreting the evidence from a dynamic systems perspective. *Developmental Psychology.* 23: 747–761.

Fonagy, I. 1983. *La vive voix: Essais de psycho-phonétique.* Paris: Payot.

Forrester, J. 1980. *Language and the origins of psychoanalysis.* New York: Columbia University Press.

Fosshage, J. 1990. Clinical protocol. *Psychoanalytic Inquiry.* 10: 461–477.

Freud, A. 1936. *The ego and the mechanisms of defense.* New York: International Universities Press.

———. 1963. The concept of developmental lines. *Psychoanalytic assessment: The diagnostic profile. An anthology of The Psychoanalytic Study of the Child.* R. Eissler, A. Freud, M. Kris, A. Solnit (eds.). New Haven: Yale University Press. 11–30.

———. (ed.) 1986. *The essentials of psycho-analysis by Sigmund Freud.* London: Hogarth.

Freud, S. 1891. *On aphasia: A critical study.* New York: International Universities Press. 1953.

———. 1893a. Some points for a comparative study of organic and hysterical motor paralyses. *S.E.*, 1: 155–172. London: Hogarth Press, 1966.

———. 1893b. Quelques considérations pour une étude comparative des paralysies motrices organiques et hystériques. *Gesammelte Werke.* 1: 37–55.

———. 1895. Project for a scientific psychology. M. Bonaparte, A. Freud, and E. Kris (eds.), *The Origins of psychoanalysis: Letters to Wilhelm Fliess, drafts and notes.* New York: Basic Books, 1954.

———. 1895a. The psychotherapy of hysteria. *S.E.*, 2: 255–305. London: Hogarth Press, 1955.

———. 1900a. The interpretation of dreams. *S.E.*, 4 & 5. London: Hogarth Press, 1953.

———. 1900b. Die Traumdeutung. *Gesammelte Werke*, 2 & 3. London: Imago, 1942.

———. 1905a. Jokes and their relation to the unconscious. *S.E.*, 8. London: Hogarth Press, 1960.

———. 1905b. Fragment of an analysis of a case of hysteria. *S.E.*, 7: 7–122. London: Hogarth Press, 1953.

———. 1909. Five lectures on psycho-analysis. *S.E.*, 11: 37–55. London: Hogarth Press, 19.

———. 1914a. On narcissism: An introduction. *S.E.*, 14: 73–102. London: Hogarth Press, 1957.

———. 1914b. On the history of the psycho-analytic movement. *S.E.*, 14: 1–66. London: Hogarth Press, 1957.

———. 1917. A difficulty in the path of psycho-analysis. *S.E.,* 17: 137–144. London: Hogarth Press, 1955.

———. 1918. From the history of an infantile neurosis. *S.E.*, 17: 7–122. London: Hogarth Press, 1955.

———. 1920. Beyond the pleasure principle. *S.E.*, 18: 7–64. London: Hogarth Press, 1955.

———. 1921a. Group psychology and the analysis of the ego. *S.E.*, 18: 69–143. London: Hogarth Press, 1955.

———. 1921b. Massenpsychologie und Ich-Analyse. *Gesammelte Werke*, 13: 71–161. Frankfurt am Main: Fischer, 1940.

———. 1923. The ego and the id. *S.E.*, 19: 12–66. London: Hogarth Press, 1961.

———. 1925a. Negation. *S.E.*, 19: 235–239. London: Hogarth Press, 1961.

———. 1925b. An autobiographical study. *S.E.*, 20: 7–74. London: Hogarth Press, 1959.

———. 1926. Inhibitions, symptoms, and anxiety. *S.E.*, 20: 87–172. London: Hogarth Press, 1959.

———. 1933. New introductory lectures on psycho-analysis. *S.E.*, 22: 5–182. London: Hogarth Press, 1964.

———. 1937. Constructions in analysis. *S.E.*, 23: 237–269. London: Hogarth Press, 1964.

———. 1938. An outline of psychoanalysis. *S.E.*, 23: 144–207. London: Hogarth Press, 1964.

———. 1950. *Aus den Anfängen der Psychanalyse.* London: Imago.

———. 1986. *Briefe an Wilhelm Fliess 1887–1904.* J. Masson (ed). Frankfurt: Fischer.

Freudenheim, M. 1994. Corporate paid psychotherapy: At what price? *New York Times.* April 12: 1.

Frye, N. 1981. The bridge of language. *Science.* 212: 127–132.

Gadamer, H.-G. 1960. *Truth and method.* New York: Seabury Press, 1975.

———. 1975. Epistemological problems of the human sciences. *Graduate Faculty Philosophy Journal.* 5: 8–14.

Gallup, G. 1977. Self-recognition in primates: A comparative approach to the bidirectional properties of consciousness. *American Psychologist.* 32: 329–338.

————. 1984. Will reinforcement subsume cognition? *Contemporary Psychology*. 29: 593–594.

Gay, P. 1988. *Freud: A life for our time*. New York: Norton.

Gedo, J. 1981. *Advances in clinical psychoanalysis*. New York: International Universities Press.

————. 1986. *Conceptual issues in psychoanalysis*. Hillsdale, NJ: The Analytic Press.

————. 1988. *The Mind in disorder: Psychoanalytic models of pathology*. Hillsdale, NJ: The Analytic Press.

————. 1993. *Beyond interpretation: Toward a revised theory for psychoanalysis*. Revised edition. New York: International Universities Press. (Orginally published in 1979.)

Gedo, J. and A. Goldberg. 1973. *Models of the mind: A psychoanalytic theory*. Chicago: University of Chicago Press.

Gedo, J., and G. Pollock. (eds.). 1976. *Freud: The fusion of science and humanism*. New York: International Universities Press.

Gedo, J., and M. Gehrie. (eds.). 1993. *Impasse and innovation in psychoanalysis: Clinical case seminars*. Hillsdale, NJ: The Analytic Press.

Geertz, C. 1973. *The interpretation of cultures*. New York: Basic Books.

Gibson, E. 1987. Introductory essay: What does infant perception tell us about theories of perception? *Journal of Experimental Psychology: Human Perception and Performance*. Special Issue: The ontogenesis of perception. Vol. 13: 515–523.

Ginzburg, C. 1983. Morelli, Freud, and Sherlock Holmes: Clues and scientific method. *The sign of three: Dupin, Holmes, Peirce*. U. Eco and T. Sebeok (eds.). Bloomington: Indiana University Press. 81–118.

Goldberg, A. 1980. Letter to the editor. *International Journal of Psycho-Analysis*. 61: 91–92.

Goldberg, C. 1984. The role of the mirror in human suffering and in intimacy. *Journal of the American Academy of Psychoanalysis*. 12: 511–528.

Gould, S. J. 1976. Human babies as embryos. *Natural History*. 84: 22–26.

Greenberg, J., and T. Pyszczynski. 1985. Compensatory self-inflation: A response to the threat to self-regard of public failure. *Journal of Personality and Social Psychology*. 43: 273–280.

Greene, G. 1951. *The end of the affair*. London: Penguin Books, 1975.

Greenson, R. 1967. *The technique and practice of psychoanalysis*. New York: International Universities Press.

Greenwald, A. 1980. The totalitarian ego: Fabrication and revision of personal history. *American Psychologist*. 35: 603–618.

Gregory, R. (ed.). 1987. *The Oxford companion to the mind*. Oxford: Oxford University Press.

Guntrip, H. 1971. *Psychoanalytic theory, therapy, and the self*. New York: Basic Books.

Hall, W. M., and R. Cairns. 1984. Aggressive behavior in children: An outcome of modeling or social reciprocity? *Developmental Psychology.* 20: 739–745.

Hanna, E. and A. Meltzoff. 1993. Peer imitation by toddlers in laboratory, home, and day-care contexts: Implications for social learning and memory. *Developmental Psychology.* 29: 701–710.

Harari, R. 1986. *Discurrir el psicoanálisis.* Buenos Aires: Ediciones Nueva Vision.

Harré, R. and G. Gillett. 1994. *The discursive mind.* London: Sage Publications.

Harris, R. 1986. *The origin of writing.* La Salle, IL: Open Court.

Haviland, J. and M. Lelwica. 1987. The induced affect response: 10-week-old infants' responses to three emotion expressions. *Developmental Psychology.* 23: 97–104.

Hegel, G. W. F. 1807. *The phenomenology of spirit.* Tr. A. Miller. Oxford: Oxford University Press, 1977.

Heidegger, M. 1947. Letter on humanism. *Martin Heidegger: Basic Writings.* D. F. Krell (ed.). New York: Harper and Row, 1977. 193–242.

———. 1950. Language. *Poetry, language, thought.* New York: Harper Colophon, 1975. 189–210.

Hemkendreis, M. 1992. Increase in self-injuries on an inpatient psychiatric unit during evening hours. *Hospital and Community Psychiatry.* 43: 394–395.

Hermann, I. 1936. Clinging—Going-in-search: A contrasting pair of instincts and their relation to sadism and masochism. *Psychoanalytic Quarterly,* 1976. 45: 5–36.

Hervey, S. 1982. *Semiotic perspectives.* London: George Allen and Unwin.

Hill, S. D., and C. Tomlin. 1981. Self-recognition in retarded children. *Child Development.* 52: 145–150.

Hirschmüller, A. 1978. *The life and work of Josef Breuer: Psychology and psychoanalysis.* New York: New York University Press, 1989.

Huesmann, L., K. Lagerspetz, and L. Eron. 1984. Intervening variables in the TV violence-aggression relation: Evidence from two countries. *Developmental Psychology.* 20: 746–775.

Innis, R. 1982. *Karl Bühler: Semiotic foundations of language theory.* New York: Plenum.

Jackendoff, R. 1994. *Patterns in the mind: Language and human nature.* New York: Basic Books.

Jacobson, S. W., and J. Kagan. 1979. Interpreting "imitative" responses in early infancy. *Science.* (205) 215–217.

Jakobson, R. 1956. Two aspects of language and two types of aphasic disturbances. *Fundamentals of language.* R. Jakobson and M. Halle (eds.). The Hague: Mouton. 53–87.

———. 1965. Quest for the essence of language. *Language in literature.* K. Pomorska and S. Rudy (eds.). Cambridge: The Belknap Press of Harvard University Press, 1987. 413–427.

————. 1974. A glance at the development of semiotics. *Language in literature*. K. Pomorska and S. Rudy (eds.). Cambridge: The Belknap Press of Harvard University Press, 1987. 436–454.

————. 1985. *Verbal art, verbal sign, verbal time*. K. Pomorska and S. Rudy (eds.). Minneapolis: University of Minnesota Press.

Jakobson, R. and M. Halle. 1956. *Fundamentals of language*. The Hague: Mouton.

Jakobson, R. and G. Lubbe-Grothues. 1985. The language of schizophrenia: Hölderlin's speech and poetry. *Verbal art, verbal sign, verbal time*. K. Pomorska and S. Rudy (eds.). Minneapolis: University of Minnesota Press. 133–140.

Johan, M. 1992. Report of the panel on enactments in psychoanalysis. *Journal of the American Psychoanalytic Association*. 40: 827–841.

Johansen, J. 1993. *Dialogic semiosis: An essay on signs and meaning*. Bloomington: Indiana University Press.

Johnston, W. 1967. Individual performance and self-evaluation in a simulated team. *Organizational Behavior and Human Performance*. 2: 309–328.

Jones, E. 1953. *The life and work of Sigmund Freud* (Vol. 1). New York: Basic Books.

Julien, P. 1987. Entre l'homme et la femme il y a l'a-mur. *Littoral*. 23/24: 25–34.

Kagan, J. 1974. Discrepancy, temperament, and infant distress. *Origins of Fear*. M. Lewis and L. Rosenblum (eds.). New York: Wiley.

————. 1979. The form of early development: Continuity and discontinuity in emergent competences. *Archives of General Psychiatry*. 36: 1047–1054.

————. 1981. *The second year: The emergence of self-awareness*. Cambridge: Harvard University Press.

Karon, B. 1992. The fear of understanding schizophrenia. *Psychoanalytic Psychology*. 9: 191–211.

Karon B. and A. Widener. 1994. Is there really a schizophrenogenic parent? *Psycholanalytic Pscyhology*. 11: 47–61.

Karpe, R. 1961. The rescue complex in Anna O's final identity. *Psychoanalytic Quarterly*. 30: 1–27.

Kaye, K. and A. Fogel. 1980. The temporal structure of face-to-face communication between mothers and infants. *Developmental Psychology*. 16: 454–464.

Keil, F. 1981. Constraints on knowledge and cognitive development. *Psychological Review*. 88: 197–227.

Kellert, S. 1993. *In the wake of chaos: Unpredictable order in dynamical systems*. Chicago: University of Chicago Press.

Kernberg, O. 1980. *Internal world and external reality: Object relations theory applied*. New York: Aronson.

Kingston, M. H. 1980. *China men*. New York: Ballentine.

Kirshner, L. 1992. The absence of the father. *Journal of the American Psychoanalytic Association*. 40: 1117–1138.

———. 1994. Trauma, the good object, and the symbolic: A theoretical integration. *International Journal of Psycho-Analysis*. 75: 235–242.

Köhler, E. 1926. *Die Persönlichkeit des dreijahrigen Kindes*. Leipzig.

Köhler, W. 1925. *The mentality of apes*. New York: Liveright, 1976.

Kohut, H. 1971. *The analysis of the self: A systematic approach to the psychoanalytic treatment of narcissistic personality disorders*. New York: International Universities Press.

———. 1977. *The restoration of the self*. Madison, CT: International Universities Press.

———. 1979. Two analyses of Mr. Z. *International Journal of Psycho-Analysis*. 60: 3–27.

———. 1984. *How does analysis cure?* A. Goldberg, and P. Stepansky (eds.). Chicago: University of Chicago Press.

Kohut, H., and E. Wolf. 1978. The disorders of the self and their treatment: An outline. *International Journal of Psycho-Analysis*. 59: 413–425.

Kolata, G. 1993. From fly to man, cells obey the same signal. *New York Times*. January 5: C1.

Kozak-Mayer, N. and E. Tronick. 1985. Mothers' turn-giving signals and infant turn-taking in mother-infant interaction. *Social perception in infants*. T. Field and N. Fox (eds.). Hillsdale, NJ: Erlbaum. 199–216.

Krampen, M. 1986. The development of children's drawings as a phase in the ontogeny of iconicity. *Iconicity: Essays on the nature of culture*. Festschrift for Thomas A. Sebeok. P. Bouissac, M. Herzfeld, and R. Posner (eds.). Tübingen: Stauffenburg Verlag. 141–191.

Kris, E. 1954. Introduction. *The origins of psychoanalysis: Letters to Wilhelm Fliess, drafts, and notes 1887–1902 by Sigmund Freud*. M. Bonaparte, A. Freud, and E. Kris (eds.). New York: Basic Books: 3–47.

Kristeva, J. 1980. *Desire in language: A semiotic approach to literature and art*. New York: Columbia University Press.

Kuhl, P. and A. Meltzoff. 1982. The bimodal perception of speech in infancy. *Science*. 218: 1138–1140.

Kuhl, P., K. Williams, F. Lacerda, K. Stevens and B. Lindblom. 1992. Linguistic experience alters phonetic perception in infants by 6 months of age. *Science*. 255: 606–608.

Lacan, J. 1938. *Les complexes familiaux dans la formation de l'individu: Essai d'analyse d'une fonction en psychologie*. Paris: Navarin Editeur-Seuil, 1984.

———. 1949. The mirror stage as formative of the function of the I as revealed in psychoanalytic experience. *Ecrits: A selection*. New York: Norton: 1–7.

———. 1951. Some reflections on the ego. *International Journal of Psycho-Analysis* 1953. 34: 11–17.

———. 1953. The function and field of speech and language in psychoanalysis. *Ecrits: A selection*. New York: Norton, 1977. 30–113.

———. 1953a. *Le Symbolique, l'imaginaial, et le réel.* Unpublished manuscript.

———. 1953–1954. *The seminar of Jacques Lacan: Book I.* J.-A. Miller (ed.). *Freud's papers on technique.* New York: Norton, 1988.

———. 1954–1955a. *The seminar of Jacques Lacan: Book II.* J.-A. Miller (ed.). *The Ego in Freud's theory and in the technique of psychoanalysis.* New York: Norton, 1988.

———. 1955–1956. *The seminar of Jacques Lacan: Book III. The psychoses.* J.-A. Miller (ed.). New York: Norton, 1993.

———. 1956. Seminar on "The Purloined Letter". *The purloined Poe.* J. Muller and W. Richardson (eds.). Baltimore, MD: Johns Hopkins University Press, 1987. 28–54.

———. 1957–1958. *The seminar of Jacques Lacan: Book V. The formations of the unconscious,* 1957–1958. C. Gallagher (Trans.). Unpublished Manuscript, 1989.

———. 1959–60. "L'éthique de la psychanalyse," Vols. I and II. Unpublished manuscript. Imprimerie BOSC Frères-Lyon. Depot legal No.7356-3rd trimester, 1981.

———. 1959–1960a. *Le séminaire: Livre VII. L'éthique de la psychanalyse.* J.-A. Miller (ed.). Paris: Seuil, 1986.

———. 1959–1960b. *The seminar of Jacques Lacan. Book VII. The Ethics of Psychoanalysis.* J.–A. Miller. (ed.). New York: Norton, 1992.

———. 1961–1962. *Le séminaire. L'identification.* Unpublished manuscript, International Research Center. New York: International General.

———. 1964. *The four fundamental concepts of psycho-analysis.* J.–A. Miller (ed.). New York: Norton, 1978.

———. 1966. *Ecrits.* Paris: Seuil.

———. 1972–1973. *Le séminaire: Liure XX.* Encore. J.–A. Miller (ed.). Paris: Seuil, 1975.

———. 1974. "La Troisième." Congrès de l'EFP, Rome. Lettres del'EFP, No. 16. Also reprinted in *Petits Ecrits et Conferences, 1945–1981.* Vol. II. Unpublished Collection. 542–568.

———. 1976. "Le Sinthome". Seminar of March 16. *Ornicar?* 9:32–40 (1977).

———. 1977. *Ecrits: A selection.* New York: Norton.

Laurent, E., and S. Schneiderman. 1977. Parcours du self. *Ornicar?* 11: 95–101.

Lauth, M.–L. 1982. Et si le Réel insiste ... *Resumé des scéances de travail pour les journées d'Avril.* S. Faladé (ed.). Groupe d'Étude sur l'Enseignement. Unpublished manuscript. Paris. 61–65.

Leonard, J. 1980. Review of *China Men* by Maxine Hong Kingston. *New York Times.* June 3.

Leroi-Gourhan, A. 1964. *Le geste et la parole: Technique et langage.* Paris: Michel.

Lester, B., J. Hoffman, and T. Brazelton. 1985. The rhthymic structure of mother-infant interaction in term and preterm infants. *Child Development.* 56:15–27.

Levin, F. 1991. *Mapping the mind: The intersection of psychoanalysis and neuroscience.* Hillsdale, NJ: The Analytic Press.

Lewis, M. and S. Lee-Painter. 1974. An interactional approach to the mother-infant dyad. *The effect of the infant on its caregiver.* M. Lewis and L. Rosenblum (eds.). New York: Wiley. 21–48.

Lewis, M., and J. Brooks-Gunn. 1979. *Social cognition and the acquisition of self.* New York: Plenum.

Lewis, M., and C. Wilson. 1972. Infant development in lower class American families. *Human Development.* 15: 112–127.

Lewisohn, P., W. Mischel, W. Chaplin, and R. Barton. 1980. Social competence and depression: The role of illusory self-perceptions. *Journal of Abnormal Psychology.* 89: 203–212.

Litowitz, B. and P. Epstein eds. 1991. *Semiotic perspectives on clinical theory and practice: Medicine, neuropsychiatry and psychoanalysis.* New York: Mouton de Gruyter.

Litowitz, B. and N. Litowitz, 1977. The influence of linguistic theory on psychoanalysis: A critical historical survey. *International Review of Psycho-Analysis,* 4: 419–448.

Lyons, J. 1982. Deixis and subjectivity: Loquor, ergo sum? *Speech, place, and action.* R. Jarvella and W. Klein (eds.). New York: Wiley. 101–124.

Loewald, H. 1960. On the therapeutic action of psychoanalysis. *International Journal of Psycho-Analysis.* 41: 16–33.

Macalpine, I. 1950. The development of the transference. *Psychoanalytic Quarterly.* 19: 501–539.

Maccoby, E. and J. Martin. 1983. Socialization in the context of the family: Parent-child interaction. *Handbook of child psychology,* Vol. 4. P.H. Mussen (ed.). New York: Wiley. 1–101.

Macmillan, M. 1990. Freud and Janet on organic and hysterical paralyses: A mystery solved? *International Review of Psycho-Analysis.* 17: 189–203.

Macmurray, J. 1957. *The self as agent.* Atlantic Highlands, NJ: Humanities Press International, 1991.

———. 1961. *Persons in relation.* Atlantic Highlands, NJ: Humanities Press International, 1991.

Mahony, P. 1989. *On defining Freud's discourse.* New Haven: Yale University Press.

Mandel, D., P. Jusczyk, and D. Pisoni. 1994. *Who ... Me?* Unpublished manuscript.

Mans, L., D. Cichetti, and L. Sroufe. 1978. Mirror reactions of Down's Syndrome infants and toddlers: Cognitive underpinnings of self-recognition. *Child Development.* 49: 1247–1250.

Maratos, O. 1982. Trends in development of imitation in early infancy. *Regressions in mental development: Basic phenomena and theories.* T. Bever (ed.). Hillsdale, NJ: Erlbaum. 81–101.

Markus. H., and S. Kitayama. 1994. The cultural shaping of emotion: A conceptual framework. *Emotion and culture: Empirical studies of mutual influence.* S. Kitayama and H. Markus (eds.). Washington, D.C.: American Psychological Association. 339–351.

Massie, H. 1982. Affective development and the organization of mother-infant behavior from the perspective of psychopathology. *Social interchange in infancy: Affect, cognition, and communication*. E. Tronick (ed.). Baltimore: University Park Press. 161–182.

Masson, J. M. (ed. and trans.), 1985. *The complete letters of Sigmund Freud to Wilhelm Fliess, 1887–1904*. Cambridge: Harvard University Press.

Masters, J. C. 1979. Interpreting "imitative" responses in early infancy. *Science*. 205: 215.

Mead, G. H. 1925. The genesis of the self and social control. *The philosophy of the present*. A. Murphy (ed.). Chicago: University of Chicago Press, 1980. 176–195.

Meissner, W. 1981. Internalization in psychoanalysis. *Psychological Issues, Monograph*. 50. New York: International Universities Press.

Meltzoff, A. 1985. The roots of social and cognitive development: Models of man's original nature. *Social perception in infants*, T. Field and N. Fox, (eds.). Norwood, NJ: Ablex. 1–30.

Meltzoff, A., and M. Moore, M. 1977. Imitation of facial and manual gestures by human neonates. *Science*. 198: 75–78.

———. 1983. Newborn infants imitate adult facial gestures. *Child Development*. 54: 702–709.

Modell, A. 1984. *Psychoanalysis in a new context*. New York: International Universities Press.

———. 1990. *Other times, other realities: Toward a theory of psychoanalytic treatment*. Cambridge: Harvard University Press.

———. 1993. *The private self*. Cambridge: Harvard University Press.

Mohatt, G. 1982. "Psychic power or spiritual power: False dichotomies and spirit phenomena in psychotherapy with native people". Unpublished manuscript. Crookston, Nebraska: Niobrara Institute.

Moran, M. 1991. Chaos theory and psychoanalysis: The fluidic nature of the mind. *International Review of Psycho-Analysis*. 18: 211–221

Morris, C. 1938. *Foundations of the theory of signs*. Chicago: University of Chicago Press.

———. 1964. *Signification and significance: A study of the relations of signs and values*. Cambridge: The M.I.T. Press.

Morris, H. 1993. Narrative representation, narrative enactment, and the psychoanalytic construction of history. *International Journal of Psycho-Analysis*. 74: 33–54.

Muller, J. 1982a. Ego and subject in Lacan. *The Psychoanalytic Review*. 69: 234–240.

———. 1982b. Cognitive psychology and the ego: Lacanian theory and empirical research. *Psychoanalysis and Contemporary Thought*. 5: 257–291.

———. 1985. Lacan's mirror stage. *Psychoanalytic Inquiry.* 5:233–252.

———. 1986. The psychoanalytic ego in Lacan: Its origins and self-serving functions. *Psychological perspectives on the self,* Vol. 3. J. Suls and A. Greenwald (eds.). Hillsdale, NJ: Lawrence Erlbaum Associates. 79–106.

———. 1987a. Language, psychosis, and spirit. *Attachment and the therapeutic Process: Essays in honor of Otto Allen Will, Jr., M.D.* J. Sacksteder, D. Schwartz, and Y. Akabane (eds.). New York: International Universities Press. 99–116.

———. 1987b. Sublimation in reverse in the treatment of the psychotic thing. *Papers of the Freudian School of Melbourne.* O. Zentner (ed.). Melbourne, Australia. 135–141.

———. 1988. Negation in "The Purloined Letter": Hegel, Poe, and Lacan. *The purloined Poe: Lacan, Derrida, and psychoanalytic reading.* J. Muller and W. Richardson (eds.). Baltimore: The Johns Hopkins University Press. 343–368.

———. 1989a. Lacan and Kohut: From imaginary to symbolic identification in the case of Mr. Z. *Self psychology: Comparisons and contrasts.* D. Detrick and S. Detrick (eds.). Hillsdale, NJ: The Analytic Press. 363–394.

———. 1989b. Imre Hermann and modern structural linguistics. *Hermann's place in contemporary psychoanalytic theory.* Memorial Conference on the centennial of Imre Hermann's birth, 11–12 November 1989. Hungarian Psychoanalytic Society, Budapest. 101–104.

———. 1990. The analyst's mythology of needs: A LAconian view. *Psychoanalytic Inquiry.* 10: 567–584.

———. 1992a. A re-reading of *Studies on Hysteria:* The Freud-Breuer break revisited. *Psychoanalytic Psychology.* 9: 129–156.

———. 1992b. Transference and Lacan's subject-supposed-to-know. *Phenomenology and Lacanian psychoanalysis.* The eighth annual symposium of the Simon Silverman Phenomenology Center. Pittsburgh: Duquesne University. 37–45.

Muller, J., and W. Richardson. 1982. *Lacan and language: A reader's guide to "Ecrits."* New York: International Universities Press.

——— (eds.). 1988. *The purloined Poe: Lacan, Derrida, and psychoanalytic reading.* Baltimore: The Johns Hopkins University Press.

Murray, L. and C. Trevarthen. 1985. Emotional regulation of interactions between two-month-olds and their mothers. *Social perception in infants.* T. Field and N. Fox (eds.). Norwood, NJ: Ablex. 177–197.

———. 1986. The infant's role in mother-infant communications. *Journal of Child Language.* 13: 15–29.

Nelson, R., and W. Craighead. 1977. Selective recall of positive and negative feedback, self-control behaviors, and depression. *Journal of Abnormal Psychology.* 86: 379–388.

Nietzsche, F. 1901. *The will to power.* New York: Vintage Books, 1968.

Nussbaum, M. 1986. *The fragility of goodness: Luck and ethics in Greek tragedy and philosophy.* Cambridge: Cambridge University Press.

Oates, J. 1983. Old Budapest. *Kenyon Review.* 5 (4): 8–36.

Ogden, T. 1986. *The matrix of the mind: Object relations and the psychoanalytic dialogue.* Northvale, NJ: Aronson.

———. 1989. *The primitive edge of experience.* Northvale, NJ: Aronson.

———. 1994. The analytical third: Working with intersubjective clinical facts. *International Journal of Psycho-Analysis.* 75: 3–19.

Ornstein, P. 1981. The bipolar self in the psychoanalytic treatment process: Clinical-theoretical considerations. *Journal of the American Psychoanalytic Association.* 29: 353–375.

———. 1990. A self psychology view. *Psychoanalytic Inquiry.* 10: 478–497.

Osofsky, J., and K. Connors. 1979. Mother-infant interaction: An integrative view of a complex system. *Handbook of infant development.* New York: Wiley. 519–548.

Ostow, M. 1979. Letter to the editor. *International Journal of Psycho-Analysis.* 60: 531–532.

Pascal, B. 1670. *Pensées.* Paris: Seuil, 1962.

Paz, O. 1974. *The monkey grammarian.* New York: Seaver Books, 1981.

Peirce, C. S. 1868. Some consequences of four incapacities. *The essential Peirce: Selected philosophical writings. Vol. 1. 1867–1893.* N. Houser and C. Kloesel (eds.). Bloomington: Indiana University Press, 1992. 28–55.

———. 1891. The architecture of theories. In *The essential Peirce: Selected philosophical writings. Vol. 1. 1867–1893.* Ed. N. Houser and C. Kloesel. Bloomington: Indiana University Press. 285–297.

———. 1940. *Philosophical writings of Peirce.* J. Buchler (ed.). New York: Dover, 1955.

———. 1966. *Selected writings.* P. Wiener (ed.). New York: Dover.

———. 1992. *The essential Peirce: Selected philosophical writings. Vol. 1 1867–1893.* N. Houser and C. Kloesel (eds.). Bloomington: Indiana University Press, 1992. 225–228.

Penman, R., J. Friedman, and R. Meares. 1986. "The temporal structure of vocalization and gaze behavior in mother-infant dyads". Unpublished manuscript, University of Melbourne: Melbourne, Australia.

Peraldi, F. 1981. Why did Peirce terrorize Benveniste? *Semiotica.* supplement: 169–179.

———. 1987. K.K.K. *Etudes freudiennes.* No. 30. 181–212.

Perris, E., N. Myers, and R. Clifton. 1990. Long-term memory for a single infancy experience. *Child Development.* 61: 1796–1807.

Person, E. 1988. *Dreams of love and fateful encounters: The power of romantic passion.* New York: Penguin.

Petitto, L., and P. Marentette. 1991. Babbling in the manual mode: Evidence for the ontogeny of language. *Science.* 251: 1493–1496.

Pettigrew, D. 1995. Peirce and Derrida: From Sign to sign. In *Pierce's doctrine of signs: Theory, applications, connections*. V. Colapietro and T. Olshewsky (eds.). Berlin: Mouton de Gruyton.

Pharies, D. 1985. *Charles S. Peirce and the linguistic sign*. Philadelphia: John Benjamins Publishing Company.

Phillips, J. 1991. Hermeneutics in psychoanalysis: Review and reconsideration. *Psychoanalysis and Contemporary Thought*. 14: 371–424.

Piaget, J. 1947. *Psychology of intelligence*. Paterson, NJ: Littlefield, Adams and Co., 1963.

Pines, M. 1984. Reflections on mirroring. *International Review of Psycho-Analysis*. 11: 27–42.

Pollock, G. 1976. Josef Breuer. *Freud: The fusion of science and humanism*. J. Gedo and G. Pollack (eds.). New York: International Universities Press. 133–163.

Posner, M., M. Rothbart, and C. Harman. 1994. Cognitive science's contributions to culture and emotion. *Emotion and culture: Empirical studies of mutual influence*. S. Kitayama and H. Markus (eds.). Washington, D.C.: American Psychological Association. 197–216.

Reeves, C. 1982. Breuer, Freud and the case of Anna O.: A re-examination. *Journal of Child Psychotherapy*. 8: 203–214.

Renik, O. 1993. Analytic interaction: Conceptualizing technique in light of the analyst's irreducible subjectivity. *Psychoanalytic Quarterly*. 62: 553–571.

Richardson, W. 1978–1979. The mirror inside: The problem of the self. *Review of Existential Psychology and Psychiatry*. 16: 95–112.

———. 1983. Lacan and the subject of psychoanalysis. *Interpreting Lacan*. J. Smith and W. Kerrigan (eds.). New Haven: Yale University Press. 51–74.

———. 1987. Ethics and desire. *American Journal of Psychoanalysis*. 47: 296–301.

Rilke, R. 1923. *Duino elegies*. (trans.) J. Leishman and S. Spender. New York: Norton, 1963.

Rizzuto, A.–M. 1989. A hypothesis about Freud's motive for writing the monograph, "On Aphasia". *International Review of Psycho-Analysis*. 16: 111–117.

———. 1993. First person personal pronouns and their psychic referents. *International Journal of Psycho-Analysis*. 74: 535–546.

Rorty, R. 1979. *Philosophy and the mirror of nature*. Princeton, NJ: Princeton University Press.

Rose, S.A. 1981. Developmental stages in infants' retention of visual stimuli. *Child Development*. 52: 227–233.

Rosenbaum, B., and H. Sonne. 1986. *The language of psychosis*. New York: New York University Press.

Rosenbaum, M., and M. Muroff. (eds.). 1984. *Anna O: Fourteen contemporary reinterpretations*. New York: The Free Press.

Rosenthal, M. 1987. *Anselm Kiefer*. Chicago and Philadelphia: The Art Institute of Chicago and the Philadelphia Museum of Art.

Rothbaum, F. M. 1976. "Developmental differences in imitation of parents and strangers on objective and subjective judgments." Unpublished doctoral dissertation, Yale University.

Rozensky, R., L. Rehm, G. Pry, and D. Roth. 1977. Depression and self-reinforcement behavior in hospitalized patients. *Journal of Behavioral Therapy and Experimental Psychiatry.* 8: 31–34.

Sacks, O. 1989. *Seeing voices: A journey into the world of the deaf.* Berkeley: University of California Press.

———. 1990. Neurology and the soul. the *New York Review of Books.* Nov. 22: 44–55.

———. 1993–1994. A neurologist's notebook: An anthropologist on Mars. *The New Yorker.* December 27/January 3: 106–125.

Sander, L.W. 1985. Toward a logic of organization in psychobiologic development. *Biologic response styles: Clinical implications.* H. Klar and L. Siever (eds.). Washington, DC: American Psychiatric Press. 19–37.

Sass, L. 1992. *Madness and modernism: Insanity in the light of modern art, literature, and thought.* New York: Basic Books.

Saussure, F. de. 1916. *Course in general linguistics.* C. Bally and A. Sechehaye (eds.). New York: McGraw–Hill, 1966.

Schafer, R. 1976. *A new language for psychoanalysis.* New Haven: Yale University Press.

Schaffer, H. 1984. *The child's entry into a social world.* London: Academic Press.

Schlessinger, N., J. Gedo, J. Miller, G. Pollock, M. Sabshin, and L. Sadow. 1976. The scientific styles of Breuer and Freud and the origins of psychoanalysis. *Freud: The fusion of science and humanism.* J. Gedo and G. Pollock (eds.) New York: International Universities Press. 187–207.

Schoenhals, H. 1995. Triangular space and the development of a working model in the analysis. *International Journal of Psycho-Analysis.* 76:103–113.

Schwartz, A. 1990. To soothe or not to soothe—or when and how: Neurobiological and learning-psychological considerations of some complex clinical questions. *Psychoanalytic Inquiry.* 10: 554–566.

Sebeok, T. 1971. Semiotics: A survey of the state of the art. *Contributions to the doctrine of signs.* Bloomington: Indiana University Press, 1976. 1–45.

———. 1976. Contributions to the doctrine of signs. Studies in Semiotics, vol. 5. Bloomington: Indiana University Press.

———. 1981. *The play of musement.* Bloomington: Indiana University Press.

———. 1983. One, two, three spells UBERTY. *The sign of three: Dupin, Holmes, Peirce.* U. Eco and T. Sebeok (eds.). Bloomington: Indiana University Press. 1–10.

———. 1994. The self: A biosemiotic conspectus. The Edith Weigert Lecture of the Forum on Psychiatry and the Humanities. *Peirce, Semiotics, and Psychoanalysis.* J. Muller and J. Brent (eds.). Baltimore: Johns Hopkins University Press, 1996.

Shapiro, E. and A. Carr. 1991. *Lost in familiar places: Creating new connections between the individual and society.* New Haven: Yale University Press.

Shapiro, E. 1994. "The boundaries are changing: Renogiating the therapeutic frame." Presented at the 75th anniversary symposium of the Austen Riggs Center, Stockbridge.

Short, T. 1992. Peirce's semiotic theory of the self. *Semiotica,* 91: 109–131.

Shotter, J. 1993. Vygotsky: The social negotiation of semiotic mediation. *New Ideas in Psychology.* 11: 61–75.

Silverman, M. 1983. Review of *Returning to Freud: Clinical psychoanalysis in the school of Lacan. Journal of the American Psychoanalytic Association.* 31: 752–758.

Singer, J., (ed.). 1990. *Repression and dissociation: Implications for personality theory, psychopathology, and health.* Chicago: The University of Chicago Press.

Singer, M. 1989. Pronouns, persons, and the semiotic self. *Semiotics, self, and society.* B. Lee and G. Urban (eds.). New York: Mouton de Gruyter. 229–296.

Smith, J. 1991. *Arguing with Lacan: Ego psychology and language.* New Haven: Yale University Press.

Sokolowski, R. 1978. *Presence and absence: A philosophical investigation of language and being.* Bloomington: Indiana University Press.

Solomon, R. 1982. Man's reach. *Journal of the American Psychoanalytic Association.* 30: 325–345.

Sterba, R. 1934. The fate of the ego in analytic therapy. *International Journal of Psycho-Analysis.* 15: 117–126.

Stern, D. 1985. *The interpersonal world of the infant: A view from psychoanalysis and developmental psychology.* New York: Basic Books.

———. 1990. *Diary of a baby.* New York: Basic Books.

Stern, D., J. Jaffe, B. Beebe, B. and S. Bennett. 1975. Vocalizing in unison and in alternation: Two modes of communication within the mother-infant dyad. *Annals of the New York Academy of Sciences.* 263: 89–100.

Stokoe, W. 1960. *Sign language structure.* Silver Springs, Md.: Linstok Press.

Stolorow, R. and G. Atwood. 1992. *Contexts of being: The intersubjective foundations of psychological life.* Hillsdale, NJ: The Analytic Press.

Strachey, J. 1934. The nature of the therapeutic action of psychoanalysis. *International Journal of Psycho-Analysis.* 15: 127–159.

Sullivan, H. 1953. *The interpersonal theory of psychiatry.* H. Perry and M. Gawel (eds.). New York: Norton.

Sullivan, L. 1988. *Icanchu's drum: An orientation to meaning in South American religions.* New York: Macmillan.

Sulloway, F. 1979. *Freud: Biologist of the mind.* New York: Basic Books.

Swales, P.J. 1986. Freud, his teacher, and the birth of psychoanalysis. *Contributions to Freud studies, Vol. 1. Freud: Appraisals and reappraisals.* P. Stepansky (ed.). Hillsdale, NJ: The Analytic Press. 3–82.

Taylor, S. 1983. Adjustment to threatening events: A theory of cognitive adaptation. *American Psychologist,* 38: 1161–1173.

Terhune, C. 1979. The role of hearing in early ego organization. *The Psychoanalytic Study of the Child.* 34: 371–383.

Thelen E. 1995. Motor development: A new synthesis. *American Psychologist.* 50: 79–95.

Thelen, E. and L. Smith. 1994. *A dynamic systems approach to the development of cognition and action.* Cambridge: MIT Press.

Thelen, M., and K. Kirkland. 1976. On status and being imitated: Effects on reciprocal imitation and attraction. *Journal of Personality and Social Psychology.* 33: 691–697.

Theunissen, M. 1977. *The other: Studies in the social ontology of Husserl, Heidegger, Sartre, and Buber.* Cambridge: The MIT Press, 1986.

Thom, R. 1973. De l'icone au symbole: Esquisse d'une théorie du symbolisme. *Cahiers Internationaux de Symbolisme.* 22/23: 85–106.

Thomas, D. 1980. Mirror images. *Scientific American.* 252: 206–229.

Thompson, M. 1985. *The death of desire.* New York: New York University Press.

Todorov, T. 1982. *The conquest of America: The question of the other.* New York: Harper, 1985.

Tolstoy, L. 1886. *The death of Ivan Ilych.* New York: The New American Library, 1960. 95–156.

Tomkins, S. 1962. The positive affects. *Affect, imagery, consciousness:* Vol. I. New York: Springer.

———. 1963. The negative affects. *Affect, imagery, consciousness:* Vol. II. New York: Springer.

———. 1981. The quest for primary motives: Biography and autobiography of an idea. *Journal of Personality and Social Psychology.* 41: 306–329.

Trevarthen, C. 1979. Communication and cooperation in early infancy: A description of primary intersubjectivity. *Before speech: The beginning of interpersonal communication.* M. Bullowa (ed.). Cambridge: Cambridge University Press. 321–347.

———. 1980. The foundations of intersubjectivity: Development of interpersonal and cooperative understanding in infants. *The social foundations of language and thought: Essays in honor of Jerome S. Bruner.* D. Olson (ed.). New York: Norton. 316–342.

———. 1982. The primary motives for cooperative understanding. *Social cognition: Studies of the development of understanding.* G. Butterworth and P. Light (ed.). Chicago: The University of Chicago Press. 77–109.

———. 1986. Form, significance, and psychological potential of hand gestures of infants. In *The biological foundations of gestures: Motor and semiotic aspects.* J. Nespoulous, P. Perron, and A. Lecours (eds.). Hillsdale, NJ: Erlbaum. 149–202.

———. 1987. Sharing makes sense: Intersubjectivity and the making of an infant's meaning. *Language topics: Essays in honour of Michael Halliday, Vol. I.* R. Steele and T. Threadgold (eds.). Philadelphia: John Benjamins.

————. 1989. Signs before speech. *The semiotic web.* T. Sebeok (ed.). New York: Mouton de Gruyter. 689–755.

Trevarthen, C., L. Murray, and P. Hubley. 1981. Psychology of infants. *Scientific foundations of paediatrics*, Second Edition. J. Davis and J. Dobbing (eds.). London: Heinemann. 211–274.

Tronick, E. 1989. Emotions and emotional communication in infants. *American Psychologist.* 44: 112–119.

Tronick. E., T. Brazelton, and H. Als. 1978. The structure of face-to-face interaction and its developmental functions. *Sign Language Studies.* 18: 1–16.

Tronick, E., H. Als, L. Adamson, S. Wise, and T. Brazelton. 1978. The infant's response to entrapment between contradictory messages in face-to-face interaction. *Journal of the American Academy of Child Psychiatry.* 17: 1–13.

Tronick, E., and J. Cohn. 1989. Infant-mother face-to-face interaction: Age and gender differences in coordination and the occurrence of miscoordination. *Child Development.* 60: 85–92.

Tronick, E., and A. Gianino. 1986. The transmission of maternal disturbance to the infant. *Maternal Depression and Infant Disturbance.* E. Tronick and T. Field (eds.). *New Directions for Child Development.* San Francisco: Jossey-Bass. 5–11.

Tsunoda, T. 1987. *The Japanese brain.* Tokyo: Daishu Shoten [Japanese].

Turkington, C. 1992. Infants do it—but what is the point? *APA Monitor.* February: 18.

Turkle, S. 1978. *Psychoanalytic politics.* New York: Basic Books.

Tursman, R. 1987. *Peirce's theory of scientific discovery: A system of logic conceived as semiotic.* Bloomington: Indiana University Press.

Urwin, C. 1984. Power relations and the emergence of language. *Changing the subject: Psychology, social regulation, and subjectivity.* J. Henriques, W. Hollway, C. Urwin, C. Venn, and V. Walderkine (eds.). London: Methuen. 264–322.

Ver Eecke, W. 1983. Hegel as Lacan's source for necessity in psychoanalytic theory. *Interpreting Lacan.* J. Smith and W. Kerrigan (eds.). New Haven: Yale University Press. 113–138.

————. 1984. *Saying "No.": Its meaning in child development, psychoanalysis, linguistics, and Hegel.* Pittsburgh, PA: Duquesne University Press.

Von Bertalanffy, L. 1968. *General system theory: Foundations, development, applications.* New York: George Braziller.

————. 1972. The history and development of general system theory. *Perspectives on general system theory: Scientific-philosophical studies.* E. Taschdjian (ed.). New York: George Braziller. 149–169.

von Uexküll, J. 1934. A stroll through the worlds of animals and men: A picture book of invisible worlds. *Instinctive Behavior: The development of a modern concept.* (trans.) C. Schiller (ed.). New York: International Universities Press. 5–80.

von Uexküll, T. 1986. From index to icon: A semiotic attempt at interpreting Piaget's developmental theory. *Iconicity: Essays on the nature of culture.* Festschrift for Thomas A. Sebeok. P. Bouissac, M. Herzfeld, and R. Posner (eds.). Tübingen: Stauffenburg Verlag. 119–140.

Voyat, G. (ed.) 1984. *The world of Henri Wallon.* New York: Aronson.

Vygotsky, L. 1962. *Thought and language.* E. Hanfmann and G. Vakar (ed. and trans.). Cambridge: The M.I.T. Press.

Wallerstein, R. 1981. The bipolar self: Discussion of alternative perspectibes. *Journal fo the American Psychoanalytic Association.* 29:377–394.

Wallon, H. 1921. La conscience et la conscience du moi. *Journal de Psychologie.* 18: 51–64.

―――. 1931. Comment se developpe, chez l'enfant, la notion du corps propre. *Journal de Psychologie.* 28: 705–748.

―――. 1934. *Les Origines du caractère chez l'enfant: Les préludes du sentiment de personalité,* 2nd Ed. Paris: Presses Universitaires de France, 1949.

Weber, S. 1982. *The legend of Freud.* Minneapolis: University of Minnesota Press.

Wernicke, C. 1900. *Grundriss der Psychiatrie in Klinischen Vorlesungen.* Leipzig: Georg Thieme.

Wertsch, J. 1991. *Voices of the mind: A sociocultural approach to mediated action.* Cambridge: Harvard University Press.

Wertsch, J., and P. Tulviste. 1992. L. S. Vygotsky and contemporary developmental psychology. *Developmental Psychology.* 28: 548–557.

Weston, D. 1990. Towards a revised theory of borderline object relations: Contributions of empirical research. *International Journal of Psycho-Analysis.* 71: 661–693.

White, G. 1994. Affecting culture: Emotion and morality in everyday life. *Emotion and Culture: empirical studies of mutual influence.* S. Kitayama and H. Markus (eds.). Washington, D.C.: American Psychological Association. 219–239.

White, R. 1960. Competence and the psychosexual stages of development. *Nebraska Symposium on Motivation.* M. Jones (ed.). Lincoln: University of Nebraska Press. 97–141.

Widlocher, D. 1985. The wish for identification and structural effects in the work of Freud. *International Journal of Psycho-Analysis.* 66: 31–46.

Wilden, A. 1972. *System and structure: Essays in communication and exchange.* Second edition. London: Tavistock Publications, 1984.

Will, O. A. 1959. Human relatedness and the schizophrenic reaction. *Psychiatry,* 22: 205–223.

―――. 1972. Catatonic behavior in schizophrenia. *Contemporary Psychoanalysis.* 9: 29–58.

Williams, R. 1992. *Recognition: Fichte and Hegel on the other.* Albany: State University of New York Press.

Wilson, A., and L. Weinstein. 1992. An investigation into some implications of a

Vygotskian perspective on the origins of mind: Psychoanalysis and Vygotskian psychology, part 1. *Journal of the American Psychoanalytic Association.* 40: 349–379.

Winnicott, D. 1951. Transitional objects and transitional phenomena. *Through paediatrics to psycho-analysis.* New York: Basic Books, 1975. 229–242.

———. 1963. Communicating and not communicating leading to a study of certain opposites. *The maturational processes and the facilitating environment: Studies in the theory of emotional development.* New York: International Universities Press, 1974. 179–192.

———. 1967. Mirror-role of mother and family in child development. *Playing and reality.* New York: Basic Books, 1971. 111–118.

———. 1974. Fear of Breakdown. *International Review of Psycho-Analysis.* 1:103–107.

———. 1975. *Through paediatrics to psycho-analysis.* New York: Basic Books.

Wolf, E. 1976. Ambience and abstinence. *The Annual of Psychoanalysis.* 4: 101–115. New York: International Universities Press.

Wolff, P. 1987. *The development of behavioral states and the expression of emotions in early infancy: New proposals for investigation.* Chicago: The University of Chicago Press.

Wright, K. 1991. *Vision and separation: Between mother and baby.* Northvale, NJ: Aronson.

Yando, R., V. Seitz, and E. Zigler. 1978. *Imitation: A developmental perspective.* Hillsdale, NJ: Erlbaum.

Yogman, M., S. Dixon, E. Tronick, L. Adamson, H. Als, and T. Brazelton. 1976. "Father-infant interaction." Paper, American Pediatric Society/Society for Pediatric Research, St. Louis.

Zetzel, E. 1970. *The capacity for emotional growth.* New York: International Universities Press.

Zuckerman, M. 1979. Attribution of success and failure revisited, or: The motivational bias is alive and well in attribution theory. *Journal of Personality.* 4: 245–287.

Name Index

Subject Index

Stereotype, 5, 7, 92, 93, 193
Still-Face, 17, 18, 29, 47, 50, 52
Stimulation, 17, 28, 29, 49
Stimulus-Boundedness, 24, 58
Stranger, 28, 52, 53, 54, 127
Subconscious, 170
Subject, 3, 8, 16, 21, 25, 36, 49, 55, 67–72,
  79, 86, 87, 105, 114, 116, 123, 130, 135,
  137, 141, 143, 153, 156, 187, 192
Substitution, 21, 28, 38, 40, 41, 60, 133, 148,
Suggestibility, 29
Summoning, 66
Superego, 129
Supposed Knowing Subject, 151, 160
Symbol, 14, 33-37, 55, 57, 58, 62, 121
Symbolic, 3, 5, 6, 8, 14, 22, 32, 46, 62, 77,
  105, 116, 117, 131, 135-186
Symbolic Castration, 148, 157
Symptom, 133, 153, 159, 169, 175
Syntax, 5, 27, 37, 38, 40, 167

Talking cure, 168
Televison, 127
Termination, 151, 159-160
Theory, 30
Things, 84
Thinking, 32
Third, 14, 21, 25, 29, 61, 70–72, 81, 85, 105,
  109, 116, 130, 132, 137, 141, 144, 148,
  158, 183, 189, 190, 193
Thirdness, 32, 41, 55, 59, 84, 99, 109, 187
Time, 69, 99, 113, 184
Touching, 20, 41, 147, 185
Tragic Man, 136
Training, 72, 135, 136
Transference, 61, 71, 98, 102, 112, 114, 116,
  129–131, 133, 148–160, 185, 189, 190
Transitional Object, 101
Transitional Space, 115, 132, 193
Transitivism, 55, 123
Translation, 39, 40, 101, 182, 188, 192
Transmuting internalization, 128, 146, 160,
Trauma, 3, 4, 72, 84, 86, 87, 142, 154, 158,
  164, 170, 175, 182
Triadic, 31, 54, 141
Turn–Taking, 21, 23, 30

Umvelt, 37, 38
Unconscious, 22, 35, 36, 41, 45, 57, 61, 66,
  69, 71, 72, 87, 114, 124, 135–137, 143,
  146, 147, 153, 161–186, 188
Undifferentiated, 32, 34, 75, 77, 93, 95, 185
Uniqueness, 144, 145

Unmediated, 62
Unnameable, 3, 4, 75, 85, 87, 100

Verbal bridge, 156, 183
Victimization, 71, 72, 182
Violation, 19, 21, 34, 111, 117
Vision Quest, 101
Visual, 4, 8, 23, 28, 35, 38, 41, 49, 57, 92,
  120, 123, 138, 185
Vocalization —see Voice
Voice, 16, 20, 21, 23, 24, 28, 34, 48, 49, 53,
  58, 68, 70, 102, 154, 192

Whole, 13, 137, 141, 148
Withdrawal, 14, 15, 49
Witness, 104, 109, 110, 137, 188
Writing, 7, 39, 40, 94, 95, 100, 105, 106,
  114, 117, 144, 171, 185

Zoosemiotics, 30